THE AMERICAN AIR MUSEUM IN BRITAIN
S. Sgt. Floyd G. Smith
1031 Kensington Dr.
Roseville, CA 95661

The Illustrated Directory of

WARSHIPS

From 1860 to the Present

D0451144

F 244

The Illustrated Directory of

WARSHIPS

From 1860 to the Present

David Miller

MBI Publishing Company

A Salamander Book

This edition first published in 2001
by MBI Publishing Company,
729 Prospect Avenue, PO Box 1,
Osceola, WI 54020-0001 USA

© Salamander Books Limited 2001

An imprint of Chrysalis Books Group plc

All rights reserved. With the exception of quoting brief passages for the purpose of review no part of this publication may be reproduced without prior written permission from the Publisher.

The information in this book is true and complete to the best of our knowledge. All recommendations are made without any guarantee on the part of the author or publisher, who also disclaim any liability incurred in connection with the use of this data or specific details.

We recognize that some words, model names and designations, for example, mentioned herein are the property of the trademark holder. We use them for identification purposes only. This is not an official publication.

MBI Publishing Company books are also available at discounts in bulk quantity for industrial or sales-promotional use. For details write to Special Sales Manager at Motorbooks International Wholesalers & Distributors, 729 Prospect Avenue, PO Box 1, Osceola, WI 54020-0001 USA.

Library of Congress Cataloging-in-Publication Data Available

ISBN 0-7603-1127-7

The Author

David Miller is a former officer in the British armed forces, who spent his service in England, the Falkland Islands, Germany, Malaysia, the Netherlands, Scotland, and Singapore. He subsequently worked as a freelance author and for three years as a journalist for Jane's Information Group. He was Editor of the two-volume *Jane's Major Warships*, and has written more than forty other works, many of them related to sea warfare and naval weapons.

Credits

Project Manager: Ray Bonds
Designers: Interprep Ltd
Reproduction: Studio Tec
Printed and bound in: Italy

Contents

Introduction

Vast numbers of warships have been built between the advent of the ironclad in 1860 and the end of the 20th Century, and it would require many volumes to cover them all. This book seeks to select and describe the majority of the important classes, particularly those which had an influence on naval development, or were of special importance to a particular navy.

During the Victorian era by far the most important naval vessel was the battleship which was the standard measure of strategic power, its position being given even greater strength with the advent of the dreadnought in 1906. During World War I the dreadnought-type battleship was supreme, although their one great clash at the Battle of Jutland in 1916 proved inconclusive. Battleships then had a long twilight ending in the middle of World War II when the aircraft carrier became the most important vessel in the fleet. The carrier continued its dominance throughout the Cold War and retains it today, although such ships – and their associated air wings – are beyond the means of all but a few rich nations. Thus, most modern navies centre around smaller ships, such as destroyers and, since the 1950s, frigates.

A recurring theme in entries concerning the 1920s and 1930s is the effect of the various naval treaties, which need to be described briefly to enable their influence to be understood. The Washington Naval Conference (November 1921 - March 1922) involved France, Italy, Japan, UK and USA, the most significant agreement being that their fleet strengths should be fixed in the ratio: UK – 5, USA – 5, Japan – 3, France – 1.75, and Italy – 1.75. It was also agreed to ban construction of battleships and battlecruisers for ten years (but Britain was allowed to build *Nelson* and *Rodney*) after which ships more than twenty years old could be replaced on a one-for-one basis. Limits on displacement and gun calibre were also agreed: battleships/ battlecruisers – 35,000 tons, 16in (406mm) guns; cruisers – 10,000 tons, 8in (203mm) guns. Limits were based on displacement rather than ship numbers, so this was defined as the displacement of a ship equipped for war, plus ammunition, but less fuel and feed-water.

Individual aircraft carriers were limited to 33,000 tons and 8in (203mm) guns, while carrier tonnage was limited to: UK and USA – 135,000 tons, Japan – 81,000 tons; France, Italy – 60,000 tons. Like other capital ships, carriers could not be replaced until they were twenty years old. The signatory powers also banned increasing existing ships offensive capability, although 3,000 tons per ship could be added to improve their anti-aircraft/submarine defences.

The 1930 London Naval Conference had the same participants, although, following disagreements, France and Italy soon withdrew. This left Japan, UK and USA to agree to continue the ban on capital ship construction to 31 December 1936, and to reduce existing battlefleets to fifteen each for UK and USA and nine for Japan. The 5:5:3 ratio was also extended to heavy cruisers, and a new ratio of 10:10:7 was introduced to cover light cruisers and destroyers.

Japan announced in 1934 that it was withdrawing from the naval treaties and the 1935 conference, also in London, ended with France, the UK and the USA agreeing (25 March 1936) to limit capital ships to 35,000 tons, and cruisers and destroyers to 8,000 tons.

Germany was limited not by the Washington and London Agreements, but by the Versailles Treaty which had formally ended World War I and left the surface fleet with eight pre-dreadnoughts, eight light cruisers, sixteen destroyers and sixteen torpedo boats; no submarines, naval aviation or coastal defences were allowed and manpower was limited to 15,000. The result was, as the Allies intended, a toothless coastal-defence force, with thoroughly antiquated equipment and very limited manpower, although a small amount of new construction was permitted. In 1935, however, the UK and Germany negotiated a separate bilateral arrangement (the Anglo-German Naval Agreement) under which Germany was permitted to built up to 35 per cent (by displacement) of the British Royal Navy in battleships, aircraft carriers, cruisers and destroyers, although they were allowed 45 per cent in submarines.

Reports of Japanese building in excess of 35,000 tons led to a revision (1938) of the treaty limits on the size of capital ships, and Hitler repudiated the Anglo-German agreement on 28 April 1939. With this the agreement structure totally collapsed.

Up to about the middle of World War II the British Royal Navy was by far the largest and most powerful in the world, setting the standards by which all others were measured. During the period 1900 to 1917 Imperial Germany attempted to challenge that dominance, but failed, while the US Navy was steadily building its strength until from about 1943 onwards it became the undisputed master of the world's oceans. Japan built a huge navy which attempted to challenge the US Navy for dominance of the Pacific in World War II, but it, too, failed totally. In the Cold War the Soviet Union built its navy at a remarkable pace and showed that it was not averse to trying new ideas which resulted in some remarkable and greatly admired ships. In the end, however, it, too, over-reached itself and collapsed both suddenly and completely, an astonishing demise considering that it was not the result of defeat in battle, but due to political and financial problems.

Entries

Entries, and in particular the specifications, are generally given for the first-of-class, as built.

Ship types. The names of ship types differ between navies and they have also changed over time. There have also been occasions when navies have deliberately placed ships in higher categories (ie, describing a destroyer as a cruiser) to deceive an enemy, or in a lower category (ie, describing a cruiser as a destroyer) to confuse their politicians. In this book ships are, with only a very few exceptions which are explained in the text, placed in the same category as that used by their own navy.

Number in class. This is the number of ships actually completed.

Displacement. Normally given as "standard" and "full load" unless specifically mentioned otherwise.

Length. Overall length of the ship but where this is not available, the figure is given as the length of the waterline (wl) or between perpendiculars (pp).

Beam. Width of the ship at its widest part.

Draught. Draught of the hull at full load (ie, excluding sonars).

Armament. "As built", in inches and then in metric down to 70mm, below which it is given in metric units only. The order of the data is: missile launchers, guns, AA weapons, ASW weapons.

Armour. Armour schemes were complicated and varied from one part of the ship to another. The figures given here show the normal maxima and minima of the main belt, which normally covered only the engines and magazines, and of other relevant areas.

Complement. This is includes crew for any embarked aircraft, but excludes admiral and staff for flagships.

Countries: Where countries are listed this is done, in accordance with international practice, in the order of the first letter of their names in the English language, thus avoiding any indication of relative importance or author's preferences.

Aircraft Carriers

Only a few years after the first appearance of aircraft, naval officers were devising methods of taking them to sea. Launching the aircraft was not the problem, since machines of the time had a very short take-off run and some planking laid along the top of a gun turret generally sufficed. The difficulty lay in the landings and it was eventually realised that a flat deck was the answer, although stopping the aircraft remained a problem for some years. Most of the problems had been solved by the late 1920s, however, and the British, Japanese and United States began to build "flat-top" carriers in large numbers. Progress gathered pace as new inventions made operations easier with the central lift, the cross-deck arrester wire, and the armoured flight deck.

In World War II carriers ousted battleships as the ultimate naval weapon. They became larger, carried more aircraft and operated in increasingly severe conditions. Such carriers played a major role in the Atlantic, but it was in the Pacific that they came into their own, with US and Japanese carrier aircraft fighting and deciding the outcome of battles without the main fleets actually coming within sight of each other.

Post-war, carrier development gathered even greater momentum as the first generation of jet-propelled aircraft went to sea. But it needed inventions like the angled-deck, steam catapult and mirror landing-aid to enable them to

Above: **Vought A-7E overflies nuclear-carrier USS *Dwight D Eisenhower* in 1988**

operate the second and subsequent generations of jet aircraft. The US Navy continued to develop ever larger carriers until it virtually standardised on the nuclear-propelled Nimitz-class, which, with a displacement of 98,235 tons, is of a size no other warship can approach let alone equal. The Soviet Navy started from scratch and then developed a series of ships with a variety of layouts until, with the *Kuznetsov*, they reached a carrier which was very nearly on a par with the Americans, but then came the collapse of the Soviet Union and all was lost. Meanwhile, other navies concentrated on developing carriers of a more moderate and affordable size, most of them in the 10-20,000 ton bracket, which was made possible by the unique V/STOL AV-8B Harrier. The French have, however, recently completed a 40,000 ton carrier which will operate conventional aircraft, although at an enormous cost. The British are also returning to large size carriers with a project which will, it is hoped, culminate in a new 40,000 ton carrier in about 2010.

Each American supercarrier has an airwing that is more powerful and capable than all but a very few national air forces. Indeed they are so important that when a US president goes into the national operations centre to deal with an overseas crisis the first question that he asks is, "Where are the carriers?" It is a question a succession of presidents will continue to ask for many years to come.

Béarn

FRANCE

Completed: May 1927.
Number in class: 1
Displacement: 22,146 tons standard; 28,400 tons full load.
Dimensions: Length 599.0ft (182.6m); beam 115.5ft (35.2m); draught 30.5ft (9.3m).
Propulsion: 2 shafts; 2 turbines; 6 boilers; 37,500shp; 21.5kt; 6,000nm at 10kt.
Armour: Main belt 3.2in (8cm), flight deck 1in (2.5cm).
Aircraft: 40.
Armament: 8 x 6.1in (155mm); 6 x 3in (76mm) AA; 8 x 37mm; 4 x 21in (533mm) TT.
Complement: 875.

History: The design for French Navy's first aircraft carrier was prepared in 1922, when, as a result of the Washington Treaty, the incomplete hull of a Normandie-class battleship became available. Work started in late 1923 and the ship was completed in May 1927. *Béarn* was of conventional design with a 591ft (180m) flight deck, an open bow and a rounded-down after end. The normal aircraft wing comprised 40 aircraft, but due to limitations in flight-deck area, only about 10 of these could be ranged at any one time.

Béarn was completely refitted in 1935, but by the outbreak of war in 1939 her maximum speed of 21.5kt was too slow for service with the fleet. When France

Jeanne d'Arc

FRANCE

Helicopter carrier/training ship
Completed: June 1964.
Number in class: 1.
Displacement: 10,000 tons standard; 12,365 tons full load.
Dimensions: Length 597.0ft (182.0m); beam 79.0ft (24.0m); draught 24.0ft (7.3m).
Propulsion: 2 geared steam turbines; 4 boilers; 2 shafts; 26.5kt; 6,000nm at 15kt.
Aircraft: 4 x Super Frelon (8 in war).
Armament: 4 x 100mm.
Complement: 627 (including 183 officer cadets).

History: The French Navy considered various proposals in the mid-1950s for a replacement for the training cruiser, *Jeanne d'Arc*, which had been in service since 1931. It was eventually decided to build a ship which could be used for training in peace but in wartime could be employed as a helicopter carrier for ASW duties, as an amphibious transport, or as a troop transport for a 700-strong infantry battalion. The hull design was based on that of the cruiser *Colbert*, but with less powerful machinery and a large flightdeck, measuring 203 x 69ft (62 x 21m), aft of the superstructure.

In peace the air wing comprises a maximum of four Super Frelon helicopters, which will be increased to eight in war by stripping out the accommodation normally used by the midshipmen trainees. In both peace and war the number of helicopters can be increased by operating smaller types such as Alouette or Lynx.

Jeanne d'Arc is normally employed as the flagship of the training squadron, undertaking a six-month cruise every year. It is a sound, sensible design,

fell in 1940 she was at Martinique, where she was de-militarised, but was returned to service as part of the Free French forces in June 1943. She was converted to an aircraft transport in the USA in 1944-45, which included installing an all-US weapons fit consisting of 4 x 5in (127mm), 24 x 40mm and 26 x 20mm. After the war *Béarn* served at Toulon for many years as an accommodation ship for submarine crews, but was sold for scrap in 1967.

Below: Béarn, completed in 1927 was the first French-built aircraft carrier

Above: Jeanne d'Arc, a training-ship in peace, was a helicopter carrier in war

producing an excellent training ship, but which also has valuable potential for alternative uses in war. It was originally planned to replace *Jeanne d'Arc* by a new ship in 2003, but in 1998 this was postponed to 2006.

Clemenceau

FRANCE

Fleet carrier
Completed: 1961-63.
Number in class: 2.
Displacement: 22,000 tons standard; 32,780 tons full load.
Dimensions: length 870.0ft (265.0m); beam 168.0ft (51.2m); draught 28.0ft (8.6m).
Propulsion: 2 shafts; Parsons geared steam turbines; 6 boilers; 126,000shp, 32kt, 7,500nm at 18kt.
Armour:
Aircraft: 40.
Armament: 8 x 100mm.
Complement: Aircraft carrier = 1,338; helicopter carrier = 984.

History: In the early post-war years the French Navy operated three carriers: an ex-British ship, *Arromanches* (1946-74), and two US carriers on loan, *Lafayette* (1950-63) and *Bois Belleau* (1953-60). These were replaced by these two all-French carriers, which entered service in 1961 *(Clemenceau)* and 1963 *(Foch)*. These were very capable ships for their size, and incorporated all the carrier developments of the 1950s, including a fully angled deck, mirror landing-sight, steam catapults and two 15 tons capacity (later increased to 20 tons) lifts.

The air group was originally planned to be 60 aircraft, but the increase in size and weight of carrier-borne aircraft in the 1950s and 60s reduced this to 40. As originally commissioned, the air group comprised two flights of Etendard IVM sea/land-attack fighters, a small number of Etendard IVP recce/tanker aircraft, with air-defence provided by Aquilons (licence-built de Havilland Sea

Charles De Gaulle

FRANCE

Completed: 1999.
Number in class: 1 (1 more to be ordered).
Displacement: 37,520 tons standard; 40,600 tons full load.
Dimensions: Length 858.0ft (261.5m); beam 211.0ft (64.4m); draught 28.0ft (8.5m).
Propulsion: Two shafts; 2 150megawatt K15 pressurised-water nuclear reactors; 2 double-reduction geared steam turbines; 82,000shp; 27kt.
Aircraft: 35-40.
Armament: 2 x Sylver vertical-launch SAAM groups(16 x 2); 32 x Aster-15 missiles), 2 x Sadral . SAM; 8 x 20mm AA.
Complement: 1,950.

History: After many years under development and construction France's nuclear carrier (CVN) entered service in 2000. The hull dimensions are virtually identical to those of the Clemenceau-class, a limit imposed by the size of the building dock at Brest, but the flight deck is much larger and is served by two 36 ton-capacity deck-edge lifts, enabling much heavier aircraft to be operated. There are two catapults, one on the forward deck, the other on the angled deck, each capable of accelerating a 22 ton aircraft to a speed of 140kt.

The nuclear propulsion system is based on that used in Le Triomphant-class SSBNs and gives a virtually unlimited range, although this does not remove the need for regular replenishment of aviation fuel, ammunition, food and stores. The total power available is such that the maximum possible speed is 27kt, somewhat slow by modern standards. One of the many innovations is the SATRAP computer-controlled stability system in which a heavy trolley moves across the ship to compensate for rolls, enabling aircraft to be launched and recovered in high sea states.

***Above: Clemenceau;* Crusader, Etendard fighters, and Alizé ASW aircraft on deck**

Venom) and ASW by Alizé turboprop aircraft. F-8E Crusaders took over the air defence role in 1963, and Super Etendard replaced the Etendard IVM in the late 1970s, while helicopters took on the ASW and planeguard duties.

The two ships remained in service much longer than expected and from the mid-1970s they alternated, with one in service as a fixed-wing carrier, while the other was either in refit or in service as a helicopter carrier with a reduced crew. *Clemenceau* left service in 1997 and was then used as a source of spares to keep *Foch* going. It was planned at one time that *Foch* would remain in service until about 2006, operating Rafale M in place of Crusaders, but that was later changed and she was decommissioned in mid-2000 and sold to Brazil.

***Above:* France's nuclear-carrier, *Charles de Gaulle,* finally entered service in 2001**

The air group comprises some 35-40 aircraft: two flights of Rafale M strike fighters, one flight of two E-2C Hawkeye AEW aircraft, and a flight of helicopters.

The final cost of this programme is estimated to be well over $US3billion and there has been lengthy discussion about whether, or not, to build a second carrier. That decision has been postponed to 2003, at the earliest.

Andrea Doria

ITALY

Helicopter cruiser
Completed: 1964.
Number in class: 2.
Displacement: 5,000 tons standard; 6,500 tons full load.
Dimensions: Length 489.8ft (149.3m); beam 56.4ft (17.3m); draught 16.4ft (5.0m).
Propulsion: Two shafts; geared turbines; 4 boilers; 60,000shp; 30kt; 5,000nm at 7kt.
Aircraft: 4 helicopters.
Armament: 1 x Terrier twin-arm SAM launcher (40 missiles), 8 x 76mm, 6 x 324mm TT.
Complement: 485.

History: These two ships, *Andrea Doria* and *Caio Duilio,* were ordered in 1957-58 and completed in 1964, and followed one of the naval fashions of the period by combining the forward elements of a cruiser with a large flight deck aft. They were essentially an enlarged version of the Impavido-class destroyer design, but with a hangar built into the after end of the superstructure and a large flight deck, which measured 98.5 x 52.5ft (30 x 16m). It was originally intended to operate Sea King helicopters, but in practice it was found that the air facilities were too small for such large aircraft and the normal air group consisted of four Agusta-Bell AB-212 ASW helicopters.

The main weapon system was a twin-armed Terrier launcher on the foredeck, which, in *Doria* alone, was replaced by the Standard SM1(ER) missile system in the mid-1970s. They also mounted eight of the then new OTO

Vittorio Veneto

ITALY

Helicopter cruiser
Completed: 1969.
Number in class: 1.
Displacement: 7,500 tons standard; 8,850 tons full load.
Dimensions: Length 589.3ft (179.6m); beam 65.6ft (19.4m); draught19.8 ft (6.0m).
Propulsion: Two shafts; geared steam turbines; 4 boilers; 73,000shp; 30.5kt; 5,000nm at 17kt.
Aircraft: 6 x SH-3D or 9 x AB-212.
Armament: 1 x Terrier twin-arm launcher (60 missiles), 8 x 76mm, 6 x 21in (533mm) TT.
Complement: 550.

History: Following early experience with *Andrea Doria* the Italian Navy decided that instead of a third ship of the same design there would be considerable benefits from building a somewhat larger ship. Thus, the *Vittorio Veneto* has a much larger hull, resulting in a flight deck measuring 60.6 x 13.3ft (18.5 x 4.0m) with a larger hangar which is underneath the flight deck rather than in the after end of the superstructure. This enables a much larger air group to be operated, consisting of six SH-3D Sea King or nine AB-212. The deeper hull forward also enabled the missile capacity to be increased from 40 to 60, and *Vittorio Veneto* is able to launch both Terrier SAMs and ASROC ASW missiles.

Vittorio Veneto served as fleet flagship until replaced by *Garibaldi* in 1985. She then took over the training ship role from *Caio Duilio* and was due to have been phased out of service in 2000, but this was later extended to at least 2005.

Above: **Italy's *Andrea Doria*, an air-capable cruiser with a large flightdeck aft**

Melara 76mm guns for close-in air defence.

Both ships were regularly refitted during their lives, but only one, *Doria*, was given a full modernisation between 1976 and 1978, while *Duilio* was converted into a training ship, instead. Both gave many years of service, *Doria* being stricken in 1991 and *Duilio* in 1992.

Above: Vittorio Veneto, **showing her flightdeck; a frigate is on her starboard side**

Giuseppe Garibaldi

ITALY

V/STOL carrier
Completed: 1985.
Number in class: 1.
Displacement: 10,000 tons standard; 13,850 tons full load.
Dimensions: Length 591.1ft (180.2m); beam 99.8ft (30.4m); draught 26.8ft (8.2m).
Propulsion: 2 shafts, 4 General Electric/Fiat LM-2500 gas turbines; 80,000shp; 29.5kt; 7,000nm at 20kt.
Aircraft: 10 x AV-8B Harrier plus one SH-3D helicopter; or 16 x SH-3D.
Armament: 4 x Otomat SSM (4x1), 2 x Albatros SAM launchers,6 x 40mm 6 x 21in 12.75in (324mm)ASW TT.
Complement: 825.

History: Construction of two aircraft carriers for the Italian Navy was started during World War Two, but neither was completed. After much discussion political agreement was given in the 1970s for a single ship with a full-length flightdeck to be built; the contract was placed in 1977 and the ship entered service in September 1985. There was then another problem since, under a law dating back to 1923, the air force was responsible for providing fixed-wing support to the fleet and in the 1980s the air force stated that it would neither operate V/STOL aircraft for the navy nor permit the navy to provide its own pilots. This impasse continued until 1989 when the navy was finally allowed to place an order for AV-8B Harrier IIs, the first operational aircraft being embarked in December 1994.

The ship is a neat design, fitting considerable capability into a relatively

Hosho

JAPAN

Completed: 1922.
Number in class: 1.
Displacement: 7,470 tons standard; 10,000 tons full load.
Dimensions: Length 541.3ft (165.0m); beam 59.0ft (18.0m); draught 20.3ft (6.2m)
Propulsion: Two shafts; geared turbines; 12 boilers; 30,000shp; 25kt
Aircraft: 26 (see notes)
Armament: 4 x 5in (127mm), 2 x 3in AA, 2 x MG
Complement: 550

History: *Hosho* was the Imperial Japanese Navy's first aircraft carrier and like many of its foreign counterparts the hull was being built for another purpose, in this case a fleet oiler, when it was decided to convert it on the ways and complete it as a carrier. As built it had a small starboard-side island but this was removed in 1923 and never replaced. The funnels were originally hinged, being normally vertical but swung to the horizontal position during flying operations; this was found to be unnecessarily complicated and they were fixed in the upright position in 1934.

The flightdeck extended from bow to stern and was originally 519ft (158.2m) long and 74.5ft (22.7m) wide, but it was extended aft in 1944 to give a length of 579.4ft (176.6m). The original aircraft complement was 26, but as aircraft became larger and heavier this was progressively reduced to 21 in 1934 and 11 in 1942. By the time that war broke out in 1941 *Hosho* had been relegated to the training role, which she continued until the war's end. She was scrapped in 1947.

small hull. The forward end of the flight deck includes a full width ski ramp, although at 6.5deg it is at half the angle of those aboard the British Invincible-class and Spanish *Principe de Asturias*. Composition of the air group is flexible and could be either all Harrier IIs or all SH-3Ds, but, in practice, a mix of the two would be embarked. The ship carries a considerable amount of weaponry, including four SSM launchers, two SAM launchers, three twin 40mm gun mounts and six torpedo tubes. Two MEN class fast personnel launches (capacity 250) can be embarked for amphibious operations or disaster relief.

A second carrier is now under construction. Designated *Nuova Unitá Maggiore* (NUM), it will displace 20,800 tons and carry a mix of AV-8B Harrier IIs and EH-101 helicopters.

***Right:* Giuseppe Garibaldi shows her sponson-mounted forward air defence guns**

***Above:* Completed in 1922, Japan's first carrier, *Hosho*, was originally a fleet oiler**

Akagi

JAPAN

Fleet carrier
Completed: 1927.
Number in class: 1.
Displacement: 36,500 tons standard; 42,750 tons full load.
Dimensions: Length 855.3ft (260.7m); beam 102.8ft (31.32m); draught 28.6ft (8.7m).
Propulsion: Four shafts, geared steam turbines, 19 boilers, 131,200shp, 31kt.
Armour: Belt 10in (25.4cm).
Aircraft: 60 (see notes).
Armament: 10 x 8in, 12 x 4.7in, 22 x MG.
Complement: 2,000.

History: Two ships laid down as Amagi-class battlecruisers in 1920 were scheduled to be converted to aircraft carriers, but one was so damaged during the 1923 earthquake that work was abandoned, leaving this ship, *Akagi*, as the only one to be completed. At that time the best form for an aircraft carrier had not been finalised, so *Akagi* had a 624 x 100ft (190 x 30m) landing-on deck atop the hangar, with two flying-off decks forward, from which aircraft could take-off direct from the hangar, an arrangement similar to that in the British *Furious*. There was no island and the two funnels were on the starboard side below flight-deck level, the larger curving downwards and the smaller upwards

Akagi was completely rebuilt between 1935 and 1938. The most obvious change was the elimination of the forward flying-off decks and the extension of the main flightdeck, which then measured 817.5 x 100ft (250 x 30m); ie, virtually the full length of the hull. Below the flightdeck the hangar was also

Kaga

JAPAN

Fleet carrier
Specifications following 1935 refit
Completed: 1928.
Number in class: 1.
Displacement: 38,200 tons standard; 43,650 tons full load.
Dimensions: Length 812.5ft (247.7m); beam 106.6ft (32.5m); draught 31.0ft (9.5m).
Propulsion: Four shafts; Brown-Curtis geared steam turbines; 8 boilers; 127,400shp; 28.3kt.
Armour: Belt 11in (30cm).
Aircraft: 90.
Armament: 10 x 8in (203mm), 16 x 5in (127mm) , 22 x 25mm.
Complement: 2,016.

History: *Kaga* was built and launched in November 1921 as a battleship, but work was then suspended due to the Washington Treaty. When the hull of the second Amagi-class battlecruiser was damaged in an earthquake during conversion work (see Hosho-class entry), it was decided to convert the unfinished *Kaga* instead. In general, *Kaga's* design was similar to that of *Akagi*, with two bow flying-off decks and a relatively short landing-on deck measuring 562.0 x 100.0ft (171.0 x 30.5m). The funnel arrangement was different with long trunks taking the exhausts along the outside of the hangar to outlets near the stern, an arrangement which proved very unsatisfactory.

The ship was totally rebuilt in 1934-35. The work included lengthening the

increased in length. Other changes included removal of the 8in gun turrets and the fitting of underwater bulges to increase stability and protection. The two funnels were replaced by a single, very large, downward-curving stack, and a small island was installed on the port side. These changes resulted in a theoretical air group of 91, although, operationally, the maximum carried was 72.

Akagi was so badly damaged by US carrier aircraft at the Battle of Midway (5 June 1942) that it had to be abandoned and scuttled.

Above: **Originally *Akagi*'s two hangars each had its own forward flying-off deck**

Above: Kaga **was generally similar to *Akagi* but the boiler uptakes were trunked aft**

hull aft by 34ft (10m), removing the forward flying-off decks and extending the flight deck, which was now 815.5ft (249m) long, and enlarging the hangar. The exhaust trunking was radically altered, being replaced by a single, downward-facing stack approximately amidships on the starboard side. The number of aircraft was increased to 90, although, in practice, no more than 81 were carried, and this was reduced to 66 in 1942. The 8in (203mm) guns, originally in single turrets, were moved to new casemates, located just above the waterline aft. A small island was installed on the starboard side of the flight-deck.

Kaga was set ablaze by four bombs from US carrier aircraft at the Battle of Midway and had to be abandoned (4 June 1942). When the fire reached the aviation fuel tanks she exploded and sank.

Ryujo

JAPAN

Fleet carrier
Specifications following 1936 refit
Completed: 1933.
Number in class: 1.
Displacement: 10,600 tons standard; 13,650 tons full load.
Dimensions: Length 590.3ft (179.9m); beam 68.2ft (20.8m); draught 23.3ft (7.1m).
Propulsion: Two shafts; geared steam turbines; 6 boilers; 65,000shp; 29kt.
Aircraft: 48 (operational maximum 37).
Armament: 8 x 5in (127mm), 4 x 25mm, 24 x 13mm MG.
Complement: 924.

History: *Ryujo* was originally planned with a single hangar, but an increase in the aircraft complement demanded by the Naval Staff resulted in an extra hangar being fitted, although without any overall enlargement of the hull. The idea of flying-off decks, as in the earlier carriers, was abandoned and there was a single flightdeck measuring 513.5 x 75.5ft (156.5 x 23.0m). The exhausts were led off through two large stacks on the starboard side, which were downward facing and supported by large brackets. There was no island, the bridge being located under the forward edge of the flightdeck. As completed, the ship proved to be overloaded, unstable, and a bad seakeeper, shipping a good deal over the bow in a seaway.

Kaiyo

JAPAN

Escort carrier (ex-liner)
Completed: 1943.
Number in class: 1.
Displacement: 13,600 tons standard; 16,483 tons full load.
Dimensions: Length 546.4ft (166.6m); beam 71.8ft (21.9m); draught 26.4ft (8.0m).
Propulsion: Two shafts; Kampon geared turbines; 4 boilers; 52,100shp; 24kt.
Aircraft: 24.
Armament: 8 x 5in (127mm) DP; 24 x 25mm AA.
Complement: 829.

History: Another example of the ex-liner conversions was *Kaiyo*, which was originally the Japanese-owned liner, *Argentina Maru*, launched in 1938 and employed on the South America run. With foreign passenger voyages impossible from December 1941 onwards, the ship was requisitioned by the government and employed for a time as a troop transport, but in late 1942 she was taken over by the Imperial Japanese Navy for conversion to an escort carrier. This involved installing a flightdeck, hangars, two lifts and an armament of eight 5in (127mm) and twenty-four 25mm cannon; in addition, the original diesel engines were replaced by destroyer-pattern boilers and turbines. A sister ship, *Brazil Maru*, was to have undergone a similar conversion, but was sunk in mid-1942 before the work could commence.

Kaiyo was commissioned in November 1943, but was employed

Ryujo was rebuilt between 1934 and 1936. The work was primarily intended to reduce the instability and improve sea-keeping, and included a reduction in armament, strengthening the hull, and considerable enlargement of the underwater bulges. This was, however, still insufficient and the bow was raised by one deck level in 1940 in yet another attempt to improve seakeeping.

This not very satisfactory carrier was sunk by four bombs and a torpedo from aircraft operating from USS *Saratoga* in the Battle of the Eastern Solomons (24 August 1942).

***Below:* Seen here as built, *Ryujo,* was unstable, overloaded and very wet forward**

mainly as an aircraft transport and flight training ship, rather than as an operational carrier. In mid 1944 the armament was increased by the addition of another twenty 25mm cannon, several 120mm rocket launchers and (curiously for a carrier) eight depth-charges. *Kaiyo* was badly damaged by British carrier-borne aircraft in July 1945 and was broken up in 1948.

***Below:* *Kaiyo,* one of the Japanese liners pressed into war service after conversion**

Soryu/Hiryu/Shokaku Taiho/Unryu

JAPAN

Fleet carriers
Specifications for *Soryu*
Completed: 1937-44.
Number in class: 5.
Displacement: 15,900 tons standard; 19,800 tons full load.
Dimensions: Length 746.5ft (227.5m); beam 69.9ft (21.3m); draught 25.0ft (7.62m).
Propulsion: Four shafts; geared steam turbines; 8 boilers; 152,000shp; 34.5kt.
Aircraft: see notes.
Armament: 12 x 5in, 28 x 25mm AA.
Complement: 1,100.

History: These closely related ships can be treated as one group. *Soryu* was the basis for all subsequent Japanese fleet carriers and was intended for the attack role, being fast, lightly built and with a large air group (63 aircraft.) *Hiryu*, completed in 1939, was slightly larger with a 3.3ft (1m) increase in beam, giving greater fuel bunkerage, and with modifications which included a bow raised by one deck level to improve sea-keeping. *Hiryu* was one of only two Japanese carriers to have an island on the port side. The Unryu-class was essentially repeat *Hiryus*, with three completed in 1944 *(Unryu, Amagi, Katsuragi)*, three abandoned incomplete on the ways, and a further eleven planned, but not started. Because of shortages created by the war, these had various different types of machinery and there were minor differences in dimensions; unlike

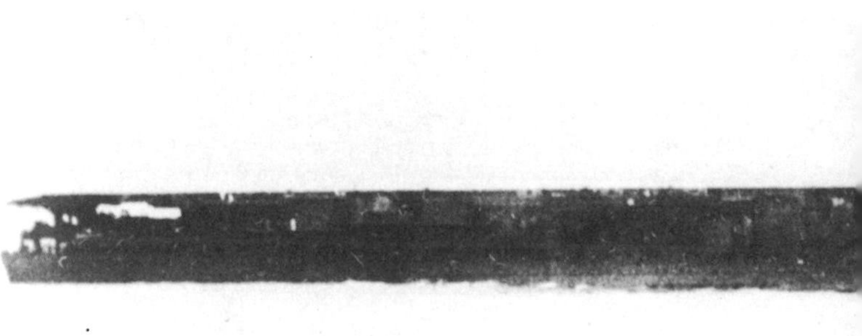

***Above: Soryu*, the model for all later Japanese carriers, was fast but lightly built**

Hiryu, however, all had an island on the starboard side.

Shokaku and *Zuikaku,* which were completed in 1941, were enlarged and improved *Hiryus* with greater armour protection, although there was still no armour for the flight deck or hangars. Carrying 72 aircraft, these were considered the most successful Japanese World War Two carriers.

Taiho was a modified *Shokaku,* incorporating lessons of the first year of war. The flight deck extended to the bow, which was enclosed on the British pattern. There was a substantial island to starboard, incorporating the funnel which was angled outwards and exhausted well clear of the flightdeck. Seven more of this class were planned but never started.

Only one of these eight carriers survived the war. Four were sunk by US carrier aircraft: *Soryu* and *Hiryu* at the Battle of Midway (4 June 1942), *Zuikaku* at the Battle of Cape Engano (25 October 1944), and *Amagi* in Japanese waters on 24 July 1945. Three were sunk by torpedoes from US submarines: two at the Battle of the Philippine Sea (19 June 1944), *Shokaku* by USS *Cavalla,* and *Taiho* by USS *Albacore,* while *Unryu* was sunk in the East China Sea by USS *Redfish* on 19 December 1944. The only survivor was *Katsuragi* which was broken up in 1947. A particular problem for these carriers was that when hit by bombs or torpedoes, poor internal design coupled with ineffective damage control procedures frequently allowed petrol vapour to spread throughout the ship, which then ignited in a massive explosion.

***Below: Shokaku,* one of a class of two completed in 1941; both were sunk in 1944**

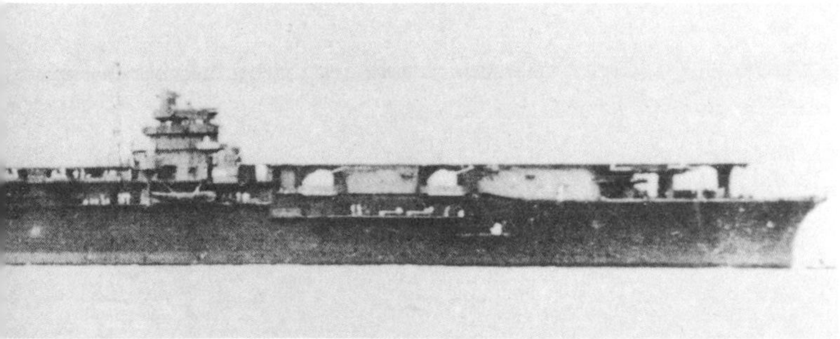

Shinyo

JAPAN

Escort carrier (ex-liner)
Completed: 1943.
Number in class: 1.
Displacement: 17,500 tons standard; 20,586 tons full load.
Dimensions: Length 621.3 ft (189.4m); beam 84.0ft (25.6m); draught 26.8ft (8.2m).
Propulsion: Two shafts; AEG turbines; 4 boilers; 26,000shp; 22kt.
Aircraft: 33.
Armament: 8 x 5in, 30 x 25mm.
Complement: 942.

History: So serious were their carrier losses and so desperate did the Japanese need for carriers become that numbers of ships built for other purposes were converted. Among these were three former submarine support ships (*Zuiho, Shoho* and *Ryuho*) and seven former passenger liners (*Junyo, Hiyo, Taiyo, Unyo, Chuyo, Kaiyo* and *Shinyo*) which had operated for a variety of merchant shipping lines, but were now lying, unused, in Japanese waters.

Representative of these ex-liners is the carrier *Shinyo*, which was originally the German Norddeutscher-Lloyd company's SS *Scharnhorst* (20,916tons) which had been trapped in Japanese waters since the outbreak of war in 1939. A modern ship, she was formally purchased by the Japanese Navy in February 1942 and work on converting it into an aircraft carrier started that

Shinano

JAPAN

Carrier group support carrier
Completed: 1944.
Number in class: 1
Displacement: 62,000 tons standard; 71,890 tons full load.
Dimensions: Length 872.7ft (266.0m); beam 119.0ft (36.3m); draught 33.9ft (10.3m).
Propulsion: Four shafts; Kampon geared turbines; 12 boilers; 150,000shp; 27kt; 10,000nm at 18kt.
Aircraft: 47.
Armour: Belt 8.1in (20.6cm); flight deck 3in (7.6cm); hangar deck 7.5in (19cm).
Armament: 16 x 5in; 145 x 25mm; 12 x 12-barrel rocket launchers.
Complement: 2,400.

History: When launched, *Shinano* was the largest aircraft carrier in the world and held that title until USS *Kitty Hawk* was commissioned in 1961. Unfortunately, *Shinano*'s size was of no avail and her operational life lasted just ten days. *Shinano* was laid down as the third of the Yamato-class battleships, but work was halted on the outbreak of war in December 1941 and then restarted in June 1942, but now as an aircraft carrier, a type urgently needed to make up for the carriers lost in the Battle of Midway (5 June 1942), The battleship hull was retained, but with an additional single long hangar, topped by an armoured flightdeck measuring 839.9 x 131.3ft (256.0 x 40.0m). Despite her enormous size, *Shinano* was not primarily intended for use as an attack carrier, but rather as a carrier group support ship, where her enormous storage capacity for aircraft, fuel and ordnance would have been of great service to the fleet.

September. It was completed as an escort carrier in December 1943. The flight deck was 590.5 x 80.5ft (180 x 24,5m) and she could carry a total of 33 aircraft. *Shinyo* was fully employed for some months but was torpedoed and sunk on 17 November 1944 by the submarine USS *Spadefish*.

Below:* Shinyo was built on the hull of the German passenger liner *Scharnhorst

Shinano was launched in October 1944 and started running trials on 19 November 1944. She was still on trials, with many parts of the work incomplete and her crew only partly trained, when she was torpedoed by USS *Archerfish* on 29 November 1944 and sank several hours later due to uncontrolled flooding. The reason for her sinking was that one of the tasks not completed was the fitting of watertight doors, although the lack of training of the crew also played a part.

***Below:* Until 1961, *Shinano* was the largest carrier built**

Principe de Asturias

SPAIN

V/STOL carrier
Completed: 1988.
Number in class: 1.
Displacement: 15,912 tons standard; 16,700 tons full load.
Dimensions: Length 642.7ft (195.9m); beam 79.7ft (24.3m); draught 30.8ft (9.4m).
Propulsion: One shaft, 2 General Electric LM-2500 gas-turbines; 46,400shp; 26kt; 6,500nm at 20kt.
Aircraft: 17 (see notes).
Armament: 4 x 20mm Meroka.
Complement: 763.

History: The first Spanish Navy carrier was *Dedalo*, a US Navy Independence-class carrier, which was obtained on loan in 1967 and purchased outright in 1973. She was employed as a V/STOL carrier, operating a mix of AV-8 Harriers and helicopters, and was so successful that the Spanish Navy decided to built a modern successor. The design was based on that of the Sea Control Ship, which was to have been ordered in large numbers for the US Navy in FY75, but was not funded by Congress, and the Spanish Navy decided on an upgraded and modernised version, which was designed in the USA but built in Spain by Bazan.

The Spanish Navy tried to keep everything as simple as in the original, but one major change was the addition of a full-width 12deg ski ramp, enabling AV-8B and EAV-8B V/STOL aircraft to carry out rolling take-offs at full load. Only a single propulsion shaft was installed, although this is backed-up by an auxiliary

Chakri Nareubet

THAILAND

V/STOL carrier
Completed: 1997.
Number in class: 1.
Displacement: 11,485 tons full load.
Dimensions: Length 599.1ft (182.6 m); beam 100.1ft (30.5m); draught 20.21ft (6.16m).
Propulsion: Two shafts, CODOG 2 Bazan-MTU 16V1163-TB83 diesels (each 5,600shp); 2 General Electric LM-2500 gas turbines (each 22,125shp); maximum 44,250shp; 26.4kt (maximum), 16.7kt (diesels); 10,000nm at 12kt.
Aircraft: Wartime, either 18 helicopters or 12 AV-8S Matador V/STOL, or a lesser mix; normal peacetime, 6 AV-8S, 4 S-70B Seahawk helicopters.
Armament: 2 x 0.50in (12.7mm) MG; fitted for but not with 3 Sadral AA missile systems.
Complement: 455 (62 officers), plus 146 aircrew; 4 Royal family; troops, normal - 450, maximum - 675.

History: In 1991 the Royal Thai Navy (RTN) placed a contract with German company Bremer Vulcan for a 7,800 t helicopter carrier. This was later abruptly cancelled and on 27 March 1992 a new contract was concluded with Spain for a larger ship to be built by *Empresa Bazan*, followed by a later announcement that AV-8S Matador aircraft would also be acquired from the Spanish Navy

The ship, which cost US$360 million, is basically similar to the Spanish *Principe de Asturias* with a 12deg ski jump and two 20t aircraft lifts, but there are also some major differences. First, the entire flight deck is offset to port, giving a distinctly asymmetric appearance and, secondly, there is a 67.3 x 23.0ft

***Above:* V/STOL carrier, *Principe de Asturias,* flagship of the Spanish fleet**

propulsion system, which provides a "return to base" service should the main system fail. Electronic and weapons fits are limited by modern standards. Overall, the Spanish navy invested well, obtaining a capable carrier at a reasonable price.

The carrier is the flagship of the Spanish fleet and is based at the main fleet base at Rota. It was originally the flagship of "Battlegroup Alfa" a NATO ASW group which was part of NATO's defences in the North Atlantic, but is now used more as a light attack carrier, normally being deployed as the flagship of *Grupo Aeronaval Alfa.* The ship's equipment includes two LCVPs, suggesting a limited amphibious capability.

***Above:* Based on *Asturias,* the Thai *Chakri Nareubet* was built in Spain by Bazan**

(20.5 x 7.0 m) docking-well with a large stern door, accommodating three 60.7ft (18.5m) landing craft, while three LCVPs can be carried on the flightdeck. Also, *Chakri Nareubet* has two propellers rather than one. Finally, to meet national requirements, special accommodation is permanently reserved for four members of the Royal family.

Special provisions are made for disaster relief, including provision for carrying containers and special vehicles in the hangar and on the flight deck, a hospital, and the ability to supply water and electrical power to the shore. The name, *Chakri Nareubet,* means "In honour of the House of Chakri" (ie, the royal family)

The ship arrived in Thai waters in 1997 and aroused great interest as it was the first aircraft carrier to be operated by a Southeast Asian navy. It has, however, proved to be very costly, not only to buy but also to operate and maintain, and in 2000 it was being operated no more than one day a month.

Moskva

RUSSIA (SOVIET UNION)

Helicopter carrier
Completed: 1967-69.
Number in class: 2.
Displacement: 14,590 tons standard; 17,500 tons full load.
Dimensions: Length 620.1ft (189.0m); beam 85.3ft (23.0m); draught 27.9ft (13.0m).
Propulsion: Two shafts; geared turbines; 4 pressure-fired boilers; 100,000shp; 31kt; 14,000nm at 29kt.
Aircraft: 14 helicopters.
Armament: 2 x SA-N-3 launchers (44 missiles), 4 x 57mm, 1 x SUW-N-1 launcher (18 missiles), 2 x RBU-6000, 10 x 21in (533mm) TT.
Complement: 850.

History: These two helicopter carriers, *Moskva* and *Leningrad*, were specifically designed to counter the threat posed by US SSBNs operating in the Mediterranean during the 1960s and 1970s. To achieve this, the Soviet naval staff required a hull capable of operating eight ASW helicopters, the minimum number needed to ensure that two were constantly on patrol. When the first ship, *Moskva*, was seen by Western experts they were surprised at the heavy armament in the forward half of the ship, which included two twin SA-N-3 SAM launchers for anti-air protection and a heavy ASW weapon fit, which comprised two RBU-6000 12-barrel rocket launchers, an SUW-N-1 missile launcher and two quintuple anti-submarine torpedo tubes. The ships were powered by a pressurised-steam system, for a design speed of 34kt.

Once the Cold War ended, the West discovered that the ships had been far less

Kiev

RUSSIA (SOVIET UNION)

V/STOL ASW carrier
Completed: 1975-87.
Number in class: 4.
Displacement: 36,000 tons standard; 42,000 tons full load.
Dimensions: Length 902.0ft (275.0m); beam 154.8ft (47.2m); draught 26.9ft (8.2m).
Propulsion: Four shafts; geared steam turbines; 140,000shp; 32kt; 13,500nm at 18kt.
Aircraft: 31 (see notes).
Armament: 4 x SS-N-12 (Sandbox) SSM launchers 24 x SA-N-9 SAM launchers; 2 x 100mm AK-100 guns (1 x 2); 8 x 30mm AK-630 Gatling AA (1 x 8); 2 x RPK-5 ASW RL.
Complement: 1,612 ship's crew; 430 air group.

History: The *Kiev* caused a tremendous impression in the West when it carried out its first cruise, in which it sailed from the Black Sea where she had been built, through the Mediterranean and then northwards through the Atlantic to join the Northern Fleet at Murmansk. As so often during the Cold War, the Soviet designers showed that they were not afraid to produce a radical design, this time with a forecastle bristling with armament, a large superstructure covered with sensors and weapons, and an angled flightdeck.

The primary mission of the Kiev-class was to deny NATO ASW forces access to the Soviet ballistic missile submarine bastions, for which they usually carried 18 Ka-27 (Hormone-A/B) AEW and ASW helicopters, twelve Yak-38 (Forger) V/STOL fighters to attack Lockheed P-3 ASW aircraft, and SS-N-12

***Above:* Innovative Soviet helicopter carrier *Moskva* caused great alarm in the West**

formidable than had appeared at the time and suffered from a number of major and many minor problems. Perhaps the most important operational problem was that the air group proved out to be too small for the intended task, but they were also poor seakeepers, particularly in heavy seas, in which they pitched badly.

The propulsion system gave many problems and had to be rebuilt several times, but they never reached their design speed; indeed, they rarely exceeded 28kt. Finally, for the crew they were very crowded and among the many measures taken to alleviate this was the complete removal of the torpedo tube installation.

Leningrad was taken out of service in 1991, but *Moskva* remained in service until the late 1990s, when she, too, was scrapped.

***Above:* Soviet carrier *Kiev* in the Western Atlantic; a dramatic and effective design**

long-range anti-ship missiles to attack surface ships, especially carriers. It had been intended that their eventual air wing would have included a number of Yak 41M (Freehand) fighter, but these never attained service status. How effective these ships might have been could only have been tested in war which never came but they were certainly large and visually impressive ships.

Kiev joined the Soviet fleet in 1975, followed by *Minsk* in 1978, *Novorossiysk* in 1982 and *Baku* (later renamed *Admiral Gorshkov*) in 1987. Improvements were incorporated into each of the later ships as they were built, with *Admiral Gorshkov* having substantially different weapons and sensors to first-of-class *Kiev*. The first three ships were stricken in 1993, with *Minsk* ending up as a gambling casino in China, while *Novorossiysk* was eventually broken up in India. Meanwhile *Kiev*'s hulk has been used as a source of spares for *Admiral Gorshkov* and there have been repeated rumours that the latter would be sold to the Indian Navy.

Kuznetsov (Orel)

RUSSIA (SOVIET UNION)

Fleet carrier
Completed: 1991.
Number in class: 1.
Displacement: 55,000 tons standard; 65,000 tons full load.
Dimensions: Length 1,005.5ft (306.5m); beam 237.2ft (72.3m); draught 29.9ft (9.1m).
Propulsion: Four shafts, TV12-4 geared turbines, 8 turbo-pressurised boilers, 200,000shp, 29kt, 12,000nm at 10kt.
Aircraft: see notes.
Armament: 12 x SS-N-19 (Shipwreck) SSM launchers; 24 x SA-N-9 (Gauntlet) SAM VLS launchers; 8 x CADS-1 CIWS (each 8 x SA-N-11 Grison SAM launchers plus 2 x 30mm gatling AA); 6 x 30mm AK-630 (1 x 6) Gatling; 2 x RPK-5 ASW/anti-torpedo rocket launchers.
Complement: 1,993 plus 626 air group.

History: The Kuznetsov-class strike carriers were a logical step in the Soviet Union's ambitions for a global power-projection capability, with two ships being laid down: the first in 1983 and the second in 1985. The names suffered from shifts in the political situation, with the first-of-class originally named *Riga*, but this was changed in 1982 to *Leonid Brezhnev*, but when the former president fell into disfavour in 1987 the name was changed yet again, this time to *Tbilisi*, then, finally to *Admiral Flota Sovetskogo Sojuza Kuznetsov* (Admiral of the Fleet of the Soviet Union Kuznetsov, usually shortened to *Kuznetsov*), which it bears today. The second carrier was launched in 1988 as *Riga*, but when the Baltic States became independent this was changed to *Varyag*.

The most unusual feature of the design is the built-in 12deg take-off ramp. The ski ramp had been developed by the British for use by V/STOL aircraft as a means of increasing their payload, but it was recognised from an early stage that there was potential for their use by conventional take-off and landing (CTOL) aircraft, but in this case as a means of shortening their take-off. The US Navy carried out a series of trials with F-14 fighters in the 1970s, but, although the take-offs were successful the idea was not pursued. The Soviet Navy showed a more continuing interest and built a shore-based trial installation which led to that aboard the *Kuznetsov*.

The forward end of the flightdeck is marked with two take-off runs, that to starboard starting just forward of the superstructure and giving the aircraft a 279ft (85m) run. The port run is longer, being some 558ft (170 m) in length, but with an interim start at the 279ft (85m) point. All three start points are equipped with catches which hold the aircraft still until their afterburners have developed full thrust. Landings on the-angled deck are conventional, with an automatic radar-controlled system, a back-up mirror landing-aid, and four arrester wires located some 46ft (14m) apart; the deck is offset at an angle of 7deg to the ship's centreline. Landings can take place at the same time as take-offs from the starboard run, but simultaneous use of the port run is obviously not possible.

The hangar is approximately 610 x 98 x 25 ft (186 x 29.8 x 7.6m) and there are two starboard side lifts. The vertical launchers for the SS-N-19 missile system are located in the centre of the flight deck forward with flush deck covers. This installation, while providing an uncluttered flightdeck means that the below-decks SS-N-19 battery and magazine take up a great deal of hangar space which otherwise could be allocated to aircraft.

The planned capacity of the ship is 58 aircraft. One possible composition is 36 Su-27K (Flanker-D) fighters, 16 Ka-271 (Helix) ASW helicopters and six other helicopters, probably a mix of Ka-29 AEW and Ka-29RLD radar-control aircraft.

By 2000, however, nothing approaching this total had ever been embarked.

Having been constructed in the Nikolayev yard in the Ukraine, *Kuznetsov* worked up and carried out trials with aircraft in the Black Sea. The ship then sailed to join the Northern Fleet where it was clearly the fleet commander's top priority. In January 1996, the ship deployed to the Adriatic, where it supported the Russian forces in the former Yugoslavia.

A further design, the nuclear-powered Type 1143.7, was laid down in November 1988 at Nikolayev. Originally named *Ulyanovsk*, this was later changed to *Pyotr Veliky* (Peter the Great), but a variety of factors led to the cancellation of the ship in 1991 and it was scrapped when only 40 per cent complete. This ship would have been equivalent in every way to contemporary large US Navy aircraft carriers, and among other differences from *Kuznetsov*, would have been fitted with conventional steam catapults.

Various attempts were made to sell *Kuznetsov* to the Indian Navy, with staff talks taking place in 1998-2000. The deal on offer was that the ship would be given free-of-charge, but that the Indians would pay for all refitting and modernisation in Russia and would also purchase an air wing of Su-27M. As of early 2001 no deal had been agreed.

***Above:* The triumph of Soviet naval designers, carrier *Kuznetsov* came late**

Ark Royal

UNITED KINGDOM

Seaplane carrier
Completed: 1914.
Number in class: 1.
Displacement: 7,080 tons standard; 7,450 tons full load.
Dimensions: Length 366.0ft (111.6m); beam 50.8ft (15.5m); draught 18.0ft (5.5m).
Propulsion: 1 shaft; triple-expansion; 2 boilers; 3,000shp; 11kt.
Aircraft: 5 floatplanes, 2 landplanes.
Armament: 4 x 12pdr, 2 x 0.303in Maxim MG.
Complement: 180.

History: The RN quickly saw the potential of aircraft at sea and the first serious trials involved an old cruiser, HMS *Hermes*, which was temporarily converted to a seaplane carrier for the 1913 naval manoeuvres. Many lessons were learnt and on the outbreak of war a number of cross-Channel ferries were requisitioned and converted as seaplane carriers. However, another ship was purchased while under construction and rebuilt to become the first purpose-designed aircraft carrier in any navy; Originally intended to be a tramp steamer, her machinery and superstructure were aft leaving the forward hull free to accommodate a 150 x 45 x 15ft (48 x 14 x 5m) "aeroplane hold" with access from the upper deck via a 40 x 30ft (12 x 9m) hatch. Named HMS *Ark Royal*, she was commissioned in December 1914.

Floatplanes were lifted out of the hold by one of two steam-powered cranes and then placed on wheeled trolleys on the foredeck; the aircraft then revved up and took off over the bows. They landed in the sea and taxied alongside *Ark Royal*, where they were picked up by the crane and returned to the hold. *Ark Royal* spent

Argus

UNITED KINGDOM

Completed: 1918.
Number in class: 1.
Displacement: tons 14,450 standard; 15,775 tons full load.
Dimensions: Length 566.0ft (172.5m); beam 68.0ft (20.7m); draught 21.0 ft (6.4m).
Propulsion: 4 shafts; Parsons geared turbines; 12 boilers; 20,000shp; 20kt.
Aircraft: 20.
Armament: 6 x 4in (102mm) AA.
Complement: 401.

History: The partially built liner, *Conte Rosso*, was bought on the stocks in August 1916, redesigned and completed as an aircraft carrier, re-named *Argus*, launched in 1917 and joined the fleet in September 1918. She was the world's first flush decked carrier, with a completely clear flightdeck, which came to a point at the bows. Aircraft of the time had no need for catapults, but *Argus* was fitted with the first type of arrester gear consisting of 54 wires, 9in (23cm) apart, laid longitudinally along the flightdeck. The primary purpose of these wires was not to stop the aircraft, but rather to prevent it being blown sideways over the edge of the flightdeck. The wires were raised 15in (38cm) above the deck and an aircraft landed into the after end of the wires, where two outward facing hooks on the undercarriage axle engaged in the wires to prevent the aircraft from either bouncing up or sliding sideways. As the aircraft continued to roll forwards, friction between the hooks and the wires brought it to a halt.

It was planned that *Argus* would have two islands, one either side of the flightdeck, but she was built with none, the bridge being under the forward end

the war in the eastern Mediterranean, including taking part in the Dardanelles campaign, not returning to England until 1920. She was renamed HMS *Pegasus* in 1934 and served in World War Two in various minor roles.

Below: **Completed in 1914, *Ark Royal* was the first purpose-built, air-capable ship**

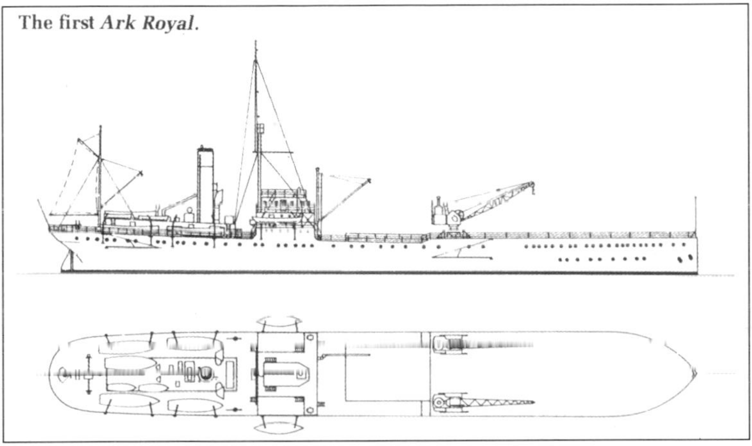

Above: **British carrier, *Argus*, completed in 1918, embarked eighteen aircraft**

of the flightdeck, with a small pilothouse which could be raised for manoeuvring in harbour and retracted during flying operations. The exhaust from the ship's engines was carried by ducts under the flightdeck to the stern, a system which worked efficiently but caused turbulence for landing aircraft.

Argus' air group comprised some 18-20 aircraft. The ship served throughout the long inter-war period and was used as an escort carrier and aircraft transport in World War Two.

Furious (1)

UNITED KINGDOM

Completed: 1917.
Number in class: 1.
Displacement: 19,513 tons standard; 22,80 tons full load.
Dimensions: Length 786.5ft (239.7m); beam 88.0ft (26.8m); draught 21.0ft (6.4m).
Propulsion: 4 shafts; Brown-Curtis geared turbines; 18 boilers; 90,000shp; 31.5kt.
Armour: 2-3in (50-75mm) belt, 2-3in (50-75mm) bulkheads, 0.75-3in (20-75mm) decks.
Aircraft: 7-10 aircraft.
Armament: 1 x 18in (457mm), 11 x 5in (140mm), 2 x 3in (75mm)AA, 4 x 3pdr (47mm), 2 x 21in (533mm) TT.
Complement: 880.

History: HMS *Furious* was originally designed as a light battlecruiser with two single 18in (457mm) guns. Doubts about the whole battlecruiser concept coincided with an urgent need for air support for the Grand Fleet and it was decided to convert *Furious* to an aircraft carrier. All the changes were made forward and involved building a hangar on the foredeck with a flight deck stretching from the bridge to the bow and which had a distinct forward slope. Two derricks were also installed for hoisting aircraft aboard. *Furious* joined the fleet in July 1917, still with the after 18in (457mm) gun, and with the specifications as given above.

Trials proved that it was impossible for aircraft to land on *Furious'* foredeck, which involved the pilot approaching from astern until he was abreast the

Eagle

UNITED KINGDOM

Completed: 1920.
Number in class: 1.
Displacement: 21,630 tons standard; 26,000 tons full load.
Dimensions: Length 667.5ft (203.5m); beam 94.0ft (28.7m); draught 24.7ft (7.5m).
Propulsion: 4 shafts; Brown-Curtis geared turbines; 32 boilers; 50,000shp; 22.5kt
Aircraft: 21.
Armament: 12 x 6in (152mm), 4 x 4in (102mm) AA, 4 x 3pdr (47mm), 6 x 21in (533mm) TT
Complement: 950.

History: The need for air cover for the Grand Fleet became more pressing as the war progressed and by mid-1917 it was clear that *Furious* had major problems (see previous entry) and that despite the much better flightdeck arrangements, *Argus* would be too slow for fleet work. As a result, the hull of the Chilean battleship, *Almirante Cochrane*, which was lying incomplete at Armstrong's yard, was purchased and redesigned as a flush-deck carrier. The original plan was to have two islands, one either side of the flightdeck, but this was dropped in favour of just one, on what then became the traditional, starboard side.

Now named *Eagle*, the new carrier underwent trials in April-October 1920 and then returned to the Portsmouth Navy Yard for final fitting out, which included conversion from coal to oil fuel and the fitting of bulges. Finally completed in 1923, *Eagle* was one of the key factors in the development of

bridge and then sideslipping and dropping onto the deck! As a result, a second conversion was set in hand which involved the removal of the remaining 18in (457mm) gun and installing a long flightdeck aft, but which left the bridge and funnel still in the middle of the ship (see picture). It was quickly found that the gases from the funnel caused strong and unpredictable draughts, while the slipstream from the bulky superstructure resulted in strong but unpredictable eddies over the flightdeck area, making landing very dangerous. Nevertheless, *Furious* became operational with the Grand Fleet, launching 7 Camel fighters on 19 July 1918 in a successful attack against Zeppelin sheds at Tondern. She went into reserve in1919 until her major rebuild (see pages 38-39).

***Below: Furious.* Ropes suspended from gallows abaft funnel created a crash barrier**

air operations at sea during the inter-war years. She then saw service in the early years of World War Two, but was torpedoed and sunk by *U-73* in the Mediterranean on 11 August 1942.

Below: Eagle* was built on the hull of incomplete battleship *Almirante Cochrane

Hermes

UNITED KINGDOM

Completed: 1924.
Number in class: 1.
Displacement: 10,850 tons standard; 13,000 tons full load.
Dimensions: Length 598.0ft (182.3m); beam 70.3ft (21.4m); draught 18.5ft (5.7m).
Propulsion: 2 shafts; Parsons geared turbines; 6 boilers; 40,000shp; 25kt.
Aircraft: 20.
Armament: 10 x 6in (152mm), 4 x 4in (102mm) AA.
Complement: 664.

History: HMS *Hermes* was the first aircraft carrier with a flush deck to be actually designed and built as such, and it was originally intended to give her two islands, although this was changed to just one while under construction. This island included the bridge and funnel and carried by a large tripod mast with a large fighting top; the island was quite long, but very narrow. To maximise the size of the

Furious (2)

UNITED KINGDOM

Completed: 1925.
Number in class: 1.
Displacement: 22,450 tons standard; 27,165 tons full load.
Dimensions: Length 786.4ft (239.7m); beam 90.0ft (27.5m); draught 28.0ft (8.6m).
Propulsion: 4 shafts; Brown-Curtis geared turbines; 18 boilers; 90,000shp; 30kt.
Aircraft: 36.
Armament: 10 x 5.5in (140mm), 2 x 4in 102mm), 4 x 2pdr pom-pom.
Complement: 1,218.

History: After her various unsatisfactory conversions, *Furious* was taken in hand in 1922 and given a complete rebuild from which she emerged in 1925 as a different ship, with a flat flightdeck, the boiler uptakes trunked back to exhaust either side of the after end of the flightdeck, and a longitudinal arrester wire system. There was no island and the bridge was under the forward end of the flightdeck, with a small charthouse which could be raised for manoeuvring in

flightdeck the hull was given considerable flare and she proved to be an excellent sea-boat. Despite her size, *Hermes* was only able to carry 20 aircraft. Like other carriers of the time, *Hermes*, as built, was fitted with longitudinal wires, but these were changed to transverse arrester wires in the early 1930s. *Hermes* was operating in the Indian Ocean when, on 9 April 1942, she was attacked and sunk by some 50 Japanese dive-bombers.

***Below: Hermes*; first ship in any navy to be designed and built as an aircraft carrier**

harbour, but lowered during flying operations. The forward end of the hangar was open, leading onto a short deck across the forecastle, from which aircraft could take-off as well as from the main flightdeck.

Furious was now considered a reasonable success, although there were many later changes. Use of the lower take-off deck was never of real value and its use was quickly discontinued, transverse arrester wires were installed in the 1930s, in 1939 a small starboard island was installed, and in 1943 the size of the flightdeck was increased. *Furious* gave good service in the early years of the war, but was now worn-out and was taken out of operational service in 1944.

***Below: Furious* in 1936; note 'flat-top,' raised quarterdeck, and guns on foredeck**

Courageous

UNITED KINGDOM

Completed: 1928-30.
Number in class: 2.
Displacement: 22,500 tons standard; 27,560 tons full load.
Dimensions: Length 786.6ft (239.8m); beam 90.5ft (27.6m); draught 28.0ft (8.5m).
Propulsion: 4 shafts; Parsons geared turbines; 18 boilers; 90,000shp; 30kt.
Aircraft: 48.
Armament: 16 x 4.7in (120mm), 4 x 2pdr pompom.
Complement: 1,216.

History: Three light battlecruisers were built during World War One: *Furious* with two 18in (457mm) guns, and *Courageous* and *Glorious*, each with four 15in (380mm) guns. The two latter ships served with the Grand Fleet as battlecruisers but were considered unsatisfactory. After the war both were placed in reserve but were then taken in hand for conversion to aircraft carriers, on similar but not identical lines to *Furious*. Like *Furious* they had a long flight-deck terminating at the forward end in a "D" and a lower take-off deck on the forecastle, but differed in having a small starboard island which incorporated the funnel.

These two ships gave good service in the inter-war years, but both were sunk early in the war. *Courageous* was sunk by two torpedoes from *U-29* on 17 September 1939, the first major unit of the Royal Navy to be lost. *Glorious* was taking part in operations off Norway when she was found by the German battlecruisers *Scharnhorst* and *Gneisenau* on 8 June 1940 and sunk by long-range gunfire.

Ark Royal

UNITED KINGDOM

Completed: 1938.
Number in class: 1.
Displacement: 22,000 tons standard; 27,720 tons full load.
Dimensions: Length 800.0ft (243.8m); beam 94.8ft (28.9m); draught 27.8ft (8.5m).
Propulsion: 3 shafts; Parsons geared turbines; 6 boilers; 102,000shp; 31kt.
Armour: 4.5in (11.4cm) belt; bulkheads 2.5-3in (6.4-7.6cm).
Aircraft: 60.
Armament: 16 x 4.5in (114mm), 32 x 2prd pompom.
Complement: 1,580.

History: When completed in 1938, this famous and much-loved ship incorporated all the lessons learnt from the trials carried out in the carriers which had been either built or converted in the early 1920s. The flight deck had a usable area of 720 x 95ft (219.5 x 29.0m) and was 56ft (17.0m) above the deep-load waterline; it had a squared-off bow and a very long stern overhang. There were two catapults and three rectangular lifts, one measuring 45 x 25ft (13.7 x 7.6m), the other two 45 x 22ft (13.7 x 6.7m), although one curious feature was that each lift-well contained two platforms, one operating between the lower and upper hangar, the other between the upper hangar and the flightdeck.

Ark Royal gave excellent service in the first two years of the war and the German propaganda machine announced on several occasions that she had been sunk. Finally, however, it came true on 14 November 1941 when she was hit by a single torpedo from *U-81*, which blew an enormous hole low down on the starboard side. Flooding gradually spread, but eventually reached the boiler

***Below:* *Courageous*, as rebuilt; she was sunk by *U-29* in August 1939**

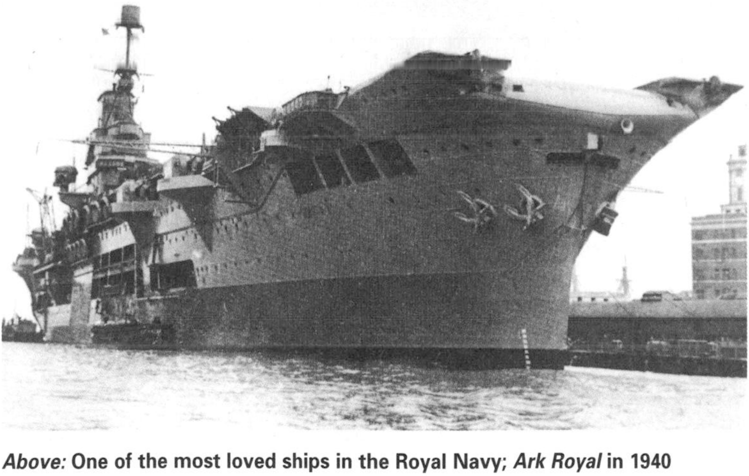

***Above:* One of the most loved ships in the Royal Navy; *Ark Royal* in 1940**

uptake ducts, which ran across the ship below the lower hangar, and she then capsized and sank. Many lessons on ship design and damage controls procedures were learnt from this loss and were implemented in all future British warship designs.

Illustrious/ Indomitable/Implacable

UNITED KINGDOM

Fleet carriers

Class	Illustrious	Indomitable	Implacable
Completed	1940-41	1941	1944
Number in class	Illustrious Victorious Formidable	Indomitable	Implacable Indefatigable
Displacement standard full load	 23,000 tons 29,240 tons	 23,000 tons 29,730 tons	 23,450 tons 32,110 tons
Dimensions length beam draught	 753.3ft (229.6m) 95.8ft (29.2m) 28.5ft (8.7m)	 754.0ft (230m) 95.5ft (29.2m) 29.0ft (8,8m)	 766.4ft (233,.m) 95.8ft (29.2m) 28.9ft (8.8m)
Propulsion shafts turbines boilers power speed	 3 Parsons geared 6 110 ,000shp 30.5kt	 3 Parsons geared 6 1110,000shp 30.5kt	 4 Parsons 8 148,000shp 32kt
Aircraft:	33	45	60
Armament	16 x 4.5in (114mm) 48 x 2pdr	16 x 4.5in (114mm) 48 x 2pdr	16x4.5in (114mm) 44 x 2pdr
Complement	1,229 later 1,997	1,392 later 2,100	1,585 later 2,300

History: These six 'fleet carriers' were the mainstay of the British carrier force throughout the war, the basic design being the three Illustrious-class, all laid down in 1937. These were followed by *Indomitable*, also laid down in 1937, which incorporated a number of improvements. Finally came the two *Implacables*, which were the final developments of the basic design, laid down in 1939 and completed in 1944.

The Illustrious-class, consisting of *Illustrious, Victorious* and *Formidable,* was the first in any navy to be built with an armoured hangar, which conferred greatly increased protection against air attack, although the weight of armour allowed only one hangar. The flightdeck was originally 620ft (189m) long in *Illustrious* and 670ft (204m) in the other two, but was later increased to 740ft (226m) in all three by alterations to the after-end round-down. All flightdecks were 95ft (29.0m) wide and were 38ft (11.6m) above the deep-load waterline. The flightdeck was served by two lifts.

The airgroup was originally 33, but by 1944 all were carrying 52-54 aircraft, while the complement grew from 1,229 to 1.997. All three carriers were repeatedly attacked throughout the war, with *Illustrious* surviving eight bombs off Crete (10 January 1941), followed by several more in Malta harbour six days later. *Formidable* and *Victorious* both served in the Far East where their armoured flightdecks enabled them to survive two *kamikaze* attacks each. Although some of these attacks resulted in the ship entering dockyards for repairs, some of them lengthy, their survival was a great tribute to the armoured deck, and to the way the lessons learnt in the loss of *Ark Royal*, concerning both design and damage control procedures, were applied.

Indomitable was a development of the *Illustrious* design, being the same overall length, but by making several alterations, including adding 6ft (1.8m) to the hull depth, moving the lifts and adjusting the distribution of armour, the designers were able to incorporate a second hangar. Originally, the effective size of the flightdeck was 680 x 95ft (207 x 29.0m), but the length was later increased to 745ft (227.0m). The air group consisted of 45 aircraft in the hangars and a further 20 parked on the flightdeck. As with the Illustrious-class, crew numbers grew; initially, 1,392 by the war's end they were 2,300.

Indomitable was subjected to very heavy attack on 12 August 1942 and was hit twice near the lifts by 1,100lb bombs which, coupled with a very near miss, put her out of action for 6 months. Back in service the following year she was hit by an air-launched torpedo on 16 July 1943 which did a great deal of damage and caused flooding, but rapid application of damage control procedures, in particular of counter-flooding, prevented her suffering a similar fate to that of *Ark Royal*.

The two Indomitable-class carriers were the final development of the Illustrious design, the major differences being four shafts instead of three, and a considerable increase in the number of sensors, such as radars. They were built without the long round-down of the earlier ships, thus giving much increased deck space, but their hangar was only 14ft (4.3m) high, making it impossible to accommodate Corsair aircraft, when these entered service. *Indefatigable's* flightdeck was hit by a *kamikaze* carrying a 500lb (227kg) bomb in 1945 which, to the astonishment of US Navy observers, caused negligible damage.

***Below: Implacable* as she appeared during World War Two**

Above: Indefatigable; **last British fleet carrier to be completed in World War Two**

Below: Fleet carrier *Illustrious*, 1953; completed in 1940 and scrapped in 1956

Campania

UNITED KINGDOM

Escort carrier
Completed: 1944.
Number in class: 1.
Displacement: 13,000 tons standard; 15,970 tons full load.
Dimensions: Length 540ft (164.6m); beam 70.0ft (21.3m); draught 22.8ft (7.0m).
Propulsion: 2 shafts; diesels; 13,250shp; 18kt; 17,000nm at17kt.
Aircraft: 18.
Armament: 2 x 4in QF HA (1 x 2), 16 x 2pdr pompom (8 x 2), 16 x 2prd pompom (4 x 4).
Complement: 639.

History: The urgent need for small carriers to extend air protection to convoys gave rise to a type of ship known as the "escort carrier," a rapid conversion of a suitable merchant ship hull, which was given a flightdeck, hangar, aircraft workshops and command facilities. In all, the British acquired 43 such ships during the war, of which 37 were supplied by the USA under Lend-Lease and 6 were converted in the UK. The first of the British-built escort carriers was

***Below: Vindex,* built on a merchant ship hull, one of the best British escort carriers**

Audacity, which was used the hull of a captured German merchant ship, followed by *Activity* and *Pretoria Castle*.

The best of the British escort carriers were the last three, all built on fast merchant ship hulls; *Vindex* and *Nairana*, which were identical, and *Campania* which was marginally smaller. All three were based on incomplete fast cargo ships lying in British yards, which enabled quite major changes to be made. *Campania* had a flightdeck measuring 515 x 70.6 (157.0 x 21.5m), which was served by two lifts, each 45 x 34ft (13.7 x 10.4m), and with a single cordite-powered catapult at the forward end. *Campania* had four arrester wires (compared to eight and six in *Nairana* and *Vindex*) which proved insufficient. *Campania's* hangar measured 198 x 63.6 x 17.6ft (60.4 x 19.2 x 5.4m), which although neither as long nor or as wide as those on "proper" carriers was considerably higher.

Campania was fitted for night flying and fighter direction and spent her entire wartime career in the Arctic. She was the only escort carrier to be retained after the war, her final mission being to serve as the flagship for the British nuclear tests in 1952.

Victorious (rebuilt)

UNITED KINGDOM

Fleet carrier
Completed: 1957.
Number in class: 1.
Displacement: 30,530 tons standard; 35,500 tons full load.
Dimensions: Length 781.0ft (38.0m); beam 157.0ft (47.8m); draught 31.0ft (9.5m).
Propulsion: 3 shafts; Parsons geared turbines; 6 boilers; 110,000shp; 31kt.
Aircraft: 36.
Armament: 12 x 3in, 6 x 40mm.
Complement: 2,400.

History: *Victorious*, one of the three original Illustrious-class carriers completed in 1941, was selected in 1950 for a major rebuild, which took no less than seven years to complete. During this process her hull was lengthened, widened and deepened, and the machinery and boilers completely replaced. The major additions were a huge sponson on the port side for a fully angled deck (8.75deg), a totally new island, and a new Type 984 "3-D" radar with its characteristic "dustbin" antenna atop the bridge. Two steam catapults were installed, together with four new-type arrester wires. The previous armament was completely removed and replaced by six US-supplied twin 3in automatic mountings and a single sextuple Bofors 40mm mounting. There were also many internal changes, including a great, and urgently needed, increase in generating capacity. *Victorious* went to sea again in 1957 and was the most up-to-date carrier in the fleet, but her aircraft capacity was not what had been hoped. It had been planned that she would carry 54, but due to the increase in

Eagle

UNITED KINGDOM

Fleet carrier
Completed: 1951.
Number in class: 1.
Displacement: 45,000 tons standard; 53,390 tons full load.
Dimensions: Length 811.8ft (247.4m); beam 171.0ft (52.1m); draught 36.0ft (11.0m).
Propulsion: 4 shafts; geared turbines; 8 boilers; 152,000shp; 31kt; 4,500nm at 24kt.
Aircraft: (1952) 60, (1964) 45.
Armament: (1952) 16 x 4.5in, 48 x 40mm AA (8 x 6), 4 x 40mm AA 2 x 2, 9 x 40mm AA (9 x 1).
Complement: 2,750 (including air group).

History: This carrier was originally laid down in 1942 as HMS *Audacious*, one of four "improved Implacables" and since, when the war ended, she was nearing completion, it was decided to carry on. Her name was changed to *Eagle* just before she was launched in 1946 and work continued at a slow pace, with trials not starting until October 1951, followed by her first operational deployment in late 1952. After service with the Mediterranean Fleet, *Eagle* underwent refit in 1954-55, which included an "interim" (5deg) angled deck and mirror deck-landing sight, and she then returned to the Mediterranean where, in 1956, her aircraft took part in the Anglo-French operations against Egypt in the "Suez War." A long and very expensive refit (1959-64) brought her fully up to modern standards, with a full (8deg)

size and weight of the latest aircraft, such as the Blackburn Buccaneer and McDonnell Phantom, this figure was never achieved and on her final deployments she carried only 18 fixed-wing aircraft and five helicopters. She was refitted in 1962-63, but when in her second refit in 1968 a minor fire offered the ideal excuse for her to be taken out of service, being scrapped the following year.

Above: **Thoroughly modernised *Victorious* after her rebuild, completed in 1957**

flightdeck, two steam catapults, Type 984 3-D radar and many lesser improvements.

During *Eagle's* life the size and weight of aircraft increased and the number in the air wing decreased accordingly. In the early 1950s she embarked 59 aircraft, including Sea Hawk day fighters, Sea Venom all-weather fighters, Wyvern strike fighters and Skyraider airborne early warning aircraft. By the 1960s, however, this had fallen to 35 fixed-wing aircraft, a mix of Scimitar fighters, Sea Vixen all-weather fighters and Gannet AEW, and ten Wessex ASW helicopters.

In 1966 the British government announced that the carrier force was to be run-down and that *Eagle*, despite her recently completed, five-year refit, would be axed. Accordingly, she was paid off in 1972 and scrapped in 1978.

Below: **Eagle, which started life as HMS *Audacious***

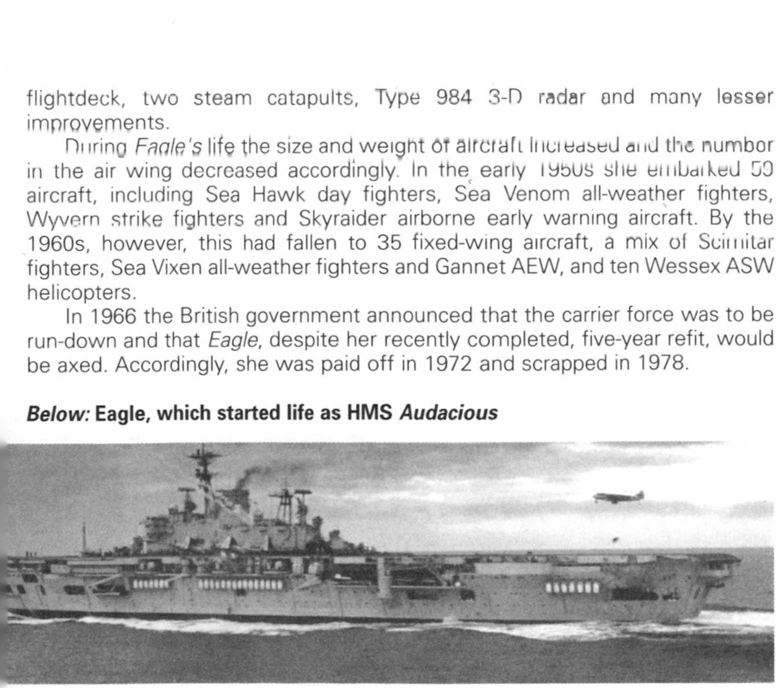

Ark Royal

UNITED KINGDOM

Fleet carrier
Completed: 1959.
Number in class: 1.
Displacement: 43,340 tons standard; 53,060 tons full load.
Dimensions: Length 811.8ft (247.4m); beam 171.0ft (52.1m); draught 36.0ft (11.0m).
Propulsion: 4 shafts; geared turbines; 8 boilers; 152,000shp; 31kt; 4,500nm at 24kt.
Aircraft: 1955 - 50; 1959 - 48; 1969 - 36.
Armament: (1955) 12 x 4.5in (6 x 2), 36 x 40mm AA (4 x 6, 2 x 2); (1959) 8 x 4.5in (4 x 2), 28 x 40mm AA (4 x 6, 2 x 2); (1969) 4 x Seacat SAM (fitted for but not with).
Complement: 2,637 including air group.

History: This new *Ark Royal* was laid down in May 1943, some 18 months after the previous holder of the name had been sunk. She was one of two "improved Implacables" (the other was *Eagle*) but work had not progressed very far when the war ended. The opportunity was then taken to incorporate improvements, including the first-ever British deck-edge lift, an "interim" (5deg) angled deck, and two steam catapults, one launching over the port bow, the other, also on the port side, over the angled deck. Building was very slow and she was not completed until February 1955, 12 years after being laid down, which was something of a record.

The deck-edge lift was never a success and was removed in 1959 and the

Light Fleet Carriers

UNITED KINGDOM

Specifications for Colossus class, as built
Completed: 1944-46.
Number in class: see table.
Displacement: 13,190 tons standard; 18,040 tons full load.
Dimensions: Length 693.2ft (211.3m); beam 80.0ft (24.4m); draught 23.4 ft (7.11m).
Propulsion: 2 shafts; Parsons geared turbines; 4 boilers; 40,000shp; 25kt.
Aircraft: 37.
Armament: 24 x 2pdr pompom.
Complement: 1,300.

History: The British "light fleet carrier" was one of the most successful and widely-used of all aircraft carriers, and brought air power to many fleets from 1945 onwards. The original design work was carried out by Vickers-Armstrong, due to shortage of capacity in the Admiralty departments, and was accepted in 1942. The main requirements were that the design should be "austere," quick to build and need only last until 1945 or the war's end, whichever was the earlier. To enable these requirements to be met some important operational limitations were set. Maximum speed was limited to 25 knots; secondary control positions and back-up machinery were eliminated (for example, the lifts had only one set of electrical machinery each); the flight-deck was unarmoured; there was no armour protection for the hull; the ships' own armament was restricted to a mix of light air defence weapons; and maximum use was made of existing designs of machinery and equipment. Finally, any design feature intended only for the comfort or convenience of the officers or crew was eliminated and anti-corrosion measures were kept to the minimum. The ship underwent a major refit in 1967-70, the primary aim of which was to prepare her to operated McDonnell F-4K Phantom fighters and Blackburn S2 Buccaneer strike aircraft. The weapons fit was progressively reduced until, from 1970 onwards, she was unarmed, being fitted for four Seacat launchers which were never actually installed.

Ark Royal's career was dogged by mechanical problems, although her engineers always managed to keep her going somehow. She achieved great public affection in the UK as a result of a 13-week television series and there was genuine feeling of national regret when she was decommissioned in 1978 and scrapped in 1980.

***Loft: Ark Royal* towards the end of her service with a fully-angled flightdeck**

designs were rushed through and it goes without saying that these 'austere' and 'interim' ships with a design life of three years gave sterling and economical service over many decades, with two of them still in service in 2001!

Despite the wartime pressures, the light fleet carrier was not a conversion,

***Below: Hermes,* largest and last of the very successful "light fleet carriers"**

Ship	Compl	Service	Scrapped
COLOSSUS Class			
Colossus	1944	France (Arromanches): 1946- 72	1978
Glory	1945	UK: 1945-1957	1961
Ocean	1945	UK: 1945-57	1962
Theseus	1946	UK: 1946-56	1962
Triumph	1946	UK (repair ship): UK (reserve): 1972	1957-65 1981
Venerable	1945	Netherlands (Karel Doorman): 1948-68 Argentina (25 de Mayo): 1968-1983	1998
Vengeance	1945	UK: 1945-52 Australia: 1952-55 UK: 1955-56 Brazil (Minas Gerais) : 1956- 2010	2010 (estimated)
Warrior	1946	Canada: 1946-48 UK: 1948- Argentina (Independencia): 1958-70	1971
PERSEUS Class			
Perseus	1945	UK (repair ship): 1946-58	1958
Pioneer	1946	UK (repair ship): 1946-54	1954
MAJESTIC Class			
Hercules	1961	India (Vikrant): 1961-1996	1996
Leviathan	-	[Cannibalised for spares]	1968
Magnificent	1948	Canada: 1946-57 UK (reserve): 1957-65	1965
Majestic	1955	[Laid-up incomplete: 1945-55] Australia (Melbourne): 1955-1982	1983
Powerful	1957	[Laid-up incomplete: 1945-52] Canada (Bonaventure): 1952-70	1970
Terrible	1949	[Laid-up incomplete: 1945-48] Australia (Sydney): 1948-73	1976

Above: Albion **seen here as a "commando carrier," operating Wessex helicopters**

HERMES Class			
Albion	1954	UK: 1954-1972	1973
Bulwark	1954	UK: 1954-76 (fixed wing) UK: 1980-81 (commando carrier)	1984
Centaur	1953	UK: 1953-66	1972
Hermes (ex-Elephant)	1959	UK: 1959-1971 (fixed wing) UK: 1971-1977 (commando carrier) UK: 1977-1984 (V/STOL strike/ASW carrier) India: 1986-2010 (V/STOL strike)	2010(?)

but was designed from the outset for its role and, while mercantile standards were applied to structural strength, the internal sub-divisions were more numerous than would be found in a merchant ship in order to achieve greater survivability. Watertight integrity was achieved by transverse bulkheads and good design, to ensure that a single torpedo hit could, at worst, only flood two adjacent sections.

There were four groups within the "light fleet carrier" category. The first was the basic Colossus-class, of which eight were completed (see table), while a further two, which started out as Colossus-class were converted to aircraft repair and maintenance ships during construction and are usually referred to as the Perseus-class.

Below: **Brazil's *Minas Gerais,* shows the benefits of the fully-angled flightdeck**

***Above: Bonaventure* (ex-*Powerful*) served the Canadian navy from 1952 to 1970**

Next came the Majestic-class, which had the same dimensions as the Colossus-class, differing principally in having strengthened decks to operate heavier aircraft, reduced fuel stowage, and improved arrangements for sailors' accommodation and messing. All these changes resulted in an increase in displacement of some 500 tons. Six Majestic-class were laid down, of which two were completed in the late 1940s, with the other four laid up after launch. One of those laid up, *Leviathan*, was subsequently used as a source of replacement machinery for the Dutch *Karel Doorman*. Of the remaining five, *Magnificent* served with the RN and was scrapped in 1965, while the other four were sold abroad. First to go was *Terrible* which went to Australia in 1948 as HMAS *Sydney*, followed by *Powerful* to Canada in 1952 as HMCS *Bonaventure*. *Majestic* then went to Australia in 1955 as that country's second carrier, becoming HMAS *Melbourne*. Finally in this group, *Hercules* was completed in 1957 and sold to India as INS *Vikrant*.

The ships of the last group, the Hermes-class, were all laid down in 1944, but were somewhat larger, having a length of 744ft (226.8m) and a full load displacement of 27,900 tons. Eight were planned, but four were cancelled in October 1944 and the remaining four were not completed until the 1950s, all of which served only with the RN. These were armed with eight 4.5in guns and 34 40mm Bofors, in place of the 2pdr pompoms in the earlier ships, and could carry up to 42 aircraft.

Virtually all the ships of the Colossus-, Majestic- and Hermes-classes that entered service were repeatedly modified during their operational lives, as their operators attempted to cope with the ever-increasing weights, size and performance of front-line naval aircraft. The advent of the steam catapult alleviated the problem for a while, as did the angled deck and other inventions, but it proved difficult for them to handle second generation jet aircraft and impossible to handle the third generation, such as the British Buccaneer, French Super Etendard and American Phantom. They were then limited to operating light second-generation jets such as the A-4 Skyhawk, V/STOL Harrier/Sea Harrier fixed-wing fighters, slower fixed-wing ASW types such as the Breguet Alizé, Fairey Gannet and Grumman Tracker, or helicopters.

Two of these fine ships will continue in service well into the 21st century: the Indian *Vikrant* and the Brazilian *Minas Gerais*.

Invincible

UNITED KINGDOM

V/STOL carrier
Completed: 1980-85.
Number in class: 3.
Displacement: 16,970 tons standard; 20,710 tons full load.
Dimensions: Length 689.0ft (210.0m); beam 118.1ft (36.0m); draught 28.9ft (8.8m).
Propulsion: 2 shafts; Combined Gas-Or-Gas (COGOG); 4 Olympus marine gas-turbines; 112,000shp; 28kt; 7,000nm at 18kt.
Aircraft: 6 x Sea Harrier FA.2 V/STOL,4 x Harrier GR.7 (RAF), 7 x Sea King HAS.5 ASW helicopters, 3 x Sea King AEW.2A, 2 x Sea King HC.4 (see notes).
Armament: 3 x Goalkeeper CIWS (1 x 3); 2 x 20mm Oerlikon GAM-B01 AA (1 x 2).
Complement: 1,051 (including air group).

History: Following the 1960s decision to cancel the proposed attack carrier (CVA-01) the British started design work on a new, large, air-capable cruiser, which was intended to operate as the flagship of a NATO ASW group operating in the Greenland-Iceland gap. These ships were described as "through-deck cruisers" and were originally intended to operate only helicopters, although provision was later made for V/STOL Sea Harriers. Three ships were completed - *Invincible* (1980), *Illustrious* (1982) and *Ark Royal* (1985) - one of which was offered for sale to the Royal Australian Navy, an offer which was hastily withdrawn as a result of the Falklands War.

The three ships remained in service throughout the 1980s and 1990s, the RN following a policy of having one in full service, one on stand-by preparing for

***Above: Illustrious* in 1983, one of three V/CTOL carriers serving in the Royal Navy**

refit (but capable of returning to service at short notice in an emergency) and one in refit. All three have undergone constant modification to bring them up-to-date with regard to the latest sensors and weapons. The greatest problem, however, has been that of space, as ever increasing demands, particularly for numbers of aircraft, have resulted in repeated adjustments to create yet more space in what are, essentially, not very large hulls. Thus, while the original (1982) air group comprised 5 Sea Harrier FRS.1, 9 Sea King HAS.5 and 2 Sea King AEW, after her latest refit, *Illustrious'* air group is now 8 Sea Harrier FA.2, 8 Harrier GR.7, 4 Sea King AEW.2 and 2 Sea King HAS.6, with a further 5 Sea Kings deployed to Royal Fleet Auxiliaries accompanying the task group.

These three ships will reach the end of their useful lives in about 2010-2015 and it is planned to replace them by two, much larger carriers, which are currently in the design stage. These are likely to displace between 30-40,000 tons, but the decision on whether they will operate conventional or vertical take-off aircraft has yet to be made. If the plan is confirmed, the contract should be placed in 2004 and the first ship laid down in about 2005-6.

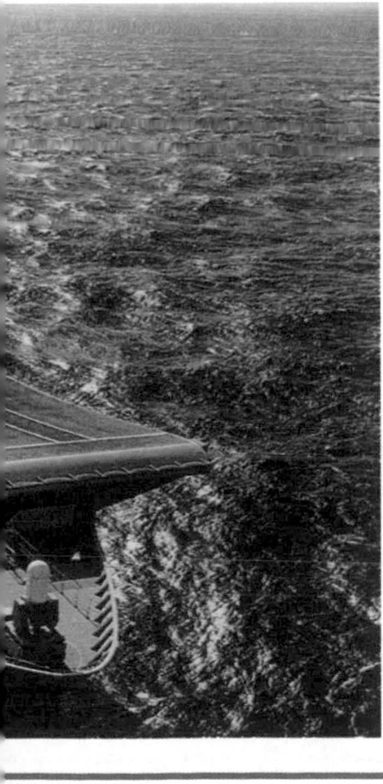

***Left: Invincible* shows her ski-jump, and the Sea Dart launcher, later removed**

Langley

UNITED STATES OF AMERICA

Completed: 1922.
Number in class: 1.
Displacement: 13,900 tons normal.
Dimensions: Length 542.3ft (165.3m); beam 65.3ft (19.9m); draught 20.7ft (6.3m).
Propulsion: 2 shafts; General Electric turbo-electric drive; 3 boilers; 6,500shp; 15.5kt.
Aircraft: see text.
Armament: 4 x 5in (127mm)/51cal.
Complement: 468.

History: From the earliest days of aviation the US Navy was interested in the potential of seaborne airpower, but it was not until 1922 that the first carrier, USS *Langley* was completed. This ship had been built at the Mare Island Navy Yard as the *Jupiter*, a Cyclops-class fleet collier, which had combined its operational function with serving as the test-bed for turbo-electric propulsion. In 1922 the superstructure, cranes and kingposts were removed and a rectangular flightdeck installed. Aircraft were stored disassembled in the hold and then raised by crane to the former maindeck, where they assembled and then raised by the single elevator to the flight deck. Although she was nowhere like fast enough to operate with the fleet, *Langley* carried out many trials and enabled

Lexington

UNITED STATES OF AMERICA

Fleet carrier
Completed: 1925.
Number in class: 2.
Displacement: 37,681 tons standard; 43,055 tons full load.
Dimensions: Length 888.0ft (270.7m); beam 105.4ft (32.1m); draught 33.4ft (10.2m).
Propulsion: 4 shafts; General Electric turbines; 16 boilers; 180,000shp; 33.3kt; 10,500nm at 15kt.
Armour: 5-7in (12.7-17.8cm) belt, 1.3in (3.3cm) deck.
Aircraft: 63.
Armament: 8 x 8in (203mm) (4 x 2), 12 x 5in (127mm) (12 x 1), 48 x 0.5in (12.7mm) (48 x 1).
Complement: 2,327.

***Above: Lexington* (CV-2) was converted from a battlecruiser**

the fledgling naval air service to gain invaluable experience in handling and controlling aircraft at sea.

At the start of World War II she was employed as an aircraft transport, but was so badly damaged in a Japanese air attack on 27 February 1942 that she had to be sunk by a US destroyer.

***Above:* The US Navy's first carrier, USS *Langley* (CV-1), here seen in 1930**

***Above: Lexington*'s sister-ship, *Saratoga*, returns to home waters in May 1945**

History: The first fleet carriers for the US Navy, *Lexington* and *Saratoga* were built on the incomplete hulls of two battlecruisers which became available due to the limitations of the Washington Naval Treaty. By far the largest aircraft carriers in the world when they were commissioned in 1927, they were also the first to have all the characteristics of the second generation of carriers: starboard island with integral funnel, straight-through flightdeck, and transverse arrester wires.

Known as "Lady Lex", *Lexington* was at sea carrying aircraft to Midway when the Japanese struck Pearl Harbor on 7 December 1941. Thereafter she was in the thick of the fighting until her luck ran out on 8 May 1942 at the Battle of the Coral Sea, where, late in the morning, she was hit by two torpedoes and three bombs. Her crew managed to bring things under control, but in the afternoon she was racked by a tremendous explosion from igniting gasoline vapour. She was abandoned and later sunk by two torpedoes from a US destroyer.

Saratoga also had a busy war, but was badly damaged in a *kamikaze* attack during the Iwo Jima landings on 21 February 1945, during which she was repeatedly hit by Japanese bombs and torpedoes. She was expended as a target in the US atomic tests at Bikini Atoll on 25 July 1946.

Ranger

UNITED STATES OF AMERICA

Fleet carrier
Completed: 1934.
Number in Class: 1.
Displacement: 14,575 tons standard; 17,577 tons full load.
Dimensions: Length 769.0ft (234,4m); beam 109.5ft (33.4m); draught 22.5ft (6.8m).
Propulsion: 2 shafts; turbines; 6 boilers; 53,500shp; 29.3kt; 10,000nm at 15kt.
Armour: side and bulkheads over magazines 2in (5cm), flightdeck 1in (2.5cm).
Aircraft: 76.
Armament: 8 x 5in (8 x 1).
Complement: 1,788.

History: *Ranger* was the first US Navy aircraft carrier to be designed as such from the outset, although her designers were constrained by the need to comply with the limitations of the Washington Naval Treaty. She was laid down in 1931 and launched in 1933, and her initial air group comprised 36 fighters, 36 bombers and 4 utility aircraft. It was originally intended that she should not have an island and to this end she had three hinged funnels on the starboard side aft; in the event she was given an island, but the hinged funnels were retained. Her original armament consisted of eight 5in (127mm) AA guns, although these were all removed in the war and replaced by 47 20mm weapons, scarcely a proper outfit for an operational carrier, but adequate for her later role as a training carrier.

Ranger was not a great success. Her seakeeping was relatively poor, heavy seas restricting flying to a significant degree, while she was not fast enough for

Yorktown

UNITED STATES OF AMERICA

Fleet carrier
Completed: 1937-41.
Number in class: 3.
Displacement: 19,875 tons standard; 25,484 tons full load.
Dimensions: Length 824.8ft (251.4m); beam 109.5ft (33.4m); draught 26.0ft (7.9m).
Propulsion: 4 shafts; Parsons turbines; 9 boilers; 120,000shp; 32.5kt.
Armour: 2.5-4in (cm) belt, 1.5in (cm) flightdeck.
Aircraft: 96.
Armament: 8 x 5in (127mm) (8 x 1); 16 x 1.1in (28mm) (4 x 4); 24 x 0.5in (12.7mm) (24 x 1).
Complement: 2,175

History: There were three ships in the Yorktown-class, the best of the US Navy's pre-war carrier designs: *Yorktown* commissioned in 1937, followed by *Enterprise* in 1938, and *Hornet* in 1941. It had been realised that *Ranger* was too small, so the new design was intended to operate virtually the same number of aircraft, but on a hull which was half as large again, in order to give better sea-keeping, a 4kt increase in speed and better protection.

The flightdeck was unarmoured and part of the superstructure rather than integral with the hull, with three centreline lifts. There were three catapults, two on the flightdeck and one athwartships on the hangar deck. One curious feature was that the ship was designed to operate almost as fast astern as ahead and there were sets of arrester wires at both ends of the flightdeck, the idea being that aircraft could land from either direction; although tested in peacetime this was never used operationally. Unlike *Ranger*, it was planned

Above: *Ranger* (CV-4) shows the open bow, typical of US carriers of the 1930s/40s

major fleet operations in the Pacific. During World War II she took part in Operation Torch, the Allied landings on North Africa, and in one raid against Norway in 1943. Thereafter, *Ranger* was used for training duties and was sold for scrap in 1947.

Above: *Hornet* returning from the Doolittle raid, April 1942

from the start to have an island, which included an integral funnel. Again in comparison with *Ranger*, the armour belt and deck were almost twice as thick and the number of watertight compartments greatly increased.

Following construction of *Yorktown* and *Enterprise*, the next carrier was constrained by the Washington Naval Treaty tonnage limits, so the next carrier, *Wasp* (see next entry) was smaller. Then, in 1938, when another carrier was required quickly, it was decided to save time by returning to the 5-year old *Yorktown* design to produce *Hornet*, although she did have a wider flightdeck.

The wooden flightdeck were a distinct liability against attack by aircraft and *kamikaze*, but all three ships had an exceptionally tight turning circle, which often enabled them to avoid attacks.

In the war *Hornet*, escorted by *Enterprise*, carried the B-25 bombers for the famed Doolittle raid. *Yorktown* was damaged at the Battle of the Coral Sea, but was repaired and able to take part in the Battle of Midway where she was sunk by Japanese submarine *I-168* (7 June 1942). *Hornet* was so heavily damaged during the Battle of Santa Cruz that she had to be abandoned, and was later sunk by the Japanese (27 October 1942). *Enterprise* took part in most of the major actions in the Pacific and survived the war, but was scrapped in 1958.

Wasp

UNITED STATES OF AMERICA

Fleet carrier
Completed: 1940.
Number in class: 1.
Displacement: 14,700 tons standard; 18,450 tons full load.
Dimensions: Length 720.0ft 219.5(m); beam 100.0ft (30.5m); draught 23.3ft (7.1m).
Propulsion: 2 shafts; Parsons turbines; 6 boilers; 70,000shp; 29.5kt.
Armour: 0.625in (1.6cm) belt, 1.25in (3.2cm) deck.
Aircraft: 76.
Armament: 8 x 5in (127mm) (8 x 1); 16 x 1.1in (28mm); 24 x 0.5in (12.7mm) (24 x 1).
Complement: 2,167.

History: *Wasp* was the last of the pre-war carriers to be limited by the Washington Treaty, the requirement being to produce the same capabilities as the Yorktown-class on a 14,500ton hull. The result was a modified and improved version of *Ranger*, which included an asymmetric hull, which was intended to offset the weight of the island and funnel. One of the main requirements was to increase the rate of launch of aircraft and the possibility of a hangar-deck flying-off platform, as in the British *Furious* and the Japanese *Akagi* and *Kaga* (qqv) was examined but rejected, although two hangar-level transverse catapults were installed, but were quickly removed. By mid-1942 *Wasp's* air group comprised 27 fighters, 37 bombers and 12 torpedo-bombers, a total of 76 aircraft.

On 15 September 1942, during operations off Guadalcanal, *Wasp* was hit by three "Long Lance" torpedoes launched by the Japanese submarine *I-19*. The crew was forced to abandon the crippled carrier, which was then finished off by torpedoes from the US destroyer, *Lansdowne*.

Above:* *Wasp* in 1942, shortly before being torpedoed by Japanese submarine *I-19

***Below:* Limited by the Washington Treaty, *Wasp*'s design had major weaknesses**

Essex

UNITED STATES OF AMERICA

Fleet carrier
Specifications for Group 1
Completed: 1942-50
Number in class: Group 1 - 5, Group 2 - 18; Group 3 - 1.
Displacement: 27,208 tons standard; 34,881 tons full load.
Dimensions: Length 872.0ft (265.0m); beam 147.5ft (45.0m); draught 27.5ft (8.4m).
Propulsion: 4 shafts; Westinghouse turbines; 8 boilers; 150,000shp; 32.7kt; 15,000nm at 15kt.
Belt: Belt 2.5-4in (6.4-10.2cm); hangar deck 2.5in (6.4cm), armour deck over belt 1.5in (3.8cm).
Aircraft: 91.
Armament: 12 x 5in (127mm) (4 x 2, 4 x 1); 32 x 40mm (8 x 4), 46 x 20mm (46 x 1).
Complement: 2,682.

History: These splendid ships formed the core of the US Navy's Fast Carrier Task Force which played a major part in the defeat of the Japanese in the Pacific War. The design was essentially an improved and enlarged Yorktown, unconstrained by the Washington Naval Treaty restrictions, and was built in three groups: Group 1 - 5 ships, Group 2 - 18 ships, Group 3 - 1 ship. The original intention was to build a total of 32, but six were cancelled in March 1945 and two were later cancelled on the slips. Rigid compliance with standardisation led to remarkably fast building time: *Essex*, for example, was laid down in April 1941, launched in July 1942 and commissioned in December 1942, a total of 20 months. As a comparison, the similar sized British *Implacable,* was laid down in February 1939, launched in December 1942 and completed in August 1944.

The carriers were of conventional design, with a long, unobstructed flightdeck, an open bow and a large superstructure to starboard. This incorporated the funnel, but due to the use of high-pressure boilers, this was

very much smaller than in previous carriers. They had much better protection than previous US carriers, including an additional armoured deck at the hangar deck level, but still did not have an armoured flightdeck, as in the British carriers. The original plan was to have three catapults, two forward on the flightdeck and one below on the hangar, athwartships. One of the two flightdeck catapults was deleted at the design stage to save weight, but the hangar-deck catapult proved of no value and was deleted in service and all carriers eventually had two flightdeck catapults. There were three large lifts, one of them a large deck-edge lift, as introduced in *Wasp* (CV 7), which proved extremely useful and popular. They had a heavy defensive armament which was increased in 1944-45 in order to deal with the threat from Japanese *kamikaze* attacks.

The wartime air group varied, but typically consisted of 36 fighters, 36 dive-bombers and 18 torpedo bombers, a total of 90. They gave extremely valuable war service, but only two suffered major damage, *Franklin* (CV 13) and *Dunker Hill* (CV17). At the end of the war a planned further five (CV 50-55) were cancelled, while work on three still under construction was halted, of which, *Reprisal* (CV 35) and *Iwo Jima* (CV 46) were cancelled and broken up.

In the post-war period the Essex-class carriers underwent a complicated series of modifications and rebuilds, almost all of them aimed at trying to keep pace with the introduction of ever larger and heavier jet aircraft. The third of the incomplete carriers, *Oriskany* (CV 34), underwent a major redesign to enable her to handle the first generation of jet aircraft and was completed in 1950. Officially designated SCB-27A, this involved a strengthened flightdeck, two powerful catapults, 23 arrester wires, a reduced armament, blisters on the hull and numerous internal changes. Eight other carriers, then in reserve, were brought up to this new standard and returned to service.

Meanwhile, more major conversions were being planned. *Antietam* (CV 36) tested the newly-invented angled deck and then several more were to converted attack carriers, which included not only the angled deck but also the plating in of the bow (the so-called "hurricane bow") and the removal of virtually all defensive armament. As the new Forrestal-class carriers came into service the Essex-class were re-roled as helicopter carriers (LPH) and anti-submarine carriers (CVS). They were progressively stricken and scrapped, the last to remain in service being *Lexington* (CV 16), which was employed as a training carrier until December 1991.

***Left:* Essex-class carrier, *Intrepid*, shortly after completion in August 1943**

Independence

UNITED STATES OF AMERICA

Light carrier
Completed: 1943.
Number in class: 9.
Displacement: 10,662 tons standard; 14,751 tons full load.
Dimensions: Length 623.0ft (189.9m); beam 109.2ft (21.5m); draught 24.3ft (7.4m).
Propulsion: 4 shafts, General Electric turbines, 4 boilers, 100,000shp, 31kt, 13,000nm at 15kt.
Aircraft: 30.
Armament: 24 x 40mm (2 x 4, 8 x 2), 22 x 20mm (22 x 1).
Complement: 1,569 (including air group).

History: When it appeared that the first of the Essex-class fleet carriers would not reach the fleet before 1944 President Roosevelt issued an order that a number of Cleveland-class light cruisers, then under construction, were to be converted on the ways into light carriers. The first of these was USS *Amsterdam* (CL59) which was completed as first-of-class carrier, USS

Right: **An American Pacific Fleet cruiser pours streams of water into the stricken light carrier USS *Princeton,* hit by Japanese bombs in October 1944. The aircraft on the forward flightdeck had been in action earlier in the day, downing 37 enemy aircraft of several hundred that had attacked the US carrier group. *Princeton* sank, but most of the crew survived**

Below: Belleau Wood **served in the US Navy 1943-1953 then went to France**

Independence (CVL22), which was actually commissioned on 1 January 1943, the day after *Essex*, (as the latter programme had been considerably speeded up) followed by the remaining eight between February and December 1943.

The original hull was retained, but with bulges to maintain stability, with an unarmoured, wooden flightdeck and open-ended hangar superimposed. There was a small island to starboard, forward of two pairs of boiler uptakes. Each of these new light carriers displaced about one-half that of an Essex but its airgroup was about one-third the size, comprising 30 aircraft (9 bombers, 12 fighters, 9 torpedo-bombers). They were generally considered to have been successful, if very cramped and with restricted maintenance facilities.

All were very active in the Pacific campaign, but only one, *Princeton* (CVL23), was lost, being sunk by Japanese aircraft during the Battle of Leyte Gulf (October 1944).

After the war the US Navy retained three, two of which were converted and had short careers as ASW carriers. Three went abroad: *Langley* and *Belleau Wood* to France in 1951 and 1953, respectively, and *Cabot* to Spain in 1967. The remaining four were scrapped between 1951 and 1970.

Midway

UNITED STATES OF AMERICA

Fleet carriers
Completed: 1945-47.
Number in class: 3.
Displacement: 47,387 tons standard; 59,901 tons full load.
Dimensions: Length 968.0ft (295.0m); beam 136.0ft (41.5m); draught 34.5ft (10.5m).
Propulsion: 4 shafts, Westinghouse turbines, 12 boilers, 212,000shp, 33kt, 15,000nm at 15kt.
Armour: Belt 7.6in (19.3cm), flightdeck 3.5in (8.9cm), hangar deck 2in (5.1cm), armour deck over belt 2in (5.1cm) bulkheads 6.3in (16cm).
Aircraft: 137.
Armament: 18 x 5in (127mm) (18 x 1), 84 x 40mm (21 x 4), 68 x 20mm (34 x 2).
Complement: 4,104.

History: The last of the US Navy's war-built carriers, these three ships were undoubtedly the most effective carriers in any navy at the time they were completed. At one time it was planned there would be six in the class, but only three were completed: *Midway* (CVB 41 - September 1945), *Franklin D Roosevelt* (CVB-42 - October 1945) and *Coral Sea* (CVB 43 - October 1947). As built, they had an axial flightdeck with two centre-line lifts and a third amidships on the port side, and could operate a huge air group, that authorised in 1945 consisting of 73 fighters and 64 bombers. They also proved of great significance in the early postwar years since they could operate the navy's first nuclear bomber, the AJ-1 Savage, with ease, and even demonstrated a capability to handle and launch a nuclear-armed twin-engined Neptune bomber, even thought it did not have folding wings.

Despite this, the original design was quickly overtaken by developments in jet aircraft, which led to a major modernisation programme for all three ships in the 1950s, in which an 8deg angled deck was installed with a side lift at its forward end. The after centreline lift would have seriously impeded landing operations, so this was moved to the starboard side, aft of the island. Two of the latest, C-11 steam catapults were also fitted to enable the ships to operate the latest and heaviest jet

***Below:* The Midway-class introduced the armoured flightdeck to US Navy service**

***Above: Midway* (CV-41) with the fully-angled flightdeck fitted in a post-war refit**

aircraft, although these were either side of the forward, centreline lift. All three ships were also fitted with a "hurricane bow" and their defensive armament considerably reduced.

Coral Sea was the last of the three to be modernised and she incorporated yet further modifications, in what proved to be a particularly successful programme. In the first two modified ships, the port side lift had been found to impede landing operations, so this was moved well aft, which not only improved landing operations and aircraft handling, but also enabled the angled deck to be extended forwards, thus increasing the usable deck area and enabling a third steam catapult to be installed. The forward centreline lift was also removed, to be replaced by a third sidelift on the starboard side, just forward of the island. All three lifts had a 74,000lb (33,636kg) capacity.

Midway was taken in hand in the late 1960s in a 4-year $US202million refit, in which the flightdeck was completely rebuilt, increasing its area by one-third, and given new lifts of much greater (130,000lb (59,100kg) capacity, which were positioned as in *Coral Sea*. The length and cost of this refit resulted in *Franklin D Roosevelt* being given a much less ambitious ($US46million) modernisation, which resulted in only a few years more service, as she was stricken in 1977.

Coral Sea was retained in service until 1990, while *Midway* served two years more.

Forrestal

UNITED STATES OF AMERICA

Super-carrier (conventionally-powered)
Specifications for Independence (CV 62) after SLEP
Completed: 1952-55.
Number in class: 4.
Displacement: 60,000 tons standard; 80,643 tons full load.
Dimensions: Length ft (326.1m); beam ft (82.3m); draught ft (11.3m).
Propulsion: Four shafts; Westinghouse geared turbines; 8 boilers; 280,000shp; 33kt; 8,000nm at 20kt.
Aircraft: Typical air group in early 1980s. 25 F4J Phantom; 24 A-7E Corsair II; 10 A-6E Intruder; 4 KA-6D Intruder (tanker); 4 E-2C Hawkeye; 4 EA-6B Prowler; 10 S-3A Viking; 6 SH-3H Sea King. Total - 87 aircraft.
Armament: 3 x Mk 29 launchers for Sea Sparrow SAMs; 3 x 20mm Mk15 Gatling CIWS.
Complement: 5,287.

History: The first US Navy post-war carrier design was for the *United States*, which would have displaced 83,249 tons (full load). This ill-fated ship was cancelled in April 1949, only 6 days after being laid down, as a result of intense political pressure from the newly independent US Air Force, which demanded exclusive control of the national nuclear deterrent force. This ship would have had a flush deck, together with a retractable bridge, and two waist catapults angled out on sponsons in addition to the usual pair of catapults forward. After intense efforts the Navy managed to reinstate its carrier programme, but with a slightly smaller design which was supposedly "multi-mission" although its overall size and aircraft-handling arrangements were still dictated by the requirement to operate the A-3 Skywarrior strategic nuclear bomber, which weighed 78,000lb (35,380kg). The outcome was the world's first "super-carrier."

The advent of the angled deck, which was tested by the US Navy in 1952 on the Essex-class carrier, *Antietam*, led to the modification of the first-of-class *Forrestal* while building. The result was a configuration which has been

***Below: Independence* at sea; these carriers have given the US Navy superb service**

***Above:* First super-carrier, *Forrestal*, with most of her airwing on the flightdeck**

followed with only minor modifications by all subsequent US aircraft carriers: a massive flight deck with considerable overhang, and a small island incorporating the funnel to starboard, and a large, uninterrupted hangar which can accommodate more than half the ship's air group.

There were four ships: *Forrestal* (CV 59), *Saratoga* (CV 60), *Ranger* (CV 61) and *Independence* (CV 62), which were completed in 1955, 1956, 1957 and 1959, respectively. As completed, the Forrestal-class was armed with eight 5in (127mm) single gun mountings, but these were steadily removed and by the late 1970s had been replaced by BPDMS and NATO Sea Sparrow missile launchers.

All four carriers followed were extremely active throughout the Cold War, but as the East-West confrontation wound down their careers came to an end. As of early 2001 all four carriers are in various grades of "storage." *Forrestal* (CV 59) became the US Navy's training carrier in February 1991, but was put into a major overhaul in 1992, but this was only half complete when it was decided that she was no longer required. As a result, she was stricken in September 1993; the hulk is still being stored and there are plans to turn her into a museum. *Saratoga* (CV-60) was stricken in September 1994 and is also in storage. *Ranger* (CV 61) underwent an extensive overhaul from May 1984 to June 1985, but was transferred to the reserve in 1993, where she is scheduled to remain until 2003 when she will be stricken. *Independence* (CV62) underwent a Service Life Extension Plan (SLEP), a major refit, from April 19 85 to February 1988 and then went to serve as the resident "forward based" carrier in Yokosuka, Japan, from September 1991 to September 1998, when she was placed in reserve, where she remains in 2001, still in excellent condition.

Kitty Hawk

UNITED STATES OF AMERICA

Supercarrier (conventionally-powered)
Specifications for Kitty Hawk (CV 63) in 2000
Completed: 1961-68.
Number in class: 4.
Displacement: 61,351 tons light; 81.985 tons full load
Dimensions: Length 1,068.9ft (325.8m); beam 130.0ft (39.6m); draught 40.0ft (12.2m).
Propulsion: Four shafts; Westinghouse geared steam turbines; 8 boilers; 280,000shp; 33kt.
Aircraft: Typical 2000 air wing, 70 aircraft: 11 F-14B Tomcat interceptors; 36 F/A-18C Hornet fighter-bombers; 4 EA-6B Prowler combat EW; 4 E-2C Hawkeye AEW; 7 S-3B Viking ASW; 7 SH-60F/HH-60H Seahawk helicopters; 1 C-2A Greyhound carrier on-board delivery.
Armament: 3 x Mk 29 launchers for Sea Sparrow SAMs; 3 x 20mm Mk 15 Phalanx CIWS.
Complement: 5,096.

History: These four conventionally-powered "super-carriers" are very powerful fighting units, second only to the US Navy's nuclear-powered carriers in combat capability. There are differences between the first two and second two ships, but they are usually considered together since they have common propulsion systems and flightdeck layouts. The two groups comprise: Group I - *Kitty Hawk* (CV 63) and *Constellation* (CV 64), both completed in 1961; and Group II - *America* (CV 66) and *John F Kennedy* (CV 67), completed in 1965 and 1968, respectively.

Kitty Hawk and *Constellation* were ordered as improved versions of the Forrestal-class, with increased flightdeck area and a different lift layout designed to improve aircraft-handling arrangements. On the Forrestals the port side lift was located at the forward end of the angled deck, making it unusable during landing operations, but on the Kitty Hawks it was repositioned to the after end of the overhang, where it no longer interfered with flying operations. In addition, the centre of the three lifts on the starboard side was repositioned ahead of the island, enabling two lifts to serve the forward catapults. A further improvement to the lifts themselves was that an additional angled section at

***Below: Constellation*, completed in 1961, will be transferred to the reserve in 2003**

***Above: Kitty Hawk* displays greater airpower than exists in most national air forces**

the forward end of the platform enabled them to accommodate longer aircraft. This flightdeck and lift arrangement was so successful that it was then used on all subsequent US "supercarriers."

The third ship of the class, *America* (CV 66), was laid down four years after *Constellation* and incorporated further improvements, the most obvious, visually, being a narrower funnel canted outwards, to carry exhaust fumes clear of the flightdeck. She was also fitted with a bow anchor in anticipation of an SQS-23 sonar dome being installed at the foot of the stem (the sonar was never fitted). It was planned by the Navy that the fourth carrier, due to be laid down in FY64, should be nuclear-powered, but Congress, shaken by the expense of the first nuclear carrier, *Enterprise*, flatly refused to fund it and the ship was built as a conventionally powered carrier to a modified Kitty Hawk design.

It was planned to modernize all four under the 28-month SLEP programme, a 28-month work programme intended to extend each ship's life by some 10-15 years, which included fitting more powerful catapults, upgrading the aircraft facilities, modernising all electronics, and extensive refurbishment of the hull, propulsion system and electrics. In the event, only two received the full SLEP, *Kitty Hawk* (1988-91) and *Constellation* (1990-93), while the third, *John F Kennedy*, received a shorter, less comprehensive, 14-month "Complex Overhaul." The fourth, *America*, was not updated at all and was stricken in August 1996.

In 2001 *Kitty Hawk*, the oldest active ship in the USN, is in the Pacific Fleet, having been homeported at Yokosuka, Japan since 1998; she is due to be deactivated in 2008. *Constellation*, serving with the Atlantic Fleet, will deactivate in 2003, transferring to the "mobilization reserve."

Enterprise

UNITED STATES OF AMERICA

Super-carrier (nuclear-powered)
Completed: 1961.
Number in class: 1.
Displacement: 73,858 tons light; 92,325 tons full load.
Dimensions: Length 1,088.9ft (331.6m); beam 257.2ft (78.4m); draught 39.0ft (11.9m).
Propulsion: Four shafts; 8 Westinghouse A2W nuclear reactors; 4 sets Westinghouse geared steam turbines; 280,000shp; 33.6kt.
Aircraft: Typical 2000 air wing, 70 aircraft: 11 F-14B Tomcat interceptors; 36 F/A-18C Hornet fighter-bombers; 4 EA-6B Prowler combat EW; 4 E-2C Hawkeye AEW; 7 S-3B Viking ASW; 7 SH-60F/HH-60H Seahawk helicopters; 1 C-2A Greyhound carrier on-board delivery.
Armament: 3 x Mk 29 launchers for Sea Sparrow SAMs; 2 RAM Mk 31 SAM systems; 3 x 20mm Mk 15 Phalanx CIWS.
Complement: 5,828.

History: Authorized in the FY58 programme, *Enterprise* (CVN 65) was laid down in February 1958 and completed in the remarkably short time of 3 years 9 months. She cost nearly twice as much to build as her oil-fuelled contemporaries of the Kitty Hawk-class, but convincing arguments were advanced to justify nuclear propulsion, including reduced life-cycle costs due to infrequent refuellings, and the ability to conduct lengthy transits and continuous operations in high threat areas at a high sustained speed. Also, the elimination of ship's bunkers made possible a 50 percent increase in aviation fuel. The technology of the time meant that no less than eight Westinghouse A2W nuclear reactors were required to provide the power needed to achieve a top speed of 33kt, although she actually achieved just over 35kt on trials.

In size and layout *Enterprise* was similar to the Kitty Hawk-class, but

Above: *Enterprise* with a conventional island after the planar arrays were removed

internally the entire centre section of the ship below hangar deck level was taken up with machinery, while she had four rudders, compared to two in all other "super-carriers." As built, *Enterprise* had a unique box-shaped island, with four huge planar arrays (known as "billboards") for the electronically scanned SPS 32/33 radars, but this was removed and replaced by a more conventional island in a subsequent refit.

Enterprise has been regularly refitted and updated, including: January 1979-March 1982, January 1991-July 1995 (which included refuelling) and, most recently, August-December 1999. *Enterprise* normally operated in the Atlantic or Middle Eastern waters and is expected to remain in service until 2013.

Below: *Enterprise* in her original form with square-sided "bill-board" radar arrays

Nimitz

UNITED STATES OF AMERICA

Super-carrier (nuclear-powered)
Specifications for *Ronald Reagan* (CVN 76)
Completed: 1984-2000.
Number in class: 9.
Displacement: 77,607 tons light; 98,235 tons full load.
Dimensions: Length 1,091.9ft (332.8m); beam 256.9ft (78.3m); draught 39.0ft (11.9m).
Propulsion: Four shafts; 2 General Electric A1G nuclear pressurized-water reactors; 4 sets geared steam turbines; 280,000shp; 31kt.
Aircraft: Typical 2000 air wing, 70 aircraft: 11 F-14B Tomcat interceptors; 36 F/A-18C Hornet fighter-bombers; 4 EA-6B Prowler combat EW; 4 E-2C Hawkeye AEW; 7 S-3B Viking ASW; 7 SH-60F/HH-60H Seahawk helicopters; 1 C-2A Greyhound carrier on-board delivery.
Armament: 3 x Mk 29 launchers for Sea Sparrow SAMs; 2 RAM Mk 31 SAM systems; 3 x 20mm Mk 15 Phalanx CIWS.
Complement: 5,621.

History: These nine nuclear-powered "super-carriers" are the mightiest warships ever built, and, together with *Enterprise* and the conventionally-powered Kitty Hawk-class, each one deploys a 70-strong airwing, which is far ahead in modernity, performance and capability of almost any national air force. The Nimitz-class carriers belong to two sub-groups, the first comprising three ships: *Nimitz* (CVAN 68),

Above: Stennis' prefabricated island is lowered into position during construction

Below: Washington (CVN-73); such huge carriers accommodate over 6,000 people

Dwight D Eisenhower (CVAN 69), and *Carl Vinson* (CVN 70), which were completed in 1975, 1977 and 1982, respectively. The second group comprises the remaining six, consisting of *Abraham Lincoln* (CVN 72), *George Washington* (CVN 73), *John C Stennis* (CVN 74), *Harry S Truman* (CVN 75) and *Ronald Reagan* (CVN 76), which were completed in 1986, 1989, 1992, 1995, 1998 and 2002.

The Nimitz-class was intended to replace the Midway-class and it was planned to use the same basic hull design as *Enterprise* (CVN 65) while the flightdeck layout, torpedo protection and electronic systems were virtually identical to those of *Kennedy* (CV 67). There had, however, been great advances in nuclear technology which meant that just two nuclear reactors could produce virtually the same power as the eight in *Enterprise*. In addition, the nuclear cores would only need to be replaced about every 13-15 years; ie, three times during the projected life span of the ships The two new reactors also required much less volume enabling the insides of the new ships to be greatly improved. The propulsion machinery is divided into two separate units, with the magazines between and forward of them, while there is a 20 percent increase in volume available for aviation fuel, munitions and general stores.

These carriers are claimed to be able to absorb three times the damage inflicted on the Essex-class carriers in 1944-45. The hull and decks are constructed of high-tensile steel, and there are numerous longitudinal as well as 23 transverse

bulkheads, and 10 firewall bulkheads, creating more than 2,000 internal compartments. In addition, 0.25in (65mm) thick Kevlar armoured plate has been installed to cover vital spaces. Passive protection is not all, however, and thirty damage-control teams are available at all times, while a 15deg list can be corrected within 20 minutes.

The second group (ie, *Roosevelt* (CVN 71) onwards) incorporates numerous improvements, including increased passive protection using Kevlar armour over the vital compartments and better hull protection.

When built, it was anticipated that each carrier would have a useful life of 50 years. This looks likely to be achieved, although it has been announced that *Eisenhower* is to be retired in 2017, ie after only 40 years).

Future plans revolve around the "CVN 77-class" which, according to plans so far announced, will be very similar in size, general layout and offensive capability to the Nimitz-class. It is, however, intended to fit new and much more efficient propulsion systems, probably new nuclear reactors and electric drive, together with the latest electronic and electrical systems. There will also be great efforts to lower the crew number from its present 5,600-odd to about 5,100.

Below: *Stennis'* empty flightdeck gives a good idea of the size of these huge ships

Battleships

The era of the great steel battleships lasted from the 1860s to the 1940s and during that time they epitomised naval power, being powerful in appearance and armed with guns which could throw huge shells over great distances. In the Victorian era battleships became increasingly complicated and grew in size as designers sought to mount an increasing number of guns of ever larger calibres. But from the 1880s onwards naval staffs and architects lost their way and the ships became cluttered with a wide variety of weapons, as a study of the armament of the British King Edward VII-class (see page 140) will show. Then came the era of the dreadnought, the "all big-gun battleship" which made every existing capital ship out-of-date, to such an extent that all battleships were immediately categorised as "pre-dreadnoughts" (and by definition obsolete) or "dreadnought" (and, thus, modern and up-to-date).

The first major engagement between battlefleets came at the Battle of Tsushima (25 May 1905) where the Japanese decisively defeated the Russians. In European waters only the German Navy posed a realistic threat to the British battlefleet and from the outbreak of World War I both sides actively sought a clash which would decide the issue. Unfortunately, when it came – at the Battle of Jutland (31 May 1916) – the issue was not decided as definitively as both sides wanted, although it was an undoubted strategic victory for the British.

After the war, the Washington and London Naval Agreements centred upon controlling the battleship fleets and their weapons, as described in the general introduction. This did not mean that there was no research – far from it – but construction was banned. Then when the agreements were abrogated, the late 1930s saw the greatest battleships being built: Bismarck-class in Germany, King George V-class in the UK, and the South Dakota- and Iowa-classes in the USA. Each of these was splendid in its own way, but the mightiest of them all were the two ships of the Japanese Yamato-class, with a displacement of just under 70,000 tons and an armament of nine18.1in (460mm) guns. The world has seen nothing like them before or since, but they were sunk by swarms of little, two-man, carrier-borne aircraft of the US Navy and the battleship era was truly at an end.

All but a few were phased-out in the decade following the end of World War II, although the British *Vanguard* and the French *Richelieu* and *Jean Bart* were completed and saw a few years of service. The greatest survivors of the lot, however, was the US Navy's Iowa-class which endured until the 1990s, albeit their primary role became shore-bombardment.

***Right:* Iowa-class battleship in the late 1980s armed with Tomahawk cruise missiles**

Rivadavia

ARGENTINA

Battleship (dreadnought)
Completed: 1914-15.
Number in class: 2.
Displacement: 28,000 tons standard; 31,000 tons full load.
Dimensions: Length 585.0ft (178.3m); beam 95.0ft (29.0m); draught 28.0ft (8.5m).
Propulsion: 3 shafts; Curtis steam turbines; 18 boilers; 45,000shp; 23kt; 7,000nm at 15kt
Armour: Belt 11-4in (280-100mm); decks 1.5in + 3in (38mm + 75mm); barbettes 12.0in (305mm); turrets 12-3in (305-75mm); conning tower 12.0in (305mm).
Armament: 12 x 12in (305mm) (6 x 2); 12 x 6in (152mm); 4 x 3in (76mm) AA; 4 x 40mm AA; 2 x 21in (533mm) TT.
Complement: 1,215.

History: These two ships, *Rivadavia* completed in 1914 and *Moreno* completed in 1915, were ordered in response to the two Minas Gerais-class battleships then being built in Britain for the Brazilian Navy. The design included a variety of influences, resulting from the way in which the orders were placed. An Argentine office was set up in London in 1908 which issued a set of rather broad requirements to a number of interested shipbuilders, fifteen of whom responded. The Argentine design office then selected the best features from each design and issued revised requirements, which caused considerable umbrage among the companies concerned, many of whom felt that commercial confidence had been breached. The discontent was increased when the contract was awarded to a US company, Fore River Shipbuilding at Quincy, Massachusetts, rather than to a European company as had been expected.

Radetzky

AUSTRIA-HUNGARY

Battleship (pre-dreadnought)
Completed: 1910-11.
Number in class: 3.
Displacement: 14,508 tons standard; 15,847 tons full load.
Dimensions: Length 455.3ft (138.8m); beam 80 .7ft (24.6m); draught 26.8ft (8.1m).
Propulsion: 2 shafts; vertical triple expansion; 12 boilers; 19,800ihp; 20.5kt; 4,000nm at 10kt.
Armour: Belt 9.0-4.0in (230-100mm); decks 2.0in (48mm); casemates 4.8in (120mm); turrets 9.8-2.3in (250-60mm); conning tower 9.8-4.3in (250-100mm).
Armament: 4 x 12in (305mm) (2 x 2); 8 x 9.4in (240mm) (4 x 2); 20 x 3.9in (100mm); 5 x 47mm; 4 x 17.7in (450mm) TT.
Complement: 890.

History: Austria-Hungary was essentially interested in exercising naval power in the Mediterranean in general and the Adriatic in particular. When war came in 1914, however, the navy found itself bottled up in the Adriatic and despite several large-scale sorties by the fleet it exercised little influence on events. Nevertheless, the quality of the ships was high.

The four Radetzky-class battleships were part of a major fleet expansion programme, with *Erzherzog Franz Ferdinand* completed in 1910, and *Radetzky* and *Zrinyi* in 1911. They were somewhat smaller than battleships in other navies, but mounted a comparatively heavy main armament, which was of typical "pre-dreadnought" mixed calibre concept, although an all-big-gun "dreadnought" layout had been considered at the design stage. The largest

Above: **Argentine battleship *Moreno* with cage foremast after her 1924-25 refit**

Main armament was similar to that mounted in recent British battleships, comprising twelve 12in (305mm) guns in six twin turrets, two each fore and aft, and two wing turrets which were capable (at least in theory) of firing through an arc of 180deg on the side they were located and 100deg on the opposite side. Secondary armament was similar to that in German ships, with twelve 6in (152mm) guns. Propulsion was on the lines of the Italian *Dante Alighieri*, with boiler rooms fore and aft of the turbine room, which was located amidships. Protection was, generally, on American lines, as was the cage foremast.

Both ships were modernised in the USA in 1924-25 when they were converted to oil-burning, a new fire-control system was added, the pole mainmast was converted to a tripod and 3in (76mm) AA guns were added. The ships served with the Argentine Navy for over 40 years, being scrapped in 1956.

Above: **Austro-Hungarian Radetzky-class battleship, *Erzherzog Franz Ferdinand***

calibre weapons were four 12.0in (305mm) in two twin, centreline turrets, with eight 9.4in (240mm) in four twin wing turrets, two either side of the bridge superstructure and two abreast the main mast. A further twenty 3.9in (100mm) guns were disposed in casemates. These ships suffered from structural weakness, since the main guns were really too powerful for the size of ship, resulting in some deformation of the hull at about one-third of its length.

The three ships took part in all the wartime operations of the Austria-Hungarian fleet, although after May 1915 this mostly involved an inactive "fleet-in-being" existence in Pola naval base. After the war all three were ceded to Italy and they were scrapped in the early 1920s.

Tegetthoff

AUSTRIA-HUNGARY

Battleship (dreadnought)
Completed: 1912-15.
Number in class: 4.
Displacement: 20,013 tons standard; 21,595 tons full load.
Dimensions: Length 499.3ft (152.2m); beam 89.7ft (27.3m); draught 29.0ft (8.9m).
Propulsion: 4 shafts; Parsons geared turbines; 12 boilers; 27,000shp; 20.3kt; 4,200nm at 10kt.
Armour: Belt 11.0-6.0in (280-150mm); decks 1.8-1.3in(48-30mm); main turrets 11.0-2.3in (280-60mm); casemates 4.8in (180mm); conning tower 11-2.3in (280-60mm).
Armament: 12 x 12.0in (305mm) (4 x 3); 12 x 5.9in (150mm); 18 x 2.6in (66mm); 4 x 21in (533mm) TT.
Complement: 1,087.

History: The only "Dreadnought" battleships actually built for the Austro-Hungarian Navy, four ships were completed: *Viribus Unitis* (1912), *Tegethoff* (1913), *Prinz Eugen* (1914), and *Szent Istvan* (1915). They were built in reply to the Italian Navy's *Dante Aligheri*, which was known to be under construction, armed with four triple 12in (305mm) turrets, but despite many political and economic difficulties the Austro-Hungarian navy actually got their ships into service first. The four *Tegetthoff*s were a neat and compact design, their twelve 12in (305mm) guns making them very powerful for their size. The last of the four, *Szent Istvan*, had some differences from the other three, mainly in the propulsion system, with AEG-Curtis turbines driving two shafts (instead of four in the others), which resulted in a slightly greater

Minas Gerais

BRAZIL

Battleships (dreadnought)
Completed: 1910.
Number in class: 2.
Displacement: 19,281 tons standard; 21,200 tons full load.
Dimensions: Length 543.0ft (165.5m); beam 83.0ft (25.3m); draught 28.0ft (8.5m).
Propulsion: 2 shafts; Vickers vertical triple expansion; 18 boilers; 23,500shp; 21kt; 10,000nm at 10kt.
Armour: Belt 9.0in (230mm); casemate 9.0in (230mm); turrets 12-9in (302-230mm); conning tower 12.0in (305mm).
Armament: 12 x 12in (305mm) (6 x 2); 22 x 4.7in (120mm); 8 x 3pdr (37mm).
Complement: 900.

History: Few ships have had as dramatic an impact as *Minas Gerais* and *São Paolo*. Built in Britain, they were not only the first dreadnoughts to be ordered by a South American navy, but at the time they were commissioned their main armament of twelve 12in (305mm) guns and the comprehensive armoured protection of Krupp steel made them the most powerful battleships in the world. In South America they gave rise to a round of orders for new ships by Argentina (Rivadavia-class) and Chile (Almirante Latorre-class), but they also had an effect far outside the southern hemisphere, since it was said in Europe that they were far too powerful for Brazil's needs and must, therefore, have been ordered for an unknown third party. The British press speculated that they would be passed on to Germany, Japan or the United States, while the German press thought that they were really intended for the British Royal Navy. None of these rumours was true, but their arrival in South American waters led the US Navy to seek increased cooperation with Brazil. A

***Above:* The Tegethoffs were the only true dreadnoughts built for Austro-Hungary**

full load displacement.

The first three ships took part in some operations in late 1914/early 1915, and all four started out to conduct in a major attack on the Allies' Otranto anti-submarine barrage in June 1918. The operation was, however, called-off when *Szent Istvan* was torpedoed and sunk by torpedoes from the Italian motor-torpedo-boat, *MAS 15*. *Viribus Unitis* was handed over to the newly independent Yugoslav National Council in late October 1918, but, unaware of this, two Italians using a "human torpedo" attacked and sank it in Pola harbour on 1 November. *Prinz Eugen* was ceded to France who used it as a target (sunk 28 June 1922), while *Tegethoff* was ceded to Italy and scrapped in 1924.

***Above:* On completion, *São Paulo* was the world's most powerful battleship**

planned third ship, which would have been even more powerful, was ordered and laid down, but for political reasons the order was cancelled when the ship was half complete and the ship was then bought by Turkey, only to be requisitioned for war service by the British as HMS *Agincourt*.

Brazil declared war on Germany on 24 October 1917 and decided to send the two battleships to join the British Grand Fleet in Scapa Flow but the repairs and modifications necessary to bring them up to the required standard took so long that the war was over before they were operational again. *Minas Gerais* underwent a major refit in 1934-37, with the boiler uptakes merged into a single, broad funnel, extra AA guns and other improvements. A similar refit was planned for *São Paolo*, but it was then decided that she was in such a poor state that it was not economically viable. *São Paolo* was stricken in 1951 and *Minas Gerais* in 1954.

Capitan Prat

CHILE

Battleship (pre-dreadnought)
Completed: 1890.
Number in class: 1.
Displacement: 6,901 tons.
Dimensions: Length 328.0ft (100.0m); beam 60.7ft (18.5m); draught 22.8ft (7.0m).
Propulsion: 2 shafts; horizontal triple-expansion; 5 boilers; 12,000ihp; 18.3kt.
Armour: Belt 11.8-7.8in (300-200mm); end 5.9-3.9in (150-100mm); citadel 3.1in (8mm); barbettes 10.8-8.0in (274-203mm); hoods 2.0in (51mm); conning tower 10.5in (267mm).
Armament: 4 x 9.4in (239mm) (4 x 1); 8 x 4.7in (119mm); 6 x 6pdr; 4 x 3pdr; 10 x 1pdr; 4 x 18in 457mm) TT.
Complement: 480.

History: Chile has always had a strong interest in naval power, which has played a key role in confrontations with its neighbours, Argentina and Peru, and in its control of its own very long coastline and off-shore territories. The war with Peru, for example, resulted in the capture of the armoured turret ship, *Huascar*, on 8 October 1879 (which is still maintained as a museum). The battleship, *Capitan Prat*, was built in France and joined the Chilean fleet in 1891. A steel-hulled ship, she had a ram bow, two masts with fighting tops, and two funnels, and was powered by two horizontal triple-expansion engines, giving her a speed of 18.3kt. Armament consisted of four 9.4in (239mm) guns in single turrets in a French-style "lozenge" layout; ie, one forward, one aft, and one on each beam, amidships. The four fixed torpedo tubes were similarly located: one

Almirante Latorre

CHILE

Battleship (dreadnought)
Completed: 1915.
Number in class: 1.
Displacement: 28,500 tons standard; 32,300 tons full load.
Dimensions: Length 661.0ft (201.5m); beam 103.0ft (31.4m); draught 30.0ft (8.8m).
Propulsion: 4 shafts; Brown-Curtis (HP)/Parsons (LP) geared steam turbines; 21 boilers; 37,000shp; 22.5kt, 4,400nm at 10kt.
Armour: Belt 9.0-4.0in (230-100mm); decks 4.0-1.0in (100-25mm); barbettes 10.0-4.0in (250-100mm); turrets 10.5-9.0in (267-229mm); conning tower 11.0in (280mm).
Armament: 10 x 14.0in (356mm) (5 x 2); 14 x 6.0in (152mm); 4 x 4.0in (102mm) AA; 2 x 40mm AA; 4 x 21.0in (533mm) TT.
Complement: 1,176.

History: When news was received of the dreadnought orders being placed by Argentina and Brazil the Chilean Navy decided that it, too, must order similar ships. The result was an order to the British shipbuilder, Armstrong, for what would be the most powerful dreadnought in any navy, her ten 14in (356mm) guns outclassing even the Brazilian *Minas Gerais*'s twelve 12in (305mm) guns. The range of these new guns was limited only by visibility and the ship had particularly comprehensive armoured protection.

The Chilean Navy ordered two ships and the first was nearing completion when war broke out. As a result the first, *Almirante Latorre*, was purchased by the Royal Navy (9 September 1914) and completed in September 1915 as HMS

***Above:* Pre-dreadnought, *Capitan Prat,* was built in France for the Chilean Navy**

in the bow, one in the stern, and one on each beam. Secondary armament consisted of four twin 4.7in (119mm) turrets, located either side of each of the masts. The *Capitan Prat* was rebuilt in 1909/10, which included new boilers and raised funnels, and an increase in speed to 19.5kt. She was stricken in the mid-1930s.

***Above: Latorre* served at Jutland as HMS *Canada,* was delivered to Chile in 1920**

Canada. She served with the Grand Fleet for the remainder of the war, being at Jutland where she was neither damaged nor received casualties. She was re-sold to Chile in 1920 taking back her previous name, *Almirante Latorre*. She was refitted at Devonport Dockyard in 1929-31 and then served on until 1959, when she was scrapped.

The second ship, *Almirante Cochrane*, was purchased by the Royal Navy in 1917 and converted into one of the first aircraft carriers, HMS *Eagle*. After the war Chile wanted this ship back, but it would have been impracticable to have re-converted her to a battleship, as Chile wanted, so the project fell through.

Herluf Trolle

DENMARK

Coastal battleship
Specifications for *Peder Skram.*
Completed: 1899-1909.
Number in class: 3.
Displacement: 3,735 tons normal; 3,785 tons full load.
Dimensions: Length 286.8ft (87.4m); beam 51.5ft (15.7m); draught 16.4ft (5.0m).
Propulsion: 2 shafts; vertical triple-expansion; 2 boilers; 5,400ihp; 16kt..
Armour: Belt 7.7-6.1in (195-155mm); decks 2.5-1.8in (65-45mm); barbettes 7.3in (185mm); casemate (face) 5.5in (140mm); turret faces 7.5in (190mm); conning tower 7.5in(190mm).
Armament: 2 x 9.4in (240mm) (2 x 1); 4 x 5.9in (150mm); 10 x 75mm; 2 x 37mm; 4 x 18in (457mm) TT.
Complement: 258.

History: There are always some types of ship which do not fit neatly into any of the major categories, one of those being the "coastal battleship," a type which found particular favour in the Nordic countries over the period approximately 1870 to 1950. This was a ship of limited displacement, but armed with several large calibre weapons and with substantial armoured protection. They were intended to patrol the coastline and not required to venture far out to sea, so they were neither fast, nor did they have great range. Thus, in most respects they could be described as a mobile coast defence battery and the Royal Danish Navy produced a series of such ships, one of the earliest being *Iver Hvitfeldt*, launched in 1886.

The Herluf Trolle-class consisted of three ships: *Herluf Trolle* completed in

Océan

FRANCE

Battleship (central battery)
Completed: 1870-75.
Number in class: 3.
Displacement: 7,775 tons full load.
Dimensions: Length 287.8ft (87.7m); beam 57.5ft (17.5m); draught 29.8ft (9.1m).
Propulsion: 1shaft; horizontal-return connecting-rod compound engine; 8 boilers; 4,180ihp; 14kt.
Armour: Wrought iron. Belt 8-7in (203-178mm); battery 6.3in (160mm); barbettes 6in (152mm).
Armament: 4 x 10.8in (274mm) (4 x 1); 4 x 9.4in (239mm); 6 x 5.5in (140mm); 12 x 1pdr revolvers. (4 x 14in (356mm) TT added later).
Complement: 778.

History: Throughout the 19th century France's main naval rival was Great Britain, but in 1868, when *Océan* was launched, the French fleet was numerically smaller than the British, although it had greater homogeneity, with twenty-six armoured ships of eight types, compared to the British twenty-nine ships of twenty-one types. On the other hand, French shipbuilders still had difficulty in working with iron-framed hulls, as a result of which their ships were wooden-hulled with wrought iron armour plating.

The *Océan*-class was designed by Dupuy de Lôme and had a full-length armoured waterline belt, with 0.6in (15mm) wrought-iron plates protecting the wooden sides above. Main armament comprised four 10.8in (274mm) breech-loading guns in the battery, which were considerably more powerful than the

***Above:* "Coastal battleships," such as *Peder Skram,* were popular in Nordic navies**

1899, *Olfert Fischer* (1903), and *Peder Skram* (1908). These ships were short and with a small draught, but a relatively wide beam and low freeboard. They had substantial protection, their main belts comprising 8.0-7.0in (203-178mm) belt of Creusot steel in *Trolle,* and 7.6-6.1in (195-155mm) of Krupp cemented steel in *Fischer* and *Skram.* Main armament comprised two single 9.4in (240mm) guns in circular turrets and four 5.9in (150mm) in amidships casemates.

Trolle and *Fischer* were scrapped in the 1930s, but *Skram* served during World War II. She was scuttled in August 1943 but raised by the Germans and given additional AA weapons to serve as a *flak* ship, renamed *Adler* (eagle). She was sunk by Allied aircraft in April 1945, but later raised and sold for scrap.

***Above:* Central battery ship, *Marengo,* was fitted with a 20 ton bronze-capped ram**

10in (254mm) rifled muzzle loaders mounted in the equivalent British ships. In the fashion of the time, there was a ram bow, which projected some 9ft (2.7m) and was tipped by a 20 ton (20.3tonne) bronze casting.

These three ships, *Océan, Marengo* and *Suffren,* were intended primarily for the protection of French colonies and overseas interests. They were stricken between 1894 and 1897.

Danton

FRANCE

Battleship (pre-dreadnought)
Completed: 1911.
Number in class: 6.
Displacement: 18,318 tons standard; 19,763 tons full load.
Dimensions: Length 481.0ft (146.6m); beam 84.7ft (25.8m); draught 30.2ft (9.2m).
Propulsion: 4 shafts; Parsons turbines; 26 boilers; 22,500shp; 19.4kt; 3,370nm at 10kt.
Armour: Belt 10.6in (270mm); upper deck 1.9in (48mm); lower deck 1.8in (45mm); barbettes 11.0in (280mm); turrets 11.8in (300mm); conning tower 11.8in (300mm).
Armament: 4 x 12in (305mm) (2 x 2); 12 x 9.4in (240mm);16 x 75mm; 10 x 47mm; 2 x 17.7in (450mm) TT.
Complement: 681 (later 923).

History: These were the French Navy's last pre-dreadnoughts, the class consisting of six ships, all completed in 1911: *Condordcet, Danton, Diderot, Mirabeau, Vergniaud,* and *Voltaire*. With a displacement some 3,000 tons greater than the previous class, the increase was devoted to improvements in armament rather than speed, although as pre-dreadnoughts, they had a main battery of four 12in (305mm) in two twin turrets, and an intermediate battery of twelve 9.4in (240mm) in six twin turrets, two abreast the bridge, two amidships and two either side of the after funnel. One innovation was that they were first French capital ships to be fitted with Parsons turbines, but while three (*Danton,*

Courbet

FRANCE

Battleship (dreadnought)
Number in class: 4.
Displacement: 23,100 tons standard; 26,000 tons full load.
Dimensions: Length 551.2ft (168.0m); beam 91.5ft (27.9m); draught 29.5ft (9.0m).
Propulsion: 4 shafts; Parson turbines; 24 boilers; 28,000shp; 21kt; 4,200nm at 10kt.
Armour: Belt 10.6-7.1in (270-180mm); decks 2.8-1.2 (70-30mm); barbettes 11in (280mm); turrets 11.4-3.9 (290-100mm); conning tower 11.8in (300mm).
Armament: 12 x 12in (305mm) (6 x 2); 22 x 5.5in (140mm); 4 x 47mm; 4 x 18in (457mm) TT.
Complement: 1,108.

History: There were two reasons for France's late entry into the dreadnought era. The first was that construction of the Danton-class pre-dreadnoughts occupied all available slips from 1906-10, and the second that the naval staffs and designers took some time to absorb the lessons of the first dreadnought "all-big-gun" ships in foreign navies. The *Courbets* included some good ideas, one being the use of super-firing turrets, which kept the overall length of the ship down, although these were combined with two wing turrets, which added to the beam and was an idea which had been dropped by most other navies. The calibre of these main guns was, however, 12in (305mm), which the French continued to use even though most other navies had already progressed, the British to to 13.5in (343mm) and the Japanese to 14in (356mm).

The ships operated in the Mediterranean during World War I, with *Courbet* scoring a very early success, sinking the Austro-Hungarian cruiser *Zenta* on 16

Above: The Danton-class were the first large French ships powered by turbines

Mirabeau and *Voltaire*) had Niclause boilers, giving them a maximum speed of 19.4kt, the others had Belleville boilers, giving a maximum of 20.7kt. All survivors were refitted in 1918, and three (*Condorcet, Diderot* and *Voltaire*) were modernised in 1922-25 for continued service as training ships.

During World War I they all served in the Mediterranean, mainly in the Aegean, while two, *Vergniaud* and *Mirabeau*, went into the Black Sea in 1918-19. *Danton* was torpedoed on 19 March 1917 but her excellent torpedo bulkheads meant that she took some forty minutes to sink, enabling most of her crew to be saved. The surviving ships were stricken in the 1930s, although *Condorcet* remained in use as a barrack ship until 1944, when she was attacked and damaged by Allied aircraft and then scuttled by the Germans.

Above: *Courbet* as she appeared in the 1930s following her major reconstruction

August 1914. *France* was lost when she hit a rock in Quiberon Bay on 26 August 1922. The other three were extensively modernised between 1921 and 1924, but from 1931 onwards all were used, first, as training ships and then as accommodation ships, with *Paris* surviving until 1955.

Provence

FRANCE

Battleship (dreadnought)
Completed: 1915-16.
Number in class: 3
Displacement: 23,230 tons standard; 28,500 tons full load.
Dimensions: Length 544.7ft (166.0m); beam 88.3ft (26.9m); draught 32.2ft (9.8m).
Propulsion: 4 shafts; Parsons turbines; 18 boilers; 29,000shp; 20kt; 4,700nm at 10kt.
Armour: Belt 10.6-6.3in (270-160mm); decks 1.6-1.2in (40-30mm); barbettes 9.8in (250mm); centre turret 15.7in (400mm), end turrets 13.4in (340mm), superfiring turrets 9.8in (250mm); conning tower 12.4in (314mm).
Armament: 10 x 13.4in (340mm) (5 x 2); 22 x 5.5in (140mm); 4 x 2.9in (75mm); 4 x 17.7in (450mm) TT.
Complement: 1,124.

History: The French Navy followed the Courbet-class with three more ships, using the same hull as the Courbets to save construction time, but with a revised layout. Although all were laid down in mid-1912 and despite the pressure from the outbreak of war the three ships were not completed until mid-1915 (*Bretagne* and *Provence*) and mid-1916 (*Lorraine*). The most important change concerned the main armament which now consisted of ten 13.4in (340mm) guns in five twin turrets, all on the centreline, two each forward and aft, and one amidships. Although firing heavier shells, these had the initial disadvantage of a shorter range (15,860yd (14,500m)) than foreign guns, although this was later increased by raising the elevation limit of the guns from 12deg to 18deg. This work was carried out on *Lorraine*'s after turrets in 1917,

Richelieu

FRANCE

Fast battleship
Completed: 1940-49.
Number in class: 2.
Displacement: 38,500 tons standard; 47,500 tons full load.
Dimensions: Length 813.3ft (247.9m); beam 108.8ft (33.0m); draught 31.8ft (9.6m).
Propulsion: 4 shafts; Parsons geared turbines; 6 boilers; 155,000shp; 32kt; 8,000nm at 15kt.
Armour: Belt 13.6-9.8in (345-250mm); main deck 6.7-5.1in (170-130mm), lower deck 1.6in (40mm); main turrets 16.9-6.7in (430-170mm); secondary turrets 5.1-2.8in (130-70mm); conning tower 13.4in (340mm).
Aircraft: 3 aircraft (see notes).
Armament: 8 x 15.0in (380mm) (2 x 4); 9 x 6.0in (152mm); 12 x 3.9in (100mm) AA; 16 x 37mm AA; 8 x 13.2mm AAMG.
Complement: 1,670.

History: No sooner were the Dunkerque-class battlecruisers under construction than the French naval authorities realised that these battlecruisers would not be powerful enough to deal with the new battleships then under construction in German and Italian yards. Thus, if the French Navy was to maintain its position it needed new, heavier armed, better armoured, and faster battleships, all of which led to the Richelieu-class, with *Richelieu* and *Jean Bart* being authorized in 1935, and *Clemenceau* and *Gascoigne* in 1938.

Design work started in 1934 and various options for main armament were considered, starting with calibre, the choices lying between 13.4in (340mm),

Right: Bretagne **after conversion to oil-burning and installation of tripod mast**

and on the remainder of *Lorraine*'s turrets and all turrets on the other two ships in 1918-19. The class had good command-and-control facilities, but one serious problem was the short forecastle, which resulted in them being very wet forward.

They served in the Mediterranean during World War I and remained in service throughout the inter-war years. *Bretagne* and *Provence* were both in Mers-el-Kebir on 3 July 1940 when the French Fleet was bombarded by the British; *Bretagne* was sunk, while *Provence* was damaged. *Provence* was later sent to Toulon for repairs, where she was scuttled by the French in November 1942, then raised by the Germans, only to be scuttled again by them in 1944. *Lorraine* was disarmed in Alexandria in July 1940 but then joined the Free French forces; she was broken up in 1954.

13.8in (350mm) and the even larger 15in (380mm). The number and disposition of the turrets was also assessed and it appears that one of the earliest decisions was to opt for a quadruple turret, in which two pairs of guns were mounted separately in a common gunhouse. The choice then lay between two turrets, both mounted forward; two turrets, one forward and one aft; and three turrets, two forward and one aft. The eventual decision was for eight of the new 15.0in (380mm), each of which could fire two 1,940lb (880kg) shells per minute to a maximum range of 49,210yd (45,000m). Each gunhouse contained two independent twin mountings, which were obviously trained together, but could be elevated separately. The secondary armament comprised three triple 6in (152mm) turrets aft of the superstructure.

The navy took the basic Dunkerque design as the start-point and scaled it up, retaining the same layout, with two superfiring turrets forward and a large tower bridge structure. Aft of the bridge was a large combined director tower/funnel, in which the exhaust gases were directed aft through an angled vent. The armour system was also identical in layout to the Dunkerque-class, although the plates were considerably thicker, being designed to defeat attack by 15in (380mm) shells. The quarterdeck was given over to two large catapults and a crane, with the hangar in the after end of the superstructure. The intention was to carry three floatplanes, but, as far as is known, these were never embarked.

Richelieu was under construction at the Arsenal de Brest and over 90 per cent complete when France surrendered in June 1940 and the ship was moved to Dakar, where she was damaged during the subsequent British attack. She joined the Allies in 1942 and went to New York for completion and refitting, emerging in October 1943 with radar, a totally modernised anti-aircraft battery, and with all the aircraft facilities removed. She spent the remainder of the war as a unit of the British Far Eastern/Pacific Fleet and then operated off French ▶

Indochina, returning to France in late 1946. She paid off in 1959 and was used as an accommodation hulk until 1964, when she was broken up.

Jean Bart, under construction at St Nazaire, was three-quarters complete in June 1940, but managed to escape under her own power to Casablanca. Work on fitting her out continued but the ship was damaged during the Allied invasion and she was returned to Brest for repair and completion in 1946. Sea trials started in 1949 but she was not fully completed until May 1955, the last new battleship to be commissioned into any navy. After a brief service life she was stricken in 1961 and scrapped in 1970.

A third ship, *Clemenceau*, was laid down in 1939, but was only 10 percent complete in June 1940. The hull was floated out of the construction dock but was destroyed by Allied aircraft on 27 August 1944. A fourth ship, *Gascoigne*, would have been built to a different design with the second main turret moved aft, in a more conventional layout, but she was never laid down.

***Right:* French battleship *Richelieu* served from late 1943 until paid off in 1959**

König Wilhelm

GERMANY (PRUSSIA)

Central battery ironclad
Completed: 1869.
Number in class: 1.
Displacement: 10,591 tons.
Dimensions: Length 368.1ft (112.2m); beam 356.3ft (18.3m); draught 28.0ft (8.6m).
Propulsion: 1 shaft; horizontal single-expansion engine; 8 boilers; 8,440ihp; 14.5kt.
Armour: Wrought iron. Belt 12.0-6.0in(305-152mm); battery 8.0-6.0in (203-152mm); deck 2.0in (51mm).
Armament: 18 x 9.5in (240mm); 5 x 8.3in (210mm).
Complement: 730.

History: In order to speed its expansion in the 1860s, the Prussian Navy purchased a number of ships from foreign yards, one of them being this ship which had been designed and laid down in England as the *Fatikh* for the Turkish Navy. The Prussian government originally intended to name her *König Wilhelm I*, although when launched in 1868 this was shortened to *König Wilhelm*. The hull was built up on the bracket frame system and had a deep double bottom, and, following the fashion of the time, a ram bow. She was ship rigged, with three masts and a long, retractable bowsprit, although this contributed very little to her performance. A full-length, wrought-iron armoured belt was fitted, which was 12.0in (305mm) thick over most of its length, reducing to 6.0in (152mm) at the ends, and covering the sides up to the main deck. At each end of the battery and standing clear of the upper deck was a narrow gallery running across the deck, each of which housed two guns. In the forward gallery the guns could fire either ahead or on the beam, while in the after structure, which overlapped the hull sides by several feet, they could fire on the beam or, in a limited arc towards the stern.

***Above: König Wilhelm* was built in England for Turkey but bought by Prussia**

At the time of its launch *König Wilhelm* was the most powerful warship in the world, and was the flagship of the Prussian Navy, although during the Franco-Prussian War she had engine problems, which prevented her from playing a major role in the conflict. On 31 May 1878 she took action to avoid several sailing craft and collided with another Prussian warship, *Grosser Kurfürst*, which sank. *König Wilhelm* was rebuilt in 1878-82, receiving new boilers, new weapons and a stronger ram. She was again refitted in 1895-96, with virtually all of her sailing rig removed, as a result of which she was reclassified as a heavy cruiser. From 1907 she was the school ship of the Naval Academy and was finally sold for scrapping in 1921.

Sachsen

GERMANY

Central citadel ironclad
Completed: 1878-83.
Number in class: 4.
Displacement: 7,677 tons.
Dimensions: Length 322.3ft (98.2m); beam 60.3ft (18.4m); draught 21.4ft (6.5m).
Propulsion: 2 shafts; two horizontal, 3-cylinder, single-expansion engines; 8 boilers, 5,000ihp; 13.5kt.
Armour: Wrought iron. Citadel 10-8in (254-203mm); deck 2-2.5in (51-64mm).
Armament: 6 x 10.25in (260mm); 6 x 3.4in (87mm); 8 x 37mm revolving cannon.
Complement: 317.

History: The Sachsen-class, originally classified as "armoured corvettes," consisted of four ships, *Sachsen*, completed in 1878; *Würtemburg* (1881); *Bayern* (1882), and *Baden* (1883). As built, they had an unusual layout with two 10.25in (260mm) guns in an open barbette forward of the bridge and a further four in a large square central barbette amidships. The appearance of this barbette, coupled with that of the four tall funnels, also arranged in a square, led to the sailors referring to the ships as *"Zementfabriken"* (cement factories). The citadel and barbettes utilised a patent sandwich wrought iron armour, which varied in thickness from 10.0in (254mm) to 8.0in (203mm).

In 1886 all were fitted with three 13.8in (350mm) torpedo tubes and all four ships were completely rebuilt in the late 1890s, with Krupp armour replacing the original, and compound engines in place of the earlier type, which increased

Kaiser

GERMANY

Battleship (pre-dreadnought)
Completed: 1898-1902.
Number in class: 4.
Displacement: 11,599 tons.
Dimensions: Length 411.0ft (125.3m); beam 67.0ft (20.4m); draught 27.0ft (8.3m).
Propulsion: 3 shafts; vertical triple-expansion engines; 12 boilers; 14,000ihp; 17kt; 3,420nm at 10kt.
Armour: Belt 12.0in (305mm); deck 2.5in (64mm); ammunition hoists 10.0in (254mm).
Armament: 4 x 9.4in (240mm); 18 x 5.9in (150mm); 12 x MG; 6 x 17.7in (450mm) TT.
Complement: 651.

History: *Kaiser Friedrich III* and *Kaiser Wilhelm II* were both completed in 1898, followed by *Kaiser Barbarossa* in 1901, and *Kaiser Karl der Grosse* and *Kaiser Wilhelm der Grosse* in 1902. These five ships were the archetypal German pre-dreadnoughts, setting a pattern that was followed until the first German dreadnoughts, the Nassau-class in 1909. The Kaisers had comparatively light main armament of four 9.4in (240mm) guns with a range of (16,900m), mounted in two twin turrets in gunhouses fore and aft. There was a very substantial secondary armament consisting of eighteen 5.9in (150mm) guns, six of which were mounted in single turrets and the remaining twelve in casemates. Power was provided by three vertical triple-expansion engines driving three 3-bladed screws, except in *Kaiser Wilhelm II* and *Kaiser Karl der Grosse*, which had two 3-bladed and one 4-bladed screws. With the exception

the speed by at least 1kt. The funnels were also reduced to one, dramatically altering the ships' appearance. The secondary armament was changed to eight 88mm.

The ships were reduced to minor roles from 1906 onwards. *Sachsen* and *Bayern* were scrapped in 1919, followed by *Würtemburg* in 1920, but *Baden* was used as a target ship and was not scrapped until 1939.

***Below:* With four tall funnels the Sachsens were called "cement factories"**

***Above:* The *Kaiser's* main armament was four (2x2) 9.4in (240mm) guns**

of *Karl der Grosse*, all were rebuilt in 1907-10, which included removing four 5.9in (150mm) guns and the stern above-water torpedo tube. The tertiary armament was then re-arranged and a further two 3.4in (88mm) guns added. Other work included cutting down the superstructure and raising the height of the funnels.

Kaiser Wilhelm II was fleet flagship from 1898 to 1906, but, despite the rebuild, none took an active part in World War I. Instead, they were all disarmed in 1916, hulked and then used as accommodation ships until being scrapped in 1920-21.

Deutschland

GERMANY

Battleship (pre-dreadnought)
Completed: 1906-08.
Number in class: 5.
Displacement: 13,993 tons.
Dimensions: Length 418.7ft (127.6m); beam 73.0ft (22.2m); draught 27.0ft (8.3m).
Propulsion: 3 shafts; vertical triple expansion engines; 24 boilers; 19,000ihp; 18.5kt; 4,800nm at 10kt.
Armour: Krupp cemented armour; belt 9.75in (280mm); decks 1.6in (40mm); turrets 11.0in (280mm); conning tower 12in (305mm).
Armament: 4 x 11.0in (280mm); 14 x 6.7in (170mm); 20 x 3.5in (88mm); 4 x machineguns; 6 x 17.7in (450mm) TT.
Complement: 743.

History: Part of the German Navy's unremitting drive to achieve parity, if not superiority, to the British Royal Navy, the five ships of the Deutschland-class were their last pre-dreadnoughts, joining the fleet in 1906 (*Deutschland*), 1907 (*Hannover* and *Pommern*), and 1908 (*Schleswig-Holstein*). They were generally similar to the previous Braunschweig-class, completed in 1902-04, but with improved armour, and a rearranged and larger tertiary armament.

All took part in the Battle of Jutland, the only pre-dreadnoughts in either fleet, where *Pommern* was hit by a single torpedo from a British destroyer and sank with the loss of 839 lives. Shortly afterwards the four remaining ships were reassigned to secondary duties. *Deutschland* was scrapped in 1920, leaving three ships which were the only capital ships permitted to the

Nassau

GERMANY

Battleship (dreadnoughts)
Completed: 1910.
Number in class: 4.
Displacement: 18,570 tons standard; 21,000 tons full load.
Dimensions: Length 479.3ft (146.1m); beam 88.4ft (26.9m); draught 29.3ft (8.9m).
Propulsion: 3 shafts; 3-cylinder vertical triple-expansion engines; 12 boilers; 22,000ihp; 19.5kt; 8,000nm at 10kt.
Armour: Belt 12.0-3.2in (300-80mm); bulkheads 8.3-3.5in (210-90mm); battery 6.3in (160mm); barbettes 11.0-2.0in (280-50mm); turrets 11.0-2.4in (280-60mm); conning tower 12.0-3.2in (300-80mm).
Armament: 12 x 11.1in (280mm) (6 x 2); 12 x 5.9in (150mm); 16 x 3.45in (88mm); 6 x 17.7in (450mm) TT
Complement: 1,139.

History: This class of four ships, *Nassau, Posen, Rheinland* and *Westfalen*, were the Imperial German Navy's answer to the British Royal Navy's *Dreadnought*, which had revolutionised the battleship world. The Nassau-class was a cautious design, based on a slight enlargement of the pre-dreadnought Deutschland-class and with reciprocating machinery, rather than the British ship's turbines.

Main armament was twelve 11.0in (280mm) guns in six twin turrets, one each fore and aft, and four in the wing positions, the latter arrangement being due to the need to leave space for the machinery below. These guns were of smaller calibre than the 12.0in (305mm) mounted in foreign dreadnoughts, but being high velocity weapons and thus having a flatter trajectory, the turret

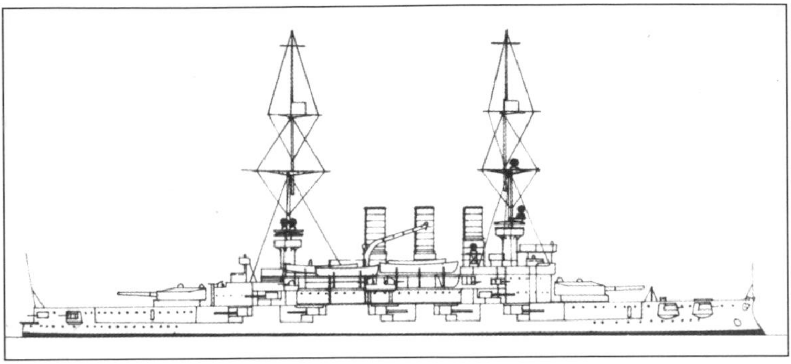

***Above:* Last German pre-dreadnoughts, the Deutschlands were completed 1906-08**

Reichsmarine (German Navy) after the Versailles Treaty. *Hannover* was scrapped in 1935, but *Schlesien* and *Schleswig-Holstein* were both rebuilt in the early 1930s and continued in service as cadet training ships, one of the major indications of the rebuild being the trunking of the forefunnel into the midships one. During the war both had their AA armament increased. Despite their age both remained in service throughout the war. *Schleswig-Holstein* was damaged at Gotenhafen by British aircraft (18 December 1944) and then scuttled (21 March 1945), but was raised after the war and used for a time as a training hulk by the East German Navy. *Schlesien* was bombed and sunk off Swinemünde in the Baltic on 4 May 1945.

***Above:* The Nassau-class was armed with twelve (6x2) 280mm (11.1in) guns**

design was simpler, and thus lighter and cheaper. These factors combined to save a considerable amount of weight, which the designers allocated to improved protection, which was notably better than that in contemporary British ships. The secondary armament was quite heavy, comprising twelve 5.9in (150mm) guns in single casemates at the main deck level, which was intended to provide heavy firepower in medium-range engagements, a tactical situation which never, in fact, came about.

All took part in the Battle of Jutland, where *Nassau* received two hits, causing moderate damage. *Westfalen* was torpedoed by a British submarine (19 August 1916), but despite heavy damage she returned to Kiel for repair. *Rheinland* ran aground at 15kt on 11 April 1918 and some 6,000 tons of armour and guns had to be removed before she could be returned to Kiel, but due to the war situation she was never repaired. All were broken up in the early 1920s.

Helgoland

GERMANY

Battleship (dreadnoughts)
Completed: 1911-12.
Number in class: 4.
Displacement: 22,800 tons standard; 24,312 tons full load.
Dimensions: Length 546.0ft (166.4m); beam 93.5ft (28.5m); draught 27.5ft (8.4m).
Propulsion: 3 shafts; three vertical triple-expansion engines; 15 boilers; 28,000ihp; 20kt; 9,400nm at 10kt.
Armour: Krupp steel. Belt 11.8-4.0in (300-102mm); bulkheads 8.3-3.5in (210-90mm); battery 6.7in (170mm); barbettes 12.0-2.4in (305-60mm); turrets 12.0-2.8in (305-70mm); conning tower 12.0-4.0in (305-100mm).
Armament: 12 x 12.0in (305mm) (6 x 2); 14 x 5.9in (150mm); 14 x 3.5in (88mm); 6 x 19.7in (500mm) TT.
Complement: 1,390.

History: Three of this class joined the fleet in 1911, *Helgoland, Ostfriesland* and *Thüringen*, followed by *Oldenburg* in 1912. These were the first battleships in the Imperial German Navy to adopt the 12in (305mm)/50-calibre gun, which was considered to have the same performance and effects as the British 13.5in (343mm)/45-calibre gun mounted in the British Orion-class. However, the German ships' apparent advantage in carrying twelve heavy guns to the British ten was negated, since, due to the lack of space for magazines, superfiring turrets could not be fitted. Thus, wing turrets were mounted which could not fire across the hull, reducing the broadside to eight guns only.

All four Helgoland-class ships served with Battle Squadron 1 of the German

Kaiser

GERMANY

Battleship (dreadnought)
Completed: 1912-13.
Number in class: 5.
Displacement: 24,300 tons standard; 27,400 tons full load.
Dimensions: Length 565.6ft (172.4m); beam 95.2ft (29.0m); draught 30.0ft (9.1m).
Propulsion: 3 shafts; Parsons/AEG-Curtis/Schichau turbines; 16 boilers; 31,000shp; 21kt; 6,000nm at 12kt (see notes).
Armour: Belt 14.0-3.2in (350-80mm); bulkheads 12.0-5.0in (305-130mm); battery 6.7in (170mm); barbettes 12.0-3.2in (305-80mm); turrets 12.0-3.2in (305-80mm); conning tower 14.0-6.0in (350-150mm).
Armament: 10 x 12.0in (305mm) (5 x 2); 14 x 5.9in (150mm); 8 x 3.5in (88mm); 4 x 3.5in (88mm) AA; 5 x 19.7in (500mm) TT.
Complement: 1,278.

History: The Kaiser-class consisted of five ships: *Kaiser*, completed in 1912, and the remainder, *Friedrich der Grosse, Kaiserin, Kînig Albert* and *Prinzregent Luitpold* in 1913. These were direct contemporaries of the British Orion-class, but mounted 12.0in (305mm) guns, as compared to the British ships' 13.5in (343mm). The layout of the five turrets was identical to that of the British Neptune- and Colossus-classes, with one turret forward, two aft (one superfiring) and two diagonally offset wing turrets amidships, although, unlike earlier German ships, these could fire across the deck on the other beam. These were the first German battleships to have turbine machinery and supplementary oil burners. It was intended that *Prinzregent Luitpold* would have a different, combined steam and diesel, system, with turbines on the two outer shafts and

Right: **In the Helgoland-class main gun calibre was increased to 305mm (12.0in)**

High Seas Fleet and all saw action at Jutland (31 May 1916). *Helgoland* and *Oldonburg* were both damaged during the battle, but were subsequently repaired. All four were stricken on 5 November 1919, disarmed and handed over to the Allies. *Helgoland, Thüringen* and *Oldenburg* were ceded to Great Britain, France and Japan, respectively, and were broken up. *Ostfriesland,* however, went to the United States, where she secured a minor place in naval history, when, on 21 July 1921, she was used for gunfire and air bombing tests. She withstood hits or near misses from some 24 shells and 80 bombs, but then she was attacked by a formation of bombers directed by Brigadier-General "Billy" Mitchell and suffered six hits by 2,205lb (1,000kg) bombs. *Ostfriesland* then rolled over and sank the first capital ship to be sunk by aircraft and the precursor of many such losses in World War II.

Above: **Kaiser-class had five twin turrets: one forward, two aft, and two wings**

the diesel on the central shaft. The latter was a 6-cylinder, 2-stroke diesel with a 12,000BHP output, made by Germania, which, it was hoped, would give a cruising range of 2,000nm at 12kt, but, in the event, it was judged unready and *Prinzregent Luitpold* spent its entire service career with only two turbines, making her about one knot slower than the others in the class.

All ships in the class were at Jutland, where *Kaiser* was hit twice but survived. All were interned after the war at Scapa Flow where they were scuttled. They were salvaged and broken up in 1929-37.

König

GERMANY

Battleship (dreadnought)
Completed: 1914-15.
Number in class: 4.
Displacement: 25,390 tons standard; 29,200 tons full load.
Dimensions: Length 575.5ft (175.4m); beam 96.8ft (29.5m); draught 30.5ft (9.3m).
Propulsion: 3 shafts; Parsons/AEG-Vulkan/Bergmann turbines; 15 boilers; 31,000shp; 21kt; 6,800nm at 12kt.
Armour: Belt 14.0-3.2in (350-80mm); bulkheads 12.0-5.0in (305-130mm); battery 6.7in (170mm); barbettes 12.0-3.2in (305-80mm); turrets 12.0-3.2in (305-80mm); conning tower 14.0-6.7in (350-170mm).
Armament: 10 x 12.0in (305mm) (5 x 2); 14 x 5.9in (150mm); 6 x 3.5in (88mm); 4 x 3.5in (88mm) AA; 5 x 19.7in (500mm) TT.
Complement: 1,315.

History: These four ships, *König, Grosser Kurfürst, Markgraf,* and *Kronprinz,* were virtual repeats of the Kaiser-class, but with rearranged main turrets, all on the centreline: two forward, two aft, and one amidships, which could fire with equal facility on either beam. The 5.9in (150mm) battery was on the upper deck. The six 3.5in (88mm) SKL/45 guns for surface warfare were later removed, while the four AA guns were reduced to two. The armoured protection, always a strong feature of German battleships, was improved compared to the Kaiser-class. *Kronprinz* was renamed *Kronprinz Wilhelm* in June 1918 to celebrate the thirtieth anniversary of his father's accession, although the new name was not to last for long.

All four ships were at the Battle of Jutland, where *König* was hit by one 15.0in

---

Bayern

GERMANY

Battleship (dreadnought)
Completed: 1916-17.
Number in class: 2.
Displacement: 28,074 tons standard; 31,690 tons full load.
Dimensions: Length 589.8ft (179.8m); beam 98.4ft (30.0m); draught 30.8ft (9.4m).
Propulsion: 3 shafts; Parsons turbines; 14 boilers; 48,000shp; 21kt; 5,000nm at 13kt.
Armour: Belt 14.0-4.7in (350-120mm); bulkheads 12.0-5.5in (305-140mm); battery 6.7in (170mm); barbettes 14.0-1.0in (350-25mm); turrets 14.0-4.0in (350-100mm); conning tower 14.0-6.7in (350-170mm).
Armament: 8 x 15.0in (380mm) (4 x 2); 16 x 5.9in (150mm); 8 x 3.5in (88mm) AA; 5 x 23.6in (600mm) TT.
Complement: 1,271.

History: The last World War I battleship class to be built for the German navy, four were launched, of which two were commissioned, *Bayern* in 1916 and *Baden* in 1917. The other two, *Sachsen* and *Würtemburg,* were slightly longer and had a diesel engine on the central shaft, but were never completed. The Bayerns marked a shift in German naval thinking, with both firepower and armour being equal to those on British ships, whereas previously the gun calibre had been less but armoured protection superior. The major element in this was the new Krupp 15.0in (380mm) gun, which, at a maximum elevation of 16deg, launched a 1,653lb (750kg) projectile to a range of 22,200yd (20,300m).

The hull was slightly longer than that of the König-class and all four turrets were placed on the centreline, there being no turret in the "Q" (amidships) position.

***Above:* König-class battleship *Grosser Kurfürst*, as completed in August 1914**

(380mm) and nine 13.5in (343mm) shells, *Grosser Kurfürst* by five 15in and three 13.5in shells, and *Markgraf* by three 15.0in, one 13.5in and one 12in (305mm), while *Kronprinz* was not hit at all. The worst damage was to *Grosser Kurfürst*, but, despite being seriously flooded, she still managed to limp home to Kiel. *Grosser Kurfürst* and *Kronprinz* were damaged on several occasions thereafter. Both were hit by torpedoes from the British submarine *J 1* on 5 November 1916, but returned to port. Later the same two ships both hit mines in the Baltic in October 1917, but the excellent internal sub-divisions prevented too much damage.

All ships were interned in 1918 and scuttled at Scapa Flow in 1919. *Grosser Kurfürst* was raised and scrapped in 1936, but the other three were not raised until the 1960s.

***Right: Baden* and *Bayern* mounted eight twin 380mm (15.0in) in four twin turrets**

Another innovation for a German ship was the use of a heavy tripod foremast, rather than a pole, to support the fire-control position. The secondary armament of sixteen 5.9in (150mm) guns was all in casemates at upper-deck level.

Bayern joined the High Seas Fleet just after Jutland and hit a mine in the Baltic in October 1917, but managed to struggle back to harbour for repairs. She was scuttled at Scapa Flow, and recovered for scrapping in the 1930s. *Baden*, which had a specially enlarged bridge, joined the fleet in March 1917 and served as fleet flagship until the end of the war. She was also scuttled at Scapa Flow, but was beached before sinking and then salved for examination in detail by the British. She was expended as a gunnery target, being sunk on 6 August 1921.

Bismarck

GERMANY

Fast battleship
Number in class: 2.
Displacement: 41,676 tons standard; 50,153 tons full load.
Dimensions: Length 823.5ft (251.0m); beam 118.1ft (36.0m); draught 29.5ft (9.0m).
Propulsion: 3shafts; 3 Blohm +Voss turbines; 12 boilers; 150,170shp; 30.1kt; 8,900nm at 17kt.
Armour: Belt 12.6-5.7in (320-145mm); bulkheads 8.7-1.8in (220-45mm); decks 4.7-1.2in (120-30mm); barbettes 8.7in (220mm); main turrets 14.1-5.1in (360-130mm); secondary turrets 3.9-0.5in (100-20mm); conning tower 13.8-1.2in (350-30mm).
Aircraft: 4.
Armament: 8 x 15.0in (380mm) (4 x 2); 12 x 5.9in (150mm); 16 x 4.1in (105mm) AA; 16 x 37mm AA; 12 x 20mm AA.
Complement: 2,092.

History: Among the most famous warships of World War II, *Bismarck* and *Tirpitz* both left their mark on naval history, albeit in different ways. The operational requirement was for a ship with a main armament of eight 15.0in (380mm) guns, disposed in four twin turrets, two forward and two aft, a well-balanced combination which would lead to good fire control. The secondary battery was to consist of 5.9in (150mm) anti-surface guns, with a separate anti-aircraft battery. Protection was to be the best possible and maximum speed was to be about 30kt.

Other battleship navies, such as those of Britain, France, Italy, Japan and the United States had, of course, carried out experimental and development programmes throughout the 1920s and 1930s, but the Versailles Treaty had

***Below: Bismarck* was an exceptionally handsome and well-balanced design**

ensured that no such continuity had been available to the German Navy. Thus, when it was decided in 1932 to begin work on a new battleship the naval staff and design offices had little choice but to take up the ideas which had prevailed in 1917-18, even though the range at which battleship engagements were likely to take place had increased considerably. The result was that, although the new German battleships were well-armoured against shells fired at relatively short range, they were considerably more vulnerable to plunging shells fired at long ranges than their more modern foreign counterparts. In addition, in the German ships the main armoured deck was placed much lower than in other contemporary designs, leaving many important compartments, particularly those housing the ship's communications and data systems, exposed to shells which penetrated the lightly armoured upper deck. In addition, the rudders and steering gear were poorly protected, making them vulnerable, particularly to air attack. Despite these shortcomings, *Bismarck* and *Tirpitz* were strongly built and, as experience would show, very difficult to sink.

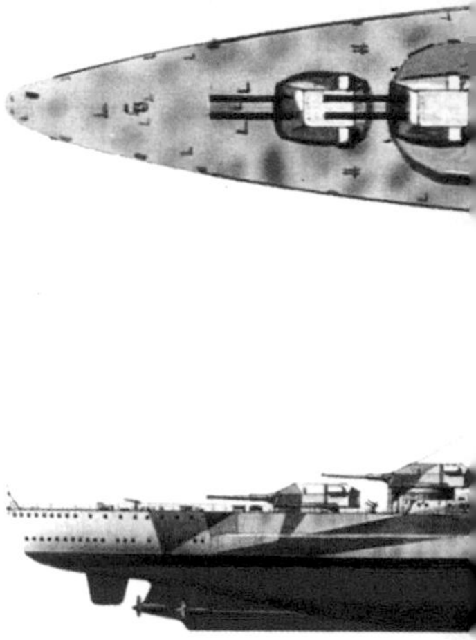

The designers started with the hull design of the World War I Bayern-class battleships, but considerably longer (823.5ft [251m] compared to 598.4ft [182.4m]) and with a much greater beam (118.0ft [36.0m] compared to 99.1ft [30.2m]). As a result, the length:beam ratio was increased from approximately 6:1 in the Bayern-class to 7:1 in the Bismarck-class. This made for a very steady gun platform and, among other benefits, much greater internal volume which provided sufficient space for an excellent system of underwater protection.

Initially, turbo-electric power, as used in some contemporary American battleships, was considered , but there was concern about the vulnerability of the

Below: Bismarck with deck camouflage

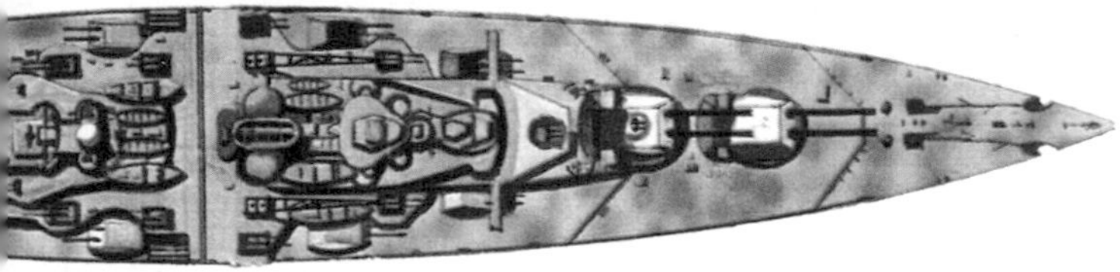

Above: Tirpitz in March 1944 with deck camouflage and many extra AA guns

power transmission cables and it was eventually decided to use the high-pressure superheated steam plant of the Scharnhorst-class, with three sets of geared turbines (Blohm+Voss in *Bismarck*; Brown, Boveri in *Tirpitz*) and twelve Wagner ultra high-pressure boilers in both. As designed, *Bismarck*'s profile was similar to that of *Scharnhorst*, but this changed during construction, when she was given a rakish funnel cowl and a clipper-bow, known in the German Navy as the "Atlantic bow".

Bismarck was completed in August 1940 and then spent a full year working up before undertaking her one and only foray into the Atlantic, escorted by the heavy cruiser, *Prinz Eugen*. The two ships left Korsfjord in Norway and met the brand-new British battleship *Prince of Wales* and battlecruiser *Hood* in the Denmark Strait. *Bismarck* sank *Hood* within minutes and damaged *Prince of Wales*, which was obliged to break off the action, but not before she had inflicted three 14.0in (356mm) hits on the German battleship. *Bismarck* then set off to seek shelter in the German-occupied port of Brest, but an armada of British ships and aircraft carriers was assembled and *Bismarck* was further hampered by an air-delivered torpedo hit on her steering gear. She was then sunk by the British battleships *King George V* and *Rodney* on 27 May 1941.

Tirpitz was deployed to Norway, where she spent most of her brief operational career, serving as a potential threat to the Allied convoys which delivered supplies to the Soviet port of Murmansk. In September 1943 she was damaged by an attack by midget submarines and then in April and August 1944 she was again damaged, this time by British carrier aircraft. She was finally disposed of by RAF Lancasters on 12 November 1944, when several hits and near misses by "Tallboy" bombs resulted in the ill-fated battleship capsizing.

Principe di Carignano

ITALY

Broadside ironclads
Completed: 1865-71.
Number in class: 3.
Displacement: 3,445 tons standard; 3,912 tons full load.
Dimensions: Length 239.4ft (73.0m); beam 49.6ft (15.1m); draught 23.5ft (7.2m).
Propulsion: 1 shaft, single-expansion, 6 cylinder engine; boilers, 1,968ihp, 10.2kt, ca 1,200nm at 10kt.
Armour: Iron. Sides 4.75in (120mm).
Armament: 10 x 72pdr (8.0in [203mm]); 12 x 6.6in (164mm).
Complement: 572.

History: There were three ships in this class. Two, *Principe di Carignano* and *Messina*, were designed by Insp. Eng. Felice Mattei and were laid down as screw frigates, but were converted into ironclads while building, their wooden sides being covered with 4.75in (120mm) thick iron plates. The third ship, *Conte Verde*, was designed from the start as an ironclad frigate by Insp. Eng. Giuseppe De Luca, although curiously, despite her designation, she was not a true ironclad since only parts of her bows and stern were protected by iron plates. There were numerous minor differences between the three, with variations in dimensions, displacement and machinery, and *Principe di Carignano* was rigged as a barquentine, the other two ships as barques. The original armament also differed, with *Principe di Carignano* mounting ten 8.0in (203mm) and twelve 6.6in (164mm), while the other two had four 8.0in and

Duilio

ITALY

Turret ship
Completed: 1880-82.
Number in class: 2.
Displacement: 10,962 tons standard; 12,071tons full load.
Dimensions: Length 358.1ft (109.2m); beam 64.8ft (19.8m); draught 27.3ft (8.3m).
Propulsion: 2 shafts; vertical engine; 8 boilers; 771ihp; 15.6kt; 3,760nm at 10kt.
Armour: Steel. Side 21.5in (546mm); deck 2.0-1.2in (51-30mm); turrets 17.0in (432mm); citadel 17.0in (432mm).
Armament: 4 x 17.7in (450mm) (2 x 2); 3 x 14.0in (356mm) TT.
Complement: 420.

History: *Duilio* and *Dandolo* were significant milestones in battleship evolution, being the first ships in any navy to combine large calibre guns in rotating turrets with a military mast and no provision for sailing. They were also the first Italian capital ships with twin screws.

The Battle of Lissa in 1866, where a superior Italian fleet was defeated by the Austro-Hungarians, inflicted a severe shock on Italian morale and led to a marked reduction in naval budgets. When the shock wore off, however, attention concentrated on producing thoroughly modern and innovative designs, of which this class was one of the most important. Such was the pace of naval development at the time, that the first guns planned for *Duilio* weighed 35 tons each, but designers then turned to weapons weighing 60 tons, before finally deciding on 100 ton Armstrongs, each capable of firing one 1,905lb (846kg) shell every 15 minutes. Protection was equally powerful, using French-made Creusot steel plates for the belt and nickel steel elsewhere. An

***Above: Messina* was converted into an ironclad by the addition of iron plates**

eighteen 6.6in. Then, in about 1870, all three had their armament modified, ending up with different batteries: *Principe di Carignano*, four 8.0in and sixteen 6.6in; *Messina*, two 10.0in and four 8.0in; and *Conte Verde*, six 10.0in one 8.0in.

Principe di Carignano took part in the Lissa campaign, bombarding Comisa on 18 July 1866, supporting the attack on Porto San Giorgio the next day, and then taking part in the major naval battle, during which she suffered slight damage. *Principe di Carignano* was discarded in 1875, the other two in 1880.

***Above: Dandolo*'s main turrets were mounted underneath the flying bridges**

interesting offensive feature was a stern compartment housing a 26.5 ton torpedo boat, which was armed with two 14in (356mm) torpedo tubes.

Duilio was modernised first in 1890, when she received and additional three 4.7in (120mm) guns, and again in 1900, when she received an additional two 3.0in (75mm), eight 2.2in (576mm) and four 1.5in (37mm) revolver guns. In 1909 she was stripped of all military weapons and equipment and converted into a coal and oil barge.

Dandolo was rebuilt between 1895-98 and rearmed with four 10.0in (254mm), seven 6.0in (152mm) and twenty-nine smaller guns, together with four 17.7in (450mm) torpedo tubes. She was used as a floating defence battery during World War I and stricken in 1920.

Conte di Cavour/ Caio Duilio

ITALY

Battleship (dreadnought)
Specifications for *Conte di Cavour,* as built.
Completed: Cavour - 1914-14; Duilio - 1915-16.
Number in class: Cavour -3; Duilio - 2.
Displacement: 22,992 tons standard; 24,250 tons full load.
Dimensions: Length 557.4ft (176.0m); beam 91.8ft (28.0m); draught 30.5ft (9.3m).
Propulsion: 4 shafts; Parsons geared turbines; 8 oil, 12 mixed boilers; 31,278hp; 22.2kt; 4,800nm at 10kt.
Armour: Terni KC. Side 10.0in (254mm); deck 4.5in (111mm); battery 5.0in (127mm); ; turrets 10.0in (254mm); conning tower 11.0in (279mm).
Armament: 13 x 12.0in (305mm) (3 x 3, 2 x 2); 18 x 4.7in (120mm); 13 x 3.0in (76mm); 3 x 17.7in (450mm) TT.
Complement: 1,200.

History: These two classes consisted of five ships, three Cavours (*Conte di Cavour, Giulio Cesare, Leonardo da Vinci*) plus two Duilios (*Caio Duilio, Andrea Doria*) which were essentially similar to the Cavours, but with a 6in (152mm) secondary armament and the amidships 12.0in (305mm) turret one deck lower. The design originated in 1908 as an improved versions of the *Dante Alighieri* and main armament comprised thirteen 12.0in (305mm) guns, mounted in one triple and one superfiring twin turret forward and aft, plus a further triple turret amidships. In the Cavours the battery housed eighteen 4.7in (120mm) quick-firing guns in nine amidships casemates on each side of the ship at maindeck level, while in the Duilios there were sixteen 6.0in (152mm) in casemates beneath the fore and aft main turrets. All five ships served in World War I, the only loss being *Leonardo de Vinci* which was sunk by a magazine explosion on 2 August 1916; she was salvaged and later scrapped.

Right: Cavour **as she appeared after her complete rebuild in the 1930s**

The four survivors were completely rebuilt in the 1930s and entered World War II as virtually new ships. In the rebuild the amidships turret was removed and the guns in the remaining four turrets were bored out and relined to a new 12.6in (320mm) calibre. The turrets and mountings were also remodelled increasing maximum elevation to 27deg, increasing range to 31,300yd (28,600m). The casemate weapons were removed and replaced by twelve 4.7in (120mm) in single turrets (twelve 5.3in [135mm]) in the Duilios. New, smaller calibre weapons were also mounted. New machinery, consisting of two-shaft geared turbines was installed and in combination with lengthened and recontoured bow and stern resulted in a new maximum speed of about 28kt. Protection was also greatly improved. Finally, a clipper-type bow, much more substantial superstructure and new, much closer funnels with cowls, totally transformed their appearance.

All four served in the Mediterranean during World War II, operating against Malta convoys, but *Conte di Cavour* was sunk in the British aerial attack on Taranto (12 November 1940). *Giulio Cesare* survived, to be handed over as reparations to the USSR who renamed it *Novorossiysk*; she served as a training ship with the Soviet Navy until 1955, when she was sunk by a mine off Sevastopol. *Caio Duilio* and *Andrea Doria* also survived, being scrapped in 1957-58.

Littorio

ITALY

Fast battleship
Specifications are for *Littorio*, as built.
Completed: 1940-42.
Number in class: 3.
Displacement: 40,724 tons standard; 45,236 tons full load.
Dimensions: Length 780.0ft (237.8m); beam 107.4ft (32.8m); draught 31.4ft (9.6m).
Propulsion: 4 shafts; Belluzo geared turbines; 8 boilers; 128,200shp; 30kt.
Armour: Belt 11.0 + 2.8in (280 + 70mm); bulkheads 8.3-2.8in (210-70mm); decks 6.4-1.8in (162-45mm); funnel uptakes 4.1in (105mm); barbettes 13.8-11.0in (350-280mm); turrets 13.8-7.9in (350-200mm); secondary turrets 11.0-2.8in (280-70mm); conning tower 10.2-2.4in (260-60mm).
Aircraft: 3.
Armament: 9 x 15.0in (381mm) (3 x 3); 12 x 6.0in (152mm); 4 x 4.7in (120mm);12 x 3.5in (90mm) AA; 20 x 37mm AA; 16 x 20mm AA.
Complement: 1,950.

History: When France laid down the Dunkerque-class battlecruisers the Italian Navy felt that it had no choice but to follow suit, placing orders for two fast battleships, *Littorio* and *Vittorio Veneto*. Both were laid down on 28 October 1934, the first battleships to be built by any major power since 1922, and were completed on 6 May 1940 and 28 April 1940, respectively. Two more were laid down in 1937, both of which were launched in 1939-40, but only one was completed, *Roma* (June 1942), while the other, *Impero*, lay incomplete until 1948, when it was scrapped.

Fuji

JAPAN

Battleship (pre-dreadnought)
Completed: 1897.
Number in class: 2.
Displacement: 12,320 tons standard; 12,533 tons normal.
Dimensions: Length 412.0ft (125.5m); beam 73.8ft (22.4m); draught 26.3ft (8.1m).
Propulsion: 2 shafts; reciprocating vertical, triple-expansion engines; 14,000ihp; 18kt.
Armour: Belt 18.0-14.0in (457-356mm); barbettes 14.0-9.0in (356-229mm); casemates 6.0-2.0in (152-51mm); deck 2.5in (63mm); conning tower 14.0in (356mm).
Armament: 4 x 12.0in (305mm) (2 x 2); 10 x 6.0in (153mm); 20 x 3-pdr; 4 x 2.5pdr; 5 x 18.0in (457mm) TT.
Complement: 637.

History: In the early 1890s it appeared to the Japanese Navy that war with China was likely in the near future and the Chinese purchase of two modern warships from Germany prompted it to place an order for its first British-built battleships. The ships, *Fuji* and *Yashima*, were ordered in 1893 and delivered in 1897, by which time the threatened war had already happened, but they took an important place in the Japanese line of battle. The design was based on that of the British *Royal Sovereign* of 1892, but was slightly smaller and with a main armament of four 12.0in (305mm) guns rather than the British ship's 13.5in (343mm). The weight thus saved was devoted to improved protection for the guns' crews by installing turrets. *Yashima* was given a smaller turning circle by cutting away the after part of the keel, although this resulted in excessive strain on the hull.

***Above: Roma,* with her high"X" turret mounting three 15in (381mm) guns**

Littorio's name was changed to *Italia* in June 1943.

Armoured protection, while substantial, was not as great as on foreign contemporaries, since the Italians preferred to depend upon speed and manouevrability. These ships gave the appearance of aggression combined with elegance.

After the war *Vittorio Veneto* was allocated to the UK and was scrapped in 1948-50. *Littorio* was damaged during the British attack on Taranto (11 November 1940), not returning to the fleet until mid-1941. While on her way to surrender in Malta she was badly damaged by a German glider-bomb; she was scrapped in 1948-50. *Roma* was also hit by glider-bombs while en route to Malta and sank, becoming the first warship to be sunk by guided missiles.

***Above: Fuji* was the first of many Japanese battleships to be built in Britain**

Yashima was lost in the Russo-Japanese War when she struck a mine off Port Arthur (15 May 1904). *Fuji* took part in the Battles of the Yellow Sea (10 August 1904) and Tsushima (25 May 1905), firing the final salvo at the latter which hit the magazine and destroyed the Russian battleship *Borodino*. *Fuji*'s British guns were replaced by Japanese models in 1910 and the ship was reclassified as a coast-defence ship, later being regraded yet again as a training ship. She played no part in World War I and was stricken in 1922.

Mikasa

JAPAN

Battleship (pre-dreadnought)
Completed: 1902.
Number in class: 1 (see notes).
Displacement: 15,140 tons standard; 15,179 tons full load.
Dimensions: Length 432.0ft (131.7m); beam 76.0ft (23.2m); draught 27.0ft (8.3m).
Propulsion: 2 shafts; reciprocating vertical triple-expansion; 25 boilers; 15,000ihp; 5,000nm at 10kt.
Armour: Krupp cemented. Belt 9.0-4.0in(229-102mm); upper belt 6.0in (152mm); deck 3.0-2.0in (76-51mm); barbettes 14.0-8.0in (356-203mm); casemates 6.0-2.0in (152-51mm).
Armament: 4 x 12.0in (305mm) (2 x 2); 14 x 6.0in (152mm); 20 x 12pdr; 8 x 3pdr; 4 x 2.5pdr; 4 x 18in (457mm) TT.
Complement: 830.

History: The battleship *Mikasa* has a firm place in naval history as Vice-Admiral Togo's flagship, when he commanded the Combined Fleet at the Battle of Tsushima (25 May 1905), where the Japanese inflicted a humiliating defeat on the Russian Navy. As flagship, *Mikasa* came under heavy fire, but her good armour, sturdy construction and skilful handling brought her through without serious damage.

Mikasa was one of four battleships ordered by the Imperial Japanese Navy from British yards under the 1896 expansion programme. Of these, the first two, *Shikishima* and *Hatsuse* were identical, while the other two, *Asahi* and

Kashima

JAPAN

Battleship (pre-dreadnought)
Completed: 1906.
Number in class: 2.
Displacement: 16,400 tons normal; 17,200 tons full load.
Dimensions: Length 473.6ft (128.0m); beam 78.2ft (23.8m); draught 26.3ft (8.1m).
Propulsion: 2 shafts; 4-cylinder vertical triple-expansion; 20 boilers; 15,800shp; 18.5kt; 10,000nm at 10kt.
Armour: Belt 9.0in (230mm); barbettes (main guns) 12.0-5.0in (305-127mm); barbettes (intermediate guns) 6.0in (152mm); turret faces (main) 9.0in (230mm); turret faces (intermediate) 8.0in (203mm); conning tower 9.0in(mm); decks 2.0in (50mm).
Armament: 4 x 12.0in (305mm) (2 x 2); 4 x 10.0in (254mm); 12 x 6.0in (152mm); 16 x 3.1in (79mm); 5 x 18in (386mm) TT.
Complement: 864.

History: At the time of their completion *Kashima* and *Katori* were among the most powerful battleships in the world, exceeding even their direct contemporaries, the British King Edward VII-class. *Kashima* was built by Vickers at Barrow and *Katori* by Armstrong at Elswick, the last battleships for the Imperial Japanese Navy to be built outside Japan. Although the design was finalised well before the Battle of Tsushima, the armament was intended specifically for long-range engagements, and, as pioneered in *Mikasa*, could be electrically-, hydraulically- or manually operated. Main armament comprised four 12.0in (305mm) guns in two twin turrets, but there was also a heavy

Above: Togos flagship at Tsushima, *Mikasa* is preserved as a national monument

Mikasa, differed slightly both from each other and from the first pair. *Mikasa* was built by Armstrong at Elswick and was armed with four 12.0in (305mm) guns in two turrets, which could be loaded at any angle of elevation, regardless of the training angle, and there were three alternative means of loading: electric, hydraulic and manual. Each gun could fire three rounds in two minutes and the ship carried a total of 240 12.0in (305mm) rounds.

Mikasa was disarmed in 1922 but survived World War Two and has since been refurbished and remains preserved as a national monument at Yokosuka.

Above: *Kashima* was for a short time the most powerful battleship in the world

intermediate battery of four 10.0in (254mm) guns in four single turrets, two on either beam. There were also twelve 6.0in (152mm) guns in a central battery, five per side at maindeck level and one at upper deck level. The armour weighed 4,439 tons and covered the length of the hull from 5.0ft (1.52m) below the waterline to the upper deck. Both ships served throughout World War I, were stricken in 1922 and broken up in 1925.

Satsuma

JAPAN

Battleship (pre-dreadnought)
Completed: 1910-11.
Number in class: 2.
Displacement: 19,372 tons standard; 19,700 tons full load.
Dimensions: Length 482.0ft (146.9m); beam 83.5ft (25.4m); draught 27.5ft (8.4m).
Propulsion: 2 shafts; vertical triple-expansion; 20 boilers; 17,300ihp; 18.3kt.
Armour: Belt 9.0-4.0in (230-102mm); decks 2.0in (50mm); barbettes 9.2-7.0in (234-178mm); turrets 9.0-7.0in (230-178mm); conning tower 6.0in (152mm).
Armament: 4 x 12.0in (305mm) (2 x 2); 12 x 10.0in (254mm); 12 x 4.7in (120mm); 4 x 3.1in (79mm); 5 x 18in (457mm) TT.
Complement: 887.

History: Designed in Japan, *Satsuma* was laid down at the Kure Naval Yard on 15 May 1905, five months before the British HMS *Dreadnought* and it was originally intended to arm her with twelve 12.0in (305mm) guns, with two twin centreline turrets (one each fore and aft), plus four turrets on each beam, one twin and two singles. This would have made *Satsuma* the world's first all-big gun ship, a type which would, presumably, have thereafter been known as "Satsumas" rather than "Dreadnoughts." Neither beam battery could fire across the ship, however, and it was then appreciated that there were few circumstances in which both beam batteries would be used simultaneously and this, coupled with the fact that the eight 12.0in (305mm) guns and their six turrets were extremely heavy and expensive. So, while the twin 12.0in (305mm) fore and aft turrets were

Settsu

JAPAN

Dreadnought (see notes)
Completed: 1910-11.
Number in class: 2.
Displacement: 20,823 tons normal; 21,900 tons full load.
Dimensions: Length 526.0ft (160.6m); beam 84.2ft (25.7m); draught 27.8ft (8.5m).
Propulsion: 2 shafts; Curtis turbines; 16 boilers; 25,0000ihp; 20.0kt; 2,700nm at 18kt.
Armour: Belt 12.0-4.0in (305-192mm); deck 1.2in (30mm); barbettes 11.0in (280mm); turrets 11.0in (280mm); conning tower 10.0in (254mm).
Armament: 4 x 12.0in (305mm)/50cal; 8 x 12.0in (305mm)/45cal; 10 x 6.0in (152mm); 8 x 4.7in (120mm); 12 x 3.1in/40; 4 x 3.1in/28; 5 x 18in (457mm) TT.
Complement: 986.

History: The next step on Japan's progress towards a true dreadnought, these two ships, *Settsu* and *Kawachi*, were modified versions of the *Aki*. Like *Aki*, they were powered by Curtis turbines, but in this case the full armament of twelve 12.0in (305mm) guns was mounted. This gave them the appearance of being "all big-gun" ships, and, in the sense that the main armament were all 12.0in (305mm) calibre, this was correct. However, there were two types of barrel, those in the fore and aft turrets being 50 calibres (ie, 50ft [15.2m]) long, while those in the beam turrets were somewhat shorter, 45 calibres (ie, 45ft [13.7m]). This resulted in significant differences in performance, particularly in muzzle velocity, which had a marked effect

retained, the beam turrets were replaced by six single-gun 10.0in (254mm) turrets, thus reverting to the pre-dreadnought concept of an "intermediate battery." The change to the lesser calibre guns also saved money, which was spent on buying Curtis turbines from the United States, which were installed in *Satsuma*'s sister, *Aki*, which followed a year later, thus making her the Japanese Navy's first turbine-powered ship. Both ships saw only limited service in World War I and were disarmed in 1922. They were then used as targets for gunnery practice by other battleships and sunk, *Aki* on 2 September 1924 and *Satsuma* one week later.

Below: *Satsuma* was named in honour of one of the greatest Japanese clans

on accuracy, particularly at longer ranges. These were the first battleships to have been totally designed in Japan, although the guns and mountings were supplied from England by Armstrong.

Kawachi was totally destroyed in an explosion on 12 July 1918 with the loss of some 700 lives, which was attributed, as were several similar disasters, to faulty cordite. *Settsu* was converted to a target ship in 1924 and radio-control was added in 1937, after which she was used for training carrier pilots in bombing techniques. She was sunk by US carrier aircraft on 24 July 1945.

Below: *Settsu* was unusual in mounting 12in (305mm) guns of different calibres

Fuso

JAPAN

Battleship (dreadnought)
Completed: 1915-17.
Number in class: 2.
Displacement: 30,600 tons standard; 35,900 tons full load.
Dimensions: Length 665.0ft (202.7m); beam 94.0ft (28.7m); draught 28.5ft (8.7m).
Propulsion: 4 shafts; Brown-Curtis turbines; 24 boilers; 40,000shp; 22.5kt; 8,000nm at 14kt.
Armour: Krupp steel. Belt 12.0-4.0in (305-102mm); casemate 6.0in (152mm); deck 3.0-1.2in (76-30mm); barbettes 12.0-8.0in (305-204mm); turrets 12.0-8.0in (305-204mm); conning tower 12.0in (305mm); director tower 6.0in (152mm)
Armament: 12 x 14.0in (356mm) (6 x 2); 16 x 6.0in (152mm); 4 x 3.1in AA; 6 x 21.0in (533mm) TT
Complement: 1,193.

History: *Fuso* and her sister-ship *Yamashiro* were laid down at Kure and Yokosuka in 1912 and 1913 and were completed in 1915 and 1917, respectively. Their size, displacement and exceptionally heavy armament confirmed Japan's status as a major Pacific power, since, with their twelve 14.0in (356mm) guns they outgunned the US Navy's Texas- and Nevada-classes, each with ten 14.0in (356mm), and were equalled only by the Pennsylvania-class, which appeared a year later. The Fuso-class's 14.0in (356mm) guns were mounted in six twin turrets, with two pairs of superfiring turrets fore and aft, and two amidships, capable of firing on either beam. These two latter turrets were, however, somewhat unusual in that the forward turret, sited between the two funnels, was at forecastle deck level, while the after

Ise

JAPAN

Battleship
Completed: 1917-18.
Number in class: 2.
Displacement: 31,260 tons standard; 36,500 tons full load.
Dimensions: Length 675.0ft (205.8m); beam 94.0ft (28.7m); draught 28.9ft (8.8m).
Propulsion: 4 shafts; Curtis turbines; 24 boilers; 45,000shp; 23kt; 9,680nm at 14kt.
Armour: Belt 12.0-4.0in (305-102mm); decks 2.2-1.3in (55-34mm); barbettes 12.0-8.0in (305-203mm); turrets 12.0-8.0in (305-203mm); forward conning tower 12.0in (305mm); aft conning tower 6.0in (152mm).
Armament: 12 x 14.0in (356mm) (6 x 2); 20 x 5.5in (140mm); 4 x 3.1in AA; 6 x 21.0in (533mm).
Complement: 1,360.

History: *Ise* and sister-ship *Hyuga* were originally going to be repeats of the Fuso-class, but so many improvements were included in the design that they became a separate class. The main armament retained the two super-firing turrets fore and aft, but there was a major change in the layout of the other two turrets, in which "P" (the forward of the two) was moved abaft the second funnel and placed atop a tall barbette where it superfired over "Q" turret, which had been lowered to maindeck level. Twenty of a new Japanese-designed 5.5in (140mm) turret were mounted in casemates, although the two foremost guns, situated far forward under the forecastle, could not be worked in bad weather. Armour and speed were the same as the Fuso-class.

Both were extensively rebuilt between the wars, being lengthened by 25.1ft (7.64m), given new machinery, which raised speed to 25.3kt, improved

***Above: Fuso* with the "pagoda" bridge, favoured by the IJN in the 1920s and 30s**

turret, between the second funnel and mainmast, was raised one complete deck level by a tall barbette.

These two ships underwent a refit in 1927-28 followed by a major reconstruction between 1930 and 1935. In the course of the latter they were given massive "pagoda" foremasts, built-up mainmasts, greatly improved deck and underwater protection and a lengthened stem.

Neither ship saw any significant action during World War II until both were present at the last battleship-versus-battleship engagement at the Battle of Surigao Strait (25 October 1944) where both were sunk by a combination of gunfire and torpedoes.

***Above: Hyuga,* of the Ise-class, in 1940; note the pagoda mast, three floatplanes aft**

secondary armament and additional armoured protection. They were also given the "pagoda masts" typical of 1930s Japanese battleship design. Following the major carrier losses at the Battle of Midway in June 1942, both ships were converted to hybrid battleship/carriers in which "X" and "Y" turrets were removed and replaced by a flat deck with a hangar below, which could house twenty-two aircraft. The flat deck had the appearance of a flightdeck, but in fact it was only used for handling aircraft and moving them forward from the lift to the two catapults. All aircraft were seaplanes or floatplanes and landed in the sea to be recovered by a crane. Both were employed as decoy carriers in the Battle of Leyte Gulf (October 1944) but they never operated aircraft in action. Both were sunk by US carrier aircraft in July 1945.

Nagato

JAPAN

Battleship
Completed: 1920-21.
Number in class: 2.
Displacement: 32,720 tons standard; 38,500 tons full load.
Dimensions: Length 708.0ft (215.8m); beam 95.0ft (28.9m); draught 30.0ft (9.1m).
Propulsion: 4 shafts; Gihon turbines; 21 boilers; 80,000shp; 26.7kt; 5,500nm at 16kt.
Armour: Belt 11.8-3.9in(300-100mm); decks 7.0-3.0in(178-76.2mm); barbettes 11.8in (300mm); casemates 1.0-0.75in (2.5-2.0mm); turrets 14.0in (356mm); conning tower 14.5-3.8in (368-97mm).
Armament: 8 x 16.0in (406mm) (4 x 2); 20 x 5.5in (140mm); 4 x 3.1in (79mm); 3 x MG; 8 x 21in (533mm) TT.
Complement: 1,333.

History: When they were completed in 1920-21, *Nagato* and *Mutsu* were the wonder of the world's naval community. They were the first battleships in any navy to be to be armed with 16in (406mm) guns, with a maximum speed of 26.7kt they were faster than any other battleship, and they also had excellent protection. Like many other Japanese battleships they did, however, suffer from one aggravating problem, because (as with contemporary British battleships) smoke and heat from the forward funnel created very unpleasant conditions in the director tower above. Various efforts were made to overcome this, starting with a clinker cowl fitted to the forward funnel shortly after

commissioning, but in 1924 more drastic action was taken by trunking the forward funnel sharply aft, but although this reduced the problem it was still not totally solved.

Both ships were thoroughly modernised between 1934 and 1936. The work included increased protection with an additional 2,636 tons of armour plate, a completely new propulsion plant and a lengthened stern. The maximum elevation of the main battery was increased to 43 deg, resulting in a considerable increase in range. The superstructure was rebuilt to include a "pagoda mast" which provided the profusion of bridges, searchlight platforms and observation posts which the Japanese naval staff considered essential in capital ships. The smoke and heat problem from the forward funnel was again addressed and the two existing funnels were removed to be replaced by a single, slightly larger funnel, which was well clear of the bridge. The torpedo tubes were removed and a catapult installed, which enabled the ship to carry three aircraft.

During the war these two ships operated in company with *Yamato* and *Musashi* as 1st Battleship Division of the Combined Fleet. They were present at the Battle of Midway but achieved little. Like at least two other Japanese battleships, *Mutsu* was totally destroyed by a magazine explosion, which occurred in Hiroshima Bay on 8 June 1943. *Nagato* was present at the Battle of Leyte Gulf, where she received some damage, which was subsequently repaired. She survived the war and was expended as a target during the Bikini atomic bomb tests, being sunk on 29 July 1946.

***Below: Nagato*, photographed in 1938, following her final refit**

Yamato

JAPAN

Battleship
Completed: 1941-42.
Number in class: 2.
Displacement: 62,315 tons standard; 69,990 tons full load.
Dimensions: Length 862.8ft (263.0m); beam 121.1ft (36.9m); draught 34.1ft (10.4m).
Propulsion: 4 shafts; geared turbines; 12 boilers; 150,000shp; 27kt.
Armour: Belt 16.1in (409mm); deck 9.1-7.9 (231-200mm); barbettes 21.5-2.0in (546-51mm); turrets 25.6-7.6 (650-193mm); conning tower 19.7-11.8 (500-300mm).
Aircraft: 7.
Armament: 9 x 18.1in (460mm) (3 x 3); 12 x 6.1in (155mm); 12 x 5.0in (127mm) DP; 24 x 25mm AA; 4 x 13,2mm AA.
Complement: 2,500.

History: These two ships have a firm place in naval history as the largest, most heavily armed and best protected battleships ever built, although when faced by US carrier air power all these attributes were to prove to be complete illusions. The Japanese naval staff considered some 23 designs between 1934, when plans for a "super-battleship" were first mooted, and 1937, when the order for the first ship, *Yamato*, was placed with Kure Dockyard. This was followed shortly afterwards by the order for the second, *Musashi*, with Mitsubishi at Nagasaki. Such large hulls required special building facilities, which included lengthening and widening existing docks, and the construction of a special ship to transport the turrets, while the security measures (which were extremely successful) included the erection of high fences, protective roofing and camouflage netting. Two more were laid down in 1939. One of these, *Shinano*, was converted to an aircraft carrier while building and was sunk by a US submarine on her maiden voyage (29 November 1944), while the other, which was only ever known as "*Hull No. 111*," was scrapped in 1942 when only 30 per cent complete. There was even talk of three more: *No 797*, a standard Yamato-class, and *Nos. 798* and *799*, which would have mounted six 20.0in (508mm) guns, the most massive ordnance ever considered for use at sea. Understandably, no orders were ever placed.

Yamato and *Musashi* had a bulbous bow, a massive (121.1ft [36.9m]) beam, but a relatively shallow draught, which was needed for deployment in Japanese coastal waters. To achieve optimum protection the machinery was concentrated into a length representing only some 54 percent of her waterline. The main armour deck was designed to withstand anything up to a 2,200lb (1,000kg) armour-piercing (AP) bomb dropped from 10,000ft (3,048m). Below that deck, 16.1in (409mm) side armour sloped outwards at 20deg and was designed to withstand an 18in (457mm) shell at 23,000-32,000yd (21,000-29,300m). It ran down for some 63.0ft (19.2m) to a 7.9-3.0in (201-76mm) anti-torpedo bulkhead. This in turn sloped down at 14deg to the outer plates of the double bottom and extended fore and aft as a 3.0-2.0in (76-51mm) screen beneath the magazines.

The three triple 18.1in (460mm) turrets each weighed 2,774 tons - ie, as much as a typical World War II destroyer. Each of the three guns was capable of firing up to two 3,240lb (1,470kg) shells per minute to a range of 45,290yd (41,400m) at a maximum elevation of 45deg. There were six 50ft (15.2m) range finders, three of which were mounted atop the main control tower, while the main turrets had one each. There was also a 32.8ft (10.0m) rangefinder on the after control tower. Japanese development of radar lagged behind that of Western navies and depended to a large extent upon information (and some hardware) supplied by Nazi Germany; nevertheless, *Yamato* and *Musashi* were given a high priority and each had five sets at the time they were sunk. The main control tower was a streamlined cylindrical structure that replaced the ugly and complicated "pagodas" of other

***Above: Yamato*'s 18.1in (460mm) guns were the largest mounted in any battleship**

Japanese capital ships. The two triple 6.1in (155mm) turrets on either side of the massive single funnel amidships were replaced by an additional 12 x 5.0in (127mm) DP in *Yamato* in 1943. Her final light AA armament in 1945 was 150 x 25mm.

Although fine sea-boats and with great potential power, *Yamato* and *Musashi* were designed and built to a totally outdated operational concept. As a result, they had undistinguished combat careers and both were sunk at sea, overwhelmed by US carrier-borne airpower. *Yamato* was launched on 8 August 1940, completed on 16 December 1941 (just a week after the Japanese attack on Pearl Harbor) and served as the flagship of the Combined Fleet, wearing the flag of Vice-Admiral Yamamoto Isoruko, from 1942 onwards.

She spent most of 1942-43 operating out of the Japanese base at Truk, but in December 1943 she was torpedoed by USS *Skate* (SS-305) and was in dockyard hands until April 1944, when she was repaired and had her AA battery considerably increased. She took part in the Battles of the Philippine Sea (June 1944) and of Leyte Gulf (October 1944), during which she fired her 18.1in (460mm) guns at US escort carriers. She was based in Japan during that winter and in April 1945 was committed to lead a task force (*Yamato* plus one cruiser and six destroyers) on a one-way "suicide mission" to attack US shipping off Okinawa, nicknamed "Operation *Ten-Go*." US Navy codebreakers knew precisely what was happening and on 7 April 1945, when some 200nm from her goal, *Yamato* was intercepted in the East China Sea by US carrier planes. At least eleven torpedo hits were recorded (possibly as many as fifteen) and there were also at least seven direct bomb hits. She sank, taking 2,498 men to their deaths, accompanied by the cruiser and three destroyers

Musashi was launched on 1 November 1940 and completed 5 August 1942. She was sunk on 24 October 1944 while in the Visayan Sea, south of Luzon, following attacks by aircraft of the US Navy's Task Force 38, which inflicted between eleven and nineteen torpedo hits and at least seventeen direct hits by bombs before the ship sank.

Ekaterina II

RUSSIA

Barbette ship
Completed: 1889-94.
Number in class: 4.
Displacement: 11,032 tons full load.
Dimensions: Length 339.5ft (103.5m); beam 69.0ft (21.0m); draught 28.8ft (8.8m).
Propulsion: 2 shafts; vertical compound engine; 14 boilers; 9,100ihp; 16kt.
Armour: Compound (steel in *Georgi Pobiedonosets*). Belt 18.0-16.0in (457-406mm); belt ends 8.0-6.0in (203-152mm); redoubt 12.0in (305mm); conning tower 9.0-8.0in (227-203mm).
Armament: 6 x 12.0in (305mm) (3 x 2); 7 x 6.0in (152mm); 8 x 3pdr; 4 x 1pdr; 7 x 15in (381mm) TT.
Complement: 674.

History: These four ships were built for the Black Sea Fleet, *Ekaterina II* and *Tchesma* being completed in 1889, followed by *Sinop* in 1890 and *Georgi Pobiedonosets* in 1894. The design was unusual in that there was a triangular central redoubt, with one twin 12.0in (305mm) gun mounting at each corner

forward and the third on the centreline aft. The mountings themselves were of the hydraulic disappearing type, made by Easton and Anderson, and were fitted with 3.0in (76mm) shields. There were some minor differences in machinery and weapons between the four ships, but nothing of major significance.

The two oldest ships, *Ekaterina II* and *Tchesma*, were both stricken in 1907, the latter, which was the heaviest of the four, having been reported to be somewhat unstable. *Georgi Pobiedonosets* was captured by the White Russian forces in 1919 and, following their defeat, was taken by them to Bizerta, where she was later scrapped. The longest to survive was *Sinop* which in 1914 had some of her armament removed, leaving with four 8.0in (203mm) and eight 6.0in (152mm) guns; the ship was then fitted with a large protective bulge and used to explode mines in a similar manner to the German World War II *sperrbrecher*. She was then relegated to guardship duties at Odessa, where she was disarmed by White Russian troops in 1917 and damaged by British interventionist forces in 1919. Finally, she was captured by the Soviet Navy and scrapped in 1922.

Below: **Imperial Russian Navy battleship, *Ekaterina II*, completed in 1889**

Petropavlovsk

RUSSIA

Battleship (pre-dreadnought)
Completed: 1899.
Number in class: 3.
Displacement: 11,354 tons full load.
Dimensions: Length (wl) 369.0ft (112.5m); beam 70.0ft (21.3m); draught 25.5ft (7.8m).
Propulsion: 2 shafts; vertical triple-expansion; 12 boilers; 11,250ihp; 16.5kt.
Armour: Harvey nickel steel. Belt 16.0-5.0in (406-127mm); deck 3.0-2.3in (76-58mm); main turrets 14.0-10.0in (356-254mm); secondary turrets 5.0in (127mm); conning tower 8.0in (203mm).
Armament: 4 x 12.0in (305mm)(2 x 2); 12 x 6.0in (152mm); 12 x 3pdr; 28 x 1pdr; 6 x 18.0in (457mm) TT.
Complement: 632.

History: The Imperial Russian Navy built a constant series of battleships in the years leading up to World War I, most in small classes of between one and three ships, and none of them of any particular merit. Among these was the Petropavlovsk-class, consisting of three ships, all of them completed in 1899: *Petropavlovsk, Poltava* and *Sevastopol*. Most Russian battleships of this period show a marked British influence, but this class was the exception, exhibiting rather more French influence. Thus, they had circular main turrets, eight of the 6.0in (152mm) guns in twin turrets mounted on sponsons, and a marked tumblehome. The main armoured belt was 240.0ft (73.0m) long and 7.5ft (2.3m) deep, but reducing to 1.2ft (0.4m) at the ends.

Peresviet

RUSSIA

Battleship (pre-dreadnought)
Completed: 1901-02.
Number in class: 3.
Displacement: 12,683 tons standard.
Dimensions: Length 434.5ft (132.4m); beam 71.5ft (21.8m); draught 26.0ft (7.92m).
Propulsion: 3 shafts; vertical triple-expansion; 32 boilers; 15,000ihp; 18kt.
Armour: Krupp cemented. Belt 9.0-5.0in (229-127mm); casemates 5.0in (127mm); ; conning tower 6.0in (152mm).
Armament: 4 x 10.0in (254mm) (2 x 2); 11 x 6.0in (152mm); 20 x 11pdr; 20 x 3pdr; 8 x 1pdr; 5 x 15.0in (381mm) TT.
Complement: 752.

History: These three ships, *Perseviet, Osliabia* and *Pobieda*, were conceived as "fast battleships" and attracted such publicity whilst under construction that the Royal Navy felt compelled to respond by building six Duncan-class battleships. As with the Petropavlovsk-class, they showed French design influence, with a high forecastle deck stretching back to the quarterdeck, and tumblehome, a feature always popular with French designers during this period. The armament also showed French influence, being mounted in twin turrets fore and aft, while the secondary and tertiary batteries were disposed mainly in casemates on the main and upper decks, though there was an unprotected 6.0in (152mm) gun which was located, somewhat optimistically, in the bows.

Peresviet was present at the Battle of the Yellow Sea in August 1904 where she was damaged heavily. She managed to regain Port Arthur only to be hit by at

Above: **Sevastopol, one of a class of three showing marked French design influence**

On the outbreak of the Russo-Japanese War all three ships were at the Far Eastern naval base of Port Arthur. On 28 May 1904 *Petropavlvosk* hit a mine which caused an explosion in her magazine, sinking her, while *Sevastopol* hit mines on 23 June and 23 August 1904, without suffering serious damage. Both *Poltava* and *Sevastopol* were present at the Battle of the Yellow Sea (10 August 1904), where both received fourteen hits from Japanese large calibre guns, but survived. *Sevastopol* received further damage at the siege of Port Arthur, and at the surrender was taken out into deep water and scuttled (2 January 1905). *Poltava* was sunk during the siege of Port Arthur, but was raised by the Japanese, repaired and put into service as the *Tan-go*, until sold back to Russia in 1916. Renamed *Tchesma*, she served for some years in the White Sea and was scrapped in 1923.

Above: **The Perseviet-class "fast" battleships provoked the British Duncan-class**

least twenty-three 11.0in (208mm) howitzer shells during the siege, forcing her crew to scuttle her (7 December 1904). She was raised by the Japanese, repaired and put into service as *Sagami* until 1916 when she was sold back to Russia. Her next mishap was to run aground off Vladivostok and the final blow came when she hit a German mine off Port Said, Egypt and was sunk (4 January 1917). *Osliabia* was part of the Russian fleet which sailed from Europe, around Africa, across the Indian Ocean and the South China Sea only to meet the Japanese Fleet in the Battle of Tsushima, where she was sunk (27 May 1915). *Pobieda* differed in various details from her sisters, but her history was very similar to that of *Perseviet*, being damaged at the Battle of the Yellow Sea, returning to Port Arthur and then so badly damaged by army howitzers that she had to be scuttled. She was raised by the Japanese and pressed into service as *Suwo*.

Gangut/Marat

RUSSIA

Battleship (dreadnought)
Completed: 1914.
Number in class: 4.
Displacement: 25,000 tons standard; 26,170 tons full load.
Dimensions: Length 549.5ft (180.0m); beam 87.3ft (26.6m); draught 30.2ft (9.2m).
Propulsion: 4 shafts; Parsons turbines; 25 boilers; 42,000shp; 23kt.
Armour: Belt 9.0-4.0in (229-102mm); decks 3.0-1.5in (76-38mm); barbettes 8.0in (203mm); turrets 8.0-5.0in (203-127mm); ; conning tower 10.0in (254mm).
Armament: 12 x 12in (305mm) (4 x 3); 16 x 4.7in (120mm); 6 x 45mm AA; 16 x 13mm AA; 4 x 17.7in (450mm) TT.
Complement: 1,277.

History: About a dozen Russian battleships survived the 1917 Revolution, but most were scrapped in the early 1920s, except for the four Gangut-class ships. *Gangut, Petropavlovsk, Poltava* and *Sevastopol*, which had been completed in 1914. They had an unusual background, design work having started in 1906-07, the navy's aim being to produce Russia's first dreadnought, armed with twelve 12in (305mm) guns and sixteen 4.7in (120mm) in casemates, but with a top speed of 21.5kt. Fifty-one designs were submitted, but the best, from

Blohm+Voss in Germany, was rejected as the government required the ships to be built in Russia. The design was then reworked with the help of British shipbuilder, John Brown, resulting in a ship which fell roughly between a battleship and a battlecruiser, and known at the time as a "Baltic-dreadnought."

The four triple 12.0in (305mm) turrets were all on the centreline, giving a broadside of twelve guns compared to eight in contemporary British and German ships. The machinery and hull design resulted in a speed of 23kt, 1.5kt above that stated in the requirement, giving a 2-3kt margin over any other dreadnought. Armoured protection was not up to the standard of the rest of the ship, several compromises being necessary to keep weight down. As the ships were to be employed in the Baltic they were given specially reinforced ice-breaking bows, but the American-style cage masts, which had been tried in the previous Imperator Pavel-class, were deleted during construction and replaced by pole masts.

They played a limited role in World War I, but in 1917 they came under Bolshevik control in July/August, but were then demobilised in January 1918 and withdrawn to Kronstadt in April. As usual, the names were changed to mark the latest political order, the names being changed in the early 1920s: *Gangut Oktyabrskaya Revoluciya; Petropavlovsk Marat, Poltava Mikhail Frunze;* and *Sevastopol Parizskaya Kommuna*. The only one to take part in the Civil War was *Petropavlovsk*, which was sunk by torpedoes from the British motor boats, then recovered, repaired and returned to service. *Poltava* was severely damaged in a fire in 1919 and stricken, only to be reinstated in 1926, but the promised repair work never started and she was scuttled in 1941. The ships received limited modification in the Inter-war years, with altered bridge arrangements, the forefunnel trunked aft to keep smoke and heat away from the fighting top, a catapult on "Q" turret and a large crane to handle the three aircraft. During World War II the three ships were used primarily for fire support, *Marat* and *Oktyabrskaya Revoluciya* in the Baltic and *Parizskaya Kommuna* in the Black Sea, and all were damaged by German bombers, but survived the war. In the late 1940s *Marat* was renamed *Volkhov* and become an artillery ship, while the other two were reclassified as training ships. All were stricken and scrapped in the mid-1950s.

***Left:* The four Gangut-class ships served throughout World Wars I and II**

Borodino

RUSSIA

Battleship
Completed: 1903-05.
Number in class: 5.
Displacement: 13,516 tons standard.
Dimensions: Length 397.0ft (121.0m); beam 76.2ft (23.2m); draught 26.2ft (8.0m).
Propulsion: 2 shafts; vertical, triple-expansion engines; 20 boilers; 16,300ihp, 17.8kt.
Armour: Krupps cemented. Belt 7.5-6.0in (191-152mm); belt ends 5.8-4.0in (147-102mm); turrets 10.0-4.0in (254-102mm); secondary turrets 6.0in (152mm); 11pdr battery 3.0in (76mm); conning tower 8.0in (203mm).
Armament: 4 x 12.0in (305mm) (2 x 2); 12 x 6in (152mm); 20 x 11pdr; 20 x 3pdr; 4 x 15.0in (380mm) TT.
Complement: 835.

History: Few battleship classes have met such disastrous ends as the Russian Borodino-class. In theory the Borodinos were an improved Russian-built version of the *Tsessarevitch*, which had been designed and built in France and had joined the Russian fleet in 1903. The Russians appear, however, to have tinkered with the design, resulting in an increase in displacement from 12,915 to 13,516 tons, and a reduction in power from 16,500hp to 16,300hp, which combined to reduce speed by at least 1k.

Imperator Aleksandr III was completed in 1903, *Borodino, Orel* and *Kniaz Suvorov* in 1904, and *Slava* in 1905. All served in European waters, but when the Russo-Japanese War broke out all except *Slava* set out on the long, slow

España

SPAIN

Battleship (dreadnought)
Completed: 1913-21.
Number in class: 3.
Displacement: 15,452 tons standard; 15,700 tons full load.
Dimensions: Length 459.2ft (140.0m); beam 78.8ft (24.0m); draught 25.5ft (7.8m).
Propulsion: 4 shafts; Parsons turbines; 12 boilers; 15,500shp; 19.5kt; 5,000nm at 10kt.
Armour: Upper belt 8.0-4.0in (203-102mm); decks 1.5in (38mm); barbettes 10.0in (254mm); turrets 8.0in (203mm); conning tower 10.0in (254mm).
Armament: 8 x 12in (305mm); (4 x 2); 20 x 4in (102mm); 4 x 3pdr; 2 x MG.
Complement: 854.

History: These three ships are noteworthy principally because, coastal battleships apart, they were the smallest and slowest dreadnought battleships ever built, although they probably also had the worst armoured protection, as well. They were built by SECN at Ferrol, one of the major limitations being the size of available dock facilities. Construction was slow and the yards were badly held up by delays in supply of equipment, particularly weapons, from Great Britain during the war years. Main armament was eight 12.0in (305mm) guns in four twin turrets, with the two echeloned turrets having arcs of fire of 180deg on the beam on which they were located and 80deg across the deck on the other beam. Secondary armament was twenty 4.0in (102mm), all in casemates. A 1913 plan to build three more battleships to a new design to be completed in 1920 was abandoned, mainly due to the difficulties of obtaining weapons and

***Above: Slava,* only Borodino-class ship not present at the Battle of Tsushima**

journey to the Far East where they met the Japanese fleet at the Battle of Tsushima (27 May 1905). The four ships were in the thick of the fighting, and suffered accordingly. *Borodino* suffered a number of shell hits which resulted in a magazine explosion, blowing the ship apart. *Aleksandr* sank as a result of shell fire alone, while *Suvorov*, was badly damaged by shells and then finished off by torpedoes. *Orel* was badly damaged during the fighting and had no choice but to surrender the following day; she was then repaired and served in the Japanese Navy as the *Iwami* until being scrapped in 1922. The only ship not at Tsushima was *Slava*, which served in the Baltic in World War I, where she met the German dreadnought *König* on 17 October 1917. The German ship inflicted such severe damage on the Russian ship that she had to be finished off with a torpedo.

***Right:* The Spanish España-class were the slowest dreadnoughts built for any navy**

equipment from overseas, primarily Great Britain, due to the war.

España ran aground on an uncharted reef off the coast of Morocco (28 August 1923); salvage attempts were abandoned after her main guns had been recovered and the ship was stricken *in situ*. *Alfonso XIII* was renamed *España* in 1931 and was on the nationalist side during the Spanish Civil War; she sank after hitting one of her own side's mines on 30 April 1937. *Jaime I* was damaged by shore artillery operated by the Riff insurgents in 1924 and was on the Republican side during the Civil War, She was badly damaged in an air attack on 13 August 1936, but was then wrecked by an internal explosion (17 June 1937); she was refloated but repairs were considered uneconomic and she was scrapped in 1939.

Sverige

SWEDEN

Coastal battleship
Completed: 1917-22.
Number in class: 3.
Displacement: 6,852 tons standard; 7,516 tons full load.
Dimensions: Length 393.7ft (120.0m); beam 61.0ft (18.6m); draught 21.3ft (6.5m).
Propulsion: 2 shafts; Curtis direct-coupled turbines; 12 boilers; 25,400shp; 22.5kt.
Armour: Belt 7.9/5.9-2.4in-(200/150-60mm); turrets 7.9-3.9in (200-100mm); conning tower 6.9in (175/100-60mm) maximum.
Armament: 4 x 11.1in (283mm) (2 x 2); 8 x 6in (152mm); 6 x 75mm; 2 x 57mm; 2 x MG; 2 x 21in (533mm) TT.
Complement: 427.

History: Like Norway and Denmark, Sweden developed a series of "coastal battleships," of which the last were these three ships: *Sverige* completed in 1917; *Drottning Victoria* (1921) and *Gustaf V* (1922). The original plan was for four ships, but the government was reluctant to start building and it was only after a nation-wide, popular fund-raising campaign had collected sufficient money to pay for one that the government felt obliged to lay down the first of class, which, in honour of the fund-raisers, was named *Sverige*. Two more, government-funded ships were laid down in 1915 which were some 5.3ft (1.6m) longer and had 117 tons greater displacement (full load), the increase being almost entirely attributable to the fact that they were given an ice-breaking capability. The fourth was never built.

These three ships gave excellent service in helping to maintain Sweden's

Warrior

UNITED KINGDOM

Broadside ironclad
Completed: 1861-62.
Number in class: 2.
Displacement: 9,137 tons full load.
Dimensions: Length 420.0ft (128.0m); beam 58.3ft (17.8m); draught 26.0ft (7.9m).
Propulsion: 1shaft, Penn horizontal, single-expansion, trunk engine; 10 boilers; 5,267ihp; 14.1kt (steam), 13kt (sail only).
Armour: Iron. Belt 4.5in (114mm); bulkheads 4.5in (114mm); teak backing 18in (457mm).
Armament: 4 x 110pdr (8in [203mm]) muzzle-loading rifled guns; 28 x 68pdr (7.0in [178mm]) muzzle loading rifled guns.
Complement: 707.

History: Anglo-French cooperation during the Crimean War quickly deteriorated to the more traditional hostility, leading, in particular, to a naval race. Thus, news of the laying-down of the French *Gloire* in 1858, led to a British order in 1859 for two new ships, *Warrior* and *Black Prince*, which were completed in 1861 and 1862, respectively. These were the world's first ocean-going, ironclad ships and at the time they were commissioned they were the most powerful ships in the world, their mission being to overtake and destroy any ship then in service; as a result, they had a battery rendered impregnable by the armoured protection and a speed greater than any comparable ship.

The bow and stern were unprotected, but amidships there was a belt of armour 4.5in (114mm) thick, 213.0ft (64.9m) long and 22.0ft (6.7m) deep, laid on teak planking 18.0in (457mm) thick. The sailing rig was based on that of

***Above: Gustav V,* one of three Sverige-class "coastal" battleships built in Sweden**

neutrality. It was always planned that they would work together as a squadron to provide concentrated firepower, the perceived threat throughout the 1920s and into the mid-1930s being the Soviet Union, and from about 1935 to 1945, Nazi Germany. Indeed, in 1944 a German naval force was detected approaching the island of Åland, upon which the battle squadron was deployed and the German ships turned away. These three ships proved to be a thoroughly worthwhile investment and exerted a strong naval influence in the restricted waters of the Baltic. They were stricken in the mid-1950s, being replaced by the Tre Kronor-class cruisers.

***Above:* Revolutionary warship, *Warrior,* can still be seen at Portsmouth, England**

contemporary 80-gun ships and consisted of three masts, with a long bow-sprit (later shortened). They could make 13kt under sail alone and just over 14kt under steam, but on one occasion, using both steam and sail *Warrior* made the speed, extraordinary for the day, of 17.5kt. Two unusual features were that these two ships had telescopic funnels and were the very last ships in the Royal Navy to carry figureheads.

The ships served with the Channel Fleet, but by 1875 had been reclassified as "coastguard ships." *Warrior* became an oil pipe-line pontoon at Milford Haven in 1923, but in the mid-1970s her historical significance was recognised and she underwent a major restoration at Hartlepool and now, fully restored to her former glory is on public display at Portsmouth, England.

Minotaur

UNITED KINGDOM

Broadside ironclad
Completed: 1867-68.
Number in class: 3.
Displacement: 10,600 tons full load.
Dimensions: Length 407.0ft (124.0m); beam 59.5ft (18.1m); draught 27.8ft (8.5m).
Propulsion: 1 shaft; Maudslay return connecting-rod engines; 10 boilers; 6,870ihp; 14.8kt;
Armour: Iron. Belt 5.5in (140mm); ends 4.5in (114mm); bulkheads 5.5in (140mm); teak backing 10in (254mm).
Armament: 4 x 9in (230mm) muzzle-loading rifles (MLR) guns; 24 x 7in (178mm) MLR.
Complement: 800.

History: With an original specification for a 50-gun frigate with all its guns behind armour, the designer, Isaac Watts, gave these ships a greater length than the previous Achilles-class and achieved a high speed relative to engine power without increasing beam or draught. The class had ram-shaped bows. They were the largest warships ever propelled by a single screw and *Northumberland* was the first ship in the Royal Navy to be fitted with steam steering gear.

Planned armament comprised forty 100pdr in the battery and ten more on pivot mounts on the upper deck, but the ships were actually completed with four 9in (230mm) on iron carriages and twenty-four 7in (178mm) on the traditional rope-worked carriages, all of them muzzle loaders. Two of the 7in (178mm) guns were mounted in the bows as chasers and a further pair were

Monarch

UNITED KINGDOM

Masted turret ship
Completed: 1868.
Number in class: 1.
Displacement: 8,322 tons full load.
Dimensions: Length 330.0ft (100.6m); beam 57.5ft (17.5m); draught 24.3ft (7.4m).
Propulsion: 1shaft; Humphreys & Tennant 2-cylinder return connecting-rod engine; 9 boilers; 7,842ihp; 14.9kt; 1,560nm at 12.5kt.
Armour: Iron. Belt 7.0-4.5in (178-114mm); bulkheads 4.5-4in (114-102mm); turrets 8.0in (203mm); conning tower 8.0in (203mm).
Armament: 4 x 12.0in (305mm) muzzle-loaders (2 x 2); 3 x 7.0in (178mm) muzzle-loaders.
Complement: 575.

History: Monitors, the first turreted ships, had very low freeboard and were essentially confined to rivers, estuaries and coastal waters, but *Monarch*, the sole ship in her class, was the first large, ocean-going turret ship, with a high freeboard and a full spread of canvas. Freeboard amidships was 14.0ft (4.3m) and the actual guns, 12in (305mm) muzzle-loaders, each weighing 25 tons (25.4 tonnes), were 17.5ft (5.2m) above the waterline. The two twin turrets were grouped close together and although the hinged bulwarks were dropped in action, the arcs of fire were limited by the superstructure and sailing rig. This was remedied to a certain extent by the three 7.0in (178mm) guns, two in the forecastle firing ahead and the third aft firing astern. A flying bridge, a feature which would be repeatedly used in British capital ships over the next fifty years, ran from the foremast to the mainmast, enabling the crew to move past the turrets.

***Above: Minotaur*, seen here in the 1890s, ended her days as a coal-hulk**

right aft, firing astern. Protection was provided by an iron belt covering the entire side (apart from a small area in the bows), and stretched from the upper deck down to 5.8ft (1.8m) below the waterline; 5.5in (140mm) bulkheads protected the bow and stern guns.

Minotaur was completed first (1865), but was then used for various tests, which led to design changes in the following two ships: *Agincourt*, completed in 1867 and *Northumberland* in 1868. *Minotaur* then became the last to be commissioned in December 1868. As built, these ships carried five masts but they were poor sailers and their rig was altered several times, but without offering much improvement. They were, however, good seaboats and steamed well.

All three ships were modified during their long service, becoming training ships in the early 1900s and later coaling hulks, *Agincourt* surviving (as hulk *C-109*) until 1960, ninety-nine years after being laid down at Birkenhead.

***Above: Monarch* seen here following her 1872 conversion to a barque-rig**

Monarch was the fastest battleship of her day, being capable of 14.9kt under steam power, and while a good sea-boat she proved difficult to handle with steam power being necessary for certain manoeuvres, although a redesigned rudder made matters better. She was rebuilt several times, being altered to barque rig in 1872 and having her sailing rig completely removed in 1890-97. She took part in the bombardment of Alexandria in 1882 and was later guard-ship at the naval base in Simon's Town, South Africa. She was then, briefly, a depot ship, renamed *Simoon*, but was broken-up in 1906.

Hotspur

UNITED KINGDOM

Ironclad ram
Completed: 1870.
Number in class: 1.
Displacement: 4,331 tons full load.
Dimensions: Length 235.0ft (71.6m); beam 50.0ft (15.2m); draught 20.8ft (6.4m).
Propulsion: 2 shafts; Napier engines; 3,500ihp; 12.7kt.
Armour: Belt 11.0-8.0in (280-203mm); breastwork 8.0in (203mm); gun house (fixed) 10.0-8.5in (254-216mm); conning tower 10.0-6.0in (254-152mm).
Armament: 1 x 12in (305mm) muzzle-loader, rifled; 2 x 64pdr muzzle-loaders, rifled.
Complement: 209.

History: *Hotspur* was designed at the time when ramming had become fashionable, following the battle between the Austro-Hungarian and Italian fleets at Lissa (16 July 1866), the first major naval battle since Trafalgar in 1805. At Lissa the tactic of ramming was employed with apparent success, resulting in many navies either building specialist "rams" or incorporating a ram in the bow of capital ships in case it might be needed. *Hotspur* was one of the first specialist rams and her primary weapon was a 10.0ft (3.05m) projection under the bow. The full length, iron armoured belt extended to 5ft (1.5m) below the waterline and was extended forwards and downwards to support the ram.

The main gun armament was a single 12in (305mm) muzzle-loader which was mounted on a turntable inside a static gunhouse, in which there were four firing ports, the gun being rotated inside the gunhouse to align it with one of the ports for firing. The reason for this extraordinary arrangement was that it was

Colossus

UNITED KINGDOM

Turret ship
Completed: 1886-87.
Number in class: 2.
Displacement: 9,420 tons full load.
Dimensions: Length 325.0ft (99.1m); beam 68.0ft (20.7m); draught 25.8ft (7.9m).
Propulsion: 2 shafts; Maudslay three-cylinder inverted compound engine; 7,488ihp; 16.5 kt.
Armour: Citadel 18.0-14.0in (457-356mm) sides; bulkheads 16.0-13.0in (406-330mm); decks 3.0-2.5in (76-64mm); turrets 16.0-14.0in (406-356mm); conning tower 14.0in (356mm).
Armament: 4 x 12in breach-loading (305mm) (2 x 2); 5 x 6in 152mm); 4 x 6pdr; 2 x 14in (356mm) TT.
Complement: 396.

History: These two ships, *Colossus* and *Edinburgh*, completed in 1886 and 1887 respectively, represent a significant watershed in British capital ship design. The hull introduced several new features, the most important being that it was constructed entirely of steel, and, secondly, it featured compound armour protection, consisting of a steel face with a wrought-iron backing. This armour was used to construct a citadel 123.0ft (37.5m) in length and with a depth of 16.0ft (4.9m), with semi-circular bulkhead ends for improved deflection of incoming shells. Both ends of the ship were compartmented to enhance flotation, with the outer compartments being filled with cork.

The 12in (305mm) guns were mounted in two twin centreline turrets amidships and it had originally been planned to use muzzle loaders, but it was

***Above: Hotspur,* designed as a "ram," was soon re-roled for coast defence**

thought that a rotating turret would not be able to sustain the shock of ramming. There were also two 64pdrs in open mounts aft.

Hotspur was a failure in most respects. She was steady and manoeuvrable but was seriously underpowered, which meant that not only was she not very fast, but also that she could not make headway in a heavy sea. In addition the firing slits in the gunhouse were so sited that she could not fire dead ahead and thus could not fire at an intended victim of her ram, even if she could catch up with it. Thus, the prospects of employing her as a ram were very small. Surprisingly, she was totally rebuilt in1881-83, being given a rotating turret containing two 12.0in muzzle-loaders, while the 64pdrs were replacing by two 6in (152mm) breech-loaders. It was all of little value and she was scrapped in 1904.

***Above:* The 1886 Colossus-class introduced steel hulls and compound armour**

decided whilst building to replace these with breech loaders, the first of such a large calibre in the British fleet. They were also the first British capital ships to have a substantial secondary armament, consisting of five 6in (152mm) guns, two on either side of the superstructure forward, one on each beam amidships, and one at the extreme after end of the superstructure.

They were not very satisfactory ships in service, rolling badly in a seaway and being difficult to manoeuvre, as a result of which they had a short service life. Both served in the Mediterranean Fleet but *Colossus* returned to the UK in 1893 followed by *Edinburgh* in 1894. Both then served as coastguard ships for some years. *Colossus* was sold for scrap in 1908 and *Edinburgh* in 1909.

Victoria

UNITED KINGDOM

Turret ship
Completed: 1890-91.
Number in class: 2.
Displacement: 10,470 tons full load.
Dimensions: Length 363.0ft (110.6m); beam 70.0ft (21.3m); draught 29.0ft (8.8m).
Propulsion: 2 shafts; two sets Humphreys 3-cylinder triple-expansion engines; 8 boilers; 14,22ihp (forced draught); 17.3kt.
Armour: Compound. Belt 18.0in (457mm); bulkheads 16.0in (406mm); ; decks 3.0in (76mm); battery screens 6.0-3.0in (152-75mm); ; turret 18.0 (475mm); conning tower 14.0in (356mm).
Armament: 2 x 16.3in (413mm) (2 x 1) breech-loaders (BL); 1 x 10in (254mm) BL; 12 x 6in (152mm); 12 x 6pdr; 9 x 3pdr; 4 x 14in (356mm) TT.
Complement: 550.

History: Despite being named after the reigning monarch, HMS *Victoria*, was an undistinguished design and met an ignominious end. Six Admiral-class ships were laid down between 1880 and 1883, with minor variations between them, but all with their main armament mounted in barbettes. The class was severely criticised, even while under construction, for having insufficient protection, which led to this new class of two ships, *Victoria* (completed in 1890), and *Sans Pareil* (1891). In these the protection was supposedly improved, and the main armament of two 16.25in (413mm) breech-loaders was mounted in a single turret forward. These very large calibre guns had a powerful blast effect, which meant that the arc of fire (in theory some 300deg) was limited by a ban on firing

Royal Sovereign

UNITED KINGDOM

First-class battleship
Completed: 1892-1894.
Number in class: 7.
Displacement: 14,150 tons load; 15,580 tons deep load.
Dimensions: Length 410.5ft (125.0m); beam 75.0ft (22.9m); draught 27.5ft (8.4m).
Propulsion: 2 shafts, 3-cylinder, triple-expansion engines; 8 boilers; 9,000ihp; 16.5kt.
Armour: Compound. Belt 18.0-14.0in (457-356mm); bulkheads 16.0-14.0in (406-356mm); decks 3.0-2.5in (76-64mm); barbettes 17.0-11.0in (432-280mm); casemates 6.0in (152mm); conning tower 14.0in (356mm).
Armament: 4 x 13.5in (343mm) (2 x 2); 10 x 6in (152mm); 16 x 6pdr; 12 x 3pdr; 7 x 18in (457mm) TT.
Complement: 712.

History: The Royal Sovereign-class was built to meet several requirements. First was the political requirement that the strength of the Royal Navy was to equal that of any two other navies combined. Second was that battleships should be built in large classes to provide a homogeneous squadron. And, thirdly, that there had to be a considerable increase in displacement to provide the protection, firepower and seakeeping necessary for modern conditions, although this brought with it a considerable increase in cost.

The design was essentially an improved version of the Admiral-class, with the guns mounted in open barbettes, but one deck higher, and with

***Above: Sans Pareil,* sister-ship to *Victoria,* which met an ignominious end in 1893**

dead ahead, which would damage the foredeck, and on firing much abaft the beam, which would damage the superstructure. In addition, the ships had a low freeboard (approximately 12.0ft [3.7m]) which meant that they were very wet forwards, adding further to the limitations on the effectiveness of the main armament. Secondary armament comprised a single 10in (254mm), also in a turret, aft and twelve 6in (152mm) mounted in two batteries in the superstructure.

Victoria was flagship of the Mediterranean Fleet from 1890 until 22 June 1893 when, due to a mistaken order by the commander-in-chief, Admiral Tryon, she was involved in a collision, being rammed by the battleship HMS *Camperdown* off the Lebanese port of Tripoli. *Victoria* flooded rapidly forwards until the level reached some forward doors, which had been left open to improve the airflow through the 6in (152mm) gun batteries. After that the ship rapidly filled, then turned turtle and sank with the loss of 284 lives, including Admiral Tryon, who refused to leave his ship. *Sans Pareil* was sold for scrap in 1907.

***Above:* Although eight Royal Sovereigns were built, the class was not a success**

tumblehomes, both of which improved seakeeping., although bilge keels had to be fitted later when it was discovered that they rolled excessively.

There was an eighth ship in the class, HMS *Hood,* which was built to a similar design, but, at the behest of the First Sea Lord, with the main guns mounted in turrets, rather than barbettes. The considerable extra topweight meant that freeboard had to be reduced by one deck, giving a return to the poor seakeeping problems of the earlier Admiral-class. These ships served in the Channel and Mediterranean Fleets until 1902, and thereafter in home waters. By 1914 only *Revenge* remained in service and she actually saw some action, being used in early 1915 to bombard the Belgian coast. Also in 1915, she was renamed *Redoubtable* and used for miscellaneous tasks at Portsmouth until being sold for scrap in 1919.

Majestic

UNITED KINGDOM

First-class battleship (pre-dreadnought)
Completed: 1895-98.
Number in class: 9.
Displacement: 14,560 tons load; 15,730 tons full load.
Dimensions: Length 421.0ft (128.3m); beam 75.0ft (22.9m); draught 27.0ft (8.2m).
Propulsion: 2 shafts, three-cylinder triple-expansion engines; 8 boilers; 10,000ihp; 17.0kt.
Armour: Belt 9.0in (229mm); bulkheads 14.0-12.0in (356-305mm); decks 4.0-2.5in (102-64mm); barbettes 14.0in(356mm); turrets 10.0in (254mm); casemates 6.0in (152mm); conning tower 14.0in (356mm).
Armament: 4 x 12.0in (304mm) (2 x 2); 12 x 6in (152mm); 16 x 12pdr; 12 x 2pdr; 5 x 18in (457mm) TT;
Complement: 672.

History: The nine ships of the Majestic-class constitute the largest single class of battleships ever built and were the major element in a massive programme which originally involved 28 cruisers and 122 other warships, intended to counter the growing naval threat from Prussia and France. Many elements of this programme were cut back but not the battleships which (with their completion dates) were: *Majestic* (1895); *Magnificent* (1895); *Prince George* (1896); *Victorious* (1896); *Jupiter* (1897); *Mars* (1897); *Caesar* (1898); *Hannibal* (1898); and *Illustrious* (1898). That nine such large, advanced and capable ships could be completed in just over two years was an extraordinary achievement and illustrates the capability of the British shipbuilding industry of the day.

King Edward VII

UNITED KINGDOM

First-class battleship (pre-dreadnought)
Completed: 1905-06.
Number in class: 8.
Displacement: 15,585 tons load; 17,290 tons full load.
Dimensions: Length 453.8ft (138.3m); beam 78.0ft (23.8m); draught 25.7ft (7.7m).
Propulsion: 2 shafts; 4-cylinder triple expansion engines; 12 boilers; 18,000ihp, 18.5kt.
Armour: Belt 9.0-8.0in (229-203mm); bulkheads 12.0-8.0in (305-203mm); barbettes 12.0in (305mm); main turrets 12.0-8.0in (305-203mm); decks 2.5-1.0in (64-25mm); conning tower 12.0in (305mm).
Armament: 4 x 12in (305mm) (2 x 2); 4 x 9.2in (234mm); 10 x 6in (152mm); 14 x 12pdr; 14 x 3pdr; 4 x 18in (457mm) TT.
Complement: 777.

History: The King Edward VII-class represents the last of a line of late-Victorian battleship designs stretching back to the Royal Sovereign-class of 1893. It consisted of eight ships: *King Edward VII* (1905); *Commonwealth* (1905); *Dominion* (1905); *Hindustan* (1905); *New Zealand* (1905, renamed *Zealandia* in 1911); *Africa* (1906); *Britannia* (1906); and *Hibernia* (1907). Obviously, the design had evolved, with an increase in displacement and this particular class introduced a much heavier secondary armament of four 9.2in (234mm) guns in four single turrets, with a tertiary armament of ten 6in (152mm) in a box battery amidships. Fire-control tops were fitted on fore and main masts, but even with this advance it proved impossible to differentiate between the shell splashes of the 12in (305mm) and 9.2in (234mm) guns, a problem which was the subject

Above: **Nine ships made the Majestics the largest class of battleships ever built**

The design was a development of the Royal Sovereign-class, but with many additional features. These ships used the newly-developed nickel-steel Harvey armour which allowed adequate protection at less cost than in earlier battleships by the provision of a lighter, deeper belt, which was 220.0ft (67.1m) long, 16.0ft (4.9m) deep and of 0.8in (229mm) thickness throughout, rising to the height of the gun deck and terminating in a 14.0in (356mm) bulkhead forward and a 12.0in (356mm) bulkhead aft.

Majestic served as Flagship Channel Fleet in 1895-1903 and all remained active until well into World War I, although four were converted into armed troopships. *Majestic* and *Prince George* took part in the Gallipoli operation in March 1915, where, on 27 May, *Majestic* was hit by two torpedoes from a U-boat and sank within seven minutes, with the loss of forty lives. All eight surviving ships were scrapped in 1920-23.

Above: Hibernia **shows a profusion of antennas after the installation of wireless**

of considerable criticism at the time.

As a class – and despite the fire control problems – these ships were successful, being considered fast and handy, and proving to be good, steady gun platforms. All served throughout World War I, but *King Edward VII* hit a mine and sank on 6 January 1916, while *Britannia* was sunk by a U-boat on 9 November 1918, just 48 hours before the war ended. The others were scrapped in 1920-21.

Dreadnought

UNITED KINGDOM

Battleship
Completed: 1906.
Number in class: 1.
Displacement: 18,110 tons standard; 21,845 tons full load.
Dimensions: Length 527.0ft (160.6m); beam 82.0ft (25.0m); draught 31.0ft (9.4m).
Propulsion: 4 shafts; Parsons turbines; 18 boilers; 23,000shp, 21kt; 6,620nm at 10kt.
Armour: Belt 11.0-4.0in (280-102mm); decks 3.0-1.5in (76-38mm); barbettes 11.0in (280mm); turret faces 11.0in (280mm); conning tower 11.0in (mm).
Armament: 10 x 12.0in (305mm) (5 x 2); 24 x 12pdr (76mm); 5 x 18in (457mm) TT.
Complement: 695-773.

History: The day that HMS *Dreadnought* joined the British Fleet she rendered every existing battleship in all other navies obsolete, her combination of "all big-gun" armament, an effective fire-control system, turbine power, four propellers and oil-fired boilers setting totally new standards, although it was her armament which stole the limelight. By the beginning of the 20th Century many thinking sailors and designers had become increasingly concerned about the rapid increase in the calibre and numbers of secondary weapons, which led to mixes such as those in the Royal Navy's King Edward VII-class (four 12in (305mm), four 9.2in (234mm)) and the Lord Nelson-class (four 12in (305mm), ten 9.2in (234mm)), while the US Navy's Louisiana-class had four 12in (305mm), eight 8in (203mm) and twelve 7in (178mm). Such combinations led to major problems of gun disposition and protection, the stowage and handling of various different types of ammunition and charges, the different maintenance procedures and spares requirements for different weapons, mountings and turrets, and, increasingly, of fire control. In the latter case, it was almost impossible for spotters in the fire direction centres to tell the difference between main and secondary weapon splashes, especially at the longer ranges.

These problems were much discussed in several navies and British Admiral 'Jackie' Fisher was by no means a lone voice in demanding major changes. What made him different, however, was that as First Sea Lord he was in a position to do something about it, while his enthusiasm and passion enabled him to overcome bureaucratic obstacles which had defeated or delayed others. While Fisher commanded the Mediterranean Fleet he started sketching designs, which he nicknamed HMS *Untakable*, for a ship which he wanted to be armed with 10in (254mm) guns, which had a much higher rate of fire (Fisher loved anything which performed *fast*) rather than the standard 12in (305mm) gun, but many experienced captains preferred the latter for its much more damaging terminal effects.

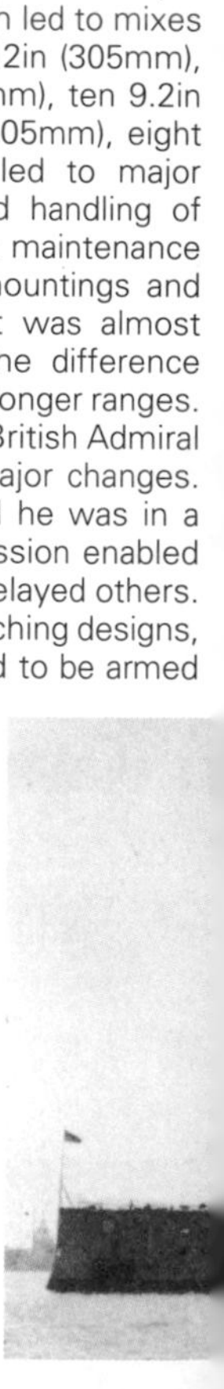

When Fisher arrived at the Admiralty as First Sea Lord in October 1904 his mind was set on what was now termed Design 'B,' with eight 12in (305mm) guns and this was the first project presented to the Committee on Designs which he set up in December 1904 with himself in the chair. The agreed requirements were for a speed of 21kt, adequate armour, a main armament of 12in (305mm) guns and some12pdr guns for anti-torpedo boat defence. Fisher had two further demands: the need for end-on fire as well as a broadside capability and his insistence on high speed, even at the expense of some protection. Various proposed designs were prepared and considered in detail, beginning with Design D, all of them powered by reciprocating machinery, except for the last (Design H), and all armed with either twelve or ten 12in (305mm) guns in twin turrets.

The Committee started work in January 1905 and perhaps its most daring step did not concern the armament at all, but was the decision to power the ship by Parsons turbines driving four rather than the then usual two or three shafts. The Committee issued its final report just seven weeks later and *Dreadnought*'s keel was laid on 2 October 1905, with progress being so rapid that she was launched on 10 February 1906 and started harbour trials on 3 October 1906, a truly astonishing achievement by the builder, Portsmouth Naval Dockyard.

An important feature of *Dreadnought* was that it was not only her all big-gun armament that was revolutionary, but also her gun-control system, which for the first time provided the equipment, instruments and communications necessary to control and direct all the guns from a central position. This required a fire direction centre with a good all-round view and a mounting for the Barr & Stroud 9ft (2.7m) optical rangefinder, all in a position which was as clear as possible of sea spray and possible damage. This resulted in it being placed atop a heavy tripod foremast, but unfortunately this placed it directly above the forward funnel. As a result the men inside had to endure extremely unpleasant working conditions, both from the heat of the exhausts and from obscuration of the view by the smoke, both of which were at their worst when steaming at high speed.

The overall impact of *Dreadnought* on battleship design was so fundamental that she started a race which would continue, with varying degrees of intensity, for the next fifty years. In the ultimate honour, this new breed of fighting ship was given the generic title "dreadnoughts," while the previous generation (ie, 1899-1906) of battleships were consigned to history under the collective and thoroughly dismissive title of "pre-dreadnoughts."

Dreadnought herself served throughout World War I, being flagship 4th Battle Squadron from August 1914 to late 1915, when she went in for a major refit. She returned to become flagship 3rd Battle Squadron in May 1916, until rejoining 4th Battle Squadron in March 1918. She paid off in July 1918, went into reserve in February 1919 and was broken up in 1920. Curiously, this unique ship has another unique achievement to her credit in that on 18 March 1915 she rammed and sank *U-29*, becoming the only battleship in any navy ever to have sunk a submarine.

Below: **The splendid *Dreadnought*, the most influential ship design ever built**

Lord Nelson

UNITED KINGDOM

First-class battleship (pre-dreadnought)
Completed: 1908.
Number in class: 2.
Displacement: 16,090 tons load; 17,820 tons full load.
Dimensions: Length 443.5ft (135.2m); beam 79.5ft (24.2m); draught 26.0ft (7.9m).
Propulsion: 2 shafts; 4-cylinder triple-expansion engines; 15 boilers; 16,750ihp, 18.0kt.
Armour: Belt 12.0-8.0in (305-203mm); bulkheads 8.0in (203mm); citadel 8.0in (203mm); barbettes 12.0in (305mm); turrets 9.2in (234mm); conning tower 12.0in (305mm); decks 4.0-1.0(102-25mm).
Armament: 4 x 12in (305mm) (2 x 2); 10 x 9.2in (234mm); 24 x 12pdr; 2 x 3pdr; 5 x 18in 457mm) TT.
Complement: 800.

History: Although they were the last of the pre-dreadnoughts, these two ships, *Lord Nelson* and *Agamemnon*, were actually completed in 1908 *after* that historic ship, since the first production of the new 12in/45 calibre guns, originally intended for the Lord Nelsons, were diverted to the *Dreadnought* to speed its entry into service. Main armament comprised four 12in (305mm) guns in two twin turrets, but with a very heavy secondary armament of ten 9.2in (234mm) guns in two single and four twin turrets. There were no 6in (152mm) guns and tertiary armament comprised twenty-four single 12pdr guns, intended for defence against torpedo boats and sited along the flying deck amidships. The hull was of a new form, with greater beam and draught than previous

Bellerophon/ St Vincent

UNITED KINGDOM

Battleship (dreadnought)
Specifications for *Bellerophon*
Completed: Bellerophons - 1909; St Vincents 1909-10.
Number in class: Bellerophon - 3; St Vincent - 3.
Displacement: 18,800 tons load; 22,102 tons full load.
Dimensions: Length 526.0ft (160.3m); beam 82.5ft (25.2m); draught 27.3ft (8.3m).
Propulsion: 4 shafts; Parsons turbines; 18 boilers; 23,000shp; 20.8kt; 5,720nm at 10kt.
Armour: Belt 10.0-5.1in (250-130mm); bulkheads 8.0in (203mm); barbettes 9.0-5.0in (230-130mm); turret faces 11.0in (280mm); conning tower 11.0-8.0in (280-203mm); decks 4.0-0.5in (100-15mm).
Armament: 10 x 12.0in (305mm) (5 x 2); 16 x 4.0in (102mm); 4 x 3pdr (47mm); 3 x 18in (457mm) TT.
Complement: 733.

History: The Bellerophon-class, consisting of *Bellerophon, Superb* and *Temeraire*, all completed in 1909, was a virtual repeat of the *Dreadnought*, with the same main armament and propulsion, but with some improvements in other areas. *Dreadnought*'s secondary battery, which had consisted of twenty-seven 12pdrs (3in [76mm]), was replaced by 16 4in (102mm) guns, a much more effective weapon, with eight on the superstructure and eight on turret roofs, although the latter proved to be useless in battle and were removed in

***Above:* Completed in 1908, the Lord Nelsons were actually pre-dreadnoughts**

designs and finer lines fore and aft, resulting in a good speed – 18kt – and excellent handling, their manoeuvrability attracting particular comment. The main armoured belt covered the entire ship along the waterline and was supplemented by an upper belt stretching as far aft as 'Y' turret barbette, and by a well-armoured citadel. Further protection was provided by a number of solid bulkheads, the first fitted in a British battleship.

Their only major shortcoming was the mixing of calibres which made direction difficult. Both ships served throughout World War I and were scrapped in 1920 (*Lord Nelson*) and 1927 (*Agamemnon*).

***Above: Bellerophon* just before the outbreak of World War I**

1916. The armoured belt was slightly thinner but was better disposed, while overall protection was considerably enhanced by a new armoured anti-torpedo bulkheads, covering the machinery spaces and magazines, and extending down to the double-bottoms, the first in a British warship. The problem of the fighting tops and funnels was also addressed, with the tripod foremast being moved ahead of the forward funnel. A new tripod mainmast was also installed carrying the after fire control position, although this proved unusable in action due to smoke interference from the forward funnel.

The next class, consisting of *St. Vincent* (1909), *Collingwood* (1910) and Vanguard (1910), again capitalised on *Dreadnought*'s revolutionary features, but with more modifications.

Neptune/Hercules

UNITED KINGDOM

Battleship (dreadnought)
Completed: 1911
Number in class: Neptune - 1; Colossus - 2.
Specifications for *Neptune*
Displacement: 19,680 tons standard; 22,720 tons full load.
Dimensions: Length 546.0ft (166.4m); beam 85.0ft (25.9m); draught 28.5ft (8.7m).
Propulsion: 4 shafts; Parsons turbines; 18 boilers; 25,000shp; 21.0kt; 6,330nm at 10kt.
Armour: Belt 10.0-2.5in (250-65mm); bulkheads 8.0-4.0in (200-100mm); barbettes 9.0-5.0in (230-130mm); turret faces 11.0in (280mm); conning tower 11.0in (280mm); decks 3.0-0.8in (75-20mm).
Armament: 10 x 12.0in (305mm) (5 x 2); 16 x 4in (102mm); 4 x 3pdr (47mm); 3 x 18in (457mm) TT.
Complement: 759.

History: Despite repeating the *Dreadnought* design in the Bellerophon- and St Vincent-classes it was evident that the layout of the main guns was not ideal. This especially applied to the wing turrets, whose position outboard of the superstructure and opposite each other prevented them from firing on the opposite beam, thus limiting the "broadside." It was attempted to overcome this in *Neptune*, completed 1911, by placing the wing turrets "*en echelon*," ie, with one forward of the other, so that they could fire across the deck onto the opposite beam. In addition, and primarily in order to save excessive hull length, "X" turret was raised to the superfiring position. Neither of these arrangements

Orion

UNITED KINGDOM

Battleship (dreadnought)
Completed: 1912.
Number in class: 4
Displacement: 22,200 tons standard; 25,870 tons full load.
Dimensions: Length 581.0ft (177.1m); beam 88.5ft (27.0m); draught 24.9ft (7.6m).
Propulsion: 4 shafts; Parsons turbines; 18 boilers; 27,000shp; 21kt; 6,730nm at 10kt.
Armour: Belt 12.0-8.0in (300-200mm); bulkheads 10.0-3.0in (250-75mm); barbettes 10.0-3.0in (250-75 mm); turret faces 11.0in (280 mm); conning tower 11.0in (280mm); decks 4.0-1.0in (100-25mm).
Armament: 10 x 13.5in (343mm) (5 x 2) 16 x 4in (102mm); 4 x 3pdr (47mm); 3 x 21in (533mm) TT.
Complement: 752.

History: These four ships, *Orion, Conqueror, Monarch* and *Thunderer*, all completed in 1912, were the first British dreadnoughts to mount all their main armament on the centreline. There were ten guns in five twin turrets, two of which were forward, two aft and one in the gap between the after funnel and superstructure, resulting in a considerable increase in both broadside and end-on fire. In addition, the main guns were the new 13.5in (343mm) which offered a considerable improvement over the 12in (305mm), with a heavier projectile, giving greater hitting power, while its lower muzzle velocity meant increased barrel life and greater accuracy. An increase in maximum elevation from 15deg to 20deg also resulted in an increase in range out to 24,000yd (21,9500m). One problem remained, however, since the sighting hoods on the forward end of

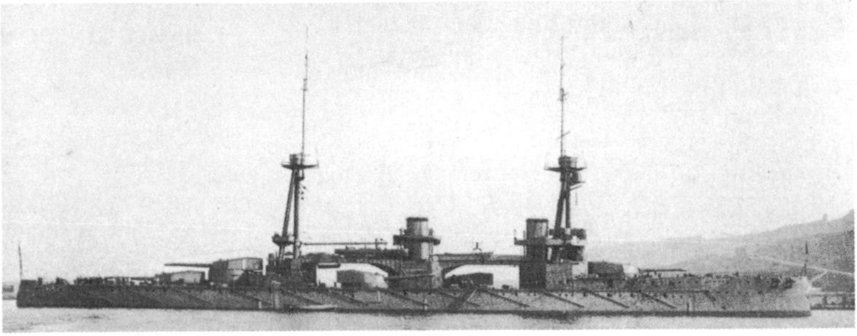

***Above:* Neptune shows the "flying bridges" over her "wing" turrets**

were satisfactory: when "P" and "Q" turrets fired on the opposite beams they strained the hull, while when firing axially the muzzle blast inflicted serious damage to the superstructure. Also, when "X" turret fired astern the muzzle blast concussed the crew in "Y" turret below. In addition, the "flying bridge," installed above "P" and "Q" turrets to carry the ship's boats, could be damaged in battle, allowing debris to fall onto the turrets, thus hampering, or even preventing, their operation.

The next two ships, *Colossus* and *Hercules*, both completed in 1911, were similar to *Neptune*, mainly because the government was under strong public pressure to increase the number of battleships, a movement whose rallying cry was "We want eight (battleships) and we won't wait." The hull and propulsion were virtually identical, and the layout of the main armament was the same.

***Above:* The Orion-class, the first to mount all its main armament on the centreline**

the turrets meant that if "B" and "Y" turrets were fired either directly ahead or astern the gun-crews in the turrets below suffered serious blast effects; as a result, the superfiring turrets were limited to the broadside arcs. Surprisingly, the foremast was again stepped abaft the forward funnel, thus continuing the smoke interference problem, although to a slightly lesser extent, since in these ships the forward funnel served only six boilers. A definite improvement was that the armoured belt was extended to the upper deck level, 17.2in (5.2m) above the waterline.

All four spent World War I with the Grand Fleet, where they sustained no damage or casualties. Indeed, their only wartime damage came from other friendly ships, with *Conqueror* and *Monarch* colliding with each other in December 1914 and *Orion* being hit by *Revenge* after the latter had broken free from her moorings. All four then fell victims to the Washington Naval Treaty, being sold for scrap between 1922 and 1926.

King George V

UNITED KINGDOM

Battleship (dreadnought)
Completed: 1912-13.
Number in class: 4.
Displacement: 23,000 tons standard; 25,700 tons full load.
Dimensions: Length 597.5ft (182.1m); beam 89.0ft (27.1m); draught 29.7ft (8.7m).
Propulsion: 4 shafts; Parsons turbines; 18 boilers; 31,000shp; 21kt; 6,730nm at 10kt.
Armour: Belt 12.0-8.0in (300-200 mm); bulkheads 10.0-4.0in (250-100mm); barbettes 10.0-3.0in (270-75mm); turret faces 11.0in (280mm); decks 4.0-1.0 (mm)
Armament: 10 x 13.5in (343mm) (5 x 2); 16 x 4in (102mm); 4 x 3pdr (47mm); 3 x 21in (533mm) TT.
Complement: 782.

History: It was originally intended that the next four battleships would be straight repeats of the Orion-class, but, benefiting from experience with the Lion-class battlecruisers, a number of changes were made. This included lengthening the hull, stepping the foremast ahead of the forward funnel and a modified version of the 13.5in (343mm) gun, firing a heavier (1,400lb [635kg]) projectile. The result was a handsome and businesslike design, although it was criticised for its secondary armament, as the 4in (102mm) gun was considered much too weak to deal with modern destroyers and torpedo boats.

Four ships were built: *King George V*, completed in 1912, and *Centurion*, *Audacious* and *Ajax*, all completed in 1913, of which *Audacious* was the only loss. This ship hit a mine on 27 October 1914 off the Scottish coast and shipped

Iron Duke

UNITED KINGDOM

Battleship (dreadnought)
Completed: 1914.
Number in class: 4.
Displacement: 25,000 tons standard; 29,560 tons full load.
Dimensions: Length 622.8ft (189.8m); beam 90.0ft (27.4m); draught 29.5ft (9.0m).
Propulsion: 4 shafts; Parsons turbines; 18 boilers; 29,000shp; 21.3kt; 7,780nm at 10kt.
Armour: Belt 12.0-4.0in (300-100 mm); bulkheads 8.0-1.5in (200-40mm); barbettes 10.0-3.0in (250-75mm); turret faces 11.0in (280mm); decks 2.5-1.0in (65-25mm).
Armament: 10 x 13.5in (343mm) (5 x 2); 12 x 6in (152mm); 2 x 3in (76mm) AA; 4 x 3pdr (47mm); 4 x 21in (533mm) TT.
Complement: 1,022.

History: The design of the Iron Duke-class was based closely on that of the King George V-class, but with a hull 25ft (7.6m) longer and with slightly greater beam and draught. Also like the King George Vs these new ships had an identical main armament of ten 13.5in (343mm) guns in five twin centreline turrets, but the secondary armament was totally recast, with a battery of 6in (152mm) replacing the unpopular 4in (102mm), but for reasons difficult to comprehend, these were extremely badly sited. Ten were in unarmoured casemates forward, five on each side, with a further two (one per side) in casemates below "Y" turret. All of these casemates were so low that the guns became unworkable in anything except the smoothest conditions, a problem not helped by the fact that the Iron Dukes tended to pitch very badly. As a

***Above:* After a long career *Centurion* was used as a Mulberry harbour blockship**

a great deal of water, which might not have been fatal had a severe storm not developed and she foundered. The other three all served in the Grand Fleet throughout the war and took part in the Battle of Jutland without casualties. *King George V* and *Ajax* were both sold for scrap in 1926, but *Centurion* had an adventurous second career. First, she was employed as a radio-controlled target ship for gunnery practice from 1926 to 1941 and then in 1942 took part in a deception operation in which she was converted to look like the newly commissioned battleship HMS *Anson* and sailed to India. She was then used as an AA battery in the Suez Canal until 1944 when she returned to the UK and was scuttled as a blockship to form a Mulberry harbour off the Canadian beach on the Normandy coast on 9 June 1944.

***Above: Emperor of India,* sunk as a target to comply with the London Treaty**

result, the two after guns were quickly resited to a new position in the forward superstructure beneath "B" turret, but the problem of the other 6in (152mm) guns was alleviated but never completely solved.

There were four ships, all completed in 1914: *Iron Duke, Marlborough, Benbow* and *Emperor of India. Marlborough* is of particular interest as the only British dreadnought in the war to be torpedoed, a hit amidships during the Battle of Jutland blowing a hole some 70ft (21m) long and 20ft (6m) deep in her side abreast the boiler room. Speed was reduced to 17kt but she remained in action until her starboard list prevented her guns from bearing on the enemy; she then proceeded under her own steam, her speed now reduced to 10kt until she reached the Humber. All four ships were with the Grand Fleet until 1919 when they went to the Mediterranean, all then moving to the Atlantic Fleet in 1926. Three were sold for scrap in 1932-33, but Iron Duke served as a depot ship in Scapa Flow from 1939-45 and was scrapped in 1946.

Queen Elizabeth

UNITED KINGDOM

Fast battleship (dreadnought)
Completed: 1915-16.
Number in class: 5.
Displacement: 27,500 tons standard; 31,500 tons full load.
Dimensions: Length 645.8ft (196.8m); beam 90.5ft (27.6m); draught 28.8ft (8.8m).
Propulsion: 4 shafts; Parsons turbines; 24 boilers; 56,000shp; 23kt; c.4,500nm at 10kt.
Armour: Belt 13.0-6.60in (330-150 mm); bulkheads 6.0-4.0in (150-100 mm); barbettes 10.0-4.0in (250-100 mm); turret faces 13.0in (330 mm); conning tower 11in (280mm); decks 13in (330 mm).
Armament: 8 x 15in (381mm) (4 x 2) 16 x 6in (152mm); 2 x 3in (76mm) AA; 4 x 3pdr (47mm); 4 x 21in (533mm) TT.
Complement: 951.

History: Knowing that foreign navies were developing 14in (356mm) which would outperform its own 13.5in (343mm) gun led the Royal Navy to develop a new 15in (381mm) gun, which turned out to be a great success. The 15in/42cal gun fired a heavier projectile to a greater range and with better accuracy than the 13.5in (343mm) and all without any increase in barrel wear. Then, when a design for a slightly modified *Iron Duke* to carry ten of the new guns was prepared it was realised that only eight guns would still give a heavier broadside than ten of the old guns, thus enabling one complete turret to be removed. This enabled six more boilers to be installed, increasing speed to 24-25kt, and it was then decided to use oil rather than coal as the fuel.

Revenge

UNITED KINGDOM

Battleship (dreadnought)
Completed: 1916-17.
Number in class: 5.
Displacement: 29,150 tons standard; 33,500 tons full load.
Dimensions: Length 620.5ft (189.2m); beam 101.3ft (30.9m); draught 32.8 ft (9.9m).
Propulsion: 4 shafts; Parsons direct-drive turbines; 18 boilers; 40,000shp; 23kt; 4,200nm at 10kt.
Armour: Belt 13.0-1.0in (330-25 mm); bulkheads 6.0-4.0in (150-100mm); barbettes 10.0-4.0in (250-100mm); turret faces 13.0in (330mm); conning tower 11.0in (280 mm); decks 2.0-1.0in (50-25 mm).
Armament: 8 x 15in (381mm) (4 x 2); 14 x 6in (152mm); 2 x 3in (76mm) AA; 4 x 3pdr (47mm); 4 x 21in (533mm) TT.
Complement: 997.

History: The last British battleships to be built during World War I, this class was originally to have comprised eight ships, but only five were actually completed: *Resolution; Revenge, Royal Oak* and *Royal Sovereign* in 1916, followed by *Ramillies* in 1917. Their dimensions were slightly smaller than the Queen Elizabeth-class, but the armour distribution was better, while the main armament of eight of the new 15in (381mm) in four twin turrets was the same. Secondary armament was fourteen 6in (152mm) guns in a single battery slightly further aft than in the *Queen Elizabeth*, and none were below the quarterdeck; these were in main-deck casemates, the last such to be fitted in the Royal Navy. They were originally to have been coal-fired, although this was

Above: Malaya **after modernisation in 1927-29 with twin funnels trunked into one**

It had originally been intended to order three battleships and one battlecruiser in the 1912 programme, but the prospect of a fast battleship was so exciting that the battlecruiser was cancelled and an additional battleship ordered, thus making it possible to form a complete four-ship Fast Division of the Grand Fleet. These were *Queen Elizabeth, Warspite*, and *Barham*, all completed in 1915, and *Valiant* completed in 1916. Then the rulers and people of the Federated Malay States funded a fifth, named which was, very appropriately, named HMS *Malaya*, which was laid down in October 1913 and completed in Febiuary 1910. A siixth chip, which would have been named *Agincourt*, was cancelled.

All were fully engaged throughout World Wars I and II, the only loss being *Barham*, which was torpedoed by *U-311* on 25 November 1941. All were broken up in the late 1940s.

Right: **The epitome of 20th century seapower: R-class on manoeuvres in the 1920s**

changed to oil-firing during construction.

These five ships were refitted but not modernised in the inter-war years and during World War II they undertook second-line, but nevertheless important duties such as protecting convoys against attacks by German surface commerce raiders. The only war loss was *Royal Oak*, which was sunk in Scapa Flow by *U-47* (14 October 1939). *Resolution* was torpedoed by a French submarine in 1940 and *Ramillies* by a Japanese minisubmarine in 1942, but both were repaired and returned to service. *Ramillies* was used for shore bombardment during the Allied landings in Normandy and the south of France. *Royal Sovereign* was loaned to the Soviet Navy as *Archangelsk* from 1944 to 1948. The four survivors were all scrapped in the late 1940s.

King George V

UNITED KINGDOM

Battleship
Completed: 1940-42.
Number in class: 5.
Displacement: 38,000 tons standard; 44,460 tons full load.
Dimensions: length 745.0ft (227.1m); beam 103.0ft (31.4m); draught 34.5ft (10.5m).
Propulsion: 4 shafts; Parsons turbines; 8 3-drum boilers; 110,000shp; 29.3kt; 13,000nm at 10kt.
Armour: Belt 15.0-4.5in (381-114mm); bulkheads 15.0in (381mm); barbettes 13.0-11.0in (330-280mm); turret faces 13.0in (330mm); decks 6.0-5.0in (152-127mm).
Aircraft: 2.
Armament: 10 x 14in (356mm) (2 x 4, 1 x 2); 16 x 5.25in (133mm); 48 x 2pdr AA.
Complement: 1,640.

History: In 1934 the British started to design a new class of battleship to be laid down in 1936 and which would comply with the constraints of the various naval treaties. After various changes of policy the Admiralty was faced with a stark choice concerning the all-important main armament: either 14in (356mm), as allowed by the 1936 London Naval Treaty, or 16in (406mm), which would be possible if one or more of the treaty signatories failed to ratify. The problem was exacerbated by the fact that the order for the guns had to be placed by mid-1936 if they were to be ready for the first two hulls, which were due to be commissioned in 1940, by which time, as the signs were beginning to indicate, Britain might well be at war with Germany. The Admiralty decided on the safer course of staying

***Left: King George V* shows the unusual combination of four- and twin-gun turrets**

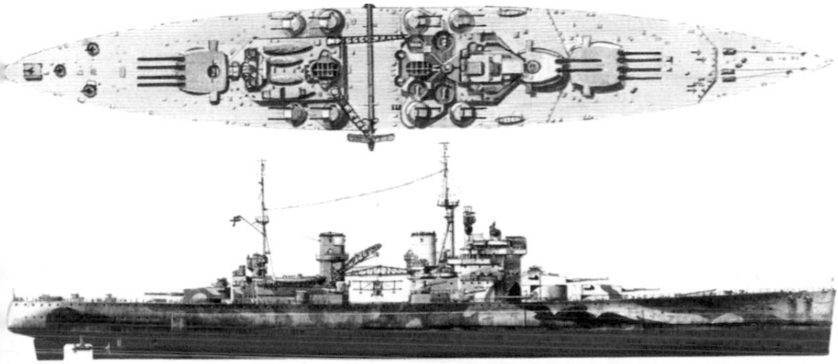

Above: Prince of Wales **in 1941; note cross-hull catapult for the Walrus seaplane**

with the 14in (356mm) gun and originally planned to mount twelve in three quadruple turrets. However, it was also decided to provide protection against 16in (406mm) shells, which meant that increased armour was required, for which weight savings had to be found elsewhere, as a result of which one turret had to be reduced from four to two guns. The end result was a quadruple turret in "A" and "X" positions and a superfiring twin turret in "B" position. These had an elevation of 40deg, but, at least initially, proved liable to mechanical problems.

Secondary armament comprised sixteen of the new 5.25in (133mm) dual-purpose guns, in two groups of four twin turrets before and abaft the catapult. Though efficient they proved too slow firing for effective anti-aircraft defence, and a larger number of 4.5in (114mm) might have provided a more effective solution. As with all battleships, considerable numbers of smaller calibre weapons were added during the war.

Protection was on the "all-or-nothing" principle as in the Nelson-class, but whereas the Nelsons had a sloping internal belt the King George V-class had a vertical external belt, which was also 1.0in (25mm) thicker over the magazines as well as much deeper below the waterline. There was no external bulge for anti-torpedo protection, but extensive internal arrangements were made to provide equivalent protection. The ships proved to be good gun platforms, although the low foredeck resulted in them shipping much water in a seaway, often forcing them to slow down.

All went to war as soon as they were completed. *King George V* served in home waters, the Atlantic (where she was flagship of the Home Fleet during the hunt for the *Bismarck*), the Mediterranean and the Pacific. *Prince of Wales* was still shaking down when she was despatched with *Hood* to confront the *Bismarck*, but had to withdraw after the loss of the battlecruiser as a result of mechanical difficulties. She then went to the Far East where, in company with HMS *Repulse*, she was attacked and sunk by Japanese aircraft on 10 December 1941. *Duke of York* served throughout the war in the Home Fleet, principally in providing distant escort for the Murmansk convoys, during one of which she sank the battlecruiser *Scharnhorst*. Once *Tirpitz* had been definitely disabled the four ships, *King George V, Anson, Howe* and *Duke of York* were all sent to the Pacific. All were decommissioned between 1946 and 1950, and then scrapped in 1957.

Vanguard

UNITED KINGDOM

Fast battleship
Completed: 1946.
Number in class: 1.
Displacement: 44,500 tons standard; 51,420 tons full load.
Dimensions: Length 814.3ft (248.2m); beam 108.0ft (32.9m); draught 34.8ft (10.6m).
Propulsion: 4 shafts; Parsons geared turbines; 8 boilers; 130,000shp; 30kt.
Armour: Belt 14.0-4.5in (355-115 mm); bulkheads 12.0-4.0in (305-102 mm); barbettes 13.0-11.0in (330-280mm); turret faces 13.0in (330mm); conning tower 3.0-2.5in (75-65mm); deck 6.0-5.0in (150-125mm).
Armament: 8 x 15in (381mm) (4 x 2); 16 x 5.25in (133mm) DP; 73 x 40mm AA.
Complement: 1,893.

History: Once the design of the King George V-class with its 14in (355mm) guns had been finalised there was still concern that foreign battleships were being built with 16in (406mm) guns. As a result, a new design was prepared, which was, in essence, an enlarged and modified *King George V* armed with nine 16in (406mm) guns. Indeed, two hulls, to be named *Lion* and *Temeraire*, were actually laid down in June/July 1939, but following the outbreak of war the work was initially suspended and then cancelled, There were two main reasons for this: first, was the need for the work-force to be employed on more urgent tasks, particularly the construction of escorts, but, secondly, there was the time it would take to design, test and produce the 16in (406mm) guns. However, a partial solution to the latter problem was quickly found, because there were four complete sets of turrets and eight 15in (381mm) guns in storage, where they had lain since being removed from the *Courageous* and *Glorious* when those two "light battlecruisers" were converted to aircraft carriers in the mid-1920s, and were enough to equip one new battleship.

These guns had, in fact, been tentatively earmarked in early 1939 for a different new ship which was under consideration for service in the Far East as a counter to the fast cruisers then being commissioned by the Japanese. This project was described at the time as a "fully-armoured battlecruiser" which term could be stood on its head to become "fast battleship" and this proved to be a suitable starting point for the new ship, for which the name *Vanguard* had now been selected.

Below: **One of the most graceful battleships ever built: HMS *Vanguard* in 1946**

***Above:* Battleship *Vanguard* closed a long and proud chapter in RN history**

The lessons of the early years of World War II were incorporated in the new design, particularly those from the loss of the *Prince of Wales*. Thus, the machinery designed for the Lion-class was used, but with four, instead of two, of the eight generators being diesel driven to avoid loss of power if the ship's boilers failed. Protection was generally similar to that of the King George V-class, but with greater splinter protection and the height of longitudinal bulkheads was increased to prevent rapid flooding. The ship was also given greater endurance than the King George V-class, presumably with Pacific service in mind.

The 15in (381mm) turrets received some modification, with elevation being increased to 30deg, thicker protection and a much improved rangefinder. *Vanguard's* secondary armament comprised sixteen 5.25in (133mm) dual-purpose guns, but, unlike the King George V-class these had full remote control.

Vanguard had no provision for aircraft, but had a full outfit of the latest radars. The forecastle was given a marked sheer which greatly improved seakeeping, although it also meant that "A" turret could not be fired dead ahead at low angles of elevation. One unusual feature was a transom stern, making *Vanguard* the only British battleship to have one.

The initial completion date was November 1943, but other projects were given greater priority and she was not launched until November 1944, which delayed commissioning until August 1946. Thus this great ship never saw war service, being employed instead on a Royal tour of South Africa and then on various NATO duties, before being placed in reserve and finally sold for scrap in 1960. She was, by any standard, a handsome ship, with a well-balanced and powerful appearance, and was noted for her excellent seakeeping and steadiness as a gun platform, and a very fitting final example of the "dreadnought" battleship, which had been pioneered by the Royal Navy half-a-century earlier.

Nelson

UNITED KINGDOM

Battleship
Completed: 1927.
Number in class: 2.
Displacement: 33,313 tons standard; 41,250 tons full load.
Dimensions: Length 710.0ft (216.4m); beam 106.0ft (32.3m); draught 33.5ft (10.2m).
Propulsion: 2 shafts; Brown-Curtis geared turbines; 8 3-drum boilers; 45,000shp; 23kt.
Armour: Belt 14.0-3.0in (356-76 mm); bulkheads 12.0-4.0in (305-102 mm); barbettes 15.0-12.0in (381-305 mm); turret faces 16.0in (406 mm); conning tower 14.0-6.5in (356-165 mm); decks 6.3-4.3in (160-109 mm).
Armament: 9 x 16in (406mm) (3 x 3); 12 x 6in (152mm); 6 x 4.7in (120mm) AA; 16/24 2pdr AA; 8 x 0.5in (12.7mm) AA; 2 x 24.5in (622mm) TT.
Complement: 1,314.

History: The 1922 Washington Naval Conference allowed the Royal Navy to build two new battleships of no more than 35,000 tons displacement and with weapons of maximum 16in (406mm) calibre. The result was these two ships, *Nelson* and *Rodney*, both completed in 1927, armed with nine 16in (406mm) guns in three triple turrets and armour sufficient to withstand similar 16in (406mm) shells. The design introduced a number of novel features, of which the most eye-catching was that all three turrets were ahead of the superstructure, which was primarily intended to shorten the length of the citadel and was necessary in order to comply with the Treaty displacement

Passaic

UNITED STATES OF AMERICA

Monitor
Completed: 1862-65.
Number in class: 10.
Displacement: 1,875 tons.
Dimensions: Length 200.0ft (70.0m); beam 46.0ft (14.0m); draught 10.5ft (3.2m).
Propulsion: 1 shaft; one Ericsson vibrating lever engine; 2 boilers; 320ihp; 7kt.
Armour: Iron. Side 5.0-3.0in (127-76mm) turret 11.0in (278mm); deck 1.0in (25mm).
Armament: 1 x 15in (381mm) Dahlgren smoothbore; 1 x 11.0in (278mm) Dahlgren smoothbore.
Complement: 75.

History: The *Monitor*, a most important milestone in warship development, was built at the Continental Iron Works and completed on 25 February 1862. She undertook her famous but inconclusive duel with *Virginia* in Hampton Roads on 9 March 1892, but foundered under tow on 31 December 1862, with the loss of sixteen of her fortynine-strong crew. Meanwhile, a new and improved design was already in production, the ten ships of the enlarged and improved Passaic-class being completed between November 1862 and April 1863. The hull was essentially an iron/wood "raft" 200ft (61.0m) long, 46.0ft (14.0m) wide and approximately 5.0ft (1.5m) deep, from which was suspended a slab-sided lower hull, made of iron. In plan view the lower hull was somewhat smaller than the raft, the "overhang" serving as a fender to provide protection for the lower hull, rudder and screws from ramming.

The turret was cylindrical in shape, with an internal diameter of 21.0ft

***Above: Nelson*'s unusual layout with all main turrets ahead of the superstructure**

limits. The turrets also allowed an elevation of 40 deg, a considerable increase on previous British designs. Not immediately visible that the protection was on the "all-or-nothing" principle pioneered by the US Navy, with the maximum armour thickness concentrated on the side belt and the single heavy armoured deck above it.

Both ships had a very active operational life in the Atlantic, where *Rodney* participated in the final destruction of the *Bismarck*, then in the Mediterranean before supporting the Normandy landings in 1944. *Nelson* then went to the Eastern Fleet while *Rodney*, which was in poor mechanical condition was put into reserve. *Nelson* was twice hit by mines and once by a torpedo, but both ships survived the war and were broken up in 1948.

Above:* USS *Passaic* was an improved version of the revolutionary *Monitor

(6.4m), and rotated on a central spindle. The original main armament comprised two Dahlgren smoothbore, muzzleloading cannon, one of 15.0in (381mm) the other of 11.0in (280mm) calibre, which were mounted side-by-side, about 7.0ft (2.1m) apart, firing though narrow slits. In most ships, however, the 11.0in (280mm) gun was replaced by an 8.0in (203mm) Parrot rifled muzzleloader in service, but later this was changed again, this time to two 15.0in (381mm) Dahlgrens.

Weehawken foundered in heavy seas (6 December 1863), while *Patapsco* was lost to a Confederate mine (15 January 1865). The others served on for many years being sold between 1899 and 1904. *Camanche* was built in Jersey City but was then immediately disassembled and sent to California aboard the transport, *Aquila*, which sank off San Francisco. The parts of the monitor were, however, salvaged and reassembled, *Camanche* finally entering service in May 1865.

Texas

UNITED STATES OF AMERICA

Second-class battleship (pre-dreadnought)
Completed: 1895.
Number in class: 1.
Displacement: 6,135 tons standard; 6,665 tons full load.
Dimensions: Length 308.8ft (94.1m); beam 64.1ft (19.53m); draught 22.5ft (6.9m).
Propulsion: 2 shafts; vertical triple-expansion engines; 4 boilers; 8,610ihp; 17.8kt.
Armour: Harvey and nickel steel. Belt 12.0-6.0in (305-152mm); 12.0in (305mm) redoubt; turret faces 12.0in (305mm); decks 3.0-2.0in (76-51mm).
Armament: 2 x 12.0in (305mm); 6 x 6in (152mm); 12 x 6pdr; 6 x 1pdr; 4 x 14in (356mm) TT.
Complement: 392.

History: *Texas* was designed in response to domestic political pressure to increase the size and power of the US Navy. The design was prepared by an English naval architect, William John, the requirement being for a ship with heavy armament, high speed and good seakeeping qualities, but on a limited displacement. The result was a single funnel ship with an unusual armament arrangement and freeboard which was high in proportion to the length, made her appear shorter than was, in fact, the case. The ship was built at the Norfolk Naval Yard and was commissioned in August 1895.

The main armament comprised two single 12.0in (305mm) guns situated fore and aft of the funnel in hydraulically-operated turrets, the forward turret offset to port and the after turret to starboard, a layout known as "*en echelon*." Both guns could fire on either beam and the ship's boats were carried on "flying bridges" above

Maine

UNITED STATES OF AMERICA

Second-class battleship (pre-dreadnought)
Completed: 1895.
Number in class: 1.
Displacement: 6,682 tons standard; 7,180 tons full load.
Dimensions: Length 318.0ft (96.9m); beam 57.0ft (17.4m); draught 21.5ft (6.6m).
Propulsion: 2 shafts; vertical triple-expansion engines; 8 boilers; 9,293ihp.
Armour: Harvey and nickel steel. Belt 12.0-7.0in in (305-178mm); barbettes 12.0-10.0in (305-254mm); turrets 3.0-2.0in (76-51mm); conning tower 10in (254mm); decks 3.0-2.0in (76-51mm).
Armament: 4 x 10in (254mm) (2 x 2); 6 x 6in (152mm); 7 x 6pdr; 8 x 1pdr; 4 x Gatling; 4 x 18in (457mm) TT.
Complement: 374.

History: In the mid-1880s the US Congress became increasingly concerned by the run-down state of the US Navy, particularly in view of the expansion of the navies of Argentina, Brazil and Chile, which were buying increasingly powerful ships from European yards.

The two immediate results of this concern were the *Texas*, which was designed by an English naval architect (see previous entry) and this ship, USS *Maine*, which was designed by the US Navy Department. *Maine* was slightly larger than the Brazilian *Riachuelo*, but the layout of the armament was remarkably similar, with the four main guns mounted in two twin turrets *en echelon* (the forward one to starboard, the after one to port) and sponsoned to enable them to fire dead ahead and astern. Both turrets were capable of firing across the deck onto the opposite beam.

***Above: Texas* was heavily armed for her size, with two 12in (305mm) guns**

the turrets. The secondary armament comprised six 6.0in (152mm) guns, four in single sponsons and two in single turrets fore and aft on the main deck.

In the Spanish-American War of 1898 *Texas* shared in the reduction of shore installations in Cuba and in the pursuit and destruction of Admiral Cervera's squadron at the Battle of Santiago (3 July 1898). By 1904 her funnel had been raised, the torpedo tubes removed and armour protection for the main ammunition hoists improved. She was decommissioned in 1911 and renamed *San Marcos*, following which she was expended as a target.

***Below: Maine* exploded in Havana harbour, starting the Spanish-American War**

This ship's place in history is secure. In January 1898, at a time of considerable US-Spanish tension *Maine* paid a good will visit to Cuba, then a Spanish possession and one of the centres of protest against Spanish rule. On 15 February *Maine* was lying at anchor in Havana harbour when she was suddenly destroyed in a massive explosion, which killed 260 of her 355-man crew. A US Court of Enquiry rapidly concluded that the cause had been the explosion of a mine placed beneath the ship and on 21 April the United States declared war on Spain. The incident has remained a source of controversy ever since, and it is now generally considered that, while absolute proof will never be possible, the balance of probability lies in an internal cause, possibly by spontaneous combustion in the coal bunker next to the magazine.

Virginia

UNITED STATES OF AMERICA

Battleship (pre-dreadnought)
Completed: 1906-07.
Number in class: 5.
Displacement: 14,948 tons standard; 16.094 tons full load.
Dimensions: Length 441.3ft (134.5m); beam 76.3ft (23.3m); draught 23.8ft (7.2m).
Propulsion: 2 shafts; vertical, triple-expansion; 12 boilers; 19,000shp; 19kt.
Armour: Krupp cement/Harvey nickel. Belt 11.0-6.0in (280-152mm); ends 6.0-4.0in (152-102mm; barbettes 10.0-6.0in (254-152mm); turrets 12.0-6.0in (305-152mm); conning tower 9.0in (229 mm).
Armament: 4 x 12in (305mm) (2 x 2); 8 x 8in (203mm); 12 x 6in (152mm); 12 x 3pdr; 4 x 21in (533mm) TT.
Complement: 812.

History: Following *Maine* and *Texas* the US Navy built a series of increasingly powerful battleships, including a new *Maine* (BB-10)-class of three ships in 1902-04. Next came the Virginia (BB-13)-class of five ships, *Virginia* (BB13), *Nebraska* (BB14), *Georgia* (BB15), *New Jersey* (BB16), and *Rhode Island* (BB17), all completed in 1906, except for *Nebraska* in 1907. Main armament was four 12in (305mm) in two twin centreline turrets, each of which had a co-rotating twin 8in (203mm) turret on its roof (ie, the 8in turret trained with the 12in turret, but the guns could be elevated independently). This was an arrangement which had already proved unsatisfactory in the Kearsarge-class, both because of its gunnery limitations, and because it resulted in considerable extra weight high in the ship, which made them roll badly; it was not repeated

Mississippi

UNITED STATES OF AMERICA

Battleship (pre-dreadnought)
Completed: 1908.
Number in class: 2.
Displacement: 13,000 tons standard; 14,465 tons full load.
Dimensions: Length 382.0ft (116.4m); beam 77.0ft (23.5m); draught 24.7ft (7.5m).
Propulsion: 2 shafts; vertical triple-expansion engines; 8 boilers; 10,000ihp; 17kt.
Armour: Krupp cemented/Harvey nickel steel. Belt 9.0-7.0in (230-178mm); ends 7.0-4.0in (178-102mm); barbettes 10.0-6.0in (254-152mm); turrets 12.0-8.0in (305-203mm); conning tower 9.0in (229mm).
Armament: 4 x 12in (mm) (2 x 2); 8 x 8in (203mm); 8 x 7in (178mm); 12 x 3in (76mm); 6 x 3pdr; 2 x 1pdr; 2 x 21in (533mm) TT.
Complement: 744.

History: The main significance of these two ships, *Mississippi* (BB23) and *Idaho* (BB24), both completed in 1908, is that they were the United States Navy's last pre-dreadnoughts. The previous two classes were the Connecticut (BB18)-class (two ships, completed 1906) and the slightly different Vermont (BB20)-class (four ships, completed 1907-08 and the aim in this new class was to reproduce the characteristics of the Vermonts in a ship displacing 3,000 tons less. Thus, the main and secondary armament was the same (4 x 12in [305mm]; 8 x 8in [203mm]), although the number of 7in (178mm) guns had to be reduced from 12 to 8 and torpedo tubes from four to two. Armoured protection was the same, although the length of the main belt was reduced to 244.0ft (74,4m). As built, the two ships had pole fore- and mainmasts, but

in subsequent classes. The other 8in (203mm) guns were in two twin turrets on the upper deck abreast the forward funnel.

The five ships were completed in 1906-07 and served throughout World War I. All were disposed of in 1923, *Virginia* and *New Jersey* being sunk as targets, the others being scrapped.

Below: **Completed in 1906-07, all five Virginias served throughout World War I**

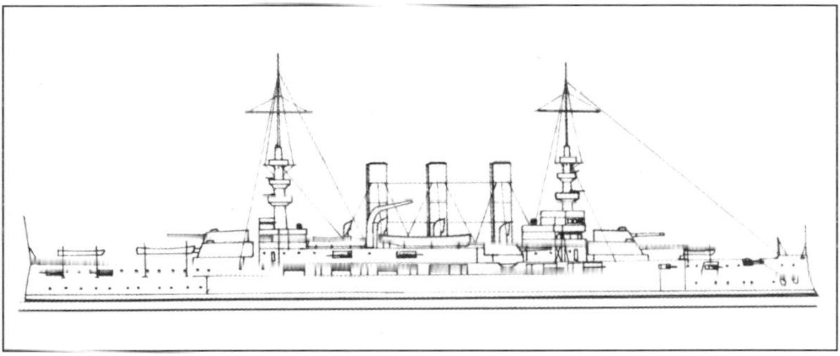

Above: **The uniquely American cage masts were fitted in the Mississippis in 1909**

these were later replaced by cage masts.

Such cost-cutting exercises are invariably counter-productive and this design was generally regarded as unsuccessful. In addition, the concept of mixed armament had been outdated at a stroke by the British *Dreadnought*, so both ships were discarded after only a brief career with the US Navy. They were sold to Greece in July 1914 where they were renamed *Lemnos* and *Kilkis*. Both were sunk on 10 April 1941, during the German invasion of Greece.

South Carolina
UNITED STATES OF AMERICA

Battleship (dreadnought)
Completed: 1910.
Number in class: 2.
Displacement: 16,000 tons standard; 17,617 tons full load.
Dimensions: Length 452.8ft (138.0m); beam 80.4ft (24.5m); draught 24.6ft (7.5m).
Propulsion: 2 shafts; vertical, triple-expansion engines; 12 boilers; 165,00ihp; 18.5kt; 5,000nm at 10kt.
Armour: Belt 10.0-8.0in (254-203mm); casemate 10.0-8.0in (254-203mm); barbettes 10.0-8.0in (254-203mm); turret faces 12.0in (305mm); conning tower 12.0in (305mm); decks 2.5in (63 mm).
Armament: 8 x 12in (305mm); 22 x 3in (76mm); 2x 21in (533mm) TT.
Complement: 869.

History: The British *Dreadnought* has gone down in history as the first battleship with an "all big-gun" armament to enter service, but the first such ship actually to be designed was USS *South Carolina* (BB26) and she only failed to win the accolade because she took longer to be laid down and in building. In fact, *South Carolina* was nearer to the ultimate battleship configuration than *Dreadnought*, since she had all four turrets on the centreline, with "B" and "X" turrets superfiring, which meant that all eight guns could fire with equal ease on either beam, unlike *Dreadnought*, whose wing turrets could not fire across the deck. This meant, in turn, that the US battleship with four turrets could fire a broadside of eight guns, precisely the same as *Dreadnought*, which had five, the one turret reduction in the American battleship resulting in a substantial saving in weight, complexity and manpower. The armour

Delaware/Florida
UNITED STATES OF AMERICA

Battleship (dreadnought)
Completed: 1910-11.
Number in class: Delaware – 2; Florida – 2.
Specifications for *Delaware*, as built.
Displacement: 20,380 tons standard; 22,060 tons full load.
Dimensions: Length 519.0ft (158.2m); beam 85.3ft (26.0m); draught 27.3ft (8.3m).
Propulsion: 2 shafts; vertical triple-expansion engines (see notes); 14 boilers; 25,000ihp; 21kt; c. 6,000nm at 10kt.
Armour: Belt 11.0-9.0in (280-230 mm); lower casemate 10.0-8.0in (254-203mm); upper casemate 5.0in (127mm); barbettes 10.0-4.0in (254-102 mm); turret faces 12.0in (305mm); conning tower 11.5in (292mm); decks 2.0in (51mm).
Armament: 10 x 12.0in (305mm) (5 x 2); 14 x 5in (127mm); 2 x 21in (533mm) TT.
Complement: 933.

History: The two Delaware-class ships, *Delaware* (BB28) and *North Dakota* (BB29) were the first battleships to be free of the Congress-imposed limitation of a maximum displacement of 16,000 tons. They were thus longer than the *South Carolinas*, enabling an additional centreline twin 12in (305mm) turret to be mounted, and with a considerable increase in internal space. They were handsome and well-armed ships, their five twin 12in (305mm) turrets, two forward and three aft, giving a ten-gun broadside, but they did have some problems with their secondary armament. This consisted of fourteen 5in (127mm) guns mounted at gun-deck level and were entirely unprotected. In addition, the two forward guns were mounted on sponsons to enable them to fire ahead, but were so far forward that they were not only very wet, but also

***Right:* South Carolina in April 1921; she served as a convoy escort during the war**

layout had also been very carefully thought out, with a main belt some 8.0ft (2.4m) deep, of which 6.8ft (2.1m) was below the waterline, while the main thickness of the belt lay from forward of "A" turret to just abaft "Y" turret.

The only major features in which *South Carolina* was inferior to *Dreadnought* were that the American ship still had reciprocating machinery and her maximum speed was 18kt, unlike the British ship's turbine machinery and maximum speed of 21kt.The South Carolina-class was the first to be fitted with the two cage masts, which made US battleships instantly recognisable for many years.

South Carolina (BB26) and *Michigan* (BB27) joined the fleet in 1910 and served in the Atlantic. They did not serve in European waters in 1917-18, although *South Carolina* did serve as a convoy escort. They were stricken and scrapped in 1924-24.

***Above:* Completed in 1910, the Delawares were the first American dreadnoughts**

broke up the bow-wave, thus wasting power.

The two ships differed, *North Dakota* being powered by Curtis turbines, while *Delaware* had traditional vertical triple-expansion engines. The turbines gave a much smoother operation, but their fuel consumption was much greater, being estimated at 45 percent at the cruising speed of 14kt. On the other hand, *Delaware's* reciprocating engines were extremely reliable, the ship being the first US Navy battleship able to steam at maximum speed for 24 hours without needing repairs, a very important consideration for the US Navy for operations across the Pacific Ocean. The two Florida-class ships (*Florida* [BB30]; *Utah* [BB31]) were virtual repeats.

Wyoming

UNITED STATES OF AMERICA

Battleship
Completed: 1912.
Number in class: 2.
Displacement: 26,00 tons standard; 27,243 tons full load.
Dimensions: Length 562.0ft (171.3m); beam 93.2ft (28.4m); draught 28.6ft (8.7m).
Propulsion: 4 shafts; Parsons turbines; 12 boilers; 28,000shp; 20.5kt; 8,000nm at 10kt.
Armour: Belt 11.0-9.0in (280-230 mm); lower casemate 11.0-9.0in (280-230mm); upper casemate 11.0-9.0in (280-230mm); barbettes 11.0in (280 mm); turret faces 12.0in (305mm); conning tower 11.5in (292 mm).
Armament: 12 x 12in (305mm); 21 x 5in (127mm); 2 x 21in (533mm) TT.
Complement: 1,063.

History: In 1908 President Theodore Roosevelt asked the Navy to consider three alternative armaments for the next class of battleships: twelve 12in (305mm) guns, eight 14in (356mm), or ten 14in (356mm) guns. The eventual decision was for the first, since the 12in (305mm) gun was already available and the 14in (356mm) was not, while the ten 14in (356mm) ship would only be able to dock at Pearl Harbor, Puget Sound or New York, and in the latter case only if the dock was extended by 5ft (1.5m). It was decided therefore to start the development of the 14in (356mm) gun and the enlargement of other docks and meanwhile to build an "interim" pair of battleships with twelve 12in (305mm) guns (albeit of a new design with a longer barrel), resulting in *Wyoming* (BB32) and *Arkansas* (BB33), both completed in 1912.

New York

UNITED STATES OF AMERICA

Battleship
Completed: 1914.
Number in class: 2 .
Displacement: 27,000 tons standard; 28,367 tons full load.
Dimensions: Length 573.0ft (174.7m); beam 95.5ft (29.1m); draught 28.5ft (8.7m).
Propulsion: 2 shafts; vertical, triple-expansion; 14 boilers; 28,100ihp; 21kt; 7,060nm at 10kt.
Armour: Belt 12.0-10.0in (305-254mm); lower casemate 11.0-9.0in (280-230mm); upper casemate 6.5in (165mm); barbettes 10in/12in (254/305mm); turret faces 14.0in (356mm); conning tower 12.0in (305mm); armour deck 2in (50mm).
Armament: 10 x 14in (356mm) (5 x2); 21 x 5in (127mm); 4 x 21in (533mm) TT.
Complement: 1,042.

History: These two battleships, *New York* (BB34) and *Texas* (BB35), were improved Wyomings, but armed with ten of the new 14in/45cal guns in five twin turrets, in place of twelve 12in (305mm) in six twin turrets. The Navy gave careful consideration to the question of machinery but decided to install vertical triple-expansion engines rather than turbines since, in their contemporary state of development, the latter could not meet the range requirement, which was essentially to reach the Philippines from the West Coast of the continental United States without refuelling.

Both ships served with 6th Battle Squadron of the Anglo-US Grand Fleet in 1917-18, where *Texas* became the first US battleship to be fitted with a flying-off platform for aircraft. Both were refitted in the mid-1920s, which included: reboilering and removing one funnel; an AA armament of 3in (76mm) guns;

***Right: Arkansas* in mid-1944 with great numbers of additional AA weapons**

Both served throughout World War I and were then expensively refitted in 1925-27. The work included replacing the original coal-burning boilers with four oil-burning units, removing the second funnel, replacing the cage mainmast by a tripod and moving the secondary armament to upper deck level. Armoured protection was also increased and a catapult and facilities for three aircraft installed.

Wyoming was converted into a gunnery training ship in the early 1930s, a role she retained until being scrapped in 1947. *Arkansas*, however, remained in operational service, supporting the US landing in Iceland in 1941 and then serving from December 1941 to April 1944 as a heavy escort for Atlantic convoys. In a 1942 refit her AA armament was considerably increased, six of her 5in (127mm) guns were removed, the cage foremast was replaced by a tripod mast, and radar was installed. After supporting the Normandy landings she was transferred to the Pacific where she supported the landings on Iwo Jima and Okinawa, before being expended as a target in the post-war atomic tests.

***Above: New York* in 1943 when employed on convoy escort duties in the Atlantic**

catapult and facilities for three aircraft; and replacing the cage masts by tripods. During World War II both served in the Atlantic from 1941 to 1944, including heavy escorts for convoys and fire support for the Casablanca landings, while *Texas* also supported the landings in Normandy and southern France. They were then transferred to the Pacific where they supported the landings on Okinawa and Iwo Jima. *New York* was damaged in a *kamikaze* attack and was later expended as a target in the atomic tests. *Texas* became a museum and remains on display at the San Jacinto State Park, near Houston.

Nevada/Pennsylvania UNITED STATES OF AMERICA

Battleship
Completed: 1916.
Number in class: Nevada – 2; Pennsylvania – 2.
Displacement: 27,500 tons standard; 28,400 tons full load.
Dimensions: Length 583.0ft (177.7m); beam 95.5ft (29.1m); draught 28.5ft (8.7m).
Propulsion: 2 shafts; Curtis turbines; 12 boilers; 26,500shp; 20.5kt; 8,000nm at 10kt.
Armour: Belt 13.5-8.0in (343-203mm); barbettes 13.0in (330mm); turret faces 18.0in (457mm); conning tower 16.0in (254mm); deck 3.0in (76mm).
Armament: 10 x 14in (356mm) (2x 3; 2 x 2); 21 x 5in (127mm) 2 x 21in (533mm) TT.
Complement: 864.

History: *Nevada* introduced the "all-or-nothing" armoured protection, based on the proposition that armour-piercing (AP) shells should be either completely stopped by thick armour, or not at all, a theory which was proved on the target ship *San Marcos* (ex-*Texas*). A main armoured belt 13.5in (343mm) thick and 17.5ft (5.3m) deep covered some 400ft (122.0m), (approximately 70 percent) of the ship's length, being closed at either end by transverse bulkheads of the same thickness, and topped by the main armoured deck. This formed a citadel above the magazines and machinery.The turrets, barbettes and funnel base were also well protected, but the only other armour was a strake aft over the steering machinery. The ten 14in (356mm) guns were mounted in two triple turrets ("A" and "Y"), with two superfiring twin turrets ("B" and "X"). These were the first oil-burning battleships in the US fleet and *Nevada* was powered by

New Mexico/ Tennessee/Colorado UNITED STATES OF AMERICA

Battleship
Specifications for *New Mexico*, as built.
Completed: New Mexico – 1917-19; Tennessee – 1920-21; Colorado – 1921-23.
Number in class: New Mexico – 3; Tennessee – 2; Colorado – 3.
Displacement: 32,000 tons standard; 33,000 tons full load.
Dimensions: Length 624.0ft (190.2m); beam 97.4ft (29.7m); draught 30.0ft (9.1m).
Propulsion: 4 shafts; General Electric turbo-electric drive; 9 boilers; 27,000shp; 21kt; 8,000nm at 10kt (see notes).
Armour: Belt 13.5-8.0in (343-203 mm); barbettes 13.0in (330mm); turret faces 18.0in (457mm); conning tower 16.0in (254mm); deck 3.0in (76 mm).
Armament: 12 x 14in (356mm) (4 x 3); 14 x 5in (127mm); 4 x 3in (76mm); 2 x 21in (533mm) TT.
Complement: 1,084.

History: Although officially three separate classes, these eight battleships, built in three groups, were closely related, with identical hulls and measurements, the differences being confined to propulsion and improved underwater protection, and, in the last group, armament. The first group of three ships, *New Mexico* (BB40), *Mississippi* (BB41) and *Idaho* (BB42), was intended to repeat the Pennsylvania-class, but with whatever improvements could be included at minimum cost. Main armament was twelve 14in (356mm) guns in four triple turrets, but, unlike previous

***Right: Nevada* having been rebuilt following very serious damage at Pearl Harbor**

Curtis turbines. *Oklahoma*, however, was built with reciprocating machinery, although this was replaced by geared turbines during a refit in 1926-27. The next class, comprising *Pennsylvania* (BB38) and *Arizona* (BB39), was essentially a slightly enlarged Nevada-class, but with twelve as opposed to ten 14in (356mm) guns in four triple turrets and a new form of anti-torpedo protection.

All four ships served in the Atlantic in World War I, were rebuilt in the 1920s and were all at Pearl Harbor on 7 December 1941. *Oklahoma* was hit by four torpedoes and capsized; she was later recovered but never repaired. *Arizona* was hit, suffered an explosion and settled on the bottom; she has been a national memorial since 1962. *Nevada* was also hit and settled on the bottom, but was raised and completely rebuilt, going on to serve as an Atlantic escort and supporting the landings in Normandy, Okinawa and Iwo Jima; she was finally expended as a target in 1948. *Pennsylvania* was in drydock at the time of the attack and suffered only minor damage. She was then completely rebuilt and employed for the remainder of the war providing fire support.

***Above: Pennsylvania* in drydock during World War II, showing her torpedo bulges**

designs, each gun could elevate independently, while the barrels were a new 14in/50calibre type, ie, 70in (1,780mm) longer than the previous model. A problem with recent US battleships had been wetness forward so the New Mexico-class was given an acutely raked clipper bow. Changes were also made to the secondary battery, which was originally intended to ▶

consist of twenty-two 5in (127mm) guns, but after practical experience with other ships in European waters in 1917-18 this was reduced to fourteen. The General Electric company had been advocating turbo-electric drive for some years and a full-scale system was installed in *New Mexico* (BB40). Two ships had originally been funded but the sale of two pre-dreadnoughts to Greece in 1914 raised enough money to pay for the third.

The next group, *Tennessee* (BB43) and *California* (BB44), both had turbo-electric drive and had two funnels in contrast to the *New Mexico*'s one. Other differences were internal and mainly concerned protection. Finally came *Colorado* (BB45), *Maryland* (BB46) and *West Virginia* (BB48), which were armed with eight of the new 16in (406mm) guns in four twin turrets. A fourth ship, *Washington* (BB47), was launched but had to be scuttled in 1924 before completion to comply with the Washington Naval Treaty.

The three New Mexicos were in the Atlantic in December 1941 but transferred to the Pacific in 1942, where they took part in support of most of the amphibious landings. All were hit by *kamikaze* attacks, but survived. Both Californias were at Pearl Harbor, where *Tennessee* was moderately damaged but *California* was sunk, then raised. Both were given substantial rebuilds, with *Tennessee* returning to in service in May 1943, although *California*, which had been much more seriously damaged, did not rejoin the fleet until January 1944. Both supported the amphibious landings and survived *kamikaze* attacks.

Maryland and *West Virginia* were also both at Pearl Harbor, where *Maryland* was slightly damaged but *West Virginia* was sunk

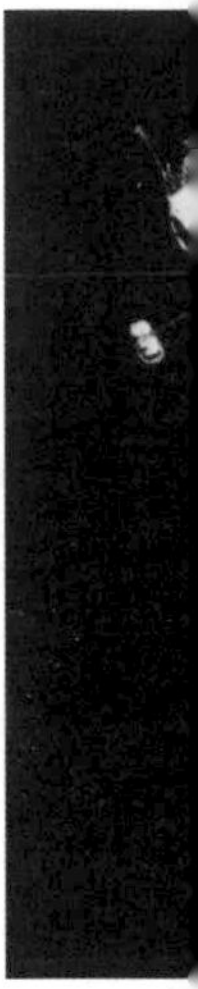

North Carolina

UNITED STATES OF AMERICA

Fast battleship
Completed: 1941.
Number in class: 2.
Displacement: 37,484 tons standard; 44,377 tons full load.
Dimensions: Length 222.1ft (728.8m); beam 108.3ft (33.0m); draught 33.0ft (10.0m).
Propulsion: 4 shafts; General Electric turbines; 8 boilers; 121,000shp; 28kt; 17,450nm at 15kt.
Armour: Belt 12.0-6.6in (305-168mm); bulkheads 11.0in (280mm); barbettes 16.0-14.7in (406-373mm); turret faces 16.0in (406mm); conning tower 16.0-14.7in (406-373mm); armoured deck 5.5-5.0in (140-127mm).
Armament: 9 x 16in (406mm) (3 x 3); 20 x 5in (127mm); 12 x 0.5in (12.7mm).
Aircraft: 3.
Complement: 1,880.

History: *North Carolina* (BB55) and *Washington* (BB56) were the first US battleships to be built after the Washington Treaty's "battleship holiday," although the US Navy waited to see what the British and Japanese intended before finalising the design. By this time it was clear that a much higher speed was required, both to operate with aircraft-carriers and to catch the fast ships, such as the Bismarck- and Scharnhorst-classes under construction in Germany and the rebuilt *Kongos* in Japan. Initially, a 30kt ship with nine 14in (356mm) guns was proposed, but this was rejected in favour of a 27kt design armed with eleven, then twelve 14in (356mm) guns, but this was then changed to nine 16in (406mm). Protection was still on the "all-or-nothing" principle, although with some modifications. The side belt was sloped and there was a 1.5in (38mm) "burster" plating on the upper deck to prevent

and then recovered. They, together with *Colorado*, then played a full role in the Pacific campaign. All eight ships were put into reserve after the war, but none saw any further active service, although *Mississippi* was used as a missile test ship in 1950s. All were scrapped in late 1950s.

Below: New Mexico **in the late 1930s following her major reconstruction**

bombs and plunging shells from penetrating the main armoured deck. New lightweight turbines were installed to achieve the high speed required and a "unit" machinery arraignment ensured that the effects of enemy action would be minimised.

The two ships commissioned in April/May 1941, but were not effective until early 1942, due in part to propeller vibration problems. *Washington* spent some months escorting Murmansk convoys, but both ships were in the Pacific by June 1942. On 13/14 November 1942 *Washington*, in company with *South Dakota*, fought and sank the Japanese battlecruiser *Kirishima*. After the war Washington was put into reserve but *North Carolina* was refitted and employed for a time as a training ship. Both were stricken in 1961, but *North Carolina* became a memorial and remains on public display, an enduring memorial to a fine pair of ships.

Right: North Carolina, **showing the two forward triple 16in (406mm) turrets**

South Dakota

UNITED STATES OF AMERICA

Fast battleship
Completed: 1942.
Number in class: 4.
Displacement: 37,970 tons standard; 44,519 tons full load.
Dimensions: Length 680.0ft (207.3m); beam 108.1ft (33.0m); draught 35.1ft (10.7m).
Propulsion: 4 shafts; General Electric turbines; 8 boilers; 130,000shp; 27.5kt; 15,000nm at 15kt.
Armour: Belt 12.2in (310mm); bulkheads 11.0in (280 mm); barbettes 11.3-17.3in (287-440mm); turret faces 18.0in (457mm); conning tower 16.0in (406 mm); armoured deck 6.0-5.8in (152-147mm).
Aircraft: 3.
Armament: 9 x 16in (406mm) (4 x 3); 20 x 5in (127mm); 12 x 1.1in (28mm); 12 x 0.5in (12.7mm).
Complement: 1,793.

History: The designers of the South Dakota-class were instructed to produce a battleship which would combine the firepower of the North Carolinas with adequate protection against 16in (406mm) shells, and all on a hull not exceeding the Washington Treaty 35,000 tons limit. Not surprisingly, this resulted in a number of compromises and resulted in a ship that was cramped and was in many ways inferior to the North Carolina. As an example of the compromises, the extra protection was obtained by using thicker side armour, whose weight was compensated for by shortening the citadel, which required a more compact machinery layout. The overall length was some 50ft (15m) less than that of the *North Carolina*, but since the beam was the same an extra 9,000shp was needed to achieve the required speed of 27.5kt.

Only two ships were ordered initially - *South Dakota* (BB57) and *Indiana* (BB58) – but a further two were ordered in 1938 - *Massachusetts* (BB59) and *Alabama* (BB60) - but all were completed in 1942.

South Dakota served at first in the Pacific where she took part in the Battle of Santa Cruz (October 1942) and then took part with *Washington* in sinking the *Kirishima*, although she received such damage that she had to return to the

USA for repairs. After a brief period in European waters, she then returned to the Pacific in mid-1943. *Massachusetts* and *Alabama* both started the war in the Atlantic but by late 1943 all four *South Dakotas* were in the Pacific, where they were employed as fast carrier escorts and on fire support missions. The ships were placed in reserve in 1946-47, but various proposals for conversion came to naught and all were sold in the early 1960s. *South Dakota* and *Indiana* were scrapped but *Massachusetts* and *Alabama* have been preserved as memorials.

Right: Aerial view of *Alabama* shows compact layout of 5in (126mm) mountings

Below: *Alabama*, sporting disruptive camouflage, joins the British Home Fleet

Iowa

UNITED STATES OF AMERICA

Fast battleship
Completed: 1943-44.
Number in class: 4.
Displacement: 48,110 tons standard; 57,540 tons full load.
Dimensions: Length 887.3ft (270.4m); beam 108.2ft (33.0m); draught 36.2ft (11.0m).
Propulsion: 4 shafts; General Electric turbines; 8 boilers; 212,000shp; 32.5kt; 15,000nm at 15kt.
Armour: Belt 12.1in (307 mm); bulkheads 11.3in (287 mm); barbettes 11.6-17.3in (295-439 mm); turret faces 19.7in (500mm); conning tower 17.5in (445mm); armour deck 6.0in (152mm).
Aircraft: 3.
Armament: 9 x16in (406mm) (3 x 3); 20 x 5in (127mm); 49 x 20mm
Complement: 1,921.

History: In 1938 rumours began to reach the United States that the Japanese were constructing battleships displacing 46,000 tons, although the radical conversion of three Kongo-class battlecruisers into fast battleships also posed a very significant threat. (The reconversion of the fourth, *Hiei*, from training ship to battleship was apparently not known at this time.) This resulted in a US order for four of a new Iowa (BB61)-class of very fast battleships, the number being set by the need to match the three Kongos, plus one to cover for a ship in refit/repair. These were duly laid down: *Iowa* (BB61) - 27 June 1940; *New Jersey* (BB62) - 16 September 1940; *Missouri* (BB63) - 6 January 1941; and *Wisconsin* (BB64) - 25 January 1941. Then in July 1940 Congress authorised a huge emergency construction programme and the Secretary of the Navy decided that rather than design a new class, an order for a further two Iowas would be placed, which were duly laid down: *Illinois* (BB65) - 6 December 1942 and *Kentucky* - 6 December 1942. In the event, only the first four were ever completed - *Iowa* and *New Jersey* in 1943 and *Missouri* and *Wisconsin* in 1944; *Illinois* was cancelled in August 1945, while *Kentucky* was eventually launched in 1950, but was never completed, being scrapped in 1958.

One of the primary reasons for the high speed required, which was extremely costly in terms of displacement and additional protection, was the fear that the Japanese would form fast carrier task forces comprising carriers escorted by heavy cruisers to harass US lines of communication in the early stages of a Pacific War. There was also a possibility that the fast battleships of the Kongo-class would be detached from the main battle fleet in support of these groups – an assessment which proved, in the event, to be absolutely correct.

The protection system was similar in principle to that of the *South Dakota*, but with important modifications. The belt, which was again tapered below the waterline and which extended to the ship's bottom, was no longer sloped internally but was attached directly to the hull plating; high-speed drag was reduced by fitting the armour plate to the inside rather than the outside of the plating. Four longitudinal torpedo bulkheads were placed inside the tapered belt thereby avoiding some of the problems experienced with underwater protection system of the South Dakotas. A remarkable feature of the design was the provision of two heavily armoured decks, with a splinter deck between them. The armoured decks had a combined thickness of about 12.0in (305mm), giving the ships unequalled protection against plunging shells and bombs.

Beam was limited by the need to pass through the Panama Canal, but length was increased considerably. Power was provided by four General-Electric geared-turbines with a combined output of 212,000shp, enabling them

Above: **Iowa-class battleship, *Missouri,* during World War II**

to reach their target speed of 33kt with ease and also making them the fastest battleships ever built.

Iowa entered service in the Atlantic in August and for the next two months was employed in escort duties off Newfoundland in anticipation of an attempted breakout by the German battleship *Tirpitz*. In January 1944, *Iowa*, in company with her recently completed sister, *New Jersey*, moved to the Pacific, where they accompanied the fast carrier task forces, and were present at the Battles of the Philippine Sea and at Leyte Gulf. *Missouri* and *Wisconsin* entered service in late 1944 and were present at the landings on Iwo Jima and Okinawa, and accompanied the fast carrier task forces on the final attacks on Japan. *Missouri* was struck by a *kamikaze* off Okinawa, but this did not prevent her from being the scene of the final total surrender of the Japanese in Tokyo Bay.

In common with other battleships, the four *Iowas* were put into reserve in the late 1940s, although *Missouri* was employed as a training ship from 1948-50. All were reactivated for the Korean War, but with minimum modifications apart from removing all aircraft facilities. One ship was on station at a time: *Missouri*, September 1950-March 1951; *New Jersey*, May-November 1951; *Wisconsin*, November 1951-March 1952; *Iowa* March-October 1952; and finally *Missouri* again, until the commitment ended in March 1953. They then remained in service, but in 1956 *Wisconsin* collided with a destroyer and had to have 70ft (20m) of her bow replaced from the uncompleted *Kentucky*. All four returned to the reserve in 1958.

New Jersey was decommissioned for service in Vietnam from 1967-69, with lighter weapons removed and some new electronic equipment added. All four were then brought back into service by the Reagan Administration to become the core element of the newly created Surface Action Groups. Modification work included the installation of eight Tomahawk and four quadruple Harpoon launchers, as well as four Phalanx close-in weapons systems (CIWS). Modern radars and other electronic gear were also added. Some of the four were deployed to the Mediterranean in support of operations in the Lebanon and *Wisconsin* and *Missouri* took part in the Gulf War in 1991. Then, in the post-Cold War rundown, they were returned to reserve status yet again: *Iowa* in 1990; *New Jersey* and *Wisconsin* in 1991 and *Missouri* in 1992.

All four were stricken in January 1995 and it was intended that they would be either offered as memorials or scrapped, but Congress intervened yet again, compelling the Navy to restore two, *New Jersey* and *Wisconsin*, to reserve

status. Subsequently this was changed, with *Iowa* being restored to reserve status in order that *New Jersey* could become a memorial in its name-state. *Missouri* was sold to a private corporation in 1998 for use as a museum at Pearl Harbor. *Iowa* is now in storage at Rhode Island. *Wisconsin* is at Norfolk, Virginia, and will eventually be open to the public. There can be no doubt that to return one or more of these ships to operational status would be a time-consuming and very expensive business, and then to maintain in service would be an equally daunting undertaking. Nevertheless, they have a very powerful public image and have strong support in Congress and it could be that the last chapter in the careers of these remarkable ships has still not been written.

***Below: Iowa* fires a broadside in the 1990s; note the Tomahawk launchers**

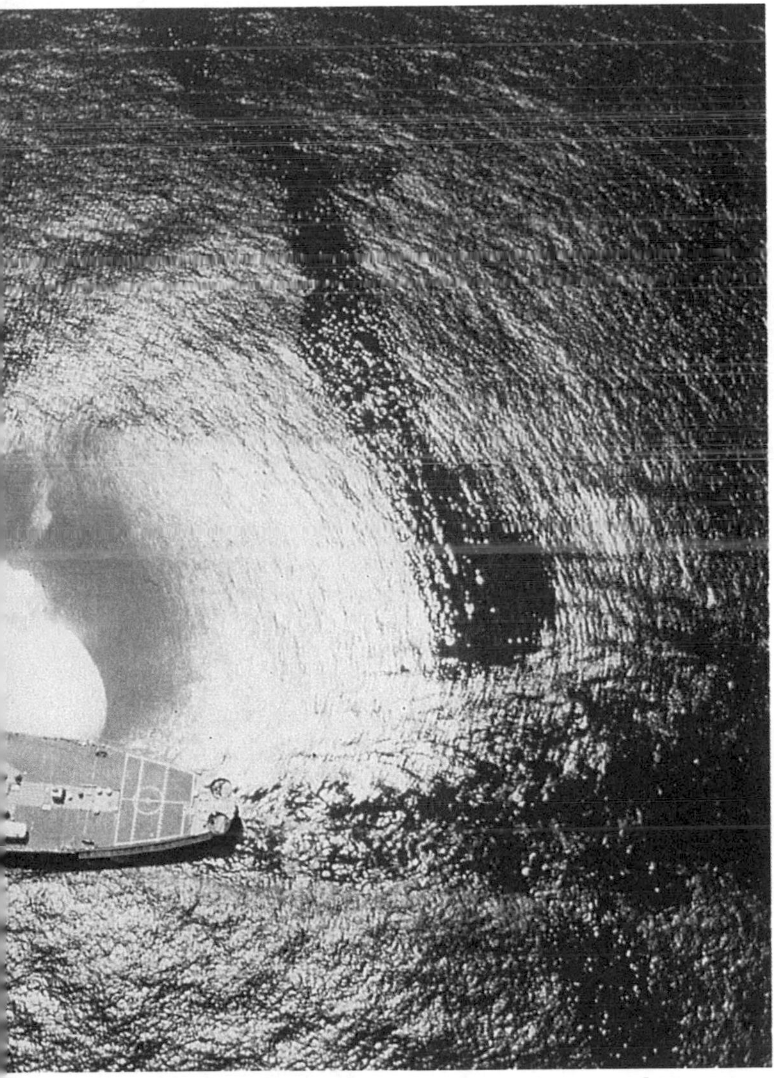

Battlecruisers

Capital ship designers had to achieve a balance between firepower, speed and protection. In the original Dreadnought and her immediate successors priority was given to firepower – the bigger guns the better – and to protection, with armour becoming ever thicker. As a result, speed was lower than the British Admiral Fisher – the battleships progenitor – wanted, and a further class of new ship emerged. Named the "battlecruiser", this design gave priority to armament – the heavier the better – and to speed – the faster they were, the happier Fisher became. Inevitably, this was achieved at the cost of armour and the great majority of British battlecruisers were singularly ill-protected.

The theory was that battlecruisers could outshoot anything that could catch them and outrun anything that outgunned them. The first British use of battlecruisers was a classic example, when two were dashed to the Falkland Islands in December 1914, where they totally defeated a force of marauding German cruisers. Unfortunately, battlecruisers were as large as battleships and were handsome ships, which gave them an aura of strength, and this, combined with glamour and "dash", led to a fatal underestimation of their weaknesses. Consequently, they were grouped together to become an integral part of the Grand Fleet, with which they participated in the Battle of Jutland – and suffered accordingly. The British never built another battlecruiser after 1920 but the type lasted in the fleet well into World War II, in which two of the best, *Hood* and *Repulse*, were both lost.

The Germans built a number of battlecruisers before and during World War I which were generally of a better quality than those of the British, but they, too,

misemployed them with the High Seas Fleet, and they never had a real opportunity for independent action outside the North Sea. The idea of the fast, lightly protected capital ship did not go away, however, and in the late 1930s the French built the Dunkerque-class, to which the Germans replied with the *Scharnhorst* and *Gneisenau* which, despite some major shortcomings, particularly in their armament, were probably the best of the breed in any navy.

The US Navy had avoided the type and concentrated instead on making their battleships faster, thus outdating the whole concept of the battlecruiser. Then, to great surprise in naval circles, they built the three Alaska-class battlecruisers towards the end of World War II. These proved to be excellent and useful ships, but the era of the big-gun ship was over and they had very short careers.

That should have been the end, but the Soviet Navy's ever-increasing influence on the balance of naval power beguiled Russian admirals into developing the largest ships, apart from aircraft carriers, to be built during the Cold War. The Kirovs were large (exactly the same length as the British battleship *Vanguard*) and their decks covered with a huge variety of weapons. However, even these have gone the way of other battlecruisers (and of the Russian Navy, as a whole), but there are rumours of the Chinese Navy building something similar, so that, even now, the day of the battlecruiser may not be entirely over.

Below: Bismarck* at anchor in a Norwegian fjord, seen from *Prinz Eugen

Dunkerque

FRANCE

Battlecruiser
Completed: 1937-38.
Number in class: 2.
Displacement: 26,500 tons standard; 35,500 tons full load.
Dimensions: Length 703.8ft (214.5m); beam 102.3ft (31.1m); draught 31.5ft (9.6m).
Propulsion: 4 shafts; Parsons geared turbines; 6 boilers; 112,500shp; 29.5kt.
Armour: Belt 9.5-7.7in (240-195mm); decks 5.0-4.5in +1.6in (125-115mm + 40mm); barbettes 13-6in (300-150mm) conning tower 10.6-6.3in (270-160mm).
Aircraft: 2 x Loire 130 seaplanes.
Armament: 8 x 13in (330mm)(2 x 4); 16 x 5.1in (130mm)(8 x 2); 8 x 37mm AA; 32 x 13.2mm AA.
Complement: 1,381-1,431.

History: These were both the first and last French battlecruisers, their intended role being to protect French merchant shipping in war from German commerce raiders, specifically the Deutschland-class *panzerschiffe* ("pocket battleships"). Thus they had a high speed - 29.5kt - and a heavy armament of eight 13in (330mm) guns in two quadruple turrets, which were both forward, but 90ft (27m) apart, to avoid them both being put out of action by a single hit from a shell or torpedo. Within the turrets the guns were mounted in pairs, each pair elevating together to a maximum of 35deg, at which they had a range of 32,800yd (30,000m). Protection was designed to resist 11in (280mm) shells at a range of 18,000yd (16,500m)

Dunkerque joined the fleet in 1937, followed by *Strasbourg* in 1938, and both

Blücher

GERMANY

Battlecruiser/armoured cruiser
Completed: 1910.
Number in class: 1.
Displacement: 15,590 tons standard; 17,250 tons full load.
Dimensions: Length 530.5ft (161.7m); beam 80.3ft (24.5m); draught 28.5ft (8.7m).
Propulsion: 3 shafts; vertical triple expansion; 18 boilers; 34,000ihp; 24.25kt; 6,600nm at 12kt.
Armour: Belt 7.0-2.4in (180-60mm); bulkheads 6.0-3.2in (150-80mm); battery 5.5in (140mm); barbettes 7.0in (180mm); turrets 7.0-2.4in (180-60mm), conning tower (10.0-3.2in (250-80mm).
Armament: 12 x 8.2in (210mm)(6 x 2); 8 x 5.9in (150mm); 16 x 3.45in (88mm); 4 x 17.7in (450mm) TT.
Complement: 1,026.

History: One of those ships which do not fit neatly into any one category, *Blücher* was built as a development of the Scharnhorst-class cruiser and was designated an "armoured cruiser" by the Germans, although her armament and displacement were significantly greater than contemporary German cruisers. Her general appearance was similar to that of a battleship, with twin funnels, a tripod mast (the first in any German warship) and a powerful armament, disposed in six twin turrets, although the 8.2in (210mm) calibre was lighter than that to be found in a capital ship. As a consequence, she has been considered internationally as the first of the German battlecruisers. *Blücher* started trials in October 1909 and, amongst other peacetime deployments, was used for gunnery experiments. In the war, she was one of the force that

***Above:* The Dunkerque-class was the French reply to Germany's "pocket battleships"**

were deployed in the Atlantic at the start of World War Two, where they took part in the operations to catch the *Deutschland* and *Graf Spee.* This was precisely the type of hunt they had been designed for, although, in the event, neither managed to catch-up with their quarries. Both transferred to the Mediterranean in April 1940 and were in the naval base at Mers-el-Kebir in July when the British demanded the surrender of the French fleet. *Dunkerque* was hit by British 15in (380mm) shells and damaged, and was subsequently further damaged in an air attack, but was repaired sufficiently to return to Toulon in November 1942, where she joined her sister, *Strasbourg,* which had escaped from Mars-el-Caber. Both were scuttled on 27 November 1942, but *Strasbourg* was later recovered and repaired by the Italian Navy, only to be sunk in an Allied air attack on 18 August 1944.

---

met the British at the Battle of Dogger Bank (24 January 1915), where a shell from the British battlecruiser *Princess Royal* caused a fire in the ammunition supply system, following which she was hit by numerous more shells and torpedoes, until she sank.

***Below:* Hard to classify, *Blücher,* sunk in 1915, was employed as a battlecruiser**

Von der Tann

GERMANY

Battlecruiser
Completed: 1911.
Number in class: 1.
Displacement: 19,064 tons standard; 21,700 tons full load.
Dimensions: Length 563.3ft (171.7m); beam 87.3ft (26.6m); draught 29.7 ft (9.0m).
Propulsion: 4 shafts; Parsons turbines; 18 boilers; 43,600shp; 24.8kts; 4,400nm at 14kts.
Armour: Belt 10.0-3.2in (250-80mm); bulkheads 7.0-4.0in (180-100mm); battery 6in (150mm); barbettes 9.0-1.2in (230-30mm); turrets 9.0-2.4in (230-60mm); conning tower 10.0-3.2in (250-80mm).
Armament: 8 x 11.1in (280mm) (4 x 2); 10 x 5.9in (150mm); 16 x 3.45in (88mm); 4 x 17.7in (450mm) TT.
Complement: 1,174.

History: The first true battlecruiser to be built for the German Navy, *Von der Tann* was of a similar size and carried similar armament to the British Invincible-class. However, she proved herself to be a somewhat better fighting ship, primarily due to the much heavier armoured protection and better internal design. Main armament was eight 11.1in (280mm) guns in four twin turrets, all on the centreline, with one forward, one aft, and two in the centre of the ship, but able to fire on either beam. A minor idiosyncrasy in the design of this ship was that she was the only German warship to be built with the officers' accommodation in the bow,

---

Moltke

GERMANY

Battlecruiser
Completed: 1912.
Number in class: 2.
Displacement: 22,216 tons standard; 25,300 tons full load.
Dimensions: Length 611.9ft (186.5m); beam 96.8ft (8.2m); draught 29.6ft (9.0m).
Propulsion: 4 shafts; Parsons turbines; 24 boilers; 52,000shp; 25.5kt; 4,120nm at 14kt.
Armour: Belt 10.7-4.0in (270-100mm); bulkheads 8.0-4.0in (200-100mm); battery 8.0-6.0in (200-150mm); barbettes 9.0-1.2in (230-30mm): turrets 9.0-2.4in (230-60mm); conning-tower 14.0-3.2in (350-80mm).
Armament: 10x 11.1in (280mm) (5 x 2); 12 x 5.9in (150mm); 12 x 3.45in (88mm); 4 x 19.7in (500mm) TT.
Complement: 1,355.

History: *Moltke* and *Goeben* were both completed in 1912 and represented a major advance on the *Von der Tann*, being considerably larger, mounting an additional twin 11.1in (280mm) turret in the superfiring position aft and with a much improved hull, which had greater beam and finer ends. They were well armed, fast, and with excellent armoured protection and internal sub-divisions.

Goeben became famous in the first few days of the war in August 1914, when she was trapped in the Mediterranean by the British, but, by a combination of skilful tactics and greater speed, her captain managed to evade the British battlecruisers, *Indefatigable* and *Indomitable*, and to reach shelter in Turkey. She was nominally transferred to the Turkish Navy as *Yavuz Sultan*

Above: **Equivalent to the British *Invincible, Von der Tann* had much better protection**

Von der Tann took part in most of the major actions in World War One, including the Battle of Jutland, where she fired the rounds which blew up *Indefatigable*. She was later hit by two 15in (381mm) and two 13.5in (343mm) shells which caused considerable damage, but she survived and returned to port for repairs. *Von der Tann* was interned with the rest of the High Seas Fleet on 24 November 1918, where she was scuttled with most other units at Scapa Flow on 21 June 1919. The hulk was raised and broken up in 1930.

Above: Goeben, **seen in 1912, became Turkey's *Yavuz Sultan* and served until 1960**

Selim and operated under the Turkish flag and with a mixed German/Turkish crew against both the Russians and British. During this period she hit no less than five mines, but survived them all. She became Turkish property after the war and was not decommissioned until 1960, the last battlecruiser in any of the world's navies.

Moltke took part in the Battle of Dogger Bank, and at the Battle of Jutland she hit the British *Tiger* on at least nine occasions and survived four 15.5in (394mm) hits herself. During the war she was twice hit by torpedoes (19 August 1915, 26 April 1918), but survived both. She went to Scapa Flow in November 1918 where she was scuttled with the other German ships. The hulk was raised in 1927 and scrapped shortly afterwards.

Seydlitz

GERMANY

Battlecruiser
Completed: 1913.
Number in class: 1.
Displacement: 25,594 tons standard; 28,100 tons full load.
Dimensions: Length 657.9ft (200.5m); beam 93.5ft (28.5m); draught 9.2ft (30.3m).
Propulsion: 4 shafts; Parsons turbines; 27 boilers; 63,000shp; 26.5kt; 4,700nm at 14kt.
Armour: Belt 12.0-4.0in (300-100mm); bulkheads 8.7-4.0in (220-100mm); battery 8.0-6.0in (200-150mm); barbettes 9.0-1.2in (230-30mm); turrets 10.0-2.75in (250-70mm); conning-tower 14.0-3.2in (350-80mm).
Armament: 10 x 11.1in (280mm) (5 x 2); 12 x 5.9in (150mm); 12 x 3.45in (88mm); 4 x 19.7in (550mm) TT.
Complement: 1,425.

History: In some respects *Seydlitz* was an enlarged version of *Moltke*, but with a different hull form and the forecastle raised by one deck level. Like *Moltke* she had tandem rudders (ie, one behind the other on the centreline) but this proved to be an unsatisfactory arrangement.

Seydlitz was part of the force that bombarded the English east coast ports in 1914 and was present at the Battle of Dogger Bank (24 January 1915) where she was hit by three shells; the two after turrets were burnt out but there was no general conflagration. She was repaired, only to hit a mine on 24 April 1916. She was particularly heavily damaged at Jutland, being hit by 21 heavy and 2

Derrflinger

GERMANY

Battlecruiser
Completed: 1914-17.
Number in class: 3.
Displacement: 26,180 tons standard; 30,700 tons full load
Dimensions: Length 690.3ft (210.4m); beam 95.1ft (29.0m); draught 31.0ft 9.5(m).
Propulsion: 4 shafts; Parsons turbines; 18 boilers; 63,000shp; 26.5kt; 5,600nm at 14kt.
Armour: Belt 11.8-3.9in (300-100mm); bulkheads 9.8-3.9in (250-100mm) ; battery 5.9in (150mm); barbettes 10.2-1.2in (260-30mm); turrets 10.7-3.2in (270-80mm); conning-tower 14.0-3.2in (350-80mm).
Armament: 8 x 12in (305mm) (4 x 2); 12 x 5.9in (15cm); 4 x 3.45in (88mm); 4 x 19.7in (500mm) TT.
Complement: 1,391.

History: *Derrflinger* entered service in 1914, followed by *Lützow* in 1916 and *Hindenburg* in 1917. The first two ships represented a marked advance over the *Seydlitz* design, being flush-decked and excellent seaboats, although they retained the somewhat ineffective tandem rudder steering system of the earlier class. Main armament was eight 12in (305mm) guns in two superfiring pairs fore and aft, and with no turrets amidships. The third ship, *Hindenburg*, was slightly different, being some 8ft (2.4m) longer and with more powerful engines, giving a 1kt increase in speed.

Lützow was finished in August 1915 but suffered turbine problems which prevented her from joining the fleet until March 1916. She was at Jutland

Above: **Repeatedly damaged during World War I, *Seydlitz* was scuttled at Scapa Flow**

medium shells, as well as by 2 torpedoes, with the same two turrets again being burnt out. She shipped some 5,300 tons of water, but after herculean efforts by her crew she eventually limped back into port under her own steam, where it was found that her forward freeboard, normally 30ft (9.1m), had been reduced to 8.8ft (2.7m)!

Despite all this, *Seydlitz* survived the war, only to be interned in Scapa Flow, where she was scuttled in June 1919. She was raised and scrapped in 1928.

Above: **The Derrflinger-class were the best battlecruisers built during World War I**

where she showed excellent gunnery but was hit by at least 24 heavy shells which caused serious flooding, leading to her being abandoned and sunk by a German destroyer. *Derrflinger* took part in the Battle of Dogger Bank, where she was hit by three 15in (380mm) shells which caused only light damage. At Jutland she was responsible for the destruction of the British battlecruiser, *Queen Mary*, but, although *Derrflinger* suffered numerous hits during the battle which resulted in severe flooding, she survived. She was interned in 1918, scuttled in 1919 and raised in 1934. *Hindenburg* was completed in October 1917 but saw no action and was interned in November 1918, scuttled in 1919 and raised for scrapping in 1930.

Deutschland

GERMANY

Panzerschiff ("pocket battleship")
Specifications for *Graf Spee*
Completed: 1929-32.
Number in class: 3.
Displacement: 12,100 tons standard; 16,200 tons full load.
Dimensions: Length 610.3ft (186.0m); beam 70.8ft (21.6m); draught 24.3ft (7.4m).
Propulsion: 2 shafts; 8 M.A.N. diesels; 54,000bhp; 28kt.
Armour: Belt 3.2-2.4in (80-60mm); deck 1.5in (45mm); barbettes 4.0in (100mm); turrets 5.5-3.3in (140-85mm); conning-tower 6-2in (150-50mm).
Aircraft: 2 x Arado Ar-196 floatplanes.
Armament: 6 x 11in (280mm) (2 x 3); 8 x 5.9in (150mm); 6 x 3.45in (88mm); 8 x 37mm AA; 8 x 21in (533mm) TT.
Complement: 1,150.

History: One of the naval lessons from World War One was that commerce raiders could exert influence out of proportion to the resources involved, so when the German Navy was expanding in the 1920s it developed a new type of fast, well-armed ship specifically for this mission. This type of ship was known in Germany as a *panzerschiff* (armoured ship), but reclassified in 1939 as a "heavy cruiser;" abroad, it was described at the time as a "pocket battleship" but is generally classified as a battlecruiser.

The Germany Navy was limited by the Treaty of Versailles to a maximum of 10,000 tons displacement for any new ship, but without any upper limit on gun calibre and the *panzerschiff* represented an ingenious maximising of capabilities within those limits. The result was a ship which could (as least in theory) outgun any ship that could catch it (ie, another cruiser) but outrun any ship that could outgun it (ie, a battleship). The publicly announced displacement was 10,000 tons (although it was later discovered outside Germany that the true figure far exceeded this) and the ships were armed with six 11in (280mm) guns in two triple turrets, and a heavy secondary armament.

The builders used the then new technique of electro-welding, saving 15 percent of the ship's weight, and armoured protection was good by cruiser standards, although not as comprehensive as that of a battleship. Power was provided by diesel engines, giving the great range required for commerce raiding, although they proved somewhat unreliable. These ships were also among the first in any navy to be fitted with radars.

The three ships - *Deutschland, Admiral Scheer* and *Admiral Graf von Spee* - joined the fleet in 1929-32. *Graf Spee*, commanded by the respected Captain Langsdorff, carried out raiding operations in the South Atlantic in 1939, but was

***Below: Admiral Graf Spee* was the last of the three Deutschland-class to be completed**

Above: Deutschland **in 1939, showing after turret and torpedo-tubes on the quarterdeck**

Below: **The Germans classified the Deutschland-class as *panzerschiff* (armoured ships)**

caught by three British cruisers off the River Plate and forced into Montevideo for repairs. Appreciating that there was no escape from the gathering British forces, Langsdorff blew up his ship, and he and his crew were interned in Argentina. The other two ships, *Lützow* (re-named from *Deutschland*) and *Scheer* also carried out a number of raiding operations, the most successful being by *Scheer* in early 1941, when she sank 17 ships (113,233grt), including the auxiliary cruiser, *Jervis Bay*. Both ships served in Norway, but were then withdrawn from active service in 1943. They were reinstated in 1944 for service in the Baltic, but both were sunk in bombing attacks. Both ships were extensively modified during the war, which included fitting prominent funnel cowls and an "Atlantic bow" to improve sea-keeping.

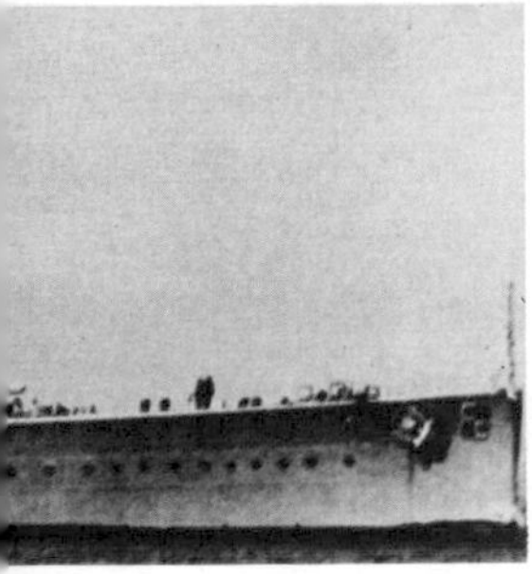

Scharnhorst

GERMANY

Battlecruiser
Completed: 1938-39.
Number in class: 2.
Displacement: 31,850 tons standard; 38,900 tons full load.
Dimensions: Length 770.7ft (234.9m); beam 98.4ft (30.0m); draught 32.5ft (9.9m).
Propulsion: 3 shafts; Brown-Boveri geared steam turbines; 12 boilers; 160,000shp; 31.5kt.
Armour: Belt 13.8-7.9in (350-200mm); decks 2in + 2in (50mm + 50mm); barbettes 13.8in-7.9in (350-200mm); turrets 14.0-6.0in (360-150mm); conning-tower 13.8-3.9in (350-100mm).
Aircraft: 4 x Arado Ar-196 floatplanes.
Armament: 9 x 11in (280mm) (3 x 3); 12 x 5.9in (150mm); 14 x 4.1in (105mm) AA; 16 x 37mm AA; 10 x 20mm AA; 6 x 21in (533mm) TT (fitted in 1942).
Complement: 1,840.

History: When the Germans built the Deutschland-class they started a naval race, since the French replied with the larger, faster, more powerful Dunkerque-class. At this, the Germans cancelled the proposed fourth and fifth Deutschland-class ships to produce a new design which was even larger, faster and more heavily armed, thus, once again, outmatching the French. The result was *Scharnhorst*, commissioned in 1939, and *Gneisenau*, which although laid down second was commissioned first in May 1938.

The ships were 160.5ft (48.9m) longer than the Deutschlands and with 22,700 tons greater displacement. They used a new type of armour which

accounted for some 40 percent of the ship's weight, providing burster armour on the upper deck and sides, with a low main armoured deck covering the ship's vitals. Diesel propulsion was considered, but the power required was so great that a superheated, high-pressure steam system was adopted instead, which was powerful and took up less volume, but proved difficult to maintain. As built, the ships had a vertical stem, but this made the ships very wet forward and was replaced in 1938-39 by a raked "Atlantic bow," although use of the forward turret was always restricted.

The calibre of the main guns was the subject of much debate, with some officers advocating 14in (356mm), while others claimed that the higher rate of fire of the 11in (280mm) guns more than compensated and, in any case, to adopt 14in guns would annoy the British, with whom the Germans were then negotiating a naval treaty. In any event, the 14in (356mm) guns would not be available until at least 1940, so nine 11in (280mm) calibre guns were mounted, but with plans to mount the larger guns in 1940, by which time, so it was thought, the war would be over.

These were large and handsome ships - particularly after the "Atlantic bow" had been fitted - and their size and looks disguised the weakness of their firepower, which was that of a heavy cruiser. Thus, they were outgunned, even by older British battleships and invariably had to withdraw when the latter were encountered.

These two ships generally operated in pairs, first in November 1939 when they steamed into the North Atlantic, where they sank the British ▶

***Below:* The Scharnhorst-class were much improved versions of the Deutschland-class**

armed merchant cruiser, *Rawalpindi*. In April 1940 they took part in the Norwegian campaign, where the British battlecruiser *Renown* damaged *Gneisenau* before the German ships used their superior speed to escape. In June they sank the British carrier, *Glorious*, together with its two escorting destroyers, although *Scharnhorst* was hit by a destroyer-launched torpedo, which caused considerable flooding, while *Gneisenau* was later hit by a torpedo from the submarine *Clyde*; both ships then spent several months under repair.

The two ships had a successful Atlantic operation in early 1941, sinking 22 ships (115,000grt) before proceeding to Brest, where they were constantly attacked by the Royal Air Force, and it was eventually decided that they should return up the English Channel to Germany, accompanied by the heavy cruiser *Prinz Eugen*. This daring voyage took place in February 1942 and all three ships reached their destination, although both battlecruisers were hit by mines and had to go into dock for repairs.

While under repair in Kiel, *Gneisenau* was again badly damaged by the RAF, her entire forecastle being demolished and although it was planned to rebuild her with a new, lengthened bow and to rearm her with nine 15in (380mm) guns, she never went to sea again.

Scharnhorst deployed to Norway in March 1943 where she posed a major threat to the

Kongo

JAPAN

Battlecruiser/battleship
Specifications for *Kongo*, as built.
Completed: 1913-1915.
Number in class: 4.
Displacement: 27,500 tons standard; 32,200 tons full load.
Dimensions: Length 704.0ft (214.5m); beam 92.0ft (28.0m); draught 27.6ft (8.4m).
Propulsion: 4 shafts; Parsons turbines; 8/11 boilers; 136,600shp; 27.5kt; 8,000nm at 14kt.
Armour: Belt 8-3in (203-76mm); decks 2.3-1.5in (57-41mm); barbettes 10in (254mm); turrets 9in (227mm) ; conning-tower 10in (254mm).
Armament: 8 x 14in (356mm) (4 x 2); 16 x 6in (152mm); 8 x 3in; 8 x 21in (533mm) TT.
Complement: 1,201.

History: These four ships were built as battlecruisers, with *Kongo* being completed in 1913 at Vickers, England, the last major Japanese warship to be built abroad; she was followed by *Hiei* in 1914, and *Haruna* and *Kirishima* in 1915, all built in Japanese yards. The Vickers design accorded to the contemporary ideas of battlecruisers, with heavy armament, high speed and limited protection. Thus, as built, they mounted eight 14in (366mm) guns, the first warships in the world to be armed with these new weapons, which were mounted in four twin turrets, with a relatively small bridge structure and two tripod masts. The armoured protection, which made up 23.3 percent of the weight of the ships, was designed to resist fire from 14in (366mm) guns at ranges of between 21,900yd (20,000m) and 27,340yd (25,000m). With their

Allied convoys to Russia. Her final sortie took place in December 1943, when she emerged to attack Convoy JB.55B. In the Battle of North Cape she was repeatedly attacked by cruisers and destroyers until she was sunk by the battleship *Duke of York* on 26 December, with the loss of 1,803 lives.

Below: Scharnhorst,* handsome but under-armed generally hunted with *Gneisenau

three funnels they were handsome and purposeful looking ships, and with a displacement of 32,200 tons they were large for their time. It has been said that the design of *Kongo* so impressed the British that, first, the design of *Tiger*, the fourth of the "Splendid Cats" (see Lion-class) was modified along the lines of the Japanese unit. Although that has never been proved, it is certainly true that in 1915 the British requested the loan of all four ships, which the Japanese politely declined.

They were very popular in the Imperial Japanese Navy and underwent two major rebuilds, the first in the late 1920s, which included fitting a massive new fighting top (known in the West as a "pagoda mast") as well as a hood on the forefunnel to reduce smoke interference. They were also given anti-torpedo bulges and additional armoured protection, while the turrets were modified to increase gun elevation from 30deg to 40deg. They were also given new boilers, but the 3,800 tons of additional armour reduced maximum speed from 27.5kt to 25.9kt.

A second and even more drastic rebuild took place in 1933-40, the main purpose of which was to restore the speed lost in the first rebuild. This involved removing the existing machinery and replacing it with lightweight turbines and new boilers, which more than doubled the available power, and reduced the number of funnels from three to two. The hull was Lengthened by 26ft (8.0m) to give a higher Length-to-beam ratio and all these improvements resulted in an increase in maximum speed to over 30kt and the ships were then officially re-classified as "fast battleships."

These ships then played a major role in World War Two, starting with the initial attacks, when *Hiei* and *Kirishima* were part of the escort for the ▶

carriers attacking Pearl Harbor, while *Kongo* and *Haruna* took part in the attacks on the Philippines, Malaya and the Dutch East Indies. *Hiei* was sunk during the Guadalcanal operation (13 November 1942) and two days later *Kirishima* was worsted in an engagement with the United States' battleships *Washington* and *South Dakota*, as a result of which she had to

Tsukuba/Ibuki

JAPAN

Battlecruiser
Specifications for *Ibuki*
Completed: 1907-1911.
Number in class: 4.
Displacement: 14,636 tons standard; 15.595 tons full load.
Dimensions: Length 485.0ft (137.2m); beam 75.3ft (23.0m); draught 26.1ft (8.0m).
Propulsion: 2 shafts; steam turbines; 24,000shp, 21.5kt.
Armour: Belt 7.0-4.0in (178-102mm); deck 3.0in (76mm); barbettes and turrets 7.0-5.0in (178-127mm); conning-tower 8.0in (76mm).
Armament: 4 x 12in (305mm) (2 x 2); 8 x 8in (203mm); 14 x 4.7in (120mm); 4 x 3in (76mm); 3 x 18in (457mm) TT.
Complement: 844.

History: *Tsukuba* and *Ikoma* were ordered in June 1904 to replace two battleships sunk by Russian mines one month earlier. It was then decided to arm them with 12in (305mm) guns, and as a result they were re-designated battlecruisers in 1912. Both were powered by vertical, triple-expansion steam engines and had a maximum speed of 20.5kt. *Tsukuba* was destroyed in an explosion in 1917, while *Ikoma* was rearmed with ten 6in (152mm) guns in 1919 and re-rated in 1921 as a first-class cruiser, although she was actually employed as a gunnery training ship until scrapped in 1924.

The Ibuki-class (*Ibuki*, completed 1909; *Kurama*, completed 1911) were improved and slightly larger Tsukubas, with a revised secondary armament, in which the 8in (203mm) guns were mounted

be scuttled. *Kongo* was sunk by a torpedo from the submarine *Sealion* on 21 November 1944 and *Haruna* was sunk by aircraft near Kure on 28 July 1945.

***Below:* Battlecruiser *Kirishima* in 1931 before her conversion to a "fast" battleship**

in turrets rather than in barbettes as in the earlier ships. *Kurama* had the same triple-expansion engines as the Tsukubas, but *Ibuki's* construction was delayed so that she could become the first Japanese ship to be fitted with Parsons steam turbines. *Ibuki* was one of the Allied warships ships escorting the Australian/New Zealand troop convoy from Australia to the Middle East in November 1914. Both ships were scrapped in 1924-25.

***Below: Tsukuba,* armed with 12in (305mm) guns, was classified as a battlecruiser**

Kirov

RUSSIA (SOVIET UNION)

Battlecruiser
Specifications for *Pyotr Velikhiy.*
Completed: 1980-98.
Number in class: 4.
Displacement: 24,300 tons standard; 26,396 tons full load.
Dimensions: Length 824.1ft (251.2m); beam 93.5ft (28.5m); draught 33.8ft (10.3m)
Propulsion: 2 shafts; Combined Nuclear and Steam Turbine (CONAS), 2 KN-3 nuclear reactors (each 300Mw); 2 oil-fired boilers; 140,000shp; 32kt; 14,000nm at 30kt (nuclear); 1,300nm at 17kt (steam).
Armour: Nuclear reactor, 3.9in (100mm) sides, 1.4in (36mm) ends; steering compartment, 2.8in (70mm) sides, 2.0in (50mm) roof; conning tower 3.2in (80mm).
Aircraft: 3 Kamov Ka-26PL ASW or Ka-27RT targeting helicopters.
Armament: 20 x SS-N-19 Shipwreck SSM launchers (20 missiles); 12 x SA-N-6 SAM launchers 96 missiles); 16 x SA-N-9 SAM launchers (128 missiles); 6 x CADS-1 CIWS (each 2 x 30mm gatling AA, 8 x SA-N-11 missiles); 2 x 130mm AK-130 guns; 10 x 21in (533mm) TT; 1 x RPK-5 ASW rocket launcher; 2 x RBU-1000 ASW rocket launcher.
Complement: 655

History: Throughout the Cold War Soviet designers regularly took Western navies by surprise, producing some novel designs which showed an eagerness to combine new equipment with innovative tactical ideas. One of the tacitly accepted naval concepts from the mid-1950s onwards was that, with the exception of aircraft carriers, the day of the large surface combatant was over and it therefore came as a considerable surprise when the Soviet Navy commissioned the first of the Kirov-class ships, whose 26,396 ton displacement, heavy armament, high speed and light protection led to the resurrection of the old term, "battlecruiser."

The operational requirement for this class was approved in 1971 and called for a ship which would be the flagship of an anti-carrier task group, combining sophisticated command-and-control facilities with a heavy offensive/defensive armament and the associated sensors. In a class of five such large ships built over an 18-year period it was to be expected that sensors and weapons systems should change, as tactical thinking changed or new systems became available, but the overall balance between anti-ship, anti-air and anti-submarine systems remained the same with the final disposition in *Pyotr Velkihiy* as shown above. Aircraft carriers apart, these ships probably represent the greatest concentration of power in a single hull in naval history.

Four of the planned five ships were completed, their names being changed on several occasions to keep pace with political changes. The first ship in the class, *Kirov* was completed in 1980 but was renamed in 1992, becoming *Admiral Ushakov,* although the West continues to refer to these ships collectively as the "Kirov-class." The second ship, *Frunze* (1984) became *Admiral Lazarev*; and the third, *Kalinin* (1988) became *Admiral Nakhimov*. The fourth ship was to have been named *Yuri Andropov*, but when it was completed in 1998 it bore the name *Pyotr Velikhy* (Peter the Great) after the tsar who created the Russian Navy. A fifth ship, originally to have been named *Dzerzhinsky*, then *Oktyabrskaya Revolutsiya* and finally *Admiral Flota Sovetskoyo Soyuza Kuznetsov,* was cancelled shortly after the keel had been laid and later scrapped.

Admiral Ushakov served in the Northern Fleet, but suffered a nuclear-related accident whilst in the Mediterranean in 1990 and, having returned to port, never put to sea again. She was stricken in 1998 for use as a source of

Above: **Soviet battlecruiser *Kirov*, one of the greatest warship designs of the Cold War**

spares for the other ships, but was then reinstated by order of the Russian parliament (Duma), although the necessary funds were not forthcoming and she has since been stricken for a second time. *Admiral Lazarev*, the only member of the class to be assigned to the Pacific Fleet, served there from 1985 but became inactive in 1994 and was decommissioned in 1998.

Admiral Nakhimov served with the Northern Fleet, but went into refit in 1999. Whether or not she will return to service is not clear. *Pyotr Velikhiy* which took thirteen years from laying down to commissioning, was originally intended for the Pacific Fleet but has never left European waters. Commissioned in 1998, the ship appeared to be still in service in early 2001, but goes to sea only rarely.

These ships represented a great achievement by Soviet naval staffs and designers, their combination of nuclear/steam power, missile/gun armament and a wide variety of sensors resulting in a ship which impressed all naval observers. Whether or not they would have been effective in combat was, never put to the test.

Invincible/ Indefatigable

UNITED KINGDOM

Battlecruisers
Specification for *Invincible*, as completed.
Completed: 1908-11.
Number in class: 6.
Displacement: 17,373 tons standard; 20,078 tons full load.
Dimensions: Length 567.0ft (172.8m); beam 78.5ft (22.1m); draught 26.2ft (8.0m).
Propulsion: 4 shafts; Parsons geared turbines; 31 boilers; 41,000shp; 25.5 kt; 3,090nm at 10kt.
Armour: Belt 6.0-4.0in (150-100mm); bulkheads 7.0-6.0in (180-150mm); decks 2.5-0.75in (65-20mm); barbettes 7.0-2.0in (180-50mm); turret faces 7.0in (180mm); conning-tower 10.0-6.0in (250-150mm).
Armament: 8 x 12in (305mm) (4 x 2); 16 x 4in (102mm); 7 x Maxim MG; 5 x 18in (457mm)TT.
Complement: 784.

History: Aggressive by nature, the British First Sea Lord, Admiral Fisher, rammed his revolutionary ideas on ship design through the Admiralty bureaucracy. The first fruits of his battlecruiser idea was the Invincible-class, which joined the fleet in 1908 (*Indomitable* and *Inflexible*) and 1909 (*Invincible*), followed by three virtually identical ships in 1911 (*Indefatigable*), 1912 (*New*

***Below:* HMAS *Australia*, one of the Indefatigable-class battlecruisers; fast but flawed**

	Dreadnought	Invincible	Indefatigable
Displacement	21,845 tons	20,078 tons	22,080 tons
Length	527ft (160.6m)	567ft (172.8m)	590.0ft (179.8m)
Main armament	10 x 12in (305mm)	8 x 12in (305mm)	8 x 12in (305mm)
Maximum armour	11in (280mm)	6in (150mm)	6in (150mm)
Power	23,000shp	41,000shp	44,000shp
Maximum speed	21kt	25.5kt	25kt

Zealand), and 1913 (*Australia*). The only significant differences between the two groups were that the Indefatigable-class were lengthened in order to enable the two midships turrets to fire on the broadside, there was some reallocation of armour and a small increase in power. *Australia* was paid for by the Australian people and became pre-war flagship of the RAN. *New Zealand* was similarly paid for by the people of New Zealand, but was pre-sented to the Royal Navy on completion.

The Dreadnought and the Invincible/Indefatigable-classes were of a similar size and displacement, and mounted similar armament, but the table shows the differences in armoured protection, power and, as a result, speed.

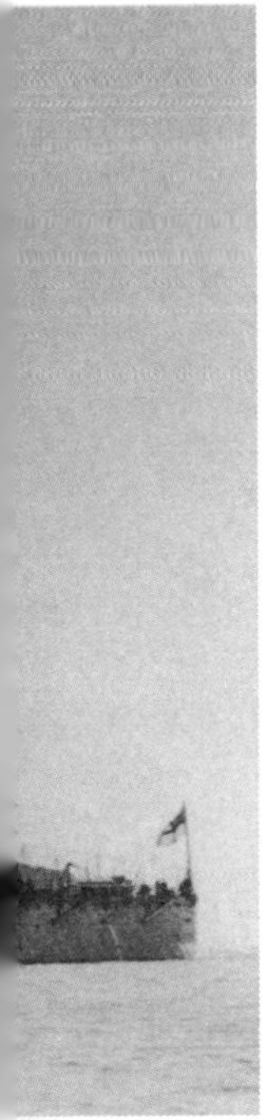

The consequence of the large calibre guns was that these ships came to be regarded as capital ships with a place in the line-of-battle, and in 1912 they were officially dubbed "battlecruisers," following which they were grouped into "battlecruiser squadrons" (BCS).

In August 1914 *Indomitable*, *Inflexible* and *Indefatigable* were in the Mediterranean where they took part in the unsuccessful hunt for the German battlecruiser *Goeben*, while *Invincible* was in home waters and took part in the Battle of Heligoland Bight (28 August 1914). *Invincible* and *Inflexible* were then sent at high speed to the Falkland Islands, where they sank all but one of Admiral von Spee's armoured cruisers on 8 December 1914. The three Invincibles were grouped into 3rd BCS in 1915 and were at Jutland, where *Invincible* blew-up with the loss of all but three of her crew, although the other two ships were undamaged.

The three Indefatigables were in 2nd BCS at time of the Battle of Jutland, where *Indefatigable* was blown up and sunk by *Von der Tann*. *Australia* was the pre-war flagship of the RAN, but returned to European waters in 1915, where she became flagship of the 2nd BCS. She missed Jutland as she was undergoing repairs following a minor collision with *New Zealand*, and after war she returned again to Australia, where she was scuttled in 1924 in compliance with the terms of the Washington Naval Treaty. *New Zealand* served throughout the war and was at Jutland but not was seriously damaged. She was sold and broken-up in 1922.

Lion

UNITED KINGDOM

Battlecruiser
Completed: 1912-13.
Number in class: 3.
Displacement: 26,270 tons standard; 29,680 tons full load.
Dimensions: Length 700.0ft (213.4m); beam 88.5ft (27.0m); draught 27.7ft (8.4m).
Propulsion: 4 shafts; Parsons turbines; 42 boilers; 70,000shp; 27kts; 5,610nm at 10kt.
Armour: Belt 9.0-4.0in (230-100mm); bulkheads 4.0in (100mm); decks 2.5-1.0in (65-25mm); barbettes 9.0-3.0in (230-75mm); turret faces 9.0in (230mm); conning-tower 10.0in (250mm).
Armament: 8 x 13.5in (343mm) (4 x 2); 16 x 4in (102mm); 4 x 3pdr (47mm); 2 x 21in (533mm) TT.
Complement: 997.

History: The Lion-class consisted of three ships: *Lion* and *Princess Royal*, which were identical and completed 1912, and the closely related but not totally identical *Queen Mary*, completed in 1913. They looked very impressive and were known collectively as the "Splendid Cats," although they were actually among the most over-rated and unsatisfactory ships built for the Royal Navy in the 20th Century. They were armed with eight of the new 13.5in (343mm) guns in four twin turrets, two forward, one aft and one amidships. In an effort to achieve the required speed of 34kt they had no less than 42 boilers, generating the remarkable figure for that period of 72,000shp, but even with this and a long hull, the greatest speed normally achieved on operations was 27kt.

Tiger

UNITED KINGDOM

Battlecruiser
Completed: 1914.
Number in class: 1.
Displacement: 28,430 tons standard; 35,710 tons full load.
Dimensions: Length 704.0ft (214.6m); beam 90.5ft (27.6m); draught 28.5ft (8.7m).
Propulsion: 4 shafts; Brown-Curtis steam turbines; 39 boilers; 85,000shp; 28kt; 4,650nm at 10kt.
Armour: Belt 9.0-3.0in (230-75mm); bulkheads 4.0-2.0in (100-50mm); decks 3.0-1.0in (75-15mm); barbettes 9.0-1.0in (230-25mm); turret faces 9.0in (230mm); conning-tower 10.0in (250mm).
Armament: 8 x 13.5in (343mm) (4 x 2); 12 x 6in (152mm); 2 x 3in (76mm) AA; 4x3pdr (47mm); 4 x 21in (533mm) TT.
Complement: 1,121.

History: A development of the *Queen Mary* design and generally considered as one of the "Splendid Cats," *Tiger* was one of the finest of the British battlecruisers, although she still suffered from some of the basic defects of the type. One of the poor points of the *Queen Mary* was overcome by moving the amidships turret to a point behind the funnels where it was, in effect, in the super-firing position although there was a considerable distance between it and X turret aft on the quarterdeck. In addition, the much criticised 4in (102mm) secondary armament was replaced by twelve of the more suitable 6in (152mm) guns. As before, the naval staffs tried to obtain every last horse-power out of the machinery, the design speed being 30kt, although in practice she never exceeded 29.1kt, at which speed her fuel consumption was excessive, to say the least.

***Above:* The Lion-class was one of the most over-rated RN designs in the 20th century**

Lion had a very active war, participating in the Battles of Heligoland Bight ((28 August 1914), Dogger Bank (24 January 1815), and Jutland (31 May 1916), where she was very nearly lost. One German hit started a fire in the midships (Q) turret and a possibly fatal explosion was only prevented by the order of a dying Marines officer to flood the magazine. *Lion* survived the war and was scrapped in 1924.

Princess Royal was hit at least nine times at Jutland, suffering 22 dead, 81 wounded and considerable damage, but remained operational and returned to port under her own power. She was scrapped in 1922.

Queen Mary took part in the Battles of Heligoland Bight and Jutland where she was hit by a succession of German shells and blew up with very heavy loss of life.

***Above:* One of the problems was that battlecruisers, such as *Tiger*, looked so powerful**

Tiger was fitted with a heavy tripod mast with a large fighting top and had three, equally-spaced funnels. This, combined with her revised main armament, gave her a well-balanced and handsome appearance, which tended to disguise the fact that she suffered from many of the defects of the earlier battlecruisers, the most important of which was that her armoured protection was inadequate for the role she was destined to play.

Tiger joined the fleet in November 1914 and took part in the action at the Dogger Bank (24 January 1915) where she suffered some damage, which was quickly repaired. She was at Jutland where she was again damaged, but not seriously, and she avoided the same fate as *Queen Mary*. Again repairs were quickly completed and she continued to serve with the Grand Fleet until the end of the war. She spent most of the post-war years as a gunnery training ship and was sold for scrapping in 1932.

Hood

UNITED KINGDOM

Battlecruiser
Completed: 1920.
Number in class: 1.
Displacement: 42,750 tons standard; 48,650 tons full load.
Dimensions: Length 860.6ft (262.8m); beam 104.1ft (31.8m); draught 32.0ft (9.7m).
Propulsion: 4 shafts; Brown-Curtis geared steam turbines; 24 boilers; 144,000shp; 30kt; 4,000nm at 10kt.
Armour: Belt 12.0-5.0in (305-125mm); decks 3.0-1.5in (75-38mm); barbettes 12.0-3.0in (305-75mm); turrets 15.0-5.0in (380-125mm); conning-tower 11.0-3.0in (280-75mm).
Armament: 8 x 15in (381mm) (4 x 2); 12 x 5in (140mm); 8 x 4in (102mm); 24 x 2pdr AA; 16 x 0.5in (12.7mm); 4 x 21in (533mm) TT.
Complement: 1,397.

History: There was a school of thought in the Royal Navy that "if a ship *looked* right, it would *be* right" and never was that proved more wrong than in the case of HMS *Hood*. The last of the British battlecruisers, *Hood* was the largest, fastest and most heavily armed capital ship in the world from 1919 to 1940, and was also by far the most handsome, having a particularly well-balanced appearance. The ship gave a very positive impression of power and naval might and was known to the admiring British Press and public as "*the mighty 'Ood.*" But, when she did eventually go into combat with a modern German battleship, *Hood*'s end was both quick and cataclysmic.

The original design dated from before Jutland, when a class of four ships was conceived as a counter to the German Mackensen-class battlecruisers, which were known to be under construction and were rumoured (incorrectly) to mount 15in (381mm) guns. The new British class followed the lines laid down by Admiral Fisher, with heavy gun armament and high speed, but with relatively light armoured protection. Following the disastrous battlecruiser losses at Jutland, however, the design was hurriedly recast, with armoured thicknesses being increased by 50 percent, adding some 5,000 tons to the displacement and reducing maximum speed by about 2kt. When it was confirmed in 1917 that all capital ship construction in Germany had ceased, three of the planned British battlecruisers were cancelled, but work continued on *Hood*, albeit at a slower pace which meant that she was not completed until 1920.

Hood had an elaborate system of internal protection, which was designed to explode large calibre shells before they could reach vital equipment deep inside the hull, but the horizontal plating was inadequate to stop plunging shells fired at long range. Vertical protection was better, with a sloped main armour belt 12in (305mm) thick and an integral torpedo bulge, which consisted of an outer destruction space, filled with hollow 1in (25cm) diameter steel tubes, each 8ft (2.4m) long and sealed at either end, an inner destruction space, normally used as an extra fuel bunker, and a series of longitudinal bulkheads.

The basic problem for *Hood* was that work had progressed too far to enable all the lessons of Jutland to be fully incorporated while the ship was under construction, but in the inter-war years the work would have taken too long and been far too expensive. In fact, a major reconstruction for *Hood* was planned to start in 1938, which would have included many improvements, including better armoured protection, a much revised secondary armament and new machinery, but the threat of war and the Royal Navy's urgent need for every capital ship it could lay its hands on resulted in the work being cancelled.

Hood was very busy from the moment war was declared, participating in the hunt for *Graf Spee*, the bombardment of the French fleet in Mers-el-Kebir, and operations with the Home Fleet. It was while serving with the latter that she was despatched, in company with the newly-completed battleship, *Prince of Wales*, to intercept the German battleship *Bismarck* and heavy cruiser, *Prinz Eugen*, which were breaking out into the Atlantic. The four ships met in the Denmark Strait on 24 May 1941, where the British commander, Vice-Admiral Holland, who was well aware of *Hood's* shortcomings, attempted to meet the German battleship head-on. In the event they met beam on and *Bismarck*'s fifth salvo resulted in a short-lived but very intense fire on *Hood*'s upper deck, leading to an explosion which blew the ship apart with the loss of all but three of her crew. Because she was held in such esteem by the British public, her loss had a major impact on British morale, which was only alleviated by the sinking of *Bismarck* a few days later.

***Below: Hood,* the last British battlecruiser, was sunk by Bismarck in a brief encounter**

Renown

UNITED KINGDOM

Battlecruiser
Specifications for both ships, as built.
Completed: 1916.
Number in class: 2.
Displacement: 27,650 tons standard; 30,835 tons full load.
Dimensions: Length 794.0ft (242.0m); beam 90.0ft (27.4m); draught 25.5ft (7.8m).
Propulsion: 4 shafts; Brown-Curtis steam turbines; 42 boilers; 112,000shp; 30kt; 3,650nm at 10kt.
Armour: Belt 6.0-1.5in (150-40mm); bulkheads 4.0-3.0in (100-75mm); decks 3.0-0.5in (75-15mm); barbettes 7.0-4.0in (180-100mm); turret faces 11.0in (280mm) ; conning-tower 10.0in (250mm).
Armament: 6 x 15in (381mm) (3 x 2); 17 x 4in (102mm); 2 x 3in (76mm); 2 x 21in (533mm) TT.
Complement: 1,260.

History: The Admiralty decided that there would be no more battlecruisers after *Tiger*, but this sensible policy was cast aside when Admiral Fisher returned as First Sea Lord in October 1914. His support of the battlecruiser idea was strengthened further when the battlecruisers despatched to the South Atlantic defeated the Germans at the Battle of the Falkland Islands, and Fisher was then able to persuade the War Cabinet to agree to two more battlecruisers.

Despite their complexity, the two ships were built with remarkable speed: *Renown* and *Repulse* were both laid down on 25 January 1915 and were completed in September and August 1916, respectively.

Alaska

UNITED STATES

Battlecruiser
Completed: 1944.
Number in class: 2.
Displacement: 29,780 tons standard; 34,250 tons full load.
Dimensions: Length 808.5ft (246.4m); beam 91.1ft (27.8m); draught 31.8ft (9.7m).
Propulsion: 4 shafts; General Electric geared steam turbines; 8 boilers; 150,000shp; 33kts; 12,000nm at 15kt.
Armour: Belt 9.0-5.0in (230-125mm); decks 1.4 + 3.8in (35 + 95mm); barbettes 13.0-11.0in (330-280mm); turrets 12.8-5.0in (325-125mm); conning-tower 10.6-5.0in (270-125mm).
Aircraft: 4.
Armament: 9 x 12in (305mm)(3 x 3); 12 x 5in (127mm); 56 x 40mm AA; 30-34 x 20mm AA.
Complement: 1,517.

History: By the end of World War Two there were just a few battlecruisers remaining in service and the type appeared destined for oblivion, so there was some surprise when the US Navy, which had kept well clear of the type during its heyday in 1906-16, suddenly introduced the Alaska-class. Six of these ships were planned and three laid down, but, in the event, only two were completed, *Alaska* (CB1) and *Guam* (CB2) both in 1944, while work on the third, *Hawaii* (CB3) was halted in April 1945 when she was almost complete.

The class was conceived as heavy cruisers armed with 12in (305mm) guns, unconstrained by the Washington Naval Treaty which had laid down that the limits for cruisers were 8in (203mm) guns and 10,000 tons displacement. A

Right: **Renown-class was a direct result of Fisher's return to the Admiralty in 1914**

From the start the light armour caused dismay and within three months of joining the fleet both ships were returned to the dockyard for 500 tons of extra armour, although all acknowledged that this was still nowhere near sufficient. Both ships were given additional armour in the early 1920s and *Renown* was given a massive rebuild in 1936-39 for a new role as a fast carrier escort; but for the war, *Repulse* would have received the same rebuild.

Both ships were busy throughout the inter-war years, their large size and handsome appearance making them effective representatives of British naval power. Both were heavily committed during the war, but *Repulse's* career was cut short when she, in company with the battleship, *Prince of Wales*, was attacked and sunk by Japanese bombers on 10 December 1941. *Renown* survived the war and was scrapped in 1948.

Above: **Construction of the US Navy's Alaska-class in 1943-44 came as a great surprise**

new type of 12in (305mm) gun was developed specially for the Alaska-class and it was originally intended to install eight in two triple and one twin turret, but to simplify production this was changed to three triple turrets. The secondary armament of 12 x 5in (127mm) was the same as for the Baltimore-class cruisers, but many more 40mm weapons were mounted due to the Alaskas' much greater length. The lack of depth in the after hull meant that there was no space for a below-decks hangar, so the four aircraft were stowed amidships, with two trainable catapults.

Alaska joined the fleet in January 1945 and took part in the assaults on Iwo Jima and Okinawa. She was then joined by *Guam* in March and they both took part in the carrier raids on Japan in the final months of the war. Their brief war service led to them being highly regarded in the fleet, establishing a reputation as ideal carrier escorts, combining high speed, excellent seakeeping, good endurance and powerful anti-aircraft batteries. Despite this success, they were placed in reserve in 1947 and scrapped in 1961.

Cruisers

The modern cruiser began its existence in the latter half of the 19th century as the steam frigate, a ship second only in size to the battleship. The role of such ships was to patrol lines-of-communication in distant waters, particularly for imperial powers such as France and Britain, who were later joined by Germany. The type had its attractions for other navies and cruisers were soon being built for the Chinese, Japanese and Russian navies, as well. So rapidly did the type develop that in 1914 Germany had some fifty heavy and light cruisers and the UK eighty-six, of which twenty-five were less than ten years old.

In World War I the cruiser developed in two different directions. One continued to be the distant-water role, operating either as an independent ship or in company with other cruisers. For this the cruiser's combination of speed, endurance and firepower proved ideal and while the Germans used their few overseas cruisers as commerce raiders, the British used theirs to first hunt down the German cruisers and then to patrol the sea-lanes. The second role for cruisers was in the North Sea, where they operated as the lighter element of the British and German fleets, carrying out reconnaissances and limited actions which did not involve clashes between the two great fleets.

During the inter-war years the size and armament of cruisers were limited by the naval treaties to 10,000 tons displacement and 8in (203mm) guns and

Above: **Nuclear-powered US missile-cruiser *Long Beach,* designed as a carrier escort**

most of the larger navies built ships which were right up to (and in some cases breached) these limits. Cruisers played an invaluable part in World War II, as the protector of trade routes, or, in the German case, as a commerce raider. British cruisers played a major role in the Mediterranean, the Atlantic and the Arctic, while US cruisers were equally busy in the Atlantic and Pacific. There were numerous classes of light cruiser, but at the heavier end the size increased inexorably, the ultimate being the US Navy's Des Moines-class with a displacement of 21,698 tons and a main armament of nine 8.0in (203mm) guns. After the war these cruisers continued in service for some years with many navies, but they proved too large, absorbed too much manpower and were generally expensive to run, so most of them had disappeared by the 1960s.

During the Cold War the US Navy built a succession of cruisers, most of them nuclear-powered and intended as missile-armed escorts for the nuclear-powered carriers. The only other navy to build cruiser-sized ships in any numbers was the Soviet Navy which produced a series of well-balanced designs that were particularly heavily armed and caused considerable alarm in the West. Today the cruiser is the largest size of surface warship that virtually all navies would consider building, but, apart from those of the US Navy, only a few remain in service.

Veinticinco de Mayo

ARGENTINA

Cruiser
Completed: 1929.
Number in class: 2.
Displacement: 6,800 tons standard; 9,000 tons full load.
Dimensions: Length 560.3ft (170.8m); beam 58.5ft (17.8m); draught 15.3ft (17.4m).
Propulsion: 2 shafts; Parsons geared turbines; 6 boilers; 85,000shp; 32 kt; 8,000nm at 14kt.
Armour: deck 1in (25mm); sides 2.8in (71mm); conning tower 2.3in (58mm) turrets 2.0in (51mm)
Armament: 6 x 7.5in (190mm) (3 x 2); 12 x 4.0in (102mm) DP; 6 x 40mm AA; 6 x 21in (533mm) TT.
Aircraft: two; one catapult.
Complement: 600.

History: Argentina had a long-standing competition with Brazil and Chile, the three of them usually being known in naval circles as the "ABC powers." These two ships, *Veinticinco de Mayo* and *Almirante Brown*, were ordered in 1926, built by the Italian company Odero Terni Orlando (OTO), and completed in July 1931. Like other contemporary Italian cruisers, the Argentine ships were lightly built, lightly protected, but fast. The main armament consisted of six guns in three twin turrets in "A" "B" and "Y" positions. The 7.5in (190mm) calibre was an unusual choice, since the only other known use was in two classes of British cruisers; the Devonshire-class of 1905 and the Hawkins-class (q.v.), completed

La Argentina

ARGENTINA

Training cruiser
Completed: 1939.
Number in class: 1.
Displacement: 6,500 tons standard; 7,500 tons full load.
Dimensions: Length 542.2ft (164.9m); beam 56.5ft (17.2m); draught 16.5ft (5.0m).
Propulsion: 4 shafts; Parsons geared turbines; 4 boilers; 54,000shp; 30kt; 10,000nm at 12kt.
Armour: deck 2.0in (51mm); sides 3.0in (76mm); turrets 2.0in (51mm).
Armament: 9 x 6in (152mm) (3 x 3); 4 x 4in (102mm); 8 x 2pdr; 12 x 1.0in (25mm) AAMG; 6 x 21in (533mm).
Aircraft: 1 seaplane.
Complement: 556 (plus 60 cadets).

History: *La Argentina* was built by Vickers-Armstrong in Britain to a modified *Arethusa* design. The ship was scheduled to be delivered in early 1938 but, due to the demands of the British rearmament programme, this was delayed until January 1939. Although designated a training ship and frequently employed as such, she was fully capable of carrying out all wartime duties of a cruiser, and served with the cruiser division of the Argentine Navy throughout World War II. Her weapons fit was well up to international cruiser standards, consisting of nine 6in (152mm) guns in three triple turrets, although the secondary armament of four 4in (102mm) guns was light, and the anti-aircraft armament of eight 2-pdr and twelve AAMG was certainly not up to the standard required by the combatant navies in 1943-45, and they were replaced by 40mm Bofors in a

***Above:* These two well-liked, Italian-built cruisers served from 1929 to 1960-61**

between 1918 and 1925. Nevertheless, the Argentine guns had a very respectable range: 29,856yd (27,300m). Each ship carried two floatplane aircraft which were housed in a hangar under the foredeck and launched from a fixed catapult over the bows; the aircraft landed in the sea and were then recovered by a crane. These handsome and powerful ships put Argentina well ahead of their two rivals in the cruiser category in the 1930s and 40s. European and American naval experts considered that the designers of these ships had tried to cram too many weapons onto too light a hull, but they were well thought of in the Argentine Navy, which they served well, until being scrapped in 1960 (*Veinticinco de Mayo*) and 1961 (*Almirante Brown*).

---

post-war refit. She also mounted six torpedo tubes and a spotter aircraft, usually a Walrus, which was launched from a midships catapult.

La Argentina joined the Argentine fleet in April 1939 and was stricken in January 1974.

***Above:* The lines of *La Argentina* immediately show the cruiser's British origin**

Bahia

BRAZIL

Scout cruiser
Completed: 1910.
Number in class: 2.
Displacement: 3,100 tons standard.
Dimensions: Length (pp) 380.0ft (115.8m); beam 39.0ft (11.8m); draught 14.5ft (4.4m).
Propulsion: 3 shafts; Parsons direct-drive turbines; 6 boilers; 18,000shp; 26.5kt; 6,600nm at 10kt.
Armour: deck 0.75in (19mm); conning tower 3.0in (76mm).
Armament: 10 x 4.7in (120mm) (10 x 1); 6 x 3pdr (47mm); 2 x 18in (457mm) TT.
Complement: 350.

History: *Bahia* and *Rio Grande do Sul* were both built by Vickers at Elswick, England, a shipyard then considered to be producing the finest cruisers in the world, and delivered in 1910. Their design was based on that of the contemporary British scout cruiser, *Adventure*, but modernised and somewhat enlarged. They were among the earliest ships to be fitted with turbines and at the time they were completed they were the fastest light cruisers in any navy, both having exceeded 27kt on their trials.

When Brazil joined the Allies in 1917 both ships served with the squadron operating off the NW African coast. Both underwent a major refit in Brazil in 1925-26, during which

Esmeralda

CHILE

Armoured cruiser
Completed: 1894.
Number in class: 1.
Displacement: 7,000 tons.
Dimensions: Length (pp) 436.0ft (132.8mm); beam 53.2ft (16.2m); draught 20.3ft (6.2m).
Propulsion: 2 shafts; Vertical, Triple-Expansion engines; cylindrical boilers; 16,000ihp; 22.3kt.
Armour: Harvey. Belt 6.0in (152mm); decks 2.0-1.5in (51-38mm); gunshields 4.5in (114mm); conning tower 8.0in (203mm).
Armament: 2 x 8in (203mm) (2 x 1); 16 x 6in (152mm); 8 x 12pdr; 3 x 18in (457mm) TT.
Complement: 500.

History: The Chilean Navy purchased a series of cruisers from 1883 onwards, all from Armstrong in Britain, except for one class of two bought from France in 1890. The first to modern European standards was *Blanco Encalada* which entered service in 1894, with *Esmeralda* following a few months later, being launched in 1894 and commissioned in 1895. She was generally similar to the earlier ship, but larger and with better armoured protection. Both ships had the same main armament of two 8in (203mm) guns in two single turrets, but *Esmeralda* had a more powerful secondary battery. In general appearance, *Esmeralda* had a ram bow, flush deck, two funnels set well apart and two heavy masts, with the foremast set well before the bridge. The two single 8in (203mm) guns were mounted in "A" and "Y" positions, with two 6in (152mm)

they were re-engined with Brown-Curtis turbines, re-boilered and converted to oil-burning, resulting in an increase of speed to 28kt. Their funnels were also considerably extended. Both saw extensive service in World War II, serving mainly as convoy escorts. On 4 July 1945 *Bahia* was serving as plane guard to a US carrier group in the mid-Atlantic when she blew up without warning and sank within three minutes, with the loss of 294 lives. *Rio Grande* was stricken in 1948.

***Below:* After 35 years service, *Bahia* blew up without warning with heavy loss of life**

guns on the foredeck and the remainder in casemates in the superstructure. There were three torpedo tubes, one on either beam, submerged, the third on the stern. The armoured belt was 325ft (100m) long, 6in (152mm) thick and 7ft (2.1m) deep, closed at both ends by bulkheads of the same thickness.

Esmeralda was refitted in 1910 and stricken in 1929.

***Above:* Like most South American warships of the time, *Esmeralda* was British-built**

Dupuy de Lôme

FRANCE

Armoured cruiser
Completed: 1895.
Number in class: 1.
Displacement: 6,676 tons.
Dimensions: Length (pp) 364.2ft (111.0m); beam 51.5ft (15.7m); draught 24.6ft (7.5m).
Propulsion: 3 shafts; 1 shaft, Vertical, Triple-Expansion engine; 2 shafts Horizontal Triple-Expansion engines; 13 boilers; 13,000ihp; 19.7kt.
Armour: Steel. Side 4in (102mm); turrets 4in (102mm); conning tower 5in (127mm).
Armament: 2 x 7.6in (193mm) (2 x 1); 6 x 6.4in (163mm); 4 x 9pdr; 8 x 3pdr; 8 x 1pdr revolvers; 2 x 18in 457mm) TT.
Complement: 526.

History: This remarkable ship was named after Stanislas Charles Dupuy de Lôme (1816-85), the most famous French warship designer in the middle of the 19th century, who had recently died. This cruiser had a long, snout-like ram bow and a sloping stern of very similar shape, and these two characteristics, allied to a marked tumblehome, two very heavy military masts and two widely separated funnels, resulted in a ship with unique appearance and quite unlike its predecessors. The sides of the ship were completely protected by the armoured belt, which extended from 4.5ft (1.4m) below the waterline to the upper deck, and there was an intricate arrangement of internal compartments to add to the protection. Main armament consisted of two 7.6in (193mm) guns,

Gloire

FRANCE

Armoured cruiser
Completed: 1903-04.
Number in class: 5.
Displacement: 10,212 tons.
Dimensions: Length 458.6ft (139.8m); beam 66.3ft (20.2m); draught 24.3ft (7.4m).
Propulsion: 3 shafts; Vertical, Triple-Expansion engines; 24 boilers; 21,800ihp; 21.5kt.
Armour: Harvey nickel. Belt 6.0-2.3in (152-58mm); main turrets 6.8in (173mm); casemates 3.3in (84mm); conning tower 6in (152mm).
Armament: 2 x 7.6in (193mm) (2 x 1); 8 x 6.4in (163mm); 6 x 3.9in (100mm); 18 x 3pdr; 2 x 18in (457mm) TT.
Complement: 615.

History: The French Navy next switched to a new series of much larger armoured cruisers, visually characterised by a long, low hull with either six or four funnels widely separated into two groups at either end of the superstructure. The first of these, *Jeanne d'Arc*, displaced 11,092 tons, which was followed by a series of generally similar vessels, the Gueydon-class (three ships) and Dupleix-class (three ships), leading to the Gloire-class of five ships, *Amiral Aube, Condé, Gloire, Marseillaise* and *Sully*, completed in 1903-04. In the Gloire-class the main armament was still two 7.6in (193mm) guns in single turrets at forecastle deck level. The secondary battery of eight 6.4in (163mm), all in casemates, was split between two at upper deck level forward below the bridge, four amidships at main deck level and two aft, also at main deck level. The armoured belt extended from the stem almost to the stern and was 11.5ft

***Above:* Dupuy de Lôme is seen here wearing a World War I camouflage scheme**

with one turret in the bows, the other on the quarterdeck aft, while the secondary battery of six 6.4in (163mm) was split into two groups with three forward and three aft.

Dupuy de Lôme was rebuilt in 1905, the changes including new boilers, an additional funnel and the removal of the mainmast. She was actually sold to Peru in 1912 but the sale was cancelled and the ship then served with the French Navy throughout World War I, being sold to a Belgian company in 1920, which converted her into a merchant ship. There were two more cruiser designs which repeated the odd appearance of the *Dupuy de Lôme*, the four-strong Amiral Charner-class and the single-ship Pothuau-class, but thereafter French ship designers reverted to slightly more conventional designs.

***Above:* Completed in 1904, *Gloire*, survived World War I to be scrapped in 1922**

(3.5m) deep extending to upper deck level for most of its length, with two armoured decks. One, *Sully*, was wrecked off the coast of Indochina in September 1905, but the remainder served throughout World War One and were stricken between 1922 and 1933.

Duguay-Trouin

FRANCE

Cruiser
Completed: 1926.
Number in class: 3.
Displacement: 7,249 tons standard; 9,350 tons full load.
Dimensions: Length 595.8ft (181.6m); beam 56.4ft (17.2m); draught 17.0ft (5.2m).
Propulsion: 4 shafts; Parsons geared turbines; 8 boilers; 100,000shp; 33kt; 3,000nm at 15kt.
Armour: box citadel 0.78in (20mm); main deck 0.78in (20mm); turrets 1.0in (30mm); conning tower 1.0in (30mm).
Armament: 8 x 6.1in (155mm) (4 x 2); 4 x 3in (76mm) AA; 4 x 13.2mm AA; 12 x 21.7in (550mm) TT
Aircraft: 2.
Complement: 578.

History: The three cruisers of the Duguay-Trouin-class, the first major warships to be designed for the French Navy after World War One, were handsome and well thought of ships. The design was the subject of much discussion within the navy in the years 1919 to 1922 and extensive studies were carried out on the foreign designs known to be building, one, which was of particular interest, being the US Navy's Omaha-class, ten of which were laid down in 1918-20. Another influence was concern about the intentions of the Italians in the Mediterranean. As always, different groups advocated additional capabilities and the size and speed requirements steadily increased. One major advance in inter-Service cooperation came with the adoption of an Army gun calibre, 6.1in

Duquesne

FRANCE

Cruiser
Completed: 1928.
Number in class: 2.
Displacement: 10,000 tons standard; 12,200 tons full load.
Dimensions: Length 626.7ft (191.0m); beam 62.3ft (19.0m); draught 20.8ft (6.3m).
Propulsion: 4 shafts; Rateau-Bretagne geared turbines; 9 boilers; 120,000shp; 33.8kt; 4,500nm at 15kt.
Armour: Box citadel 1.0in (25mm); turrets 1.0in (30mm); conning tower 1.0in (25mm).
Armament: 8 x 8in (203mm) (4 x 2); 8 x 3in (76mm); 8 x 37mm AA; 12 x 13.2mm AA; 6 x 21.7in (550mm) TT.
Aircraft: 2.
Complement: 605.

History: One of the warship types created by the Washington Naval Treaty was a new category of cruiser with an 8in (203mm) gun armament on a 10,000 ton displacement hull. France felt compelled to produce a series of such "Treaty cruisers" of which *Duquesne* and *Tourville*, both completed in 1928, were the first. An immediate difficulty was that there was no 8in (203mm) gun in the French naval armoury so an entirely new weapon had to be developed. A more fundamental problem was that the limitations of the "Treaty cruiser" posed many challenges to the designers in all navies, and in France, as in many others, they decided to emphasise speed and firepower at the expense of protection. Thus, they produced a cruiser that was well armed, with eight 8in (203mm)

Above: **After ugly pre-war designs, *Duguay-Trouin* introduced a new Gallic elegance**

(155mm), using the military barrel and breech mechanism in a naval twin mounting, each weapon being in an individual cradle. Three ships, *Duguay-Trouin, Lamotte-Picquet* and *Primaguet,* were approved in April 1922 and completed in 1926-27. The three ships had a long, rotating catapult installed on the quarterdeck and normally carried two floatplanes, later reduced to one.

The ships proved very satisfactory in service and in the peacetime years one was generally in the Atlantic fleet, one in the Mediterranean and one in the Far East. *Duguay-Trouin* was the only one to survive the war. *Lamotte-Picquet* was sunk by US aircraft in Saigon in January 1945 while *Primaguet* was sunk at Casablanca, also by US aircraft, in November 1942.

Above: **Completed in 1928, the Duquesne-class were the first French "Treaty" cruisers**

guns, and was certainly very fast, with a designed speed of 33.8kt (which both ships easily exceeded on trials), but protection was weak, to say the least, amounting to no more than a 1.0in (30mm) box around the machinery and magazines. Indeed, their lack of protection was severely criticised within the navy and at one stage it was proposed to convert them into small aircraft carriers, but this was rejected. On the more positive side, their large size allowed a more powerful secondary battery.

Both ships spent the pre-war years on cruises or based in the Mediterranean and they were still there in 1939, when they were employed for a time in contraband-control patrols. Both were in Alexandria from July 1940 until June 1943 when they joined the Allies. Post-war both ships spent tours of duty in Indochina, primarily engaged in shore bombardment in support of ground forces fighting the Viet Minh. Both were removed from the active list in late 1947 and then employed in miscellaneous harbour tasks until being scrapped, *Duquesne* in 1955 and *Tourville* in 1962.

Suffren

FRANCE

Cruiser
Completed: 1930-32.
Number in class: 4.
Specifications for *Suffren*, as built.
Displacement: 9,938 tons standard; 12,780 tons full load.
Dimensions: Length 643.0ft (196.0m); beam 65.7ft (20.0m); draught 24.0ft (7.3m).
Propulsion: 3 shafts; Rateau-Bretagne geared turbines; 9 boilers; 90,000shp; 31kt; 4,500nm at 15kt.
Armour: Belt 2.0in (51mm); upper and main decks 1.0in (25mm); turrets 1.0in (25mm); conning tower 11.0in (280mm).
Armament: 8 x 8in (203mm) (4 x 2); 8 x 3.0in (76mm); 8 x 37mm AA; 12 x 13.2mm AAMG; 12 x 21.7in (550mm) TT.
Aircraft: 2.
Complement: 605.

History: These four ships, *Suffren*, completed in 1930, *Colbert* and *Foch* both completed in 1931, and *Dupleix*, completed in 1932, were, in effect, modified Tourvilles, in which the designers sought to rectify the imbalance in that design by increasing protection at the expense of speed. Indeed, this process continued throughout their construction with *Suffren* having 951 tons of armour, double that in *Tourville*, but this was increased to 1,374 tons in the next two and to 1,533 tons in *Dupleix*. The result was that no two ships in the class were identical, with *Colbert* and *Foch* slightly shorter and with less beam than

---

Algérie

FRANCE

Cruiser
Completed: 1934.
Number in class: 1.
Displacement: 10,000 tons standard; 13,900 tons full load.
Dimensions: Length 610.9ft (186.2m); beam 65.6ft (20.0m); draught 20.2ft (6.2m).
Propulsion: 4 shafts; Rateau-Bretagne geared turbines; 6 boilers; 84,000shp; 31kt; 8,700nm at 15kt.
Armour: Belt 4.8in (122mm); main deck 3in (76mm); turret faces 3.8in (97mm); conning tower 3.8-2.8in (97-71mm).
Armament: 8 x 8in (203mm) (4 x 2); 12 x 3.9in (100mm) AA; 8 x 37mm AA; 6 x 21.7in (550mm) TT.
Aircraft: 3.
Complement: 748.

History: *Algérie* is generally recognised as not only the best "Treaty cruiser" built by the French Navy but also as among the very best built in any navy. She was ordered in response to the Italian Zara-class (q.v.) and at last the designers faced up to the criticisms of a lack of protection in previous "Treaty cruisers," not only using 2,657 tons of armour but also greatly improving the distribution with a 4.8in (122mm) belt and a 3in (76mm) main deck. The turbines provided 84,00shp compared to 90,000shp in the Suffrens, but a more refined hull form ensured that the speed remained at 31kt. Main armament was eight 8in (203mm) but the secondary armament was increased to twelve 3.9in (100mm) guns in six twin turrets. Two seaplanes were normally carried, which were

Above: **France's second "Treaty cruisers", the Suffren-class were improved Tourvilles**

Suffren, the differences being mainly attributable to rearrangements of the armour.

Suffren was part of the French squadron interned at Alexandria from June 1940 until June 1943, when she joined the Allies. In the immediate post-war years she served in Indochina and was paid off in 1962 and scrapped in 1974. The other three were all at Toulon on 27 November 1942, where *Foch* and *Dupleix* were both scuttled and then raised the following year; *Foch* was scrapped but *Dupleix* was destroyed by Allied bombing. Instead of being scuttled, the third, *Colbert*, was destroyed by fire, becoming a total loss on 7 December 1942.

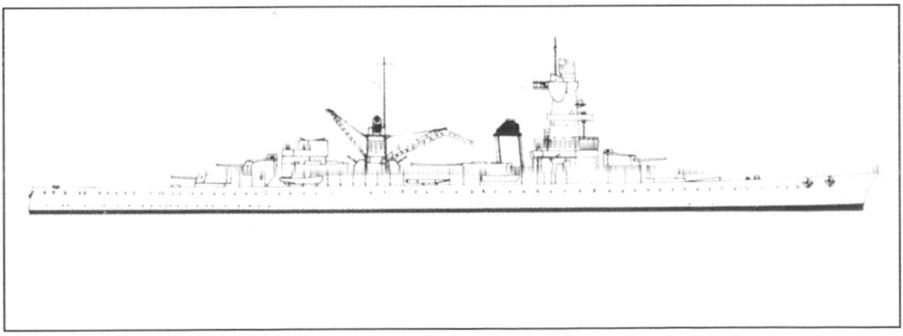

Above: Algérie **is accepted as one of the finest "Treaty cruiser" designs in any navy**

stored in the open, with one on the catapult (which was operated by explosives rather than compressed-air in previous systems), the other on the spar deck. One notable feature of the design was the massive tower above the bridge, reminiscent of the German Deutschland-class, then building. She underwent several refits, that in 1940-41 including the removal of the mainmast and of all aviation facilities.

Algérie served, always as a flagship, in the Mediterranean up to the outbreak of war, when she first led a task group in the Atlantic, and then transported a large consignment of gold to Canada. She then returned to operate in the Mediterranean until the French collapse, where her most active duty was to escort the battleship *Provence*, following the latter's escape from Oran. When the Germans occupied Vichy France in November 1942 *Algérie*'s crew set fire to her and she sank. The wreck was raised in March 1943 and scrapped.

Emile Bertin/ La Galissonniére

FRANCE

Cruiser
Specification for *La Galissonniére*, as built.
Completed: Emile Bertin - 1934; La Galissonniére - 1935-37.
Number in class: Emile Bertin - 1; La Galissonniére - 6.
Displacement: 7,600 tons standard; 9,100 tons full load.
Dimensions: Length 558.9ft (179.5m); beam 57.3ft (17.5m); draught 17.6ft (5.4m).
Propulsion: 2 shafts; Parsons geared turbines; 4 boilers; 84,000shp; 34kt; 7,000nm at 12kt.
Armour: Main belt 4in (102mm); main deck 1.5in (38mm); turret faces 4in (102mm); conning tower 3.8in (97mm).
Armament: 9 x 6.0in (152mm) (3 x 3); 8 x 3.5in (89mm) AA; 8 x 37mm AA; 12 x 13.2mm AA; 4 x 21.7in (550mm) TT.
Aircraft: 4.
Complement: 764.

History: *Emile Bertin* was a very fast cruiser, usually employed as a squadron flagship for twelve of the "super-destroyers". She displaced 8,480 tons (full load) and was armed with nine of a new model 6.0in (152mm) gun in three triple turrets. The La Galissonniére-class was essentially a slightly larger version of the *Emil Bertin* and is generally regarded as the most successful of the French pre-war cruiser designs, consisting of six ships: *La Galissonniére*, *Jean de*

De Grasse/Colbert

FRANCE

Cruiser
Completed: De Grasse - 1956; Colbert - 1959.
Number in class: De Grasse - 1; Colbert - 1.
Specifications for *De Grasse*, as completed.
Displacement: 9,380 tons standard; 11,545 tons full load.
Dimensions: Length 618.0ft (188.3m); beam 61.0ft (18.6m); draught 18.0ft (5.5m).
Propulsion: 2 shafts; Rateau-Bretagne geared turbines; 4 boilers; 110,000shp; 33kt.
Armament: 16 x 5in (127mm) (8 x 2); 20 x 57mm AA.
Complement: 950.

History: *De Grasse* was laid down in 1938 as the first of three "improved La Galissonniäres" but on the outbreak of war the other two were cancelled and work on *De Grasse* was suspended. Work recommenced in 1946 to the original conventional light cruiser design, but following the launch in late 1946 work was again stopped while the design was recast as an AA cruiser. Work restarted in 1951 and was completed in 1954, although her travails were not yet over as she sank on leaving drydock (the seacocks had been left open); she was refloated but was not finally handed over until 1956. Displacement was 11,545 tons and armament comprised sixteen 5.0in (127mm) guns in eight twin turrets and twenty 57mm guns in ten twin turrets, with a complex radar-controlled fire direction system. It appears, however, that topweight was too great, since in the early 1960s four 57mm mounts and two fire-control directors were removed. In 1966 *De Grasse* was converted to become flagship of the force carrying out the French atomic trials in the Pacific, a role she performed

***Above: Montcalm* of the La Galissioniére-class, seen here in the Mediterranean in 1953**

Vienne, *Marseillaise*, *Gloire*, *Montcalm*, and *Georges Leygues*. The design speed was 32.5kt but they all exceeded this by a fair margin on trials, all achieving at least 35kt. The design included a long, uncluttered quarterdeck, with the catapult mounted on the roof of "Y" turret. There was a large hangar, which accommodated four aircraft.

Emile Bertin took part in the Norwegian campaign (April 1940) where she was damaged. After some time at the French islands of St Pierre et Migneton she declared for the Allies in August 1943 and went to the USA for a refit. She then operated in the Mediterranean, carried out one postwar tour in Indochina and was scrapped in the 1950s.

The La Galissonniére-class spent most of the war in Toulon, where *La Galissonniére*, *Jean de Vienne* and *Marseillaise* were all scuttled by their crews.

***Above: De Grasse*, laid down in 1938 but completed in 1956 as an air defence cruiser**

until 1973 when she was stricken, being scrapped in 1976.

Colbert was a post-war development of *De Grasse*, being laid down in 1953 and completed in 1959. The armament was the same as for the earlier ship, but none had to be removed until she underwent a major refit in 1970-72 from which she emerged as a guided-missile cruiser with a twin-arm Masurca SAM launcher on the quarterdeck, two single 3.9in (100mm) guns forward, and six 57mm mounts, three on each beam amidships. Four MM38 Exocet launchers were added forward of the bridge in 1980. She then served as the flagship of the Mediterranean squadron until stricken in 1991, the last of a long line of French cruisers.

Gazelle

GERMANY

Light cruiser (fourth class)
Specifications for second-of-class, *Niobe*, as built.
Completed: 1900-04.
Number in class: 10.
Displacement: 2,916 tons.
Dimensions: Length 344.8ft (105.0m); beam 40.1ft (12.2m); draught 18.2ft (5.5m).
Propulsion: 2 shafts; Triple Expansion; 8,000ihp; 22kt.
Armament: 10 x 4.1in (105mm) (10 x 1); 2 x 17.7in (450mm) TT.
Complement: 249.

History: The German Navy built a series of medium-sized warships from the 1850s onwards, their designations including frigate, corvette, even the French *aviso*, but finally settling on the term cruiser. The most outstanding design was the Gazelle-class of ten ships (1900-04) and their successors the very similar seven-ship Bremen-class (1904-07), which were the first modern cruisers in any navy. They had a long ram bow and two raked funnels, their armament being ten 4.1in (105mm) guns in single mounts and three 17.7in (450mm) torpedo tubes. First-of-class *Gazelle* was slightly different from the remainder and there were minor differences in length, beam and displacement between most of them. The earlier ships were transferred to coastal defence duties in 1914 but all took part in the war, three being sunk: *Ariadne* (1914), *Undine* (1915) and *Frauenlob* (1916), while *Gazelle* was hulked in 1916 (scrapped 1920). Because of their age, the seven survivors were among the very few warships allowed to Germany in the Versailles Treaty and of those *Amazone*, *Niobe*, and *Nymphe*

Dresden

GERMANY

Light cruiser
Completed: 1908-09.
Number in class: 2.
Displacement: 3,606 tons standard; 4,200 tons full load.
Dimensions: Length 386.8ft (117.9m); beam 44.3ft (13.5m); draught 18.0ft (5.5m).
Propulsion: 2 shafts; 4 Parsons turbines; 12 boilers; 15,000shp; 24kt; 3,600nm at 14kt.
Armour: Deck 0.75-1.75in (20-30mm); gunshields 2.0in (50mm); conning tower 4.0in (100mm).
Armament: 10 x 4.1in (105mm); 8 x 2.0in (52mm); 2 x 17.7in (450mm) TT.
Complement: 322.

History: These two ships, *Dresden* and *Emden*, were developed from the very similar Königsberg-class, completed in 1907-08. *Emden* deployed to the Far East in 1909 and was at the German colony of Tsingtao when war broke out. She carried out a series of daring raids against British targets until being caught by HMAS *Sydney* in the Cocos Islands. Following a gun battle she was beached (9 November 1914), after which most of the survivors sailed in a captured schooner to Arabia, then trekked overland through Syria and Turkey until they reached Germany again. When war broke out *Dresden* was in the Caribbean and followed orders to sail south and around Cape Horn to join Admiral Graf Spee in the Pacific. *Dresden* was still

were completely rebuilt, with a clipper bow and other improvements. *Niobe* was sold to Yugoslavia in 1925 and the remainder were stricken between 1929 and 1932.

***Above:* German Gazelle-class cruiser, *Nymphe*, after her post-World War One rebuild**

with the admiral when his squadron met the British at the Battle of the Falkland Islands, but this cruiser managed to escape destruction and was then systematically hunted down until she was cornered by British ships, as a result of which she was scuttled (14 March 1915).

***Below:* Both *Emden* and *Dresden* (seen here) established fine reputations in 1914-15**

Magdeburg

GERMANY

Light cruiser
Completed: 1912.
Number in class: 4.
Displacement: 4,498 tons standard; 5,500 tons full load.
Dimensions: Length 455.0ft (138.7m); beam 43.9ft (13.4m); draught 16.9ft (5.1m).
Propulsion: 3 shafts; 3 Bergmann turbines; boilers; 29,904shp; 27.6kt.
Armour: Belt 2.3-0.8in (60-18mm); deck 1.5-2.3in (40-60mm); gunshields 2.0in (50mm); conning tower 4.0in (100mm).
Armament: 12 x 4.1in (105mm); 2 x 19.7in (500mm) TT; 120 mines.
Complement: 354.

History: The design of these four ships, *Magdeburg, Breslau, Strasburg* and *Stralsund,* marked yet further important steps in German cruiser development. The underwater hull profile was totally redesigned to give a new level of hydrodynamic efficiency, while above the waterline a new form of clipper bow and a more refined bow shape gave better seakeeping and a drier forecastle. Also, since the cruisers were required to carry mines, a minedeck was formed by cutting down the quarterdeck. Protection was increased by adding an armoured belt at waterline level, which was incorporated into the hull's construction rather than bolted on. Another feature was that while all were turbine-powered, each ship had a different make of turbine to enable comparisons to be made: *Breslau,* four shafts, two AEG-Vulkan turbines; *Magdeburg,* three shafts, three Bergmann turbines; *Stralsund,* three shafts, three Bergmann turbines; and *Strasburg,* two shafts, two German Admiralty-pattern turbines.

Pillau

GERMANY

Light cruiser
Completed: 1914-15.
Number in class: 2.
Displacement: 4,320 tons standard; 5,170 tons full load.
Dimensions: Length 443.9ft (135.3m); beam 44.6ft (13.6m); draught 19.7ft (6.0m).
Propulsion: 2 shafts; German Admiralty-pattern turbines; 10 boilers; 30,000shp; 27.5kt; 4,300nm at 12kt.
Armour: deck 0.75-3.0in (20-80mm); conning tower 2.0-3.0in (50-75mm).
Armament: 8 x 5.9in (150mm) (4 x 2); 2 x 3.5in (88mm); 2 x 19.7in (500mm) TT; 120 mines.
Complement: 442.

History: At the start of both world wars one of the first things warship-building countries did was to see what ships were under construction for foreign countries and expropriate them. Thus, in August 1914 these two ships were under construction for the Russian Navy at the Schichau yard in Danzig and were immediately taken over by the German authorities. Their intended main armament was eight Russian 5.1in (130mm) guns, but this was changed, not to the German standard cruiser weapon, the 4.1in (105mm), but to the much more powerful 5.9in (150mm). Secondary armament was to have been four Russian 2.5in (63mm) guns, but four German 2.0in (54mm) guns were actually mounted, although these were soon changed to two 3.5in (88mm) in service. Both served with the High Seas Fleet and were at Jutland,

***Above: Stralsund* survived World War I, but went to France in the peace settlement**

All served in World War I, but only *Magdeburg's* name is known to history. When laying mines off Russia's Baltic coastline, this ship was attacked and damaged by Russian cruisers, as a result of which she ran aground (16 August 1914). Russian specialists found the German codebooks in the wreck and, in a most altruistic act, passed them on to British naval intelligence, giving the latter a priceless advantage throughout the war. *Breslau* was escort to the battlecruiser *Goeben* when the latter escaped the British Mediterranean Fleet in August 1914 and the two ships found safety in Turkey, where *Breslau* was incorporated into the Turkish Navy as *Midilli*. She was sunk by mines (20 January 1918). The other two survived the war and both were then handed over to Allies, *Stralsund* to France and *Strasburg* to Italy.

where *Elbing* collided with the battleship *Posen* and had to be scuttled. *Pillau* survived the war and went to Italy as *Bari* in 1921. She was sunk off Livorno by US aircraft in September 1943

***Below:* The two Pillaus, built in Danzig for Russia in 1914, were seized by Germany**

Emden

GERMANY

Light cruiser
Completed: 1925.
Number in class: 1.
Displacement: 5,600 tons standard; 6,900 tons full load.
Dimensions: Length 508.8ft (155.1m); beam 46.9ft (14.3m); draught 19.0ft (5.8m).
Propulsion: 2 shafts; Brown-Boveri geared-turbines; 10 boilers; 45,900shp; 29.4kt; 5,300nm at 18kt.
Armour: Belt 1.5in (38mm); deck 0.8in (20mm); gunshields 2.0in (51mm); conning tower 4.0-2.0in (102-51mm).
Armament: 8 x 5.9in (150mm); 3 x 3.5in (88mm); 4 x 20mm; 4 x 21in (533mm) TT.
Complement: 650.

History: The cruiser *Emden* was of great symbolic importance to the post-World War I German Navy - the *Reichsmarine* - as the first major warship to be built under the limitations imposed by the Versailles Treaty. That had laid down very stringent limits on Germany's post-war forces, those concerning light cruisers being that the navy was allowed eight, of which only six could be in commission at any one time, with a maximum standard displacement of 6,0000 tons. Further, new ships could only be built to replace old ones, and then only when they were twenty years old. *Emden* was laid down in 1921 and completed in 1925, her design being based on that of the *Köln*, the last cruiser to be built during the recent war. *Emden*'s main purpose, however, was not as a fighting ship, but to train the young officers and cadets needed to form nucleus of the new navy and this she did very well, conducting many overseas

Königsberg

GERMANY

Light cruiser
Completed: 1929-30.
Number in class: 3.
Displacement: 6,650 tons standard; 8,130 tons full load.
Dimensions: Length 570.8ft (174.0m); beam 50.2ft (15.3m); draught 18.3ft (5,6m).
Propulsion: 2 shafts; Admiralty-pattern geared-turbines, 6 boilers, 65,000shp; plus 2 M.A.N. diesels, 1,800bhp; 32kt; 3,100nm at 13kt.
Armour: Belt 2.8-2.0in (71-51mm); deck 1.5 -0.8in (38-20mm); turrets 1.3in (33mm); conning tower 4.0-1.0in (102-25mm).
Armament: 9 x 5.9in (150mm) (3 x 3); 2 x 3.5in (88mm); 8 x 37mm; 8 x 20mm; 12 x 19.7in (500mm) TT.
Aircraft: 2.
Complement: 850.

History: Although superficially similar to *Emden*, the three K-class cruisers, *Königsberg*, *Karlsruhe* and *Köln*, were built to a completely new design. Parts of the hull were fabricated using the newly-developed electro-welding techniques, whose main benefit was a reduction in weight. The new 5.9in (150mm) guns were mounted in a new triple turret, one in "A" position, the other two aft. An unusual feature of the latter two was that "X turret was offset slightly to port and "Y" to starboard, apparently to give them greater arcs of fire, although since such an arrangement was never repeated, it presumably offered few benefits.

The machinery was also innovative in that it was composed of two disparate elements in what would today be described as a COSOD system; ie,

***Above: Emden,* first warship built by Germany after World War I, designed for training**

cruises in the inter-war years. One of her commanding officers during this period was Karl Dönitz, the future commander-in-chief of, first, the U-boat arm and, later, of the whole navy. During World War II she continued in her, still very necessary role as a training ship but also took part in several operational missions. These included the occupation of Norway and bombarding the Russian coast during Operation Barbarossa, but she ran aground in Oslofjord in December 1944 and was eventually seriously damaged by RAF bombs and paid off, after which her crew blew her up (3 May 1945).

***Above:* Like her sisters, *Karlsruhe,* was overloaded and had an inherently weak hull**

combined steam or diesel. In this, the diesels were used only for cruise, giving a speed of some 10kt, while the steam plant gave a maximum of 32kt, but the different systems could not be used in combination. The Germans were, naturally, trying to squeeze everything they could into the design and a major consequence was that the hulls were inherently weak. Indeed, on one world cruise *Karslruhe* suffered damage which was so substantial that she had to put into San Diego, California for dockyard work to repair and strengthen the hull.

Like *Emden*, these ships were used for training young officers and cadets, and undertook numerous pre-war cruises. All three were sunk in World War II; two by British action, one by scuttling.

Leipzig/Nürnberg

GERMANY

Light cruiser
Specifications for *Leipzig*, as built.
Completed: Leipzig - 1931; Nürnberg - 1935.
Number in class: Leipzig - 1; Nürnberg - 1.
Displacement: 6,515 tons standard; 8,250 tons full load.
Dimensions: Length 581.0ft (177.1m); beam 53.2ft (16.2m); draught 16.0ft (4.9m).
Propulsion: 3 shafts; outer shaft - 2 Admiralty-pattern geared turbines, 8 boilers, 60,000shp, 31kt; centre shaft4 M.A.N. diesels, 12,400bhp, 18kt; all three - 32kt; 3,800nm at 15kt.
Armour: belt 2.5-1.5in (63-38mm); deck 0.8in (20mm); turrets 1.3-0.8in (33-20mm); conning tower 4.0-1.3in (102-33mm).
Armament: 9 x 5.9in (150mm)(3 x 3); 2 x 3.5in (88m); 8 x 37mm; 12 x 19.7in (500mm) TT.
Complement: 850.

History: *Leipzig* was laid down in 1928 and completed in 1931, followed by *Nürnberg*, the first warship to be ordered by the new Nazi regime in 1934, which was completed in 1935. Both ships featured another variation on the steam/diesel power plant, in this case COSAD (combined steam and diesel). There were three shafts, with the steam turbines (Admiralty-pattern in *Leipzig*, Parsons in *Nürnberg*) driving the outer two, while the eight M.A.N. diesels were coupled to the central shaft via a common gearbox. The diesels drove the ship at cruising speed (10kt), with the outer shafts being turned over by small electric motors, and for maximum speed both steam and diesel were used. The inner propeller had variable-pitch

Hipper/Prinz Eugen

GERMANY

Heavy cruiser
Specifications for *Hipper*, as built.
Completed: Hipper - 1939; Prinz Eugen - 1940.
Number in class: Hipper - 2; Prinz Eugen - 1.
Displacement: 14,050 tons standard;18,200 tons full load.
Dimensions: Length 665.7ft (205.9m); beam 69.8ft (21.3m); draught 19.0ft (5.8m).
Propulsion: 3 shafts; Blohm+Voss geared-turbines; 12 boilers; 132,000shp; 32.5kt; 6,500nm at 17kt.
Armour: Belt 3.3-1.5in (84-38mm); deck 1.3-0.5in (33-13mm); main turrets 6.3-2.3in (160-58mm); conning tower 6.0-2.0in (152-51mm).
Armament: 8 x 8in (203mm) (4 x 2); 12 x 4.1in (105mm); 12 x 37mm; 8 x 20mm; 12 x 21in (533mm) TT.
Aircraft: 3.
Complement: 1,600.

History: Although Germany was not a party to the Washington Naval Treaty, these three ships were, in effect, German versions of the "Treaty cruiser" with 8in (203mm) guns mounted in a (theoretically) 10,000 ton hull. The first two, *Admiral Hipper* and *Blücher*, were both completed in 1939, and were followed by *Prinz Eugen* in 1940, which had a greater displacement (19,042 tons) and was slightly longer (679.1ft [207.7m]) but was otherwise identical (the greater length was due to the "Atlantic bow," a curved clipper bow replacing the straight stem which had proved to result in a very wet foredeck.)

It was planned that there would be three ships in the second group, but

***Above: Nürnberg* served in the German Navy until 1945 and then went to the USSR**

blades which could be set to the most efficient angle according to the speed.

Nürnberg was slightly the larger of the two, with an overall length of 594.8ft (181.3m) and a displacement of 8,380 tons, while the main armament of nine 5.9in (150mm) was identical. *Leipzig's* secondary armament altered between 1931 and 1934, with six 3.5in (88mm) being added and the torpedo tubes changed from 19.7in (500mm) to the international standard 21in (533mm) type, and these changes were implemented in *Nürnberg* while under construction. The later ship did, however, mount eight 20mm cannon which were not fitted in the earlier ship at all. Both ships had a large single funnel, but *Nürnberg* differed in having a much larger block-shaped bridge superstructure. Both ships were busy on secondary tasks during the war and *Leipzig* was very nearly lost when she was rammed by *Prinz Eugen* in 1944. After the war *Leipzig* was scrapped, while *Nürnberg* was passed to the USSR (*Admiral Makharov*) and is believed to have been operated into the 1950s as a training ship.

***Above: Admiral Hipper*, as completed in 1939; note no funnel cap**

only *Prinz Eugen* was completed for the German Navy. The second, *Seydlitz*, was 90 percent complete when it was decided to convert her to an aircraft carrier, but this work was later cancelled and the still incomplete hulk was scuttled in 1945. *Lützow* was some 80 percent complete when she was sold to the USSR in early 1940 and towed to Leningrad for completion and where she was used as a floating battery during the siege of that city. Damaged by German artillery fire, she was later refloated and then used for some years as an accommodation hulk. All these ships employed a high-pressure steam system, which proved to be extremely troublesome.

Admiral Hipper made two successful forays into the Atlantic on commerce-raiding operations, and also took part in the invasion of Norway. She spent most of 1942 based in Norway and made several attacks on Allied convoys, but was severely damaged in December by the British cruisers *Jamaica* and *Sheffield* and had to return to Germany for repairs. She was badly damaged by RAF bombs in 1945 and was scuttled by her crew. *Blücher* led the German attack on Oslo and was sunk by the defending Norwegian forts on the approach to the city. *Prinz Eugen* led a charmed life throughout the war. She partnered *Bismarck* on the latter's ill-fated voyage into the Altantic, but survived to reach Brest and then took part, with *Scharnhorst* and *Gneisenau*, in the "Channel Dash" in which, despite being attacked several times, she was the only one to escape damage. After the war she was allocated to the United States and took part in several atomic tests, which she survived. Her hulk still lies on Enubui Reef, but due to nuclear radiation hazards cannot be recovered and scrapped.

Spetsai

GREECE

Armoured cruiser
Completed: 1889-90.
Number in class: 3.
Displacement: 4,808 tons.
Dimensions: Length 334.7ft (102.0m); beam 51.8ft (15.8m); draught 18.0ft (5.5m).
Propulsion: 2 shafts; Vertical, Triple-Expansion engines; 6,700ihp; 17kt.
Armour: Creusot/compound. Belt 12.0-4.0in (305-102mm); battery 14.0-12.0in (356-305mm); barbette 12in (305mm).
Armament: 3 x 10.8in (275mm) (3 x 1); 5 x 5.9in (150mm); 4 x 3.4in (86mm); 4 x 3pdr; 4 x 1pdr; 6 x 1pdr revolvers; 3 x 14in (355mm) TT
Complement: 440.

***Above:* *Prinz Eugen* survived many actions only to be destroyed in atomic tests in 1946**

History: These three cruisers, *Spetsai*, *Psara* and *Hydra*, were built in France for the Royal Hellenic Navy and were handsome ships, but with an armament layout not known to have been used by any other navy. The main armament comprised three 10.8in (275mm) guns, but these were of two different barrel lengths, two being 34 calibres (30.7ft [9.4m]) long, the other one 28 calibres (25.2 [7.7m]). The two long-barrel guns were mounted in single barbettes on either bridge wing, while the third, with the shorter barrel, was mounted aft. The 5.9in (150mm) guns were also mounted singly, with one right forward as a bow chaser, one beneath each of the forward 10.8in (275mm) guns and two more under the foredeck. All three ships served until 1919 when they were deleted from the navy list and all were broken up in 1929.

***Below:* Greek cruiser, *Psara*; armament layout was unlike that of any other warship**

Tripoli

ITALY

Torpedo cruiser
Completed: 1886.
Number in class: 1.
Displacement: 835 tons standard; 952 tons full load.
Dimensions: Length 240.8ft (73.4m); beam 25.8ft (7.9m); draught 12.0ft (3.7m).
Propulsion: 2 shafts; double-expansion engines; 6 boilers; 2,543ihp; 17.5kt; 1,000nm at 10kt.
Armour: protective deck 1.5in (38mm).
Armament: 1 x 4.7in (120mm); 6 x 57mm; 2 x 37mm; 3 x 37mm revolvers; 5 x 14in (357mm) TT.
Complement: 111.

History: This elegant, steel-hulled vessel was the first successful ship in a very long line of Italian cruisers, her predecessor, *Pietro Micca*, completed in 1877, having been placed in reserve immediately after her rather unsuccessful trials. *Tripoli* was a long, low ship, with a ram bow, two raked funnels and two raked masts, giving more of the appearance of an expensive private yacht rather than a warship, although she gained a more purposeful look later when the masts were removed, the tunnels lowered and fitted with caps, and a proper charthouse installed. She was fitted to carry mines in 1897 and was employed in that role in World War I but, possibly due to some bureaucratic oversight, was not reclassified as a minelayer until 1921. Her armament was changed on several ocassions during her long operational life, that shown above being changed in 1904 to one 3in (76mm), six 57mm; one 47mm and three 14in

Garibaldi

ITALY

Armoured cruiser
Specifications for *Varese*, as built.
Completed: 1901-05.
Number in class: 3.
Displacement: 7,234 tons standard; 7,972 tons full load.
Dimensions: Length 366.7ft (111.8m); beam 59.9ft (18.3m); draught 23.2ft (7.1m).
Propulsion: 2 shafts; Vertical, Triple-Expansion; 24 boilers; 13.655ihp; 19.3kt; 4,400nm at 10kt.
Armour: belt 4.8in (122mm); gunshields 2.0in (51mm); deck 1.5in (38mm); conning tower 4.8in (122mm).
Armament: 1 x 10in (254mm); 2 x 8in (203mm); 10 x 3in (76mm); 6 x 47mm; 2 x Maxim MGs; 4 x 17.7in (450mm) TT.
Complement: 510

History: These ships were designed to be able to fight as part of the main battle fleet or to conduct independent operations, in which case they had the speed to escape from any more powerfully armed enemy. They were well-armed, although it was with the mix of weapons customary in the era: one 10in (254mm) and two 8in (203mm), with a secondary armament of ten 3in (76mm) and six 47mm. The design created an immediate impression and attracted export orders for seven from Argentina, Japan and Spain. This commercial success was helped by the fact that the Italian Navy was prepared to release ships already under construction against its own order to be supplied to overseas customers first, so that the first ship actually to be received by the home navy was the sixth to have been laid down. The Argentine Navy ordered

(357mm) torpedo tubes. This was changed again in 1910 when her torpedo tubes were removed in order to enable her to carry many more mines (64), the remainder of her armament then being two 3in (76mm) and four 57mm. She was stricken in 1923.

***Above:* The first effective cruiser in the Italian Navy, *Tripoli* was a very elegant design**

***Above:* Garibaldi-class armoured cruiser, *Varese*; the type served in four navies**

a total of six, of which it received four, which were named *General Belgrano, General Garibaldi, General Pueyrredon*, and *General San Martin*. Delivered in 1896-98, two survived until 1935, one to 1948 and the last until 1954. Argentina also ordered a further two of an Improved-Garibaldi design, but these were transferred to Japan while under construction, becoming *Kasuga* and *Nisshin*. The final export order was to Spain, *Cristóbal Colón*, which was delivered in 1897 and sunk the following year at the Battle of Santiago (3 July 1898). Finally, the Italian Navy received three: *Varese* and *Giuseppe Garibaldi* in 1901, and *Francesco Ferrugio* in 1905. *Garibaldi* was sunk by the Austro-Hungarian *U-4* (18 July 1915), while *Varese* was stricken in 1923 and *Feruccio* in 1930.

Pisa

ITALY

Armoured cruiser
Completed: 1909.
Number in class: 2.
Displacement: 9,832 tons standard; 10,600 tons full load.
Dimensions: Length 461.0ft (140.5m); beam 68.9ft (21.0m); draught 23.0ft (7.1m).
Propulsion: 2 shafts; Vertical, Triple-Expansion engines; 22 boilers; 20,808ihp; 23.5kt; 2,500nm at 12kt.
Armour: Vickers. belt 7.9in (200mm); deck 5.2in (130mm); main gun turrets 10in (160mm); conning tower 7.1in (180mm).
Armament: 4 x 10.0in (254mm) (2 x 2); 8 x 7.5in (190mm); 16 x 3in (76mm); 8 x 47mm; 4 x MG; 3 x 17.7in (450mm) TT.
Complement: 684.

History: These large and fast ships were heavily armed for their size. Indeed, the Royal Italian Navy originally classified them as second class battleships and in some ways they were similar in concept to the British Invincible-class battlecruisers (q.v.), although their main armament of four 10in (254mm) guns was by no means as formidable as the latter's eight 12in (305mm). Two were built, *Pisa* and *Amalfi*, both being completed in 1909.

Amalfi was on patrol in the Northern Adriatic on 7 July 1915 when she was torpedoed and sunk by the supposedly Austro-Hungarian submarine *U 26*, although this was, in fact,

Trento

ITALY

Cruiser
Completed: 1928-29.
Number in class: 2.
Displacement: 10,344 tons standard; 13,334 tons full load.
Dimensions: Length 646.2ft (197.0m); beam 67.6ft (20.6m); draught 22.3ft (6.8m).
Propulsion: 4 shafts; Parsons geared turbines; 12 boilers; 150,000shp; 36kt; 4,160nm at 16kt.
Armour: Belt 2.8in (70mm); decks 2.0-0.8in (50-20mm); barbettes 2.8-2.4in (70-60mm); turrets 3.9in (100mm); conning tower 3.9-1.6in (100-40mm).
Armament: 8 x 8in (203mm) (4 x 2); 16 x 3.9in (100mm) AA; 4 x 40mm AA; 4 x 0.5in (12.7mm) MG; 8 x 21in (633mm) TT.
Aircraft: 2
Complement: 781.

History: The two ships of the Trento-class, *Trento* and *Trieste*, were the first of the Royal Italian Navy's "Treaty cruisers" and while they mounted the permitted eight 8in (203mm) guns they actually exceeded the 10,000 ton limit (although by no means the only navy to do so). As with many Italian designs, very high speed was emphasised at the expense of protection. There were four shafts, the two outer shafts driven by the forward engineroom and the two inner shafts by the after engineroom, with the design power of 120,000shp sufficient for 34kt, although they achieved 36kt on trials. Maximum speed at full load in the open ocean was about 31kt. As was Italian practice at the time, there were two aircraft in a hangar under the foreck. These were launched from a fixed catapult

the German *UB 14*, with a German captain and crew, and Italy and Germany were not at that time at war with each other. *Pisa* survived the war and in 1921 was reclassified as a coastal battleship, although for the rest of her career she was employed as a training ship. She was stricken in April 1937.

***Below: Amalfi,* sunk in 1915 by a German U-boat flying Austro-Hungarian colours**

on the foredeck centreline and recovered from the sea by a crane.

Trento was at the Battles of Calabria (July 1940), Cape Matapan (March 1941) and Second Sirte (March 1942), but was sunk by British submarine *Umbra* in June 1942. *Trieste* was also at Matapan but was torpedoed by British submarine *Utmost* in November 1942. Although badly damaged, she was able to reach port but was later sunk in an air raid (10 April 1943).

***Below:* The Trento-class was the first attempt by the Italian Navy at a "Treaty cruiser"**

Zara

ITALY

Heavy cruiser
Completed: 1931-32.
Number in class: 4.
Displacement: 11,680 tons standard; 14,300 tons full load.
Dimensions: Length 557.2ft (182.8m); beam 62.8ft (20.6m); draught 21.9ft (7.2m).
Propulsion: 2 shafts; Parsons geared turbines; 8 boilers; 95,000shp; 32kt; 4,480nm at 16kt.
Armour: belt (150-100mm); decks (70-20mm); barbettes (150-120mm); turret (150-120mm);conning tower 150-70mm).
Armament: 8 x 8in (203mm) (4 x 2); 16 x 3.9in (100mm); 4 x 40mm; 8 x 13.2mm MG.
Aircraft: 2.
Complement: 841.

History: This class was the Italian Navy's second attempt at a "Treaty cruiser" design, the balance in the Trento-class having gone too far in achieving speed at the expense of protection. The class consisted of four ships, *Fiume*, *Gorizia*, *Pola*, and *Zara*, which joined the fleet in 1931-32. The aim was to produce a cruiser within the laid-down limits of eight 8in (203mm) guns and 10,000 tons displacement, but with a speed of 32 knots and an armour belt of 7.9in (200mm), but when this proved impossible to achieve major steps were taken to reduce weight. Thus, the belt was reduced to 5.9in (150mm), the hull was stepped abreast the foremast, the torpedo tubes were deleted, and a twin-screw, lightweight propulsion system was installed. When the weight still proved to be some 1,500 tons over the limit, the Italians just decided to go ahead.

Condottieri Groups I-V

ITALY

Light cruisers
History: The Condottieri light cruisers consisted of twelve ships in five groups built over a period of six years. They provide an excellent example of the progressive development of a reasonably sound basic design, with every step achieving improvements in capability or protection, but with displacement increased inexorably from 6,844 tons in Group I to 11,575 tons in Group V, a seventy percent increase!

The series started with the Giussano-class (Group I), consisting of *Giussano*, *Barbiano*, *Colleoni* and *Banda Nere*. The Italian naval staff's aim was to produce a ship which could catch and destroy ships such as the large, fast and powerful French destroyers (eg, the Jaguar-class) which were posing a major threat to Italian interests in the Mediterranean. Weight was kept down by providing minimal facilities for the crew and by measures such as the use of welding, while protection was very limited. All this enabled *Barbiano* to attain the extraordinary speed of 42 knots for half-an-hour and to sustain 39 knots for eight hours, although a more usual speed in open waters was about 32 knots.

The Group II design sought to rectify some of the problems, with two being built: *Cadorna* and *Diaz*. There was no tumblehome (thus improving stability and increasing accommodation space), the bridge structure was simplified and lowered, and an improved model of the 6in (152mm) turret was mounted. In addition, the aircraft facilities were moved from the bow, with the catapult being resited on the after shelter deck and angled out to starboard. Again these ships were very fast and on trials *Cadorna* achieved 38.1kt and *Diaz* 39.7kt. Both were fitted to lay mines, carrying between eighty-four and 138 depending upon the type.

***Above:* All four Zara-class cruisers were lost in the war, three of them on the same day**

All four ships were lost in the war, three of them on the same day, during the Battle of Cape Matapan (29 March 1941). The sequence began late in the evening of 28 March 1941 when *Pola* was torpedoed and immobilised by British carrier aircraft. Her sister-ships *Fiume* and *Zara* were detached to assist her, but during the night the British battle fleet came upon the three ships and *Fiume* and *Zara* were immediately sunk by close-range gunfire from the battleships *Barham*, *Valiant* and *Warspite*, following which, *Pola*, still without power, was torpedoed and despatched by British destroyers. The fourth ship, *Gorizia*, took part in various engagements and was repeatedly damaged, eventually being taken to La Spezia for major repairs. She was still lying there at the Italian surrender (9 September 1943) and was captured by the Germans, but was later sunk by Italian human torpedoes (26 June 1944).

***Above: Luigi Cadorna* pre-war, one of two in Group II of the Condottieri design**

Group III also comprised two ships: *Montecuccoli* and *Attendolo*. These were larger than Group II with an additional 200 tons in displacement. This increase, plus weight saving measures, meant that a total of 1,350 tons could be devoted to protection compared to 575 tons in Group II. The aviation facilities were again altered and this time there was a rotating catapult amidships, so that the after boiler uptakes had to be trunked aft, resulting in considerable separation between the two funnels. The bridge structure was also greatly simplified, consisting essentially of a circular tower, topped by the main director.

Group IV, *D'Aosta* and *Savoia*, were generally similar to Group III, but were again larger to give yet further improvements to the protection. Group V was probably the best and consisted of two ships, *Abruzzi* and *Garibaldi*, with ▶

ITALIAN CONDOTTIERE-SERIES LIGHT CRUISERS			
Class Name **Group**		**Giussana** **I**	**Cadorna** **II**
Completed		1931-32	1933
No. in class		4	2
Displacement	Standard	5, 110 tons	5,232 tons
	Full load	6,844 tons	7,001 tons
Dimensions	Length	555.4ft (169.3m)	555.4ft (169.3m)
	Beam	50.8ft (15.5m)	50.8ft (15.5 m)
	Draught	17.8ft (5.3m)	18.0ft (5.5m)
Propulsion	Shafts	2	2
	Turbines	Belluzo	Parsons
	Boilers	6	6
	Power	95,000shp	95,000shp
	Speed	36.5kt	36.5kt
	Range	3,800nm/18kt	2,930nm/16kt
Armour	Main belt	0.9in (24mm)	0.9in (24mm)
	Deck	0.8in (20mm)	0.8in (20mm)
	Turrets	0.9in (23mm)	0.9in (23mm)
	Conning tower	1.6in (40mm)	1.6in (40mm)
Armament	Main	8 x 152mm	8 x 152mm
	AA	6 x 100mm	6 x 100mm
	AA	8 x 37mm	2 x 40mm
	MG	8 x 13.2mm	8 x 13.2mm
	TT	4 x 533mm	4 x 533mm
Aircraft	Catapult	1	1
	Aircraft	2	2
Complement		520	544

Montecuccoli III	Duca d' Aosta IV	Abruzzi V
1935	1935-36	1937
2	2	2
7,405 tons	8,317 tons	9,440 tons
8,853 tons	10. 3 74 tons	11,575 tons
597.8 (182.2m)	613.2ft (186.9m)	613.5ft (187.0m)
54.5ft (16.6m)	57.4ft (17.5m)	62.0ft (18.9m)
19.7ft (6.0m)	21.3ft (6.5m)	22.3ft (6.8m)
2	2	2
Belluzo	Parsons	Parsons
6	6	8
106,000shp	110,000shp	100,000shp
37kt	36.5kt	34kt
4,122nm/18kt	3,900nm/14kt	4,125nm/12.7kt
2.4in (60mm)	2.8in (70mm)	3.9in (100mm)
1.2in (30mm)	1.4in (35mm)	1.6in (40mm)
2.8in (70mm)	3.5in (90mm)	5.3in (135mm)
3.9in (100mm)	3.9in (100mm)	5.6in (140mm)
8 x 152mm	8 x 152mm	10 x 152mm
6 x 100mm	6 x 100mm	8 X 100mm
8 x 37mm	8 x 37mm	8 x 37mm
8 x 13.2mm	12 x 13.2mm	8 x 13.2mm
4 x 533mm	6 x 533mm	6 x 533mm
1	1	2
2	2	4
650	694	692

a 1,000 ton increase in displacement and a 4ft (1.2m) increase in beam. Protection was again improved and main armament consisted of ten of a new model of 6in (152mm) gun. Two catapults were fitted amidships and the funnels were noticeably closer than in any of the previous groups. By now the requirement for speed had moderated somewhat and these ships were required only to do about 34 knots on trials and 31 knots at sea.

A Group VI was planned, which would have consisted, again, of two ships. They would have been slightly larger, with improved protection and carried four aircraft, but were cancelled in June 1940 before the keels had been laid.

Exactly half the ships were war losses, including all four of Group I: *Colleoni* was sunk off Crete by the Australian cruiser, HMAS *Sydney* (19 July 1940); *Barbiano* and *Giussano* by three British and one Dutch destroyer in the action off Cape Bon (13 December 1941); and *Banda Nere* by the submarine *Urge* (1 April 1942). The other war losses were *Diaz* (Group II), sunk by the submarine *Upright* (25 February 1941) and *Attendolo* (Group III) by air attack (4 December 1942).

The others all survived the war, with the two Group IV ships being transferred to foreign navies: *D'Aosta* to the USSR in 1949 as *Stalingrad*, and *Savoia* to Greece in 1951 as *Helle*. Both were stricken in the 1960s. The remainder continued to serve in the Italian Navy and were eventually stricken: *Cadorna* (Group II) in 1951; *Montecuccoli* (Group III) in 1964; and *Abruzzi* (Group V) in 1961. *Garibaldi* (Group V) was completely rebuilt between 1957 and 1962 as a guided missile cruiser and remained in service until 1972.

***Top Right:* A Group IV ship, *Luigi di Savoia duca degli Abruzzi,* shown after the war**

***Bottom Right: Garibaldi,* totally rebuilt 1957-62, became an early guided-missile ship**

Asama

JAPAN

Armoured cruiser
Completed: 1899.
Number in class: 2.
Displacement: 9.700 tons standard; 10,520 tons full load.
Dimensions: Length 442.0ft (134.7m); beam 67.3ft (20.5m); draught 24.5ft (7.4m).
Propulsion: 2 shafts; Vertical, Triple-Expansion engines; 8 boilers; 18,000ihp; 21.5kt; 10,000nm at 10kt.
Armour: Belt 7.0- 3.5in (178-89mm); deck 2.0in (51mm); barbettes 6.0in (152mm); turrets 6.0in (152mm); conning tower 4.0-3.0in (102-76mm).
Armament: 4 x 8in (203mm) (2 x 2); 14 x 6in (152mm); 12 x 12pdr; 7 x 2.5pdr; 5 x 18in (457mm) TT.
Complement: 726.

History: These two ships, *Asama* and *Tokiwa*, had extraordinarily long service lives, both serving in the Russo-Japanese war, World War I, the Sino-Japanese War and World War II. They were designed and built by Armstrongs at Elswick, England, on the banks of the River Tyne, both being completed in 1899. Their design was based on that of the Armstrong cruisers recently delivered to Chile (the O'Higgins-class), but were slightly larger, with a better-balanced secondary armament and improved protection. Design speed was 21.5 knots but this was exceeded on trials by some 2 knots, although poor maintenance once in service resulted in a significant loss of speed.

Both ships played a full part at the Battle of Tsushima, where they formed part of the line of battle and were employed, in effect, as second-class battleships. Both were damaged in the battle but were then repaired. Both

***Above: Asama,* built in 1899, survived three wars and was finally scrapped in 1947**

served throughout World War I but in 1921 they were reclassified as coastal defence ships. *Asama* was converted to a training ship for midshipmen in 1937, a role in which she continued to the end of World War II. *Tokiwa*, however, spent only a year as a coastal defence ship, being converted to a minelayer in 1922, carrying up to 300 mines. She suffered a major explosion in 1927, which caused considerable damage (thirty-eight dead), but was repaired and returned to service. In 1937 she was refitted and modernised with her mine-carrying capacity increased to 500 Type 5 mines, as well as eighty depth-charges. She was damaged by a US-laid mine in April 1945 and repaired, but was then sunk by US carrier aircraft on 8 August 1945.

Suma

JAPAN

Protected cruiser
Completed: 1896-99.
Number in class: 2.
Displacement: 2,657 tons.
Dimensions: Length (pp) 306.8ft (93.5m); beam 40.0ft (12.2m); draught 15.3ft (4.6m).
Propulsion: 2 shafts; Vertical, Triple-Expansion engines; 8,500ihp; 20kt.
Armour: deck 2.0-1.0in (51-26mm); gun shields 4.5in (114mm).
Armament: 2 x 6in (152mm) (2 x 1); 6 x 4.7in (120mm); 10 x 3pdr; 4 x 2.5pdr; 4 x Maxim MGs; 2 x 15in (381mm) TT.
Complement: 310.

History: In its first decades of expansion the Imperial Japanese Navy depended upon ships built abroad, but a national shipbuilding base was established, which gradually expanded its capabilities and the size of its projects. Thus, the cruiser *Akitsushima* was designed by a British naval architect, but assembled at Yokosuka Naval Yard from imported components and completed in 1894. The Suma-class represents the next step, as they were designed in Japan and built entirely from Japanese materials and in Japanese yards. The initial design was, in fact, generally similar to that of the *Akitsushima*, first-of-class *Suma*, having the same type of somewhat cluttered upper deck. When she ran trials, however, *Suma* was found to be very wet and lacking in stability, so urgent corrective action was taken with the second ship, *Akashi*, which was still on the stocks, making her flush-decked and thus increasing the freeboard. In addition,

Chikuma

JAPAN

Light cruiser
Completed: 1912.
Number in class: 3.
Displacement: 5,000 tons standard; 5,040 tons full load.
Dimensions: Length 475.0ft (144.8m); beam 46.6ft (14.2m); draught 16.8ft (5.1m).
Propulsion: 2 shafts; Curtis turbines; 16 boilers; 22,500shp; 26kt; 10,000nm at 10kt.
Armour: Krupp steel. Belt 3.5-2.0in (89-50mm); deck 2.3-1.5in (57-38mm); conning tower 4.0in (102mm).
Armament: 8 x 6in (152mm) (8 x 1); 4 x 3.1in (79mm); 2 x MG; 3 x 18in (457mm) TT.
Complement: 414.

History: The second-class cruiser *Tone* was built in Sasebo Naval Yard, the design being based on that of the British Town-class; she was completed in 1910 and the Chikuma-class was an improved version. It consisted of three ships: *Chikuma*, *Yahagi* and *Hirado*. As built, they were armed with a main battery of six 6.0in (152mm), with a secondary battery of eight 3.0in (79mm), but soon after commissioning four of the 3.0in (79mm) were removed from the waist and replaced by two more 6.0in (152mm) guns, bringing the total of the latter up to eight. There were further minor changes to their armament during the inter-war years.

***Above:* Suma-class were the first major warships designed and built entirely in Japan**

the fighting tops on both main and foremasts were removed in an effort to improve stability, but this was presumably insufficient as the mainmast was subsequently removed altogether, leaving a plain pole foremast. The same modification was also implemented in Suma. The machinery was also different from *Akitsushima*, which had been powered by horizontal triple-expansion engines, the Sumas having the vertical type. However, the latter were reboilered several times, suggesting that all was not well.

Both ships took part in the Russo-Japanese war, in which *Akasho* was mined but subsequently repaired. They were disarmed in 1922 and *Suma* was scrapped in 1928, while *Akashi* was expended as a target in 1930.

All three saw service throughout World War I, at the beginning of which they took part in the search for Admiral von Spee's Pacific squadron and the lone raider, *Emden*. *Chikuma* was stricken in 1931 and *Hirado* in 1940, while *Yahagi* became a training ship.

***Below:* Chikuma-class cruiser, *Yahagi*, in the 1920s; she later became a training ship**

Kuma

JAPAN

Light cruiser
Completed: 1920-21.
Number in class: 5.
Displacement: 5,500 tons standard; 5,832 tons full load.
Dimensions: Length 532.0ft (162.1m); beam 46.5ft (14.2m); draught 15.8ft (4.8m).
Propulsion: 4 shafts; Gihon geared turbines; 12 boilers; 90,000shp; 36kt; 9,000nm at 10kt.
Armour: Belt 2.5in (63mm); deck 1.3in (32mm).
Armament: 7 x 5.5in (140mm) (7 x 1); 2 x 3.1in (79mm); 8 x 21in (533mm) TT; 48 mines.
Complement: 450.

History: The Kuma-class, consisting of *Kuma*, *Tama*, *Kitakami*, *Oi* and *Kiso*, was intended to serve in both scouting and flotilla roles, with first-of-class completed in 1920, the balance in 1921. They were the first of what was known as the "5,500-series" and main armament comprised seven 5.5in (140mm) guns in single mounts: two on the foredeck; two abreast the bridge; two between the after funnel and the mainmast; and the last abaft the mainmast. As built, they had three straight sided funnels of equal height, but the forward funnel was raised in the 1920s and all three funnels were fitted with flare-suppressors in the 1930s. They did not have aviation facilities when launched, but these were installed later, with all being fitted with a flying-off platform on the foredeck in the 1920s; this was, however, removed from all in the late '20s, but *Kuma* and *Tama* were rebuilt with a rotating catapult aft in 1934-35.

Nagara

JAPAN

Light cruiser
Completed: 1922-25.
Number in class: 6.
Displacement: 5,570 tons.
Dimensions: Length 532.0ft (162.1m); beam 46.5ft (14.2m); draught 15.8ft (4.8m).
Propulsion: 4 shafts; Gihon geared turbines; 12 boilers; 90,000shp; 36kt; 5,000nm at 14kt.
Armour: Belt 2.5in (63mm); deck 1.75in (32mm).
Armament: 7 x 5.5in (140mm); 2 x 3in (76mm); 8 x 24in (610mm) TT; 48 mines.
Complement: 450.

History: This class of six ships, *Nagara*, *Abukuma*, *Isuzu*, *Kinu*, *Natori* and *Yura*, was intended to provide flagships for cruiser and destroyer squadrons, an idea pioneered by the Royal Navy in World War I, and was the second in the "5,500-series," the design being developed from that of the Kuma-class (see previous entry). They were the first Japanese warships to mount the newly-developed 24in (610mm) torpedo tubes and, as built, all had a fixed flying-off platform above the "A" and "B" gun mounts, with the hangar inside the bridge superstructure. This arrangement meant that they had tall, slab-sided forward superstructure, which was retained even after the aviation facilities were removed fairly soon after completion. Catapults of the 15 metre-type (49ft) were installed between the after funnel and mainmast in *Yura* and *Kinu* in 1929-31 but, following accidents, they were removed and all ships in the class were then given rotating catapults, together with a tripod mainmast, incorporating a crane for handling the aircraft.

***Above: Kuma;* note the flare-suppressors on the funnels and the large aircraft catapult**

Two of the class, *Oi* and *Kitakami*, were given a unique conversion in 1941, when they were converted into "torpedo cruisers" with no fewer than forty 21in (533mm) torpedo tubes. To make this possible they were given two 200.0ft (61.0m) sponsons stretching from the forefunnel to the mainmast, upon which were mounted ten quadruple torpedo tubes, five to each side. Later, eight of *Kitakami's* quad mounts were removed to enable her to carry landing craft but four of the torpedo mounts were replaced in early 1944. Then, having been damaged by a British submarine she was rebuilt yet again, this time with all the torpedo tubes and one of her turbines removed, becoming a *kaiten* (suicide craft) carrier, with eight (four per side) on the sponsons. Four were lost during the war, one survived and was scrapped in 1947.

***Above: Yura,* one of a class designed as flagships for cruiser or destroyer flotillas**

As with all Japanese warships, these received several inter-war refits, leading to modifications of weapons and equipment. In the 1930s *Abukuma* was specially fitted-out as a leader for night-attack destroyers, while during the war *Isuzu* became a flotilla leader for an ASW group, for which role she was given a heavy anti-aircraft armament of eleven triple and six single 25mm automatic cannon and three twin 0.5in (12.7mm) AAMG mounts.

The major peacetime event for this class was that in a collision with *Kitakami* (Kuma-class) on 20 October 1930, *Abukuma* lost most of her forecastle, which was replaced in Kure dockyard. Three were sunk by US submarines: *Nagara* by USS *Croaker* (7 August 1940; *Isuzu* by USS *Char* and *Gabilan* (7 April 1945); and *Natori* by USS *Hardhead* (18 August 1944). *Kinu* was sunk by US aircraft (10 November 1942) as was *Abukuma* (26 October 1944), while *Yura* was so badly damaged by aircraft off Guadalcanal that she had to be finished off by Japanese destroyers the following day (25 October 1942).

Furutaka

JAPAN

Heavy cruiser
Completed: 1926.
Number in class: 2.
Displacement: 7,100 tons standard; 9,540 tons full load.
Dimensions: Length 607.5ft (185.2m); beam 51.8ft (15.8m); draught 18.3ft (5.6m).
Propulsion: 4 shafts; Parsons geared turbines; 12 boilers; 102,000shp; 34.5kt; 6,000nm at 14kt.
Armour: Belt 3in (76mm); deck 1.4in (36mm); turrets 1.0in (25mm).
Armament: 6 x 8.0in (203mm) (6 x 1); 4 x 3.0in (76mm); 2 x MG; 12 x 24.0in (600mm) TT.
Aircraft: 1.
Complement: 625.

History: Although these two ships, *Furutaka* and *Kako*, are generally regarded as the first to meet the Washington Treaty standards for cruisers, the design was actually finalised before the treaty was signed. There were a number of unusual features in the design. First, there are good reasons in a ship for having a high forecastle and a low quarterdeck, which is usually achieved by a step in the hull, but this tends to cause stresses at the step-point. In the Furutaka-class the designers tried to get around this by having a flush deck (which is strong) but with a decided "kink" at about two-thirds of the way from bow to stern. Not normally visible from photographs, but, to achieve the speed required by the navy, the designers gave the ship a very high length:beam ratio of 11.7:1, compared to (for example), the contemporary US Pensacola-class where the

Aoba

JAPAN

Cruiser
Completed: 1927.
Number in class: 2.
Displacement: 7,100 tons standard; 8,760 tons full load.
Dimensions: Length 607.5ft (185.2m); beam 51.9ft (15.8m); draught 18.8ft (5.7m).
Propulsion: 4 shafts; Parsons geared turbines; 12 boilers; 102,000shp; 34.5kt; 6,000nm at 14kt.
Armour: Belt 3in (76mm); deck 1.4in (36mm); turrets 1.0in (25mm).
Armament: 6 x 8.0in (203mm) (3 x 2); 4 x 4.7in (120mm); 2 x 13mm MG; 12 x 24in (610mm) TT.
Aircraft: 1.
Complement: 625.

History: These two ships, *Aoba* and *Kinugasa*, were improved versions of the *Furutaka*, with same length and marginally greater beam (2.0in [51mm]), and with the six 8.0in (203mm) guns in three twin turrets. The calibre of the secondary armament was greater - 4.7in (120mm) compared to 3.0in (76mm) - but the torpedo tubes were again fixed. These were the first Japanese ships to have an aircraft catapult included in the initial design, although the actual machinery was not available until some time after completion. Both ships underwent a limited refit in 1938-40with bulges increasing the beam to 57.8ft (17.6m) with a consequent fall in speed to 33kt. The aircraft complement was increased from one to two. AA defences were increased by eight 25mm cannon and four 13.2mm machine guns, but this was still totally inadequate for the attacks that were to come, and it was to be substantially increased as the war progressed.

ratio was 8.73:1. Further oddities were the disposition of the six main guns in single turrets and the twelve torpedo tubes were fixed.

In the late 1930s the ships underwent refits where some of these problems were put right. The six single 8in (203mm) turrets were replaced by three twin turrets, rotating torpedo mountings were installed, and bulges were fitted, increasing the beam to 55.6ft (16.9m) and standard displacement to 8,700 tons. *Kako* was sunk by three torpedoes from US submarine *S-44* (10 August 1942) and *Furutaka* by gunfire from US surface ships (11 October 1942).

***Above: Kako,* in her original configuration, with six 8in (203mm) guns in single turrets**

Both ships had a very busy war, starting with participating in the attack on Wake Island and various landings in the period December 1942 to April 1943, followed by the Battle of the Coral Sea, Battle of Savo Island and the Guadalcanal campaign, during which *Aoba* was severely damaged. while *Kinugasa* almost sank USS *Boise*. While *Aoba* was being repaired *Kinugasa* was sunk by aircraft from USS *Enterprise* (15 November 1942) and when *Aoba* returned she was nearly sunk by torpedoes from USAAF B-17 aircraft and after further repairs she was sent to Singapore and then to the former Dutch East Indies. In October 1944 she was again damaged by a torpedo, this time from the submarine USS *Bream*, but managed to make her way back to Kure where she was hit by US Navy aircraft (24 April 1945) and then by USAAF aircraft (28 July 1945), the last of these causing her to settle on the bottom.

***Above: Kinugasa;* the Aoba-class was a much improved version of the Furutaka design**

Nachi/Takao

JAPAN

Heavy cruiser
Specifications for Nachi-class, as built.
Completed: Nachi - 1928-29; Takao - 1932.
Number in class: Nachi - 4; Takao - 4.
Displacement: 10,000 tons standard.
Dimensions: Length 668.5ft (203.8m); beam 56.9ft (17.3m); draught 19.3ft (5.9m).
Propulsion: 4 shafts; geared turbines; 12 boilers; 130,000shp; 35.5kt; 8,000nm at 14kt.
Armour: Belt 3.9in (100mm); deck 1.4in (36mm); turrets 1.0in (25mm); barbettes 3.0in (76mm).
Armament: 10 x 8.0in (203mm) (5 x 2); 6 x 4.7in (120mm); 2 x 13.2mm MG; 12 x 24.0in (610mm) TT.
Aircraft: 2.
Complement: 773.

History: These were four-ship classes, the earlier of the two, the Nachi-class (*Nachi, Myôkô, Haguro, Ashigara*) being the first Japanese cruisers built to the Washington Naval Treaty limits. The second group , the Takao-class (*Takao, Atago, Maya, Chokai*) was essentially similar, but with some improvements. In the Nachi-class the hull was essentially an enlarged version of that used in the Aoba-class, with a similar slope towards the stern. The main armament was mounted in five twin turrets, three of them on the foredeck in an arrangement pioneered by the British Nelson-class battleships. Protection was much improved from the *Aoba* and the bridge structure was much more massive.

Mogami

JAPAN

Light cruiser
Completed: 1935-37.
Number in class: 4.
Displacement: 8,500 tons standard; 10.993 tons full load.
Dimensions: Length 661.1ft (201.5m); beam 59.1ft (18.0m); draught 18.1ft (5.5m).
Propulsion: 4 shafts; geared turbines; 10 boilers; 152,000shp; 37kt; 8,150nm at 14kt.
Armour: Belt 4.9-3.9in (124-10mm); deck 2.4-1.4in (61-36mm); turrets 1in (25mm).
Armament: 15 x 6.1in (155mm) (5 x 3); 8 x 5in (127mm) DP; 4 x 40mm AA; 12 x 24in (mm) TT.
Aircraft: 3.
Complement: 850.

History: In order to appear to comply with the 1930 London Navy Treaty the Imperial Japanese Navy (IJN) designated these ships, *Mogami, Mikuma, Suzuya* and *Kumano*, as "light" cruisers, when their nearly-11,000 ton displacement would have made them a "heavy" cruiser in virtually every other navy. Major efforts were made to keep displacement down, including the use of a considerable amount of electric welding, while the hulls were of very light construction, but there was a very heavy armament, and the result was nearly a major disaster, since on trials it was discovered that stability was dangerously poor, there were many welding defects and hull distortions prevented the turrets from training. Indeed, the situation was so bad that the first three were decommissioned and returned to the yards, where, together with the nearly

***Above: Ashigara*; note turret arrangement, massive bridge and heavy funnel trunking**

Although displacement was published as the 10,000 tons stipulated in the treaty, the actual figure was 10,980 tons, a 10 percent overshoot. The Takao-class had an identical hull, but the bridge structure was even more massive and the torpedo tubes were rotating rather than fixed. All eight ships underwent major refits in the mid-1930s

Only one survived the war, and she, *Myoko* was crippled, having been torpedoed twice, first in Leyte Gulf and secondly by submarine USS *Bergall*; she survived, only to be laid up in Singapore for the rest of war. Four were sunk by submarine action: *Atago* by USS *Darter*, and *Maya* by USS *Dace* (both on 23 October 1944), *Ashigara* by British submarine HMS *Trenchant* (8 June 1945) while *Takao* survived two torpedo hits from USS *Darter* (23 October 1944) and was then finished off by British X-craft in Singapore roads (31 July 1945). *Chokai* was sunk by US aircraft and gunfire (25 October 1944), *Nachi* by US aircraft on 5 November 1944, and *Haguro* by torpedoes from British destroyers (16 May 1945).

***Above: Mogami* on trials; she was so unstable that she had to be redesigned and rebuilt**

complete *Kumano*, they were redesigned and rebuilt, the work including adding bulges, strengthening the hull, replacing much welded plating and reducing the number of torpedo reloads.

The original main armament consisted of fifteen 6.1in (155mm) guns in five triple turrets - in itself a very heavy battery - but, and despite the stability problems - these were replaced by ten 8.0in (203mm) guns in five twin turrets in 1939-40. At the same time the complement of torpedoes returned to twenty-four. By this time full load displacement had risen to 13,668 tons.

Mogami was given an unsightly and unsatisfactory conversion to seaplane carrier during the war. All four were sunk by US carrier aircraft: *Mikuma* at Midway on 6 June 1942; *Mogami* and *Suzuya*, both on 25 October 1944; and *Kumano* on 25 November 1944.

Tone

JAPAN

Heavy cruiser
Completed: 1938-39.
Number in class: 2.
Displacement: 11,215 tons standard; 15,200 tons full load.
Dimensions: Length 661.1ft (201.5m); beam 60.7ft (18.5m); draught 21.2ft (6.5m).
Propulsion: 4 shafts; geared turbines; 8 boilers; 152,000shp; 35kt; 9,000nm at 18kt.
Armour: Belt 4.9-3.9in (125-100mm); deck 2.5-1.2in (64-31mm); turrets 1.0in (25mm).
Armament: 8 x 8.0in (203mm) (4 x 2); 8 x 5.0in (127mm) DP; 12 x 25mm AA; 12 x 24in (610mm) TT.
Aircraft: 6.
Complement: 850.

History: *Tone* and *Chikuma* were designed to provide forward reconnaissance for the cruiser force and combined a heavy armament with unusually large aviation facilities. They were nominally "light" cruisers and were designed with twelve 6.1in (155mm) guns in four triple turrets, all of which were on a long foredeck, with "A," "C" and "D" turrets at deck level and "B" turret superfiring. This arrangement enabled the entire after part of the ship to be devoted to aircraft; designed capacity was six but no more than five were ever carried. There were two catapults at the forward end of the aircraft deck and a system of rails and turntables to enable the aircraft to be moved easily, but no hangars. Then Japan withdrew from the naval treaty arrangements, enabling these

Agano

JAPAN

Light cruiser (destroyer flagship)
Completed: 1942-44.
Number in class: 4.
Displacement: 6,652 tons standard; 8,534 tons full load.
Dimensions: Length 571.2ft (174.1m); beam 49.8ft (15.2m); draught 18.5ft (5.6m).
Propulsion: 4 shafts; geared turbines; 6 boilers; 100,000shp; 35kt; 6,300nm at 18kt.
Armour: belt 2.2in (56mm); deck 0.7in (18mm); turrets 1.0in (25mm).
Armament: 6 x 6.0in (152mm) (3 x 2); 4 x 3.0in (76mm); 32 x 25mm AA; 8 x 24in (610mm) TT.
Aircraft: 2.
Complement: 730.

History: In most navies destroyer flotillas were commanded by the senior commanding officer, exercising overall control from his own destroyer, but the IJN pursued an idea which was adopted for some years by the Royal Navy and developed a special type of light cruiser to serve as a destroyer flagship.This class of four ships, *Agano*, *Noshiro*, *Yahagi*, *Sakawa*, was built for such a role, for which they were required to be lightly protected, fast and well armed. Four were ordered but only the first-of-class seems to have been treated with any sense of urgency, being completed in October 1942, while *Noshiro* and *Yahagi* were completed in 1943 (June and December, respectively) and *Sakawa* was so late (November 1944) that, in the chaotic conditions of the time, she never became operational.

Agano led 4th Destroyer Flotilla in the battles around Guadalcanal in

ships, even though under construction, to be almost totally redesigned with eight 8in (203mm) guns, but still all on the foredeck, increasing displacement to some 12,500 tons.

Tone and *Chikuma* operated together for most of the war and were part of the forces attacking Pearl Harbor, Wake Island, the Dutch East Indies, Darwin and Ceylon. Both were damaged in 1942 and 1943, but not seriously, and both took part in a second foray into the Indian Ocean in early 1944. Both were sunk by US carrier aircraft, *Chikuma* on 25 October 1944 and *Tone* on 24 July 1945. For some unexplained reason no known photograph of *Chikuma* exists, while the only picture of *Tone* was taken from a US aircraft during the attack which resulted in her loss.

Below: **Heavy cruiser, *Tone*, armed with eight 8in (203mm), carried six floatplanes**

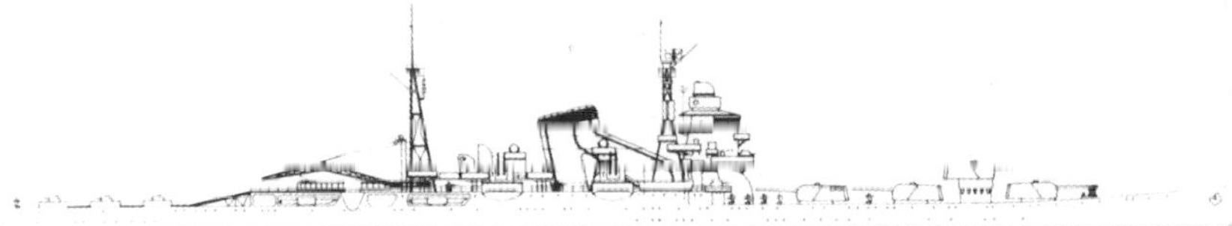

January-February 1943; she was later badly damaged in an air attack on Rabaul harbour and was on her way home for repairs when she was sunk by USS *Skate* (17 February 1944). *Noshiro* commanded 2nd Destroyer Flotilla, with which she took part in the battles of the Philippine Sea (18-22 June 1944), Leyte Gulf (October 1944) and Samar, but immediately after the latter she was sunk by US carrier aircraft (26 October 1944). *Yahagi* led 10th Destroyer Flotilla, with which she saw much action in 1944 and early 1945. Her final trip was as one of the escorts to battleship *Yamato* on the abortive attack on the US invasion fleet around Okinawa; like the battleship, *Yahagi* was subjected to relentless aerial attack, and having been hit by seven torpedoes and a dozen bombs she, too sank (7 April 1945).

Below: **Cruiser/destroyer leader *Sakawa*, the only ship in her class to survive the war**

De Ruyter

NETHERLANDS

Cruiser
Completed: 1935.
Number in class: 1.
Displacement: 6,000 tons standard; 7,548 tons full load.
Dimensions: Length 560.3ft (170.8m); beam 51.5ft (15.7m); draught 16.8ft (5.1m).
Propulsion: 2 shafts; Parsons geared turbines; 6 boilers; 66,000shp; 32kt; nm at kt.
Armour: Belt 2.0-1.2in (50-30mm); barbettes 1.2in (30mm); turrets 1.2in (30mm); decks 1.2in (30mm); conning tower 1.2in (30mm).
Armament: 7 x 5.9in (150mm) 3 x 2; 1 x 1); 10 x 40mm AA; 8 x 0.5in (12.7mm) AAMG.
Complement: 435.

History: The Dutch had a long-standing requirement for three cruisers to operate in the Dutch East Indies, which had been partially met by the *Java* (completed 1925) and *Sumatra* (1926), but the third, *Celebes*, was cancelled. The requirement, however, remained and was eventually met by a new ship, *De Ruyter*, whose design and armament were subjected to the most rigorous financial constraints. Indeed, the original design was so small that some enlargement was eventually agreed, although, as in other navies in the 1920s, weight was saved by a combination of careful design and the use of welding. The main armament consisted of the slightly unusual combination of twin 5.9in (150mm) turrets in "A," "X" and "Y" positions, with a single 5.9in (150mm) superfiring in "B" position. There was a large bridge tower and a catapult abaft the large single funnel. Two Dutch-built Fokker CX aircraft were carried. Despite

De Ruyter

NETHERLANDS

Cruiser
Completed: 1952.
Number in class: 2.
Displacement: 9,529 tons standard; 11,850 tons full load.
Dimensions: Length 615.0ft (187.3m); beam 57.0ft (17.3m); draught 22.0ft (6.7m).
Propulsion: 2 shafts; de Schelde-Parsons geared turbines; 4 boilers; 85,000shp; 32kt.
Armament: 8 x 6in (152mm) (4 x 2); 8 x 57mm AA; 8 x 40mm AA
Complement: 926.

History: These two ships started life as enlarged versions of the 1936 *De Ruyter* design (see previous entry), being laid down in May and September 1939. Work continued very slowly during the German occupation, but after the war the design was totally revised in the light of lessons learned during the conflict before work started again in the late 1940s, with both being finally completed in 1953. During this process the names were changed several times. The first-of-class was originally named *De Zeven Provincien*, but was renamed *De Ruyter* prior to entering service in 1954. The second ship was originally named *Eendraght*, but this was changed, first to *Kijkduin* and subsequently to *De Zeven Provincien*. Both served as flagships of the ASW task group provided by the Dutch Navy under NATO plans and *De Zeven Provincien* was converted to an air defence cruiser in the 1960s, in which her after end was totally rebuilt (including the removal of two 6.0in [152mm] and one twin 57mm turret) to accommodate a single Terrier SAM launcher, with the associated magazines (40 missiles) and radars.

Above: **Dutch cruiser, *De Ruyter*, sunk by the Japanese in the Battle of the Java Sea**

the financial stringency the fire control systems were very sophisticated for that era and included some automation, remote control and stabilisation.

De Ruyter served in the East Indies from 1937 onwards and in February 1942 became the flagship of the Dutch Admiral Doorman, commanding the naval striking force, which had been set up by the short-lived Australian-British-Dutch-American (ABDA) command. *De Ruyter* commanded during the battle of the Java Sea in which she was hit by torpedoes from the Japanese heavy cruiser *Haguro* and sank shortly afterwards with heavy loss of life (27 February 1942).

Right: **The second *De Ruyter*, laid down in 1939, completed in 1953, scrapped in 1999**

Both ships were sold to Peru. *De Ruyter* was sold in 1973, becoming the *Aguirre*, and was fitted out as a helicopter carrier. She was scrapped in 1999. *De Zeven Provincien* was sold in 1976 after her Terrier installation had been removed and returned to the United States. Named *Almirante Grau*, she is still in service in 2001, her eight 6.0in (152mm) guns making her the last gun-armed cruiser in any navy.

General Admiral

RUSSIA

Armoured cruiser
Completed: 1875-77.
Number in class: 2.
Displacement: 5,031 tons
Dimensions: Length (wl) 285.8ft (87.1m); beam 48.0ft (14.6m); draught 24.0ft (7.32m).
Propulsion: 1 shafts; Vertical Compound engine; 12 boilers; 4,470ihp; 12.3kt.
Armour: Wrought iron. Belt 6.0-5.0in (152-127mm); deck 1.0in (25mm)
Armament: 6 x 8.0in (203mm) (6 x 1); 2 x 6.0in (152mm); 4 x 3.4in (86mm); 8 x 1pdr revolvers.
Complement: 480.

History: These two ships, *General Admiral* and *Gerzog Edinburgski* were the first armoured cruisers to be built and created a strong impression among other modern navies. The 7.0ft (2.1m)-wide wrought iron armoured belt covered virtually the entire length of the ship and stretched to 5.0ft (1.5m) below the waterline, with a 1in (25mm) deck. There was also an armoured coaming around the engineroom hatch. As built, the main battery consisted of four 8.0in (203mm) guns mounted amidships at upper deck level, with a secondary battery of two 6.0in (152mm) and four 3.4in (86mm), but this was changed during their long careers. Two 15.0in (305mm) above-water torpedo tubes were added soon after commissioning and in 1889 *Gerzog Edinburgski* is recorded as having four 8.0in (203mm), five 6.0in (152mm), and six 4.0in 102mm).

They had a full ship rig, but unlike many contemporaries were not fitted

Admiral Nakhimov

RUSSIA

Armoured cruiser
Completed: 1888.
Number in class: 1.
Displacement: 8,524 tons.
Dimensions: Length (wl) 333.0ft (101.5m); beam 61.0ft (18.6m); draught 27.5ft (8.4m).
Propulsion: 2 shafts; Vertical Compound engines; 12 boilers; 9,000ihp; 17kt.
Armour: Compound. Belt 10.0-6.0in (254-152mm); barbettes 8.0- 3.0in (203-76mm); conning tower 6.0in (152mm).
Armament: 8 x 8.0in (203mm) (4 x 2); 10 x 6.0in (152mm); 4 x 3.4in (86mm); 6 x 3pdr revolver; 4 x 1pdr revolver; 3 x 15.0in (381mm) TT; 40 mines.
Complement: 570.

History: At some time in the early 1880s the Russian Navy managed to obtain copies of drawings of the French *Imperieuse* and British *Warspite* and used these as the basis for a new ship of their own, *Admiral Nakhimov*, which was laid down in 1884 and completed in 1888. The result was a handsome ship with four twin 8.0in (203mm) guns in four turrets, one each in "A" and "Y" positions, and one on each side on a sponson, amidships. The secondary armament comprised ten 6.0in (152mm) in casemates. She was originally rigged as a brig. *Nakhimov* was modernised in 1899, which included new boilers, the removal of the sailing rig to leave two, relatively short, military masts and changes to the secondary armament. *Nakhimov* was part of the Russian fleet at the Battle of Tsushima (27

***Above: General Admiral* had a service life from 1875 to 1938, a total of 63 years**

with a ram. They were both re-engined in the 1890s and were re-roled as training ships in the 1890s. In 1909 they were re-roled again, this time as minelayers, each carrying 600 mines, for which they were given new names: *General Admiral - Narova* and *Gerzog Edinburgski - Onega*. The latter was hulked in 1915, but *Narova* survived the revolution to become *25 Oktiabriya* and survived until 1938, a service life of sixty-three years.

May 1905) where she escaped serious damage during the main battle, but was torpedoed in the night engagement which followed. She was in a sinking condition, so her captain ordered the seacocks to be opened before surrendering.

The magnitude of the naval disaster at the Battle of Tsushima tends to overshadow the fact that the Imperial Russian Navy had a large warship design and building capability, and produced many good designs, of which *Admiral Nakhimov* was but one. In their day, many of the ships were highly regarded abroad and Russian naval architects were considered the equal of those in Western European countries.

***Below: Admiral Nakhimov,* following the removal of the original sailing rig**

Riurik

RUSSIA

Armoured cruiser
Completed: 1908.
Number in class: 1.
Displacement: 15,190 tons.
Dimensions: Length 529.0ft (161.2m); beam 75.0ft (22.9m); draught 26.0ft (7.92m).
Propulsion: 2 shafts; Vertical, Triple-Expansion engines; 28 boilers; 19,700ihp; 21.0kt.
Armour: Krupps. Belt 6.0-4.0in (152-102mm); turrets 8.0-7.3in (203-185mm); conning tower 8.0in (203mm).
Armament: 4 x 10.0in (254mm) (2 x 2); 8 x 8.0in (203mm); 20 x 4.7in; 4 x 3pdr; 2 x 18in (457mm) TT.
Complement: 899.

History: *Riurik* was a handsome and well-balanced ship, and generally acknowledged to be one of the finest armoured cruisers built for any navy. Her design was the outcome of an international competition, which was won by the British firm of Vickers at Barrow-in-Furness. This took place at the time of the Russo-Japanese war and numerous improvements were worked into the design to incorporate the lessons from that disastrous conflict, particularly in damage control and counter-flooding arrangements. She was completed by Vickers in 1908 and delivered to the Russian Navy in 1909. She was armed with four 10.0in (254mm) guns in two twin turrets, one noteworthy feature being the magazine flooding arrangements which were considerably advanced over contemporary British arrangements. The armoured belt

Pallada (Aurora)

RUSSIA

Protected cruiser
Completed: 1902-03.
Number in class: 3.
Displacement: 6,823 tons.
Dimensions: Length 425.6ft (126.7m); beam 55.0ft (16.8m); draught 20.8ft (6.4m).
Propulsion: 3 shafts; Vertical, Triple-Expansion engines; 24 boilers; 12,000ihp; 19.0kt.
Armament: 8 x 6.0in (152mm) (6 x 1); 24 x 11pdr; 8 x 1pdr; 3 x 15in 381mm) TT.
Complement: 571.

History: One of these ships, *Aurora*, is of major historical importance, since it remains fully preserved at St Petersburg, one of the very few authentic relics of the pre-dreadnought warship era. All three ships, *Pallada*, *Diana* and *Aurora*, were built in Russian yards and completed in 1902-03.

The main armament consisted of eight 6in (152mm) guns, five forward and three aft. The forward guns were positioned with one on the foredeck, and four on separate sponsons, two abreast the bridge, two abreast the forefunnel. Aft there was one gun on the quarterdeck and two on sponsons either side of the mainmast. The guns were in open mounts in *Pallada* and *Diana*, but with shields in *Aurora*.

Pallada was serving in the Far East on the outbreak of the Russo-Japanese War and was torpedoed on 9 February 1904 but not badly damaged. She was, however, sunk during the Japanese bombardment of Port Arthur (8 December 1904) but was later raised and repaired by the Japanese, being renamed *Tsugaru*. She was not one of the ships returned to Russia and was stricken

***Right:* A handsome design, *Riurik* was considered one of the finest cruisers of her day**

was fabricated from Krupp plate and was 6.0in (152mm) thick, 13.1ft (4.0m) deep. The main belt extended from the forward to the after 10.0in (254mm) gun barbettes, a distance of some 500ft (152.4m) and was then extended forward t the bow and aft to the sternpost by thinning plates, first of 4.0in (102mm) and then of 3.0in (76mm).

A plan to build two more ships to the same design in Russian yards was cancelled, as was a Vickers' plan to produce a new version powered by Parsons turbines, which had rapidly become essential for modern warships. *Riurik* served as the flagship of the Baltic Fleet in peacetime and had an active role in World War I, carrying out several minelaying operations, as well as taking part in a major engagement off Gotland island. She ran aground in February 1915 and was hit by a mine in November 1916, but was repaired on both occasions. She was placed in reserve in 1918 and broken up in 1922.

***Above: Aurora,* seen here in 1910, is still afloat in St Petersburg, Russia in 2001**

from the Japanese Navy in 1922. *Diana* served in the Baltic during the war and revolution, but was laid up in 1918 and sold for scrap in 1922. *Aurora's* guns fired the salvo which started the Revolution on 7 November 1917 and has held a very special place in Russian history ever since.

Admiral Nakhimov

RUSSIA (Soviet Union)

Cruiser
Completed: 1927-32.
Number in class: 2.
Displacement: 7,000 tons standard.
Dimensions: Length 535.5ft (163.2m); beam 51.5ft (15.7m); draught 18.3ft (5.6m).
Propulsion: 4 shafts; Brown-Curtis turbines; 14 boilers; 55,000shp; 29.5kt.
Armour: Belt 3.0in (76mm); deck 1.5in (38mm); conning tower 3.0in (76mm).
Armament: 15 x 5.1in (130mm) (15 x 1); 4 x 63mm AA; 4 x MG; 2 x 18.0in (457mm) TT; 100 mines.
Aircraft: 1.
Complement: 630.

History: Originally intended to consist of four ships, two were laid down in 1913 and two in 1914, but their completion was seriously effected by the Revolution. Two ships were never completed: the hull of the *Admiral Kornilov* was launched in 1922 to clear the ways and immediately broken up. The hull of the second, *Admiral Istomin*, lay incomplete at Nikolayev from 1914 to 1938, when it was finally broken up, still on the slipway. The other two were completed, but only after a long wait. *Admiral Nakhimov* was launched in 1915, *Admiral Lazarev* in 1916 and both were being fitted out when the Revolution took place, following which the port was over-run by the Germans in 1918. The Germans handed the ships over to the Allies, who then passed them on to the White Russians under General Wrangel, but both were eventually recaptured by the Red forces. The two ships were then given revolutionary names and work carried on, albeit slowly, with the first,

Kirov

RUSSIA (Soviet Union)

Cruiser
Completed: 1938-40.
Number in class: 2.
Displacement: 7,880 tons standard; 9,436 tons full load.
Dimensions: Length 626.7ft (191.0m); beam 57.9ft (17.7m); draught 23.8ft (7.2m).
Propulsion: 2 shafts; geared steam-turbines; 6 boilers; 113,000shp; 36kt (plus diesels for cruising).
Armour: Belt 2.0in (52mm); main deck 2.0in (52mm); turrets 3.0in (76mm); conning tower 6.0in (152mm).
Armament: 9 x 7.1in (180mm) (3 x 3); 6 x 3.9in (100mm); 6 x 45mm; 4 x 0.5in (12.7mm) MG; 6 x 21in (533mm) TT; 100 mines.
Aircraft: 2.
Complement: 734.

History: These were the first two major warships to be built following the Russian Revolution and were designed with the help of the Genoa-based Ansaldo company, which explains their resemblance to contemporary Italian cruisers. The design was approved in 1934 and the two ships, *Kirov* and *Voroshilov*, were completed in 1938 and 1940, respectively. There were some differences between the two, with *Voroshilov* having a greater displacement (9,950 tons at full load) and with ten 37mm AA in place of the six 45mm AA guns. During the war *Kirov* served in the Baltic and *Voroshilov* in the Black Sea, both being employed almost exclusively in the shore bombardment role. Both were slightly damaged by German air attacks but were quickly repaired, while *Voroshilov* was also damaged by a mine (November 1942). Both served well

Above: *Chervona Ukraina*, laid down in 1913, was completed in 1927, sunk in 1941

Chervona Ukraina (formerly *Admiral Nakhimov*) being completed in 1927. The second, *Krasni Kavkaz* (formerly *Admiral Lazarev*) was completed in 1932, but with a longer 556.1ft (169.5m) hull, two (as opposed to three) funnels, with the forecastle deck extended aft to the second funnel, and a lattice mainmast. The main armament was also completely recast, now consisting of 180mm (7.1in) guns in four single turrets. Both took part in the defence of Sevastopol, during which *Chervona Ukraina* was sunk by Stuka dive-bombers (13 November 1941). *Krasnyi Kavkaz* survived the war, was employed as a training ship form 1945 to 1958, and was sunk as a target in the SS-N-1 missile trials programme in 1960.

Above: *Voroshilov*, one of two Italian-designed but Soviet-built cruisers

into the Cold War, with *Voroshilov* being scrapped in the1960s and *Kirov* in the 1970s.

A second group of four, the Maxim Gorkiy-class (*Maxim Gorkiy, Molotov, Kaganovich, Kalinn*), were laid down in 1936 (two) and 1939 (two) and were virtual repeats of the Kirov-class. These were then followed by the Chapayev-class, laid down in 1938-40, was an enlarged version of the Kirov-class, lengthened in order to accommodate a fourth triple 7.1in (180mm) turret. Seven were laid down in 1938-40, of which five were completed in 1949-50, and these had relatively short operational careers, three being scrapped in the 1960s, while the other two were relegated to the training role.

Sverdlov

RUSSIA (Soviet Union)

Cruiser
Specifications for *Sverdlov,* as completed.
Completed: 1951-55.
Number in class: 14.
Displacement: 13,600 tons standard; 16,640 tons full load.
Dimensions: Length 689.0ft (210.0m); beam 72.0ft (22.0m); draught 22.6ft (6.9m).
Propulsion: 2 shafts; geared turbines; 6 boilers; 100,000shp; 32.5kt; 9,000nm at 18kt (plus diesels for cruising).
Armour: side 4.0in (100mm); bulkheads 4.75in (120mm); deck 2.0in (50mm); conning tower 6.0in (152mm).
Armament: 12 x 6.0in (152mm) (4 x 3); 12 x 3.9in (100mm); 32 x 37mm AA; 10 x 21in (533mm) TT.
Complement: 1,250.

History: The British suffered greatly during World War II from attacks on Atlantic convoys by *Scharnhorst, Gneisenau, Admiral Scheer* and other German surface raiders. Thus, the threat posed by these large, modern and powerful-looking ships was taken very seriously by NATO in the 1950s and '60s. Soviet post-war naval plans originally required thirty modern cruisers and it seems that the five Chapaevs (see previous entry) counted towards this figure, with twenty-five Sverdlovs to follow. Four of these were cancelled in 1953, so that twenty-one were laid down, but work on seven was halted in 1959, of which six were scrapped by 1962, while one, which had been virtually complete, was retained as a hulk. The fourteen actually completed resembled the Chapaev-

Kynda

RUSSIA (Soviet Union)

Missile cruiser (rocket cruisers)
Completed: 1962-65.
Number in class: 4.
Displacement: 4,400 tons standard; 5,600 tons full load.
Dimensions: Length 464.9ft (141.7m); beam 51.8ft (15.8m); draught 17.4ft (5.3m).
Propulsion: 2 shafts; geared steam turbines; 4 pressure-fired boilers; 100,000shp; 34kt; 7,000nm at 15kt.
Armament: 2 x launchers for SS-N-3 missiles (2 x 4); 1 x SA-N-1 (1 x 12); 4 x 76mm guns (2 x 2); 2 x RBU-6000 ASW RL; 6 x 21.0in (533mm) TT.
Complement: 375.

History: The Soviet Navy converted several existing ships to take missiles, but the Kynda-class was the first to be purpose built. The *Kynda* had a new, distinctive hull-form with a long forecastle, a low quarterdeck and a square, cut-away stern, a pattern followed in later missile cruisers. There was a modern block superstructure and two tower masts to carry the heavy antenna arrays for the air surveillance and missile guidance radars. There were two massive four-tube launchers for the SS-N-3 missiles, one forward, one aft, with one reload missile for each tube in magazines

***Above:* The last Russian gun-cruisers, the Sverdlovs were handsome, powerful ships**

class in appearance, but with the forecastle deck carried much further aft and large funnel caps; fewer than half were ever operational at any one time, the remainder being either in refit or in lightly-manned reserve.

One, *Ordzhonikidze*, was transferred to Indonesia in 1962, her arrival causing some initial alarm among South-East Asian navies, but she quickly became unserviceable. The remaining Soviet ships were repeatedly modified, with the torpedo tubes all being removed in the 1960s and new electronic sensors constantly added until the early 1970s. Several were converted to missile ships, while two (*Zhdanov* and *Admiral Senyavin*) were converted to command ships in 1970-72, with some armament being replaced by deckhouses for admirals and their staffs. Another four (*Oktybrskaya Revolutsiya, Admiral Ushakov, Aleksandr Suvarov* and *Mikhail Kutusov)* were given limited modernisations in the 1970s. The survivors were stricken in the late 1980s, the last to go being *Murmansk* in 1992.

housed in the superstructure. The ships operated in conjunction with land-based aircraft or submarines, which provided the target acquisition and mid-course and terminal guidance for the missiles. The design suffered from excessive topweight and thus poor stability, which led to a stop after the fourth ship had been built, although ten had originally been planned. Three were decommissioned in the early 1990s, but one (*Admiral Golovko*) remained in service in 2001, having been employed as flagship of the Black Sea fleet since 1995.

***Below:* The Kynda-class were the first purpose-built missile ships in the Soviet Navy**

Kresta I/II

RUSSIA (Soviet Union)

Missile cruiser (large ASW ships)
Specifications for Kresta I, as built.
Completed: Kresta I - 1967-69; Kresta II - 1969-77.
Number in class: Kresta I - 4; Kresta II - 10.
Displacement: 5,600 tons standard; 7,535 tons full load.
Dimensions: Length 521.5ft (159.0m); beam 55.1ft (16.8m); draught 17.4ft (5.3m).
Propulsion: 2 shafts; pressure-fired steam turbines; 4 boilers; 91,000shp; 32kt; 5,200nm at 18kt.
Armament: 2 x SS-N-14 launchers (8 missiles); 2 x SA-N-3; 2 x RBU-6000; 2 x RBU-1000; 4 x 57mm guns; 4 x AK-630 gatling; 10 x 21in (533mm) TT.
Aircraft: 1 helicopter.
Complement: 343.

History: The Kresta I-class of four ships (*Admiral Zozulya, Vitse-Admiral Drozd, Vladivostok, Sevastopol*) were originally to have had a primary mission of anti-ship operations, but this was changed in the "crash" ASW ship programme of the late 1960s, when the Soviet Navy began to concentrate on the threat posed by US Navy strategic submarines armed with Polaris (and later Poseidon) missiles. The Kresta-Is were designated "large ASW ships" although their armament and sensors were still primarily anti-surface.

The ten Kresta IIs were a major redesign with a greatly improved ASW capability. A Bull Nose sonar was mounted in the bow, resulting in a more sharply raked clipper bow, while the missile-guidance Hormone-B helicopter was replaced by the Hormone-A ASW version with a dipping sonar. The anti-

Kara

RUSSIA (Soviet Union)

Anti-submarine cruiser
Completed: 1971-79.
Number in class: 7.
Displacement: 6,700 tons standard; 8,565 tons full load.
Dimensions: Length 568.8ft (173.4m); beam 60.7ft (18.5m); draught 17.4ft (5.3m).
Propulsion: 2 shafts; COGAG; 4 M-5 gas-turbines; 120,000shp; 32kt; 6,500nm at 18kt.
Armament: 8 x launchers for SS-N-14 (2 x 4); 2 x SA-N-3 launchers; 2 x SA-N-4 launchers; 4 x 76mm guns; 4 x AK-630 gatling; 2 x RBU-6000 ASW rocket launchers; 2 x RBU-1000 ASW rocket launchers; 10 x 21.0in (533mm) TT.
Aircraft: 1 helicopter.
Complement: 380.

History: The Kara-class was a development of the Kresta II (see previous entry), but with gas-turbine propulsion, which resulted in a major redesign of the midships section. Thus, the gas-turbine uptakes were led up a very large, square funnel, and this, in turn, meant that the Headnet-C surveillance antenna had to be moved to a new position atop the bridge. The Kara-class also had a 50ft (15m) section added amidships, which enabled 76mm guns to replace the 57mm guns and two of the new SA-N-4 missile systems to be mounted in bins abreast the tower mast. A variable depth sonar (VDS) was installed at the stern beneath the flightdeck. Another significant change compared to the Kresta II was a major enlargement of the bridge, providing the much improved facilities required for Cold War ASW command-and-control. Once again, these handsome, purposeful-looking ships, with their multitude of sensors and weapons systems created a major impression in the West. All were stricken in the 1990s

ship SS-N-3 missiles were replaced by two SS-N-14 ASW missile launchers, and two of the new SA-N-3 launchers gave a much improved air defence capability. All four Kresta Is and ten Kresta IIs served until the early 1990s, when they were all stricken.

***Below:* Kresta I cruiser, *Vitse-Admiral Drozd,* on exercise in Caribbean waters**

***Right:* Kara-class cruisers were enlarged Kresta IIs, with gas-turbine propulsion**

Sovremenny

RUSSIA (Soviet Union)

Cruiser
Completed: 1980-97.
Number in class: 18.
Displacement: 6,200 tons standard; 7,800 tons full load.
Dimensions: Length 511.8ft (156.0m); beam 56.8ft (17.3m); draught 21.3ft (6.5m).
Propulsion: 2 shafts; geared steam turbines; 4 pressure-fired boilers; 100,000shp; 32kt; 10,500nm at 14kt.
Armament: 2 x SS-N-22 missile launchers (2 x 4); 2 x SA-N-7 missile launchers; 4 x 5.1in (130mm) DP guns (2 x 2); 4 x 30mm gatling; 2 x RBU-1000 ASW rocket launchers; 4 x 21in (533mm) TT.
Aircraft: 1 helicopter.
Complement: 350.

History: In 1980 the first of a new series of Soviet cruisers, known to the US and NATO navies as BAL-COM 2 (= BALtic COMbatant #2), ran trials in the Baltic. These trials were conducted without her main armament (although most of her radars were in place), but it was clear to naval experts that the ship's primary role was anti-surface warfare. The Sovremennys are, in fact, lineal successors to the Kresta-class, being of almost identical size and using the same pressure-fired steam propulsion system. One of the class's main missions was the support of amphibious landings for which it mounted four 5.1in (130mm) guns in two twin-gun, fully-automated turrets. The main, long-range weapon is the SS-N-22 anti-ship missile, with four launch tubes either side of the bridge superstructure, while the defensive armament comprised the

Udaloy I/II

RUSSIA (Soviet Union)

Cruiser
Specifications for Udaloy I, as built.
Completed: Udaloy I - 1980-94; Udaloy II - 1999.
Number in class: Udaloy I - 14; Udaloy II - 1.
Displacement: 6,200 tons standard; 7,900 tons full load.
Dimensions: Length 531.5ft (162.0m); beam 63.3ft (19.3m); draught 20.3ft (6.2m).
Propulsion: 2 shafts; COGAG; 4 gas-turbines; 120,000shp; 35kt; 10,500nm at 14kt.
Armament: 2 x launchers for SS-N-4 SSM/ASW; 8 x SA-N-9 SAM launchers; 2 x 100mm guns (2 x 1); 2 x RBU-6000 ASW rocket launchers; 8 x 21in (533mm) TT.
Aircraft: 2.
Complement: 300.

History: The Soviet Navy's Udaloy-class bore a remarkable resemblance in both size and concept to the US Navy's Spruance-class (q.v.). The ship, originally known to NATO as "BAL-COM 3" is optimised for the ASW mission, with no anti-ship systems and only a minimal short/medium range SAM system. The ASW armament includes two of the standard quadruple SS-N-14 launchers abreast the bridge, with two RBU-6000 rocket launchers on the hangar roof and two quadruple ASW torpedo tubes amidships. The Udaloys have a large hangar and flightdeck for two Kamov Ka-27 (Helix-A) ASW helicopters. There is a large low-frequency sonar in the bow (hence the dramatically curved clipper bow) and a low-frequency Horse Tail variable-depth sonar in the stern. Fourteen were completed, which were then split equally between the Northern and Pacific fleets, but by 2001 only seven remained in service and it is doubtful whether more than three are operational at any one time.

Above: **Powerful ships, the last two Sovremennys were sold to China in 2000/2001**

SA-N-7 SAM system, two pairs of ASW torpedo tubes, and two RBU-1000 close-in ASW rocket launchers. Unlike the *Kresta* II, these ships have one main radar tower carrying a large back-to-back unit.

The original plan was to build twenty-eight, of which a total of twenty was laid down, but one was hulked before completion. Of the nineteen completed, the last two were sold to China and delivered in 2000/2001. A proposal to sell one to Cuba was not pursued, and of the seventeen built for the Soviet Navy ten remained in service by 2001, the others having been cannibalised or scrapped.

A slightly modified version, Udaloy II, was designed for the KGB Border Guard, Maritime Division, and two were under construction in 1991. In the aftermath of the 1991 revolution, however, both were handed over to the navy, of which one was scrapped and the other completed as *Admiral Chabanenko*.

Below: **Udaloy cruiser, designed to a similar specification to US Navy Spruance-class**

Slava

RUSSIA (Soviet Union)

Cruiser
Completed: 1982-93.
Number in class: 4.
Displacement: 10,000 tons standard; 12,500 tons full load.
Dimensions: Length 613.5ft (187.0m); beam 68.2ft (20.8m); draught 24.6ft (7.5m)
Propulsion: 2 shafts; COGOG; boost - 4 M8KF gas-turbines, each 27,500shp cruise - 2 M70 gas-turbines, each 10,000shp; 32.5kt; 9,000nm at 15kt.
Armament: 16 x launchers for SS-N-12 SSM (16 x 1); 8 x SA-N-6 SAM launchers; 2 x SA-N-4 launchers; 2 x 5.1in (130mm) guns (1 x 2); 6 x 30mm gatling; 2 x RBU-6000 ASW rocket launchers; 10 x 21in (533mm) TT.
Aircraft: 1 helicopter.
Complement: 600.

History: These large and impressive ships were originally nicknamed BLK-COM-1 by NATO (= BLacK Sea COMbatant 1) and unconfirmed reports suggest that they were a simplified "fail-safe" alternative to the Kirov-class battlecruisers. The main battery consists of sixteen SS-N-12 anti-ship missiles in single tubes mounted in four sets of pairs either side of the forward superstructure, with the SA-N-6 vertical launch groups in the deck immediately abaft the funnel. There is a twin 5.1in (130mm) fully automated mount on the foredeck and the torpedo tubes are behind sliding doors in the hull below the hangar.

It was originally planned to build six, but with the end of the Cold War and the collapse of the Soviet Union this was reduced to three for the Russian Navy: *Moskva* (ex-*Slava*); *Marshal Ustinov* (ex-*Admiral Flota Lobov*); *Varyag* (ex-

---

Mendez Nunez

SPAIN

Light cruiser
Completed: 1924-25.
Number in class: 2.
Displacement: 4,650 tons standard.
Dimensions: Length 462.0ft (140.8m); beam 46.0ft (14.0m); draught 15.5ft (4.7m).
Propulsion: 4 shafts; Parsons geared turbines; 12 boilers; 45,000shp; 29kt; 5,000nm at 13kt.
Armour: Belt 3.0-1.25in (76-38mm); deck 1.0in (25mm); conning tower 6.0in (152mm).
Armament: 6 x 6in (152mm) (6 x 1); 4 x 3pdr AA; 4 x MG; 12 x 21in (533mm) TT.
Complement: 343.

History: These two ships were built to a design generally similar to that of the British Cambrian-class light cruisers, but shortages of building materials both during and immediately following World War I meant that having been laid down in 1917 they were not completed until 1924 - *Mendez Nunez* - and 1925 - *Blas de Lezo*. It was initially intended to build four, but two were cancelled in 1919. The propulsion system was mixed, with six coal-fired boilers and six oil-fired boilers. Main armament comprised six single 6in (152mm) guns, with one on the foredeck, one either side of the forward funnel, one on either beam atop the shelter deck and one on the quarterdeck.

Both ships were involved in a serious incident in 1932 when sailing off Cape Finisterre: due to a miscalculation both grounded on the Centollo Reef. *Mendez Nunez* was refloated and repaired, but when *Blas de Lezo* was hauled off, she flooded and sank (11 July 1932). *Mendez Nunez* was rebuilt as an anti-aircraft

Above: **Four of the impressive Slava-class were completed: Russia -3, Ukraine -1**

Chervona Ukraina). These ships have often been used for foreign visits by the Soviet/Russian Navy, where their large size and multiplicity of sensors and weapons always creates a favourable impression. In 2001 all three were nominally in service, but no more than one at a time is fully operational. After a great deal of discussion between the new Russian and Ukrainian authorities, mainly over costs, the fourth was eventually completed in 2000 for the Ukrainian Navy as *Ukrayina*.

cruiser in 1944-45, armed with eight 4.7in (120mm) guns, three forward and three aft in a triple-tier arrangement similar to the British Dido-class (q.v.), and the remaining two abreast the mainmast. There were also four twin 37mm and two quadruple 20mm mounts. The bridge structure was completely remodelled and the number of funnels reduced from three to two. She was stricken in 1963.

Below: **Spanish cruiser, *Mendez Nunez*, demonstrates her firepower in 1939**

Canarias

SPAIN

Cruiser
Completed: 1936.
Number in class: 2.
Displacement: 10,113 tons standard; 13,070 tons full load.
Dimensions: Length 635.8ft (193.6m); beam 64.0ft (19.5m); draught 17.3ft (5.3m).
Propulsion: 4 shafts; Parsons geared turbines; 8 boilers; 90,000shp; 33kt; 8,700nm at 15kt.
Armour: Belt 2.0in (56mm); magazine sides 4.5in (114mm); decks 1.5-1.0in (38-25mm); conning tower 1.0in (25mm).
Armament: 8 x 8.0in (203mm) (4 x 2); 8 x 4.7in (120mm) AA; 8 x 40mm AA; 4 x 12,.5mm AAMG; 12 x 21in (533mm) TT.
Complement: 780.

History: The design of these two ships, *Baleares* and *Canarias*, was based on that of the British Kent-class cruiser (q.v.), which the British naval architect reworked to Spanish requirements. Thus, they had the same hull as the Kents and retained the bulges, but by narrowing the beam, making the hull slightly longer and increasing the power by 10,000shp they could attain 33kt. It was originally intended to install two funnels, but whilst building was in process this was altered to one very long and instantly recognisable funnel, although why this should have been thought necessary has never been explained. *Canarias* was almost completed when the Civil War broke out and she was quickly made combat worthy, although it then took several years to get everything straightened out. *Baleares* was slightly behind *Canarias* and was

Tre Kronor

SWEDEN

Cruiser
Specifications for *Tre Kronor*, as built.
Completed: 1944-45.
Number in class: 2.
Displacement: 8,200 tons standard; 9,200 tons full load.
Dimensions: Length 597.1ft (182.0m); beam 54.8ft (6.7m); draught 21.3ft (6.5m).
Propulsion: 2 shafts; de Laval geared steam turbines; 4 boilers; 90,000shp; 33kt.
Armour: Belt (25-20mm), (80-70mm) over vitals; decks (30mm); turrets (125-50mm); conning tower (25-20mm).
Armament: 7 x 6.0in (152mm) (1 x 3; 2 x 2); 27 x 40mm AA; 6 x 21in (533mm) TT; 160 mines.
Complement: 610.

History: These two ships, *Tre Kronor* and *Göta Lejon*, were laid down in 1943 and completed in 1947. The main armament was slightly unusual, comprising seven 6in (152mm) Bofors guns, with one triple turret in "A" position, and two twin turrets in "X" and "Y" positions. These were fully automatic and had a maximum elevation of 70deg, enabling them to be used in the anti-aircraft role. *Göta Lejon* was modernised twice, in 1950-52 and 1957-58, the latter including a new bridge superstructure, revised radars and a new secondary armament. *Tre Kronor* had a refit in the early 1950s, but a major rebuild on the same lines as her sister was cancelled for financial reasons, and because the Swedish Navy had decided to concentrate on small warships. *Tre Kronor* was sold to became a pontoon bridge in 1964, but *Göta Lejon* was sold to Chile in 1971, where she served as *Latorre* until being stricken in 1984.

***Above:* Canarias' huge single funnel was replaced by two funnels in the 1950s**

also rushed to completion, although she actually served for a while without "Y" turret, which was eventually installed in mid-1937. Both ships played a very active role in the naval Civil War on the Nationalist side and sank numerous Republican warships and merchant ships. *Baleares* was, however, sunk by three Republican destroyers when a torpedo hit her forward magazine (6 March 1938). *Canarias* was steadily improved over the years and in a major refit in the early 1950s she reverted to the originally-planned two funnel layout, much improving her appearance. She was stricken in December 1975.

***Above:* Sweden's Tre Kronor-class were among the most handsome cruisers ever built**

Arethusa

UNITED KINGDOM

Frigate (fourth Rate)
Specifications for *Arethusa*, as converted to steam.
Converted: 1860-62.
Number in class: 4.
Displacement: 3,708 tons.
Dimensions: Length 252.3ft (76.9m); beam 52.7ft (16.3m); draught 22.3ft (6.8m).
Propulsion: 1 shaft; John Penn Horizontal Simple Expansion engine; 3,165ihp; 11.7kt.
Armament: 10 x 8in (203mm); 40 x 32pdr muzzle-load; all muzzle-loading, smooth-bore.
Complement: 525.

History: These four ships, *Arethusa*, *Constance*, *Octavia* and *Sutlej*, were all built by the Pembroke Naval Dockyard as fourth-rate sailing frigates, being launched between 1846 and 1855. They were then all lengthened by some 70.0ft (21.3m) and converted to steam propulsion between 1860 and 1862, being redesignated steam frigates, approximately equivalent to latter day cruisers. In an interesting experiment, they were given different types of engine to see how they compared: *Arethusa* - horizontal simple expansion; *Octavia* and *Sutlej* - return connecting-rod type; and *Constance* - compound. Once in service *Arethusa*, *Constance* and *Sutlej* were set to race from Plymouth Sound to Madeira, which *Constance* won, covering the greatest distance with the most economical consumption of coal. But although the

Inconstant

UNITED KINGDOM

Iron frigate
Specifications for *Inconstant*, as built.
Completed:1869-76.
Number in class: 3.
Displacement: 5,780 tons.
Dimensions: Length 337.3ft (102.8m); beam 50.3ft (15.3m); draught 25.5ft (7.8m).
Propulsion: 1 shaft; John Penn Horizontal Simple-Expansion engine; 11 boilers; 7,360ihp; 16.2kt.
Armament: 10 x 9.0in (mm); 6 x 7.0in; all muzzle-loading rifled guns.
Complement: 600.

History: *Inconstant* and her two sisters, *Raleigh* and *Shah*, were designed and built as a direct response to the United States' Wampanoag-class and when she ran trials *Inconstant* proved herself to be the fastest warship afloat. The ships had an iron hull which was completely clad in a double layer of 3in (76mm) timber, and all three were coppered. The engines were of greater size and power than in any other existing cruiser and provided an unprecedented speed, *Inconstant* logging 15.5kt for 24 hours. All three had telescopic funnels and hoisting screws, and were ship-rigged with a fixed bowsprit. The main broadside battery consisted of ten 9in (229mm) guns while the 7in (178mm) guns were mounted on the upper deck, with two as chase guns firing through forward embrasures. *Raleigh* was sold in 1905 and *Shah* in 1919, but *Inconstant* lasted until 1956, when she was broken up.

victory of the compound engine was clearly demonstrated, it was judged that the complexities and unreliability of such engines were beyond the capabilities of the engineroom staffs of the day.

***Below: Constance*, apart from the funnel, the picture of a traditional sailing frigate**

***Above:* The Inconstant-class (this is *Shah*) had a speed of 16.5kt - very fast for the day**

Volage

UNITED KINGDOM

Iron screw corvette
Specifications for *Active*, as built.
Completed: 1870-75.
Number in class: 3.
Displacement: 3,080 tons.
Dimensions: Length 270.0ft (82.3m); beam 40.0ft (12.8m); draught 22.0ft (6.7m).
Propulsion: 1 shaft; Humphreys & Tennant Horizontal Simple Expansion engine; 5 boilers; 4,130ihp; 15.0kt.
Armament: 6 x 7.0in (178mm); 4 x 64pdr; all muzzle-loading, rifled.
Complement: 340.

History: After a number of large frigate designs the Royal Navy changed its policy for cruisers and produced a series of rather smaller ships, now designated corvettes. Among the first of these was this three-strong class, consisting of *Active* and *Volage*, which were virtually identical and the later *Rover*, which incorporated a number of improvements. One of the main requirements was for speed which was achieved by a mixture of greater power and a length:beam ratio appreciably greater than in any previous ships. Another requirement was for manoeuvrability, which was achieved by refining the ends to enable the rudder to have maximum effect on the water. The result was a fast manoeuvrable ship, as requested, but which pitched and rolled to make them difficult gun platforms, which was partially remedied by fitting large bilge-keels. They were ship-rigged.

Rover followed some five years later and incorporated lessons learnt with

Cressy

UNITED KINGDOM

First-class armoured cruiser
Completed: 1901-04.
Number in class: 6.
Displacement: 12,000 tons load.
Dimensions: Length 472.0ft (143.9m); beam 64.5ft (21.2m); draught 26.0ft (7.9m).
Propulsion: 2 shafts; 4-cylinder Triple-Expansion engines; 30 boilers; 21,000ihp; 21kt.
Armour: Krupp. Belt 6.0-2.0in (152-56mm); decks 3.0-1.0in (76-25mm); casemates 5.0in (127mm); turrets 6.0in (152mm); conning tower 12.0in (305mm).
Armament: 2 x 9.2in (234mm); 12 x 6.0in (152mm); 12 x 12pdr; 3 x 3pdr; 2 x 18in (457mm) TT.
Complement: 760.

History: Three of this class were to achieve an unfortunate degree of notoriety, which ensures their place in any naval history. The class started innocuously enough as the latest in a long series of armoured cruisers which were required to impose the *Pax Britannica* on the world's oceans. They were enlarged versions of the previous Diadem-class, but with much improved armoured protection using hard-faced Krupp steel and more powerful weapons. The main armament included two 9.2in (234mm) guns in single turrets, which were hydraulically-operated and could be reloaded at any angle of elevation or training.

They served in the Channel and West Indies fleets in peacetime and in August 1914 all except *Sutlej* were part of Cruiser Force-C, responsible for patrols in the southern North Sea. On 22 September 1914 they were on patrol

***Above: Volage* is seen here with her retractable funnel in the stowed position**

the first two. Thus, she had a straight stem (as opposed to a clipper bow), more powerful compound engines, ten boilers, two (as opposed to one) funnels, and revised lines aft. *Rover* was stricken in 1893, while her two sisters survived until 1904 (*Volage*) and 1906 (*Active*).

Above:* Three Cressys were sunk in a matter of minutes on 22 September 1914 by *U-9

and utterly oblivious to the threat posed by submarines when their course took them across the path of *U-9*, which promptly torpedoed *Aboukir*; she sank very quickly, leaving many survivors in the water. The other British ships, not realising what had caused the disaster, milled about trying to rescue their comrades, presenting ideal targets to *U-9*, which then sank first *Cressy* and then *Hogue*. It was a major catastrophe, involving the loss of well over a thousand men and three relatively modern cruisers, and an unprecedented victory by a submarine over surface warships.

Drake

UNITED KINGDOM

Armoured cruisers (first-class)
Completed: 1902-03.
Number in class: 4.
Displacement: 14,150tons.
Dimensions: Length 533.5ft (162.6m); beam 71.3ft (21.7m); draught 26.0ft (7.9m).
Propulsion: 2 shafts; 4-cylinder Triple-Expansion engines; 43 boilers; 30,000ihp; 23kt.
Armour: Belt 6.0-2.0in (152-51mm); decks 2.5-1.0in (75-25mm); barbettes 60in (152); turrets 60in (152mm) conning tower 12.0in (305mm).
Armament: 2x 9.2in (234mm) (2 x 1); 16 x 6in (152mm); 14 x 12pdr; 3 x 3pdr; 2 x 18in (457mm) TT.
Complement: 900.

History: The Drake-class continued the steady increase in the size of British first-class cruisers, being essentially an enlarged version of the Cressy-class (see previous entry), with thicker and redistributed armour to give greater protection, and an increase of four 6in (152mm) guns. They also had an additional thirteen boilers, giving them a maximum speed of 23kt, which was very fast for the day, but their greatest achievement lay in their steaming ability, with all four being capable of consistently running for long periods at high speed.

There were four ships, *Good Hope*, completed in 1902, and *Drake, King Alfred* and *Leviathan*, all completed in 1904. Up to the outbreak of war, two were usually employed as cruiser squadron flagships in the Far East or Mediterranean, while the other two were either in refit or operating in home waters.

Warrior

UNITED KINGDOM

Armoured cruiser (first-class)
Completed: 1906-07.
Number in class: 4.
Displacement: 13,550 tons load.
Dimensions: Length 505.3ft (154.0m); beam 73.5ft (22.4m); draught 25.0ft (7.6m).
Propulsion: 2 shafts; Triple Expansion engines; 19 boilers; 23,000ihp; 23kt.
Armour: Belt 6.0-3.0in (152-76mm); barbettes 6in (76mm); turrets 7.5-4.5in (190-114mm); decks 1.5-0.8in (38-20mm); conning tower 10.0in (254mm).
Armament: 6 x 9.2in (234mm) (6 x 1); 4 x 7.5in (191mm); 26 x 3pdr; 3 x 18in (457mm) TT.
Complement: 712.

History: These four ships, *Achilles, Cochrane, Natal* and *Warrior*, were a follow-on from the two-ship Duke of Edinburgh-class, completed in 1906, but with some important modifications. The main armament was the same, comprising six single 9.2in (234mm) turrets, one in "A" position, one in "Y" position and two on either beam, one pair abreast the forefunnel and the other pair just forward of the mainmast. The ten 6in (152mm) of the *Duke of Edinburgh* were, however, omitted in favour of four 7.5in (191mm) in single turrets amidships and with the same protection as the 9.2in (234mm) guns. With other measures, this resulted in greater topweight, which lowered the centre of stability, as a result of which they were very steady ships and excellent seaboats, making them very popular in service.

All served with the Grand Fleet during the war. *Natal* was lying at Cromarty when she was totally destroyed by an internal explosion, one of several in the

***Above: Good Hope* was lost with all hands at the Battle of Coronel in 1914**

Two were sunk during the war. *Good Hope* was Admiral Cradock's flagship during the disastrous Battle of Coronel (1 November 1914) where the British squadron was virtually wiped-out. Towards evening, Good Hope suffered a catastrophic magazine explosion and then sank; there were no survivors. Second loss was *Drake*, which was torpedoed by U-79 on 2 October 1917. The other two survived, but were sold for scrap in 192014 March 1915.

***Above: Achilles* was the only ship of the Warrior-class to survive World War I**

British fleet due to faulty cordite, with the loss of 404 lives (31 December 1915). *Achilles* was in refit at the time of Jutland, but both *Cochrane* and *Warrior* both took part in the battle (31 May 1916), which the former survived. *Warrior*, however, was badly damaged in the opening engagement and foundered next day while under tow (1 June 1916). The sole survivor, *Achilles*, was sold in 1921.

Leander

UNITED KINGDOM

Cruiser (second-class)
Completed: 1885-87.
Number in class: 4.
Displacement: 4,300 tons load.
Dimensions: Length 315.0ft (96.0m); beam 46.0ft (14.0m); draught 20.5ft (6.3m).
Propulsion: 2 shafts; Horizontal, Direct-Acting, Compound engines; 12 boilers; 5,500ihp; 16.5kt; 11,000nm at 10kt.
Armour: Deck 1.5in (38mm); gunshields 1.5in (38mm).
Armament: 10 x 6.0in (152mm) breech-loading, rifled; 16 x MG; 4 x TT.
Complement: 278.

History: *Iris* and *Mercury*, completed in 1879, were the Royal Navy's first warships to be built of steel and were originally given the somewhat imprecise description of "despatch vessels," but this was later changed to "second-class cruiser." The Leander-class - *Amphion*, *Arethusa*, *Leander* and *Phaeton* - were repeats, but with some modifications, including revised protection and main armament, and a vertical as opposed to curved stem. These new ships also had a rather surprising secondary armament, consisting of no less than sixteen machine guns - two Gatlings, four Gardners and ten Nordenfelds - which suggests an anticipated requirement to deal with attacks by small boats and to repel large numbers of boarders, although where these might have been encountered is not clear. Following trials the funnels were raised by 6.0ft (1.8m) which then enabled all four to exceed the design speed, while the efficient engines and large coal bunkers gave them a range of 11,000nm at 10kt, both

Archer

UNITED KINGDOM

Cruiser (third-class)
Completed: 1888-91.
Number in class: 8.
Displacement: 1,770 tons load; 1,950 tons full load.
Dimensions: Length 240.0ft (68.6m); beam 36.0ft (11.0m); draught 14.5ft (4.4m).
Propulsion: 2 shafts; 2 cylinder Horizontal, Direct-Acting, Compound engines; 4 boilers; 2,500ihp; 15kt.
Armour: Deck 0.4in (9.5mm); gunshields 1.0in (25mm).
Armament: 6 x 6.0in (152mm) breech-loading rifles; 8 x 3pdr; 2 x MG; 3 x 14in (356mm) TT.
Complement: 176.

History: In 1884 the Royal Navy laid down two ships, *Fearless* and *Scout*, officially described as "torpedo cruisers," whose purpose was to carry out torpedo attacks on the enemy fleet on the high seas, and to protect the British fleet from similar attacks by enemy torpedo boats. The requirement to operate on the high seas meant that they needed to be larger than the torpedo boats of the time, but they, themselves, turned out to be bad seaboats, as a result of which they were soon relegated to other duties, such as scouting for the fleet and trade protection and were reclassified as "3rd class cruisers." The Archer-class were based on the Scout-class, but larger and better armed, and although described as "torpedo cruisers" whilst building they were reclassified as "3rd class cruisers" shortly after commissioning. *Serpent* was wrecked in November 1890 and all the remainder were sold in 1905-06.

***Above: Leander*, as built; these large ships had a somewhat imprecise mission**

very respectable figure for the era. As built, they were barque rigged, but the yards were removed in the late 1890s.

Amphion and *Arethusa* were stricken in 1906 and 1905, respectively, while *Leander* became a depot ship in 1904 and was stricken in 1920. *Phaeton*, however, had a somewhat odd career, being sold in 1913 to become the civilian training ship *Indefatigable*, only to be repurchased by the Royal Navy in 1941, with which she served as the training ship *Carrick II* until sold for scrap in 1947.

***Above: Brisk*, an Archer-class "torpedo cruiser" later reclassified as a "3rd class cruiser"**

Gem

UNITED KINGDOM

Cruiser (third-class)
Completed: 1904-05.
Number in class: 4.
Displacement: 3.000 tons load.
Dimensions: Length 373.8ft (113.9m); beam 40.0ft (12.2m); draught 14.5ft (4.4m).
Propulsion: 2 shafts; 4 cylinder Triple Expansion; 10 boilers; 9,800ihp; 21.8kt.
Armour: Deck 2.0-0.8in (51-20mm); gunshields 1.0 (25mm); conning tower 3.0in (76mm).
Armament: 12 x 4.0in (102mm) (12 x 1); 8 x 3pdr; 4 x MG; 2 x 18.0in (457mm) TT.
Complement: 296.

History: This was the last class to be classified as third-class cruisers and consisted of four ships: *Amethyst*, *Diamond*, *Sapphire* and *Topaz*. As so often happens, the preceding designs had become better armed and faster, resulting in larger ships, which were difficult to distinguish from other types of cruiser. Main armament comprised twelve 4.0in (102mm) guns, all in single mounts, with two in "A" and "Y" positions and the remainder five per side equally spaced between the fore- and mainmasts.

Three of the class were powered by triple-expansion engines, but *Amethyst*, the last to be completed, was the first ship larger than a torpedo-boat destroyer to be powered by Parsons turbines in order that the two forms of propulsion could be fairly compared. The trials demonstrated that *Amethyst* was faster than her sisters (23.4kt compared to 21.8kt), more economical at high power (3,000nm compared to 2,000nm at 20kt), and also proved to be

Bristol/Weymouth

UNITED KINGDOM

Light cruisers
Specifications for *Bristol*, as built.
Completed: Bristol - 1910, Weymouth - 1911-12.
Number in class: Bristol - 5, Weymouth - 4.
Displacement: 4,800 tons standard; 5,300 tons full load.
Dimensions: Length 453.0ft (138.1m); beam 47.0ft (14.3m); draught 15.5ft (4.7m).
Propulsion: 4 shafts; Parsons turbines; 12 boilers; 22,000shp; 25kt; 5,000nm at 16kt.
Armour: Deck 2.0-0.8in (51-20mm);
Armament: 2 x 6in (152mm) (2 x 1); 10 x 4in (102mm); 4 x 3pdr; 2 x 18in (457mm) TT.
Complement: 480.

History: The Royal Navy suffered from some muddled thinking over cruisers in the first decade of the 20th century, with the larger cruisers becoming virtually small battleships, while the traditional cruiser role was being performed (not very well) by larger destroyers. The Admiralty therefore decided to build the Bristol-class of five ships (*Bristol*, *Glasgow*, *Gloucester*, *Liverpool* and *Newcastle*), all completed in 1910, which, whilst good in many respects, proved to be lively gun platforms and overcrowded, as well having an unsuitable mixed armament. This led to the "Improved Bristol-class" (Weymouth-class), which had a uniform main battery of eight 6in (152mm) and a greatly extended forecastle, with a bulwark to protect the waist guns. There were four ships, *Dartmouth*, *Falmouth*, *Weymouth* and *Yarmouth*, which proved to be robust and popular in service, and led the way to even more successful designs.

Above: **Sapphire, a Gem-class 3rd-class cruiser, here wearing the flag of a rear-admiral**

much more reliable. At the start of World War I *Diamond*, *Sapphire* and *Topaz* served as command ships for senior officers of destroyer flotillas. All later moved to the Mediterranean and Far Eastern waters, and *Diamond* was employed for a time as a transport for six CMBs (coastal motor boats). All were scrapped in 1920-21.

Above: Weymouth, **lead ship of the "Improved Bristol-class" seen here in 1916**

All nine ships had a very busy war, spending most of their time in the South Atlantic, Pacific and Indian Oceans, where they chased a variety of German warships, raiders and merchant ships with considerable success. The exception was *Falmouth*, which operated in the North Sea and was the only one to be lost, being torpedoed and damaged by *U-66* on 19 August 1916, but was then finished off by a second torpedo from *U-52*. The *Bristols* were scrapped in 1921-27, followed by the Weymouths in 1928-30.

Chatham/Birmingham UNITED KINGDOM

Light cruisers
Specifications for *Chatham*, as built.
Completed: Chatham - 1912-16; Birmingham - 1914-22.
Number in class: Chatham - 6; Birmingham - 4.
Displacement: 5,400 tons standard; 6,000 tons full load.
Dimensions: Length 458.0ft (139.6m); beam 49.0ft (14.9m); draught 16.0ft (4.9m).
Propulsion: 4 shafts; Parsons turbines; 12 boilers; 25,000shp; 25.5kt; 4,500nm at 16.0kt.
Armour: Belt 2.0in (50mm), deck 1.5-0.4in (40-15mm); conning tower 4.0in (102mm).
Armament: 8 x 6.0in (152mm) (6 x 1); 4 x 3pdr; 2 x 21.0in (533mm) TT.
Complement: 475.

History: The Chatham-class were improved versions of the Weymouth-class, the major visual change being an extension of the forecastle aft until it was level with the mainmast and a graceful, clipper bow, while measures were also taken to reduce the rolling and thus improve shooting. Weight-saving measures also enabled additional armour to be worked in to protect the waterline. In addition, the new type of guns in the Weymouth-class had proved unpopular in service and these were replaced by an older, lighter and more accurate model. Three Chatham-class (*Chatham*, *Dublin* and *Southampton*) were built for the Royal Navy, while another three were built for the newly-created Royal Australian Navy. Of these, two (*Sydney* and *Melbourne*) were built in the UK, while the third, *Brisbane*, was the first major warship to be built in Australia.

Arethusa/Caroline/Calliope UNITED KINGDOM

Light cruisers
Specifications for *Arethusa*, as built.
Completed: Arethusa - 1914-15; Caroline - 1914-15; Calliope - 1915.
Number in class: Arethusa - 8; Caroline - 6; Calliope - 2.
Displacement: 3,750 tons load; 4,400 tons full load.
Dimensions: Length 436.0ft (132.9m); beam 39.0ft (11.9m); draught 13.4ft (4.1m).
Propulsion: 4 shafts; Parsons turbines; 8 boilers; 40,000shp; 28.5kt.
Armour: Belt 3.0-1.0in (76-25mm); deck 1.0in (25mm).
Armament: 2 x 6.0in (152mm) (2 x 1); 6 x 4.0in (102mm); 1 x 3pdr AA; 4 x 21in (533mm) TT.
Complement: 276.

History: The concept of employing light cruisers (also known as "scouts") as flotilla leaders and for immediate support for destroyers depended upon those cruisers being able to keep up with their charges. By 1911 it was clear that not only was this no longer possible but that the gap would grow wider with new destroyer types about to enter service. As a result a new class of light cruisers was ordered, with a maximum speed of 28.5kt and the new ships entered service in 1914-15 as the Arethusa-class. The armament consisted of two 6in (152mm) and six 4in (102mm) which seems odd, since the main justification for the *Dreadnought*, which had been launched only six years previously, was that it was

The Birmingham-class was a virtual repeat of the Chatham-class, the only differences being an additional 6in (152mm) gun and slightly greater flare in the bows. Three (*Birmingham, Lowestoft, Nottingham*) were built for the Royal Navy and one (*Adelaide*) was built in Australia for the RAN, not being completed until 1922.

All except *Adelaide* served throughout World War I, the only loss being *Nottingham*, which was hit by three torpedoes from *U-52* on 19 August 1916 and sank with the loss of 38 lives. *Sydney* took part in the famous action against the German cruiser *Emden*, which was sunk on 9 November 1914. All surviving ships were scrapped in 1926-36, except for the much newer *Adelaide*, which was scrapped in 1949.

***Right: Sydney*, one of four Chatham/ Birmingham-class cruisers in the Australian Navy**

***Above: Champion* of the Calliope-class, one of a successful pre-war series of cruisers**

unwise to mix calibres because of complications over splash-spotting, different shells in the logistic chain and so on. This problem was made worse in these ships because the 4in (102mm) was a new type which proved to be unreliable.

The Caroline-class consisted of six ships to a modified design, which was10ft (3.0m) linger and with 2.5ft (0.8m) greater beam, while the armament was rearranged, with two 4in (102mm) on the foredeck and both 6in (152mm) aft. This was altered during the war, the two foredeck guns being replaced by a single 6in (152mm) in 1916-17, with a fourth 6in (152mm) being mounted abaft the funnels. The last two were fitted with two different versions of the newly-developed Parsons geared turbines. Known as the Calliope-class, they had only two funnels compared to three in the previous two classes.

Hawkins

UNITED KINGDOM

Cruiser
Completed: 1919-25.
Number in class: 4.
Displacement: 9,750 tons standard; 12,190 tons full load.
Dimensions: Length 605.0ft (184.4m); beam 65.0ft (19.8m); draught 19.3ft (5.9m).
Propulsion: 4 shafts; Parsons geared turbines; 12 boilers; 60,000shp; 30.0kt; 5,400nm at 14kt.
Armour: Belt 3.0-1.5in (76-40mm); deck 1.3in (40mm); conning tower 3.0in (76mm).
Armament: 7 x 7.5in (190mm) (7 x 1); 6 x 12pdr (76mm); 4 x 3in (76mm); 4 x 3pdr (47mm); 6 x 21in (533mm) TT.
Complement: 712.

History: In 1914-15 the German cruisers and armed raiders in distant waters caused problems out of proportion to their small numbers and in 1915 the Royal Navy stated a requirement for a new class of cruiser, well armed and with good endurance, able to undertake lengthy independent patrols in distant waters to deal with such problems. After some consideration, the unusual armament of 7.5in (190mm) guns was chosen, which had previously been used only in the 1904 Devonshire-class; this gave excellent range (22,000yd [20,117m]), although the 200lb (91kg) shell had to be hand loaded. The machinery was originally intended to be mixed coal- and oil-fired, since oil was still not widely available in distant oceans, but this was changed to oil only in some, while under construction, the others being converted later. Four ships were built - *Effingham,*

Kent/London/Norfolk

UNITED KINGDOM

Heavy cruisers
Completed: Kent - 1928; London - 1929; Norfolk - 1930.
Number in class: Kent - 7; London - 4; Norfolk - 2.
Specifications for *Kent*, as built.
Displacement: 9,750 tons standard; 13,400 tons full load.
Dimensions: Length 630.0ft (192.0m); beam 68.3ft (20.8m); draught 20.5ft (6.3m)
Propulsion: 4 shafts; Parsons geared turbines; 8 boilers; 80,000shp; 31.5kt; 9,400nm at 12kt.
Armour: Box around ammunition spaces 4.0-1.0in (102-25mm); turrets 1.0in (25mm).
Armament: 8 x 8.0in (203mm) (4 x 2); 4 x 4.0in (102mm); 4 x 3pdr; 4 x 2pdr pompom; 8 x 21.0in (533mm) TT.
Aircraft: 1.
Complement: 685.

History: These thirteen ships, all completed in 1928-30, were the British response to the Washington Naval Treaty, with a 10,000 ton displacement and guns of no more than 8in (203mm) calibre. Known as "Treaty cruisers" (and also as the "County-class) all three groups were essentially to the same design, their appearance being unmistakable, with a high freeboard, flush deck and three, slightly raked funnels. Main armament was the newly-designed 8.0in (203mm) gun disposed in four twin turrets, which gave some trouble for several years, although this had been resolved by 1939.

The first seven ships, all completed in 1928, comprised two for the Royal Australian Navy (*Australia, Canberra*) and five for the Royal Navy (*Berwick, Cornwall, Cumberland, Kent, Suffolk*). The second group of four (*Devonshire,*

Above: Hawkins **was designed to deal with commerce raiders in distant waters**

Frobisher, Hawkins and *Raleigh* - a planned fifth, which would have been named *Cavendish,* was completed as an aircraft carrier and renamed *Vindictive.* When they appeared in 1918, these ships caused quite a stir in naval circles since they outclassed all existing cruiser designs in every other navy.

Effingham underwent a substantial refit in the late 1930s, which included replacing the 7.5in guns with eight 6in (152mm) guns, three in "A," "B," and "C" positions forward, two amidships, one on either beam, and three in "X," "Y" and "Z" positions aft. In addition, the engine uptakes were trunked into one very large funnel.

Unusually, two of the class were wrecked; *Raleigh* in Canadian waters in 1922 and *Effingham* off the Norwegian coast in 1940.

Above: **The County-class was the British reply to the "Treaty cruiser" requirement**

London, Shropshire, Sussex), all for the RN and completed in 1929, were virtually identical except that they did not have bulges, reducing the beam by 2.3ft (0.7m) and increasing speed by 0.8kt. The final two (*Dorsetshire, Norfolk*) differed only in internal improvements to the turrets and shell supply systems. All ships were updated in refits, but *London* was virtually rebuilt in 1938-41, which involved a much more substantial bridge structure, similar to that in the Fiji-class, and a reduction of one funnel, although not visually apparent was that the greatly increased weight overstressed the hull, which had to be strengthened.

There were three war losses. *Cornwall* and *Dorsetshire* were sunk by Japanese carrier-based bombers on 5 May 1942, while *Canberra* was sunk by shellfire from Japanese warships (9 August 1942).

York/Exeter

UNITED KINGDOM

Cruisers
Specifications for *York*, as launched.
Completed: York - 1930; Exeter - 1931.
Number in class: York - 1; Exeter - 1.
Displacement: 8,250 tons standard; 10,350 tons full load.
Dimensions: Length 540.0ft (175.3m); beam 57.0ft (17.4m); draught 20.3ft (6.2m).
Propulsion: 4 shafts; Parsons geared turbines; 8 boilers; 80,000shp; 32.3kt; 10,000nm at 14kt.
Armour: Side 3.0in (76mm); box protection to ammunition spaces 4.0-1.0in (102-25mm); turrets 1.0in (25mm).
Armament: 6 x 8.0in (203mm) (3 x 2); 4 x 4.0in (102mm); 2 x 2pdr pompom; 6 x 21in (533mm) TT.
Complement: 623.

History: The County-class cruiser programme proved a very major expense at a time of national austerity and great pressure on the defence budget, forcing the Admiralty to seek a cheaper alternative, termed a "Class B cruiser." The result was *York* which was, in essence, a scaled-down Norfolk, armed with six 8in (203mm) guns, but the same turrets and ammunition supply system. She was followed by *Exeter*, which was almost identical, but with upright funnels and a 12.0in (305mm) increase in beam. *York* was given one aircraft and a catapult in 1931, while *Exeter* was fitted with facilities for two aircraft in 1932.

York was lying in Suda Bay when she was hit by an Italian explosive motor-boat (MTM) operated by 10MAS (26 March 1941), forcing her to be beached

Leander/Perth

UNITED KINGDOM

Light cruisers
Specifications for *Leander*, as built.
Completed: Leander - 1933-35, Perth 1935-36.
Number in class: Leander - 5, Perth - 3.
Displacement: 6,985 tons standard; 9.000 tons full load.
Dimensions: Length 554.5ft (169.0m); beam 55.2ft (16.8m); draught 19.0ft (6.0m).
Propulsion: 4 shafts; Parsons geared turbines; 6 boilers; 72,000shp; 32.5kt; 5,700nm at 13kt.
Armour: Belt 3.0in (76mm); turrets 1.0in (25mm); ammunition spaces 3.5-1.0in (89-25mm).
Armament: 8 x 6.0in (152mm) (4 x 2); 4 x 4.0in (102mm); 8 x 21in (533mm) TT
Aircraft: 1.
Complement: 570.

History: The Leander-class (*Achilles*, *Ajax*, *Leander*, *Neptune*, *Orion*) were the first in a series of "light" cruisers for the Royal Navy. Main armament consisted of eight 6in (152mm) guns in four twin turrets, the guns being a manually-rammed version of the guns mounted in the battleships *Nelson* and *Rodney*. As built, all had a single catapult and a spotter floatplane, but these were removed during the war. *Leander* and *Achilles* were both loaned to the newly-formed Royal New Zealand Navy (RNZN), which operated them throughout World War II. The Perth-class (*Hobart*, *Perth*, *Sydney*), also known as the "Modified Leander-class" were identical in virtually all respects except for the machinery arrangement, which resulted in two, instead of one, funnels; all three were operated by the Royal Australian Navy (RAN).

and abandoned. *Exeter* was the heaviest of the three cruisers involved in the action with *Graf Spee* in December 1941 and was very seriously damaged, leaving her with no main guns operating. She was repaired but was sunk by Japanese surface ships on 1 March 1942.

Above: *Exeter*, badly damaged at the River Plate was sunk by the Japanese in 1942

Above: *Achilles*, one of the victors at the River Plate, seen post-war as INS *Delhi*

There were three war losses. *Neptune* sank in an Italian minefield on 19 December 1941, all but one of her crew being lost. The RAN lost two of its ships: *Sydney* was sunk in an unusual, mutually fatal, engagement with the German raider *Kormoran* (19 November 1941), while *Perth* was hit by at least four torpedoes in the Battle of Sunda Straits (1 March 1942).

These were the only single-funnel cruisers in the Royal Navy during World War II, which led to a classic example of misidentification when the German raider *Graf Spee* spotted *Ajax* and *Achilles* off the River Plate in December 1939. The German bridge staff decided that the single funnels meant that the two ships were destroyers and by the time it was realised that they were actually cruisers the German ship was already committed to battle, with fateful consequences for them. *Ajax*, *Leander* and *Orion* were scrapped in 1949, but *Achilles* was sold to India (INS *Delhi*) in 1948 and was scrapped in 1978.

Arethusa

UNITED KINGDOM

Light cruiser
Completed: 1935-37.
Number in class: 4.
Displacement: 5,220 tons standard; 6,665 tons full load.
Dimensions: Length 506.0ft (154.2m); beam 51.0ft (15.5m); draught 16.5ft (5.0m).
Propulsion: 4 shafts; Parsons geared turbines; 4 boilers; 64,000shp; 32.3kt; 5,300nm at 13kt.
Armour: belt 2.3in (58mm); turrets 1.0in (25mm); ammunition spaces 3.0-1.0in (76-25mm).
Armament: 6 x 6.0in (152mm) (3 x 2); 4 x 4in (102mm); 6 x 21in (533mm) TT
Aircraft: 1.
Complement: 500.

History: These four ships (*Arethusa, Aurora, Galatea, Penelope*) represent an attempt to build the smallest possible cruiser capable of operating with the fleet and was, in effect, a slightly reduced version of the Modified Leander (Perth-class), but armed with six instead of eight 6.0in (152mm) guns. As built, all had a catapult and one floatplane, but aviation facilities were removed in 1940-41.

All four had a very busy war, in which two were lost, both sunk in the Mediterranean by German U-boats: *Galatea* on 14 December 1941 and *Penelope* on 18 February 1944. *Arethusa*, however, survived serious damage from an aerial torpedo, while *Aurora* was hit on separate occasions by a mine and a bomb, and survived both. After the war *Arethusa* was scrapped in 1950, while *Aurora* was transferred to Nationalist China as *Chungking* in 1948 and

Southampton/Gloucester

UNITED KINGDOM

Cruisers
Specifications for *Southampton*, as built.
Completed: Southampton - 1937, Gloucester - 1938-39.
Number in class: Southampton - 5, Gloucester - 3.
Displacement: 9,100 tons standard; 11,350 tons full load.
Dimensions: Length 591.0ft (180.3m); beam 61.7ft (1808m); draught 20.3ft (6.2m).
Propulsion: 4 shafts; Parsons geared turbines; 4 boilers; 75,000shp; 32kt; 7,850nm at 13kt.
Armour: Belt 4.5in (114mm); box protection for ammunition spaces 4.5in-1.0in (114-25mm); turrets 1.0in (25mm).
Armament: 12 x 6in (152mm) (4 x 3); 8 x 4in (102mm); 8 x 2pdr pompom; 6 x 21in (533mm) TT.
Aircraft: 3.
Complement: 748.

History: Sometimes regarded as a single class of eight ships, with minor differences in the last three, these were 6.0in (152mm) gun ships designed in response to intelligence reports concerning new cruisers under construction in Japan with fifteen 6.1in (155mm) guns on a displacement of 8,500 tons (this was the Mogami-class [q.v.]). The Royal Navy demanded a "reply," which would have similar characteristics as to size, armament, range and speed, and, in addition, be capable of carrying five aircraft. In the event, these criteria could not all be met and main armament comprised twelve 6.0in (152mm) guns in a new triple mount with 45deg elevation, only three aircraft could be embarked and displacement was well above that laid down. The first five (*Birmingham,*

then captured by the Communists in 1949, who renamed her *Huang Ho*. She is believed to have been sunk at Taku by Nationalist aircraft in 1949-50.

Above: *Penelope*, most famous of the Arethusa-class, on builders' trials in 1936

Above: *Liverpool*, one of eight of a very handsome and powerful group of cruisers

Glasgow, Newcastle, Sheffield, Southampton) were all completed in 1937. They were followed by the remaining three (*Gloucester, Liverpool, Manchester*) a year later, which had improved protection to the turrets and other minor changes.

These were particularly handsome and powerful-looking ships, all of which played a very active role in World War II, during which three were sunk, all in the Mediterranean, each of them being so badly damaged by enemy action that they had to be abandoned and sunk by friendly fire. This happened to *Southampton* in the Sicilian Narrows (11 January 1941) and to *Gloucester* off Crete (22 May 1941) both of which were hit by enemy aircraft and had to be torpedoed by friendly forces, while *Manchester* was hit by torpedoes from an enemy MTB and had to be scuttled off Tunisia (13 August 1942).

Edinburgh

UNITED KINGDOM

Cruiser
Completed: 1939.
Number in class: 2.
Displacement: 10,550 tons standard; 13,175 tons full load.
Dimensions: Length 613.5ft (187.0m); beam 63.3ft (19.3m); draught 21.3ft (6.5m).
Propulsion: 4 shafts; Parsons geared turbines; 4 boilers; 80,000shp; 32.5kt; 8,500nm at 14kt.
Armour: Belt 4.5in (114mm); turrets 4.0-2.0in (102-52mm).
Armament: 12 x 6.0in (152mm) (4 x 3); 12 x 4.0in (102mm); 16 x 2pdr pompom; 6 x 21.0in (533mm) TT.
Aircraft: 3.
Complement: 850.

History: These two ships, *Belfast* and *Edinburgh*, were generally similar to the Southampton-class. However, the after gun turrets were both raised by one deck level and the funnels were moved aft, although this was not due to a different machinery arrangement but because of the siting of the magazine for the 4.0in (102mm) ammunition and to create space for the athwartships fixed catapult. In the early stages of design a quadruple turret with power loading was under consideration, but early trials of this very complex piece of machinery did not go well and the idea was dropped.

Edinburgh spent most of her wartime career in northern waters, but with two brief visits to the Mediterranean. However, she was off the Norwegian coast when she was torpedoed by *U-456* and was proceeding slowly

Dido/Bellona

UNITED KINGDOM

Anti-aircraft cruisers
Specifications for *Dido*, as built.
Completed: Dido - 1940-42; Bellona - 1943-44.
Number in class: Dido - 11, Bellona - 5.
Displacement: 5,600 tons standard; 6,850 tons full load.
Dimensions: Length 512.0ft (156.1m); beam 50.5ft (15.4m); draught 16.8ft (5.1m).
Propulsion: 4 shafts; Parsons geared turbines; 4 boilers; 62,000shp; 32.2kt; 4,900nm at 11kt.
Armour: side 3.0in (76mm); bulkheads 1.0in (25mm).
Armament: 10 x 5.25in (133mm) (5 x 2); 8 x 2pdr pompom; 8 x 0.50in (12.7mm) MG.
Complement: 480.

History: These cruisers were intended for fleet air defence and the fact that they were designed in 1935-36 and the first laid down in 1937 shows that the Royal Navy clearly understood the nature of the coming air threat, well before the outbreak of war. They were designed to mount ten 5.25in (133mm) semi-automatic guns with power loading, but these new weapons were subject to serious production delays. As a result, some were completed with four instead of five turrets, while two had four twin 4.5in (114mm) guns in open mounts. The Bellona-class differed only in having four twin 5.25in (133mm) mounts and upright funnels.

Five were lost in the war, four of them in the Mediterranean. Three of these were torpedoed by submarines: *Bonaventure* by Italian submarine *Ambra* (31 March 1941), *Naiad* by *U-565* (11 March 1942) and *Hermione* by *U-205* (16 June

***Above: Belfast,* seen here in the 1950s, is still afloat in the River Thames in London**

homewards when she was attacked by destroyers and again damaged. Without power and flooding rapidly she was abandoned and sunk by a British destroyer (2 May 1942). *Belfast* took part in Arctic operations including the Battle of North Cape (26 December 1943) and was then involved in the D-day landings. Post-war she served off Korea, but was then preserved and remains as a national memorial, berthed opposite the Tower of London.

***Above: Cleopatra* with two turrets forward (top) and *Sirius* with three (bottom)**

1942). The fourth, *Spartan*, was hit and sunk by a Henschel-293 guided bomb off the Anzio beachhead (29 January 1944). The exception was *Charybdis* which was hit by torpedoes from the German torpedo boats *T-23* and *T-27* off the Brittany coast on the night of 23/24 October 1943. The majority of the surviving ships were scrapped in the late 1950s, except for *Diadem* which went to Pakistan in 1956 as *Babur* and was scrapped in 1985.

Fiji

UNITED KINGDOM

Cruiser
Completed: 1940-43.
Number in class: 11.
Displacement: 8,530 tons standard; 10,450 tons full load.
Dimensions: Length 555.5ft (169.3m); beam 62.0ft (18.9m); draught 19.8ft (6.0m).
Propulsion: 4 shafts; Parsons geared turbines; 4 boilers; 72,500shp; 31.5kt; 6,520nm at 13kt.
Armour: Belt 3.5-3.3in (89-84mm); turrets 2.0-1.0in (51-25mm).
Armament: 12 x 6.0in (152mm) (4 x 3); 8 x 4.0in (102mm); 8 x 2pdr pompom; 6 x 21.0in (533mm) TT.
Aircraft: 2.
Complement: 920.

History: This design, also known as the "Colony-class," was, in effect, the "County-class" design adapted to the limitations imposed by the 1937 London Naval Treaty, the main limitation being a displacement of 8,000 tons. Eleven were built: *Bermuda, Ceylon, Fiji, Gambia, Jamaica, Kenya, Mauritius, Newfoundland, Nigeria, Trinidad, Uganda.* Main armament was twelve 6in (152mm) guns, but, compared with the Edinburgh-class, the two after guns were one deck lower, as in the original Southampton-class, although "X" turret was removed from four of the class between 1942 and 1944, mainly in order to increase the air defence armament. *Fiji* and *Kenya* did not have aviation facilities when they were built and these were removed from the rest during the course of the war. For many years a characteristic of British cruisers had been the "cruiser stern," in which the hull came to a graceful point, but this was discontinued in the "Colony" and subsequent classes, which had a transom

Swiftsure/Superb

UNITED KINGDOM

Cruiser
Specifications for Swiftsure, as built.
Completed: 1944-45.
Number in class: 3.
Specifications for *Swiftsure*, as built.
Displacement: 8,800 tons standard; 11,130 tons full load.
Dimensions: Length 555.5ft (169.3m); beam 63.0ft (19.2m); draught 20.7ft (6.3m).
Propulsion: 4 shafts; Parsons geared turbines; 4 boilers; 72,500shp; 31.5kt; 6,250nm at 13kt.
Armour: Belt 3.5-3.3in (89-84mm); turrets 2.0-1.0in (51-25mm);
Armament: 9 x 6.0in (152mm) (3 x 3); 10 x 4.0in (102mm); 16 x 2pdr pompom; 6 x 21.0in (533mm) TT.
Complement: 960.

History: The final chapter of British World War II cruisers is somewhat complicated. The Swiftsure-class design was very similar to that of the Fiji-class, but with 1.0ft (25mm) increase in beam, no aviation facilities, increased bunkerage and heavier air defence armament. Two ships were built to this design: one for the Royal Navy (*Swiftsure*) and one for the Royal Canadian Navy (RCN), originally to be named *Minotaur*, but commissioned as *Ontario*. The next class was originally to have been a minor development of the Swiftsure design with another 1.0ft (25mm) increase in beam and with further improvements in protection and in air defence armament. Only one ship, *Superb*, was completed

Above: *Kenya* in 1949; main armament was nine 6in (152mm) guns in triple turrets

stern, giving a significant increase in internal space aft.

Two were lost in the war. *Fiji* survived a torpedo attack by *U-32* in 1940 but was hit by bombs off Crete and sunk (22 May 1941). *Trinidad* was hit by one of her own torpedoes whilst en route to Russia (29 March 1942) but reached Murmansk, where she was patched. On the return voyage, however, she was hit by bombs, starting a fire and demolishing one of the patches; she had to be abandoned and scuttled (15 May 1942). The remainder survived the war and served in the post-war navy well into the 1950s. Peru bought *Ceylon* and *Newfoundland* in 1959, which became *Coronel Bolognesi* and *Capitan Quinones*, respectively; they were scrapped in 1979-82. India bought *Nigeria* in 1957; she served as *Mysore* until being scrapped in 1986. The remainder were scrapped in 1960-68.

***Above:* Last of the wartime cruisers to be completed, *Superb* had classic British lines**

to this design.

Swiftsure joined the fleet in mid-1944 and went to the Pacific where she took part in the Okinawa campaign and took the Japanese surrender in Hong Kong. She was scrapped in 1962. *Ontario* served in the Pacific at the end of the war and was later employed as a training ship; she was scrapped in 1960. *Superb* was too late for the war and was scrapped in 1960.

Tiger

UNITED KINGDOM

Cruiser
Specifications for *Tiger*, as built.
Completed: 1959-61.
Number in class: 3.
Displacement: 9,550 tons standard; 11,700tons full load.
Dimensions: Length 555.5ft (169.3m); beam 64.0ft (19.5m); draught 23.0ft (7.0m).
Propulsion: 4 shafts; geared steam turbines; 4 boilers; 80,000shp; 31.5kt; 6,500nm at 13kt.
Armour: Belt 3.0 (76mm); turrets 2.0-1.0in (51-25mm).
Armament: 4 x 6.0in (152mm) (2 x 2); 6 x 3.0in (76mm).
Complement: 880.

History: These three ships, laid down in 1941-42, were originally to have been sister ships to *Superb* (see previous entry) but their construction was slowed down and they were launched in 1944-45 and then allowed to lie incomplete until their future had been decided. It was not until 1951 that a plan was agreed under which the three hulls would be completed as modernised gun-armed cruisers to the specification shown above. There were several changes of name, the three eventually being completed as: *Blake* (ex-*Tiger*, ex-*Blake*); *Lion* (ex-*Defence*); and *Tiger* (ex-*Bellerophon*).

Their completion took some time and they joined the fleet between 1959 and 1961 with an armament of four 5.0in (152mm) and six 3.0in (76mm) AA. Both types of weapon were water-cooled and fully-automated, but in practice they were very unreliable and incapable of firing more than a few round without

Trenton

UNITED STATES OF AMERICA

Wooden screw frigate
Completed: 1877.
Number in class: 1.
Displacement: 3,900 tons.
Dimensions: Length (pp) 253.0ft (77.1m); beam 20.5ft (14.6m); draught 20.5ft (6.3m).
Propulsion: 1 shafts; Compound, Return Connecting-Rod engine; 3,100ihp; 12.8kt.
Armament: 10 x 8.0in (203mm) rifled, muzzle-loaders.
Complement: 416.

History: *Trenton* was built of liveoak and, following the practice of the time, was fitted with a cast-iron ram, whose point was 9.0ft (2.7m) below the waterline and 8.0ft (2.4m) ahead of the stem. She was considerably shorter than her immediate predecessors in the United States fleet, the Java-class, for example, having been 312.5ft (95.3m) in length. The 8in (203mm) battery was all on the main deck, and all were rifled. *Trenton* was lost in a double tragedy, which took place in Apia harbour in Samoa during a typhoon. In the storm, another screw frigate, *Vandalia*, was driven onto a reef and her crew were trying to save her when *Trenton* was driven onto exactly the same spot, with the result that both ships were total losses (16 March 1889).

The designation "frigate" typifies the changes that have occurred in naval designations. Until the middle of the 19th century, large ships intended for long range patrols were designated "frigates" but the name fell into disuse. At the end of the century the name "cruiser" was coined for the type and then, in

Above: Lion **was armed with four highly-automated 6in (152mm) guns in twin turrets**

a stoppage. The ships were, in fact, already out-of-date and after only a few years service were converted to helicopter cruisers, *Blake* (1965-69) and *Tiger* (1968-72), while *Lion* was cannibalised for spares and then scrapped in 1975. The helicopter conversion involved removing the after 6.0in (152mm) and 3.0in 76mm) turrets and constructing a huge hangar and flightdeck, which enabled them to operate four Westland Wessex ASW helicopters. Such large and complex ships, with their large crews and high operating costs, proved a very expensive method of taking four helicopters to sea and their second career was also short, being stricken in 1979 (*Tiger*) and 1980 (*Blake*) and scrapped shortly afterwards.

---

the middle of the 20th century the name "frigate" was resurrected, but for a much smaller, escort vessel.

Above: Trenton, **built for Pacific patrols, met her end driven ashore in a Samoan storm**

Chicago

UNITED STATES OF AMERICA

Cruiser
Completed: 1889.
Number in class: 1.
Displacement: 4,500 tons standard; 4,864 tons full load.
Dimensions: Length 342.1ft (104.3m); beam 48.3ft (14.7m); draught 19.0ft (5.8m).
Propulsion: 2 shafts; Compound, Overhead-Beam engine; 5,000ihp; 14kt.
Armament: 4 x 8.0in (203mm); 8 x 6.0in (152mm); 2 x 5.0in (127mm); 2 x 6pdr; 2 x 1pdr.
Complement: 409.

History: *Chicago* was authorised and laid down in 1883, and launched in 1885, but was not completed until 1889. There was a curious mix of armament, with a main battery of four 8in (203mm) in individual sponsons on the upper deck, eight 6.0in (152mm) on the main deck amidships and two 5.0in (127mm), also on the maindeck, but aft. She was rigged as a three-masted barque rig (but without the usual royals), with steam power being supplied by a compound engine, which, when running trials, gave an indicated 5,084 horsepower and a speed of 15.4kt. She was rebuilt between 1895 and 1898, being given new machinery and improved weapons, while the sailing rig was removed.

From 1910 to 1917 she was operated by various East Coast

New York

UNITED STATES OF AMERICA

Armoured cruiser
Completed: 1893.
Number in class: 1.
Displacement: 8,200 tons standard; 9,021 tons full load.
Dimensions: Length 384.0ft (117.0m); beam 23.8ft (19.8m); draught 23.8ft (7.3m).
Propulsion: 2 shafts; Vertical, Triple-Expansion engines; 12 boilers; 16,000ihp; 20kt.
Armour: Nickel steel. Belt 4.0in (102mm); barbettes 10.0-5.0in (254-127mm; turrets 5.3in (135mm); conning tower 7.5in (191mm).
Armament: 6 x 8.0in (203mm) (2 x 2; 2 x 1); 12 x 4.0in (102mm); 4 x 1pdr; 3 x 14in (356mm) TT.
Complement: 566.

History: When built, *Maine* (q.v.) and *New York* were both classified as armoured cruisers (ACR) but the former was soon reclassified as a second-class battleship, leaving *New York* as the first such ship, but with the hull number of ACR-2. As built, *New York* was armed with two twin 8.0in (203mm) in "A" and "Y" positions, with one single 8.0in (203mm) on each beam amidships. In a rebuild between 1905 and 1908, however, the armament was changed. In the main armament, the twin 8.0in (203mm), 35-calibre tubes in the fore and aft turrets were replaced by 45-calibre tubes, while the two amidships 8.0in (203mm) guns were deleted. In the secondary armament

militias and then served for six years as a submarine depot ship, after which she went to Pearl Harbor as an accommodation ship. She was being towed back to San Francisco for sale when she foundered on 8 July 1936.

Below: *Chicago* was completed with barque rig, but this was removed ten years later

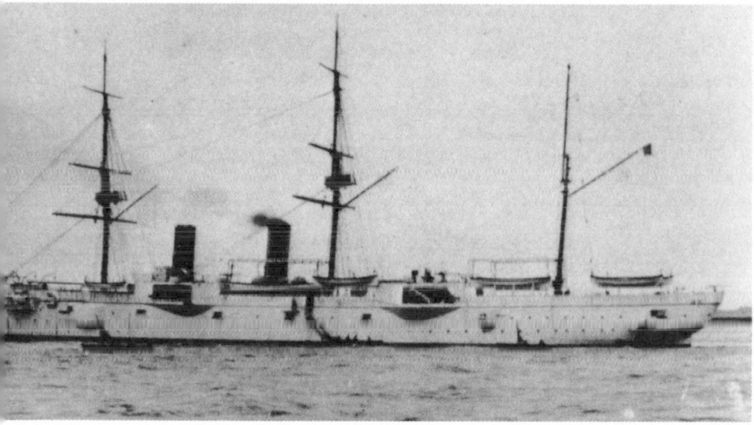

the twelve 4.0in (102mm) were replaced by ten 5.0in (127mm) and eight 3.0in (76mm), and the torpedo tubes were completely removed. Protection was also increased and the boilers replaced. The ship's name was changed to *Saratoga* in 1911 and to *Rochester* in 1917. She had an extraordinarily long career, ending her days in the Philippines, where, despite having been stricken in 1938 it was still felt necessary to scuttle her in December 1941 to avoid capture by the Japanese.

Below: *New York* was the first of a long line of armoured cruisers for the US Navy

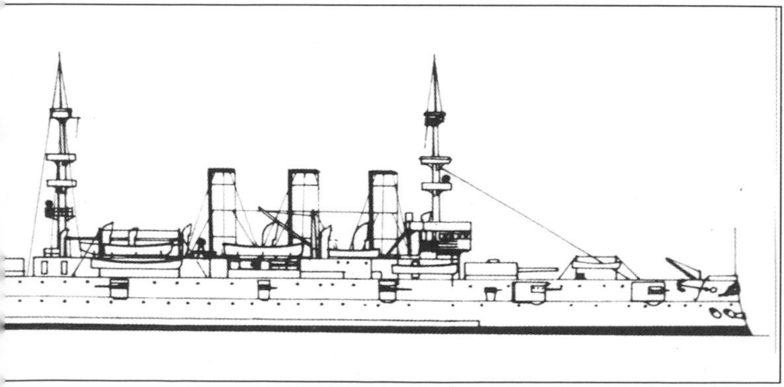

Brooklyn

UNITED STATES OF AMERICA

Armoured cruiser
Completed: 1896.
Number in class: 1.
Displacement: 9,215 tons standard; 10,068 tons full load.
Dimensions: Length 402.6ft (122.7m); beam 64.7ft (19.7m); draught 24.0ft (7.3m).
Propulsion: 2 shafts; Vertical, Triple-Expansion engines; 16,000ihp; 20kt.
Armour: Harvey and nickel steel. Belt 3.0in (76mm); barbettes 8.0-3.0in (203-76mm); turrets 5.5in (140mm); conning tower 8.5in (216mm).
Armament: 8 x 8.0in (203mm) (4 x 2); 12 x 5.0in (127mm); 12 x 6pdr; 4 x 1pdr; 5 x 18in (457mm) TT.
Complement: 561.

History: Although built after *New York*, *Brooklyn* appeared to be from an earlier era, with three extremely tall funnels, and French-style tumblehomes. Main armament comprised eight 8.0in (203mm) guns in four twin turrets, one each in "A" and "Y" positions, and two wing turrets on midships sponsons. For some obscure reason training the forward and the starboard wing turrets was done by electrical power and by steam power in the other two. The twelve 5.0in (127mm) guns were split between two levels, with eight on the main deck, all in sponsons, and four on the upper deck, of which the forward two were sponsoned out under the forecastle. Taken altogether, the armament was an untidy mixture of calibres, sited in a manner lacking in method.

Brooklyn took part in the Spanish-American War and was out of service

Columbia

UNITED STATES OF AMERICA

Commerce-raiding cruiser
Completed: 1894.
Number in class: 2.
Displacement: 7,375 tons standard; 8,270 tons full load.
Dimensions: Length 413.1ft (125.9m); beam 58.2ft (17.7m); draught 22.6ft (6.9m).
Propulsion: 3 shafts; Vertical, Triple-Expansion engines; 21,000ihp; 21kt.
Armour: Deck 4.0-2.5in (102-64mm); conning tower 5.0in (127mm).
Armament: 1 x 8.0in (203mm); 2 x 6.0in (152mm); 8 x 4.0in (102mm); 12 x 6pdr; 4 x 1pdr; 4 x 14in (356mm) TT.
Complement: 477.

History: There is a long tradition in maritime warfare of attacks on enemy merchant ships, often known as *guerre de course*, but not many ships have been designed specifically for that role, the US Navy's Columbia-class being among that small group. The class consisted of two ships built at the same time and in the same yard, but there were some differences, among them that *Columbia* had four funnels and 14in (356mm) torpedo tubes, while *Minneapolis* had two funnels and 18in (457mm) tubes. Despite their aggressive role their main armament was fairly light; as built, it consisted of one 8.0in (203mm) in a shield on the quarterdeck and two 6.0in (152mm) side-by-side on the foredeck just below the bridge, but the sole 8.0in (203mm) was replaced by a single 6.0in (152mm) about 1910. The 4.0in (102mm) guns were in

from 1908 to 1914, which included a period in refit, which included some necessary improvements and removal of the torpedo tubes. She spent a year in the Pacific in 1920 and was sold for scrap in 1922.

Below: **Completed in 1896, *Brooklyn*'s tall funnels seemed to be from an earlier era**

sponsons at main deck level. The torpedo tubes were also removed from both ships during their careers. Both ships spent long period in reserve: *Columbia* from 1906 to 1915 and *Minneapolis* from 1906 to 1917. Both then returned to service for a short period before being sold for scrap in the early 1920s.

Below: **Columbia-class cruisers were designed for *guerre de corse* (commerce raiding)**

Pensacola

UNITED STATES OF AMERICA

Cruiser
Completed: 1929-30.
Number in class: 2.
Displacement: 9,097 tons standard; 11,512 tons full load.
Dimensions: Length 585.7ft (178.5m); beam 65.3ft (19.9m); draught 19.5ft (5.9m).
Propulsion: 4 shafts; Parsons turbines; 8 boilers; 107,000shp; 32.5kt; 10,000nm at 15kt.
Armour: Belt 2.5in (64mm); barbettes 0.75in (19mm); turret faces 2.5in (64mm).
Armament: 10 x 8.0in (203mm) (2 x 3, 2 x 2); 4 x 5.0in (127mm); 6 x 21.0in (533mm) TT.
Aircraft: 4.
Complement: 631.

History: The US Navy built no cruisers between the Salem-class in 1905 and the ten-strong Omaha-class, which were laid down 1918-20 and completed between 1923 and 1925. There was then another, albeit shorter, gap before the first "Treaty cruisers" were completed in 1929-30: *Pensacola* and *Salt Lake City*. These were armed with ten 8.0in (203mm) guns, with twin mounts in "A" and "Y" positions, and triple mounts in "B" and "X" positions, it being somewhat unusual to mount the triple turrets above the twins. Secondary armament comprised four 5.0in (127mm), with six torpedo tubes mounted in the waist, although the latter were deleted in the mid-1930s. Four aircraft were carried, all in the open, with two catapults but no hangars.

Both ships were extremely active throughout World War II. *Pensacola* took

Portland

UNITED STATES OF AMERICA

Cruiser
Completed: 1932.
Number in class: 2.
Displacement: 10,258 tons standard; 12,755 tons full load.
Dimensions: Length 610.0ft (185.9m); beam 66.0ft (20.1m); draught 21.0ft (6.4m).
Propulsion: 4 shafts; Parsons turbines; 8 boilers; 107,000shp; 32.5kt; 10,000nm at 15kt.
Armour: Belt 2.3in (58mm); barbettes 1.5in (38mm); turret faces 2.5in 64mm).
Armament: 9 x 8.0in (203mm) (3 x 3); 8 x 5.0in (127mm); 8 x 0.5in (12.7mm) MG.
Aircraft: 4.
Complement: 807.

History: The Pensacola-class was followed by the six-ship Northampton-class in which the main armament was reduced to nine guns in three triple turrets and the forecastle was extended to improve seakeeping. These were followed by the generally similar two-ship Portland-class, which was slightly longer (610.0ft [185.9m] compared to 600.3ft [183.0m]) and with a revised bow shape. Both had better protection than their predecessors and both were outfitted as fleet flagships.

Both ships had a very busy war in the Pacific. *Portland* was hit by three dud air-launched torpedoes at the Battle of Santa Cruz but was less fortunate at Guadalcanal when she was hit by a destroyer-launched torpedo and severely damaged (13 November 1942). Following repairs she returned to the fray but completed the war unscathed. She was in reserve for many years and was scrapped in 1959. *Indianapolis* had a similarly active war, but just before the

part in many engagements, but her first serious damage being at Tassafaronga on the night of 30 November 1942 when she was hit by a torpedo, which caused numerous casualties. The ship was repaired, refitted and returned to action and was hit by shore batteries during the Okinawa landings (17 February 1945). *Salt Lake City* had a similarly energetic war and also incurred damage from time to time. Both survived the war and were used as targets during the Bikini atomic tests in 1946; *Pensacola* was sunk during the tests but *Salt Lake City* survived and was later scuttled off the western seaboard of the United States.

***Above:* The Pensacola-class was the US Navy's first design for a "Treaty cruiser"**

very end she carried critical components of the first atomic bombs from the United States to Tinian, arriving on the 26 July 1945. She then sailed for Leyte but, by chance, ran across the path of Japanese submarine *I-58*, which hit the cruiser with three torpedoes; she sank in just twelve minutes. It is estimated that some 800 of the 1,119 aboard survived the sinking, but due to errors and misunderstandings they were not found for five days, by which time only 320 were still alive. Her captain survived and was court martialled, where he was given a reprimand, but he later committed suicide.

***Above:* Northampton-class cruiser *Louisville*; worked hard in the war, scrapped in 1960**

Cleveland

UNITED STATES OF AMERICA

Cruiser
Completed: 1941-44.
Number in class: 27 (see notes).
Displacement: 11,744 tons standard; 14,131 tons full load.
Dimensions: Length 610.1ft (186.0m); beam 66.3ft (20.2m); draught 24.5ft (7.5m).
Propulsion: 4 shafts; General Electric turbines; 4 boilers; 100,000shp; 32.5kt; 11,000nm at 15kt.
Armour: Belt 5.0-3.5in (127-89mm); deck 2.0in (52mm); barbettes 6.0in (152mm); turret faces 6.5in (165mm); conning tower 5.0in (127mm).
Armament: 12 x 6.0in (152mm) (4 x 3); 12 x 5.0in (127mm); 28 x 40mm; 10 x 20mm.
Aircraft: 4.
Complement: 1,285.

History: This was probably the largest class of cruisers ever ordered, although changes in plans reduced the number actually completed. A total of fifty-two were ordered, of which fourteen were cancelled at various stages of construction, while another nine were converted while under construction and completed as light aircraft carriers (CVL). Another two were completed to such a different cruiser design that they constitute the separate Fargo-class, leaving twenty-seven to be completed as the Cleveland-class cruisers. Such a large order did not stem from any inherent superiority, however, but was due to the 1940 decision to concentrate on existing designs, in order to get as many ships as possible to sea for the clearly discernible future war. Thus, the Cleveland

Des Moines

UNITED STATES OF AMERICA

Heavy cruiser
Completed: 1948-49.
Number in class: 3.
Displacement: 17,255tons standard; 20,934 tons full load.
Dimensions: Length 716.5ft (218.4m); beam 75.3ft (23.0m); draught 26.0ft (7.9m).
Propulsion: 4 shafts; General Electric turbines; 4 boilers; 120,000shp; 33kt; 10,500nm at 15kt.
Armour: Belt 6.0-4.0in (152-102mm); deck 3.5in (89mm) plus 1in (25mm) weather deck; barbettes 6.3in (160mm); turret faces 8.0in (203mm); pilot house 6.5-5.5in (165-140mm)
Armament: 9 x 8.0in (203mm) (3 x 3); 12 x 5.0in (127mm); 24 x 3.0in (76mm) AA; 24 x 20mm AA.
Aircraft: 4.
Complement: 1,799.

History: A long-standing shortcoming of the existing design of 8in (203mm) gun was its very slow rate of fire, which had caused operational problems, especially in fast-moving night engagements. Fortunately, a programme had been in hand to improve the rate of fire of the 5.0in (152mm) gun and the work done there was carried over into the larger calibre gun with equal success. It was decided that the new triple turret merited a totally new ship design, giving rise to these large and sophisticated ships, which were the culmination of US Navy gun-armed cruiser design. These were large ships with a length of 716.5ft (218.4m) and a displacement of almost 21,000 tons, and their main armament of nine of the new 8.0in (203mm) Mark 16 guns each tube firing at ten rounds

Above: **Twenty-seven Cleveland-class cruisers were completed; this is *Dayton* (CL105)**

design was based on that of the *Helena*, the last of the Brooklyn-class, which had been built to a slightly different design to that of her sisters. The Clevelands were given extra beam, but despite that they were always bothered by stability, possibly because the original plan was for the superstructure to be made from aluminium, but this proved to be unavailable in the war, and steel had to be used, instead. Also while *Helena* was armed with fifteen 6in (152mm) guns in five triple turrets, one complete turret was removed in the Cleveland design and replaced by two extra twin 5in (127mm) turrets, to increase the air defence capabilities.

They all played a major role in the Pacific war, in which not one was lost. After the war they were quickly placed in reserve, but six were converted to guided-missile ships in the late 1950s.

Above: Des Moines, **armed with nine of the new rapid-firing 8in (203mm) guns**

per minute made them formidable adversaries for any existing surface warship, particularly their main potential enemy in the 1950s and '60s, the Soviet Sverdlov-class cruisers (q.v.).

Four were planned, but one was cancelled, the other three - *Des Moines*, *Salem* and *Newport News* - joining the fleet in 1948-49, where their principal use was as fleet flagships. *Salem* decommissioned in 1959, followed by *Des Moines* in 1961, but they were not stricken until 1991. *Newport* News remained in service longer, not being decommissioned until 1975, but she was stricken in 1978 and scrapped in 1993. *Salem* is now a museum and *Des Moines* was scrapped in the late 1990s

Worcester

UNITED STATES OF AMERICA

Light cruiser
Completed: 1948.
Number in class: 2.
Displacement: 14,700 tons standard; 17,997 tons full load.
Dimensions: Length 679.5ft (207.1m); beam 70.7ft (21.5m); draught 24.8ft (7.5m).
Propulsion: 4 shafts; General Electric turbines; 4 boilers; 120,000shp; 33kt; 8,000nm at 15kt.
Armour: Belt 5.0-3.0in (127-76mm); barbettes 5in (127mm); turret faces 6.5in (165mm).
Armament: 12 x 6.0in (152mm) (6 x 2); 24 x 3.0in (76mm); 12 x 20mm.
Complement: 1,401.

History: The Worcester-class ships were given "CL" hull numbers so that, with a displacement of just under 18,000 tons, they must rate as by far the largest "light" cruisers ever built. They were designed to take advantage of the recently perfected automatic 6.0in (152mm) gun, which was originally needed to protect the fleet against high-flying bombers, but later was seen as being vital for defence against the new anti-ship guided-missiles introduced by the Germans in 1943.

It was planned to order four, but with the end of the war clearly in sight this was reduced to two - *Worcester* and *Roanoke* - which were completed in mid-1948. The ships mounted no less than twelve of the new guns in six twin turrets, three forward and three aft, all on the centreline, and the main reason for the very long hull was the need to accommodate the large magazines

---

Boston

UNITED STATES OF AMERICA

Missile cruiser conversion
Converted: 1955/56.
Number in class: 2.
Displacement: 13,589 tons standard; 17,947 tons full load.
Dimensions: Length 673.4ft (205.3m); beam 69.7ft (21.3m); draught 24.9ft (7.6m).
Propulsion: 4 shafts; geared turbines; 4 boilers; 120,000shp; 33kt; 7,300nm at 20kt.
Armament: 2 x Mk 10 launcher for Terrier SAM (2 x 2); 6 x 8.0in (203mm) (2 x 3) guns; 10 x 5in (127mm) AA; 8 x 3in (76mm) AA.
Complement: 1,544.

History: *Boston* and *Canberra* were built as Baltimore-class gun cruisers, both being completed in 1943. After World War II missile development proceeded at a steady, but not spectacular pace, with the former Allies absorbing the work that had been done in Germany in 1941-45, but the outbreak of the Korean War in July 1950 and an intensification of the Cold War resulted in an acceleration of all programmes, including the Terrier (then designated BY-3, but later RIM-2), which was showing great promise. These two ships were then selected to be rebuilt in order to get the system to sea as quickly as possible, the work being completed in 1955-56. The entire after superstructure was removed to enable two twin-arm Mark 10 missile launchers to be installed, each sitting atop a seventy-two round revolving magazine. The rebuild also included the radars and other sensors associated with the missile system. A plan was made for a second rebuild in which the forward guns would also have been replaced by a

Above: **Displacing 18,000 tons, *Worcester* (CL144) was a very heavy "light" cruiser**

needed to supply such a large number of rapid-firing guns.

The ships entered service in 1949. Both ships spent most of their short active service careers in the Pacific and Mediterranean, and *Worcester* also saw service in Korean waters during the war there. Both were placed in reserve in 1958 and sold for scrap in 1972-73.

Above: Boston **after her rebuild, with two twin-arm Terrier missile launchers aft**

Mark 10 launcher and missile magazine, thus making the ships "double-ended" but this was shelved. The Terrier systems were completely removed in the late 1960s and the ships reclassified as cruisers (CA), but they were decommissioned in 1970 and stricken later in the decade.

Missile cruiser conversions

UNITED STATES OF AMERICA

Modified Cleveland
Converted: 1958-60.
Number in class: 6.
Displacement: 11.066 tons light; 15,152 tons full load.
Dimensions: Length 610.0ft (186.0m); beam 65.7ft (20.0m); draught 25.7ft (7.8m).
Propulsion: 4 shafts; geared turbines; 4 boilers; 100,000shp; 32kt; 8,000nm at 15kt.
Armament: 1 x Mark 12 launcher for Talos SAM (1 x 2); 3 x 6.0in (152mm) guns (1 x 3); 2 x 5.0in (127mm) guns.
Complement: 1,382.

Albany
Converted: 1962-64.
Number in class: 3.
Displacement: 14,394 tons light; 18,777 tons full load.
Dimensions: Length 674.9ft (205.8m); beam 69.8ft (21.3m); draught 25.8ft (7.9m).
Propulsion: 4 shafts; General Electric geared turbines; 4 boilers; 120,000shp; 32kt; 7,000nm at 15kt.
Armament: 2 x Mark 12 launchers for Talos SAM (2 x 2); 2 x Mark 10 launchers for Tartar SAM (2 x 2); 1 x ASROC ASW missile launcher; 2 x 5.0in (127mm) guns (1 x 2); 6 x 12.75in (324mm) ASW TT.
Complement: 1,266.

History: *Boston* and *Canberra* were quickly followed by six more conversions, this time six former Cleveland-class cruisers. Three of these, *Galveston*, *Little Rock* and *Oklahoma City* were converted to take the Talos system, and the other three, *Providence*, *Springfield* and *Topeka* to take the Terrier system. As with the Boston-class (see previous entry) the conversion affected mainly the after end, where one of the new launchers was mounted on the quarterdeck, which was fed with missiles from a magazine in the deckhouse immediately behind it. In two ships, *Galveston* and *Topeka*, the fore part of the ship remained unchanged, retaining the two 6.0in (152mm) turrets on the foredeck and the three 5.0in (127mm) turrets, one before and two abreast the bridge. In the other four only one 6.0in (152mm) and one 5.0in (127mm) mounting were retained, allowing space for a much enlarged bridge, which included extensive new command and staff facilities for their role as fleet flagships. *Galveston* and *Topeka* were decommissioned in 1969 and 1970, respectively, followed by the others in the mid-1970s.

Three Baltimore-class cruisers underwent the most radical of the post-war missile conversions, the work being completed in 1962 (*Albany* and *Columbus*) and 1964 (*Chicago*). The original plan called for an entirely missile armament, with one twin-arm Talos launcher at either end, each with fifty-two missiles, and two Tartar launchers in the waist, each with forty-two missiles. In addition, to comply with the contemporary doctrine of task groups sailing in a dispersed formation to avoid destruction by a single nuclear attack, the ships also had an ASW system consisting of an ASROC launcher with eight missiles and the associated SQS-23 sonar system. Unfortunately for the designers, President Kennedy attended a demonstration where a Terrier missile missed its target and he insisted that the ships mount two single 5in (127mm) guns

***Above: Albany* (CA123) as a gun-armed cruiser, following completion in 1946**

in open mounts as a last-ditch defence. These ships had a disproportionately high bridge structure, the reason being that the two SPG-9 radar scanners had to be mounted above and behind the forward launcher and it was necessary to bring the bridge crew's sightline clear of the topmost array.

Chicago was the primary air defence ship during the operation to mine Haiphong harbour in North Vietnam and when hostile fighters prepared to attack the mining aircraft she launched a Talos at a range of 48 miles, which downed one aircraft, following which the remainder departed rapidly. All three ships were given limited modernisations during their service. All were decommissioned between 1976 and 1985 and were scrapped in the 1990s.

***Below: Albany's* sister-ship, *Columbus* (CG-12) as a "double-ended" missile cruiser**

Long Beach

UNITED STATES OF AMERICA

Missile cruiser, nuclear powered
Completed: 1961.
Number in class: 1.
Displacement: 15,111 tons standard; 16,602 tons full load.
Dimensions: Length 721.3ft (219.9m); beam 73.3ft (22.3m); draught 23.8ft (7.3m).
Propulsion: 2 shafts; nuclear; 2 C1W nuclear reactors; 2 General Electric turbines; 80,000shp; 30+kt.
Armament: 1 x launcher for Talos SAM (1 x 2); 2 launchers for Terrier SAM (2 x 1); 1 x launcher for ASROC ASW missiles (1 x 8); 6 x 12.75in (234mm) ASW TT.
Complement: 1,107.

History: *Long Beach* was the first surface warship in the world with nuclear propulsion and the US Navy's first purpose-built missile warship. It was designed as an air defence escort for the nuclear-powered carrier, *Enterprise* and, as built, was armed with two Mark 10 Terrier launchers forward with one Mark 12 Talos launcher aft. The depth of the hull enabled large magazines to be accommodated giving the ship a total capacity of 166 SAMs. There was also an ASROC launcher amidships. Electronics were designed to be fully compatible with those of *Enterprise* and one of the major visual characteristics of the ship was her huge SPS-32/33 "billboard" antenna arrays. The Talos system was removed in 1979 and the after launcher replaced by four Harpoon launchers. and she underwent a major refit between 1980 and 1983, which included removing the SPS-32/33 arrays (although the flat-faced surfaces remained) and installing two Phalanx CIWS systems; a proposal to install launchers for

Leahy

UNITED STATES OF AMERICA

Guided-missile cruiser
Completed: 1962-64.
Number in class: 9.
Displacement: 5,146 tons standard; 7,590 tons full load.
Dimensions: Length 555.0 ft (162.5m); beam 53.3ft (16.3m); draught 19.0ft (5.8m).
Propulsion: 2 shafts; geared turbines; 4 boilers; 85,000shp; 32kt; 8,000nm at 20kt.
Armament: 2 x Mark 10 launchers for Terrier SAM (2 x 2); 1 x launcher for ASROC ASW system; 4 x 3in (76mm) guns; 6 x 12.75in (324mm) ASW TT.
Complement: 377.

History: The conventionally-powered Leahy-class ships, together with their nuclear-powered half-sister *Bainbridge*, were the second generation of AAW escorts and were designed at a time when it was thought that the naval gun would totally disappear. The class consisted of nine ships: *Dale, England, Gridley, Halsey, Leahy, Reeves, Richmond, Turner, Worden* and *Yarnell*. They were "double-ended", ie with missile launchers both fore and aft, although locating missiles on the foredeck was considered by many at the time to make them vulnerable to damage by the sea. It was for this reason that the Leahy-class was given a "knuckle," intended to divert spray away from the foredeck, which had not previously been a characteristic of US ship design. There were two Mark 10 launchers, each with a forty-round magazine and an ASROC ASW missile launcher was also carried (the launcher contained eight rounds and there were no reloads) with an SQS-23 sonar dome in the bow.

The class underwent a major modernisation between 1967 and 1972 to bring their electronic systems up-to-date, and were later fitted with two Phalanx CIWS. They were all stricken in 1993-94.

***Above: Long Beach*, the first nuclear-propelled surface warship in the world**

Tomahawk was not implemented.

During the Vietnam War, *Long Beach* shot down two North Vietnamese MiG fighters, one in May 1968, the second a month later. The ship was deactivated in July 1994.

***Above: Halsey*, eighth of nine, conventionally-powered, Leahy-class cruisers**

Bainbridge

UNITED STATES OF AMERICA

Guided-missile cruiser (nuclear-powered)
Completed: 1962.
Number in class: 1.
Displacement: 7,250 tons light; 7,982 tons full load.
Dimensions: Length 565.0ft (172.3m); beam 56.0ft (17.0m); draught 19.4ft (5.9m).
Propulsion: 2 shaft nuclear; 2 D2G reactors; 2 geared turbines; 60,000shp; 30kt.
Armament: 2 x Mark 10 launcher s for terrier SAM; 1 x launcher for ASROC ASW system; 4 x 3.0in (76mm) guns; 6 x 12.75in (324mm) ASW TT.
Aircraft: 1.
Complement: 459.

History: *Bainbridge* was a near-sister of the Leahy-class (see previous entry) and like them she was "double-ended" but, since her nuclear unit did not require exhausts, she did not have the prominent "macks". The layout of the main armament was identical with the Leahy-class, with twin-arm Mark 10 launchers fore and aft, each with a forty-missile magazine. There was also an ASROC box launcher before the bridge (no reloads) and an SQS-23 sonar dome in the bow.

The ship underwent major modernisation between 1974 and 1976, which included updating all electronic systems and the addition of a large deckhouse between the two masts, which housed the new NTDS (Naval Tactical Digital System) command-and-control system. The 3in (76mm) guns were also removed, and quadruple Harpoon launchers and two Phalanx CIWS installed.

Belknap

UNITED STATES OF AMERICA

Guided-missile cruiser
Completed: 1964-67.
Number in class: 9.
Displacement: 5,409 tons light; 7,890 tons full load.
Dimensions: Length 547.0ft (166.8m); beam 54.8ft (16.7m); draught 18.2ft (5.5m).
Propulsion: 2 shafts; geared turbines; 4 boilers; 85,000shp; 32kt; 7,100nm at 20kt.
Armament: 1 x Mark 10 launcher for Terrier SAM/ASROC ASW; 1 x 5.0in (127mm) gun; 2 x 3.0in (76mm); 6 x 12.8in (324mm) ASW TT (not in all).
Aircraft: 1.
Complement: 388.

History: The Belknap-class, together with their nuclear-powered half-sister, *Truxtun*, constitute the final group of AAW "frigates" completed for the US Navy during the 1960s, and like the Leahy-class, also consisted of nine ships: *Belknap*, *Biddle*, *Daniels*, *Fox*, *Horne*, *Jouett*, *Standley*, *Sterret*, and *Wainwright*. The Belknaps shared a common hull form and superstructure with the Leahy-class, but there was a major shift in emphasis in the weapons systems embarked.

In the Belknap-class the "double-ended" concept was dropped, with the one remaining missile launcher on the foredeck. This single twin-arm Mark 10 launcher was served by three twenty-round magazines which were capable a carrying Talos or Standard SAMs, or, in a major advance, ASROC ASW missiles, thus doing away with the separate box launcher previously required. The weather deck area saved by these changes enabled a 5in (127mm) gun to be mounted on the quarterdeck, and a hangar and flightdeck for the

***Above:* Bainbridge was a nuclear-propelled version of the Leahy-class**

The helicopter-based LAMPS-1 ASW system was also installed.

Bainbridge was decommissioned in 1995 after a long career escorting carrier battle groups in the Pacific.

***Above:* Belknap, name-ship of a class of nine conventionally-powered cruisers**

LAMPS-1 ASW helicopter ASW system to be installed immediately abaft the second "mack."

Belknap collided with the carrier *John F Kennedy* in November 1975, resulting in very serious damage to the smaller ship, but she survived and was rebuilt. Several of these ships had live engagements with hostile aircraft during the Vietnam War and *Biddle* and *Sterret* are both known to have downed MiGs, while the latter may also have shot down a Styx missile, which, if correct, would have been the first ever operational anti-missile engagement. All these ships were stricken in the mid-1990s.

Truxtun

UNITED STATES OF AMERICA

Guided-missile cruiser (nuclear-powered)
Completed: 1967.
Number in class: 1.
Displacement: 8,149 tons light; 8,927 tons full load.
Dimensions: Length 564.0ft (172.0m); beam 57.8ft (17.6m); draught 19.8ft (6.0m).
Propulsion: nuclear; 2 shafts; 2 D2G nuclear reactors; 2 geared turbines; 60,000shp; 30kt.
Armament: 1 x Mark 10 launcher for Terrier SAM/ASROC ASW; 1 x 5.0in (127mm) gun; 2 x 3.0in (76mm); 6 x 12.8in (324mm) ASW TT.
Aircraft: 1.
Complement: 490.

History: *Truxtun* was originally included in the US Navy's Belknap-class programme as a conventionally-powered ship, but was given nuclear propulsion at the insistence of the US Congress. She carried an identical weapons outfit to her half-sisters, but major modifications were made to the layout., the most marked being that the positions of the missile launcher and gun were reversed. Thus, the single 5.0in (127mm) gun was on the foredeck, while the twin-arm Mark 10 launcher was on the quarterdeck, with its magazines under the helicopter flightdeck. A further change was that instead of the two triple ASW torpedo launchers on rotating mounts *Truxtun* had two fixed tubes, located in the superstructure amidships. The helicopter hangar was wider but shorter than that in the Belknap-class. As built, *Truxtun* mounted two twin 3in (76mm) mounts amidships, but these were replaced in the late

California

UNITED STATES OF AMERICA

Guided-missile cruiser (nuclear-powered)
Completed: 1974-75.
Number in class: 2.
Displacement: 9,561 tons standard; 11,100 tons full load.
Dimensions: Length 596.0ft (181.7m); beam 61.0ft (18.6m); draught 20.5ft (6.3m).
Propulsion: nuclear; 2 shafts; 2 D2G nuclear reactors; 60,000shp; 30+kt.
Armament: 2 x Mark 13 single-arm launchers for Standard SAM; 1 x launcher for ASROC ASW system; 2 x 5.0in (127mm) (2 x 1) guns; 4 x 12.8in (234mm) ASW TT.
Complement: 533.

History: These two ships, *California* and *South Carolina*, were built to meed the need for a new class of nuclear escort to accompany the new Nimitz-class CVNs, and a third ship was approved in FY68, but later cancelled in favour of the improved Virginia design. The California-class was considerably larger and even more sophisticated than *Truxtun* and returned to the "double-ended" concept, although using single-arm Mark 13 launchers. This had several disadvantages, because, first, ASROC could not be launched from the Mark 13, so a separate box launcher and magazine were required for the ASW missiles, and, secondly, the later extended-range version of the Standard missile (SM-ER) could not be handled. *California* was the first ship in the navy to mount the new lightweight 5in (127mm) gun and the first to have the SPG-51D digital (as opposed to analogue) missile-control system. These ships had a flightdeck aft, but did not have a hangar. These ships had a new version of the D2G nuclear

1970s by two quadruple Harpoon SSM launchers. Two Phalanx CIWS were also mounted.

Truxtun spent all her service as part of the *Enterprise*'s escort group, together with *Long Island* and *Bainbridge*. She was decommissioned in 1995.

Below:* Congress forced the US Navy to install nuclear-propulsion in *Truxtun

reactor whose core had three times the life of that fitted in *Truxtun*.

They were both recored in 1993, at which time their ASROC was removed. They were both stricken in the late 1990s.

***Above: South Carolina,* one of two nuclear-powered California-class cruisers**

Virginia

UNITED STATES OF AMERICA

Guided-missile cruiser (nuclear-powered)
Completed: 1976-80.
Number in class: 4.
Displacement: 8,625 tons standard; 10,420 tons full load.
Dimensions: Length 596.0ft (181.7m); beam 61.0ft (18.6m); draught 20.5ft (6.3m).
Propulsion: nuclear; 2 shafts; 2 D2G nuclear reactors; 2 geared turbines; 60,000shp; 30+kt.
Armament: 2 x Mark 26 twin-arm launchers for Standard MR SAM and ASROC ASW missiles (see notes); 2 x 5in (127mm) guns (2 x 1); 4 x 12.8in (324mm) ASW TT.
Aircraft: 2 helicopters.
Complement: 519.

History: The Virginia-class was originally intended to be a nuclear-powered counterpart to the Spruance-class DDGs, but they were eventually built as modified versions of the California-class CGNs (see previous entry). There were, however, some significant improvements, which included the new Mark 26 twin-arm launcher, of which the forward one handled both Standard SAMs and ASROC ASW missiles, thus doing away with the separate ASROC launcher and magazine. The elimination of the separate facilities for ASROC enabled the hull to be shortened by 10.0ft (3.1m). As with most other surface warships, eight launch canisters for Harpoon anti-ship missiles were installed in the 1980s.

One unusual feature was the helicopter hangar beneath the quarterdeck. Such an arrangement was used in many wartime cruisers, but was then discontinued, to reappear in this class. A lift transferred the helicopters from the flightdeck to the hangar. All Virginia-class cruisers were retired in the late 1990s.

Above: Virginia's **foredeck, with twin-arm Mark 26 launcher and 5in (127mm) gun**

Left: Mississippi **aft, with same weapons as forward, plus helipad but no hangar**

Ticonderoga

UNITED STATES OF AMERICA

Guided-missile cruisers
Completed: 1983-94.
Number in class: 27.
Specifications for *Ticonderoga*, as built.
Displacement: 7,019 tons light; 9,589 tons full load.
Dimensions: Length 565.9ft (172.5m); beam 55.1ft (16.8m); draught 24.6ft (7.5m).
Propulsion: 4 shafts; COGAG; 4 General Electric LM-2500 gas-turbines; 100,000shp; 30+kt; 6,000nm at 20kt.
Armament: 2 x Mark 26 twin-arm launchers for Standard SM-2 MR SAM; 8 x launchers for Harpoon SSM; 2 x 5in (127mm) gun (1 x 2); 2 x 20mm Vulcan Phalanx CIWS; 2 x 25mm Bushmaster cannon; 6 x 12.8in (324mm) ASW TT
Aircraft: 1 LAMPS-III ASW helicopter.
Complement: 380.

History: The Ticonderoga-class cruisers use the same basic hull and gas-turbine propulsion system as the Spruance-class destroyers, the difference lying in their combat systems. In the 1970s the major threat to US and NATO fleets, but particularly to US carrier battle groups, came from omni-directional saturation missile attacks launched from a combination of Soviet surface warships, submarines and aircraft. Conventional radar systems could not cope with such a threat, so the Aegis system had to be developed specifically to counter it, resulting in this planar array system, with each of the four SPY-1 fixed antennas covering one quarter of the airspace around the ship. The required 360deg coverage is then achieved by sequential illumination using electronic control, rather than by mechanical rotation of the entire antenna used by conventional systems.

The ships were built in two major groups. The first group of five ships (*Ticonderoga* [CG 47] to *Gates* [CG 51]) are armed with two Mark 26 twin-arm

launchers, each served by a below-decks rotating magazine, containing forty-four Standard SM-2(MR) missiles. The remainder, from *Bunker Hill* (CG 52) onwards, are armed with two Mark 41 vertical launcher groups, one forward, the other aft, containing a total of 122 missiles, the majority Standard SM-2(MR) SAMs, but with a number of Tomahawk anti-ship/land-attack missiles also being carried. All ships have two 5.0in (127mm) guns (one forward, one aft), eight Harpoon anti-ship missile launchers on the transom, and a flightdeck and hangar for the LAMPS-III helicopter. All also have two 20mm Vulcan Phalanx CIWS which are mounted on platforms immediately abaft the forward funnel, one on each side.

One other difference from the Spruance-class is that the Ticonderoga-class ships are fitted with a large bulwark, which was necessary because the greatly increased weight causes the hull to sit rather deeper in the water and without the bulwark the foredeck would be extremely wet.

The earlier ships are now just over twenty years old and a plan has been developed for major upgrades (Cruiser Conversion Program [CCP]) during the period 2001-2010. The original plan included the first four ships, which would have had their twin-arm launchers replaced by Mark 41 vertical launch groups. The programme has, however, been changed and it is now likely that the first four ships will simply be retired, with sixteen further ships being modified, which will include an updating of all weapons systems (including the replacement of Vulcan Phalanx by RAM [rolling airframe missile] and modernisation of all electronic systems. A later plan will be made for the remaining (newest) ships, but meanwhile it has been announced that four of these ships will be modified to incorporate a limited ballistic missile defence system and will return to service with this capability in 2005.

***Below:* Ticonderoga-class missile cruiser, *San Jacinto*; twenty-seven have been built**

Destroyers

The modern destroyer owes its existence to the sudden emergence of small and very fast torpedo-boats in the 1880s, which threatened to devastate battle fleets in a myriad of pin-prick attacks. The answer lay in the "torpedo-boat destroyer" which was soon shortened to "destroyer", a vessel of about 800-1,000 tons displacement which, in order to deal with the torpedo boats, was armed with guns and very fast. Thus, in most fleets destroyer men became a race apart, their dashing ships and small crews making for a much closer camaraderie than existed on the bigger ships.

In World War I it was realised that destroyers were excellent ships in their own right, so they were armed with torpedo tubes and assembled in flotillas to take part in fleet actions. In addition to this, the emergence of the U-boat as a highly dangerous enemy raised the requirement for large numbers of smaller warships to deal with them and the destroyer was one of the major answers.

As with most types of warship, the size of the destroyer continued to increase, as did the number and complexity of the weapons it carried. Thus, by the outbreak of World War II they were fast and capable ships capable of acting independently or grouped together in flotillas. As in World War I they served as anti-submarine ships, especially on long-distance convoys, but also as general-purpose warships, taking part in numerous surface actions. Some outstanding

designs were produced, of which the German 1936 type, British Battle-class and US Gearing-class were probably the best, the latter being produced in great numbers.

During the Cold War, the size of what was described as a destroyer increased yet again, until there was a split in most navies, with ships displacing 2-5,000 tons with a predominantly ASW role being classified as frigates, while ships displacing 4,000 tons and over and with a mainly air defence or anti-surface role were classified as destroyers. Indeed, there is such reluctance to use the term "cruiser" that the US Navy's Arleigh Burke-class, displacing 8,000 tons, and the Japanese Kongo-class, displacing 9,000 tons, are both classified as destroyers, even though they are larger than many World War II cruisers. Concerning Japanese destroyers, it should be noted that, although produced with remarkably little publicity or fuss, the post-war Japanese destroyers are among the most numerous and best designed in any navy.

One aspect that is very apparent from this book is that modern destroyers have come a long way from the British "30-knotters", when they were small and inexpensive "maids-of-all-work". Today, they are large, very well-equipped and highly sophisticated – and, as a consequence, very expensive – warships.

Below:* H.M.S. *Devonshire a British Country-class destroyer

St Laurent

CANADA

Completed: 1955-57.
Number in class: 7.
Displacement: 2,000 tons standard; 2,600 tons full load.
Dimensions: Length 366.0ft (111.6m); beam 42.0ft (12.8m); draught 13.2ft (4.2m).
Propulsion: 2 shafts; English Electric geared steam-turbines; 2 boilers; 30,000shp; 28kt.
Armament: 4 x 3in (76mm) DP (2 x 2); 2 x 40mm AA; 2 x Limbo Mk 10 ASW mortars.
Complement: 290.

History: These ships were designed at a time when NATO had a pressing requirement for escorts to keep merchant shipping moving across the Atlantic in the event of war with the Soviet Union. The design was prepared in Canada by a British naval architect on loan, and was based generally on the British Whitby-class escort then building for the Royal Navy, but it incorporated the lessons learnt by the Royal Canadian Navy during World War Two, when it had provided a large proportion of the Allied escort force fighting the German U-boats. The many curved surfaces, for example, were designed to prevent the formation of ice, always a major hazard in northern waters. They were excellent seaboats, but only a few years after entering service their short-range ASW armament was no longer adequate to deal with nuclear-powered submarines. As a result, they were all rebuilt in the mid-1960s, being given a helicopter platform and hangar, and variable-depth sonar; the single funnel was replaced

Restigouche

CANADA

Completed: 1958-59.
Number in class: 7.
Displacement: 2,000 tons standard; 2,600 tons full load.
Dimensions: Length 366.0ft (111.6m); beam 42.0ft (12.8m); draught 13.2ft (4.2m).
Propulsion: 2 shafts; English Electric geared steam-turbines; 2 boilers; 30,000shp; 28kt.
Armament: 2 x 3.0in (76mm) Mk 6 DP (2 x 1); 2 x 3.0in (76mm) Mark 22 DP; 2 x 40mm AA; 2 x Mark 10 Limbo ASW mortars.
Complement: 290.

History: The Restigouche-class was ordered in 1952, and was essentially a modified St Laurent design. Forward of the bridge, a British 3.0in/70cal Mk 6 mounting replaced the US weapon, although the after mounting remained unchanged. As with the St Laurent-class it became necessary to upgrade these ships in the mid-1960s to cope with the threat from SSNs, and all seven ships were given the US ASROC (anti-submarine rocket) system, which replaced the after gun mounting and one of the two Limbo ASW mortars. Due to financial constraints, only four could be converted and the remaining three were placed in reserve in 1974. The four that were converted served on in the Pacific and were given a DELEX in the early 1980s. *Terra Nova* and *Restigouche* both served in the Gulf War in the early 1990s for which they were fitted with two Phalanx Mk 15 CIWS, two quadruple Harpoon launchers (in place of ASROC), two 40mm Bofors (in place of the ship's boats),

***Above: Skeena* shows the unique design features of Canadian Cold War destroyers**

by twin exhaust uptakes. The helicopter was the Canadian version of the Seaking and at that time was by far the largest ASW helicopter in service aboard a 3,000 ton escort. The first of these ships was scrapped in 1979, but the others were given a Destroyer Life Extension (DELEX) which kept them in service until 1989-94.

---

two 0.5in (12.7mm) MGs, and upgraded electronics and communications equipment. All were laid off as the City-class destroyers entered service.

***Below: Terra Nova* of the Restigouche-class, seven ships built in the late 1950s**

Mackenzie

CANADA

Completed: 1962-63.
Number in class: 4.
Displacement: 2,000 tons standard; 2,600 tons full load.
Dimensions: Length 366.0ft (111.6m); beam 42.0ft (12.8m); draught 13.2ft (4.2m).
Propulsion: 2 shafts; English Electric geared steam-turbines; 2 boilers; 30,000shp; 28kt.
Armament: 2 x 3in (76mm) Mk 6 DP (2 x 1); 2 x 3in (76mm) Mark 22 DP; 2 x 40mm AA; 2 x Mark 10 Limbo ASW mortars.
Complement: 290.

History: These four destroyers were ordered in 1957 and were essentially a repeat of the Restigouche-class, but with many minor improvements, primarily intended to improve habitability. In addition, yet further improvements were made to the bridge and weather-deck fittings to improve their suitability for cold-weather operations in northern Atlantic and Arctic waters, while the pre-wetting system for washing-off nuclear fall-out was also upgraded. They remained unmodified for many years in service, except for the fitting of Mark 32 12.8in (324mm) ASW torpedo tubes. In the early 1980s, however, they all underwent a limited DELEX updating refit,

Annapolis

CANADA

Completed: 1964.
Number in class: 2.
Displacement: 2,400 tons standard; 3,000 tons full load.
Dimensions: Length 366.0ft (111.6m); beam 42.0ft (12.8m); draught 13.2ft (4.2m).
Propulsion: 2 shafts; English Electric geared steam turbines; 2 boilers; 30,000shp; 28kt.
Armament: 2 x 3in (76mm) Mark 33 DP (1 x 2); 6 x 12.8in (324mm) Mark 32 ASW TT; 1 x Limbo Mark 10 ASW mortar.
Aircraft: 1 helicopter
Complement: 228.

History: These two ships, *Annapolis* and *Nipigon*, were the final sub-group in the 20-strong St Laurent-series of ships, which represented a major success for the Royal Canadian Navy. The hull form and machinery were identical to the earlier classes, but the upperworks underwent a major redesign and a radically new armament was fitted. These were the first Canadian destroyers to be designed from the outset for helicopter operation and, unlike foreign designs which tended to place the hangar and flightdeck aft, the Canadians mounted them virtually amidships, where the effects of pitch were much reduced. The forward end of the hangar embraced the twin exhaust uptakes, thus saving space which then

when they were given SQS-505 sonar and some of the electronic systems were replaced. They spent the latter part of their service in the Pacific Training Group and were disposed of between 1992 and 1995.

***Below: Mackenzie*, one of a class of four; note curves designed to prevent ice forming**

allowed a Mark 10 Limbo ASW mortar to be mounted. The ships had a good sonar fit which included the stern-mounted SQS-504 variable-depth sonar. To compensate for the increased topweight, only one twin 3in (76mm) mounting was fitted, the US Navy's Mark 33 being preferred to the British model fitted in earlier ships, because it was lighter. Both ships were modernised in 1977-79 and underwent a DELEX in 1982-85. Both were stricken in the mid-1990s.

***Below: Annapolis*; this class of two was the final development of the St Laurent design**

Iroquois

CANADA

Completed: 1970-73.
Number in class: 4.
Displacement: 3,551 tons standard; 4,700 tons full load.
Dimensions: Length 423.0ft (128.9m); beam 50.0ft (15.2m); draught 14..5ft (4.4m).
Propulsion: 2 shaft; COGOG; 2 Pratt & Whitney FT4A2 gas-turbines (boost), 50,000shp; 2 Pratt & Whitney FT12AH3 gas-turbines (cruising),7,400shp; 29kt; 4,500nm at 20kt.
Armament: 1 x 5in (127mm) Super Rapid; 1 x Mark 41 vertical launch system for Standard SM-2 (MR); 1 x Phalanx 20mm CIWS; 6 x 12.8in (324mm) ASW TT.
Aircraft: 2 helicopters.
Complement: 285

History: The design of these four ships, collectively known as the "Tribal-class" derived from that of a projected "air defence missile frigate" prepared for the Canadian navy in the early 1960s. In the event, the planned Tartar missile system proved far too expensive and the design was recast to produce an ASW ship, incorporating the necessary sonars and ASW torpedo tubes, as well as a hangar and flightdeck for two CH-124 Seaking helicopters. As a result of a decision late in the design process, these were the first Western ships to be built with an all-gas turbine propulsion system. The result was a ship that was widely acknowledged to be the finest ASW destroyer of its generation.

The four ships underwent a major rebuild designated "TRUMP" (Tribal Update and Modernisation Programme) which was intended to convert them into the long-awaited area-defence missile ships. On the foredeck the 5.0in

Almirante Riveros

CHILE

Completed: 1960.
Number in class: 2.
Displacement: 2,730 tons standard; 3,300 tons full load.
Dimensions: Length 402.0ft (122.5m); beam 43.0ft (13.1m); draught 13.3ft (4.0m).
Propulsion: 2 shafts; Parsons Pametrada geared turbines; 2 boilers; 54,000shp; 34.5kt.
Armament: 4 x 4.0in (102mm) DP (4 x 1); 6 x 40mm AA; 5 x 21in (533mm); 2 x Squid ASW mortar.
Complement: 266.

History: The Chilean Navy has had a long and close relationship with the British Royal Navy and until recently bought many British warships, some of them second-hand, but many, as in this case of *Almirante Riveros* and *Almirante Williams*, brand-new. The hull and propulsion system were virtually identical with the British Daring-class, but the armament was different, consisting of four automatic 4.0in (102mm) guns in single turrets. which were specially designed for these Chilean ships by Vickers. Secondary armament comprised six 40mm Bofors amidships and five 21.0in (533mm) torpedo tubes in a single mounting abaft the after funnel. After some four years in service two quadruple Seacat SAM launchers were mounted in place of two of the 40mm guns. Both ships underwent a major modernisation between 1971 and 1975, which included a completely new sensor fit and some changes to the armament. This comprised the removal of the 21.0in (533mm) torpedo tubes, and their replacement by four MM38 Exocet launchers and six 12.8in (324mm) Mark 32 ASW tubes. Two of the Exocet launchers were later removed and installed in other Chilean ships. These two very handsome and capable ships were stricken in the late 1990s.

Right: **The Iroquois-class aviation facilities, showing large hangar and flightdeck close to centre of pitch**

(127mm) gun was removed and replaced by a Mark 41 vertical launcher for the Standard SM-2 (MR) missile system, for which twenty-nine missiles are carried. A much lighter 76mm gun was mounted atop the forward deckhouse and the bifurcated exhausts were replaced by a single funnel. Internally, the cruise engines being replaced by two new GM-Allison 570KF gas-turbines. They are due to remain in service until about 2004, although one may be decommissioned earlier, as part of the naval contribution to a 1999 defence cutting proposal.

Below: **Handsome lines of *Almirante Riveros* are of unmistakable British origin**

Luda I/II

PEOPLE'S REPUBLIC OF CHINA

Specifications for Luda I, as built.
Completed: 1972-92.
Number in class: Luda I - 17; Luda II - 1.
Displacement: 3,760 tons standard; 3,960 tons full load.
Dimensions: Length 433.1ft (132.0m); beam 42.0ft (12.8m); draught 14.5ft (4.4m).
Propulsion: 2 shafts; geared steam turbines; 4 boilers; 72,000shp; 32kt; 4,000nm at 15kt.
Armament: 6 x HY-2 SSM (2 x 3); 4 x 5.1in (130mm) guns (2 x 2); 8 x 57mm or 37mm AA; 4 x 25mm AA; 2 ASW rocket launchers; 2 or 4 depth-charge throwers.
Complement: ca. 300

History: These were the first ocean-going warships to be built for the People's Liberation Army - Navy (PLAN), the design being based on that of the Soviet Neustrashimmy-class (known to NATO as the Talinn-class). Only one of those Soviet ships was completed in 1955 and the project was then not pursued any further, so presumably the Soviet Navy was not reluctant to pass the design on to the PLAN. The latter copied most of the features of the original, the major innovation being the main armament, which comprised four HY-2 anti-ship missiles, mounted in two pairs on trainable mounts, replacing the torpedo tubes in the original Soviet *Neustrashimmy*.

Sixteen of the first version, Luda I, were completed between 1972 and 1981, of which one was destroyed in an explosion in 1978. The surviving fifteen were all in service in 2001. One ship of a modified design, designated Luda II in

Luhu

PEOPLE'S REPUBLIC OF CHINA

Completed: 1993-96.
Number in class: 2.
Displacement: 4,800 tons standard; 5,700 tons full load.
Dimensions: Length 485.6ft (148.0m); beam 52.5ft (16.0m); draught 24.6ft (7.5m).
Propulsion: 2 shafts; CODOG; 2 General Electric LM–2500 gas-turbines, 53,600shp, 31.5kt; 2 MTU 12V1163 diesels, 8,840bhp, 20kt; 4,000nm at 16kt..
Armament: 8 x C-802 or C-801 SSM (4 x 2); 1 x HQ-7 (Crotale) SAM; 2 x 3.9in (100mm) guns (2 x 1); 8 x 37mm AA; 6 x 12.8in (324mm) ASW TT; 2 x Type 74 ASW rocket launchers.
Aircraft: 2 helicopters.
Complement: 230.

History: These two ships, *Harbin* and *Qingdao*, were completed in 1991 and 1993 respectively, and represented a major leap forward for both the PLAN and the Chinese shipbuilding industry. Anti-ship armament comprises eight C-802 or C-801A anti-ship missiles in box launchers, which, as in Luda II, are fixed and angled outwards. There is also one twin 100mm mount in "A" position. The air defence missile system is the Hong Qian-7 (HQ-7), which is thought to be a locally-produced version of the French Crotale Modulaire; this is in an eight-round launcher, with an adjacent magazine containing a further eight rounds. Close-in air defence is provided

Above: **Luda I-class of the PLAN; China's first ocean-going warship design**

the West, was completed in 1992. This mounts eight YJ-1 SSM launchers, which are much smaller than the earlier HY-2 and are mounted in simple, fixed box launchers, the forward group of four being angled out to port and the after group to starboard. The Luda II also has a number of Western electronic systems.

Many Western reports claim that these ships are "primitive" and not up to Western standards, but that was not the point. They have given the PLAN invaluable experience in operating destroyer-size ships in the open ocean and enabled it to impose an increasing dominance over the South China Sea. In addition, they gave Chinese naval architects and ship builders experience in working on modern designs, which has been utilised to the full in subsequent designs, which are of wholly Chinese origin.

---

by eight 37mm guns in four, fully automatic twin mounts, which, as in Italian ships, are sited to give 360deg coverage, with two immediately before the bridge and two at the after end of the hangar roof, all are mounted on small sponsons. There is also a hangar and flightdeck for two ASW helicopters; the flightdeck is fitted with a French Samahe helicopter recovery system. Although these two ships appear satisfactory for the PLAN's needs, only two were built and production then moved on to an enlarged version, the Luhai-class.

Below: **Luhu-class destroyer, designed in China but with much Western equipment**

Arquebuse/Claymore

FRANCE

Specifications for Arquebuse-class, as built.
Completed: Arquebuse - 1902-05; Claymore - 1905-08.
Number in class: Arquebuse - 20; Claymore - 13.
Displacement: 298 tons.
Dimensions: length 190.9ft (58.2m); beam 21.0ft (6.4m); draught 10.4ft (3.2m).
Propulsion: 2 shafts; Triple-Expansion engines; 2 boilers; 6,300ihp; 28kt.
Armament: 1 x 2.6in (65mm); 6 x 47mm; 2 x 15in (381mm) TT.
Complement: 60.

History: Starting in 1899 the French Navy built a series of *contre-torpilleurs* (torpedo-boat destroyers) known as the *300 tonne* design, the first three groups, each of four ships, being the Durandal-class, Framée-class and Rochfortais-class. There were some differences between each of these groups, but all were very minor, all being identically armed and powered. They did, however, suffer from a number of problems, including instability and an inability to reach their design speeds. As a result, the fourth group, the Arquebuse-class, were slightly larger and were given higher boiler pressure

***Below: Arbalète,* one of the twenty-strong Arquebuse-class built in 1902-05**

which enabled them to reach their design speed, while a reorganisation and increase in the superstructure made life at sea slightly more comfortable for the crew. In addition, the deletion of the mainmast reduced the topweight problem. The result was a more satisfactory ship and apart from two war losses (*Mousquet* in 1914 and *Catapulte* in 1918) they all survived World War One. All were then scrapped between 1919 and 1921.

The next group, the Claymore-class, had a yet further minor increase in beam and a rise in propulsive power to 6,800ihp, but the main difference was that they mounted two tubes for the new 17.7in (450mm) torpedoes, which, for such small boats, represented an appreciable increase in topweight. This gave rise to renewed problems over topweight, which could only be overcome by reducing the upperworks and replacing the closed bridge by an open one. Perhaps surprisingly, they all survived the war and were stricken in the 1920s, although one, *Trident*, served on until 1931.

These *contre-torpilleurs* were lightly constructed and were very poor seaboats, as a result, they were not only unsuitable for fleet actions but were also not very good as escorts, either.

Bouclier

FRANCE

Specifications for Bouclier, as built (see notes).
Completed: 1910-12.
Number in class: 12.
Displacement: 692 tons.
Dimensions: Length 237.0ft (72.2m); beam 24.9ft (7.6m); draught 9.6ft (2.9m).
Propulsion: 3-shafts; Parsons turbines; 4 boilers; 13,000shp; 35.5kt; 1,600nm at 14kt.
Armament: 2 x 3.9in (100mm) (2 x 1); 4 x 65mm; 4 x 17.7in (450mm) TT.
Complement: 80

History: These twelve ships were nominally 800 tonners, but the six shipyards involved in their construction were given the general specification required by the French Navy and then allowed to produce their own designs. The armament was standard, but the yards were simply told that the ships were to be powered by turbines and the boilers were to be oil-fired, and were given outline requirements as to size and crewing, and, not surprisingly, this resulted in some noticeable differences. For propulsion, two had three shafts and Parsons turbines, while the remainder had two shafts and turbines made by Breguet (2), Parsons (4), Rateau (3) and Zoelly (1). All twelve ships had four boilers, but over the class as a whole, four different makes were installed. All had three funnels, except *Casque*, which had three. There were several consequences, one of which was that performance differed markedly, with the three-screw *Bouclier* being the fastest at 35.5 knots, while the twin-screw ships did 30 knots, although *Commandant Bory* never managed more than 24 knots. The ships had

Le Fantasque

FRANCE

Completed: 1933-34.
Number in class: 6.
Displacement: 2,569 tons standard; 3,400 tons full load.
Dimensions: Length 434.3ft (132.4m); beam 40.5ft (12.5m); draught 16.4ft (5.0m).
Propulsion: 2 shafts; geared steam-turbines; 4 boilers; 74,000shp; 37kt; 4,000nm at 15t.
Armament: 5 x 5in (127mm) (5 x 1); 4 x 37mm AA; 4 x 13.2mm AA; 9 x 21.7in (550mm) TT; 50 mines.
Complement: 210.

History: These extremely handsome ships, the first of the French twin funnel "super destroyers," were, for the whole of their operational careers, the fastest flotilla craft afloat. Three (*L'Indomptable, Le Malin, Le Triomphant*) were powered by Parsons, the three others (*Le Audacieux, Le Fantasque, Le Terrible*) by Rateau geared turbines and all were quite capable of sustaining 37 knots at full load, while *Le Terrible* demonstrated a maximum speed of 45.03 knots, and 42.93 knots for eight hours. They were armed with the new Model 1929 5.5in (140mm) gun, which had a theoretical rate of fire of twelve rounds per minute and a maximum range of 21,900yd (20,000m). Late in their careers (about 1944) the survivors were re-rated as light cruisers, although their range was not that of a true cruiser.

Two of the class were lost during the war: *L'Indomptable* being scuttled (27 November 1942) and *L'Audacieux* being sunk by Allied bombers at Bizerta (7 May 1943). The remaining four spent most of the war with the

***Above:* *Francis Garnier*, one of twelve destroyers designed and built in six shipyards**

a very active time during the war, nine being in the Mediterranean throughout the period, while three served in the Channel. There were four war losses: two to mines, one to an Austrian U-boat, and one was lost in a collision with another French destroyer. The surviving ships were stricken between 1927 and 1933.

free french forces and were refitted in the United States in 1943-44. These four served on into the post-war period and were eventually stricken between 1954 and 1964.

***Below:* The superb lines of French "super destroyer" *Le Terrible*, capable of 37kt**

Surcouf (T 47)

FRANCE

Completed: 1955-57.
Number in class: 12.
Displacement: 2,750 tons standard; 3,740 tons full load.
Dimensions: Length 422.0ft (128.6m); beam 42.0ft (12.7m); draught 18.0ft (5.4m).
Propulsion: 2 shafts; Rateau geared turbines; 4 boilers; 63,000shp; 34kt; 5,000nm at 18kt.
Armament: 6 x 5.0in (127mm) Mod 1948 (3 x 2); 6 x 57mm AA; 4 x 20mm; 12 x 21.6in (550mm) TT.
Complement: 347

History: These twelve ships were lineal descendants of the French inter-war "super-destroyers" and were somewhat larger than most destroyers completed in the 1950s. The primary missions for these ships, which were designated *escorteur d'escadre*, was as anti-aircraft escorts for the French Navy's new aircraft carriers, for which they were originally armed with six 5.0in (127mm) guns, a calibre deliberately chosen to enable them to use the widely-available US ammunition.

Between 1962 and 1965 four ships - *Dupetit-Thouars, Kersaint, Bouvet* and *Du Chayla* - were re-armed with the US Navy's Tartar air defence missile system, with one single-arm Mark 13 launcher and its magazine replacing the two after gun mounts. In the same refit one of the forward guns ("B" position) was replaced by a 14.8in (375mm) Bofors six-tube ASW rocket launcher, and the two funnels were both heightened. The Tartar installation was upgraded in the late 1960s with a new US radar and a French SENIT 2 command-and-control

DuPerré (T53)/ La Galissonniere (T56)

FRANCE

Specifications are for DuPerré, as built
Completed: DuPerré - 1957-58; La Galissonniere - 1962.
Number in class: DuPerré - 5; La Galissonniere - 1.
Displacement: 2,750 tons standard; 3,740 tons full load.
Dimensions: Length 422.0ft (128.6m); beam 42.0ft (12.7m); draught 18.0ft (5.4m).
Propulsion: 2 shafts; Rateau geared steam-turbines; 4 boilers; 63,000shp; 34kt; 5,000nm at 18kt.
Armament: 6 x 5.0in (127mm) Mod 1948 (3 x 2); 6 x 57mm Mod 1951; 2 or 4 x 20mm AA; 1 x 14.1in (357mm) Bofors ASW rocket launcher; 6 x 21.7in (550mm) TT.
Complement: 346.

History: The five destroyers of the DuPerré-class used the same hull as the Surcouf (T47)-class, the main difference being an increased capability for tracking and controlling aircraft, coupled with a change to the ASW armament. A height-finding radar was installed on the foremast, displacing the air search radar to the mainmast, while 1 x 14.1in (375mm) ASW mortar was mounted aft just ahead of "X" turret. *DuPerré* was converted to a sonar trials ship in 1967, but between 1972 and 1974 she was completely rebuilt for the ASW role, with a hangar and flightdeck aft, a single 100mm gun forward, four Exocet MM38 launchers and two catapults for L5 torpedoes replacing the previous tubes. Additional command facilities were also installed enabling *DuPerré* to be

***Above:* The post-war Surcouf design was directly based on pre-war "super-destroyers"**

system. First to retire was *Bouvet* in 1982, whose missile system was transferred to the new AA destroyer, *Cassard*, and *Kersaint* followed in 1983, in order to pass her missile system to *Jean Bart*. The remaining two ships stayed in service until relieved by the new AA ships: *Dupetit-Thouars* by *Cassard* in 1988 and by *Du Chayla* by *Jean Bart* in 1991.

Five more underwent a different conversion in 1968-70, becoming specialist ASW ships. This involved a virtually complete replacement of their weapons and sensors, including the addition of the Malafon ASW missile system and a bow sonar, which, in turn, required a more clipper bow and a stem anchor. These ships remained in service until relieved by the Georges-Leygues-class ASW frigates in the mid-1980s.

***Above:* The DuPerré-class used the Surcouf hull, but were optimized for air defence**

employed as a flagship. All ships in the class were stricken between 1976 and 1992.

La Galissonniere was completed as an experimental ship, designed to lead into a new class of specialised ASW escorts. She had an identical hull to the T47 and T53 classes, but was armed with a Malafon ASW missile launcher, six 21.7in (550mm) torpedo tubes, a 14.8in (375mm) mortar and an ASW helicopter. The hangar roof doubled as the flightdeck, the hangar being provided by a complicated system of folding panels, an arrangement with a passing similarity to that in the contemporary British Tribal-class, and equally unsatisfactory. She was stricken in 1990.

Suffren

FRANCE

Completed: 1967-70.
Number in class: 2.
Displacement: 5,090 tons standard; 6,090 tons full load.
Dimensions: Length 517.0ft (157.6m); beam 51.0ft (15.5m); draught 24.0ft (7.3m).
Propulsion: 2 shafts; Rateau geared steam turbines; 4 boilers; 72,500shp; 34kt; 5,100nm at 18kt.
Armament: 1 x Masurca SAM twin-arm launcher; 2 x 100mm Mod 1964 (2 x 1);4 x 20mm AA; 1 x Malafon ASW missile launcher; 4 x catapults for L5 torpedoes.
Complement: 355.

History: These were the first French warships designed from the outset to carry SAMs, their role being to provide both air defence and ASW protection for the new Foch-class aircraft carriers. At least three ships were planned but budgetary restraints limited the total to two. The ships and their systems are of exclusively French design and manufacture, the principal missile system being the Masurca medium-range SAM, which is similar in configuration and performance to the US Navy's Terrier. The twin-arm launcher is located on the quarterdeck with the 48-round magazine housed in the superstructure immediately ahead. The original Masurca was a beam-rider, but the Mod 3 has semi-active guidance. The air search radar is the three-dimensional DRBI-23 which is housed in the huge, instantly recognisable radome above the bridge. The Malafon ASW missile launcher is located immediately abaft the mainmast, with thirteen missiles in an adjacent deckhouse. The two ships are scheduled to retire in 2003 (*Suffren*) and 2005 (*Duquesne*).

Tourville (F67)

FRANCE

Completed: 1974-77.
Number in class: 3.
Displacement: 4,850 tons standard; 5,800 tons full load.
Dimensions: Length 501.0ft (152.5m); beam 50.0ft (15.3m); draught 21.0ft (6.5m).
Propulsion: 2 shafts; Rateau geared steam-turbines; 4 boilers; 54,400shp; 31kt; 5,000nm at 18kt.
Armament: 6 x Exocet MM.38 anti-ship missiles; 1 x Crotale SAM launcher; 1 x Malafon ASW missile launcher; 2 x 100mm Mod 1968 (2 x 1); 2 x 20mm AA; 2 catapults for L5 torpedoes.
Aircraft: 2 helicopters.
Complement: 282.

History: These three guided-missile destroyers, *Tourville, Duguay-Trouin* and *De Grasse*, were originally to have been built to the same design as *Aconit*, a single ship which was completed in 1973. However, *Aconit* had a single shaft, which proved unpopular and the Tourville-class was slightly enlarged to enable it to accommodate a doubled-up version of the Aconit propulsion system. This resulted in an increase in speed of 4kt, while the extra space also enabled a hangar and flightdeck to be added, resulting in a much more satisfactory ship. Two Lynx ASW helicopters are carried, and these, together with the Malafon ASW missile system give these ships a good ASW capability, while six Exocet launchers atop the Malafon magazine add a considerable anti-ship capability. These were also among the first ships to be fitted with the Crotale air defence SAM system. Once in service the hull was found to suffer from slight bending and cracking, so two large steel strakes were added just below the upper deck

Below: **The DRBI-23 3-D radome made *Suffren* and *Duquesne* instantly recognisable**

level in the 1970s. *Duguay-Trouin* was retired in 1999, while the other two, which were modernised in the early 1990s, will serve on until 2000-2011.

Below: De Grasse, **one of three Tourville-class guided missile destroyers built 1970-77**

Georges Leygues (C70) FRANCE

Completed: 1979-90.
Number in class: 7.
Displacement: 3,550 tons standard; 4,350 tons full load.
Dimensions: Length 456.0ft (139.1m); beam 46.0ft (14.0m); draught 19.0ft (5.7m).
Propulsion: 2 shafts; CODOG; 2 Rolls-Royce Olympus TM-3B gas-turbines, 52,000shp, 30kt; 2 SEMT-Pielstick 16PA6-CV280 diesels, 10,400bhp, 21kt; 9,500nm at 17kt.
Armament: 4 x MM.38 Exocet anti-ship missiles; 1 x Crotale air defence missile launcher; 1 x 3.9in (100mm) Mod 1968 gun; 2 x 20mm AA; 2 x catapult for L5 ASW torpedoes.
Aircraft: 2 helicopters.
Complement: 216.

History: The George Leygues-class is a smaller, less costly version of the Tourville-class, but the design also made one major innovation with its propulsion machinery. A number of similar-sized contemporary warships, such as the British Type 42 and Dutch Kortenaer-class, used a COGOG arrangement, in which Olympus gas-turbines were used for maximum power in combination with the lower-powered Rolls-Royce Tynes for cruising. The French, however, rejected this for two main reasons, the first being the Tyne's relatively high fuel consumption and the second what they considered to be its insufficient power when running astern, particularly in the tropics. Otherwise, however, the layout was the same as the British and Dutch ships, with the main propulsion machinery grouped centrally in adjacent compartments and the auxiliary machinery rooms fore and aft.

Cassard (C70AA) FRANCE

Completed: 1988-91.
Number in class: 2.
Displacement: 3,900 tons standard; 4,500 tons full load.
Dimensions: Length 456.0ft (139.1m); beam 46.0ft (14.0m); draught 18.0ft (5.6m).
Propulsion: 2 shafts; 4 SEMT-Pielstick 18 PA 6 V280 BTC diesels; 42,300bhp; 29.6kt; 8,000nm at 18kt.
Armament: 1 x Mark 13 launcher for Standard SM-1 SAM; 2 x SADRAL SAM launchers; 1 x 3.9in (100mm) Mod 1968 gun; 2 x 20mm AA; 2 x catapults for L5 ASW torpedoes
Aircraft: 1 helicopter.
Complement: 225.

History: These guided-missile destroyers were intended to replace the air defence versions of the T47 type and shared a common hull with the Georges Leygues-class, being referred to nu the French Navy as the C70AA type. The original plan was for a class of four, but the last two were cancelled in February 1984. Apart from the hull, the very different roles mean that there was little commonality between the two classes and the adoption of an all-diesel propulsion system was dictated mainly by space requirements, since the air intakes and exhausts for the gas-turbines would have limited the space available on the upper deck, and it was also thought that the corrosive exhausts from a gas-turbine would damage the numerous antennas required for the air defence systems. Particular attention was paid to the effectiveness of the flexible engine mountings in order to reduce the noise level compared to traditional diesel installations. To reduce topweight, much of the superstructure was made from lightweight aluminium alloy, but it is claimed

Above: Primauguet, **a Georges Leygues-class (C70ASW) destroyer**

The adoption of gas-turbines, which require extensive intake and exhaust trunking in a hull some 45.0ft (14m) shorter than the Tourville-class placed severe limitations on the space available on the upper deck for weapons systems. As a result it was decided not to mount the Malafon ASW missile system in order to accommodate the facilities required for two Lynx ASW helicopters. For similar reasons, only one 3.9in (100mm) gun could be mounted, and only four Exocet launchers compared to six in the Tourville-class. One shortcoming in the design was that the bridge was found to be too low in rough seas; as a result, in the last three to be built it was raised by one deck level.

It was originally planned to build eight ships, but the last was cancelled as an economy measure. *Georges Leygues* was retired in 2000 and the others will be progressively stricken between 2004 and 2014.

Above: **The two Cassard-class ships, used the C70 hull, but optimised for air defence**

that considerable attention has been paid to fire resistance.

The primary weapons system is the US Navy Standard SM-1 missile and these are the last ships to employ this missile which has been retired from other navies. Forty missiles are carried, being launched from a single-arm Mark 13 launcher, which is mounted just ahead of the helicopter hangar. The complete SAM installations for these two ships were transferred from two of the T47-class AA conversions. The two ships are due to remain in service until 2013 (*Cassard*) and 2015 (*Jean Bart*).

S 138

GERMANY

Completed: 1906-07.
Number in class: 11.
Displacement: 533 tons standard; 684 tons full load.
Dimensions: length 231.9ft (70.7m); beam 25.6ft (7.8m); draught 9.0ft (2.8m).
Propulsion: 2 shafts; Vertical Triple-Expansion engines; 4 boilers; 11,000ihp; 30.3kt; 1,830nm at 17kt.
Armament: 1 x 3,.5in (88mm) gun; 3 x 2in (52mm) guns; 3 x 17.7in (450mm) TT.
Complement: 80.

History: In the early years of the 20th century, the Imperial German Navy produced a series of ships designated *Hochseetorpedoboote*, which translates as "high seas torpedo boats" which were ocean-going warships, capable of operating with the fleet. Indeed, their major war role was to accompany the High Seas Fleet into battle and to attack enemy capital ships with their torpedoes; attacking enemy destroyers was not part of their function. The requirement was for ninety-six units (144 from 1906 onwards) and the practice was to build one class of boats each year. The classes were known as G 132-class, S 138-class V 150-class, and so on, but although the pennant numbers ran sequentially, the letter prefixes had no tactical significance, referring instead to the shipyard responsible for construction: B = Blohm + Voss; G = Germaniawerft; H = Howaldtswerke; S = Schichau; V = AG Vulkan; and Ww = Imperial Yard, Wilhelmshaven. Thus, the S 138-class succeeded the Germania-

1936-type

GERMANY

Completed: 1938-39.
Number in class: 6.
Displacement: 1,811 tons standard; 3,415 tons full load.
Dimensions: Length 404.2ft (123.2m); beam 38.7ft (11.8m); draught 13.1ft (4.0m).
Propulsion: 2 shafts; Wagner geared turbines; 6 boilers; 70,000shp; 38.2kt.
Armament: 5 x 5.0in (127mm) C34 (5 x 1); 4 x 37mm AA; 7 x 20mm AA; 8 x 21in (533mm) TT.
Complement: 313.

History: Germany's first post-World War One destroyers were the 1934-type, of which the first Z1 (Z = *Zerstörer* [destroyer]) was launched in 1935. This class of four was so successful that all further destroyers built up to 1945 were developments of this basic design. The 1934-type was succeeded by the 12-strong 1934A-type (Z5-Z16), which, in turn, was succeeded by the 1936-type. These six ships, Z17-Z22, were very handsome, with a clipper bow, long forecastle, low bridge and two funnels. Armament comprised five 5.0in (127mm) guns in single mounts and ten torpedo tubes, with an increasing number of anti-aircraft weapons as the air threat increased. A problem common to all these destroyers was the propulsion machinery, which employed a high-pressure steam system, which was intended to achieve maximum power in a small space, but, despite much effort on the parts of both designers and engineers, it never achieved a satisfactory degree of performance, and no German destroyer ever achieved its design speed. The *Kriegsmarine's* destroyer force was the victim of one of the major naval disasters of World War Two when ten (out of twenty-one in service) were sunk by the British in the two

built G 137 class and was built by Schichau at Elbing in Fiscal Year 1906. They were small by international standards, one of the major design criteria laid down by the redoubtable Admiral Tirpitz being that the crew had to be no greater than could be commanded by one officer. Two were lost in World War One, the remainder being scrapped in 1920 or 1928.

***Below:* An early German destroyer *(Hochseetorpedoboote)*, S 143 of the S 138 class**

Above:* Z 38 of the 1936A (Mob) type, here seen post-war as HMS *Nonsuch

Battles of Narvik on 10 and 13 April 1940: those lost being Type 1934 - four; Type 1934A - four; Type 1936 - five. Thus, just one of this six-strong class remained - Z20 - which survived the war and was then ceded to the Soviet Union in 1946 and served in the Baltic Fleet for some years.

Hamburg (Type 1010) GERMANY

Completed: 1964-68.
Number in class: 4.
Displacement: 3,340 tons standard; 4,330 tons full load.
Dimensions: length 438.8ft (133.7m); beam 44.0ft (13.4m); draught 17.0ft (5.2m).
Propulsion: 2 shafts; Wahodag steam turbines; 4 boilers; 72,000shp; 36kt; 6,000nm at 13kt.
Armament: 3 x 3.9in (100mm) (3 x 1); 4 x MM.38 Exocet anti-ship missiles; 8 x 40mm AA; 4 x 21.0in (533mm) TT; 3 x 14.8in (375mm) ASW mortars.
Complement: 284.

History: These were the first destroyers to be built for the Federal German Navy (FGN) after World War II. The peace treaty ending the war had prohibited the FGN from building warships of more than 3,000 tons and NATO plans originally called for twelve destroyers, each displacing some 2,500 tons, but when it proved impossible to accommodate the desired capabilities in such a small hull the Western European Union simply raised the limit to 6,000 tons. The design was then recast to produce a ship displacing some 3,400 tons and four were built as the Type 101 or Hamburg-class.

At a time when other navies were already building destroyer-sized ships armed with guided missiles, the German design was very conservative, with an all-gun main armament, and a secondary armament of torpedoes and two Bofors ASW mortars. The Hamburg-class was intended primarily to meet the

***Above: Hessen*, one of four Hamburg-class destroyers of the Federal German Navy**

FRG's NATO-assigned commitment in the Baltic, resulting in a design with a low freeboard and a somewhat "top-heavy" appearance. Despite this the Hamburg-class frequently deployed outside the Baltic and sometimes operated as the FGN's contribution to NATO's Standing Naval Force Atlantic (STANAVFORLANT). These ships were replaced by the Brandenburg Type 123 frigates and were scrapped in the early 1990s

***Below: Schleswig-Holstein* on NATO operations in a Norwegian fjord**

Rajput

INDIA

Completed: 1980-88.
Number in class: 5.
Displacement: 4,050 tons standard; 4,870 tons full load.
Dimensions: Length 479.7ft (146.2m); beam 51.8ft (15.8m); draught 16.1ft (4.9m).
Propulsion: 2 shafts; 4 Type M-3 gas-turbines; 94,000shp; 32kt; 4,000nm at 18kt.
Armament: 4 x P-20 Termit (SS-N-2C Styx) anti-ship missile launchers; 2 x Volna (SA-N-1 Goa) SAM launcher; 2 x 76.2mm AK-726 DP guns (2 x 1); 4 x 30mm AK-630 gatling AA; 5 x 21.0in (533mm) TT; 2 x RBU-6000 ASW rocket launcher.
Aircraft: 1 helicopter.
Complement: 345.

History: For several decades after Independence from Britain the Indian Navy used British-built ships. However, it then started to build its own, the biggest programme being the construction of four British-designed Leander-class frigates, followed by three Godavari-class, which were Indian-designed developments of the Leander design, and then three Improved Godavari class. Meanwhile, increasingly strong links were established with Russia, which included the supply of a number of submarines, but also the provision of the Rajput-class, which is a modified version of the Soviet Navy's Kashin-class. The ships for India were not surplus Soviet Navy ships, but were built specially for the Indian Navy at the Nikolayev yard in Russia between 1977 and 1986. The initial order was for three (*Rajput, Rana, Ranjit*), but this was increased by a further two (*Ranvir, Ranvijay*) after the first-of-class had been in service for two

Nembo

ITALY

Completed: 1901-04.
Number in class: 6.
Displacement: 352 tons standard; 380 tons full load.
Dimensions: length 210.0ft (64.0m); beam 19.5ft (5.9m); draught 7.5ft (2.3m).
Propulsion: 2 shafts; Triple-Expansion engines; 3 boilers; 5,200ihp; 30.2kt.
Armament: 5 x 57mm (5 x 1); 4 x 14.0in (356mm) TT.
Complement: 51.

History: The first Italian-built destroyer was *Fulmine*, an experimental vessel, commissioned in 1900, with a displacement of 337 tons and a design speed (which was never reached) of 26.5 knots. Next came the Nembo-class, which were designed by an Italian naval architect, but in association with the British company, Thornycroft, and built in Naples. The result was much more successful. All were given new oil-fired boilers between 1908 and 1912 and minelaying gear was added during World War I. There were three war losses, *Nembo's* being an unusual double affair. The Italian destroyer was torpedoed by the Austro-Hungarian U-boat, *U-16*, but as *Nembo* descended to the bottom the fuzes on her depth-charges acted, sinking the U-boat

***Above:* The Rajput-class, built in Russia to a specially-modified Kashin-class design**

years; an order for a further five was discussed but never confirmed. There are a number of significant differences from the original Soviet navy ships, the most visible being that the four SS-N-2C missile launchers are located abreast the forward superstructure and fire forward, while a flightdeck for the a single Ka-25 Hormone ASW helicopter has replaced the after 3.0in (76mm) gun mount, with a ramp leading down to a below decks hangar. *Rana* was involved in a collision in 1999 and has not been repaired. The remainder were to have undergone a major refit in the Ukraine in the late 1990s but this has not yet started.

---

which was nearby (17 October 1916). Both *Turbine* and *Borea* were sunk in separate actions with Austro-Hungarian destroyers in May 1915. The three survivors were scrapped in 1923-24.

***Below: Fulmine,* the Italian Navy's first-ever destroyer design, was not a great success**

Audace

ITALY

Completed: 1916.
Number in class: 1.
Displacement: 922 tons standard.
Dimensions: length 287.1ft (87.5m); beam 27.3ft (8.3m); draught 8.2ft (2.5m).
Propulsion: 2 shafts; Brown-Curtis steam-turbines; 3 boilers; 22,000shp; 30kt; 2,180nm at 15kt.
Armament: 7 x 4.0in (102mm) (7 x 1); 2 x 40mm; 2 x 6.5mm MG; 4 x 17.7in (450mm) TT.
Complement: 118.

History: A ship with an unusual history, she was one of a pair ordered by the Imperial Japanese Navy from the British yard, Yarrow, in 1912. Range had been a problem for destroyers and both ships were designed with an unusual propulsion system of steam-turbines for full speed, but with two diesels for cruising, coupled to the main shafts by German-built transformers, which could also reverse the propellers. When war broke out in August 1914 the two transformers were prevented from leaving Germany and, as a result, the power system was never put to the test, as both ships had to be completed without their diesels. *Urukaze* was eventually delivered to Japan in 1919, but the other, *Kawakaze*, was transferred to Italy in July 1916 and two days later was renamed *Intrepido*. On 30 August, however, another destroyer, *Audace*, was sunk in a collision with a merchant-ship and to perpetuate the name, *Intrepido* was renamed *Audace* at her launch on 27 September 1916. The new *Audace* served during the remainder of World War I and throughout the inter-war years, serving

Freccia/Folgore

ITALY

Specifications for Folgore-class, as built.
Completed: Freccia - 1930-32; Folgore - 1931.
Number in class: Freccia - 4; Folgore - 4.
Displacement: 1,205 tons standard; 2,116 tons full load.
Dimensions: length 315.4ft (96.2m); beam 32.0ft (9.8m); draught 10.3ft (3.2m).
Propulsion: 2 shafts; Parsons geared turbines; 3 boilers; 44,000shp; 38kt.
Armament: 4 x 4.7in (120mm) (2 x 2); 2 x 40mm AA; 4 x 13.2mm MG; 6 x 21.0in (533mm) TT.
Complement: 185.

History: These two classes show how designers sometimes simply do not get things right. In the inter-war years the Royal Italian Navy placed great emphasis on speed and the Freccia-class was designed as escorts for the new, fast cruisers then joining the fleet.They were handsome ships, with a clipper bow, an enclosed bridge and a single funnel, and on trials they proved capable of reaching the design speed of 38kt. However, the machinery proved incapable of sustaining such speed under operational conditions, they were poor seaboats, particularly so once about half the fuel had been consumed, when they became dangerously unstable. Corrective action was attempted, with large bilge keels and some 90 tons of ballast being added, and matters were so arranged that empty oil tanks could be filled with seawater. These led, in their turn, to fuel contamination problems and a reduction in speed to 30kt, so the ships spent most of their wartime careers as convoy escorts.

The Fulgore-class attempted to cure these faults. They had a narrower beam to improve the speed, but this simply reduced the range without solving

Right: **Built in a British yard for Japan, *Audace* was bought by Italy before delivery**

under the Italian flag until 12 September 1943 when she was seized by the Germans in Venice harbour. She was commissioned into the *Kriegsmarine* as TA 20 and was sunk in the Adriatic by two British destroyer-escorts on 1 November 1944.

---

the speed problem and they were also poor seaboats. Not one of these eight ships survived the war: six were sunk by the Allies, one was mined, and one was seized by the Germans and later scuttled.

Below: Fulmine, **an Italian destroyer of the modified Folgore group**

Soldati

ITALY

Completed: Group I - 1938-39; Group II - 1942-43.
Number in class: Group I - 12; Group II - 6.
Displacement: 1,690 tons standard; 2,250 tons full load.
Dimensions: Length 350.0ft (106.7m); beam 33.6ft (10.2m); draught 11.5ft (3.5m).
Propulsion: 2 shafts; Belluzzo geared turbines; 3 boilers; 48,000shp; 38kt.
Armament: 4 or 5 x 4.7in (120mm) (2 x 2 plus 1 x 1); 12 x 13,2mm MG; 6 x 21.0in (533mm) TT; 2 depth-charge throwers.
Complement: 206.

History: Following the unsatisfactory Freccia- and Folgore-classes, great care was taken with next design, the Maestrale-class (four ships), which proved to be much better. As a result, the virtually identical Oriani- (four ships) and Soldati-classes followed, the latter consisting of two groups: Group I, twelve ships completed in 1938-39 and Group II, six ships completed in 1942-43, which were simply repeats of the same design. The war years saw minor variations in armament and an increase in air defence weapons. Of the eighteen ships, eleven were lost in the war: three were sunk at sea (surface ships - one, submarines - two); three were destroyed in Allied air raids while under the Italian flag, and another two, having been taken over by the Germans, were then also lost to Allied air raids. There were three more war losses, two being mined and one capsized in a violent storm. Seven survived the war, of which two were handed over to the Soviet Navy and three to the French Navy as part of the peace treaty, leaving two in Italian hands, one of which was stricken in 1958, the other in 1963.

Impetuoso

ITALY

Completed: 1958.
Number in class: 2.
Displacement: 2,775 tons standard; 3,810 tons full load.
Dimensions: Length 418.8ft (127.6m); beam 43.2ft (13.2m); draught 14.8ft (4.5m).
Propulsion: 2 shafts; geared steam-turbines; 4 boilers; 65,000shp; 34kt; 3,000nm at 16kt.
Armament: 4 x 5.0in (127mm) (2 x 2); 16 x 40mm AA; 1 x Menon, triple-tube ASW mortar; 2 x 21.0in (533mm) TT
Complement: 315.

History: After World War II the Italian Navy had to cede a number of ships to foreign navies as part of the 1947 Peace Treaty, principally to France and the USSR, leaving it with just ten destroyers. Italy was, however, one of the early members of NATO and a requirement was quickly established for an expansion of the navy. Four elderly ex-US Navy destroyers were acquired (1951 - 2; 1964 -1; 1975 - 1) but, with its traditions, it was clear that Italy needed to restart building its own warships. Among the early fruits of this programme were the two destroyers of the Impetuoso-class, which were ordered in 1950, but not completed until 1958. The hull design was based on that of the Commandante-class, some of which had been laid down in 1943, but none of which were completed. This design was essentially a repeat of the Soldati-class (see previous entry), but enlarged and modified to incorporate lessons learned in the war. Strong US influence was seen in the armament, which consisted of four US Navy 5.0in (127mm) guns in twin turrets and a strong air defence complement of sixteen 40mm guns. The major ASW weapon was, however,

Above: Grecale **was one of only two Soldati-class to survive the war in Italian hands**

the Italian designed Menon, three-tube mortar. The machinery was identical to that used in the US Navy's Gearing-class destroyers, and the sensors (radars and sonars) were also of US origin.

There was a proposal for a mid-life modernisation of these two ships, which would have involved removing both twin 5.0in (127mm) turrets, replacing the forward mount by a new single lightweight 5.0in (127mm) gun and the after mount by a Tartar surface-to-air missile launcher and magazine. This never took place, although some elements of the sensor systems were upgraded from time to time. *Indomito* was stricken in 1980, followed by *Impetuoso* in 1983.

Below: **Italy's first post-war destroyers, the Impetuoso-class took eight years to build**

Impavido

ITALY

Completed: 1963-64.
Number in class: 2.
Displacement: 3,201 tons standard; 3,990 tons full load.
Dimensions: Length 430.9ft (131.3m); beam 44.8ft (13.7m); draught 14.5ft (4.4m).
Propulsion: 2 shafts; geared steam-turbines; 4 boilers; 70,000shp; 33kt; 3,300nm at 20kt.
Armament: 1 x Mark 13 launcher for Tartar SAM; 2 x 5.0in (127mm) (1 x 2); 4 x 3.0in (76mm); 6 x 12.8in (324mm) ASW TT.
Complement: 340

History: Derived from the conventional gun-armed destroyers of the Impetuoso-class (see previous entry), these were the first Italian warships to carry guided missiles. They retained the forward twin 5.0in (127mm) mounting of their predecessors, but the after mounting was replaced by a US Mark 13 single-arm launcher and a magazine for forty missiles. The funnels were heightened to keep the corrosive exhausts clear of the radar arrays on the after deckhouse. Short-range anti-aircraft armament comprised four new, Italian-designed 3.0in (76mm) guns, the Italian Navy having decided that 40mm was no longer adequate for dealing with modern aircraft. The only ASW armament was a pair of triple ILAS-3 tubes for Mark 44 or Mark 46 torpedoes. A helicopter flightdeck was located on the quarterdeck; there were no hangar facilities, but aircraft could be refuelled.

Audace

ITALY

Completed: 1972.
Number in class: 2.
Displacement: 3,600 tons standard; 4,400 tons full load.
Dimensions: Length 448.3ft (136.6m); beam 47.3ft (14.4m); draught 15.1ft (4.6m).
Propulsion: 2 shafts; geared steam-turbines; 4 boilers; 73,000shp; 33kt; 3,000nm at 20kt.
Armament: 1 Mark 13 launcher for Tartar SAM; 2 x 5.0in (127mm) (2 x 1); 4 x 3.0in (76mm) AA; 4 x 21.0in (533mm) TT; 6 x 12.8in (324mm) ASW TT.
Aircraft: 2.
Complement: 380.

History: Ordered in the late 1960s, this design was a progressive development of the *Impavido*, but with a number of major advances. A new hull design was adopted, whose higher freeboard gave much improved seakeeping, and all weapons and electronic systems were of Italian origin, with the exception of the US Standard missile system, Mark 44/46 ASW torpedoes and the Dutch sonar. The gun armament, all produced by Italian company, OTOBreda - was unusually heavy for contemporary destroyers, with two single 5.0in (127mm) forward and four 3.0in (76mm) AA in single turrets amidships. In addition, full aviation facilities were provided, the hangar being capable of accommodating either one SH-3D Seaking or two AB-212 helicopters. The four 21.0in (533mm) torpedo tubes were all in fixed mounts in the stern, launching wire-guided "fish" through the transom.

Both ships were modernised, work on *Ardito* being completed in 1988 and on *Audace* in 1991. The Mark 13 SAM launcher was upgraded to the latest Mod

Both ships were modernised in the mid-1970s, during which the Terrier system was replaced by Standard SM-1(MR) and all electronic systems were upgraded. *Intrepido* was stricken in 1991 and *Impavido* in 1992.

***Below:* The Impavido-class had a flightdeck and refuelling facilities but no hangar**

***Below:* The Audace-class were large and sophisticated missile-armed destroyers**

5 version and the new Italian short-range AA system was added; this used Aspide missiles, with the box launcher replacing the "B" position 5.0in (127mm) gun. In addition, the original 3.0in (76mm) AA weapons were replaced by the new "Super Rapid" version. They were due to be retired in 2000, but their service has now been extended until the arrival of the two promised Common New-Generation Frigates (formerly known as Project Horizon), possibly in about 2006-07.

De La Penne

ITALY

Completed: 1993.
Number in class: 2.
Displacement: 4,500 tons standard; 5,400 tons full load.
Dimensions: Length 484.6ft (147.7m); beam 52.9ft (16.1m); draught 16.4ft (6.7m).
Propulsion: 2 shafts; CODOG; 2 GM/Fiat LM-2500 gas-turbines, 55,000shp, 31.5kt; 2 GMT BL230 diesels, 12,600bhp, 21kt; 7,000nm at 18kt (diesels).
Armour: Mirex.
Armament: 8 x Otomat SSM; 1 x Albatros launcher for Aspide SAM; 1 x 5.0in (127mm); 3 x 3.0in (76mm) OTOBreda DP; 6 x 12.8in (324mm) ASW TT.
Aircraft: 2 helicopters.
Complement: 400.

History: These two large and capable ships were ordered in 1986 to replace the Impavido-class and were launched with the names *Animoso* and *Ardimentoso*. In 1992, however, it was decided to change their names to commemorate two World War II heroes, both of whom had been honoured for their very gallant service with the famous 10th MAS (also known as "Decima"): *Luigi Durand de la Penne*, and *Francesco Mimbelli*. The 5.0in (127mm) guns came from the Audace-class which had given up one turret each during their modernisation. Primary anti-ship system is the Otomat SSM (8 missiles), while the 3.0in (76mm) guns, Aspide missiles and the four related SPG-76 fire directors form an integrated short/close-range air defence system. The helicopter facilities comprise a flightdeck and hangar which are large enough to accommodate not

Ikazuchi/Marakumo/ Akatsuki

JAPAN

Specifications for Ikazuchi-class, as built.
Completed: Ikazuchi - 1899-1900; Marakumo - 1898-1900; Akatsuki - 1901-02.
Number in class: Ikazuchi - 6; Marakumo - 6; Akatsuki - 2.
Displacement: 305 tons.
Dimensions: Length 220.8ft (67.3m); beam 20.5ft (6.3m); draught 5.3ft (1.6m).
Propulsion: 2 shafts; Vertical Triple-Expansion engines; 6,000hp; 31kt.
Armament: 1 x 12pdr; 5 x 6pdr; 2 x 18.0in (457mm) TT.
Complement: 55.

History: Following the Sino-Japanese war in 1894 the Imperial Japanese Navy (IJN) prepared a major new building plan, which was promulgated in 1896 as the Ten-Year Naval Expansion Programme, and included, amongst many other items, the need for twenty-three destroyers. The Japanese shipbuilding industry was growing rapidly at the time but could not cope with plans on this scale, so orders for sixteen destroyers were placed with British yards. The six-strong Ikazuchi-class was built by Yarrow to a design developed from the *Corrientes*, which that company had recently built for Argentina; these were all launched in 1899 and completed 1899-1900. The Murakumo-class, also of six ships, was built by Thornycroft to a design based on that of the recently-completed British destroyer, *Angler*; these were all launched and completed between 1898 and 1900. These two classes were generally very similar, with a turtleback foredeck, open bridge and four funnels, with the Murakumo-class

only the current SH-3D Seaking but also the future EH-101. Some areas of the hull and superstructure are protected by a layer of Mirex armour, a derivative of Kevlar. A second pair of ships was cancelled when Italy joined the (then) Anglo-French Horizon programme

Below: De la Penne, Mimbelli* are named after brave officers of World War II *Decima

***Above: Kasumi,* one of a follow-on order placed with the British Yarrow shipyard**

being marginally larger. Both had an identical armament, with the 12-pdr sited aft, although later in their careers both had their forward 6-pdr replaced by a second 12-pdr. The Akatsuki- and Shirakumo-classes were slightly enlarged versions of the Ikazuchi- and Murakumo-class, respectively, and built by the same British yards. Finally, Japanese yards built the remaining seven ships - the Harusame-class.

Fubuki

JAPAN

Completed: 1927-31.
Number in class: 20.
Displacement: 1,750 tons standard; 2,057 tons full load.
Dimensions: Length 378.3ft (115.3m); beam 34.0ft (10.4m); draught 10.5ft (3.2m).
Propulsion: 2 shafts; geared steam-turbines; 4 boilers; 50,000shp; 38kt.
Armament: 6 x 5.0in (127mm) DP (3 x 2); 2 x 13mm AA; 9 x 24.0in (610mm) TT; 18 x depth charges.
Complement: 197.

History: These twenty ships were ordered in four batches and were known originally by their numbers - Destroyer Numbers 35 to 54, inclusive, but names were allocated in 1928. They were known to the IJN as the "Special Type" and at the time the first were completed they had the most powerful armament of any destroyer in the world, while their 5.0in (127mm) guns were the first totally enclosed turrets to be mounted in a destroyer. As with several other Japanese types this class had to be rebuilt between 1935 and 1937 to improve stability and strengthen the hull, which increased displacement to: standard - 2,050 tons and full load - 2,400 tons. In common with most World War II warships the AA armament was steadily increased throughout the war, with "X" turret being removed in 1943-44 in order to create space and topweight for yet more. Final armament for the survivors in 1945 was 4 x 5.0in (127mm) DP, 14 x 25mm AA, 4 x 13.2nn AA and 36 depth-charges.

One ship was lost in a collision in 1934 and eighteen were sunk during the war: mines - 2; surface ships - 3; submarines - 5; carrier-borne aircraft - 7. The sole survivor, *Ushio*, was scrapped in 1948.

Asashio

JAPAN

Completed: 1936-37.
Number in class: 10.
Displacement: 1,961 tons standard; 2,330 tons full load.
Dimensions: Length 388.0ft (118.3m); beam 33.9ft (10.4m); draught 12.1ft (3.7m).
Propulsion: 2 shafts; geared steam-turbines; 3 boilers; 50,000shp; 35kt.
Armament: 6 x 5.0in (127mm) DP (3 x 2); 4 x 25mm AA; 8 x 24.0in (610mm) TT; 16 depth-charges.
Complement: 200.

History: This class marked the end of Japanese compliance with the limits laid down by the various interwar naval treaties; as a result, the ships were somewhat larger than the preceding types. Major efforts were made to reduce topweight, which included a much simpler and uncluttered bridge structure, although it still proved possible to mount a superfiring twin 5.0in (127mm) turret aft. They were the first IJN ships to be armed with the new 25mm Type 96 machinegun. A new type of advanced steam turbine was also installed, which proved to be very unreliable at first, while poor rudder design resulted in a lack of manoeuverability; both problems had,

***Below:* When first commissioned, these were the most powerful destroyers in the world**

however, been resolved by the time of the attack on Pearl Harbor in December 1941. During the war "X" turret was removed to provide the space and topweight to mount a much enhanced anti-aircraft armament.

All ten ships were lost during the war, all to US forces. Two were sunk by submarines; four were sunk by US surface warships, three of them on the same night during the Battle of Surigao Strait (4/5 March 1943); and the remaining four were sunk by land- and carrier-based aircraft.

***Below:* Every one of the ten Asashio-class destroyers was sunk by enemy action**

Murasame

JAPAN

Specification for Murasame, as built.
Completed: 1959.
Number in class: 3.
Displacement: 1,838 tons standard.
Dimensions: Length (wl) 360.8ft (110.0m); beam 36.0ft (11.0m); draught 12.2ft (3.9m).
Propulsion: 2 shafts; Mitsubishi/Escher-Weiss geared steam-turbines; 2 boilers; 35,000shp; 32kt; 6,000nm at 18kt.
Armament: 3 x 5in (127mm) DP (3 x 1); 4 x 3.0in (76mm) AA; 2 x ASW torpedo racks; 1 x Hedgehog ASW mortar; 2 x Y-guns; 1 x depth-charge rack.
Complement: 220.

History: The JMSDF started building new warships in the early 1950s, the destroyers starting with the Harukaze-class (two ships, completed 1956), followed by the Ayanami-class (seven ships, completed 1958-60) and then the Murasame-class. The primary mission of these three ships was anti-air warfare (AAW) for which their principle weapon was three 5.0in (127mm) Mark 39 guns in single turrets, which had been removed from the US Navy's Midway-class carriers in a refit. They had a disappointing rate of fire and were far from ideal AAW weapons. The rate of fire was, however, sufficiently

Amatsukaze

JAPAN

Completed: 1965.
Number in class: 1.
Displacement: 3,050 tons standard; 4,000 tons full load.
Dimensions: Length (pp) 429.8ft (131.0m); beam 43.9ft (13.4m); draught 13.8ft (4.2m).
Propulsion: 2 shafts; General Electric/Ishikawajima turbines; 2 boilers; 60,000shp; 33kt; 7,000nm at 18kt.
Armament: 1 x Mark 13 launcher for Standard SM-1 (MR) SAM; 4 x 3.0in (76mm) (2 x 2); 1 x ASROC ASW missile system; 2 x Hedgehog ASW mortar; 6 x 12.8in (324mm) ASW TT.
Complement: 290.

History: This was the first guided-missile ship to be built for the JMSDF, being laid down in November 1962 and completed in February 1965, a construction time of 27 months - a remarkable achievement. At first glance, the ship, with its flush deck and twin tall funnels, bears a resemblance to the contemporary US Navy Charles F Adams-class, but there were many differences, including the characteristically Japanese superstructure and the gun armament, which was two twin 3.0in (76mm), both mounted forward in the Japanese ship and two single 5-0in (127mm), one forward, one aft, in the American ships. Both missile systems, Standard and ASROC, including missiles, launchers and sensors/directors, were supplied from the United States. The ship had a very long, uncluttered quarterdeck which is occasionally reported to have been a helicopter flightdeck, but this was not the case, and the crane mounted on the transom was for handling boats which were stowed in a below-decks hangar. *Amatsukaze* was decommissioned in 1995.

great to demand rather large magazines and handling spaces, which made them very crowded ships. In compliance with then current JMSDF policy, the three ships, while all having two shafts, had different types of geared steam-turbine: *Murasame* - Mitsubishi/Escher-Weiss; *Yudachi* - Kanpon-Ishikawajima; and *Harusame* - Ishikawajima. All three were converted to auxiliaries in1984-85 and then deleted in 1987-89.

Below: **The Murasame-class were among the last gun-armed air defence ships**

Below: ***Amatsukaze,*** **here running trials, was the first Japanese missile-armed ship**

Yamegumo/Minegumo

JAPAN

Completed: Yamegumo - 1966-67, 1972-78; Minegumo - 1968-70.
Number in class: Yamegumo - 6; Minegumo - 3.
Displacement: 2,100 tons standard; 2,700tons full load.
Dimensions: Length (pp) 376.9ft (114.9m); beam 38.8ft (11.8m); draught 13.2ft (4.0m).
Propulsion: 2 shafts; 6 Mitsui diesels, 26,500bhp; 27kt; 7,000nm at 20kt.
Armament: 4 x 3.0in (76mm) DP (2 x 2); 1 x ASROC ASW launcher; 1 x 14.8in (375mm) ASW rocket launcher; 6 x 12.8in (324mm) ASW TT.
Complement: 210.

History: These unusual destroyer escorts (DE) officially belong to two separate classes, but were closely related, having the same hulls and propulsion system and were, in essence, updated versions of the destroyer escorts (DE), such as the Dealey- and Claud Jones-classes, built for the US Navy in the 1950s. All were designed for the ASW role and were powered by six diesels on two shafts and were well-equipped for ASW operations, with a number of effective sonars. The major difference between them was that the Yamagumo-class was armed with ASROC, with the single, eight-cell box launcher located amidships, between two funnels. The Minegumo-class, however, was equipped with the DASH ASW drone, which required the after superstructure to be moved forward and a single funnel fitted, so that the drone helicopter flightdeck and hangar could be installed aft. DASH was, however, a failure and was removed and some years later an ASROC launcher was installed on what had been the DASH flightdeck. The six Yamagumo-class ships were built in two groups, the

Takatsuki

JAPAN

Completed: 1967-70.
Number in class: 4.
Displacement: 3,100 tons standard; 4,500 tons full load.
Dimensions: Length 446.2ft (136.0m); beam 43.9ft (13.4m); draught 14.4ft (4.4m).
Propulsion: 2 shafts; Mitsubishi geared steam-turbines; 2 boilers; 60,000shp; 32kt; 7,000nm at 20kt.
Armament: 2 x 5.0in (127mm) (2 x 1); 1 x ASROC ASW launcher; 1 x Bofors 14.8in (375mm ASW rocket launcher; 6 x 12.8in (324mm) ASW TT.
Aircraft: 3 DASH drones.
Complement: 270.

History: The JMSDF was very keen on the US Navy's DASH system, which employed a remotely-piloted, rotary-winged drone to carry an ASW torpedo to a remote launch point. The system proved a failure in the US Navy and was removed, but the JMSDF persisted with the system for several more years. These four units were built for the fleet ASW role and carried three DASH, which operated from a large flightdeck on the quarterdeck, with a hangar immediately forward. Unlike other ASW ships, the Takatsuki-class carried an ASROC launcher as well as DASH, and also had a four-barrelled 375mm Bofors ASW rocket launcher in the bows, as well as two triple Mark 32 tubes for 324mm ASW torpedoes.

The DASH was eventually discarded in the late 1970s and two of the class, *Takatsuki* and *Kikizuki*, were rebuilt in the mid-1980s. This involved the removal of the DASH facility and the after 5.0in (127mm) gun, and the installation of a

first three being completed in 1966-67 followed by the three Minegumo-class in 1968-70, and then the second three Yamagumo-class in 1972-78. By 2001 none of the nine ships remained on the active list; several were still in service as training ships, the remainder have been stricken.

***Below:* *Yamegumo* and *Minegumo* classes shared the same hull and propulsion systems**

***Above:* The Takatsuki-class was designed to operate the DASH helicopter ASW drone**

Mark 29 launcher for Sea Sparrow missiles on the quarterdeck (with the magazine below), two quadruple Harpoon launchers amidships, and one Mark 15 CIWS atop the after deckhouse. Of the two unmodernized units, *Nagatsuki* was stricken in the mid-1990s, while *Mochizuki* continues to serve but as an auxiliary.

Haruna/Shirane

Specifications for *Haruna*, as built.
Completed: Haruna - 1973-74; Shirane 1978-79.
Number in class: Haruna - 2; Shirane - 2.
Displacement: 4,700 tons standard; 6,300 tons full load.
Dimensions: Length (pp) 501.9ft (153.0m); beam 57.4ft (17.5m); draught 16.7ft (5.1m).
Propulsion: 2 shafts; geared steam-turbines; 2 boilers; 70,000shp; 32kt.
Armament: 2 x 5.0in (127mm) (2 x 1); 1 x ASROC ASW launcher; 6 x 12.8in (324mm) Mark 32 ASW TT.
Aircraft: 3 helicopters.
Complement: 340.

History: The entire after part of these two ships, *Haruna* and *Hiei*, is dedicated to aviation facilities for three large HSS-2B Seaking ASW helicopters, with a very spacious flightdeck and a capacious hangar which extends forwards beside the single "mack" (combined mast and stack) which is offset to port. Inset in the flightdeck is a Canadian Beartrap hauldown system and there is a heavy-duty aircraft-handling crane on the roof of the hangar. For medium- and close-range ASW work there is an 8-cell ASROC launcher (no reloads) and two triple Mark 32 torpedo tubes amidships. As built, the only air defence weapon were the two 5.0in (127mm) guns on the foredeck, but a Mark 29 launcher for NATO Sea Sparrow was installed on the hangar roof and two Mark 15 CIWS were added in a late 1980s modernisation refit. The same refit should also have included the addition of Harpoon missiles, but this was cancelled.

The two-strong Shirane-class, *Shirane* and *Kurama*, is an improved version of the Haruna-class, slightly larger and with more advanced electronics. They can be distinguished visually from their half-sisters by their two separate funnels, which are fitted with large cowls, designed to keep the corrosive exhaust gasses away from the radar arrays and other sensors. There is a similar large hangar for the three helicopters, but in this case the Mark 29 launcher on the hangar roof was included in the initial build rather than added later.

All four ships serve as flagships of escort flotillas, for which they embark a rear-admiral and his staff of twenty officers and ratings. These ships are large and spacious, and are among the best helicopter-carrying destroyers in any navy.

Below: **The Haruna-class helicopter carriers were designed for fleet ASW duties**

Tachikaze

JAPAN

Completed: 1976-82.
Number in class: 3.
Displacement: 3,850 tons standard; 4,800 tons full load.
Dimensions: length (pp) 469.2ft (143.0m); beam 46.8ft (14.3m); draught 15.1ft (4.6m).
Propulsion: 2 shafts; geared steam-turbines; 2 boilers; 70,000shp; 32kt.
Armament: 1 x Mark 13 Mod 4 launcher Standard SM-1(MR) SAM; 2 x 5.0in (127mm) (2 x 1) guns; 1 x Mark 112 ASROC ASW launcher; 6 x 12.8in (325mm) Mark 32 ASW TT.
Complement: 277.

History: The three Tachikaze-class guided-missile destroyers are enlarged versions of the Amatsukaze-class, with a more powerful gun armament of two 5.0in (127mm), which are located in "A" and "Y" positions, thus releasing "B" position for the Mark 112 ASROC launcher with a reload magazine to its immediate rear, below the bridge. Their propulsion plant is identical with that of the Haruna-class. The Tachikaze-class also represented a major step in the steady move towards Japanese electronic sensors and systems, replacing the US-designed equipment which had been used in JMSDF ships up to that time. The three ships were completed at three year intervals and it is not, therefore, surprising that the two later vessels were each completed with a number of improvements, which were then incorporated into the earlier ships in the course of routine refits. Thus, second-of-class, *Asakaze*, introduced a new Japanese electronic countermeasures (ECM) outfit and was the first to be fitted

Hatsuyuki

JAPAN

Completed: 1982-87.
Number in class: 12.
Displacement: 2,850 tons standard; 3,700 tons full load.
Dimensions: length (pp) 432.3ft (131.7m); beam 44.1ft (13.7m); draught 14.3ft (4.3m).
Propulsion: 2 shafts; COGOG; 2 Kawasaki/Rolls-Royce Olympus TM-3B gas-turbines, 56,780shp, 30kt; 2 Kawasaki/Rolls-Royce Tyne RM-1C gas-turbines, 10,68shp, 195kt.
Armament: 8 x Harpoon SSM; 1 x Mark 29 launcher for NATO Sea Sparrow SAM; 1 x 3.0in (76mm) OTOBreda gun; 1 x Mark 112 launcher for ASROC; 6 x 12.8in (324mm) Mark 32 ASW TT.
Aircraft: 1 helicopter.
Complement: 190.

History: The Hatsuyuki-class ASW destroyers were a completely new design, representing a major break from the earlier Takatsuki-and Yamagumo-classes, with a totally new hull and a greatly altered armament. One of the major visual features is the very large funnel, which incorporates not only the four uptakes from the gas-turbines, but also passive infrared cooling and water-spray systems. The first seven ships of the class had aluminium superstructures, but once the lessons of the Falklands (Malvinas) War had been absorbed this was changed to steel in the last four.

Greater attention was paid to anti-air warfare than in previous Japanese ASW ships, with a Mark 29 launcher for NATO Sea Sparrow missiles installed on the quarterdeck, and an OTOBreda 3.0in (76mm) on the foredeck. Two

***Above:* Sawakaze, a Tachikaze class, missile-armed, fleet air defence destroyer**

with the new Japanese OPS-11 air surveillance radar. All three ships should remain in service until about 2006-2010.

***Above:* No less than twelve Hatsuyuki-class ASW destroyers were built in the 1980s**

20mm Mark 15 CIWS were added later. A large hangar and flightdeck accommodate an HSS-2B Seaking helicopter. This was the largest ASW helicopter in service at the time and the JMSDF built the flightdeck and hangar at 01 deck level and as far forward as possible, unlike many other navies which have the flightdeck on the quarterdeck where the effects of pitch are much greater. One ship of this class, *Shimayuki*, has been reclassified as a training ship, while the remaining eleven are in service with the various escort squadrons.

Asagiri

JAPAN

Completed: 1988-90.
Number in class: 8.
Displacement: 3,500 tons standard; 4,200 tons full load.
Dimensions: Length 449.4ft (137.0m); beam 48.0ft (14.6m); draught 14.6ft (4.5m).
Propulsion: 2 shafts; COGAG; 4 Kawasaki/Rolls-Royce Spey SM-1A gas-turbines; 53,300shp; 30kt.
Armament: 8 x Harpoon SSM; 1 x Mark 29 launcher for Sea Sparrow SAM; 1 x 3.0in (76mm) OTOBreda DP gun; 2 x 20mm Phalanx CIWS; 1 x ASROC ASW launcher; 6 x 12.75in (324mm) ASW TT
Aircraft: 1 helicopter.
Complement: 220.

History: Another in the seemingly endless series of post-war Japanese destroyers, the eight-strong Asagiri-class is an improved version of the *Hatsuyuki* design. They are slightly larger and have a new propulsion system using four Kawasaki/Rolls-Royce Speys in a COGAG arrangement, as opposed to the earlier ships' COGOG, the visual evidence of the different engines being the two separate funnels. The newer ships also have much improved electronics, including the OPS–24 air search radar which uses a planar array, incorporating hundreds of tiny transmitters antennas.

The Asagiri-class was designed to operate the HSS-2B Seaking, but these have been replaced by the SH-60J, the Japanese-built version of the Sikorsky Seahawk. *Umugiri*, the last to be completed, was the first to be fitted with

Kongo

JAPAN

Completed: 1993-98.
Number in class: 4.
Displacement: 7,250 tons standard; 9,485 tons full load.
Dimensions: Length 528.2ft (161.0m); beam 68.9ft (21.0m); draught 20.3ft (6.2m).
Propulsion: 2 shafts; COGAG; 4 IHI/General Electric LM-2500 gas-turbines; 100,000shp (approx); 30kt; 4,500nm at 20kt.
Armament: 8 x Harpoon SSM; 2 x Mark 41 vertical launch systems (90 x Standard SM-2 MR SAM and VL ASROC ASW missiles); 1 x 5.0in (127mm) OTOBreda DP gun; 2 x 20mm Mark 15 Phalanx CIWS; 6 x 12.8in (324mm) Type 68 ASW TT.
Aircraft: 1 helicopter (no hangar).
Complement: 310.

History: These guided-missile destroyers are very large ships, their displacement (9,485 tons) and length (528.2ft [161.0m]) making them larger than many World War Two cruisers, but they were designated "destroyers" for political reasons. Their design was based on that of the Arleigh Burke-class (see entry below), although they are actually somewhat larger, and they are by far the most sophisticated warships in any navy other than that of the United States. The programme was slowed down by two factors: one was US reluctance to release the full extent of Aegis technology, and the other was national resistance to the vast expense involved, each ship costing $US1.48billion at 1995 prices.

These ships have two distinct roles. First, they provide at-sea air cover for

towed-array sonar and this is now being retrofitted to the earlier seven ships. A recent decision to install two 0.50in (12.7mm) or 20mm machineguns is evidence of the seriousness with which the terrorist and pirate threat is now taken.

***Below: Yamagiri,* an Asagiri-class destroyer; eight were completed 1988 - 1990**

***Above:* Each of the four Kongo-class destroyers cost $US 1.48billion (1995 prices)**

JMSDF escort groups and, secondly, they are integrated into the Japanese national air defence system, which includes protection against incoming tactical ballistic missiles. The one, relatively minor, shortcoming is that they only have a flightdeck and have neither a hangar nor the Beartrap haul-down system for a helicopter.

It was originally intended that there would be eight ships, but the costs reduced this to four, the last of which was completed in 1998. Later, however, the JMSDF managed to work a fifth ship back into the programme and this is due to join the fleet in 2006-07.

Murasame

JAPAN

Completed: 1990-2002.
Number in class: 9.
Displacement: 4,400 tons standard; 5,100 tons full load.
Dimensions: Length 495.4ft (151.0m); beam 55.6ft (17.0m); draught 17.1ft (5.2m).
Propulsion: 2 shafts; COGAG; 2 Rolls-Royce Spey SM1C gas-turbines; 2 General Electric LM-2500 gas-turbines; 84,630shp; 30 kt; 4,500nm at 18kt.
Armament: 8 x Harpoon SSM; 1 x Mark 41 VLS group forward (16 cells) for VL ASROC; 1 x Mark 48 VLS group amidships (16 cells) for Sea Sparrow SAMs; 1 x 76mm OTOBreda 3.0in (76mm) Compact DP gun; 2 x 20mm Mark 15 CIWS; 6 x 12.8in (324mm) ASW TT.
Aircraft: 1 helicopter.
Complement: 170.

Right: Murasame-class destroyers will be fitted with a 64-missile system

History: These ships are the successors to the Asagiri-class, but are somewhat larger, and in many respects fit in between that class and the Kongo-class. They currently have two groups of vertical launchers: one 16-cell Mark 41 group forward of the bridge and one 16-cell Mark 48 group aft of the second funnel. However, it is intended to purchase the Evolved Sea Sparrow missile (ESSM) which will be installed in the Mark 48 VLS in "quad-packs" giving a total of 64 close-in missiles compared to the current 16. In addition, a second Mark 41 VLS is to be installed and Standard SM-2 missiles will be carried, as well as VL ASROC. The SM-2s will be launched and controlled in flight by a Kongo-class destroyer, which means that the Murasame-class will be acting, in effect, as floating magazines. Nine of these large and capable destroyers are to be built.

Holland/Friesland

NETHERLANDS

Specifications for Holland-class, as built.
Completed: Holland - 1954-55; Friesland - 1956-58.
Number in class: Holland - 4; Friesland - 8.
Displacement: 2,215 tons standard; 2,765 tons full load.
Dimensions: Length 371.0ft (113.1m); beam 37.0ft (11.4m); draught 17.0ft (5.1m).
Propulsion: 2 shafts; Werkspoor-Parsons geared steam-turbines; 4 boilers; 45,000shp; 32kt.
Armament: 4 x 4.7in (120mm) (2 x 2); 1 x 40mm AA; 2 x 14.8in (375mm) Bofors ASW rocket-launchers; 2 x depth-charge racks.
Complement: 247.

History: These destroyers, built in two batches of four and eight respectively, were specifically designed for ASW operations in the North Atlantic, where they were required to protect NATO task forces or convoys against attack by Soviet submarines. They also had a number of secondary tasks, including air defence and countering surface attacks by light forces. Their ASW armament comprised a twin Bofors rocket launcher and depth-charges, while their main surface/air armament was two twin 4.7in (120mm) Bofors guns, which were fully-automated and radar-controlled. The first batch was originally to have consisted of six ships, but it was too soon after the war and with the two De Ruyter-class cruisers also under construction the Dutch shipbuilding industry was overstretched. As a result the order was reduced to four and some equipment from the uncompleted pre-war Isaac Sweers-class was utilised, particularly the engines, which were not really powerful enough for these ships.

Tromp

NETHERLANDS

Number in class: 2.
Displacement: 3,665 tons standard; 4,308 tons full load.
Dimensions: Length 453.0ft (138.3m); beam 49.0ft (14.8m); draught 22.0ft (6.6m).
Propulsion: 2 shafts; COGOG; 2 Rolls-Royce Olympus TM-3B gas turbines, 44,000shp, 28kt; 2 Rolls-Royce Tyne RM-1A gas-turbines, 8,200shp, 18kt; 5,000nm at 18kt.
Armament: 8 x Harpoon SSM; 1 x Mark 13 launcher for Standard SM-1 MR SAM; 1 x Mark 29 launcher for NATO Sea Sparrow SAM; 2 x 4.7in (120mm) guns (2 x 1); 6 x 12.8in (324mm) ASW TT.
Aircraft: 1 helicopter.
Complement: 306.

History: These two ships, *Tromp* and *De Ruyter*, were built as replacements for the De Ruyter-class cruisers, their mission being to serve as air defence flagships for the Dutch ASW squadron which the Netherlands provided as part of their commitment to NATO. They were designated "frigates" by the Royal Netherlands Navy and wore "F-" pennant numbers, but in overall size and mission they were fully on a par with guided-missile destroyers in other navies, and are, therefore, included in this section.

As part of an Anglo-Dutch agreement, they were originally to have been armed with the British Sea Dart SAM system, in return for which the British would have purchased Dutch radars for their Invincible-class aircraft carriers and Type 82 destroyers. The deal fell through, in part because Sea Dart proved to be too bulky and costly, and the Dutch purchased the US Navy Tartar system, instead. There was a single Mark 13 launcher aft, atop a

Once life had returned to normal in the Netherlands work started on the second batch, which were slightly larger (381.0ft [116.0m] overall, 3,070 tons full load displacement) and had more powerful machinery (60,000shp). This extra size enabled them, to carry an increased secondary AA armament of six 40mm Bofors guns.

One ship of the first group and seven of the second group were sold to Peru in 1978-82, where two were taken out of service in 1985-86 and used as a source of spares for the others which survived until 1990-91.

***Below:* Dutch destroyer *Friesland*. Twelve were built; eight later went to Peru**

***Above:* The two Tromp-class served as flagships of the Dutch Atlantic ASW group**

deckhouse which contained the magazine for forty Standard SM-1 MR missiles. For close-range air defence the ships carried a Mark 29 launcher, mounted forward, with sixty missiles. The fully-automated twin 4.7in (120mm) gun mounts came from the first two of the Holland/Freisland-classes to be scrapped. The most prominent feature of their design was the huge radome atop the bridge, which housed the Signaal SPS-01, three-dimensional air surveillance radar. There was a hangar and flightdeck aft for a single Westland WG.13 Lynx ASW helicopter.

The combination of high freeboard and broad hull-form resulted in a ship with excellent sea-keeping qualities, and they were popular and successful in service. *Tromp* was stricken in 1999 and scrapped in 2000 and was followed by *De Ruyter* in 2001.

Leitenant Ilin/ Orfej/Gavriil

RUSSIA

Completed: 1914-16.
Number in class: 8.
Displacement: 1,260 tons normal.
Dimensions: length 321.5ft (98.0m); beam 30.5ft (9.3m); draught 9.8ft (3.0m).
Propulsion: 2 shafts; AEG turbines; 4 boilers; 30,000shp; 32kt.
Armament: 4 x 4.0in (102mm) (4 x 1); 1 x 40mm AA; 2 x MG; 9 x 18.0in (457mm TT; 50 mines.
Complement: 150.

History: The Imperial Russian Navy had to split its resources between four fleets - Northern, Baltic, Black Sea and Far East - none of which were mutually supporting, but they could sometimes assist each other in other ways. Thus, when it was decided to build a new series of destroyers for the Baltic, the Bespokoiny-class, which had recently been completed for the Black Sea Fleet, was used as the basis of the new design. The same hull was retained, but more powerful machinery was installed and the torpedo armament was altered to suit the Baltic conditions, with two 4.0in (10-2mm) guns and twelve 18.0in (457mm) torpedo tubes. The Naval Staff duly accepted the design, which was then built at three separate yards: Lieutenant Ilin-group (8 ships) at the Putilov Yard, Petrograd; Orfei-group (8 ships) at Metal Works, Petrograd; and Gavriil-group (6 ships) at the Russo-Baltic Yard, Reval. The early hulls were nearing completion when the Navy Staff issued instructions for alterations to the armament, with one set of triple torpedo tubes being removed and replaced by a third 4.0in (102mm) gun; the number of guns was later increased yet again,

***Above: Grom,* one of a number of the class built at the Metal Works, Petrograd**

by adding a fourth 4.0in (102mm) gun, which was mounted on the quarterdeck.
Fourteen of the twenty ships ordered were actually completed in the period 1915 to 1917, of which one was lost during the war against Germany and three more in 1919 during the Civil War. These three - *Gavriil, Konstantin* and *Vladimir* - met a particularly tragic end, when on 21 October 1919 they blundered into a British-laid minefield off Kronstadt, and of their combined crews of 450 men only 25 survived. A few ships were stricken during the interwar years, but some survived until the 1950s.

***Below:* Russia's first destroyer, *Novik,* attained 37.2kt during 1913 trials**

Skory (Project 30B)

RUSSIA (Soviet Union)

Completed: 1949-53.
Number in class: 68.
Displacement: 2,316 tons standard; 3,066 tons full load.
Dimensions: Length 395.4ft (116.0m); beam 39.3ft (12.0m); draught 12.8ft (3.9m).
Propulsion: 2 shafts; geared steam-turbines; 4 boilers; 60,000shp; 36.5kt; 3,500 nm at 15.7kt.
Armament: 4 x 5.1in (130mm) (2 x 2); 2 x 3.3in (85mm); 7 x 37mm; 10 x 21.0in (533mm) TT; 2 x depth-charge mortars; two depth-charge racks (either 52 depth charges or 60 mines could be carried).
Complement: 286.

History: The appearance of large numbers of these elegant, Soviet-designed destroyers in the early 1950s put the West on notice that the Soviet Navy had begun a major expansion plan. In fact, the decision had been made by the Soviet dictator, Stalin, in 1945 and his plan for the navy included a massive 250 of these "2,500-ton" destroyers. As a result design work started in late1945 and was based on an earlier Type 30 design, which had not been built due to the pressures of the Great Patriotic War. The new design was approved in January 1947, the first keel laid in May 1948 and the first ship completed in October 1949. In the event, Stalin's grandiose plan was not realised, but even so, no less than sixty-eight were built, the work being split, almost equally, between the four fleet areas: sixteen at Severodvinsk in the Arctic, sixteen at Zhdanov in the Baltic; eighteen at Nikolayev on the Black Sea, and eighteen at Komsomol'sk on the Pacific coast.

Kotlin/Kildin

RUSSIA (Soviet Union)

Specifications for Kotlin-class, as built.
Completed: 1955-58.
Number in class: Kotlin - 27; Kildin - 4.
Displacement: 2,662 tons standard; 3,230 tons full load.
Dimensions: Length 413.8ft (126.1m); beam 41.7ft (12.7m); draught 13.8ft (4.2m).
Propulsion: 2 shafts; geared steam turbines; 4 boilers; 72,000shp; 38kt; 4,000nm at 14kt.
Armament: 4 x 5.1in (130mm) (2 x 2); 16 x 45mm; 10 x 21.0in (533mm) TT, 6 x depth-charge throwers, 2 x depth charge racks; 50 mines.
Complement: 284.

History: The ships of the Kotlin-class were the last non-missile destroyers to be built for the Soviet Navy, joining the fleet between 1955 and 1957. They were slightly larger than the Skory-class, but had a similar layout, albeit updated with the latest weapons, including two new twin 5.1in (130mm) fully automatic guns in fully-stabilised turrets, and sixteen 45mm cannon in four new quadruple mounts. Unlike the Skory-class they had a flush deck, with high bows which made the rather more seaworthy than their predecessors, while their superstructure was made of aluminium-magnesium alloy, a common enough material at the time, but one which would never be used in a post-Falklands War design. In line with the grandiose ideas of the early 1950s it was originally planned to build 110, but this was quickly reduced to 100 and in the event only twenty-seven were completed, which, as in the *Skory* building programme. were split between the four major fleet areas. Twelve of these ships were converted in 1958-60 to improve their ASW capability.

***Above:* Skory-class destroyer visits a British port; she created an excellent impression**

The design included lessons learnt from the recently-ended war and was heavily armed for its size, with two twin 5.1in (130mm) guns and ten 21.0in (533mm) torpedo tubes and were heavily employed by the Soviet Navy for some 20 years. They were not, however without some shortcomings, being poor seaboats and with a very large turning circle. Eight of the class were modernised in the late 1950s, with a greater emphasis on ASW, but most served on unchanged. Six were transferred to Egypt (1956 - two; 1962 - two; 1968 - two) and seven to Indonesia (1959 - four; 1962 - one; 1964 - two), and two to Poland (1957 - one; 1958 - one). The remainder were stricken in the 1970s and 1980s.

***Above:* The Kotlins were the last Soviet destroyers built without missile armament**

Another four ships were completed as the Kildin-class, armed with an SS-N-1 launcher atop a deckhouse aft, which contained six missiles, with a massive girder launcher on the quarterdeck. Three of these were later modified to take the newer SS-N-2 missile, while the fourth remained unconverted.

One Kotlin-class was transferred to Poland in 1970 and one was modified by the addition of a hangar to carry out the first Soviet helicopter landings at sea. All the Soviet ships were stricken in the late 1980s.

Krupny

RUSSIA (Soviet Union)

Completed: 1960-61.
Number in class: 9.
Displacement: 3,500 tons standard; 4,192 tons full load.
Dimensions: Length 455.8ft (138.9m); beam 48.7ft (14.8m); draught 13.8ft (4.2m).
Propulsion: 2 shafts; geared steam-turbines; 4 boilers; 72,000shp; 34.5kt; 3.000nm at 18kt.
Armament: 2 x SS-N-1; 16 x 57mm; 6 x 21.0in (533mm) TT; 2 x RBU-2500 ASW RL.
Complement: 310.

History: These eight guided missile destroyers were originally "rocket ships" armed with the SS-N-1 (Scrubber) missile, whose role was to attack surface warships or land targets. There were two single-arm launchers, one on the foredeck, the other atop a deckhouse, aft, with six missiles for each. The SS-N-1 became obsolete in the mid-1960s (ie, very soon after they joined the fleet) and all eight ships were modified for the ASW role, after which they were known as the Kanin-class. This work involved a new bow-mounted sonar and the installation of three RBU-6000 ASW mortars, one on either side of the mainmast and one on the foredeck.The number of torpedo tubes was increased by replacing the triple tubes by quintuple mounts. A helicopter flightdeck was installed aft, but there was no hangar. This conversion proved to be extremely expensive

Kashin/Kashin Mod

RUSSIA (Soviet Union)

Completed: 1962-73.
Number in class: 20.
Displacement: 3,400 tons standard; 4,390 tons full load.
Dimensions: Length 472.4ft (144.0m); beam 51.8ft (15.8m); draught 15.1ft (4.6m).
Propulsion: 2 shafts; COGAG; 4 M-3 gas-turbines; 72,000shp; 34kt; 3,500nm at 18kt.
Armament: 2 x launchers for SA-N-1 SSM; 4 x 3.0in (76mm) (2 x 2); 5 x 21.0in (533mm) TT; 2 x RBU-6000 ASW RL; 2 x RBU-10000 RL.
Complement: 266.

History: By the 1960s, Western naval experts had learnt to await the appearance of each new Soviet warship design with a mixture of enthusiasm and anxiety, and the Kashin-class did not let them down. It was a long, low and graceful design, but every part of the decks and masts seemed to be covered with a multitude of weapons and sensors, many of them never seen in the West before. Not so immediately obvious was that the propulsion plant set totally new standards, comprising four M-3 gas-turbines and made the Kashin the first all-gas turbine warship in the world. The total weight of the powerplant was about half that of an equivalent steam plant, but what was more important was that it could work up to cruising speed from rest in 10 minutes and to full speed in about 20 minutes. A growing problem in warships of the time was the enormous increase in the electrical power requirements caused by a proliferation of electronic devices, coupled with ever-increasing standards of accommodation for the crew, and the Soviet Navy adopted gas-turbines to produce this "domestic power" as well.

and the Soviet Navy never again attempted such a major rebuild, preferring instead to build new ships for new missions.

***Below:* Krupny-class destroyer, with smoky exhausts typical of Soviet warships**

***Above:* Kashin Mod, with six SS-N-2C launchers aft; six were built or converted**

The final ship, *Sderzhanyy*, was completed to a modified design with four SS-N-2C (Styx) fixed launchers. Known as "Kashin-Mod" five earlier ships were upgraded to this new standard. Production of the Kashin-class ended in 1972, but was restarted some years later to produce five new ships (see Rajput-class).

Oquendo/Roger de Lauria SPAIN

Specification for Oquendo, as built.
Completed: Oquendo - 1960; Roger de Lauria - 1969-70.
Number in class: Oquendo - 1; Roger de Lauria - 2.
Displacement: 2,050 tons standard; 2,765 tons full load.
Dimensions: Length 382.1ft (116.5m); beam 36.4ft (11.1m); draught 11.8ft (3.6m).
Propulsion: 2 shafts; Rateau-Bretagne geared steam-turbines; 3 boilers; 60,000shp; 39kt; 5,000nm at 15kt.
Armament: 6 x 4.7in (120mm) (3 x 2); 4 x 20mm AA; 2 x Hedgehog; 2 x side-launching torpedo racks.
Complement: 267.

History: These three ships had a troubled genesis. Spain had, on several previous occasions, purchased French designs for construction in Spanish shipyards and in this case the design was based on that of the French pre-war Le Hardi-class, ten of which had been completed for the French Navy in 1938-41. The Royal Spanish Navy ordered nine of these ships in 1947 but after the first three had been laid down in 1951, the remaining six were cancelled in 1953. It had been planned to install eight 4.1 (104mm) guns (4 x 2) and seven 21.0in (533mm) torpedo tubes, but this was changed during construction to six 4.7in (120mm) guns and two torpedo-launching racks. The result was that when *Oquendo* ran trials in 1960-61 she was found to be dangerously unstable and had to return to the dockyard to have her armament reduced and any unnecessary topweight removed. She returned to sea in 1963 less both "X" turret and her 20mm guns, and with a considerable amount of ballast, her full

Alvaro de Bazan SPAIN

Completed: 2002-06.
Number in class: 4.
Displacement: 4,555 tons standard; 5,802 tons full load.
Dimensions: Length 481.3ft (146.7m); beam 57.4ft (17.5m); draught 15.7ft (4.8m).
Propulsion: 2 shafts; CODOG; 2 General Electric LM-2500 gas-turbines, 46,648dhp, 28.5kt; 2 Bazan-Caterpillar 3600-series diesels, 12,000bhp; 28.5kt; 5,000nm at 18kt.
Armament: 8 x Harpoon SSM; 1 x 48-cell Mark 41 vertical launcher for Standard SM-2 Block IV SAM, Evolved Sea Sparrow Missile (ESSM) SAM; 1 x 5.0in (127mm) gun; 1 x 20mm Meroka CIWS; 2 x 20mm AA; 4 x 12.8in (324mm) ASW TT
Aircraft: 1 helicopter.
Complement: 250.

History: Although rated as a frigate, the new Spanish F-100 class is included here because they have a displacement of 5,802 tons and are equal in every respect to destroyers in other navies. Their origins lie in a 1994 agreement between Germany, the Netherlands and Spain for a new air defence ship, in which the partners agreed to standardise as much as was possible, but without actually producing a single design, as happened, for example, with the abortive Project Horizon design. Despite the less restrictive nature of this agreement, Spain still felt it necessary to withdraw in 1995 and to pursue its own course, resulting in the Alvaro de Bazan (F-100) class. The contract for four ships was placed in 1997 and the first-of-class will enter service in 2002, at a cost of about $US540million each. Main armament is the Standard SM-2 Block IV SAM

load displacement having increased to 3,005 tons.

The remaining two ships, *Roger de Lauria* and *Marques de la Ensenda*, were virtually dismantled and then rebuilt to a greatly amended design, not being completed until 1969-70, some eighteen years after their keels had been laid. The new design resulted in a longer, broader hull and, apart from a French propulsion plant virtually all the weapons and sensors were of US origin. They were armed with six 5.0in (127mm) guns and were fitted with the first flightdecks in the Spanish Navy. *Oquendo* was stricken in 1978 after only eighteen years service, while the other two served on until the 1980s.

***Below:* Marqués de la Enseñada, last of the class of three to remain in service**

***Above:* The Aegis-equipped F100 air defence destroyers; Spain is building four**

system, which gives air defence coverage out to a range of some 93miles (150km) and launched from the Mark 41 vertical launch system. Close-area air defence is the responsibility of ESSM missiles, which will be housed in "quadpacks;" ie, four missiles in each of sixteen tubes for a capacity of 64 missiles. The main electronic system is the Lockheed Martin SPY-1D Aegis three-dimensional tracking and targetting system, which is substantially the same as that now being installed in the US Navy's Arleigh Burke-class destroyers and includes elements of the very latest Baseline 6 version. These are remarkable ships which are destined to remain in service for some thirty years.

Halland

SWEDEN

Completed: 1955-56.
Number in class: 2.
Displacement: 2,630 tons standard; 3,400 tons full load.
Dimensions: Length 397.1ft (116.0m); beam 41.3ft (12.6m); draught 18.0ft (5.5m).
Propulsion: 2 shafts; de Laval geared steam-turbines; 2 boilers; 58,000shp; 35kt; 3,000nm at 20kt.
Armament: 1 x Mark 20 launcher for Saab Rb-08A SSM; 4 x 4.7in (120mm) (2 x 2); 2 x 57mm AA; 6 x 40mm AA; 8 x 21.0in (533mm) TT; 2 x 14.8in (375mm) ASW RL; mines.
Complement: 290.

History: Ever anxious to protect its neutrality, Sweden built a succession of destroyers throughout the inter-war years, with four classes - a total of ten ships - built between 1926 and 1940. In March 1940, however, the naval high command become anxious about events in mainland Europe and purchased four somewhat elderly destroyers from Italy, which reached Sweden in July 1940, having been temporarily impounded by the British en route. The Italian ships were not a success, not least because it proved very difficult to convert them for cold weather operations. After this brief foray into foreign purchases, Sweden reverted to building its own, with eight ships being completed in 1942-43.

The first true post-war destroyers were the Halland-class, two were ordered in 1948 and completed in 1955-56. *Halland* and *Småland* were powerful for their size and were kept constantly busy - along with the rest of the Swedish Navy - in dealing with numerous incursions by unidentified intruders. In a 1967

Ostergötland

SWEDEN

Completed: 1958-59.
Number in class: 4.
Displacement: 2,150 tons standard; 2,600 tons full load.
Dimensions: Length 367.5ft (112.0m); beam 36.8ft (11.2m); draught 12.0ft (3.7m).
Propulsion: 2 shafts; de Laval geared steam turbines; 2 boilers; 47,000shp; 35kt; 3,000nm at 20kt.
Armament: 4 x Bofors 4.7in (120mm) (2 x 2); 7 x 40mm AA; 6 x 21.0in (533mm) TT; 1 x Squid Mark 3 ASW mortar; 60 mines.
Complement: 244.

History: The significance of these four ships is that they were the last major warships to be built for the Royal Swedish Navy. They were slightly smaller than the Halland-class and flush-decked, but had the same armament of four 4.7in (120mm) fully automatic guns. In 1963 three of their seven 40mm guns were removed and replaced by a single British Seacat SAM launcher. All four were stricken in 1982-83.

These were the last large warships because the Swedish Navy had decided that its future lay in a larger number of smaller warships, particularly fast attack craft (FAC) such as the Spica-I, -II and -III, and Hugin-classes, with full load displacements of some

Above: **The Halland-class destroyers were built to bolster Sweden's neutrality**

refit they were armed with the Saab Rb08A surface-to-surface missile, becoming the first non-Soviet destroyers to carry such a weapon.

Two more Halland class ships were built to meet an order from Colombia. These mounted a different armament, with six twin 4.7in (120mm) turrets, a much lighter AA armament and only four torpedo tubes. Named *Trece de Junio* (later *Siette de Agosto*) and *Veinte de Julio*, they were delivered in 1958 and were stricken in the mid-1980s.

---

300 tons and armed with a mix of guns and missiles. When such vessels were not at sea they were berthed in large shelters hewn out of rocky cliffs to protect them from attack and nuclear explosions.

Below: **The Ostergötland-class were the last large warships built for the Swedish Navy**

30-Knotters

UNITED KINGDOM

Specifications for Palmer-built ships.
Completed: 1897-1902
Number in class: 66.
Displacement: 390 tons light; 440 tons full load.
Dimensions: length 220.0ft (67.1m); beam 20.8ft (6.3m); draught 9.8ft (3.0m).
Propulsion: 2 shafts; triple-expansion; 6,200ihp; 30kt.
Armament: 1 x 12pdr; 5 x 6pdr; 2 x 18.0in (457mm) TT.
Complement: 63.

History: The menace posed to late Victorian battle fleets by small, fast torpedo-boats became so severe that in the mid-1890s the Royal Navy started building a new type of ship to attack them. These were originally known as "torpedo-boat destroyers" but this was soon shortened to "destroyers." These early British destroyers were known collectively by their design speed, the first group being the "27-knotters" which were completed between 1894 and 1896, and these were succeeded by the group described here: the "30-knotters." A total of sixty-six were built at ten yards, being completed between 1897 and 1902: Brown - three; Doxford - four; Earle - two; Fairfield - six; Hawthorn Leslie - five; Laird - thirteen; Palmer - thirteen; Thomson - five; Thornycroft - ten; and Vickers - five. The specifications given above are for the Palmer-built ships, which were generally considered to be the best in the class; the others differed marginally in dimensions and displacement.

The Admiralty policy was to lay down the general size and performance, the armament (one 12-pdr, five 6-pdrs and two 18.0in (457mm) torpedo tubes) and the crew (63), and then to leave the yards to submit their own designs for approval by the Board of Admiralty. The "30-knotters" were long, slim boats with

***Above: Sylvia*, completed in 1899; note the turtle foredeck, typical of early destroyers**

a turtle foredeck, open bridge and either two or three funnels, and all employed triple-expansion engines, except those built by Thornycoft, which had four-cylinder compounds. They were lightly built to help achieve the design speed, but despite this they stood up remarkably well to the strains of war service between 1914 and 1918, during which they were worked hard, mainly on coastal escort duties. Four were lost to enemy action, while another ten were lost during their service: wrecked - four; collision - four, and foundered - two. The survivors were scrapped in the early 1920s.

***Below:* A century's difference between *Victory* and *Petrel*, an 1899 30-knot destroyer**

V-and-W class

UNITED KINGDOM

Specifications are for V-class, as built.
Completed: V - 1917-18; W - 1917 -18; Modified W - 1919.
Number in class: V - 25; W - 21; Modified W - 16.
Displacement: 1,100 tons standard; 1,490 tons full load.
Dimensions: Length 312.0 ft (95.1m); beam 29.5ft (9.0m); draught 10.5ft (3.2m).
Propulsion: 2 shafts; Brown-Curtis single-reduction geared turbines; 3 boilers; 27,000shp; 34kt.
Armament: 4 x 4.0in (102mm) (4 x 1); 1 x 3.0in (76mm); 4 x 21.0in (533mm) TT.
Complement: 134.

History: During World War One there were constant demands for ever increasing numbers of destroyers, which, apart from their duties with the battle fleet, proved to be excellent "maids-of-all-work." As a result, large numbers were built, the Admiralty's policy being to build classes to form a number of homogeneous flotillas, each led by a specially-built "flotilla-leader," which was based on the class it was intended to lead, with equal if not slightly superior performance and extra facilities for the Captain "D" (the flotilla commander) and his small staff. Several classes were built, including the five-strong V-class, completed in 1917, which were leaders for the R-class destroyers. These were very successful and when a need arose for a new and more powerful type of destroyer to be built in large numbers, it was decided to save design time by simply taking the V-class flotilla leader design and repeating it, but with the incorporation of a few modifications, such as strengthened decks and bridges, and the deletion of the staff facilities and the amidships compass platform. They were handsome ships, instantly recognisable by their long forecastle, very tall thin forefunnel and short squat after funnel. Twenty-five were ordered in June 1916, of which four were completed as minelayers, with another six being converted to minelayers later.

In December 1916, before the first-of-class had even been launched, an order for twenty-three "repeat V-class" was placed; designated the W-class, the only difference was that they were armed with two triple torpedo tubes instead of two twins, as in the earlier ships. The orders for two were cancelled in 1917, resulting in twenty-one being built, of which five were completed as minelayers. Further demands for yet more destroyers led to a demand for "repeat Ws" with orders for sixteen being placed in January 1918 and a further thirty-eight three months later. They were built to the same dimensions as the earlier "V-and-Ws" but with a slightly altered stern, 4.7in (120mm) guns in place of the earlier 4.0in (102mm), revised boiler-room layout (which resulted in a broader fore funnel and narrow after funnel) and other minor changes. The end of the war resulted in many cancellations and only sixteen actually being completed, most between April 1919 and July 1920, although it was 1924 before the last joined the fleet. The sixty-two ships were so similar that they were always known to the Royal Navy as the "V-and-W class" and were regarded with great affection throughout their long service lives.

All except the "Modified Ws" saw service in the last months of World War One, but with only one loss, *Vehement* being sunk by a mine (1 August 1918). *Warwick* was very nearly lost whilst serving as flagship on the Zeebrugge raid on 10 May 1918, when her back was broken by a mine on the return voyage, but she managed to reach Dover and was repaired. A number of these ships served in the Baltic in 1918-19, where *Verulam* was lost to a mine (4 August 1919) and *Vittoria* to a torpedo (1 September 1919).

In 1933 four - *Vampire, Vendetta, Voyager* and *Waterhen* - were transferred to the Royal Australian Navy. Many underwent conversions prior to or during World War Two. Fifteen were converted to anti-aircraft ships in 1938-40, with their original 4.0in (102mm) QF Mark V guns being replaced by a new, high-angled version, the 4.0in (102mm) Mark VI, with four 20mm Oerlikons being added later. Then, in 1942, there was a desperate need to close the escort gap in mid-Atlantic, as a result of which twenty-one V-and-Ws were converted into long-range escorts, with the forward boilers being replaced by additional oil bunkers, resulting in a small loss of speed but a great increase in range; they were also given a much larger outfit of depth-charges. There was another bitter campaign being fought in British coastal waters and eleven ships were converted into short-range escorts, primarily in order to fight German E-boats, for which they were armed with two 4.0in (102mm) guns, two 6-pdrs, three 2 pdr pompoms, two 20mm Oerlikons, three 21.0in (533mm) torpedo tubes and twenty depth-charges.

Despite their age, all the survivors fought hard throughout World War Two. Eight were lost to bombs, two to mines; and five to torpedoes (U-boats - three, E-boats - two). The remaining ships were all scrapped in the late 1940s.

Below: *Valentine*, one of five V-class flotilla leaders, completed in 1917

Below: *Windsor*; the V-and-W-classes were very popular in the Royal Navy

E and F-class

UNITED KINGDOM

History: It was Admiralty policy for many years to build destroyers in batches, which then formed one or more flotillas, all with the same performance and armament. At the same time, the appropriate number of flotilla leaders were designed and built, with additional facilities for Captain "D" and his small staff. Typical of such ships were these two, *Exmouth* and *Faulknor*, which were built a leaders for the E- and F-classes, each of eight ships, all of them identical and completed in 1934. The table above shows the specifications of the flotilla ships (centre column) and the leaders (right column) , showing that the latter were larger, mounted on extra gun and had additional power, giving them slightly greater speed.

Exmouth was sunk by a U-boat (21 January 1940), while *Faulknor* survived the war to be scrapped in 1946.

***Right: Fame* during the war; this ship went to the Dominican Navy in 1949**

Tribal

UNITED KINGDOM

Completed: Australia - 1942-48; Canada - 1942-48; UK - 1938-39.
Number in class: Australia -3; Canada - 8; UK - 16.
Displacement: 1,959 tons standard; 2,519 tons full load.
Dimensions: Length 377.0ft (114.9m); beam 36.5ft (11.1m); draught 13.0ft (4.0m).
Propulsion: 2 shafts; Parsons geared-turbines; 3boilers; 44,000shp; 36.3kt.
Armament: 8 x 4.7in (120mm) (4 x 2); 4 x 2-pdr pompom; 4 x 21.0in (533mm) TT.
Complement: 190.

History: The Tribal-class was the very epitome of British destroyer design, being graceful, well-balanced, heavily-armed and fast, one memorable description of them being that they were "magnificent in appearance, majestic in movement and menacing in disposition". The original requirement stemmed from the appearance in the early- and mid-1930s of large and heavily-armed destroyers in foreign navies, such as the Japanese Fubuki-class (2,057 tons, six 5.0in (127mm) guns) and German 1934-type (3,156 tons, 5 x 5.0in (127mm) guns). The resulting British design was characterised by a sharply angled stem; a large bridge; two raked funnels, the forward one being the thicker of the two; a large deckhouse aft; and an armament of no less than eight 4.7in (120mm) guns.

Sixteen ships were built for the Royal Navy, all of which were launched in 1937 and commissioned in 1938-39. A further three were built in Australia for the Royal Australian Navy, while the Royal Canadian Navy received eight, of which the first four were built by Vickers-Armstrong in England, and the second four in Canada.

There were variations in the main armament. The British ships originally

	E/F-class destroyers	Destroyer leaders
Completed	1934	1934
Number in class	16	2
Displacement		
standard	1,405 tons	1,495 tons
full load	1,940	2,049 tons
Dimensions		
length	329.0ft (100.3m)	343.0ft (104.5m)
beam	33.3ft (10.1m)	33.8ft (10.3m)
draught	12.5ft (3.8m)	12.5ft (3.8m)
Propulsion		
shafts	2	2
engines	steam-turbines	steam-turbines;
boilers	3	3
power	36,000shp	38,000shp
speed	36kt	36.8kt
Armament		
guns	4 x 4.7in (120mm)(4x1)	5 x 4.7in (102mm)(5x1)
TT	8 x 21.0in (533mm)	8 x 21.0in (533mm)
Complement	145	175

Above: **The splendid lines of the British Tribal-class; this is HMCS *Micmac***

mounted eight 4.7in (120mm) guns in four twin, open-backed gunhouses, but during the war those ships not already sunk had their "X" turret replaced by a new turret mounting two 4in (102mm) guns. All the RAN and the first four RCN ships were fitted with only six 4.7in (102mm) guns from the time of completion. The second batch of RCN ships never mounted the 4.7in (120mm) gun at all, being armed with eight 4.0 (102mm) guns. All ships had additional anti-aircraft armament installed during the war, and the load-out of depth-charges was increased from thirty to forty-six.

Twenty-two served during the war, of which twelve British and one Canadian were sunk. One of the Australian ships foundered in 1969 and all but one of the remainder were broken up after the war. The one exception was HMCS *Haida*, which is preserved at Toronto, Canada.

J/K/N-classes

UNITED KINGDOM

Completed: 1939-42.
Number in class: 24.
Displacement: 1,760 tons standard; 2,330 tons full load.
Dimensions: Length 356.5ft (108.7m); beam 35.7ft (10.9m); draught 13.7ft (4.2m).
Propulsion: 2 shafts; Parsons geared steam turbines; 2 boilers; 40,000shp; 36kt.
Armament: 6 x 4.7in (120mm) (3 x 2); 4 x 2-pdr pompom; 10 x 21.0in (533mm) TT; depth-charges.
Complement: 183.

History: These were the first of a long line of British single-funnel destroyers and were also the first to be built with longitudinal framing. They were actually one large class of identical ships, built in a constant stream, but the first eight had names beginning with the letter "J" the second eight with "K" and the last eight with "N." In this case there was no separate group of slightly larger flotilla leaders, but three - *Jarvis, Kelly* and *Napier* - were given special fittings to suit them for the role. During the war four ships - *Napier, Nestor, Nizam* and *Norman* - were operated by the Royal Australian Navy, two by the Dutch navy - *Van Galen* and *Tjerk Hiddes*, and one - *Piorun* - by the Polish Navy.

The twin 4.7in (120mm) mounts were identical with those in the Tribal-class. The original AA armament of one quadruple 2-pdr pompom was increased as the war progressed, by the end of which some had four 40mm Bofors and other ten 20mm Oerlikons. The usual depth-charge load-out was forty-five.

O/P-classes

UNITED KINGDOM

Completed: 1942-43.
Number in class: 16.
Displacement: 1,540 tons standard; 2,220 tons full load.
Dimensions: Length 345.0ft (105.2m); beam 35.0ft (10.7m); draught 13.5ft (4.1m).
Propulsion: 2 shafts; Parsons geared steam-turbines; 2 boilers; 40,000shp; 37kt; 3,850nm at 20 knots.
Armament: 4 x 4.0in (102mm) (4 x 1); 4 x 2-pdr pompom; 8 x 21.0in (533mm).
Complement: 176.

History: The design for the O-class was produced prior to World War Two and was intended to meet a requirement for a slightly smaller destroyer optimised for escort work, which did not need to be as heavily armed as the fleet destroyer. The hull was based on that of the J-class, but was 11.5ft (3.5m) shorter, although it retained the same machinery. The main armament was lighter, consisting of four single 4.7in (120mm) in four of the class, but the others had four 4.0in (102mm) in anti-aircraft mounts and were fitted to carry up to sixty mines. The P-class were repeats of the O-class, except that all were armed with 4in (102mm) guns in AA mounts in somewhat inelegant gunhouses, and none were fitted to carry mines.

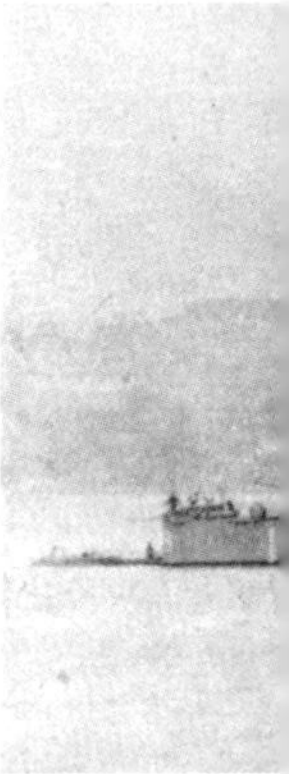

Like destroyers in all major navies, they all had a very busy war, but, somewhat surprisingly, not a single O-class ship was lost in the war. However, five P-class were lost: two were torpedoed by German U-boats, one was sunk by gunfire from

***Above: Javelin* served throughout the war and was scrapped in 1949**

Khartoum was destroyed by an internal explosion initiated by a ruptured torpedo air-vessel (20 June 1940), but eleven were lost due to enemy action: three by mines, two by torpedoes (one from a U-boat the other from an aircraft), and six by bombing. One of the most noteworthy of the latter was HMS *Kelly*, commanded by Earl Mountbatten, which was lost during the Battle for Crete (23 May 1941).

Italian ships, and two were sunk by bombs. *Petard* had the distinction of sinking three enemy submarines - one German, one Italian and one Japanese - a record not equalled by any other Allied warship. In addition, *Petard* rescued the Enigma codebooks from the sinking U-boat which played a major role in the British codebreaking activities.

***Below: Offa*, one of sixteen O- and P-class destroyers, all of which had a very busy war**

C-class

UNITED KINGDOM

Completed: Ca - 1943-44; Ch - 1944-45; Co - 1944-45; Cr - 1944-45.
Number in class: Ca - 8; Ch - 8; Co - 8; Cr - 9.
Displacement: 1,710 tons standard; 2,510 tons full load.
Dimensions: Length 362.8ft (11.6m); beam 35.7ft (10.9m); draught 14.3ft (4.3m).
Propulsion: 2 shafts; Parsons geared steam-turbines; 2 boilers; 40,000shp; 36.8kt.
Armament: 4 x 4.5in (114mm) (4 x 1); 2 x Bofors 40mm AA; 4 x 21.0in (533mm) (8 in Ca-class).
Complement: 186.

History: This class comprised thirty-two ships for the Royal Navy, which are usually described as the "Ca-" "Ch-," "Co-," and "Cr-" classes, the designations being taken from the two initial letters used for the names in each group; eg, *Cavendish, Chaplet, Cockade, Creole*. In fact the only major difference between the groups was that the first group, the Ca-class, had eight 21.0in (533mm) torpedo tubes in two quadruple mounts, whereas the other three groups were fitted with Remote Power Control (RPC) for the main guns, whose additional topweight had to be offset by the deletion of one quadruple torpedo mounting. All of these ships were effected by the navy's problems over weaponry which built up from 1943 onwards, where production of guns failed to keep pace with the construction of new ships; as a result, these were many deviations from the standard fit and numerous delays and none of the Ch-, Co- and Cr- groups were completed before the end of the war. One of the Co-class, *Comet*, was the first British destroyer to be of all-welded construction. A thirty-seventh ship was built for the Royal Canadian Navy: HMCS *Crusader*.

Weapon-class

UNITED KINGDOM

Completed: 1947-48.
Number in class: 4.
Displacement: 1,965 tons standard; 2,825 tons full load.
Dimensions: Length 365.0ft (111.3m); beam 38.0ft (11.6m); draught 14.7ft (4.5m).
Propulsion: 2 shafts; Parsons geared steam-turbines; 2 boilers; 40,000shp; 34kt; 5,000nm at 20kt.
Armament: 6 x 4.0in (102mm) (3 x 2); 6 x 40mm Bofors AA; 10 x 21.0in (533mm) TT.
Complement: 255.

History: Most British shipyards were involved in 1944-45 in constructing Battle-class destroyers, but there were a number of yards which could not accommodate such large ships. To maintain the flow of work the "Weapon-class" design was prepared, which in essence, used the same hull as the "S-", "Z-" and "C-classes" but with updated weapons and equipment. They were intended to be fleet ASW escorts, for which their anti-submarine outfit consisted of six 12in (305mm) Squid mortars, while their main gun armament was six 4.0in (102mm) AA in three twin mounts, a weapon which the navy considered very light for a fleet unit. It was decided to adopt the "unit arrangement" for the machinery, with two engine and two boiler rooms arranged alternately, which provided for far better damage control and was standard in larger warships and contemporary US destroyers, as it dramatically reduced the possibility of one round resulting in the total loss of main power. This did, however, result in slight increases in hull length and beam, and necessitated the use of two funnels, one inside the mast, the other a thin,

Four ships were transferred to Norway in 1946 and four to Pakistan (1954 - one; 1958 - three). The remainder served in the Royal Navy throughout the 1950s and 1960s, many of them being converted to ASW frigates. They were scrapped in the 1960s but one, HMS *Cavalier*, has been preserved as a memorial.

***Below: Chevron,* one of thirty-two very similar destroyers completed 1943-45**

***Above:* The Battleaxe class, completed 1947-48, were later converted into radar pickets**

upright tube, which was unpopular with some elements of the Royal Navy who felt strongly that their destroyers should have elegant lines.

All four ships were converted into radar pickets in 1958-59 and were given a second lattice mast immediately forward of the second funnel to carry the new radar array. The torpedo tubes were removed to make way for a new deckhouse which accommodated the new equipment and operators.

The original order was for twenty ships, but with the end of the war sixteen were cancelled and the four that were completed joined the fleet in 1947-48. *Battleaxe* was involved in a serious collision with the British frigate, *Ursa*, in 1962 and was never repaired; she was scrapped in 1964. The others did not last much longer, *Broadsword* being stricken in 1968, followed by *Scorpion* in 1971 and *Crossbow* in 1972.

Daring

UNITED KINGDOM

Completed: 1952-54.
Number in class: 8.
Displacement: 2,830 tons standard; 3,580 tons full load.
Dimensions: Length 390.0ft (118.9m); beam 43.0ft (13.1m); draught 13.6ft (4.1m).
Propulsion: 2 shafts; double-reduction geared steam-turbines; 2 boilers; 54,000shp; 34.8kt; 4,400nm at 20kt.
Armament: 6 x 4.5in (114mm) (3 x 2); 6 x 40mm Bofors AA; 10 x 21.0in (533mm) TT; 3 x 12.0in (305mm) Squid ASW mortars.
Complement: 278.

History: The Daring-class started as a progressive development of the Battle-class, but when it was finalised in February 1945 the design had been reworked to incorporate all the lessons learnt during the war. As a result the hull had a beam:depth ratio greater than in previous ships and was of all-welded construction, although some yards did not have the necessary facilities and their hulls used a mixture of rivetting and welding. The 4.5in (114mm) guns were in a totally new design of turret which offered greater protection than any used previously in British destroyers. These ships were so much larger and more heavily armed than previous British destroyers but were not quite large enough to be described as cruisers, so, for most of their careers they were described as "Daring-class ships," a unique category all their own.

One of the noteworthy innovations was that British warships had traditionally used d.c. (direct current) power supplies and four of the class had such systems. The other four, however, used a.c. (alternating current), which

County

UNITED KINGDOM

Completed: 1962-70.
Number in class: 8.
Displacement: 6,200 tons normal; 6,800 tons full load.
Dimensions: Length 521.5ft (158.9m); beam 54.0ft (16.4m); draught 20.5ft (6.2m).
Propulsion: 2 shafts; COSAG: geared steam-turbines, 2 boilers, 30,000shp; 2 Metrovick G6 turbines, 30,000shp; 30kt; 3,500nm at 28kt.
Armament: 1 x twin launcher for Seaslug SAM; 4 x 4.5in (120mm) (2 x 2); 2 x four-arm Seacat launcher; 2 x 20mm Oerlikon.
Aircraft: 1 helicopter.
Complement: 440.

History: If any ships epitomised the confusion over warship terminology it was the British County-class. With a length of 521.5ft (158.9m) and a displacement of 6,800 tons they were as large as many World War Two cruisers, but the name "cruiser" had an aura of a big ship and since the Admiralty had perforce to obtain political and financial approval for these ships the term "destroyer" sounded much more modest. (A similar subterfuge was employed some years later when the Invincible-class were described as "through-deck cruisers" until they were actually in service, when they suddenly became aircraft-carriers.)

These larger and impressive ships were required to carry the Seaslug missile, an early SAM which required a large magazine to hold thirty-six vertically stored missiles. The missiles were lifted into a long, tunnel-like working area, turned through 90 degrees and then progressed along the tunnel, first undergoing a series of checks to ensure that they were serviceable, then the aerodynamic surfaces were fitted, and then, after a final checkout, they

***Right:* Completed 1952-54, the Daring-class incorporated the lessons of World War II**

quickly became the standard in the Royal Navy.

The original British order was for sixteen ships but eight were cancelled at the end of the war, leaving eight to be completed, with construction continuing at a much slower pace. The first was launched in March 1949 and the last in May 1952, the names being: *Dainty; Daring; Decoy, Defender; Delight; Diamond; Diana*; and *Duchess*.

The Royal Australian Navy ordered four to the same design to be built in Australian yards, but one was cancelled before construction began. The first to be launched was HMAS *Voyager* in 1952, followed by *Vendetta* (May 1954) and *Vampire* (October 1956). However, *Voyager* was lost in a tragic collision with the carrier, HMAS *Melbourne*, on 11 February 1964, and the Royal Navy transferred *Duchess* to make good the loss. *Decoy* and *Diana* were transferred to Peru in 1970, where they served until the mid-1990s. Meanwhile, the remaining British ships were stricken in the 1970s.

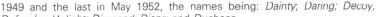

***Right:* The County-class were built around the Sea Slug air defence missile system**

were fed out to the twin launcher on the quarterdeck. This launcher was a unique device, consisting of a maze of girders and tubing, which was excessively complicated for the purpose it was required to fulfil.

The County-class were powered by a Combined Steam-And-Gas (COSAG) system, consisting of a set of high-pressure and low-pressure turbines, with a gas-turbine geared to the same shaft for boost. This system enabled the ships to get underway quickly and also gave a reasonable maximum speed of 30 knots. The ships had a flightdeck and hangar for a single Wessex helicopter. They were later fitted with Exocet missiles, with four canisters replacing "B" turret.

Two ships, *Antrim* and *Glamorgan* took part in the Falklands War in 1982, where both survived damage from Argentine forces. *London* was sold to Pakistan in 1982, but has since been scrapped. The last four to be built, *Antrim, Fife, Glamorgan* and *Norfolk* went to Chile in the mid-1980s, where they continue to serve in 2001.

Type 42 (Sheffield/ Manchester classes)

UNITED KINGDOM

Specifications for Sheffield-class, as built.
Completed: Sheffield - 1975-82; Manchester - 1982-85.
Number in class: Sheffield - 10; Manchester - 4.
Displacement: 3,850 tons standard; 4,350 tons full load.
Dimensions: Length 410.0ft (125.0m); beam 46.0ft (14.0m); draught 19.0ft (5.8m).
Propulsion: 2 shafts; COGOG; 2 Rolls-Royce Olympus TM3B gas-turbines, 50,000shp, 30kt; 2 Rolls-Royce Tyne RM1A gas-turbines, 8,000shp, 18kt; 4,750nm at 18kt.
Armament: 1 x twin-arm launcher for Sea Dart GWS.30 SAM; 1 x 4.5in (120mm); 2 x 20mm AA; 6 x 12.8in (324mm) ASW TT.
Aircraft: 1 helicopter.
Complement: 299.

History: These guided-missile destroyers were designed to provide area defence for a British task force, their principle armament being the very effective Sea Dart missile, with a single, twin-arm launcher on the foredeck. It was originally intended that they should have been somewhat larger, but financial pressure from the Treasury resulted in a cramped ship, with no space for the Ikara ASW system, although there was a flightdeck and hangar for a Lynx helicopter. Power was provided by four Rolls-Royce gas-turbines, two Olympus for main power and two Tynes for cruising, but the financial stringencies led to reduced bunkerage, which, in its turn, resulted in relatively limited endurance. Nevertheless, with a total of ten ships, it was the largest class built for the Royal Navy for many years and naturally played an important part in the Falklands War in 1982. Two of the class were the major British casualties during that war, with *Sheffield* being scuttled on 10 May 1982 after being seriously damaged by an Exocet missile six days earlier, while *Coventry* was sunk by bombs on 25 May.

***Below:* Manchester, a Type 42 Batch 3, incorporating all the lessons of the Falklands War**

***Above: Hercules,* one of two Sheffield-class ships built for the Argentine Navy**

The shortcomings of the Sheffield-class had been recognised before the Falklands War and the first of a "stretched Type 42" - the Manchester-class - was launched on 27 November 1980 and completed on 16 December 1982. These are 53.0ft (16.2m) longer, although the armament and general layout is little changed from the earlier ships, the extra length being devoted to improved accommodation, better seakeeping and greater endurance. This extra length did, however, give rise to problems and long strakes have been added since completion to stiffen the hull. During the Gulf War *Gloucester* shot down a Silkworm missile heading for a combined US/British task group (25 February 1991). Another ship of the class, *Southampton,* was damaged in a collision in the Gulf some years later (3 September 1988) and had to be taken back to the United Kingdom aboard a transporter and repaired at very considerable expense. The surviving British ships will serve on to the end of this decade when they will be progressively replaced by the new Type 45 destroyers.

Argentina bought two Type 42 destroyers: *Hercules* was built in the United Kingdom and completed in 1976; *Santisima Trinidad* was built in Argentina and completed, after lengthy delays in 1981. Attempts were made to sell them in the mid-1980s, but without success and both are still in reserve.

Cassin

UNITED STATES OF AMERICA

Completed: 1912-13.
Number in class: 8.
Displacement: 1,010 tons normal; 1,235 tons full load.
Dimensions: length 305.4ft (93.1m); beam 30.2ft (9.2m); draught 9.8ft (3m).
Propulsion: 2 shafts; Parsons steam-turbines; reciprocating engine for cruising; 4 boilers; 16,000shp; 29kt.
Armament: 4 x 4.0in (102mm); 8 x 18.0in (457mm) TT.
Complement: 98.

History: The United States Navy built a small number of destroyers every year, their primary role always being seen as defending the battlefleet against attack by torpedo boats. Thus, there was the Smith-class (1908-9, 5 boats, 900 tons, 28kt), followed by the Paulding-class (1909-10, 10 boats, 887 tons, 30kt), and then the Monaghan-class (1910-12, 11 boats, 883 tons, 30kt), All had triple screws and were armed with five 3.0in (76mm) guns, but the number of torpedo tubes increased from three in the Smith-class to six in the Paling- and Monaghan-classes.

The Cassin-class, however, introduced a number of changes, mainly because the General Board, a committee of senior officers, whose attention had previously concentrated on the battleships and cruisers of the battlefleet now took a direct interest in destroyer design. The result was a somewhat larger ship, displacing 1,235 tons to the Monaghan's 883 tons, and with a major increase in firepower, mounting 4.0in (102mm) guns, although the number had to be reduced from five to four in order to accommodate an increase in the

Wickes

UNITED STATES OF AMERICA

Completed: 1917-19.
Number in class: 111.
Displacement: 1,090 tons standard; 1,247 tons full load.
Dimensions: length 314.3ft (95.8m); beam 30.8ft (9.4m); draught 9.2ft (2.8m).
Propulsion: 2 shafts; Parsons steam-turbines (plus geared cruising turbine); 4 boilers; 24,200shp; 35kt; 2,500nm at 20kt.
Armament: 4 x 4.0in (102mm); 2 x 1-pdr AA or 1 x 3.0in (76mm) AA; 12 x 21.0in (533mm) TT.
Complement: 114.

History: The first fifty of these ships were authorised as part of the US Navy's 1916 programme, which was designed to prepare for inevitable involvement in World War One. The main design criterion was to keep pace with the planned new battlecruisers and cruisers, which necessitated a speed of 35 knots, which could only be achieved by a fifty percent increase in power, which meant more (and heavier) machinery in a relatively small hull. The result was the famous "flush-decker" which was built at eight yards: Bath iron Works - 8; Chesapeake Navy Yard - one; Cramp - twenty-one; Fore River - twenty-six; Mare Island Navy Yard - eight; New York Ship Building - ten; Newport News - eleven; and Union Iron Works - twenty-six. The ships were built to two slightly different detailed designs, one prepared by Bethlehem Steel for its Fore River and Union Iron Works shipyards, the other by Bath Iron Works for the remainder, this latter being dubbed, albeit unofficially, as the "Liberty" type.

***Above:* Cassin-class *Aylwin*, the result of General Board interest in destroyer design**

number of torpedo tubes to eight. The General Board was also concerned that the destroyers must keep up with the bigger ships and so emphasised seakeeping and range. This latter was increased by an unusual arrangement with Parsons turbines driving the two shafts at higher speeds, but with a single reciprocating engine being clutched to one shaft when the speed fell below 15 knots. All served in the Atlantic Fleet in 1917-18, and three were transferred to the Coast Guard in 1924-31. The complete class was scrapped in 1934-35.

Only a few were completed in time to take part in World War One, but the type provided the bulk of the US Navy's destroyer force throughout the 1920s and 1930s, although twenty-five were disposed of, mainly due to mechanical shortcomings. Fourteen were converted to fast minelayers in 1920, all their torpedo tubes being removed to provide space for the mines. Even so, a large number remained in 1939, and although olderly they still played a full part in World War Two. Twenty-seven were handed over the Royal Navy and RCN in 1940 in order to provide those two navies with desperately-needed escorts. A number were lost in the war and the survivors were scrapped in 1946-47.

***Below: Fairfax*, a Wickes-class destroyer, wearing a World War I camouflage scheme**

Mahan

UNITED STATES OF AMERICA

Completed: 1935-36.
Number in class: 18.
Displacement: 1,488 tons standard; 2,103 tons full load.
Dimensions: Length 341.3ft (104.0m); beam 35.4ft (10.7m); draught 12.3ft (3.8m).
Propulsion: 2 shafts; General Electric steam-turbines; 4 boilers; 49,000shp; 36.5kt; 6,500nm at 12kt.
Armament: 5 x 5.0in (127mm) (5 x 1); 4 x 0.5in (12.7mm); 12 x 21.0in (533mm) TT.
Complement: 158.

History: The Farragut-class, completed in 1934-35, were built within the London Naval Treaty's 1,500-ton limits for destroyers, and also saw a return to the high forecastle in US Navy destroyers in order to improve seakeeping, since the "flush-deckers" had proved to be so wet. This class was followed by the eight-strong Porter-class, which were built as specialist flotilla leaders on the lines of those in other navies. Next came the Mahon-class, which used a virtually identical hull to the Farragut-class, but with a number of significant innovations.

There were three sets of quadruple torpedo tubes, with one set on the centreline between the two funnels, where "Q" gun (No 3 gun in the US Navy system) had been in the Farragut-class, but with the two waist sets moved to either beam and abreast of each other. The displaced turret was then relocated on the after end of the shelter deck. Thus, the number of tubes had been increased by four, the number of guns had been retained and there had been no increase in the length of the ship. A further change was that the superimposed guns were given gun shelters for the crew, but in the last two

Benson/Gleaves

UNITED STATES OF AMERICA

Specifications for Benson class, as built.
Completed: 1939-42.
Number in class: Benson - 30; Gleaves - 71.
Displacement: 1,839 tons standard; 2,395 tons full load.
Dimensions: Length 348.3ft (106.2m); beam 36.1ft (11.0m); draught 13.2ft (4.0m).
Propulsion: 2 shafts; Westinghouse steam-turbines; 4 boilers; 50,000shp; 35kt; 6,500nm at 12kt.
Armament: 5 x 5.0in (127mm) (5 x 1); 6 x).5in (12.7mm) MG; 10 x 21.0in (533mm) TT.
Complement: 208.

History: The differences between the two classes were minimal, the most notable being that the Gleaves-class had 10 tons greater displacement and had round, as opposed to flat-sided, funnels. There were many minor differences between the two classes, between construction batches within the classes, and between different groups as wartime modifications were introduce. Thus, in 1943 twelve ships were fitted with three Mousetraps (ahead-throwing ASW rocket launchers), while another group was converted into air defence ships, with AA armament greatly increased and all torpedo tubes eliminated. Another group of twelve, all in the Atlantic Fleet, were converted into destroyer-minesweepers (DMS) in 1944, followed by a second group of twelve in 1945.

They all led very active lives during the war, in the course of which thirteen were sunk. After the war all except the twelve 1945 DMSs were put into reserve. In the 1950s a number were passed to friendly countries, recipient navies including those of Taiwan, Greece, Italy, Japan and Turkey.

***Above: Drayton*, a Mahan-class destroyer on builder's trials in mid-1936**

ships the two forward guns were housed in proper gunhouses.

As in all warships, wartime experienced led to major changes in armament and sensors, and by 1945 these ships had four 5.0in (127mm), two twin 40mm Bofors, five 20mm Oerlikon and a variety of radars. Two were virtually destroyed at Pearl Harbor (7 December 1941) but were completely rebuilt at Mare Island; six more were sunk during the war. That left ten, all of which were broken up in the late 1940s.

***Above: Baldwin*; the Benson/Gleaves-class was the last before the definitive Fletchers**

Fletcher

UNITED STATES OF AMERICA

Completed: 1942-44.
Number in class: 181.
Displacement: 2,325 tons standard; 2,924 tons full load.
Dimensions: Length 356.4ft (114.7m); beam 39.6ft (12.1m); draught 13.8ft (4.2m).
Propulsion: 2 shafts; General Electric steam-turbines; 4 boilers; 60,000shp; 38kt; 6.500nm at 15kt.
Armour: 0.75in (19mm) sides; 0.5in (13mm) over machinery.
Armament: 5 x 5.0in (127mm) (5 x 1); 4 x 1.1in (28mm); 4 x 20mm; 10 x 21.0in (533mm) TT; 6 x depth-charge throwers; 2 x depth-charge racks.
Complement: 272.

History: A total of 175 of these outstanding destroyers were launched between 1942 and 1944 (another six were cancelled), making this by far the largest single class of destroyers ever built for the US Navy. It was also one of the most successful and was particularly popular with the destroyer men themselves. There was a great jump in displacement from 2,325 tons in the Benson-class to 2,924 tons in the Fletchers, which not only enabled a heavier armament to be mounted "as-built," but also allowed considerable extra armament - particularly anti-aircraft weapons - to be added during the war, without a serious loss in stability. Unlike the Bensons, the Fletchers had a flush deck which added to the structural strength of the hull, although this made them somewhat cramped internally.

Three were built with an aircraft catapult, which displaced "Q" (Number 3) turret and one quintuple torpedo mounting, one of which served in an operational theatre. The idea was not a success and was not repeated. The air defence armament was increased during the war, most having three twin 40mm Bofors plus ten 20mm Oerlikon, which was later changed to five twin 40mm and seven 20mm. A few were modified in 1945 by removing one

***Above:* In typical destroyer fashion, *Conway*, hastens towards the sound of the guns**

torpedo tube mounting in order that two twin Bofors could be replaced by two quadruple Bofors.

Seventeen were lost in the war, but once hostilities had ended almost all of the Fletchers were placed in reserve, although many were returned to active duty for the Korean War, during which thirty-nine were given a refit which reduced the armament to four main guns and five torpedo tubes. From the mid-1950s onwards many were passed to friendly navies: Argentina - five; Brazil - seven; Chile - two; Colombia - one; Germany (West) - six; Greece - six; Italy - three; Japan - two; Korea (South) - three; Mexico - two; Peru - two; Spain - five; Taiwan - four; Turkey - five. Those that remained were stricken and broken-up in the 1970s.

***Below: Rowe*; the Fletcher-class was one of the finest destroyer designs of the war**

Allen M Sumner

UNITED STATES OF AMERICA

Completed: 1944-45.
Number in class: 58.
Displacement: 2,610 tons standard; 3,218 tons full load.
Dimensions: Length 376.5ft (114.8m); beam 40.8ft (12.5m); draught 14.2ft (4.3m).
Propulsion: 2 shafts; General Electric steam-turbines; 4 boilers; 60,000shp; 36.5kt; 3,300nm at 20kt.
Armament: 6 x 5in (127mm) (3 x 2); 12 x 40mm Bofors AA; 11 x 20mm Oerlikon; 10 x 21.0in (533mm) TT; six depth-charge throwers; two depth-charge racks.
Complement: 336.

History: The Sumner-class had virtually the same hull and machinery as the Fletcher-class, but differed in having as its main armament three twin 5.0in (127mm) mounts in place of the earlier ships' five single mounts. There were still two turrets forward, but the new arrangement made a great deal of difference aft where there was just one twin turret in "Y" position, in place of three single turrets. This freed both space and topweight for additional anti-aircraft armament. At the time the design was being prepared the General Board was considering an even heavier destroyer, with more powerful armament and greater speed, so the Sumner-class was considered to be an "interim" design; thus, as seems invariably to happen when something is labelled "interim" the Sumners and their very close relatives the Gearings (see next entry) were produced in vast numbers.

Although generally satisfactory, the Sumner-class suffered from a number

Gearing

UNITED STATES OF AMERICA

Completed: 1945-47.
Number in class: 97.
Displacement: 2,616 tons standard; 3,460 tons full load.
Dimensions: Length 390.5ft (119.0m); beam 40.9ft (12.5m); draught 14.3ft (4.4m).
Propulsion: 2 shafts; General Electric steam-turbines; 4 boilers; 60,000shp; 36.8kt; 4,500nm at 20kt.
Armament: 6 x 5.0in (127mm) (3 x 2); 12 x 40mm Bofors AA; 11 x 20mm Oerlikon; 10 x 21.0in (533mm) TT; six depth-charge throwers; two depth-charge racks.
Complement: 336.

History: Gearing-class ships were lengthened by 14.0ft (4.3m), resulting in their name of "long-hull Sumners." This increase created additional internal volume for greater bunkerage; an extra 240 tons extending the range, always an essential factor in the Pacific, by some 1,200nm at 20kt. The longer waterline also gave a small increase in speed. The original order was for 116, or which 97 were actually completed, 93 to the original design. A further four were completed post-war as prototypes of a new type of ASW escort. Five others lay in various stages of completion for some ten years after the war and were then scrapped. One other ship, *Timmerman* (DD-828), served as a trials ship for a new type of lightweight, but very high powered machinery with an output of 100,000shp; she was completed in 1951, but the trials were unsuccessful and she was stricken in 1958.

One of the urgent needs in the final stages of the Pacific campaign was for radar pickets and twenty-four were converted in 1945, the work involving removing the forward torpedo mounting and replacing it with a tripod mast

***Right:* Sumner-class destroyer, *Putnam*, armed with six 5in guns in three twin mounts**

of problems. Because so much space seemed to be available, too much anti-aircraft armament was added, eventually comprising two quadruple and two twin 40mm, plus eleven 20mm mounts. This resulted in excessive topweight, making them less seaworthy and requiring extra power to maintain fleet speeds, which resulted in a shorter than designed range. The other drawback was a partially-enclosed bridge, which proved so unpopular with commanding officers that it had to be replaced. Twelve ships were completed as destroyer-minelayers, with 120 mines in place of the torpedo tube mountings.

Three were lost in the war and one was lost in a collision in 1969 (*Frank E Evans* [DD-754], 2 June 1969). The remainder spent most of the post-war years in reserve, but, like the Fletchers, a number were passed to friendly navies in the 1970s, and the remainder were scrapped.

***Above:* The Gearings, this is *William C Lawe*, were known as "long-hulled Sumners"**

carrying a radar array. Also in 1945 the need for additional air defence armament was great to counter Japanese attacks, particularly for kamikaze, and all Gearings had their after torpedo tubes removed to create space for a third quadruple 40mm mount. All Gearings remained on active duty after the war, but in the early 1950s the radar picket role was so important that a further dozen were converted. Most of the remainder became ASW escorts and all underwent a major modernisation under the FRAM programme.

Mitscher

UNITED STATES OF AMERICA

Completed: 1953-54.
Number in class: 4.
Displacement: 3,642 tons standard; 4,855 tons full load.
Dimensions: Length 490.0ft (149.4m); beam 47.5ft (14.5m); draught 14.7ft (4.5m).
Propulsion: 2 shafts; geared steam-turbines; 4 boilers; 80,000shp; 36.5kt; 4,500nm at 20kt.
Armament: 2 x 5.0in (127mm) (2 x 1); 4 x 3.0in (76mm); 8 x 20mm; 4 x 21.0in (533mm) TT; 2 x Weapon Alfa ASW; 1 x depth-charge rack.
Complement: n.k.

History: These fleet escorts represent one of the early steps in the steady increase in destroyer size in the post-1945 period; indeed, the Mitschers' displacement of 4,855 tons was so great by 1950s standards that after a initial period when they were known as destroyers they were redesignated as "frigates," a name which had not been used in the US Navy for over a century. The four ships - *Mitscher, John S McCain, Willis A Lee* and *Wilkinson* - were designed as escorts for fast carrier task groups, and had a particular emphasis on air defence and air direction. The design originated in 1944-45, but construction was delayed in part by the post-war slow-down in defence spending, but also by the regular changes to the requirement and thus to the design.

Anti-submarine warfare was not considered too important in the design since it was thought that the high speed of the task group would provide sufficient protection, even from the new, much faster Soviet submarines then entering service. Despite this, they become involved in ASW experiments,

Forrest Sherman

UNITED STATES OF AMERICA

Completed: 1955-59.
Number in class: 18.
Displacement: 2,800 tons standard; 4,916 tons full load.
Dimensions: Length 418.5ft (127.6m); beam 44.9ft (13.7m); draught 15.0ft (4.6m).
Propulsion: 2 shafts; geared steam-turbines; 4 boilers; 70,000shp; 33kt; 4,500nm at 20kt.
Armament: 3 x 5.0in (127mm) (3 x 1); 4 x 3.0in (76mm); 2 x hedgehog ASW mortars; 4 x 21.0in (533mm) TT; 6 x 12.8in (324mm) ASW TT.
Complement: 324.

History: This eighteen-strong class started life as the first US Navy post-war, gun-armed destroyers, but there were successive changes to their mission and armament as the US Navy tried to keep pace with modern developments. As built, they were armed with three fully-automatic 5.0in (127mm) guns, unusually arranged with one forward and two aft. Also unusual were the 21.0in (533mm) torpedo tubes mounted in the first two ships, which did not the traditional anti-ship role nor were they mounted on a traversing mounting, being instead anti-submarine weapons launched from four fixed tubes. This idea was, however, quickly rejected and they were deleted from the third ship onwards, being later replaced by 12.8in (324mm) ASW torpedo tubes in two triple mounts.

A succession of review bodies eventually decided that the ships should be reroled as air defence ships armed with a single-arm Mark 13 missile launcher aft, which, with its attendant magazine, replaced the two 5.0in (127mm) guns. The three year refit also involved a large deckhouse for the SPG-51

***Above: Wilkinson*; the Mitschers were first major step In an increase in destroyer size**

Mitscher becoming the first destroyer in the US Navy to operate a helicopter in 1957, following which *Wilkinson* became the first ship to operate a DASH rotary-winged drone in 1960.

In 1964 two units were converted to take the Tartar SAM system, with a single-arm launcher aft and a forty-round missile magazine. The same conversion also involved the installation of an ASROC launcher forward with sixteen missiles, together with two triple 12.8in (375mm) ASW torpedo tube mountings in the waist. The outcome was a ship that suffered from being top heavy and the other two in the class were not converted. The class had a relatively short life, *Mitscher* and *McCain* being stricken in 1968, followed by *Lee* in 1972 and *Wilkinson* in 1974.

---

tracker/illuminator and two massive lattice masts. It had been intended that the entire class would receive this conversion, but the Secretary of Defense stopped the programme after four ships on the grounds that it was very expensive and of limited operational value. The four ships then became known, after the lead-ship in the conversion programme, as the Decatur-class.

The remaining ships were given a limited ASW conversion and a number were used as trials platforms: *Barry* testing the SQS-23 bow-mounted sonar; *Hull* the Mark 71 8in (203mm) gun and *Bigelow* the Vulcan Phalanx CIWS. They were all decommissioned in the early 1980s, following which two were sunk as targets, two became museum ships, and the remainder were stricken in the early 1990s.

***Right:* Forrest Sherman, as built, with three, fully automatic 5in (127mm) guns**

Farragut

UNITED STATES OF AMERICA

Completed: 1959-60.
Number in class: 10.
Displacement: 4,167 tons standard; 5,648 tons full load.
Dimensions: Length 512.5ft (156.3m); beam 52.3ft (15.0m); draught 17.8ft (5.3m).
Propulsion: 2 shafts; geared steam-turbines; 4 boilers; 85,000shp; 32kt; 5,000nm at 20kt.
Armament: 1 x Mark 13 launcher for Terrier missiles; 1 x 5in (127mm); 1 x launcher for ASROC missiles; 6 x 12.8in (324mm) ASW TT.
Complement: 360.

History: The ten Farragut-class guided-missile destroyers underwent a series of redesigns whilst on the drawing-board, as the US Navy sought to define the mission for such Fast Task Group Escorts. At first, it was decided that their primary role should be air defence, with a secondary capability of submarine *detection* (ie, leaving it to some other ship in the group to carry out the 'kill.') To fulfil these missions they would be armed with four of the new rapid-fire 5.0in (127mm) guns in single turrets, two twin 3.0in (76mm), while their ASW capability was limited to two Hedgehogs and a depth-charge rack, which meant that the real ASW work would have to be undertaken by other ships in the group. At this time - the mid-1950s - the Terrier SAM system was reaching operational status and it was decided that the last five of the class would be armed with this system, with a twin-arm launcher on the quarterdeck and a forty-round magazine in a deckhouse. Shortly afterwards this decision, too, was changed and the Chief of Naval Operations instructed that all ships in the class

Charles F Adams

UNITED STATES OF AMERICA

Completed: 1960-64.
Number in class: 23.
Displacement: 3,277 tons standard; 4,526 tons full load.
Dimensions: Length 437.0ft (133.2m); beam 47.0ft (14.3m); draught 15.0ft (4.6m).
Propulsion: 2 shafts; geared steam-turbines; 4boilers; 70,000shp; 33kt; 4,500nm at 20kt.
Armament: 1 x twin-arm launcher for Tartar SAM system; 2 x 5.0in (127mm) (2 x 1); 1 x ASROC launcher; 6 x 12.8in (324mm) ASW TT.
Complement: 333.

History: The Charles F Adams-class was the first post-war US Navy destroyer to be built in significant numbers, with twenty-nine ships: US Navy - twenty-three; Royal Australian Navy - three; and West German Navy - three. The first thirteen ships were fitted with the Mark 11 twin-arm launcher, but later ships had the Mark 13 single-arm, lightweight version, which was mechanically simpler and thus much more reliable; it was also capable of a higher launch rate. An ASROC eight-round "pepperbox" launcher, was mounted between the two funnels.

The US Navy ships served until the late 1980s when they were decommissioned; four were supplied to Greece and one to Australia (for use solely as a source of spares), and the remaining US ships have since been scrapped. The three Australian new-buy ships - the Perth-class - were completed in 1965-67 and were virtually identical to the US Navy version, except that they were fitted with the Australian-developed Ikara system in place of the ASROC. In 2001 only one remained in service. The West German

***Above: Luce,* a late 1950s Farragut-class guided-missile destroyer**

were to have the Terrier system. It was also recognised that confining the ships' ASW role to mere detection was no longer sufficient, so the forward "B" position 5.0in (127mm) gun was replaced by an ASROC box-launcher and they were given a much more capable sonar. As a result of all these changes, when the first Farragut-class ship was commissioned in 1959, she was the first in the US Navy ships to have actually been built (as opposed to converted) as a missile-ship.

The ships were modernised between 1969 and 1977, and among the new systems they received were Harpoon anti-ship missiles and the Vulcan Phalanx close-in weapons system. They were also rearmed with Standard SM-2 missiles and *Mahan* was the first ship to carry the extended range version of the missile - SM-2(ER). None was sold abroad and all were decommissioned between 1989 and 1993.

***Above:* HMAS *Hobart,* an Adams-class destroyer; the Australian navy operated three**

Navy also purchased three ships - Lütjens-class - which differed only in their funnels, which had side exhausts, and modified masts. Two of these remained in service in 2001 and both are due to be retired in 2002-03.

Spruance/Kidd

UNITED STATES OF AMERICA

Specifications for Caron (DD 970) onwards (see notes).
Completed: Spruance - 1975-81; Kidd 1981-83.
Number in class: Spruance - 31; Kidd - 4.
Displacement: 7,410 tons light; 9,250 tons full load.
Dimensions: Length 563.3ft (171.7m); beam 55.0ft (16.8m); draught 20.5ft (6.3m).
Propulsion: 2 shafts; COGAG; 4 General Electric LM-2500 gas-turbines; 80,000shp; 30kt; 6,000nm at 20kt.
Armament: 8 x Harpoon SSMs; 1 x Mark 41 vertical launcher for Tomahawk SSM and VLASROC ASW missiles; 1 x Mark 29 launcher for NATO Sea Sparrow SAM; 2 x 5.0in (127mm) guns (2 x 1); 2 x 20mm Mark 15 Phalanx CIWS; 4 x 0.5in (12.7mm) MG; 6 x 12.8in (324mm) ASW TT.
Aircraft: 1 helicopter.
Complement: 393.

History: By the early 1970s, the Gearing- and Sumner-class destroyers were reaching the end of their useful lives, despite regular updates and modifications, and, after much discussion, the US Navy settled on the Spruance-class design to replace them. At the time they joined the fleet, the design epitomised the US Navy philosophy of the time, which concentrated on three features. The first of these was for large hulls and a block superstructure in order to maximise internal volume. The second was for machinery which

Below: Elliott **appears to have few weapons or sensors, but is a capable, effective ship**

***Above:* *John Young*, a Spruance-class destroyer; early criticism has given way to praise**

combined power and fuel economy with ease-of-maintenance and, when necessary, ease-of-replacement. The third was a weapon system which combined high technology and combat effectiveness with modular design, so that individual elements could be repaired or replaced easily. Taken together, it was hoped that these measures minimise "platform" costs and maximise "payload" during the ships' anticipated thirty-year life.

Their appearance was, however, greeted with a storm of criticism. The first cause of these adverse comments was that the ships were extremely expensive and double the size of the ships they were replacing. The criticism then intensified when the ships entered service, since to the amateur observer they *appeared* to have very little armament - only two guns and the ASROC launcher - and few sensors, particularly when compared with contemporary Soviet ships, whose decks were covered with weapons and whose masts were bedecked with antennas of every description. The Spruance-class has, however, overcome such ill-informed criticism and has given many years of excellent service. It has gradually become clear that the apparently few launchers on the deck are served by large magazines which are hidden from view below decks, while the antennas serve radars, sensors and other electronic devices which are far more capable and flexible than those in Russian ships. Finally, the inherent flexibility of the design has been shown by the ease with which it was adapted to become the Ticonderoga-class cruiser for the US Navy and the Kidd-class air defence destroyer for Iran (see below).

The first seven ships were completed with Mark 26 rail launchers forward, but these were replaced from the eighth ship onwards by the Mark 41 Vertical Launcher System (VLS). This VLS is capable of launching Standard SM-2 SAMs, Tomahawk land-attack missiles and Vertical-Launch ASROC, and is also capable of a much higher rate of fire, giving the ships much greater operational flexibility. As a result the first seven ships were retired in FY97, even though they had many years of service left.

The remaining ships have undergone many modernisations and modifications. Twelve are currently being fitted with RAM (rolling-airframe missiles) launchers on the stern. *Arthur W Radford* (DD-968) was fitted with an

Advanced Enclosed Mast Sensor System in 1997, which is a very large, square-sided, experimental mainmast, totally enclosing the antenna arrays. This structure, which is 88.0ft (26.8m) high and weighs 35.7 tons (36.3 tonnes), is intended to reduce the radar cross-section and to provide easier maintenance for the sensors inside. *Radford* was badly damaged in a collision with a merchant ship in 1999 and was rebuilt at a cost of $US32.7million.

The Spruances have a large hangar which is sited almost amidships and is integrated with the after exhaust uptakes. This accommodates a single Sikorsky SH-60 LAMPS-III ASW helicopter, but Congress tried to force the navy into building an "air-capable" ship, *Hayler* (DD-997), which would have had facilities for four helicopters. This proved to be such an expensive project, however, that the ship, the last Spruance to be built, was completed almost to the standard design, although it does have some differences; for example, it is the only ship in the class to have the SPS-49 air-search radar.

In the early 1970s the (then) Shah of Iran ordered four modified versions of the Spruance-class and the allowances made in the Spruance design for spaciousness and modular installation made redesign to meet the Shah's requirements an easy matter. The ships were optimised for air defence with Mark 26 twin-arm SAM launchers in place of the ASROC and Sea Sparrow launchers in the Spruance-class, although, since the Mark 26 could launch the ASROC missile, very little capability was actually been lost. The Iranians also required additional air-conditioning and sand filters for operations in the Gulf, but on his expulsion by Ayatollah Khomeini the order was cancelled and they were eventually acquired by the United States Navy as the Kidd-class. These served in the US Navy from 1981 to the late 1990s when they were offered for sale. Various navies examined the possibilities very closely, including those of Australia and Greece, but in the end both turned them down. In late 2000 the Taiwanese declared an interest in the ships, declaring that the increasing threat from mainland China, coupled with the US Navy's known reluctance to release Aegis technology, made these ideal ships for its navy. President Bush approved this proposal in early 2001 but it is likely to be bitterly opposed by the Chinesen Government in Beijing.

***Left: Kidd,* a ship built for Iran, adopted by the US Navy, now on offer to Taiwan**

Arleigh Burke

UNITED STATES OF AMERICA

	Flight I	Flight II	Flight IIA
Completed	1991-97	1998-99	2000-2008 (est)
Number in class	21	7	29
Displacement Light Full Load.	 6,624 tons 8,315 tons	 6,914 tons 9,033 tons	 n.k. 9,238 tons
Dimensions Length Beam Draught	 504.6 (153,8m) 66.6 ft (20.3m) 20.7ft (6.3m)	 504.6 (153.8m) 66.6ft (20.3m) 21.7ft (6.6m)	 509.5 ft(155.3m) 66.6ft (20.3m) 21.0ft (6.4m)
Propulsion: Shafts Gas-turbines Power Speed Range	 2 4 x General Electric LM-2500 90,000shp 30+kt 4,400nm at 20kt		
Armament Launchers Missiles Harpoon Gun CIWS TT	 2 x Mark 41 VLS 90 8 1 x 5in (127mm) 2 x 20mm Phalanx 6 x Mark 32		 2 x Mark 41 VLS 96 - 1 x 5in (127mm) - 6 x Mark 32
Aircraft	-	-	2 x SH-60R
Complement	337	380	380

History: Like the Spruance-class, the Arleigh Burke-class, designed as a replacement for the aging missile destroyers, was the subject of much debate before the design was finalised and authorised by Congress. They are very comprehensively equipped compared with equivalent ships in other navies, but they still lack some of the facilities available in the Ticonderoga-class cruisers. One of the design criteria was that the Arleigh Burkes would provide about 75 percent of the air defence capability of a Ticonderoga at 66 percent of the price, although whether this has been achieved in practice is impossible to discover.

The first twenty-seven ships were designated " Flight I" which forms the basis for all subsequent versions. The hull and superstructure are made of steel, the only aluminium being used for the funnels. The hull form is unusually broad in relation to its length in comparison with earlier warships, which has resulted in excellent seakeeping qualities. The structure includes some 130 tons of Kevlar, of which approximately 70 tons is used around the command-and-control spaces. Many stealth features are included in the design, with all outside surfaces angled and corners rounded to reduce the radar signature, while infra-red suppressors are fitted to the exhaust uptakes, and the Prairie/Masker device suppresses propeller noises. All electronics are hardened ▶

Top: Stethem. **Forward armament is 5in gun, 16-cell Mark 41 VLS and 20mm CIWS**

Above: **Two Arleigh Burkes, *Mitscher* (nearest) and *Russel,* at speed in the Atlantic**

against electromagnetic pulses (EMP), one of the side effects of a nuclear explosion.

This is the first class of US Navy warship to include a comprehensive collective protection system for defence against nuclear fallout or chemical/biological attack, with access to the ship's interior being through double air-locked hatches (of which there are many fewer than in most other ships of this size) and the entire interior is protected by positive pressurisation to exclude contaminants. In addition as much reliance as possible is placed on recirculated air within the ship, with any incoming air being carefully controlled and filtered.

The sensor and weapons control system centres on the Aegis SPY-1D three-dimensional, with four planar arrays mounted on the forward superstructure to give 360deg coverage. The ship is commanded from the operations room which is below the waterline.

One of the major shortcomings of the Flight I ships is that they do not have a hangar for a helicopter. There is, however, a flightdeck, and the ship is provided with refuelling and rearming facilities for a visiting helicopter. There is also a full LAMPS-III data-link to receive operational ASW information.

The second production standard was Flight II, which consisted of seven ships, from *Mahan* (DDG-72) to *Porter* (DDG-78). In general, these ships are identical to Flight I, but with the following exceptions. The ship can handle the extended range version of the Standard SAM - SM2(ER) - and is fitted with the Joint Tactical Information Data (JTIDS) and other more advanced electronic systems, including the SLQ-32(V)3 EW suite and the Link 16 tactical data information exchange system. The specifications above show that Flight II has a greater full load displacement, which is due to the allocation of greater volume to fuel bunkers, thus increasing the range. The only visible difference between Flights I and II is that in the former the topmast follows the same angle as the mast, whereas in the latter the topmost is vertical.

Flight III was to have been a major advance but was dropped, principally on grounds of expense. However, the Japanese Kongo-class gives some impression of what a US Navy Arleigh Burke Flight III might have looked like and been capable of.

Having lost Flight III, the US Navy developed Flight IIA, which is essentially a 5ft (1.5m) longer version of the Arleigh Burke Flight II, but with a number of significant changes, the most important of which is that it is fitted with two hangars, thus enabling it to embark two SH-60 Seahawk helicopters. The transom has also been extended to enable a dual RAST to be fitted in the

***Below: Mitscher*, two of the four Aegis SPY-1D radar arrays can be seen on the bridge**

***Above: Ramage*; the Arleigh Burke is the most powerful destroyer in the world today**

flightdeck, which means that the SQR-19 TACTAS towed-array can no longer be shipped. One consequence of this new hangar is that the after pair of SPY-1D arrays have had to be raised by 7.9ft (2.4m) to enable their beams to clear the hangar roofs.

There are several changes with regard to the missiles. First, the navy has decided that there is little value in the ability to replenish the missile stock at sea, which means that the cranes, which took up the space of three cells in each of the two launcher groups, are no longer required. Thus, six more vertical launch cells per ship are available for missiles - a valuable addition. Also, the vertical launcher can handle the new Evolved Sea Sparrow Missile (ESSM), which is supplied in "Quad Packs" (ie, four ESSMs in each cell normally allocated to one missile); six cells are allocated to ESSM for a total of twenty-four missiles. Once ESSM is available the 20mm Phalanx CIWS mounts will be removed. As with Flight II ships, the deck fittings for Harpoon launchers have been installed but the missiles will not normally be shipped. From 2003 onwards Tactical Tomahawk and Land-Attack Standard Missiles (LASM) will be carried.

Nueva Esparta

VENEZUELA

Completed: 1953-56.
Number in class: 3.
Displacement: 2,600 tons standard; 3,300 tons full load.
Dimensions: Length 402.0ft (122.5m); beam 43.0ft (13.1m); draught 12.8ft (3.9m).
Propulsion: 2 shafts; Parsons geared steam-turbines; 2 boilers; 50,000shp; 34.5kt; 5,000nm at 11kt.
Armament: 6 x 4.5in (120mm) (3 x 2); 16 x 40mm AA; 3 x 21.0in (533mm) TT; 2 x depth-charge throwers; 2 x depth-charge racks.
Complement: 254.

History: For many years Venezuela had a "gunboat navy" which used small elderly ships and was mainly responsible for riverine operations. In 1946, however, the country's natural resources started to be developed and the navy began a process of expansion, starting with the acquisition of seven ex-British Flower-class corvettes. The process was then continued with the purchase of these three brand-new destroyers, which were designed and built by Vickers-Armstrong at Barrow-in-Furness: *Aragua, Nueva Esparta* and *Zulia*. These were very handsome ships, with the designers being able to take the best of British practice without the usual constraints of the Admiralty design departments.

Nueva Esparta and *Zulia* were both refitted in England in 1959, when, among other work, the torpedo tubes were removed and replaced by two Squid ASW mortars. All three ships then went to New York Naval Dockyard in 1960 where various items of US electronics were installed. *Nueva Esparta* again visited England in 1968-69, this time Cammel-Laird at Birkenhead, where

---

Dubrovnik

YUGOSLAVIA

Completed: 1931.
Number in class: 1.
Displacement: 1,880 tons standard.
Dimensions: Length 371.4ft (113.2m); beam 35.0ft (10.7m); draught 13.5ft (4.1m).
Propulsion: 2 shafts; Parsons geared steam-turbines; 3 boilers; 48,000shp; 37kt.
Armament: 4 x 5.5in (140mm) (4 x 1); 2 x 3.3in (84mm); 6 x 40mm AA; 2 x MG; 6 x 21.0in (533mm) TT.
Complement: 220.

History: In August 1929 the Royal Yugoslav Government placed a contract with the British shipyard, Yarrows, to design and build *Dubrovnik*, a destroyer leader. With a standard displacement of 1,800 tons she was the largest destroyer in the world at the time she was completed and reflected current British destroyer design practice. Main armament was four 5.5in (140mm) guns in single mounts, a rather unusual calibre for naval use.

Dubrovnik took King Alexander on his State visit to France in 1934, but then, only a few days later, had the sombre task of taking his body home, following his assassination. The ship was captured by the invading Italians in 1941 and impressed into the Italian Navy as the *Premuda*. She was then captured by the Germans on 8 September 1943 and impressed into the *Kriegsmarine* as *TA-32*, who rearmed her with four 4.1in (105mm), four 37mm AA, thirty-six 20mm AA, and removed three of the torpedo tubes. She was then employed in various night actions and was eventually scuttled at Genoa on 24 April 1945.

twelve 40mm Bofors were removed and replaced by two Seacat SAM launchers. It does not appear that either of her two sister ships were ever fitted with Seacat. *Aragua* was stricken in 1975, followed by both her sisters in 1978.

Below: Nueva Esparta, **one of three destroyers bought by Venezuela in the mid-1950s**

Above: **Destroyer *Dubrovnik,* built in Britain in the 1930s for the Yugoslav navy**

Split

YUGOSLAVIA

Completed: 1958.
Number in class: 1.
Displacement: 2,400 tons standard; 3,000 tons full load.
Dimensions: Length 393.6ft (120.0m); beam 39.3ft (12.0m); draught 12.2ft (3.7m).
Propulsion: 2 shafts; Parsons geared steam-turbines; 2 boilers; 50,000shp; 31.5kt.
Armament: 4 x 5.0in (127mm) (4 x 1); 12 x 40mm; 5 x 21.0in (533mm); 2 x Hedgehog ASW rocket launcher; 6 x depth-charge throwers; 2 x depth-charge racks; 40 x mines.
Complement: 240.

History: Few ships have had such a long construction time as this Yugoslavian

destroyer. She was designed before World War Two by the French company, Chantiers de la Loire, with the keel being laid in July 1939. At that time her planned armament was five 5.5in (140mm) (the same calibre as Dubrovnik), ten 40mm, eight 13mm MG and six 21.0in (533mm) torpedo tubes, and her design speed was 37 knots. The hull was incomplete at the time of the Italian invasion, but they failed to complete her and she was reclaimed by Tito's forces in 1944. The plans were then redrawn to take a mixture of US and British weapons and sensors, but she was not launched until 1950 and even then completion was not achieved until 1958. She was a useful ship and served her navy well until being stricken in 1980 and sold to Indonesia.

***Below: Split*; laid down in 1939 she was not fully completed until 1958**

Escorts

Navies have always needed a small warship to undertake the many minor tasks that arise in both peace and war, and at the start of the 20th Century this task was being performed by torpedo boats and destroyers, although the British also developed a type known as a "colonial sloop" and the French a general-purpose ship known as an "*aviso*". During World War I this requirement increased with the need for escort vessels, particularly once the U-boat had become a major threat; this was met by a mixture of smaller, older destroyers and minor vessels such as patrol craft and converted trawlers.

As seen in the previous section, during the inter-war years destroyers became larger and more sophisticated until, when war came in 1939, although many destroyers had to be employed as escorts, there was a need for a smaller, simpler and less expensive type of ship. This was met by types such as the British 1,200-ton Flower-class corvette, but, as always happens, the size was soon forced to increase, there being two main reasons in the early war years. First was the need for a longer range ship carrying more weapons and sensors, and therefore more crew, and second the requirement to improve the crew's living conditions, which were abysmal. This led to a type of second-class destroyer, known in the United States as a Destroyer-Escort (DE), while in Britain the traditional title of "frigate" was resurrected.

The next major influence on size came at the very end of the war and

Above: **The US Navy has built many post-war escorts; this is Garcia-class, *Davidson***

continued into the Cold War. This was the dramatic increase in the speed of the submarines to be hunted, which stemmed from the German Type XXI *elektroboot*. These U-boats increased submerged speeds from about 3-4 knots to a normal 10-12 knots with short bursts of 15-20 knots, which required a hunting ship that could travel at much greater speeds than previously, and in all but the most exceptional weather conditions. Such speed and seakeeping requirements led, once again, to the need for a larger, longer, and more stable hull, with much more powerful engines.

In the first two decades after the war this requirement was met by converting World War II destroyers, of which vast numbers were available. When these had to be replaced, however, the modern frigate became a warship specialising in ASW, but with some air defence and anti-ship capability. Then came yet another major influence on size, as the helicopter emerged as an excellent ASW weapon system and frigates needed to be to accommodate one, or sometimes two, which meant that space, volume and topweight were required for a flightdeck, hangar, magazine, aviation fuel and the manpower to operate them.

Thus, today's frigates are ships of between 3-4,000 tons displacement, which have a primary mission of ASW, either as task force or convoy escorts. But they also have to be capable of a wide range of other missions, thus filling the gap left by the destroyer as it has become ever larger and more sophisticated.

Yarra/Swan

AUSTRALIA

Frigate
Specifications for Yarra-class, as built.
Completed: Yarra - 1961-64; Swan - 1970-71.
Number in class: Yarra - 4; Swan - 2.
Displacement: 2,150 t tons standard; 2,560 tons full load.
Dimensions: Length 370.0ft (112.8m); beam 41.0ft (12.5m); draught 17.3f t (5.3m).
Propulsion: 2 shafts; geared turbines; 2 boilers; 30,000shp; 30 kt; 4,500nm at 12 kts.
Armament: 2 x 4.5in (114mm) (1 x 2); 2 x 40mm Bofors AA; 12 x 21in (533mm) TT; 2 x Limbo Mk 10 ASW mortar.
Complement: 234.

History: Built in Australia, these were the last in a long line of British ship designs operated by the Royal Australian Navy (RAN). The first four, the Yarra-class, were virtual repeats of the Royal Navy's Type 12 (Whitby-class) frigate design, but with the improvements of the Rothesay-class and further modifications to suit the RAN's own requirements. It was originally intended to build six, but in the event only four were completed: *Yarra* (F45) (1961); *Parramatta* (F46) (1961); *Stuart* (F48) (1963); and *Derwent* (F49) (1964).

In the second pair the forecastle deck was extended to the stern, which gave additional accommodation. *Stuart* was the first to be fitted with the Australian-developed Ikara ASW missile system, while *Derwent* was the first to have a British Seacat surface-to-air missile system in place of the

Wielingen (E71)

BELGIUM

Frigate
Completed: 1975-77.
Number in class: 4.
Displacement: 1,880 tons light; 2,283 tons full load.
Dimensions: Length 349.0ft (103.0m); beam 40.0ft (12.3m); draught 17.0ft (5.3m).
Propulsion: 2 shafts; CODOG; 1 Rolls-Royce Olympus gas-turbine, 28,000shp; 2 Cockerill diesels, 6,000bhp; 25kt, 4,500nm at 18kt.
Armament: 4 x MM38 Exocet SSM (4 x 1); 1 x NATO Sea Sparrow; 1 x 3.9in (100mm) gun; 1 x 12.8in (375mm) ASW rocker-launcher; 2 x torpedo launchers.
Complement: 160.

History: In the 1960s the Belgian naval staff prepared a requirement for a new frigate to replace the ex-British Algerine-class ships then in service. The new class was intended for the protection of merchant shipping in the North Sea, the English Channel and its Western Approaches, for which it had to possess a full ASW capability in combination with limited anti-air and anti-surface capabilities. The naval staff also laid down that only mission-essential features were to be provided, that only NATO standardized weapons and sensors would be installed, and, finally, that the ships must be built in Belgian yards. The programme was approved in June 1971, design was completed by July 1973 and the order was placed in October 1973, with the four ships being completed, all in 1978: *Wielingen* (F910); *Westdiep* (F911); *Wandelaar* (F912); and *Westhinder* (F913).

twin 40mm Bofors. All ships in the class were subsequently fitted with both systems. Nine years later the RAN ordered two more ships, *Swan* (F50) and *Torrens* (F53), which employed the same hull as the Yarra-class, but incorporated most of the improvements made by the RN in their Leander-class. These included a continuous two-deck superstructure and a new stump-mast for the air-warning radar, but did not include a helicopter flightdeck.

Yarra, Parramatta and *Stuart* were transferred to the reserve in the early 1980s and later scrapped, while *Derwent* was scuttled to form an artificial reef. *Swan* and *Torrens* were laid off and scrapped in the late 1990s.

***Below:* HMAS *Derwent*, fourth of the Yarra-class frigates, as completed in 1964**

These compact and well-armed frigates had a good a combination of anti-air, anti-surface and ASW capabilities, the only major deficiency being the lack of a helicopter.

The ships are based at Zeebrugge. *Westdiep* (F 911) and *Westhinder* (F 913) deployed to the Adriatic in 1993 as part of the UN embargo forces. *Westhinder* (F 913) subsequently hit rocks off the Norwegian coast in mid-1993 and was then deleted. From the mid-1990s one ship was kept operational, with a second in refit and a third on unmanned standby. It is planned to replace them in the 2010-2015 timeframe.

***Below: Wandelaar,* one of the three remaining Belgian Navy Wielingen-class frigates**

Niteroi

BRAZIL

Frigate
Completed: 1976-80.
Number in class: 6.
Displacement: 3,200 tons standard; 3,800 tons full load.
Dimensions: Length 424.0ft (129.2m); beam 44.2ft (13.5m); draught 18.2ft (5.6m).
Propulsion: 2 shafts; CODAG; 2 Rolls-Royce Olympus gas-turbines, 56,000shp; 4 MTU diesels, 18,000bhp; 30kt; 5,300nm at 17kt.
Aircraft: 1 Westland Lynx helicopter (not in GP version).
Armament: 2 x Seacat SAM (2 x 3); 1 x Branik ASW; 1 x DC rack 1 x 4.5in (114mm) gun; 2 x 40mm Bofors; 1 x 375mm Bofors ASW RL; 6 x 324mm Mk 32 ASW TT (see notes).
Complement: 200.

History: This class was designed by Vosper Thornycroft of Woolston, England for the Brazilian Navy. Following acceptance of the design, four were built in England - *Niteroi* (F40) (1974); *Defensora* (F41) (1977); *Constitução* (F42) (1978) and *Liberal* (F43) (1978) - while the other two were built in Brazil - *Independencia* (F44) (1979); and *Uniao* (F45) (1980). These were all to the same basic design, but two, *Constitução* and *Liberal* had a weapons and sensor fit optimised for general purposes (ie, surface warfare), while the other four were fitted for ASW duties. The weapons for the ASW version are shown above, but in the general warfare ships the Branik (a Brazilian version of the Australian Ikara system) ASW launchers were replaced by four Exocet MM38 SSM launchers and a second 4.5in (114mm) turret was mounted aft in place of the VDS

Inháuma

BRAZIL

Corvette
Completed: 1989-94.
Number in class: 4.
Displacement: 1,670 tons standard; 1,970 tons full load.
Dimensions: Length 314.3ft (95.8m); beam 37.4ft (11.4m); draught 12.1ft (5.5m).
Propulsion: 2 shafts; CODOG; 1 GE LM-2500 gas-turbine, 23,000shp; 2 MTU diesels, 7,800bhp; 27kt; 4,000nm at 15kt.
Aircraft: 1 Westland Lynx helicopter.
Armament: 4 x Exocet MM40 SSM; 1 x 4.7in (115mm) Vickers Mk 8 gun; 2 x 40mm Bofors; 6 x 12.8in (324mm) TT.
Complement: 162.

History: This was intended to have been a class of twelve corvettes for the Brazilian coastguard service, designed with the help of the German company, Marine Technik, and all to be built in Brazil. The first two were ordered in 1982 and in 1986 the order was increased to sixteen units, but this was later cut-back to a total of just four: *Inháuma* (V30) (1986); *Jaceguay* (V31)(1987); *Julio de Noronha* (V32) (1992); and *Frontin* (V33) (1994). The programme suffered a number of difficulties, among the most important being that building was delayed by labour problems and bankruptcy in the shipyard. It was also reported that the ships proved somewhat top-heavy on entry into service, which may explain why the planned Vulcan Phalanx CIWS has not been installed, and that they are very "wet" forward.

After a long gap, plans for a fifth ship were announced in 1994, with

Above: Niteroi, **nameship of a class of six; five were built in the UK, the sixth in Brazil**

installation. All were modernized in Brazil in the late 1990s, which involved installing four Exocet MM40 launchers in all six ships and removing the outdated Branik ASW system. The work also included replacing the command-and-control systems and electronic sensors with modern French and Italian systems.

---

possible further orders to follow. This ship, to be named *Barrosso* (V34), is due to be completed in 2002 and is a lengthened version of the *Inháuma* design, with a 13.8ft (4.2m) longer hull to accommodate more powerful diesels, a larger flightdeck and improved accommodation, while the freeboard and bow rake are to be increased in an effort to reduce the wetness forward.

Above: Inháuma, **one of four ships built in Brazil to a German design in 1983 - 1994**

City

CANADA

Frigate
Completed: 1992-96.
Number in class: 12.
Displacement: 45,305 tons standard; 4,761 tons full load.
Dimensions: Length 440.3ft (134.2 m); beam 53.8ft (16.4m); draught 16.4ft (5.0m).
Propulsion: 2 shafts; CODOG; General Electric LM-2500 gas-turbines, 46,000shp; 1 SEMT-Pielstick diesel, 8,800bhp; 28kt; 7,100nm at 15kt.
Armament: 1 x 57mm SAK Mk2 gun; 8 x Harpoon SSM, 2 x Mk 48 VL Sea Sparrow SAM systems; 1 x Mk 15 Vulcan Phalanx CIWS; 3 x 324mm ASW TT; 8 x 0.5in (12.7mm) MG.
Aircraft: 1 CH-124A Sea King helicopter.
Complement: 225.

History: It was originally planned to build twenty of these ships, but the order for the first six was not placed until June 1983, followed by the order for a further six in December 1987 and the last eight will not now be built. Ships and completion dates were: *Halifax* (330) (1991); *Vancouver* (331) (1992); *Ville De Quebec* (332) (1993); *Toronto* (333) (1993); *Regina* (334) (1994); *Calgary* (335) (1994); *Montreal* (336) (1993); *Fredericton* (337) (1994); *Winnipeg* (338) (1994); *Charlottetown* (339) (1995); *St John's* (340) (1995); *Ottawa* (341) (1996).

The Canadians have extensive experience of North Atlantic operations and the high freeboard, flush deck and broad beam (which was carried well forward) to reduce "wetness," while the deep draught and fine bow lines prevented the sonar dome lifting clear of the water. These all combined to reduce slamming and minimise pitch and roll, which were of considerable benefit to helicopter operations, as well as to general crew comfort and efficiency. The hull and

Hvidbjørnen/Beskytteren

DENMARK

Frigate
Specifications are for Hvidbjørnen-class, as built.
Completed: 1962-63.
Number in class: 4.
Displacement: 1,345 tons standard; 1,650 tons full load.
Dimensions: Length 238.2ft (72.0m); beam 38.0ft (11.5m); draught 16.0ft (5.0m).
Propulsion: 1 shaft; 4 General Motors diesels; 6,400hp, 18kt; 6,000nm at 13kt.
Aircraft: 1 helicopter.
Armament: 1 x 3in (76mm) DP; depthcharge thrower
Complement: 85.

History: The four Hvidbjørnen-class ships were specially designed and equipped for fishery protection duties in waters under Danish sovereignty around Greenland and the Faroe islands, and in the North Sea. Names were: *Hvidbjørnen* (F348), completed in 1962; and *Vædderen* (F349), *Ingold* (F350) and *Fylla* (F351), all completed in 1963. Their Danish designation was as "inspection vessels" but they were also rated as "frigates" although their armament of one 3in (76mm) gun and a few depth-charges would not have made them particularly effective in a war situation.

One more ship, *Beskytteren* (F340), was completed in 1976 to a "modified-Hvidbjörnen" design. This was some 5.86ft (1.8m) longer and was powered by three Burmeister & Wain diesels; the sole armament consisted of a single 3in (76mm) gun on the foredeck.

***Above:* The City-class was the subject of intense national debate before building started**

superstructure were fabricated mainly from high-tensile steel, with high-yield steels giving additional strength in areas of major stress and for ballistic protection. Considerable efforts were also been made to enhance the ship's stealth characteristics. Primary mission was ASW, so special attention was paid to underwater radiated noise, with the propellers designed to maximise the speed at which cavitation begins. There were problems on first-of-class trials, mainly due to radiated noise levels, but these were quickly rectified. Plans to lengthen the second group of six hulls to increase SAM capacity and to improve living conditions were shelved. *Vancouver, Regina, Calgary, Winnipeg* and *Ottawa* are based in the Pacific, the remainder in the Atlantic.

The four original Hvidbjørnen-class ships were stricken in the early 1990s, but *Beskytteren* remains in service.

***Below:* Danish frigate *Vaedderen,* designed for deployment in Arctic waters**

Peder Skram

DENMARK

Frigate
Completed: 1966-67.
Number in class: 2.
Displacement: 2,200 tons standard; 2,720 tons full load.
Dimensions: Length 396.4ft (112.6m); beam 39.4ft (12.0m); draught 14.1ft (4.3m).
Propulsion: 2 shafts; CODOG: 1 MTU diesel, 4,800bhp; 1 General Electric LM-2500 gas-turbine, 18,400shp; 28kt; 2,500nm at 18kt.
Armament: 4 x 5in (127mm) (2 x 2); 4 x 40mm Bofors; 3 x 21in (533mm) TT; DC.
Complement: 200

History: These two ships were designed in Denmark and built in the Danish shipyard at Helsingör, but were financed with US "offshore" funds, being completed in 1966, *Peder Skram* (F352), and 1967, *Herluf Trolle* (F353). The Terne ASW system, which was in the original design, was never installed and the original triple torpedo tube mounting was replaced by two twin mounts amidships soon after completion, although these were later removed during modernization in 1976-78. The modernization work included the removal of "B" turret and its

Thetis

DENMARK

Frigate
Completed: 1991-92.
Number in class: 4.
Displacement: 2,600 tons standard; 3,500 tons full load.
Dimensions: Length 369.1ft (112.5m); beam 47.2ft (14.4m); draught 19.7ft (6.0m).
Propulsion: 1 shaft; 3 MAN/Burmeister & Wain diesels; 10,800 hp(m); 20kt; 8,500nm at 15.5kt.
Armament: 1 x OTO Melara 76mm gun; 1 x 20mm; 2 x DC racks.
Aircraft: 1 helicopter.
Complement: 61.

History: A preliminary study by British design consultancy YARD in 1986 led to Dwinger Marine Consultants being awarded a contract for a detailed design, completed in mid-1987. Four ships were ordered in late 1987: *Thetis* and *Triton*, completed in 1990; followed by *Vaedderen* and *Hvidbjørnen*, completed in 1992. The hull was some 98ft (30m) longer than the earlier Hvidbjørnen-class to improve sea-keeping qualities and to allow extra space for additional armament. The design allows the use of containerised equipment to be shipped depending on role and there is some commonality with the Danish StanFlex 300 ships. The hull is ice-strengthened to enable penetration of 3ft (1m) thick ice and efforts have been made to incorporate stealth technology, for instance by placing anchor equipment, bollards and winches below the upper deck. There is a double skin up to 6,6ft (2.0m) below the waterline. The flight deck

replacement by two quadruple Harpoon SSM launchers, while an 8-cell NATO Sea Sparrow SAM launcher was installed on the quarterdeck and two triple ASW torpedo launchers amidships.

There was a serious engine room fire in *Herluf Trolle* in 1982, but she was repaired and returned to service in 1983. Both ships were placed in reserve in 1987 and scrapped in the 1990s.

Below: *Herluf Trolle*, one of two Danish-designed and -built Cold War frigates

Above: *Hvidbjørnen*; the Thetis-class is one of the most elegant warship designs ever

measures 92 x 46ft (28 x 14m) and will accept Sea King or Merlin helicopters.

The primary role is fishery protection and the ships are also employed for seismological surveys, particularly in the Greenland EEZ. The design was deliberately made flexible so that these ships could be developed into fully armed frigates later, with possible equipment including: surface-to-surface missiles (eg, Harpoon), surface-to-air missiles (eg, vertical launch Sea Sparrow and RAM), and ASW torpedo tubes, together with the associated sensors and arrays.

Le Corse (E50)/ Le Normand (E52)

FRANCE

Frigate
Specifications for *Le Corse*, as built.
Completed: Le Corse - 1955-56; Le Normand - 1956-60.
Number in class: Le Corse - 4; Le Normand - 14.
Displacement: 1,250 tons standard; 1,702 tons full load.
Dimensions: Length 327.0ft (95.1m); beam 34.0ft (10.3m); draught 14.0ft (4.3m).
Propulsion: 2 shafts; Rateau geared turbines; 2 boilers; 20,000shp; 28kt; 4,000nm at 15kt.
Armament: 6 x 57mm Mod 1951 (3 x 2); 2 x 20mm; 1 x 9.0in (357mm) ASW RL; 2 x DC mortars; 1 x DC rack; 12 x 21.6in (550mm) TT.
Complement: 174.

History: The first French-designed warships to be produced after World War II, the four E50-class ships were produced as part of France's commitment to NATO, with three of them being financed by the United States under the Mutual Defense Assistance Pact (MDAP). The four ships were: *Le Corse, Le Boulonnais* and *Le Bordelais*, all completed in 1955, and *Le Brestois*, completed in 1956. They were flush-decked ships, with a passing similarity to the US Navy's Dealey-class destroyer-escorts (DE), although this was no more than coincidence.

The E50-class had some shortcomings and these were rectified in the E52

Commandant Riviere (A69)

FRANCE

Aviso
Completed: 1962-70.
Number in class: 9.
Displacement: 1,750 tons standard; 2,230 tons full load.
Dimensions: Length 338.0ft (98.0m); beam 38.0ft (11.5m); draught 14.0ft (4.3m).
Propulsion: 2 shafts, 4 SEMT-Pielstick 12-cylinder diesels; 16,000bhp; 25kts; 7,500nm at 16kt.
Armament: 3 x 100mm Mod 1953 (3 x 1); 2 x 30mm/40mm; 1 x 305mm ASW mortar; 6 x 550mm ASW TT.
Complement: 166.

History: The French Navy long had a mission for patrolling France's colonial possessions in Africa, the Far East and the Pacific, a role for which a corvette-sized vessel known as an *aviso* had been devised pre-war, a type which was equivalent to the British "colonial sloop." During the Cold War the requirement for such ships continued, but it was combined with a wartime role as a NATO convoy escort under the designation *avisos escorteurs*. Nine of the Commandant Riviére-class were completed between 1962 and 1970, and with a full load displacement of 2,230 tons they mounted an armament of three 100mm guns and two 30/40mm, while ASW armament comprised a 305mm mortar (which also had a special shore-bombardment round) and two triple sets of 550mm torpedo tubes. Somewhat surprisingly, considering the small hull, the ship could also accommodate either an

***Above:* *Le Corse,* lead ship of a class of eight light frigates for the French Navy**

(Le Normand)-class, fourteen of which were completed between 1956 and 1960, seven being paid for by the MDAP and seven by France. The major difference was that the twelve 550mm torpedo tubes in the E50-class were in a somewhat vulnerable position on the 01 deck immediately ahead of "B" gun, whereas in the E52-class they were moved back to the upper deck amidships. The last five ships (*L'Agenais, Le Bearnais, L'Alsacien, Le Provençal, Le Vendéen*) all had a completely rebuilt bridge, a single, large, square block compared to the previous tiered structure, but the last three of these had other differences, mainly concerning ASW armament, leading them to be designated the E52B-class.

The four E50s were stricken in 1975-77, while the E52s had some five years further service and were stricken between 1979 and 1985

---

admiral and his staff or an eighty-man marine detachment, for whom two 30ft (9m)-long landing craft were carried on davits.

These very useful ships also served as trials platforms for new weapons and sensors, and as test beds for new forms of propulsion. Three were sold to the Uruguayan Navy between 1988 and 1991, where they are still in service. The remainder were all stricken from the French Navy in the mid-1990s and later scrapped.

***Below:* France has long employed *avisos,* frigates designed specially for colonial duties**

D'Estienne d'Orves (A69) FRANCE

Aviso escorteur
Completed: 1976-1986.
Number in class: 17.
Displacement: 1,100 tons standard; 1,250 tons full load.
Dimensions: Length 262.0ft (80.0m); beam 34.0ft (10.3m); draught 17.0ft (5.3m).
Propulsion: 2 shafts, 2 SEMT-Pielstick diesels; 11,000shp; 23.5kts; 4,500nm at 15kt.
Armament: 2 x MM38 Exocet SSM; 1 x 100mm Mod 1968; 2 x 20mm; 1 x 12.8in (375mm) ASW rocket launcher; 4 launchers for torpedoes.
Complement: 105.

History: The original intention was to produce thirty-five ships to replace the E 50, E 52 and Commandant Riviére classes, using a common hull but with two sensor/armament fits: Type A 69 - coastal ASW; Type A 70 - surface operations. In the event, only the Type A 69 was built, with the French Navy taking seventeen, while three were sold to Argentina. The requirement was for a ship which could undertake lengthy patrols in colonial waters, but in general war could be used for ASW in coastal waters; ie, within the 200m (100 fathom) line) ASW. It was also required to be suitable for use in sea training. Where performance was concerned, the emphasis was on endurance, resulting in a maximum speed of 23kt, but a range of 4,500nm at 15 kt and an endurance of 30 days. The emphasis throughout the design was on simplicity, ruggedness and reliability, which are essential in distant waters, where the ships had to be self-reliant for long periods.

There were problems with funnel emissions in the early ships and the fifth

Floreal FRANCE

Surveillance frigate (Fregate de Surveillance)
Completed: 1992-94.
Number in class: 6.
Displacement: 2,600tons standard; 2,950tons full load.
Dimensions: Length 306.8ft (93.5m); beam 45.9ft (14.0m); draught 14.1ft (4.3 m).
Propulsion: 2 shafts; CODAD; 4 SEMT-Pielstick diesels; 8,820hp(m) (6.5MW);20kt; 10,000nm at 15 kt; 50 days.
Aircraft: 1 light helicopter.
Armament: 2 x MM38 Exocet SSM; 1 x 100mm Model 1968CADAM gun; 2 x 20mm.
Complement: 86 (plus 24 Marines).

History: This class was ordered in three pairs, *Floreal* and *Prairial* in January 1989, *Nivose* and *Ventose* in January 1990 and *Vendemaire* and *Germinal* January 1991. All were built at Chantiers de l'Atlantique at St Nazaire, with the weapon systems being fitted by DCAN Lorient. The ships were designed for operations in distant waters, with the hull, accommodation and most facilities being built to mercantile standards, one example being that all four engines are in one large engine room to reduce watchkeeping and maintenance requirements. Critical items such as damage control, magazines and helicopter facilities are to full Service standards.

The ships have two screws and a bow thruster, making them extremely manoeuvrable, and also have stabilisers and air-conditioning. There is a large flight deck and the funnel was designed to improve airflow over the flight deck, so that, although the embarked helicopter is usually a Dauphin or Alouette,

Above: *Commandant l'Herminier* an *aviso* of the d'Estienne d'Orves-class

had a raised funnel, which cured the problem and was then fitted to all others in the class. At one stage there was a proposal to install a flight deck and hangar for a light helicopter, but this would have stretched them beyond their limits.

Above: The latest colonial frigates are the Floreal-class, built to commercial standards

larger types such as Puma/Cougar can also be operated. The good medical facilities include a small hospital and there is also a 100ton cargo hold aft. It is planned to replace the manually-operated 20 mm guns with two Matra Simbad twin launchers in due course. Normal deployment is three in the Pacific, one in the Indian Ocean, one in the Caribbean, and one as tender to the training ship *Jeanne d'Arc*.

La Fayette/Arriyad/ Kang Ting

FRANCE

Surveillance frigate
Completed: 1995-2002.
Number in class: 5.
Displacement: 3,100 tons standard; 3,600 tons full load.
Dimensions: Length 410.1ft (125.0m); beam 50.9ft (15.5m); draught 13.45ft (4.1m).
Propulsion: 2 shafts; CODAD; 4 SEMT-Pielstick diesels; 21,000bhp; 25kt; 9,000nm at 12kt.
Armament: 8 x MM40 Exocet SSM; 1 x Crotale SAM system; 1 x 100mm Model 1968 CADAM gun; 2 x).5in (12.7mm) MG.
Aircraft: 1 helicopter.
Complement: 86 (plus 24 Marines).

History: French analysis in the mid-1980s indicated a requirement for a ship for: national or international naval operations, including shadowing, deterrence and, when required, attack on hostile ships; intelligence collection; rescue of threatened French citizens; landing special forces; support of amphibious operations; humanitarian missions; and, finally, search and rescue. The result was the La Fayette-class and ten were originally planned for the French Navy, but this was later reduced to five. The design criteria were: stealth, reduced vulnerability to hits; good seakeeping; flexibility; a high degree of automation;

Köln (Type 120)

GERMANY

Frigate
Completed: 1961-64.
Number in class: 6.
Displacement: 2,090 tons standard; 2,750 tons full load.
Dimensions: Length 360.3ft (109.8m); beam 36.1ft (11.0m); draught 15.1ft (4.6m).
Propulsion: 2 shafts; CODAG; 4 MAN diesels, 12,000bhp; 2 Brown-Boveri gas-turbines, 24,000shp; 32kt; 3,450nm at 12kt.
Armament: 2 x 100mm (2 x 1); 6 x 40mm; 4 x 21in (533mm) ASW TT; 2 x 375mm ASW mortars.
Complement: 238.

History: These six frigates were the first ships of any size to be designed and built in Germany after 1945, the design originally being known as "*Geleitboot-55*" (escort ship-1955). Orders were placed in 1957 and they were delivered: *Köln* - 1961; *Emden* - 1961; *Augsburg* - 1962; *Karlsruhe* - 1962; *Lübeck* - 1963; and *Braunschweig* - 1964.

They were regularly refitted whilst in German service, modifications including additional protection, increased stability, updated electronics and enhanced armament. The original full-size 21in (533mm) twin torpedo tubes were replaced by four tubes for the shorter 21in (533mm) ASW torpedoes. Of the German ships, one was broken up in 1989, while the last, ex-

***Above:* The La Fayette-class's unique shape is designed to minimise radar signature**

and moderate costs. The result is a ship with a unique appearance. Six have been built for Taiwan (Kang Ting-class) and were delivered between 1996 and 1998, and a further three are under construction for the Saudi Navy (Arriyad-class) for delivery between 2002 and 2005.

Köln, was decommissioned in 1989 and is now used as a training hulk for damage control and firefighting. The remaining four were all sold to Turkey: two in 1983, one in 1988 and the last in 1989. Of these, two were cannibalised to keep the other two in service, but all were scrapped in the late 1990s.

***Below:* The Köln-class were the first frigates built in West Germany after World War II**

MEKO

GERMANY

Frigates

Country	Argentina	Australia/ New Zealand	Greece
National class name	Almirante Brown	ANZAC	Hydra
Completed	1980-1984	1993-2004	1990-1997
Built: Germany In-country	4 0	0 10	1 3
Displacement standard (t) full load (t)	2,900 3,360	3,300 3,600	2,710 3,200
Dimensions length (oa) beam (m) draught (m)	412.1ft (125.6m) 49.2ft (15.0m) 14.1ft (4.3m)	380.2ft (115.9mm) 48.6ft (14.8m) 13.5ft (4.1m)	383.8ft (117.0m) 48.6ft (14.8m) 13.5ft (4.1m)
Propulsion	COGOG. 2 Olympus GT; 2 Tyne GT; 30.5kt; 4,500nm at 18kt.	CODOG. 1 LM2500 GT; 2 MTU diesel; 27kt; 6,000nm at 18kt.	CODOG. 2 LM2500 GT; 2 MTU diesel; 31kt; 4,100nm at 18kt.
Weapons SSM	8 x Exocet	-	8 x Harpoon
SAM	Albatros/ Aspide	Mk 41 VLS SeaSparrow	Mk48 VLS SeaSparrow
Main Gun	1x127mm	1x127mm	1x127mm
Close-in	8 x 40mm	-	2x k 15
Torpedo tubes (all 324mm)	6	6	6
Aircraft	2xAlouette III	1xSH-60B (Aus); 1xSH-2B (NZ)	1xS70B-6
Crew	200	163	189

Nigeria	Portugal	Turkey	Turkey
Aradu	Vasco da Gama	Yavuz	Barbaros
1979-1982	1989-1991	1985-1989	1993-2000
1 -	3 0	2 ?	2 2
- 3,680	2,700 3,300	2,414 2,919	3,100 3,350
412.1ft (125.6m) 49.2ft (15.0m) 14.1ft (4.3m)	380.2ft (115.9m) 48.6ft (14.8m) 13.5ft (4.1m)	380.2ft (115.9m) 46.6ft (14.2m) 13.5ft (4.1m)	380.2ft (115.9m) 48.6ft (14.8m) 13.5ft (4.1m)
CODOG. 2 Olympus GT; 2 MTU diesel; 30.5kt, 4,500nm at 18kt	CODOG. 2 LM 2500 GT; 2 MTU diesel; 32kt;4,900nm at 18kt.	CODAD. 4 MTU diesels; 27kt; 4,100nm at 18kt.	CODOG. 2 LM 2500 GT; 2 MTU diesels; 32kt; 4,100nm at 18kt
8 x Otomat	8 x Harpoon	8 x Harpoon	8 x Harpoon
Albatros/ Aspide	Mk 29 SeaSparrow	Mk29 Aspide	Mk 29 Aspide
1x127mm	1x100mm	1x127mm	1x127mm
8x40mm	2x0mm	3x25mm	3x25mm
6	6	6	6
1xLynx	2xSuper Lynx	1xAB212ASW	1xAB212
230	184	180	186

History: MEKO (*Merhzwecks Kombination* = Multi-Role Combination) is a ship construction system for destroyers and frigates devised by German builders Blohm+Voss. System flexibility enables customers to select a hull and superstructure from a common design, but with variable length, and then to specify their own requirements for weapons, propulsion, sensors, command-and-control equipment and other electronics. Such a system avoids many of the costs usually involved in a new class of ship. Weapons and electronic systems are installed in Functional Units, which are mounted in a container or framework, or on a pallet. Standardized installation and removal routes facilitate construction and make it easier to remove units for overhaul or replacement. One of many advantages is that hull construction is decoupled. Some functional units (eg, guns) are hard mounted to the ship platform, with the unit being placed in position, levelled, bedded down using a quick-setting resin and then bolted down. Other units which require shock absorption have shock mounts at the interface between the platform and the functional unit, enabling all equipment within the unit to be hard mounted.

Australia

Having bought British warships for many years, the Royal Australian Navy (RAN) switched to US ships in the 1960s, purchasing three Adams-class destroyers (1962-67) followed by six Perry-class frigates (1977-93), so it came as a surprise when the 1980s competition for a new class of frigate was won by Blohm+Voss. The contract was signed in November 1989 to build ten MEKO 200ANZ frigates, eight for Australia and two for New Zealand. Construction started in March 1992, with modules being constructed at Newcastle and Whangarei, and then shipped to Melbourne for assembly. Ships #1, #3 and #5-#10 were for the RAN, while #2 and #4 were for the RNZN. The total contract was scheduled to run for fifteen years and at $US 3.8 billion (1988 dollars) was the largest defence programme ever undertaken in Australia.

Designated MEKO 200ANZAC, the design is based on the Portuguese MEKO 200PN, but one unusual feature is the propulsion system, with two MTU diesels but only one LM 2500 gas-turbine, giving a lower maximum speed of 27 knots, but a very considerable increase in range. The RAN's plan to install a 76 mm gun had to be altered when the Army insisted on a 127mm weapon, to obtain improved terminal effects in the shore bombardment missions.

The RAN has commissioned a "Warfighting Improvement Programme" (WIP) which, as the name implies, will result in a major enhancement to their combat capabilities, particularly in weapons systems and surveillance/command facilities. The programme has been funded at $Aus610million and the contract was due to be placed in 2001.

Greece

Greece ordered four MEKO200 Mod3HN in April 1988, in a complicated deal with NATO and seven of its members. One element concerns German offsets for tanks and aircraft, while US Foreign Military Sales credits were used for the electronics and some of the weapon systems. *Hydra*, the first-of-class, was built by Blohm+Voss and completed in November 1992, while the other three, *Spetsai, Psara* and *Salamis*, were built in Greece with German assistance and delivered between 1996 and 1998. Like the ANZAC ships, the design followed that of the Portuguese Da Gama-class, but with a single hangar and a prominent bulwark around the bows. The Greek ships differ from other MEKO 200s in having two Mk 15 CIWS (Vulcan Phalanx), one in "B" position forward of the bridge.

New Zealand

The Royal New Zealand Navy (RNZN) ordered two ships as part of the MEKO ANZAC programme. These are generally very similar to the RAN version, although the RNZN uses Kaman SH-2F SeaSprite helicopters rather than the SH-60 used by the Australians. The RNZN has made repeated efforts to persuade its government

***Right:* Hydra, one of four MEKO200HN built for the Hellenic Navy**

to obtain a third ship, one plan being for a new-build ship and another to purchase one of the RAN's eight ships, but no agreement has yet been reached.

Portugal

The three Portuguese ships (MEKO200PN) were ordered in July 1986 and all were completed in 1991. Seven NATO countries (Canada, France, Germany, Luxembourg, Netherlands, Norway, USA) shared 60 percent of the costs, the remainder being met by Portugal. This was the first to incorporate "MEKO Mod 2" concepts such as greatly increased compartmentalisation, and is designed primarily for the ASW mission. It has full facilities for two Westland Lynx helicopters, with a French 100 mm gun, but with only one Mark 15 CIWS, which is located on the hangar roof. The ships are fitted with stabilisers and have full RAS facilities, with space left for a towed sonar array and VLS Sea Sparrow in due course.

Turkey - MEKO 200TN Track I/Track II

The Turkish Navy signed a contract in December 1982 and four ships were constructed by Blohm + Voss - *Yavuz;* Howaldtswerke - *Turgut Reis,* and Golcük, Turkey - *Fatih* and *Yildirim* with the US Navy providing training in US systems and the Federal German Navy the operational training. Although these arrangements were complicated they worked very well and the time from contract signing to commissioning the fourth ship was six years and four months.

The contract for the MEKO 200TN Track II was signed in January 1990 and four were built, *Barbaros* and *Salihreis* by B+V in Germany, and *Oruçreis* and *Kemalreis* by GolcÅk in Turkey. These are longer than the Track I ships, making them the same length as the MEKO 200s built for Australia, Greece, New Zealand and Portugal; and were built to the latest MEKO Mod 3 standards.

***Below:* MEKO frigate of the Turkish Navy, which now operates eight of these ships**

Brandenburg (Type 123) GERMANY

Frigate
Completed: 1994-96.
Number in class: 4.
Displacement: 3,660 tons standard; 4,700 tons full load.
Dimensions: Length 455.5ft (138.9m); beam 54.8ft (16.7m); draught 14.3ft (4.4m).
Propulsion: 2 shafts; CODOG; 2 General Electric LM-2500 gas-turbines, 25,840shp each; 2 MTU diesels, 5,535bhp each; 29+kt; 4,000nm at 18kt.
Aircraft: 2 helicopters.
Armament: 8 x Harpoon SSM; 1 x Mk41 VL Sea Sparrow SAM; 2 x Mk49 RAM SAM; 1 x 76mm gun; 2 x 20mm Rheinmetall Rh-202 cannon;4 x 324mm ASW TT.
Complement: 219.

History: The order for these four large and capable frigates was placed in June 1989; the design was by Blohm+Voss, but one ship was built in each of the four major German shipyards. It is not a MEKO design, as such, but it employs the MEKO principle, with fourteen modules, each easily removable and shock-mounted, containing outfits such as communications, sonar equipment and weapons. The design was based on German analysis of the naval engagements in the 1981 Falklands (Malvinas) War, which concluded that while it was necessary to try to destroy all incoming missiles, some hits were inevitable; thus, survivability after a missile hit is an essential requirement. This was achieved in the Brandenburg design by the use of three large, continuous box girders at the strength-deck level, with the ship divided laterally into twelve independent compartments, each with its own ventilation module and NBC

Godavari/Improved Godavari GERMANY

Frigate
Specification for Godavari-class, as built.
Completed: Godavari - 1983-86; Improved Godavari - 1999-2006.
Number in class: Godavari - 3; Improved Godavari - 1 (+2).
Displacement: 3,700 tons standard; 4,300tons full load.
Dimensions: Length 412.1ft (125.6m); beam 47.2ft (14.4m); draught 13.5ft (4.1m).
Propulsion: 2 shafts; Bhopal Engineering steam turbines; 2 boilers; 30,000 hp; 27kt; 4,500 at 12kt.
Aircraft: 1 ASW helicopter.
Armament: 4 x SS-N-2C Styx SSM launcher; 1 x SA-N-4 SAM launcher; 2 x 57mm gun (2 x 1); 8 x 30mm AK-230 CIWS; 6 x 324mm ASW TT.
Complement: 313.

History: The Indian Navy built four of the British-designed Leander-class frigates between 1971 and 1981, and this led to a much-modified version, the three-strong Godavari-class (Indian Navy Type 16), *Godavari, Gomati* and *Ganga*, which were completed between 1983 and 1986. This had a larger hull and the same propulsion plant, but with Russian weapons systems; indigenously-produced components amounted to 72 per cent of the whole. This then led to a yet further modified version, the Improved Godavari (Type 16A), which has the similar hull and propulsion characteristics, but carries eight Kh-35 Uran SAM

***Above:* The Brandenburg-class is not a MEKO design, but uses the same principles**

filter station. The design is spacious, with sufficient volume, electrical power and displacement available for growth during the ships' planned 30-year lives.

Another design criterion was stealth, with the superstructure and hull carefully angled, which, in combination with classified measures, reduces radar cross section by about 90 percent compared to the Type 122. Type 123s also have a large room on the starboard side, separate from the bridge and accommodates a CTG (commander task group) and a staff of ten, with their own combat information centre (CIC).

These four frigates were originally to have been known as the 'Deutschland' class, but this was changed to the names of four *Länder* (states). The ships and completion dates are: *Brandenburg* (1994); *Schleswig-Holstein* (1995); *Bayern* (1996); *Mecklenburg-Pommern* (December 1996).

***Above: Gomati,* an Indian-built Godavari-class frigate, developed from the Leander**

launchers on the foredeck, which area is considerably modified from the original, the CIWS is replaced by the much-improved 30mm AK-630 gatling and the electronics systems are all much more advanced. The three ships and their completion dates are: *Brahmaputra* (1999); *Betwa* (2002); and *Beas* (2006).

These ships have a unique combination of Russian, Western and Indian weapon and electronic systems, which has inevitably led to some equipment compatibility problems. Such problems have been exacerbated by supply delays in the delivery of Russian-made equipment. The result has been considerable delays in overall delivery and the final ship of the three Improved Godavaris is not due for delivery before 2006.

Saam (Vosper Mk5)

IRAN

Frigate
Specifications for class in 1990s.
Completed: 1971-72.
Number in class: 4.
Displacement: 1,250 tons standard; 1,540 tons full load.
Dimensions: Length 310.0ft (94.5m); beam 36.4ft (11.1m); draught 10.8ft (3.3m).
Propulsion: 2 shafts; CODOG; 2 Rolls-Royce Olympus gas-turbines, 46,000shp; 2 Paxman Valenta diesels, 3,800bhp; 39kt; 5,000nm at 15kt.
Armament: 4 x C-202 SSM; 1 x 114mm Vickers Mk8 gun; 2 x 35mm Oerlikon AA; 3 x 20mm Oerlikon AA; 2 x 0.5in (12.7mm) AAMG; 2 x 82mm mortar; 1 x Limbo ASW mortar.
Complement: 135.

History: This class of four Vosper Mk 5 frigates was one of many British naval systems ordered by the Shah in the later years of his rule, being delivered: *Saam* - 1971; *Zaal* - 1971; *Rastam* - 1972; *Faramarz* - 1972. They were originally fitted with the British semi-automatic Mk6 gun, but this was replaced by the Vickers Mk8 during their first refit in the 1970s. As built, the ships had almost entirely British equipment, but, following the revolution, Iran became almost totally cut-off from Western sources of supply and replacement equipment has been mounted whenever it has become available. Thus, Chinese-supplied C-202 missile

Bergamini

ITALY

Frigate
Completed: 1961-62.
Number in class: 4.
Displacement: 1,410 tons standard; 1,650 tons full load.
Dimensions: Length 308.3ft (94.0m); beam 37.3ft (11.4m); draught 10.2ft (3.1m).
Propulsion: 2 shafts, 4 Fiat/Tosi diesels; 16,000bhp; 25kt; 3,000nm at 18kt.
Aircraft: 1 x ASW helicopter.
Armament: 2 x 76mm (2 x 1); 1 x Menon ASW mortar; 6 x 324mm ASW TT
Complement: 163.

History: These small escorts were originally rated as *Corvette Veloci Tipo* 2 (corvettes, fast, type 2), although their maximum speed of 25kt was relatively slow by Italian standards. Four were built: *Luigi Rizzo*, completed in 1961; and *Carlo Bergamini, Virgilio Fasan*, and *Carlo Margottini*, all of which were completed in 1962. However, they possessed a powerful ASW weapons fit, which led to them being re-rated as frigates. They were powered by four high-speed diesels, made by Fiat (*Fasan and Margottini*) and Tosi (*Bergamini* and *Rizzo*).

They underwent considerable changes in service. The original armament comprised three 76mm and one twin 40mm guns, fixed torpedo tubes and two Menon ASW mortars. Then the Italian Navy concluded that 76mm was the minimum calibre for effective AA fire, so the twin 40mm was removed. The main ASW weapon was the Menon, a long-barrelled mortar in a fully trainable and elevating turret, with two mounted side-by-side, both on the 01 deck abaft "B" gun. When the twin 40mm was removed from "X" position, however, one of

launchers have replaced the I Sea Killer missiles, while the original Seacat SAM launchers were replaced first by twin ZU-23-2 AA cannon and later by the current single 20mm mounts.

All ships were renamed after the Revolution, the new names being: *Alvand* (ex- Saam); *Alborz* (ex-*Zaal*); *Sabalan* (ex-*Rastam*); and *Sahand* (ex-*Faramarz*). These four ships have taken part in many of the Gulf conflicts and confrontations, in one of which *Sahand*) was hit and destroyed by US-launched Harpoon missiles (19 April 1988).

***Below: Saam,* lead-ship of a class of four built in the UK for the Shah of Iran's navy**

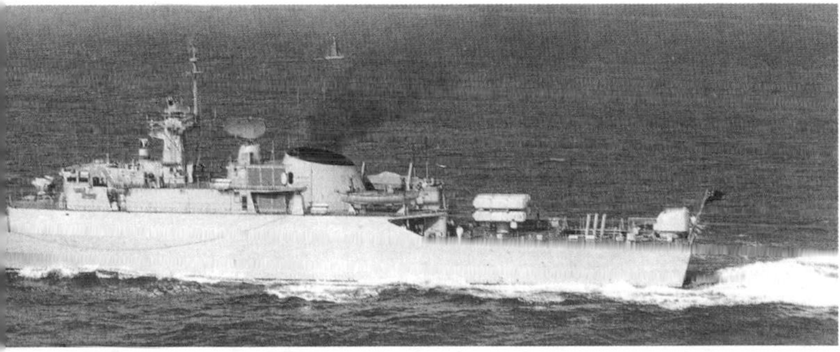

***Above: Carlo Bergamini,* the first of many Italian post-war frigates**

the two Menons was moved aft to take its place. Then it was decided that the modern fast submarine threat was such that a helicopter - the Agusta-Bell AB-204 - was needed, so the after Menon was removed, the funnel trunked into the mast to form a "mack"and the upper deck area thus cleared was used to install a telescopic hangar and flight deck. Later it was decided that a larger, heavier helicopter - the Agusta-Bell AB-212- was needed. so the 76mm gun in "Y" position was also removed to enable the hangar and flightdeck to be enlarged. The ships were stricken: *Rizzo* - 1980; *Bergamini* - 1981; *Fasan* and *Margottini* - 1988.

Alpino

ITALY

Frigate
Completed: 1968.
Number in class: 2.
Displacement: 2,000 tons standard; 2,700 tons full load.
Dimensions: Length 371.8ft (113.3m); beam 43.0ft (13.1m); draught 12.3ft (3.8m).
Propulsion: 2 shafts; CODAG; 2 Tosi-Metrovick gas-turbines, 15,000shp; 4 Tosi diesels, 16,800bhp; 29kt; 3,500nm at 18kt.
Aircraft: 2 helicopters.
Armament: 6 x 76mm (6 x 1); 1 x Menon ASW mortar; 6 x 324mm ASW TT.
Complement: 263.

History: These two ships were originally named *Circe* and *Climene*, but were later renamed *Alpino* and *Carabiniere* respectively, which were "destroyer" names in Italian Navy traditions. There were originally intended to be four ships in a follow-on version of the Centauro-class of four ships, which were completed between 1957 and 1959, but many changes were made and the two ships eventually completed were very different ships. The hull was very similar, but the intended steam plant was replaced by a new CODAG installation and this enabled the number of funnels to be reduced from two to one. Then, as in the Bergamini-class (see previous entry) the 40mm was rejected and six 76mm mounted, two forward in "A" and "B"

Lupo/Artigliere

ITALY

Frigate
Specifications for Lupo-class, as built.
Completed: 1977-87.
Number in class: 8.
Displacement: 2,208 tons standard; 2,500 tons full load.
Dimensions: Length 370.2ft (112.8m); beam 39.3ft (12.0m); draught 12.0ft (3.7m).
Propulsion: 2 shafts; CODOG; 2 General Electric/Fiat gas-turbines, 50,000shp; 2 GMT diesels, 8,490bhp; 35kt; 4,350nm at 16kt (on diesels).
Aircraft: 1 helicopter.
Armament: 8 x Otomat SSM (8 x 1); 1 x 127mm gun; 1 x Sea Sparrow SAM launcher; 4 x 40mm guns; 6 x 324mm ASW TT.
Complement: 263.

History: Originally conceived as a follow-on to the Alpino-class and taking the place of the two cancelled units, these emerged as rather different. The two forward 76mm guns and the single Menon ASW mortar on the foredecks of the Lupo-class were replaced by a single 127mm dual-purpose lightweight gun, while the helicopter and the 324mm ASW torpedoes removed the requirement for the Menon ASW mortar removed. The Lupos were also the first ship in the Italian Navy to mount the Otomat SSM, with four launchers mounted either side of the foremast. Another change from the Alpino-class was that the propulsion system was CODOG as opposed to CODAG.

The Lupo-class was the first post-war Italian design to achieve significant overseas sales, with six being sold to Venezuela, four to Peru and four to Iraq. The orders from the first two countries posed no problems but the latter order

positions, two amidships either side of the funnel, and two either side of the hangar. They were the first Italian ASW ships to mount a Variable-Depth Sonar (VDS). *Carabiniere* became a trials ship in 1993 and both ships were stricken and scrapped in the late 1990s.

Below: _Alpino_ and _Carabiniere_ were the first Italian ships with a variable-depth sonar

Above: Lupo-class, _Orsa_; note the AB-212 ASW helicopter on the flightdeck aft

eventually fell through, although the ships had actually been completed. They lay unused for some years, the Italian Navy having little interest in them as they were fitted with a great deal of non-Italian equipment, but they were eventually purchased by the Italian government and allocated to the navy. Designated the Artigliere-class, the navy has removed as much as possible of the non-standard equipment and employs them as gunboats (*pattugliatori*), roughly, the equivalent of US Coastguard cutters, principally in patrolling the Adriatic. All eight Lupo-class and four Artigliere-class were in service in 2001.

Maestrale

ITALY

Frigate
Completed: 1982-85.
Number in class: 8.
Displacement: 2,500 tons standard; 3,200 tons full load.
Dimensions: Length 405.0ft (122.7 m); beam 42.5ft (12.9m); draught 15.1ft (4.6m).
Propulsion: 2 shafts; CODOG; 2 Fiat/GE LM 2500 gas-turbines, 50,000shp; 2 GMT diesels, 10,146bhp(m); 33kt; 3,800nm at 22kt.
Aircraft: 2 helicopters.
Armament: 4 x Teseo SSM launcher; 1 x Albatros SAM launcher; 1 x 127mm DP gun; 4 x 40mm Dardo AA; 2 x 533mm TT; 6 x 324mm ASW TT.
Complement: 232.

History: This is an enlarged and improved version of the Lupo-class. Eight were built: *Maestrale*, completed in 1982; followed by *Grecale, Libeccio, Scirocco,* and *Aliseo*, all completed in 1983; then *Euro*, completed in 1984; and finally *Espero* and *Zeffiro* completed in 1985.

There is a large hangar and flightdeck for two AB-212 ASW helicopters, which are supplemented by six 324mm ASW torpedo tubes, mounted amidships in two groups of three on either beam. Anti-surface weaponry comprises four Teseo launchers on the hangar roof and a single 127mm gun mounted in "A" position. The main surface-to-air system is the Albatros launcher, mounted in "B" position with twenty-four Aspide missiles, supplemented by four OTOBreda 40mm Dardo gun systems.

Matsu

JAPAN

Destroyer escort
Completed: 1944.
Number in class: 18.
Displacement: 1,262 tons standard; 1,506 tons full load.
Dimensions: Length 328.0ft (100.0m); beam 30.7ft (9.4m); draught 10.8ft (3.3m).
Propulsion: 2 shafts; geared-turbines; 2 boilers; 19,000shp; 28kt.
Armament: 3 x 5in (127mm) (1 x 2; 1 x 1); 24 x 25mm AA; 4 x 24in TT; 36 DCs.
Complement: *c.* 150.

History: These World War II ships were the first destroyer-escorts (DE) built for the Imperial Japanese Navy (IJN). A total of eighteen was built, construction taking some eight-nine months, with all completed between February and November 1944. They were built in answer to the IJN's urgent need for convoy escorts, a category that had been ignored in pre-war planning, and were both fast and heavily armed. Main armament was three 5in (127mm) guns, one single with a shield forward and a twin mounting without a shield aft. Anti-aircraft weaponry comprised no less than twenty-four 25mm cannon as

***Above:* *Espero*, note 5in (127mm) and octuple Albatros SAM launcher on foredeck**

They are not due to receive a mid-life modernisation and are scheduled to remain in service until 2010-2015.

---

built, although most had "acquired" at least five more by the end of the war.

Seven of the class were lost during the war, all to US forces: submarine - *Momo* (15 December 1944); mine - *Sakura* (11 July 1945); aircraft - *Ume* 31 January 1945 , *Momi* (5 January 1945); surface warships - *Matsu* (4 August 1944), *Kuwa* (3 December 1944) *Hinoki* (7 January 1945). Of the survivors, two each were allocated to China, USSR, UK and USA, and most were scrapped in the late 1940s. Those not allocated to specific Allies were scrapped in Japan shortly after the war.

Below:* Like other wartime navies, the IJN needed escorts; this is Matsu-class *Momo

Chikugo

JAPAN

Destroyer escort
Completed: 1970-77.
Number in class: 11.
Displacement: 1,470 tons standard; 1,700 tons full load.
Dimensions: Length 305.0ft (93.0m); beam 35.5ft (10.8m); draught 11.5ft (3.5m).
Propulsion: 2 shafts; 2 Mitsubishi/Burmeister, Wain or Mitsui diesels; 16.000bhp; 25kt; 10,700nm at 12kt.
Armament: 2 x 3in (76mm) (1 x 2); 2 x 40mm; 1 x ASROC ASW; 12 x 12.75in (324mm) Mk32 ASW TT.
Complement: 165.

History: The post-war Japanese navy, known as the Japanese Maritime Self Defense Force (JMSDF), started by acquiring a large number of US Navy vessels, among them eighteen Tacoma-class "patrol frigates." These foreign ships were quickly supplemented and then replaced by Japanese-designed and -built ships, with the four Isuzu-class, completed in 1961-64 being the first DEs. These were followed by the Chikugo-class of eleven ships completed between 1970 and 1977. A neat design, their main claim to fame was as the smallest ships ever to carry the US ASROC system, with one eight-cell launcher mounted amidships. In common with many IJN and JMSDF ships they had a large superstructure for their size, and as a result had to be given a

Ishikari

JAPAN

Destroyer escort
Completed: 1981.
Number in class: 1.
Displacement: 1,200 tons standard; 1,450 tons full load.
Dimensions: Length 277.3ft (84.5m); beam 32.8ft (10.0m); draught 11.5ft (3.5m).
Propulsion: 2 shafts; CODOG; 1 Kawasaki/Rolls-Royce Olympus gas-turbine, 28,390shp; 1 Mitsubishi diesel, 5,000bhp; 25kt 10,700nm at 12kt.
Armament: 8 x Harpoon SSM (2 x 4); 1 x 76mm OTO Melara gun; 1 x 375mm ASW rocket launcher; 6 x 12.8in (324mm) ASW TT.
Complement: 90.

History: Unusual in being a "one-off", *Ishikari* was built by Mitsui at Tamano and completed in March 1981. It is somewhat smaller than the previous Chikugo-class, approximating to corvettes in other navies, and introduced a high degree of automation, which enabled a much smaller crew (ninety compared to 164) to be carried. It is powered by a CODOG system, in which either the single gas-turbine or the single diesel are able to power both propellers. Although fitted to carry eight Harpoon missiles only four are normally

larger than usual beam to ensure adequate stability. The ships were stricken as they reached 25-26 years of service, with only two remaining in service in 2001 and the last due to strike in 2002/3.

***Below:* Chikugo-class escort *Yoshino*; note the ASROC launched abaft the funnel**

carried in peacetime. It is generally considered that the JMSDF tried to achieve too much on too small a displacement in this design and this may explain why only one was built and the next class was somewhat larger

***Below:* *Ishikari*, the only vessel in its class, proved too small for the ASW mission**

Yubari

JAPAN

Destroyer escort
Completed: 1983-84.
Number in class: 2.
Displacement: 1,470 tons standard; 1,690 tons full load.
Dimensions: Length 298.5ft (91.0m); beam 35.4ft (10.8m); draught 11.5ft (3.5m).
Propulsion: 2 shafts; CODOG; one Kawasaki/Rolls/Royce Olympus gas-turbines, 28,400shp; one Mitsubishi diesel, 4,650bhp; 25kt.
Armament: 8 x Harpoon SSM launchers; 1 x 786mm OTO Melara Compact; 1 x 375mm ASW rocket launcher; 6 x 12.8in (374mm) ASW TT.
Complement: 98.

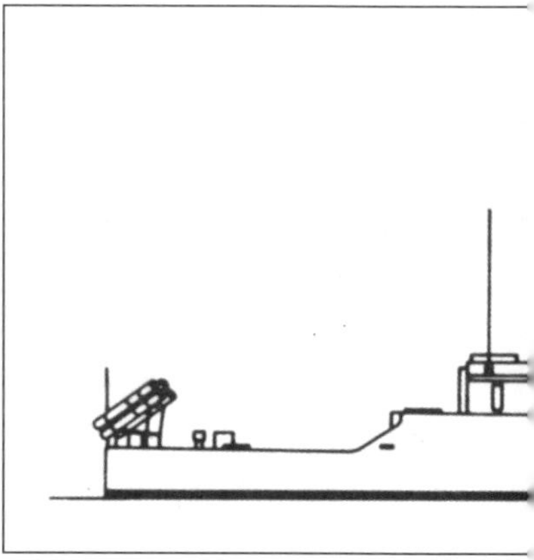

History: After the very small Ishikari-class, the JMSDF reverted to a larger design, which was, in essence, a larger hull with improved accommodation and greater fuel capacity, but identical weapons and sensor fits. Main armament is the Harpoon SSM, with two groups of four canisters mounted on the transom, with a single 76mm OTO

Abukuma

JAPAN

Destroyer escort
Completed: 1989-93.
Number in class: 6.
Displacement: 2,050 tons standard; 2,550 tons full load.
Dimensions: Length 357.6ft (109.0m); beam 44.0ft (13.4m); draught 12.5ft (3.8m).
Propulsion: 2 shafts; CODOG; 2 x Kawasaki/Rolls-Royce Spey gas-turbines, 27,000shp; 2 x Mitsubishi diesels, 10,000bhp; 27kt.
Aircraft: 1 helicopter.
Armament: 4 x Harpoon SSM; 1 x 76mm OTOBreda Compact gun; 1 x 20mm Vulcan Phalanx CIWS; 1 x ASROC ASW system; 6 x 12.8in (324mm) ASW TT.
Complement: 115.

History: The first pair of this six-ship class was approved in the 1986 estimates, ordered in March 1987, and entered service in 1989/90. These were followed by four more, the last of which was completed in 1993; a seventh ship was requested but funding was not authorised.

These ships show how growth has become an inevitable part of modern naval development and Japanese destroyer escorts have grown from the 1,450 ton displacement in the Ishikari to 2,550 tons in this class, which made them virtually the

Melara Compact on the foredeck. Two ships, *Yubari* and *Yubetsu*, were completed in 1983-84 and a third was requested but not funded. Both remain in service in 2001 and, together with Ishikari, form the 27th Escort Squadron, based at Ominato.

Below: **The two Yubaris were essentially slightly larger versions of the *Ishikari***

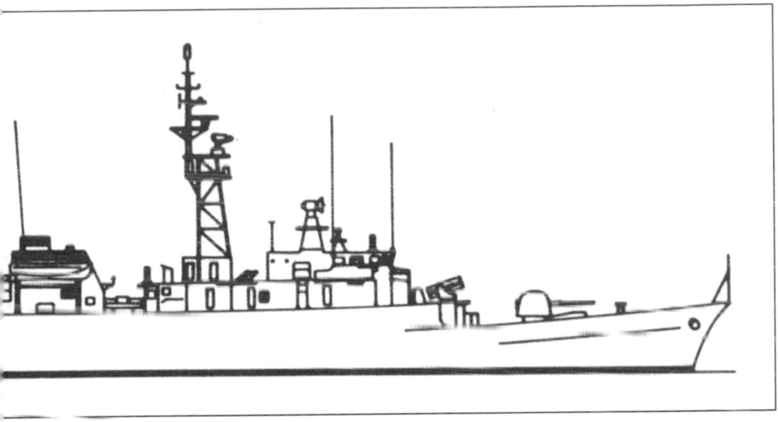

same size as the contemporary British "broad-beamed" Leander- and US Bronstein- classes. These Japanese ships appear to have incorporated some early "stealth" features such as sloping surfaces, which would otherwise have been vertical, and rounding corners, which would usually have been "squared-off." A noteworthy feature of the naming of these ships is that they all carry names last used for cruisers in the Imperial Japanese Navy in the Second World War: *Abukuma*; *Jintsu*; *Ohyodo*; *Sendai*; *Chikuma*; and *Tone*. They are very well equipped, but the only helicopter facility is a VERTREP station aft; there are no landing facilities.

Below: **The Abukuma-class is well-equipped for ASW but has no helicopter facilities**

Kortenaer/Bremen

NETHERLANDS

Frigate
Completed: 1978-83.
Number in class: 10.
Displacement: 3,000 tons standard; 3,786 tons full load.
Dimensions: Length 427.0ft (130.2m); beam 47.0ft (14.4m); draught 20.0ft (6.0m).
Propulsion: 2 shafts; COGOG; 2 Rolls-Royce Olympus gas-turbines, 51,600shp; 2 Rolls-Royce Tyne gas-turbines, 9,800shp; 30kt; 4,000nm at 20kt.
Aircraft: 2 helicopter.
Armament: 8 x Harpoon SSM launchers; 1 NATO Sea Sparrow SAM launcher; 1 x 76mm OTO Melara Compact gun; 1 x 40mm or 1 x 30mm Goalkeeper CIWS; 4 x 324mm ASW TT.
Complement: 200.

History: The Dutch had a requirement in the early 1970s for a ship which would operate in the North Atlantic in any weather and under threat from air, surface and submerged attack; be capable of 30kt, with a cruising speed of 20kt and a range of 4,000nm; be fitted with the latest weapons, sensors and an ASW helicopter; and have maximum NATO standardisation. After discussions with various NATO allies in search of a collaborative programme, the Dutch decided that they should proceed independently and placed an order for the first four Kortenaer-class ships in October 1974, followed by an order for a further four a month later, then for the final four in 1976. The Greek Navy then asked to purchase two ships and, to ensure the sale, two ships already fitting out were sold to the Greeks, and two more ships were ordered for the RNethN, but to be air defence rather than ASW ships (Jacob van Heemskerk-class). With the end of the Cold War the RNethN ran down its Kortenaer force, selling four to Greece (three in 1992, one in 1997) and two the the United Arab Emirates in 1996. All were refitted prior to delivery. Thus, in 2001 the position was: Netherlands - four

Below: **Kortenaer ASW version; the first *Pieter Florisz,* before being sold to Greece**

Left: **Close-up of the major sensors aboard *Witte de With*, a Heemskerck-class ship**

ships in reserve, all available for sale; Greece - six ships (two from original order plus four bought later); UAE - two ships.

The Federal German Navy (FGN) ordered six Kortenaer-class ships in 1977 as the Bremen-class (Klasse 122A), which were the same size as the Dutch ships but with differences in weapons and sensors. All six are due to serve on to about 2010, when they will be stricken; they are not due to be given a service-life extension refit.

***Below:* *Jacob van Heemskerck*, first of two air defence versions of the Kortenaer-class**

Karel Doorman

NETHERLANDS

Completed: 1989-94.
Number in class: 8.
Displacement: 2,800 tons standard; 3,320 tons full load.
Dimensions: Length 401.0ft (122.3m); beam 47.0ft (14.4m); draught 20.0ft (6.1m).
Propulsion: 2 shafts; CODOG; 2 Rolls-Royce SM-1A Spey gas-turbines, 37,550shp, 30kt; 2 Stork-Werkspoor 12 SWD 280 V-12 diesels, 8,450bhp, 21kt; 5,000nm at 18kt.
Armament: 8 x Harpoon SSM; 1 x Mark 48 Vertical Launch System for NATO Sea Sparrow SAM; 1 x 3.0in (76mm) gun; 1 x 30mm Goalkeeper CIWS; 2 x 20mm; 4 x 12.8in (324mm) ASW TT
Aircraft: 1 helicopter.
Complement: 154.

History: This guided-missile frigate design, originally known as the "M-class," started out as a replacement for the Roofdier-class, with a role of peacetime surveillance and fishery protection, mainly in the North Sea, but with occasional forays into the North Atlantic. However, the role changed resulting in an increase in size, mainly due to the decision to operate a helicopter, originally the Westland Lynx, but in due course the NH-90. A further problem arose when it was realised that there was going to be a three-year gap at the Royal Schelde shipyard, between the completion of the last Kortenaer-class frigate and the scheduled start of work on the first of the M-class. As a result the latter event was brought forward and the keel of the first ship was laid before a contract was signed.

Despite these early problems they have turned out to be excellent ships and well-suited to their task. They were among the first warships to included accommodation for women, and also can carry thirty marines. One unusual feature is the Mark 48 Mod 1 vertical launcher for NATO Sea Sparrow SAMs, which consists of sixteen tubes mounted along the port side of the hangar. This

***Below: Willem van der Zaan,* second of the Karel Doorman-class to be completed**

***Above: Van Galen*; note the large number of antenna and radar arrays**

is a very simple and straightforward mounting, with the rocket exhausts venting straight over the side, but it was realised that the installation was vulnerable to terrorist action and a large sheet of Kevlar now protects the launchers from close-range attack. The Dutch Labour Party has suggested that four of these ships should be sold as an economy measure.

***Below: Van Galen*; note vertical launchers for Sea Sparrow missiles on side of hangar**

Oslo

NORWAY

Frigate
Completed: 1966-67.
Number in class: 5.
Displacement: 1,450 tons standard; 1,760 tons full load.
Dimensions: Length 318.0ft (96.6m); beam 36.6ft (11.2m); draught 17.3ft (5.3m).
Propulsion: 1 shaft; double-reduction, geared turbines; 2 boilers; 20,000shp; 25kt; 4,500nm at 15kt.
Armament: 6 x Penguin SSM (2 x 3); 1 NATO Sea Sparrow SAM launcher; 4 x 3in (76mm) (2 x 2) guns; 1 x Terne III ASW rocket launcher; 6 x 324mm ASW TT.
Complement: 150.

History: These ships were built under a five-year naval construction programme approved by the Norwegian Storting (Parliament) in 1960. All were constructed in the Norwegian Naval Dockyard at Horten, with half the cost being borne by Norway, the remainder by the United States. The hull and propulsion system were based on the contemporary US Navy Dealey-class destroyer escorts, but incorporated many modifications to suit Arctic conditions and Norwegian operational requirements. All ships were modernised between 1985 and 1990, the work including improved weapons control and habitability; new countermeasures equipment; new sonar and the replacement of the after 76mm mounting by a Bofors 40mm/70. The sonar fitted during this programme used a variable-depth "fish" and towing this in the heavy seas to be found in the region resulted in the hulls becoming over-stressed and a strengthening programme was started in 1995. A new Plessey AWS-9 radar was also fitted in 1995.

Krivak I/II/III

RUSSIA (Soviet Union)

Frigate
Specifications for Krivak I, as built.
Completed: Krivak I - 1969-81; Krivak II - 1976-81; Krivak III - 1984-93.
Number in class: Krivak I - 21; Krivak II - 11; Krivak III - 9.
Displacement: 3,300 tons standard; 3,575 tons full load.
Dimensions: Length 405.3ft (123.5m); beam 46.3ft (14.1m); draught 15.1ft (4.6m).
Propulsion: 2 shafts; CODAG; 2 M-8K gas-turbines, 40,000shp; 2 M-62 gas-turbines (cruise), 14,950shp; 31kt; 4,995nm at 14kt.
Armament: 4 x SS-N-14 SSM launchers; 2 x SA-N-4 SAM launchers; 4 x 76.2mm AK-726 DP guns (2 x 2); 2 x RBU-6000 ASW rocket launchers; 8 x 21in (533mm) ASW TT; 16 mines.
Complement: 190.

History: Built as a successor to the Riga-class, the Krivak-class first appeared in 1970 and was built in three major versions. Twenty-one Krivak Is, built from 1969-1981 were the standard Soviet Navy ASW ship of their time, and were followed by eleven Krivak IIs, built from 1976 to 1981, which were developed versions with modified weapons and sensors. The Soviet Navy initially designated these ships *bol'shoy protivolodochny korabl* (large anti-submarine ship), but this was changed in 1977 to *storozhevoy korabl* (escort ship) but it was later changed back to *bol'shoy protivolodochny korabl* again. The third version, Krivak III, nine built between 1984-93, was a special design with a helicopter hangar and flightdeck for the KGB Maritime Border Guards. Two Krivak Is were given a major modernisation between 1987 and 1994, but shortage of funds prevented the others from being similarly modernised.

Above: **Norwegian frigate, *Bergen*; design was based on the Dealey (see page 472)**

Above: **The only serious shortcoming in Krivak I/II was the lack of an ASW helicopter**

In the 1990s the Krivaks Is and IIs started to be stricken and by 2001 there were six Krivak Is, two Krivak I (modernised), four Krivak IIs and seven Krivak IIIs left in Russian service, with a further two Krivak Is, one Krivak II and one Krivak III with the Ukrainian Navy. However, as with all Russian and Ukrainian ships the state of maintenance and manning of all these is very poor, and many less than the numbers given are actually seaworthy. ▶

Koni (Project 1159)

RUSSIA (Soviet Union)

Frigate
Specification for Koni I, as built.
Completed: 1978-84.
Number in class: 13.
Displacement: 1,440 tons standard; 1,660 tons full load.
Dimensions: Length 311.7ft (95.0m); beam 42.0ft (12.8m); draught 13.8ft (4.2m).
Propulsion: 3 shafts; CODAG; 1 gas-turbine, 15,000shp; 2 diesels, 15,000bhp; 27kt; 1,800nm at 14kt.
Armament: 1 x SA-N-4 SAM launcher; 4 x 76mm (2 x 2) guns; 4 x 30mm; 2 x RBU-6000 ASW rocket launcher; 2 DC racks; 20 mines.
Complement: 110.

History: A design developed specifically for export. Of the thirteen built, only one was operated by the Soviet Navy in the Black Sea, and that was employed solely to demonstrate the ship to potential foreign customers and to train crews in its operation. Of the remainder, three went to Algeria, two to Cuba, three to East Germany, two to Libya and two to Yugoslavia, and finally the Soviet demonstrator was sold to Bulgaria. There were three versions, which had minor differences. Both the Libyan and Yugoslav ships are armed with four SS-N-2C, surface-to-surface missiles, while

***Left:* The *Krivak* was one of the best designs in the Soviet Navy (on previous page)**

the Libyan ship also has 400mm torpedo tubes, the only known export customer for this weapon

In 2001 the status was: Algeria - all three in service; Bulgaria - sole ship still in service; Cuba - one in service, two have been sunk to create breakwaters for skin-divers; Libya - two in service, one in reserve; Yugoslavia (Serbia/Montenegro) - one in service, one being cannibalised for spares.

***Below:* The Koni-class light frigates were built solely for export to foreign navies**

Al Madinah

SAUDI ARABIA

Frigate
Completed: 1985-86.
Number in class: 4.
Displacement: 2,000 tons standard; 2,870 tons full load.
Dimensions: Length 377.3ft (115.0 m); beam 41.0ft (12.5 m); draught 16.1ft (4.9m) (sonar).
Propulsion: 2 shafts; 4 SEMT-Pielstick diesels; 32,500bhp; 30 kt; 8,000nm at 15kt.
Armament: 8 x Otomat SSM launchers (4 x 2); 1 x Crotale SAM launcher; 1 x 100mm Compact DP; 4 x 40mm OTOBreda AA; 4 x 21in (533mm) TT.
Aircraft: 1 helicopter.
Complement: 179.

History: The four Al Madinah-class ships (also known as "F2000") were ordered from France in 1980, with the first completed by DCN International in 1985, followed by the other three in 1985 to 1986. The primary mission of these ships is anti-surface warfare, albeit with good anti-air and ASW capabilities. They are built with a continuous ("flush") deck with the upper deck, which extends to the after end of the flight deck, as the strength deck, giving a deep hull girder, with a high resistance to longitudinal stress. The ships operate exclusively in a hot, dry, sandy environment and are, therefore, fitted with three very powerful air-conditioning plants, together with a wash-down system which cleans the superstructure of fine-grained sand. The CODAD propulsion system consists of four reversible SEMT Pielstick diesels, two on each shaft, which results in a simple and economical system.

Descubierta

SPAIN

Frigate
Completed: 1976-82.
Number in class: 9.
Displacement: 1,233 tons standard; 1,666 tons full load.
Dimensions: Length 291.3ft (88.8m); beam 34.0ft (10.4m); draught 12.5ft (3.8m).
Propulsion: 2 shafts; 4 MTU-Bazan diesels; 15000 hp(m);
sustained; 25kt; 4,000nm at 18 kt.
Armament: 4 x Harpoon SSM (2 x 2); 1 x Mk29 Sea Sparrow SAM launcher; 1 x 76mm gun; 2 x 40mm Bofors; 1 x 375mm Bofors ASW rocket launcher; 6 x 324mm ASW TT.
Complement: 118 (plus 30 marines).

History: This design has its origins in the Portuguese *Joao Coutinho*, which was developed by Blohm+Voss and then considerably modified by the Spanish shipyard Bazan, which included the unusual Y-shaped funnel. The first four were ordered from Bazan, Cartagena, on 7 December 1973 followed by four more from Bazan, Ferrol on 25 May 1976.

Whilst under construction F 37 and F 38 were sold to Egypt prior to completion as *Abuqir* and *El Suez*, respectively, but were not replaced by a further two for Spain. A further unit was built for Morocco (*Lieutenant-Colonel Errhamani*) in 1983. The Spanish units (and dates of completion) were: *Descubierta* (1978); *Diana* (1979); *Infanta Elena* (1980); *Infanta Cristina* (1980); *Cazadora* (1981); and *Vencedora* (1982).

It was planned at one stage that the 40mm gun aft of the mainmast would be replaced by the Spanish Meroka CIWS, together with its associated fire

***Right:* The Al Madinah-class was designed and built in France for the Saudi Navy**

Al Madina suffered a major engine-room fire in August 1991, but repairs were completed in December 1993 and the ship was operational again in May 1994. DCN International carried out a major major refit/modernisation project between 1995 and 1999. Known as "Project Mouette" the programme included all four frigates, plus two replenishment ships supplied by France to Saudi Arabia in the early 1980s. The major changes to the frigates involved upgrading the TAVITAC command system, the Otomat missiles and the sonar system, and replacing the existing helicopter-handling system with the DCN Samahe. All other systems, including the engines, were refurbished.

---

control radars but this update was shelved. In addition to the crew there is accommodation for up to thirty troops, while the crew accommodation has been modified to accept female personnel. All six Spanish ships are based at Cartagena, where they form 21st Escort Squadron.

***Below:* Descubiertas are in service with the Egyptian, Moroccan and Spanish navies**

Nareusan (Type 25T)

THAILAND

Frigate
Completed: 2.
Number in class: 2.
Displacement: 2,500 tons standard; 2,980 tons full load.
Dimensions: Length 393.7ft (120m); beam 42.7ft (13m); draught 12.5ft (3.8m).
Propulsion: 2 shafts; CODOG; two General Electric LM-2500 gas-turbines, 55,000hp; two MTU diesels, 14,730 hp(m); 32kt; 4,000nm at 18kt.
Aircraft: 1 helicopter.
Armament: 8 x Harpoon SSM launchers; 1 x 127mm US Mk 32 Mod 5 DP gun; 4 x 37mm Type 76A AA 6 x 324mm Mk 32 ASW TT.
Complement: 150.

History: The Royal Thai Navy (RTN) had some unsatisfactory experiences with the Chao Praya-class (Chinese Jianghu III [Type 053]) frigates, but in spite of this they later signed another contract for two larger Chinese frigates to a new design. The contract, signed in September 1989, was for the China State Shipbuilding Corporation (CSSC) to deliver the basic ships in 1994, following which US and European weapon systems would be fitted in Thai shipyards. By early 1993 the programme had slipped by 12 months and the first ship eventually sailed for Bangkok in January 1995.

The basic ship design was prepared jointly by the RTN and the CSSC and incorporates a considerable amount of Western machinery and equipment, providing enhanced capabilities in comparison with the earlier Jianghu III (Type 053) ships. For example, power is provided by US gas-turbines and German

Hunt

UNITED KINGDOM

Escort destroyer
Specifications for Type II, as built.
Completed: 1939-45.
Number in class: Type 1 - 23; Type 2 - 33; Type 3 -28; Type 4 - 2.
Displacement: 1,050 tons standard; 1,580 tons full load.
Dimensions: Length 280.0ft (85.3m); beam 31.5ft (9.6m); draught 12.4ft (3.8m).
Propulsion: 2 shafts; Parsons geared turbines; 2 boilers; 19,000shp; 27kt; 2,100nm at 20kt.
Armament: 6 x 4in (102mm) QF guns (3 x 2); 4 x 2pdr pompom;.
Complement: 168.

History: In World War II there was a constant need for both fleet and escort destroyers and insufficient of either. One attempt to fill this gap was the British World War II Hunt-class escort destroyers, which ran through four series. The original Type I design was based on the pre-war sloop, *Bittern*, but with 8ft (2.4m) less beam and much greater power, while the main armament was the same (six 4in (102mm) guns) but with an additional quad 2pdr AA mount. Unfortunately, on first-of-class trials it turned out that the design was dangerously unstable (the result of a major error in the calculations) and the "Y" position twin 4in (102mm) had to be removed and the quad 2pdr moved to its place. Twenty-three of the Type Is were completed in 1939-40 until the Type II, with 2.5ft (0.8m) greater beam, resolved the problems and the original weapon fit was restored.

There were, however, further difficulties, since the Hunts had a short range and could not be used on ocean escort work, while if, as often happened, they

diesels, while the radars are a mix of US, Dutch and Chinese types. The main gun is a US type, but anti-aircraft guns are Italian OTOBreda 40 mm, controlled by a Chinese-manufactured RTN-20 Dardo tracker.

***Below:* The Nareusan-class was built in China to a joint Chinese/Thai design**

***Above:* The Hunt-class were the British equivalents of the US Navy's destroyer-escorts**

were used with fleet destroyers, their lack of torpedoes was a major drawback. This was overcome in the Type III by replacing one twin 4in (102mm) with a twin 21in (533mm) torpedo tube installation. The two Type IVs were completely different with a long forecastle deck, which became the pattern for frigates in the 1950s and '60s. As usually happens in war, there were wide variations in armament both between and within the four "types," one of the more unusual being a 2pdr mounted in the eyes of the ship as a "bow chaser" (a term redolent of Nelson and the Napoleonic wars) in ships engaged in chasing German E-boats in the Channel. There were a large number of war losses and after the war most survivors were passed on to Allied navies and the few remaining scrapped.

Bridgwater/Hastings

UNITED KINGDOM

Sloop
Specifications for *Hastings*, as built.
Completed: Bridgwater - 1929; Hastings - 1931.
Number in class: Bridgwater - 2; Hastings - 4.
Displacement: 1,045 tons standard; 1,640 tons full load.
Dimensions: Length 266.3ft (81.2m); beam 34.1ft (10.4m); draught 12.5ft (3.8m).
Propulsion: 2 shafts; Parsons geared turbines, 2 boilers; 2,000shp; 16.5kt
Armament: 2 x 3in (102mm) (2 x 1); 2 x 3pdr.
Complement: 100.

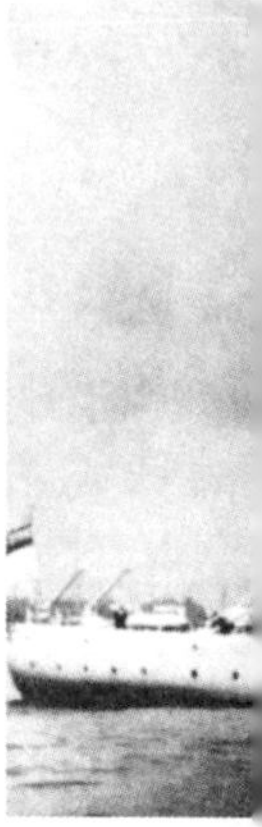

History: These ships, sometimes known as "colonial sloops" were intended for duties in the oceans around the countries of the British Empire in peace and as ASW escorts in war. The first two, *Bridgwater* and *Sandwich*, were the first such sloops built since World War I and were followed by a further four, *Folkestone, Hastings, Penzance* and *Scarborough*, which were virtually identical except that one of the 4in (102mm) guns was in an HA (high-angle) mounting. During the war depth-charge racks were added and up to eight 20mm Oerlikon were mounted, while the 3pdr saluting gun was removed. There was one war loss, *Penzance* (24 August 1940) and the remainder survived the war to be stricken in 1946-47. Eight

Black Swan/Modified Black Swan

UNITED KINGDOM

Sloop
Specifications for *Black Swan*, as built.
Completed: Black Swan - 1939-41; Modified Black Swan - 1943-45.
Number in class: Black Swan - 4; Modified Black Swan - 29.
Displacement: 1,300 tons standard; 1,945 tons full load.
Dimensions: Length 299.5ft (91.3m); beam 37.5ft (11.4m); draught 10.9ft (3.3m).
Propulsion: 2 shafts; Parsons geared turbines; 2 boilers; 4,300shp; 19.8kt; nm at kt.
Armament: 6 x 4.5in (114mm) (3 x 2); 4 x 2pdr pompom; DC racks.
Complement: 180.

History: Following from the Shoreham-class (see previous entry) the RN produced a series of small classes (Grimsby (12 built), Bittern (3) and Egret (3), each an improvement on its predecessor, culminating in the very successful Black Swan/Modified Black Swan-classes, which were built throughout the war, the last being launched in February 1946. The difference between the two was, in fact, relatively minor, the most noticeable being a 1ft (0.3m) increase in the beam. The armament varied throughout the war, with some receiving additional 2pdr pom-poms, some 40mm Bofors and others 20mm Oerlikons. All carried 110 depth charges, but an additional 50 could be carried in place of one of the 40mm Bofors. The Hedgehog ASW mortar appeared during the war and at least four of these ships were fitted.

All these sloops fought a very hard war, especially in the Atlantic, where they were particularly successful when employed in the "escort groups," which

further ships of the Shoreham- and Repeat Shoreham-classes were completed in 1931-33 had a 15ft (4.6m) longer hull, but were otherwise very similar to the Hastings-class.

***Below:* British pre-war sloops were intended for colonial duties in peace, ASW in war**

***Above:* The Black Swan-class were one of the outstanding ASW platforms of the war**

were groups of ASW ships whose sole employment was in hunting and destroying U-boats. There was one war loss among the original Black Swans, *Ibis*, which was hit by an aircraft-launched torpedo (10 November 1942), while the Modified Black Swans suffered five war losses (*Chanticleer, Kite, Lapwing, Lark* and *Woodpecker*), all to U-boats. The survivors were retained well into the 1950s, with most being sold for scrap between 1958 and 1965, although three were supplied to the fledgling Federal German Navy in 1958-59.

Flower/ Modified Flower

UNITED KINGDOM

Corvette
Completed: 1940-44.
Number in class: 288.
Displacement: 1,170 tons standard; 1,245 tons full load.
Dimensions: Length 205.0ft (62.5m); beam 33.2ft (10.1m); draught 13.6ft (4.1m).
Propulsion: 1 shaft; Vertical, Triple Expansion; 2 boilers; 2,750ihp; 16.5kt.
Armament: 1 x 4in (102mm); depth charges (40).
Complement: 48.

History: These small warships, with minimal armament, and, although excellent seaboats, desperately cramped and uncomfortable for their crews (almost entirely reservists), played a crucial role in the Allied victory in the Battle of the Atlantic. The Admiralty requirement, stated in January 1939, was for an escort which could be constructed in large numbers, at reasonable cost, and in yards not normally involved in warship work, which would combine seaworthiness, manoeuverability, endurance, survivability and a good weapons and sensor fit. The actual design originated at the Smith's Dock Co in early 1939, who took the design of their latest Antarctic whaler, *Southern Pride*, lengthened it by 30ft (9m) and added weapons, depth charges and the latest Asdic (sonar). The emphasis was on simplicity and ease of production, and the

Castle

UNITED KINGDOM

Corvette
Completed: 1943-45.
Number in class: 46.
Displacement: 1,060 tons standard; 1,590 tons full load.
Dimensions: Length 252.0ft (76.8m); beam 36.7ft (11.2m); draught 13.5ft (4.1m).
Propulsion: 1 shaft; Vertical, Triple-Expansion engines; 2 boilers; 2,750ihp; 16.5kt.
Armament: 1 x 4in (102mm); 1 x Squid; depth charges (15).
Complement: 120.

History: Once the Flower-class corvettes were in service it was clear that they were too small and uncomfortable for their crews, one of the problems being that their length did not fit in with the normal distance between waves in the North Atlantic. Smith's Dock therefore suggested that the length should be increased significantly, from 205ft (62.5m) to 252ft (76.8m) and this resulted not only in greater comfort but also in greater space for weapons, enabling the Squid to be mounted.

Well over one hundred were originally planned, but only forty-six were completed in Canadian and UK yards, the remainder being cancelled. Three were lost, two to U-boats and one to a mine. The Canadian survivors were sold between 1947 and 1949 and the British ships were scrapped in the 1950s.

Above: **Based on a whaler design, Flower-class corvettes established a splendid record**

first keels were laid down in late 1939. The design, weapons and sensors were constantly modified as the war progressed, which included extending the forecastle, altering the forward hull profile, fitting radar, deepening the bilge keels to reduce rolling, improving the bridges, and enhancing the living conditions for the crew. The number of depth charges was also increased, first to forty and then to seventy-two, and Hedgehog was also fitted from 1942 onwards, although it never replaced the depth charges. All this resulted in a doubling of the crew, which by 1943 amounted to some 108 men, which only served to increase the overcrowding and discomfort. Thirty-six Flower-class corvettes were lost in action, half of them to enemy submarines, but they were involved in the destruction of over fifty U-boats.

Below: **Castles were a little larger but better laid out and equipped than the Flowers**

River

UNITED KINGDOM

Frigate
Completed: 1943-46.
Number in class: Australian-built 12; Canadian/UK-built - 127.
Displacement: 1,310 tons standard; 1,920 tons full load.
Dimensions: Length 301.3ft (91.8m); beam 36.7ft (11.2m); draught 11.8ft (3.6m).
Propulsion: 2 shafts; Vertical, Triple-Expansion; 2 boilers; 5,500ihp 21kt.
Armament: 2 x 4in (102mm) (2 x 1); Hedgehog ASW spigot mortar; depth-charges (126, later 150).
Complement: 140.

History: The River-class was one of the successors to the ubiquitous Flower-class corvettes, which although effective proved to be too small and very uncomfortable for Atlantic conditions. The River-class was some 93ft (28m) longer and proved to be an altogether more effective deepwater escort. A total of 139 of these ships were built between 1943 and 1945 in yards in Australia, Canada and the UK, and served in the RAN, RCN and RN, with a few also serving in the US Navy. As an added complication, some were built in Canada for supply to the US Navy, but were then re-allocated to the RN under Lend-Lease!

All were built to the same basic design, but there were minor differences in armament, both as built and then in service. They were constructed to First Class merchant ship practice, but with scantlings based on those of light warships. The great majority was powered by Vertical, Triple-Expansion Engines (VTE) of the same type as installed in Flower-class corvettes, but with two sets,

Loch/Bay

UNITED KINGDOM

Frigate
Specifications for Loch-class, as built.
Completed: 1944-46.
Number in class: Loch - 30; Bay - 26.
Displacement: 1,435 tons standard; 2,260 tons full load.
Dimensions: Length 307.0ft (93.6m); beam 38.6ft (11.8m); draught 12.4ft (3.8m).
Propulsion: 2 shafts; Vertical, Triple-Expansion engines; 2 boilers; 5,500ihp; 19.5kt.
Armament: 1 x 4in (102mm); 4 x 2pdr pompom; 10 x 20mm Oerlikon; 2 x Squid; depth charges (15)
Complement: 114.

History: The Loch-class was an improved and slightly longer version of the River-class, with a much improved ASW armament. As with the Rivers, the great majority had reciprocating machinery, but two were completed with turbines. It was originally planned to build 110, but 26 were converted to Bay-class and 54 were cancelled when it was clear that the Battle of the Atlantic had been won. Of the thirty completed three were supplied to the South African Navy in 1944 and two were completed as depot ships. None were lost in the war; six were transferred to New Zealand in 1948-49 and one to Malaysia in 1964; the remainder were scrapped in the 1960s.

The Bay-class were all laid down as Loch-class but were converted while under construction to have a different weapons fit, with greater emphasis on anti-air capability. Thus they had two twin 4in (102mm) guns in high-angle mounts, plus two twin 40mm Bofors and two (four in some) single Bofors. This was achieved at the expense of a reduced ASW capability, with Hedgehog in

one on each shaft, but five of the original production batch were given two Parsons geared turbines, instead. All were armed with two single 4in (102mm) guns, and all were fitted with hedgehog ASW mortars and carried 126 (later 1250) depth charges. Five were lost to enemy action, all to U-boats.

***Below:* A Canadian River-class frigate; 130 were built in Australia, Canada and the UK**

place of Squid. The class was twenty-five strong, but two of these were completed as despatch vessels and four as survey vessels. None were lost in the war, four were supplied to Portugal in 1959-61 and one to Finland in 1962; the remainder were scrapped between 1957 and 1962.

***Below:* Loch-class frigate *Loch Fyne*, a slightly larger and improved River-class design**

Rapid (Type 15)

UNITED KINGDOM

Fast frigate
Converted: 1952-57.
Number in class: 23.
Displacement: 2,240 tons standard; 2,850 tons full load.
Dimensions: Length 358.3ft (109.2m); beam 35.7ft (10.9m); draught 13.8ft (4.2m).
Propulsion: 2 shafts; Parsons geared turbines; 2 boilers; 40,000shp; 36.8kt; 4,750nm at 15kt.
Armament: 2 x 4in (102mm) (1 x 2); 2 x 40mm AA; 2 x 21in (533mm) TT; 2 x Squid.
Complement: 195.

History: In the late 1940s there was a growing threat from the rapidly-expanding Soviet Navy, particularly against the lines-of-communication between North America and Western Europe across the Atlantic. A significant element of this threat was posed by the Whiskey-class submarines, whose submerged speed rendered the existing ASW ships, such as the River-class, too slow. The need for much faster ASW ships was met in the first instance by converting twenty-three existing war-built destroyers, whose value in their original role was now minimal. The outcome, known as the Type 15 or "Full Conversion" was a great success, with the two prototypes, *Rocket* and *Relentless* being converted in 1952-53, followed by the others over the next five years. The forecastle deck was extended almost to the stern, creating much greater internal space and a new operations room complex was inserted below the bridge. The bridge was completely redesigned and, unlike all previous RN destroyers and frigates, was totally enclosed, providing shelter from the weather for the watchkeepers,

Tenacious (Type 16)

UNITED KINGDOM

Fast frigates
Converted: 1952-53.
Number in class: 10.
Displacement: 1,793 tons standard; 2,593 tons full load.
Dimensions: Length 358.3ft (109m); beam 35.8ft 11(m); draught 20.5ft (6.25m).
Propulsion: 2 shafts; 2 Parson geared turbines; 2 boilers; 40,000shp; 32kt; 5,225nm at 15kt.
Armament: 2 x 4in (102mm) (2 x 1); 5 x 40mm Bofors; 4 x 21in (533mm) TT; 2 x Squid Mk3.
Complement: 180.

History: Although the Type 15 "Full Conversion" proved such a success it was also an expensive and time-consuming undertaking and so pressing was the need that it was decided to produce a "Limited Conversion" as well, which was allocated the number, Type 16. This involved ten destroyers of the wartime O-, P-, and T-classes and the work was completed in a relatively short space of time. Unfortunately, the result was not very satisfactory since the ships were not given the ideal ASW outfit, while the anti-surface and anti-air capabilities were not very good, either. The alterations to the hull and superstructure were minimal, and, unlike the "Full Conversions" the outward appearance of the

***Above:* Londonderry, one of the very effective Rothesay-class frigates**

coxswain and lookouts, resulting in much increased efficiency. The ASW outfit was very sophisticated and included the latest search and attack sonars and two Squid mortars, which were replaced by the ASW mortar Mk10 in later ships. These conversions served until the late 1960s, covering the gap until the new generation of purpose-built ASW frigates became operational, and proved most successful. *Wrangler*, was transferred to the South African Navy (as *Vrystaat*), but all other served only in the RN and most were scrapped between 1965 and 1972, although *Ulster* and *Grenville* survived until 1980 and 1983, respectively.

ships changed little. The work was completed in 1952-53 and the ships remained in service until the mid-1960s, when they were all broken up.

***Below:* The Blackwoods were armed and equipped for ASW, and nothing else**

Whitby/Rothesay (Type 12)

UNITED KINGDOM

Frigate
Specifications for Whitby class, as built.
Completed: Whitby - 1956-58; Rothesay - 1960-61.
Number in class: Whitby - 6; Rothesay - 9.
Displacement: 2,150 tons standard; 2,560 tons full load.
Dimensions: Length 370.0ft (112.7m); beam 41.0t (12.5m); draught 17.0ft (3.9m).
Propulsion: 2 shafts; geared steam turbines; 2 boilers; 30,000shp; 29kt; 4,500nm at 12kt.
Armament: 2 x 4.5in (mm)(1 x 2); 2 x 40mm STAAG Mk2 AA;12 x 21in (533mm) TT; 2 x Limbo Mk10.
Complement: 152.

History: The Type 12 was the first of the new-build, post-war frigates for the Royal Navy and the hull, which was designed specifically for ASW operations in the North Atlantic, proved to be one of the RN's great successes and provided the basis for all its subsequent Cold War frigate designs. The forward part of the hull had a sharp "V"-form, which was designed to enable the ship to be driven hard into a head sea without the "slamming" which would have been experienced with traditional destroyer designs, while above the waterline was a high forecastle which kept green water off the gun and enclosed bridge and also served to minimise (although it could never eliminate) spray. This forward "V" merged into a square midships section, which was optimised for the high

Blackwood (Type 14)

UNITED KINGDOM

Frigate
Completed: 1956-57.
Number in class: 12.
Displacement: 1,180 tons standard; 1,535 tons full load.
Dimensions: Length 310.0ft (94.5m); beam 35.0ft (10.7m); draught 15.5ft (4.7m).
Propulsion: 1 shafts; 1 Parsons turbine; 2 boilers; 15,000shp; 27kt; 4,500nm at 12kt.
Armament: 3 x 40mm Bofors (3 x 1); 2 x Limbo Mk10; 4 x 2in (533mm) TT.
Complement: 140.

History: The high unit cost of the Type 12s (UK£3.5million) led the RN to design a more economical alternative, which emerged as the Type 14 Blackwood-class. These twelve ships had the same ASW capability as the Type 12, but at virtually half the price, the economies being achieved by reducing the propulsive power (one turbine and one propeller compared to two of each in the Type 12) and with all other capabilities ruthlessly curtailed. Such "single mission" ships were good at ASW, but at very little else, since their only anti-surface or anti-air armament was three 40mm Bofors, and this apparent inflexibility made them unpopular in the RN, although the fact was that had war come the Type 14s would have been very good at their job of convoy escorts.

One of the class, *Exmouth*, took part in a very significant trial, when it was fitted with an entirely novel propulsion system consisting of a single Rolls-Royce Olympus gas-turbine (23,200shp), with two Rolls-Royce Proteus gas-

***Above:* *Wrangler*, one of many destroyers converted to ASW frigate in the 1950s**

sustained speed required when attacking a submarine, whilst also providing maximum internal volume.

The Rothesay class was a repeat Type 12, outwardly indistinguishable, except for the removal of the twelve torpedo tubes, but with internal rearrangements. Later they were modernised to include a flightdeck for a light helicopter. None were sold abroad, but the design was used as the basis for the Australian-built Yarra-class (qv). All were scrapped or sunk as targets in 1985-89, except for *Plymouth*, which is preserved as a memorial.

turbines (8,500shp) for cruising, all geared to the single shaft. The outcome was a great success and most subsequent RN warships have had gas-turbine propulsion. The ships were later relegated to fishery protection and other second-line duties. The first three were stricken in 1971, the last in 1985.

***Below:* Full conversions proved costly, so ten were given a cheaper partial conversion**

Leopard (Type 41)

UNITED KINGDOM

AA frigate
Completed: 1957-59.
Number in class: 4.
Displacement: 2,300 tons standard; 2,520 tons full load.
Dimensions: Length 340.0ft (103.6m); beam 40.0ft (12.2m); draught 11.8ft (3.6m).
Propulsion: 2 shafts; 8 diesels; 14,400shp; 25kt; 7,500nm at 16kt.
Armament: 4 x 4.5in (114mm) (2 x 2); 2 x 40mm Bofors AA; 1 x Squid.
Complement: 205.

History: Admiralty plans in the 1950s were for escort task groups made up of a max of Type 12 Whitby-class ASW frigates, Type 61 air defence ships (see following entry) and Type 41 anti-aircraft frigates. These Type 41s had a Type 960 long-range air warning radar and a Mk 6M fire-control system which controlled two twin 4.5in (114mm) automatic mountings for area air defence. The air defences were supported by a STAAG twin 40mm system for close-in defence, but this latter proved ineffective and was replaced by a single, manually-controlled 40mm. One of the problems encountered with these ships was that the diesel exhausts were brought up into the lattic masts, one effect of which was to cause corrosion on the radar antennas and other equipment on the masthead. This was virtually the same problem as that experienced with the dreadnought battleships where exhaust fumes caused such problems with the fired direction tops and shows, once again, that those who forget the lessons of the past are fated to repeat them.

The four ships, *Leopard, Lynx, Puma* and *Panther,* were completed

Salisbury (Type 61)

UNITED KINGDOM

Air defence frigate
Completed: 1957-60.
Number in class: 4.
Displacement: 2,170 tons standard; 2,350 tons full load.
Dimensions: Length 340.0ft (103.6m); beam 40.0ft (12.2m); draught 11.8ft (3.6m).
Propulsion: 2 shafts; 8 diesels; 14,400shp; 25kt; 7,500nm at 16kt.
Armament: 2 x 4.5in (114mm) (2 x 2); 2 x 40mm Bofors AA; 1 x Squid.
Complement: 207.

History: The Type 61 air-direction frigates shared a common hull and propulsion system with the Type 41 (Leopard-class) and although eight were originally planned, only four were completed. The primary mission of these ships was to steam just outside the limit of the aircraft carrier's radar coverage, to acquire incoming targets while they were still "over-the-horizon" from the fleet, and then to call on and control either two simultaneous aircraft interceptions by day or one by night. Thus their principal "weapons systems" were their radars rather than their guns or missiles and among the sets they carried as built were Type 960 long-range, Type 982 narrow-beam air search, Type 277Q height-finder, and Type 293Q short-range air-search. Later they were converted to carry the Type 965 air-search radar which included a huge "bedstead" antenna array mounted on a plated mainmast.

One was sold to the newly-formed Bangladesh Navy, *Llandaff* in 1976 (*Umar Farooq*); at one stage it was proposed that *Lincoln* would also be sold to Bangladesh in 1982, but this never took place. In 2001 *Umar Farooq* remained in service. The British units were scrapped in 1981-82.

Above: **Type 41 were specialised air defence frigates, but their guns were out-of-date**

between 1957 and 1959. A fifth ship, *Panther*, was sold to India while under construction and was to have been replaced by a new *Panther*, but this was cancelled. Two ships were sold to the newly created Bangladesh Navy, *Jaguar* in 1978 and *Lynx* in 1982, becoming *Ali Haider* and *Abu Bakr* respectively. The two remaining British ships were sold for scrap in 1976-77. As of 2001 both Bangladeshi ships were still in service, although a replacement was being sought; when the new ship joins, *Abu Bakr* will continue to serve as a training ship, while *Ali Haider* will be stricken.

Above: **Type 61s were air direction ships, tasked with controlling carrier aircraft**

Tribal (Type 81)

UNITED KINGDOM

Frigate
Completed: 1961-64.
Number in class: 7.
Displacement: 2,300 tons standard; 2,700 tons full load.
Dimensions: Length 360.0ft (109.7m); beam 42.3ft (12.9m); draught 13.3ft (4.0m).
Propulsion: 1 shaft; COSAG; geared steam turbine, 1 boiler, 12,500shp; 1 AEI G6 gas-turbine, 7,500shp; 27kt; 4,500nm at 12kt.
Armament: 2 x 4.5in (114mm) (2 x 1); 2 x 40mm Bofors or 2 x 20mm Oerlikon; 1 x Limbo Mk 10.
Aircraft: 1 helicopter.
Complement: 253.

History: The designation of these ships followed a tortuous path. They were originally called "Common-Purpose Frigates" but when this was seen to suggest that specialist frigates such as the Types 12, 41 and 61 were ill-advised, this was changed to the pre-war category of "sloop" to indicate a ship with a general anti-surface role but with a tendency to serve in the tropics. Then came the need to replace Loch-class ships in the Gulf and since the name "frigate" was perceived to have a greater public impact, the Tribals became frigates once again.

The Tribals did, in fact, have a general purpose armament, with two single, hand-loaded, semi-automatic 4.5in guns, primarily intended for shore bombardment, either two 40mm or two 20mm for short-range air defence and a single Limbo ASW mortar. These ships also embarked a single Wasp

Leander

UNITED KINGDOM

Frigate
Specifications for original British *Leander*, as built.
Completed: 1963-73.
Number in class: 48.
Displacement: 2,350 tons standard; 2,860 tons full load.
Dimensions: Length 372.0ft (113.4m); beam 41.0ft (12.5m); draught 18.0ft (5.5m).
Propulsion: 2 shafts; geared steam turbines; 2 boilers; 30,000shp; 28kt; 4,000nm at 15kt.
Armament: 2 x 4.5in (114mm) (1 x 2); 2 x 40mm AA; 2 x 20mm Oerlikon; 1 x Limbo.
Aircraft: 1 helicopter.
Complement: 251.

History: Sixteen Leanders were built for the RN, followed by ten "Broad Beam Leanders" with a 2.0ft (0.61m) wider hull. Large numbers were exported, four being built in the UK Chile - 2; New Zealand - 2), while the design was built under licence in India (six Niligiri-class) and the Netherlands (six Van Speijk-class) and the two Swan-class built in Australia (qv) are also normally accounted as being 'Leander' class ships.

The original RN Leanders were separated into two groups for major upgrading programmes. In Batch 1 (eight ships) the gun was replaced by an Ikara ASW system, radars upgraded and two Seacats installed. In Batch 2TA (four ships) the main gun was replaced by four MM38 Exocet launchers, the Limbo was removed, the flightdeck enlarged, and a towed sonar array installed, with one Seacat and the Type 965 radar being removed to reduce topweight.

helicopter, with a tiny flightdeck aft, which doubled as the lift which lowered the aircraft into the hangar. For those who tried it, taking off and landing on a Tribal at sea was an unforgettable experience.

Below: **Type 81s were general-purpose ships; all now serve with the Indonesian Navy**

Right: **Chilean ship, *Condell*; the Leander was the outstanding British post-war design**

Batch 2B (four ships) was similar but without the towed array and an extra SeaCat and two triple 324mm TT added. In Batch 3 five Broad Beam Leanders were gutted and rebuilt, with the main gun and Limbo ASW mortar removed and various items resited to reduce topweight; a six-cell Sea Wolf SAM launcher and four MM 38 Exocet launchers were then installed forward of the bridge, and the hangar and the flight deck adapted to take Lynx helicopters. That left five unmodified "Broad-Beam Leanders" of which four were given a standard mid-life refit, while *Bacchante* was sold to the RNZN.

Of the 26 Leanders which served with the RN, 17 were either scrapped or expended as targets, while nine were sold to foreign customers: Chile - 2; Ecuador - 2; India - 1; New Zealand - 2; Pakistan - 2. The Dutch operated six Van Speijk-class all six of which were sold to Indonesia between 1986 and 1989.

Mermaid

UNITED KINGDOM

Frigate
Completed: 1973.
Number in class: 1.
Displacement: 2,300 tons standard; 2,520 tons full load.
Dimensions: Length 339.3ft (103.4m); beam 40ft (12.2m); draught 12.2ft (3.7m).
Propulsion: 2 shafts; 8 diesels; 12,380shp; 24kt; 4,800nm at 15kt.
Armament: 2 x Vickers 4.0in (102mm) (1 x 2); 2 x Bofors 40mm; one Limbo Mk10 mortar.
Complement: 210.

History: In the late 1950s President Nkrumah of Ghana developed a very ambitious plan to create a navy, starting with two minesweepers acquired in 1959, followed by two corvettes, with another two planned, but the centrepieces were two new-build frigates. The first (*Black Star*) was intended to be a combined fleet flagship and training ship, but was also required to serve as a presidential yacht. Built by Yarrow, the hull and machinery were virtually identical with the British Type 41 (q.v.) but the superstructure was quite different to accommodate large staterooms on the weather deck. This pushed the bridge forward, eliminating the forecastle and resulting in a notably small foredeck, almost totally taken up by the twin 4in gun turret and a flush deck, an unusual feature in a British-built warship at the time.

Nkrumah was overthrown in a coup (February 1966) and the frigate order was cancelled. The ship was completed and launched and then offered for sale by the builders, but was eventually purchased by the RN in 1972 and

Amazon (Type 21)

UNITED KINGDOM

Amazon (Type 21)
Frigate
Specifications for *Amazon*, as built.
Completed: 1974-78.
Number in class: 8.
Displacement: 3,100 tons standard; 3,700 tons full load.
Dimensions: Length 384.0ft (117.0m); beam 41.7ft (12.7m); draught 19.5ft (5.9m).
Propulsion: 2 shafts; COGOG; 2 Rolls-Royce Olympus gas-turbines, 50,000shp; 2 Rolls-Royce Tyne gas-turbines, 9,900shp; 30kt; 4,000nm at 17kt.
Armament: 4 x MM38 Exocet SSM (not Amazon, Antelope); 1 x 4.5in (114mm) gun, 2 x 20mm Oerlikon; 1 x Seacat SSM launcher.
Complement: 175.

History: The Type 21 was the outcome of lobbying by private shipbuilders demanding to supply a frigate to the RN to their own rather than to an "official MoD" design, and free of what they claimed to be the latter's "excessively high" standards. Their proposals would, the designers claimed, result in a ship which was both cheaper and attractive to export customers. The case was accepted and eight ships were constructed, although they were no cheaper than contemporary RN frigates, were overweight (despite widescale use of aluminium in the superstructure), proved unable to accept the next generation of RN weapons and sensors, and won no export orders. They were, however, initially popular with the RN since they were very handsome ships and had an excellent performance, being both fast and very manoeuvrable. All took part in the Falklands (Malvinas) War, in which two were sunk: *Ardent* (22 May) and

commissioned in 1973 as HMS *Mermaid*. She served as a training ship from 1973-77, but was then sold to the Royal Malaysian Navy as *Hang Tuah*, who operated it until it was sold for scrap in the late 1990s.

***Below: Mermaid* was originally built for Ghana as a presidential yacht/training ship**

***Above: Ambuscade*; the Type 21 was popular in peace, but not so effective in war**

Antelope (24 May). After the war the surviving six all had to have their hulls strengthened and served for a few more years with the RN but were then sold en bloc to the Pakistan Navy. In Pakistan Chinese LY-60N SSMs have been fitted in three ships and US Harpoon SSMs in the other three, which also have the Vulcan Phalanx CIWS. Other steps have been taken to modernise them, particularly with improved sensors and they seem likely to remain in service for some years to come.

Broadsword (Type 22) **UNITED KINGDOM**

Frigate
Completed: Batch 1- 1979-82; Batch 2 - 1984-88; Batch 3 - 1988-90.
Number in class: Batch 1- 4; Batch 2 - 6; Batch 3 - 4.
Displacement: 4,000 tons standard; 4,400 tons full load.
Dimensions: Length 430.0ft (131.2m); beam 48.5ft (14.8m); draught 129.8ft (6.1m).
Propulsion: 2 shafts; COGOG; 2 Rolls-Royce Olympus gas-turbines, 54,600shp; 2 Rolls-Royce Tyne gas-turbines, 9,700shp; 30kt; 4,500 at 18kt.
Armament: 4 x MM38 Exocet SSM; 2 x SeaWolf SAM launchers; 2 x 40mm AA; 6 x 12.8in (324mm) TT.
Aircraft: 2 helicopters.
Complement: 222.

History: The Type 22 was intended to replace the Leander-class, but turned out to be a much larger ship due to the need to accommodate additional weapons systems and sensors to meet new threats (eg, the Soviet SS-N-7 missile) as well as to give space for maintainers to work and to accept new equipment in mid-life rebuilds. Like the Leander-class, the Type 22 was required to operate in northern latitudes, which demanded a seaworthy hull capable of high speed in rough seas. *Broadsword* and *Brilliant* took part in the Falklands (Malvinas) War, in which the latter shot down two Argentine Skyhawks with her SeaWolf missiles.

The original four were succeeded in production by the Batch 2 (Boxer-class), which was 485ft (148.1m) long and displaced 4,800 tons at full load. Thus, despite the extra space allowed for in the Batch 1 design, extra size was

Duke (Type 23) **UNITED KINGDOM**

Frigate
Completed: 1990-2002.
Number in class: 16.
Displacement: 3,600 tons standard; 4,300 tons full load.
Dimensions: Length 436.4ft (133.0m); beam 52.8ft (16.1m); draught 18.5ft (5.5m).
Propulsion: 2 shafts; CODLAG; 2 Rolls-Royce Spey gas-turbines, 18,770shp; 4 Paxman-Valenta diesels, 5,200kW; 2 electric cruise motors, 4,000shp; 28kt; 7,800nm at 17kt.
Armament: 8 x Harpoon SSM launchers; 1 x SeaWolf SAM vertical launcher; 1 x 4.5in (114mm) DP gun; 2 x 30mm DES-30B AA guns; 4 x 12.8in (324mm) ASW TT.
Aircraft: 1 helicopter.
Complement: 181.

History: The Type 22 was very successful but also very expensive and once again there was a call for a cheaper frigate, which led to the Type 23 (Duke-class), although the original design grew as a result of the lessons learnt from the Falklands (Malvinas) War. These ships are primarily intended for towed-array operations, albeit using the Type 2031Z system, which is smaller than the Type 2050 in the Type 22. To date the Type 23s have used the Westland Lynx ASW helicopter but this will be replaced by the considerably larger EH.101 Merlin when this enters service. The Type 23 is armed with SeaWolf SAMs but these are fired from a 32-cell vertical launcher in the foredeck, rather than the six-missile swing-arm launcher used in earlier ships.

The Type 23 is the first British warship to incorporate radar-defeating "stealth" features in its design, which include a flared hull, elimination of 90deg

***Right: Brave*, a Type 22 Batch 2 frigate, designed for the rigours of the North Atlantic**

still needed to accommodate the Type 2031Z towed-array sonar. Also, the Type 2016 sonar was moved to the bow, resulting in a much more steeply raked stem. Six were completed between 1984 and 1988.

Next came four Batch 3 ships (Cornwall-class), whose dimensions were the same as Batch 2, although full load displacement increased to 4,900 tons. These incorporated the lessons of the Falklands War, which included the return of the 4.5in (114mm) gun, improved command-and-control facilities and a Goalkeeper CIWS. Four of these very handsome ships were completed between 1988 and 1990.

***Above: Somerset*; one of the Type 23s now providing the RN's front-line force**

corners and infra-red filters in the exhaust system. It was originally intended that these ships would serve for eighteen years without a mid-life update; not surprisingly, this has proved over-optimistic and they will start such an update in 2005. Ships have been given names of British Dukes and were allocated pennant numbers in sequence until it was realised that *Somerset*'s number, F-232, was the same as that of a well-known RN form used to report mishaps such as collisions or groundings; the form's number being sacrosanct, the ship's pennant number was changed to F-82.

GMT/TE/TEV/WGT/DFET/FMR

UNITED STATES OF AMERICA

Destroyer escorts
Completed: 1942-45.
Number in class: see table
Specification for GMT (Evarts-class), as built.
Displacement: 1,192 tons standard; 1,416 tons full load.
Dimensions: Length 289.4ft (88.2m); beam 35.2ft (10.7m); draught 10.1ft (3.1m).
Propulsion: 2 shafts; diesel-electric; 2 General Motors diesels; 6,000bhp; 19.5kt; 6,000nm at 12kt.
Armament: 3 x 3in (76mm) (3 x 1)4 x 1.1in; 9 x 20mm; 1 x Hedgehog; 8 x DC throwers; 2 x DC racks.
Complement: 156.

Type	Class Name	Hull	Drive	Speed
GMT	Evarts	289.4ft (88.2m)	Diesel-electric; 2 GM diesels	21kt
TE	Buckley	306.0ft (93.3m)	Turbo-electric; 2 GE turbines	24kt
TEV	Rudderow	306.0ft (93.3m)	Turbo-electric; 2 GE turbines	23kt
WGT	Butler	306.0ft (93.3m)	Turbo-electric; 2 Westinghouse turbines	23kt
DET	Cannon	306.0ft (93.3m)	Diesel-electric; 2 GM diesels	21kt
FMR	Edsall	306.0ft (93.3m)	Diesel-electric; 2 Fairbanks-Morse diesels	20kt
TOTALS				

History: No fewer than 500 destroyer escorts (DEs) were built between 1942 and 1945, 423 for the US Navy and 77 for the RN. There were six variants on the same basic design, the differences being principally attributable to hull lengths, main weapons and propulsion systems; although all had electric drive, the differences lay in how the power was produced. The origin lay in a British request for a "second-rate" destroyer on the lines of the Hunt-class and President Roosevelt gave the go-ahead in August 1941. The original design was the GMT (= General Motors, tandem) which had a short hull with diesel-electric drive, but diesels were wanted for many other uses. As a result a new version was produced powered by two GE steam-turbines with two boilers in a turbo-electric system; designated the TE (= turbo-electric), this had a slightly longer hull and more were produced than any other variant. Next came the TEV (= turbo-electric; 5 inch [ie "V"] guns) which had the same longer hull and propulsion system as the TE, but was armed with two 5in (127mm) guns. The fourth version was simply a variant on the TEV, being powered by Westinghouse (as opposed to General Electric) geared turbines, hence the designation WGT. The fifth version, designated DET, had the original General

***Above: Manuel,* a WGT version (Butler-class) of the ubiquitous destroyer-escort**

Guns	USN	RN
3 x 3in	65	31
3 x 3in	102	46
2 x 5in (127mm)	22	
2 x 5in (127mm)	83	
3 x 3in (76mm)	66	
3 x 3in (76mm)	85	
	423	77

Motors tandem diesel drive and three 3in (76mm) guns as the GMT, but in the longer hull. Finally came the FMR (= Fairbanks-Morse) powered by submarine-type diesels with reduction gearing. Many of these were converted for other uses, both during and after the war, such uses including troop transports, radar pickets.

A total of 77 was supplied to the RN - thirty-one GMT and forty-six TE - where they were known, collectively, as the Captain-class. All survivors were returned to the United States after the war.

Thus, the US Navy found itself in 1946 with hundreds of these small escorts, which were now referred to by the name of the first-of-class, rather than by the initials.

Some were scrapped at once, some were put into reserve and others were geadually sold or given to friendly navies. A few remain in service in 2001.

***Above: Poole;* Edsall-class, a type which served on with smaller navies into the 1980s**

Dealey

UNITED STATES OF AMERICA

Destroyer escorts
Completed: 1954-57.
Number in class: 13.
Displacement: 1,314 tons standard; 1,877 tons full load.
Dimensions: Length 315.0ft (96.0m); beam 36.7ft (11.2m); draught 11.8ft (3.6m).
Propulsion: 1 shaft; geared-turbine; 2 boilers; 20,000shp; 27kt; 6,000nm at 12kt.
Armament: 4 x 3in (76mm) (2 x 2); Weapon Alfa ASW system.
Complement: 173.

History: These ships were the US Navy's first post-war destroyer escorts (DE) and the design was deliberately prepared so that it could be placed into large-scale production with the minimum of fuss in the event of war. Thus, the hull was of simple construction and there was only one screw to minimise demands on the gear-making industry. Despite this, they needed to be able to cope with the modern threat which, in the mid-1950s was a large fleet of Soviet Whiskey-class submarines. This meant that they had to be fast, 27kt, and were fitted with modern sonars and carried the latest US Navy ASW weapon, the

Weapon Alfa. They were seaworthy ships but were considered to be underarmed and in the 1960s ten of the class were fitted with SQS-23 sonar, and their after 3in (76mm) turret was removed and replaced by a hangar and flightdeck for the DASH ASW drone, a remotely-controlled helicopter which carried an ASW torpedo to the vicinity of an enemy submarine and then dropped it.

Eight ships were built abroad, five in Norway and three in Portugal, which were based on a modified Dealey design. The two designs were, however, somewhat different from each other, since the Norwegian Oslo-class was intended for operations in the Arctic, while the Portuguese Da Silva-class was intend for tropical waters.

Only two Dealeys were sold abroad, both in 1972: Dealey to Uruguay as 18 De Julio, and Hartley to Colombia as Boyaca. All the remainder were sold for scrap in1972-74.

***Below: Dealey,* name ship of a class of thirteen ocean escorts built in the 1950s**

Claud Jones

UNITED STATES OF AMERICA

Frigate
Specifications are for Turkish Berk-class, as built.
Completed: 1959-68.
Number in class: 6
Displacement: 1450 tons standard; 1950 tons full load.
Dimensions: Length 311.7ft (95.0m); beam 38.7ft (11.8m); draught 18.1ft (5.5m).
Propulsion: 1 shaft; 4 Fiat-Tosi diesels; 24,000 hp(m); 25 kt; 10,000nm at 9kt.
Armament: 4 x 76mm Mk 33 DP (2 x 2); 2 x Mk11 fixed Hedgehog ASW mortar; 6 x 324mm Mk 32 ASW TT; 1 x Mk 9 depth-charge rack.
Complement: 164

History: The Dealey-class DEs, built for the US Navy in the mid-1950s proved to be rather expensive and the Claud Jones-class was built in 1959-60 in an attempt to obtain a less expensive ASW escort vessel. They were, therefore, given diesel engines, a limited speed (22kt) and a minimal weapons system, comprising a pair of fixed Hedgehogs, a lightweight torpedo system and a single depth-charge rack at the stern. Four were built, completed between 1958 to 1960, but they were thoroughly unpopular in the US Navy and spent most of their service as electronic surveillance ships in the Pacific.

Two were built in Turkey in the late 1960s and the four US Navy ships were sold to Indonesia in 1973-74, where they have proved economical to run and easy to maintain. The Indonesian Navy has removed all the Hedgehog mortars and some ex-Soviet weapons have been installed. The Indonesian ships are *Samadikun*, *Martadinata*, *Mongishisidi* and *Ngurah Rai*, while the Turkish ships are named *Berk* and *Peyk*.

Knox

UNITED STATES OF AMERICA

Destroyer escort/frigate
Completed: 1969-74.
Number in class: 46.
Displacement: 3,020 tons light; 4,066 tons full load.
Dimensions: Length 438.0ft (133.5m); beam 47.0ft (14.3m); draught 25.0ft (7.6m).
Propulsion: 1 shaft; Westinghouse geared turbines; 2 boilers; 35,000shp; 27kt; 4,500nm at 20kt.
Armament: 1 x 5in (127mm) gun; 1 x Sea Sparrow SAM launcher; 1 x ASROC ASW system; 2 x 21in (533mm) TT; 4 x 12.8in (324mm) ASW TT.
Aircraft: DASH.
Complement: 224.

History: The successor to the Garcia/Brookes-classes, Knox-class ships were longer, but retained the single propeller and single 5in (127mm) gun. Like the previous class they were originally classified destroyer escorts (DE) but redesignated frigates (FF) in 1975. Forty-six were built, entering service between 1969 and 1974, while a further ten were cancelled. The ship was dominated by the tall 'mack' intended as a mounting for billboard antennas, but in practice only normal radar arrays were ever used. As built, the ships were armed with a 5in (127mm) gun, four 12.8in (324mm) ASW torpedo tubes, DASH helicopter drone, and an eight-cell Mk 16 ASROC launcher, the latter having a newly-developed reloading capability.

During their service DASH was replaced by the SH-2 SeaSprite helicopter (LAMPS-I) and thirty-one ships were fitted with Sea Sparrow, but a 1970s plan to fit Sea Chapparal in the remainder was cancelled. Thirty-five were modified to take the

Above: **The Jones-class DEs were built as simpler, cheaper alternatives to the Dealeys**

Below: **Forty-six Knox-class were built for the US Navy, plus five for Spain**

TACTAS variable-depth sonar, with a new computerised system to cope with the dramatic increase in data flow. The original plan to fit two 533mm (21 in) torpedo tubes was never implemented, but the ships were given an anti-ship capability in 1972 when the two port cells of the ASROC launcher were modified to accept Harpoon, with two more Harpoons in the missile magazine.

The Knox-class was criticised from the start for having only one propeller, while during their service they were considered too wet forward. The former could not be rectified, but all ships received bulwarks and spray strakes in the early 1980s, adding 9.1 tons to the displacement.

The only early export order was for five, which were built in Spain (Baleares-class) and completed in 1973-76. With the end of the Cold War Knox-class ships were taken out of US service and some were leased/sold to selected friendly navies: Egypt - 2; Taiwan - 9; Greece - 3; Thailand - 2; Turkey - 8. The remainder were scrapped.

Bronstein/Garcia/Brooke

UNITED STATES OF AMERICA

Destroyer escort/frigates
Specifications for *Garcia*, as built
Completed: Bronstein - 1963; Garcia - 1964-67; Brooke - 1965-68.
Number in class: Bronstein -2; Garcia - 10; Brooke - 7.
Displacement: 2,441 tons standard; 3,371 tons full load.
Dimensions: Length 414.0ft (126.2m); beam 44.0ft (13.4m); draught 24.0ft (7.3m).
Propulsion: 1 shaft; Westinghouse geared turbines; 2 pressure-fired boilers; 35,000shp; 27kt; 4,000nm at 20kt.
Armament: 2 x 5in (127mm) (2 x 1); ASROC ASW system; 2 x 21in (533mm) TT; 6 x 12.8in (324mm) ASW TT.
Aircraft: DASH.
Complement: 209.

History: Following the unsatisfactory Claud Jones-class, the search for an effective ocean ASW escort led inexorably towards a larger hull, more powerful propulsion machinery to provide greater speed, more effective sensors and a powerful weapons fit. The first step in this process was the Bronstein-class of just two ships, both completed in 1963, a totally new design with a length of 372.0ft (113.4m) and a displacement of 2,723 tons. They carried three 3in (76mm) guns, an ASROC launcher, the DASH drone helicopter and the new SQS-26 sonar, but their maximum speed of 27.5kt was no better than that of the Dealey-class. Both ships were stricken in 1990.

One of the major concerns remained the speed of the escorts, since not only were modern Soviet submarines capable of 30kt submerged, but if war came the Allied convoys would also be steaming at speeds of 25-28kt. One potentially effective power plant was the lightweight, pressure-fired boiler then

***Above: Julian A Furer*, a Brooke-class frigate, now serving with the Pakistan Navy**

under development. Another important factor in the early 1960s was that the large stocks of World War II destroyers and destroyer escorts held in reserve were now very elderly, increasingly unsuitable for modern conditions and needed replacement.

The outcome was a new DE, with pressure-fired boilers, which was built in two groups. The ten-strong Garcia-class was the anti-submarine version with an ASW armament of an ASROC system, six 12.8in (324mm) ASW torpedo tubes and a DASH drone, together with an anti-surface armament of two 5in (127mm) guns and two 21in (533mm) torpedo tubes. The Brooke-class were missile ships with an identical hull and machinery to the Garcia. Their armament consisted of a single Terrier SAM launcher (sixteen missiles) in place of the after 5in (76mm) gun and no 21in (533mm) torpedo tubes, but was otherwise the same as that of the Garcias. The Brookes were, however, considered to be rather expensive for a fairly limited capability and only six were built. The final ship of this group, *Glover*, was built to test a pump-jet propulsion system and while she had a 5in (76mm) gun and an ASROC launcher forward, she had neither a 5in (76mm) gun nor a Tartar launcher aft.

The Garcias and Brookes proved successful in service. In the 1970s the DASH facilities in all except two were enlarged to enable them to operate the LAMPS manned helicopter system, and all the 21in (533mm) torpedo tubes were removed from the Garcias. All were redesignated frigates in June 1975, the Garcias becoming "FF-" and the Brookes "FFG-". All were decommissioned in 1988-89 and eight were leased to Pakistan, but had to be returned in 1993-94 as a result of a political dispute and were scrapped. Four went to Brazil, also in 1988, and the remaining US Navy ships were scrapped in 1993.

Above: Bronstein, **one of two ships which started a long line of US Navy frigates**

Oliver Harzard Perry UNITED STATES OF AMERICA

Frigate
Completed: 1979-2003.
Number in class: 71.
Displacement: FFG 9-19 - 2,769 tons light; 3,658 tons full load; remainder 3,010-3,210 tons light; 3,900-3,2310 tons full load.
Dimensions: Length FFG 7-35, as built, 453.0ft (138.1m); others, as built, 455.0ft (135.6m),; beam 45.0ft (13.7m); draught (hull) 14.8ft (4.5m).
Propulsion: 1 shaft; 2 General Electric LM-2500 gas-turbines; 41,000shp; 29kt; 4,200nm at 20kt. Plus 2 retractable electric propulsors; total 720p; 6 kt.
Armament: 1 Mk 13 launcher (4 x Harpoon; 36 x Standard SAM); 1 x 3in (76mm) OTOMelara gun; 1 x 20mm Vulcan Phalanx CIWS; 2 x 25mm Bushmaster low-anglecannon; 2 or 4 0.5in (12.7mm) MG; 6 x 12.8in (324mm) ASW TT.
Aircraft: 1 or 2 helicopters.
Complement: 214.

History: In the 1970s some expensive and sophisticated specialised ASW and AAW ships were being built to protect carrier and surface action groups and the Perry-class was intended as the "low-technology" counterpart. The primary mission was ASW protection of amphibious forces, merchant ship convoys and underway replenishment groups, but strict limits were placed on cost, displacement and manpower. They were intended to be built in smaller yards, so efforts were made to use simple techniques, for example, by using flat panels wherever possible and keeping internal passageways straight. Propulsion was also simplified, using two gas-turbines to drive one propeller. It was recognised that these limitations would reduce overall capabilities, but the result was a capable and well-liked ship, which has played a major role in many conflicts.

The weapon fit reflected the design philosophy. There was a single Mk 13 launcher on the foredeck with the magazine below containing 40 missiles, ▶

Above: Kaman SH 2F helicopter on the flightdeck of a US Navy Perry-class frigate

Below Left: Australian Perry-class frigate, *Newcastle*, launches Standard SM-1 missile

Below Right: *Santa Maria*, one of six Perry-class frigates built in Spain for the Spanish Navy

***Above:* The Perry-class has been a success, with seventy-one built in four countries**

usually 36 Standard SAM and four Harpoon SSM. The gun was an OTOBreda 76mm Compact located atop the superstructure, with a single Mk 15 20mm Vulcan Phalanx CIWS added later on the hangar roof. ASW capability included two triple torpedo tubes and two helicopters (LAMPS I in the earlier ships, LAMPS III in others), but, unlike previous frigate classes, ASROC missiles were not carried.

Propulsion was by two gas-turbines, the ships attaining 25kt on one engine and 28kt on both, although Perry achieved 31kt on trials. One unusual feature was two retractable propulsion pods, each containing a 325hp engine, to provide a "get-you-home" facility and to assist in docking.

The original ships had a vertical transom and a flightdeck designed for the LAMPS I (SH-2F) helicopter. When it was decided to operate the LAMPS III (SH-60) helicopter from these ships a slightly larger flightdeck was needed, which was achieved by angling out the transom, thus increasing overall hull length from 435.0ft (138.1m) to 455.0ft (135.6m). FFG 36 onwards were built with this longer hull and four of the earlier ships were later rebuilt to the same standard.

When construction in Taiwan ends a total of seventy-one Perrys will have been built. Fifty-five were built in the USA, fifty-one for the US Navy and four for Australia (Adelaide-class). A further two were then built in Australia (Adelaide-class) and six in Spain (Baleares-class). Taiwan (RoC) is building eight (Cheung Kung-class), the last of which will be completed in 2003; plans to build a "Batch II" of a more advanced design have been cancelled.

As of 2001 a number of the Perry-class had been sold to foreign navies including Bahrein, Egypt and Turkey, while one has been presented as a gift to the Polish Navy. Not all the intended recipients have accepted the offer. More are due to be sold and the remaining seventeen will spend some years with the US Navy's National Reserve Fleet. Although built as ocean escorts, these ships have proved very valuable to the US Navy as general-purpose warships; they have, for example, been deployed in the Gulf since the early 1980s and no fewer than fourteen took part in the Gulf War.